SPORTS ETHICS FOR SPORTS MANAGEMENT PROFESSIONALS

Patrick K. Thornton
Rice University, Sport Management Program
IE Business School, Madrid, Spain, Professor of Sport Law
University of Houston Law Center, South Texas College of Law,
Adjunct Professor

Walter T. Champion Jr.
George Foreman Professor of Sports and Entertainment Law
Thurgood Marshall School of Law
Texas Southern University

Lawrence S. Ruddell
Associate Professor of Business
Belhaven University
President and Founder
The Global Institute for Ethical Leadership

JONES & BARTLETT
LEARNING

World Headquarters
Jones & Bartlett Learning
40 Tall Pine Drive
Sudbury, MA 01776
978-443-5000
info@jblearning.com
www.jblearning.com

Jones & Bartlett Learning
Canada
6339 Ormindale Way
Mississauga, Ontario L5V 1J2
Canada

Jones & Bartlett Learning
International
Barb House, Barb Mews
London W6 7PA
United Kingdom

Jones & Bartlett Learning books and products are available through most bookstores and online booksellers. To contact Jones & Bartlett Learning directly, call 800-832-0034, fax 978-443-8000, or visit our website, www.jblearning.com.

Production Credits

Publisher, Higher Education: Cathleen Sether
Senior Acquisitions Editor: Shoshanna Goldberg
Senior Associate Editor: Amy L. Bloom
Editorial Assistant: Prima Bartlett
Production Manager: Julie Champagne Bolduc
Production Editor: Jessica Steele Newfell
Production Assistant: Sean Coombs
Associate Marketing Manager: Jody Sullivan
V.P., Manufacturing and Inventory Control:
    Therese Connell

Photo Research and Permissions Supervisor:
    Christine Myaskovsky
Composition and Project Management:
    Glyph International
Cover Design: Kate Ternullo
Cover Image: (top) © Amy Myers/ShutterStock, Inc.;
    (bottom) © sylvaine thomas/ShutterStock, Inc.
Printing and Binding: Malloy, Inc.
Cover Printing: Malloy, Inc.

Library of Congress Cataloging-in-Publication Data
Thornton, Patrick K.
  Sports ethics for sports management professionals / Patrick K. Thornton,
Walter T. Champion, Jr., Lawrence S. Ruddell.
      p. cm.
  Includes bibliographical references and index.
  ISBN 978-0-7637-4384-0 (alk. paper)
  1. Sports—Management. 2. Sports—Moral and ethical aspects.
I. Champion, Walter T. II. Ruddell, Larry. III. Title.
  GV713.T565 2012
  796.06'9—dc22

                                            2011002393

6048

Printed in the United States of America
15 14 13 12 11   10 9 8 7 6 5 4 3 2 1

To my wife, Alison, and our sons, George and Samuel.

— PT

*To my son Charles who will be in the 400 in the 2020 Olympics—Son,
watch out for lane changes, Love, Dad*

— WTC

*I dedicate this to my dad, Joe Ruddell, who was a star performer on the
Virginia Tech basketball team of the 1940s, and brothers Pres (who played
Minor League Ball with the Twins), Jim, and Bill, for the love of sports that we
all share, and my kids, Preston and Anna, that they may share the passion
and "run the race!"*

— LR

CONTENTS

PREFACE

The term *ethics* covers a broad spectrum of disciplines in today's society. Business ethics, medical ethics, legal ethics, environmental ethics, and, yes, even sports ethics are prevalent in today's culture. Sports ethics confronts many issues common in our society within the context of the sports world. Race and discrimination, gender equity issues, privacy, intellectual property, gambling, violence, and drug use and drug testing are all significant topics in the study of sports ethics.

Sports management professionals (SMPs) will be confronted with many ethical decisions during their careers. It is essential that they be equipped to make the right decision when faced with a difficult situation. This book was written with an eye toward the sports management professional, who will certainly encounter many tough decisions during his or her career. It is one of the goals of this book to assist the SMP in making the right decision when the situation arises. Ethical situations can arise for the sports manager in a variety of circumstances: in the employment process, in the administration of an athletic program at both the amateur and professional levels, in youth sports, and in the everyday decisions an SMP must make in fulfilling his or her duties and responsibilities.

In Chapter 1, several ethical models are presented that the SMP may use as a platform to make ethical decisions. No one likes a cheater; that is a simple proposition. The concept of cheating is explored in the first chapter. How is cheating actually defined, and what should be done to avoid cheating in sports? Chapter 1 also presents several practical cases ("tough calls") for the SMP relating to discrimination in the workplace, eligibility and participation issues, disability issues in sports, and ethical issues confronting the SMP in collegiate and professional sports. Each case allows the student to apply the ethical decision-making process to a sports-related ethical dispute.

In Chapter 2, the concepts of sportsmanship and gamesmanship are examined. Is there a difference between the two? If so, what are the differences, and how are they applied in the sporting world? Every sport has rules that all participants (fans, players, coaches, referees, and parents) must abide by. However, rules are often broken, particularly by the participants. Sometimes this is even done intentionally. Should sports tolerate the intentional breaking of the rules of the game or sport? America's national pastime of baseball seems to tolerate the concept of gamesmanship more than other sports, and Chapter 2 further explores the differences between sportsmanship and gamesmanship in this context. Spying and espionage have always been present in sports. Trying to figure out the "secrets" of another athlete's success can be valuable information for a competitor. Those concepts are developed and discussed fully in Chapter 2. "Trash talking" and profanity have become prevalent in both professional and amateur sports. Is it ever acceptable to engage in either, and, if so, under what circumstances? The limits of this kind of behavior are also discussed for all levels of sports.

Gambling has been present in sports ever since participants have thrown or passed a ball. It is a simple, but true, statement: individuals like to play games of chance with the hope of winning money. But is gambling good for a sport? Every professional sports league regulates gambling to a certain extent. Many experts agree that gambling diminishes the integrity of the sport. Chapter 3 explores the influence gambling has had on players, teams, referees, and leagues at both the professional and amateur levels and what has been done to reduce the influence of gambling in sport.

All those involved in sports have an ethical calling. Participants should play the game within the rules; coaches should perform their duties ethically and responsibly. Sports officials and umpires have a moral and ethical duty to be fair and unbiased in all their rulings. These concepts are explored in Chapter 4. Participants must comply with a code of conduct during play, and they should not engage in unsportsmanlike conduct or violent behavior. It is incumbent on coaches to provide for the safety of participants. Coaches must supervise and instruct athletes properly to prevent injury, and they must refrain from violent and abusive behavior towards the athletes they coach. It is an understatement that sports officials have a tough job, but they must perform it without bias and with consideration for the safety of all participants and fans.

Chapter 5 discusses two of the most important participants at any sporting event—parents of youth sports participants and fans. Parents are becoming more involved in their children's sporting events, and along with that increased involvement come ethical duties. Parents should conduct themselves appropriately and be good examples for youth sports participants at all events. "Parental rage" has become a major issue, both legally and ethically, at the youth sports level. Chapter 5 discusses this concept in depth. Every sporting event needs enthusiastic fans. Without fans, no sport can survive. Fans love to cheer their team to victory, but it must be done in an ethical and certainly a nonviolent manner. Fans at sporting events owe an ethical duty to others at the sporting event to conduct themselves appropriately, while still enjoying the sporting event and to refrain from "fan rage," violent behavior, "over the top" heckling, or stalking athletes. All of these concepts and ethical issues are explored in Chapter 5.

Violence in sports is a major ethical issue facing almost every major sport. Violence is tolerated in many sports and even encouraged in others. Issues of how much violence at all levels of sports should be tolerated are explored in Chapter 6. Both civil and criminal sanctions can be levied against violent athletes to attempt to curb inappropriate behavior. The sport of professional hockey tolerates, and in some cases even encourages, fighting and has clearly stated so. Unfortunately, athletes sometimes also engage in "off-the-field" violence. Leagues, teams, and managers may have to deal with off-the-field violent and nonviolent issues as well, determining appropriate punishment for the offenders.

It seems no topic has been explored and discussed more in the sporting world in the last few years than drug use and drug testing. Chapter 7 explores drug testing and use and its ethical implications in the context of both professional and amateur sports. Steroid use has become prevalent in sports and is a controversial issue. This topic presents major ethical dilemmas for athletes and for the SMP.

Congress has become involved in professional sports leagues to try to "clean up" the sport. Ethical issues abound in this area for the sports manager, athlete, coach, and athletic association as well as for professional teams and leagues.

Race has a long history in sports. In Chapter 8 race and discrimination issues are discussed. Racial issues are present at all levels of sports and involve all participants, sports officials, coaches, and parents. In this chapter, cases and case studies explore issues dealing with race in the employment context as well as with eligibility issues.

Sports agents arrived on the sports scene in the late 1960s, primarily because of the increasing salaries for professional players. In Chapter 9, numerous ethical issues facing sports agents are examined. Agents are in a trust or fiduciary relationship with clients, and they must abide by certain ethical and legal rules when performing their duties. Agents have many responsibilities and obligations to their clients, including contract negotiations, endorsements, tax advice, and legal advice. All of these duties must be performed in an ethical and legal manner. The issue of attorneys also acting as agents is explored. Many entities regulate sports agents: the NCAA, states, player unions, and universities. Any regulation of agents must be fair and ethical, and any discipline levied against unethical agents must comport with the agent regulatory system.

Chapter 10 discusses women in sports, gender discrimination, and Title IX. For many years women did not have the same opportunities as men to participate and be involved in sports. Many antiquated attitudes existed, and some still do, about the "fragile" woman who is unable to participate in sports and "can't keep up with the boys." Unfortunately, discrimination and abuse against women in sports have become very significant issues for all involved in sports. An SMP will be called upon to make ethical decisions dealing with both sexual harassment and sexual abuse of women athletes. Title IX has done a lot to make women's sports "equal" to men's sports, but there is still room to grow. An SMP working at the collegiate level will certainly be faced with ethical issues related to Title IX and must understand the reasons behind its implementation. Compliance issues dealing with Title IX are also explored.

Intellectual property rights and licensing are significant issues for anyone involved in sports, especially the SMP. Cable television, the Internet, Twitter, Facebook, and other forms of broadcasting and social media dominate the sports landscape. Professional teams, universities, and players all have ethical concerns dealing with the protection of trademarks, copyrights, trade secrets, and the licensing of intellectual property. Ethical issues involving the fair use of copyrighted material, infringement of trademarks, ethics in sponsorship agreements, and protecting the athlete's image and rights of publicity are all explored in Chapter 11.

In Chapter 12 sports ethics is discussed in the context of sports media. Sports fans can access sports games and news in a wide variety of forms. Reporters, writers, and producers all owe a duty to perform their jobs in an ethical manner including producing factually accurate and truthful stories and to verify the facts of any story. The production of the story must be done in a truthful and forthright manner, presenting all sides of an issue. Ethical and legal issues can arise in reporting stories of athletes. The media must immediately issue a retraction for any statement or story that is untrue and also issue an apology. That is the ethical thing to do. Media outlets should be aware of how the individuals in a story are portrayed and refrain from stereotyping any groups or individuals during their presentation of the news or a journalistic piece. Social media has now become a form of art, and ethical issues abound in this area. These are explored in depth as well.

It is our hope that this book will assist you in furthering your understanding of ethics and more specifically sports ethics. We also hope it provides you with some practical decision-making skills to assist you in your career in the sports industry.

Good luck in your study of sports ethics.

ACKNOWLEDGMENTS

A good book needs input from a variety of people, and this book is no exception. There are many people to thank for this project. First, to my beautiful wife, Alison, who has listened to me talk about sports for 20 years. To my father, Jack, and my mother Jennie, who were always concerned with making good moral decisions. To my sister, Candy, and brother-in-law, Brad, as well.

Jackie Faccini, attorney Michael Flint, and Emma K. Tsai, MLS, all deserve special acknowledgments for their valuable contributions of research and for reviewing the manuscript. Their insights were invaluable. A special acknowledgment goes to my longtime friend Mark Schwartz, with whom, next to my father, I have shared more conversations about sports than anyone. Thanks to professor James "Jimmy" Disch, (Sports Ethics Fellow, 2011) Rice University, who has taught me much about sportsmanship and ethics both in sports and in life. Also, to my father-in-law, Gene Hewett (U.S. Air Force), for his thoughtful insights. A special thanks to my colleagues at Rice University for their support and encouragement during this project: Dr. Jimmy Disch, Dr. Nicholas Iammarino, Dr. Clark D. Haptonstall, Dr. Jason Sosa, Tom Stallings, Dr. Bruce Entyre, Dr. Heidi Perkins, Dr. Augusto Rodriguez, Wendy Schell and Teresa Arellano.

I was also fortunate to receive contributions and advice from several outstanding legal scholars. They are in no particular order: Dr. Mark Willis, Dr. Rick Nash, Mike McDonald, Steve Elkington, Joe Branch, Dr. Mike Bourke, Massimo Coccia, Seth Daniel, Dr. Doni Wilson, super lawyer Nick Nichols, Gil Fried, Ronnie Wren, G. Ray Thornton, Mike Janecek, Matt Mitten, Dr. Richard "Hutch" Divorak, Doug Gerhman, Mike Laramie, Kenny Waldt, Joseph Promo, Waco Thornton, David Brickey, Cheryl Thornton, Dennis Chalupa, Sam Webb, Dr. Yuri Yatsenko, Oliver Luck, Jessie Marcos, E. Brian McGeever, Jack Dolphin, Kathleen Stischer-Burnette, Jon Maire, Dr. William Little, Kurt Kilman, Kevin Erwin, Steve Moniaci, Sally Richardson, and Vanessa Gionis. Also, many thanks to my colleagues at Columbia Southern University for their continued support: Dr. Karen Smith, Dr. Mark Pantaleo, Doug Marker, Dr. Sonya Rogers, Veronica Hurd, and Alexis Banks.

Thanks to the many law school, university deans, and department chairs who hired me to teach a variety of legal and sports related courses over many years, including Dean John Nussbaumer at the Thomas M. Cooley Law School; Richard Alderman at the University of Houston Law Center; Lylene Pilkenton, South Texas College of Law; Marian Dent at Pericles Law in Moscow, Russia; my good mate Gordon Walker at

Latrobe Law School in Melbourne, Australia; Itziar Murillo and Pilar Villar at ISDE in Madrid, Spain; Gabriela Sonato at the IE Business School in Madrid, Spain; and Mandi Gibson, South Texas College of Law.

Much of the information in this book has been collected through research as well as experiences I have had in the sports industry, classroom teaching, and even by watching sports. I have been fortunate to teach sports ethics and law courses to undergraduate, graduate, and law students, and to LLMs in a variety of countries. Those experiences have assisted me immensely in writing this book. I am very proud of the many outstanding students to whom I have taught law and ethics over the past 20 years in the United States and across the globe in South Korea, Vietnam, Australia, Russia, and Spain. They all have contributed to the book in some fashion. It has been a pleasure to teach each one of them.

I would also like to thank the reviewers of this book, whose input was invaluable: Donnie Andrews, PhD, Jackson State University; Ronald W. Quinn, PhD, Associate Professor, Xavier University; Jennifer L. VanSickle, EdD, University of Indianapolis; Jeff Vessely, EdD, Chair and Professor of Physical Education, Indiana University–Purdue University Indianapolis; and James Zarick, EdD, High Point University.

Of course, a great deal of thanks and credit goes to my co-authors in *Sports Ethics*, Walter T. Champion Jr. and Lawrence S. Ruddell. It is always great working with both of these fine scholars.

I was taught sportsmanship very early in life by my family and through youth sports. In youth sports I received the Mike Driscoll sportsmanship award four times. I never gave it much thought until later in life when I discovered the award was named after a young Marine who lived in my neighborhood who died in the Vietnam War in 1967 at the age of 22. Any acknowledgment to him would seem to not be enough, but I felt compelled to mention it.

Finally to the fantastic people at Jones & Bartlett Learning. I cannot say enough about all of them: Shoshanna Goldberg, Julie Bolduc, Jody Sullivan, Prima Bartlett, and Rebecca Ritter. Thanks are also due to Anupriya Tyagi at Glyph International for her careful work with the manuscript. Thank you for all your hard work and patience in producing a quality product!

—Pat Thornton

I mostly observed sports ethics, or the lack thereof, while watching fans misbehave at an Eagles game. Other instances were in my 8th grade physical education class and as a participant in little league and school athletics. As far as someone who was ethical and exhibited sportsmanship at all times, my hat has to go off to Walter Payton.

—Walter T. Champion Jr.

I'd like to thank my colleagues Patrick Thornton and Walter Champion for including me on this important project; Chip Mason, the Dean of the College of Business at Belhaven University for his support and encouragement to write; and my coaches throughout the years (Sink, Purcell, Holland, and many others) who taught sports ethics and sportsmanship as a way of life.

—Larry Ruddell

CASE STUDY RUBRIC

We have prepared many case studies for your use in the study of sports ethics. We believe the case studies in the book will assist you greatly in your study and teaching of sports ethics. The following guidelines will assist you with the case studies in the book. Most of the studies are based on actual events in the sporting world. We have referenced each one so you can do further research and study if you so desire. You should find them very helpful in developing your own ethical decision-making skills. For the professor, they are arranged so they can be assigned to students to write papers, develop questions, or used as extra credit assignments that will further develop knowledge of sports ethics. When examining the case studies, the following questions should be asked:

1. What is the ethical dilemma or dilemmas posed in this case study?
2. What should the goal of the sports management professional (SMP) be when first addressing this problem?
3. What is the best ethical model to use to approach the ethical situation posed?
4. As an SMP, what other information would you need to have to make an ethical decision?
5. What other individuals would you need to consult to achieve a fair and ethical decision?
6. Does this ethical problem require a form of alternate dispute resolution such as a mediator? If so, how should you proceed, and what should be the goal of the mediator?
7. If this ethical problem cannot be resolved between the parties, what specific compromises can be offered in an attempt to resolve the problem?
8. Does this situation present legal issues that require the assistance of an attorney to arrive at a fair and ethical decision?
9. What cultural, social, or race issues need to be addressed by the parties involved in the scenario?
10. What are the possible consequences of making an unethical decision in this situation?

Good luck with the case studies and your study of sports ethics.

ETHICAL CONCEPTS IN SPORTS

SPORTS IN SOCIETY

America is a sports crazed culture, but Americans are not alone in their love of sports. The world is connected in a sports culture with millions of individuals in Spain, India, Australia, New Zealand, Canada, Colombia, China and many other countries watching and participating in sports each year. Participating in sports can bring new challenges to an individual and teach valuable life lessons along the way. Americans participate in a variety of sports including golf, basketball, cycling, tennis, baseball, soccer, and ice hockey. Parents are enrolling their children in youth sports at an ever-increasing rate so they might learn time honored concepts such as hard work, dedication, team building, competition, and sportsmanship and hopefully transfer those skills to their personal life. All are good societal values and build character in youth.

Youth sports have never been more popular. In the United States millions of kids participate in a variety of sports beginning at the toddler stage. Before their children can even bounce a ball, swing a club, or run in a straight line, overzealous parents have them in the sports arena learning how to kick a ball, take a charge or throw a spiral. Kids participate in sports for a variety of reasons, some healthy and some not so healthy. Many participate because their friends are playing, others because their parents insist, and some even participate just for fun! When sports stop being fun, kids tend to drop out. The benefits of youth sports include increased confidence, increased fitness (less time for video games), increased social awareness, moral development, and improved problem-solving skills. Choosing sides, nominating a team captain, and shaking hands with an opponent after a match are all good character traits for a young athlete to develop, although organized sports has taken some of these basic tasks away from the youth participant. Many youth sports programs involve "select teams" or All-Star teams, in which certain players are picked to play additional games.

Sports at the high school level are increasing in popularity, and watching collegiate sports is extremely popular in the United States. With universities offering scholarships in a variety of sports including basketball, bowling, lacrosse, football, rodeo, riflery, ice hockey, and swimming, parents are hoping that their child will be a superstar.

Spectators flock to stadiums around the world to watch sports. American fans love to watch football, both amateur and professional; collegiate and professional basketball; ice hockey; and of course, America's national pastime, baseball. Athletes in professional sports can earn millions of dollars playing their favorite sport. Sports franchises are valued at more than $1 billion, and collegiate football games can draw more than 110,000 fans. The New York Yankees are valued at $1.2 billion, and some football coaches at major universities can earn more money than the university president.[1]

Some fans seem to take sports a little too seriously, and this can include many youth sports parents. Ardent fans spend hours each day ruminating over statistics for their individual fantasy leagues while others paint their bodies and "tailgate" for up to 6 hours before the NFL game of their favorite team. The contemporary sports world is fraught with "over-the-top parents" and fans alike.[2]

Christopher Noteboom fits well into the dedicated category. He was an enthusiastic Philadelphia Eagles football fan, some may believe just a little too enthusiastic. In November 2008 he was arrested for running onto the field during a Philadelphia Eagles football game. Before judging him too harshly, consider his calling that day. Noteboom ran onto the field with a plastic bag under his right arm that contained the ashes of his recently deceased mother who herself was a long time Eagles fan. When Noteboom reached the 30-yard line, he dropped to his knees, made the sign of the cross, and lay on his stomach. Now that's a fan and a good son![3]

Before you cast aspersions on Noteboom, consider the following comments that appeared in the *New York Times* in 1895 concerning Americans' infatuation with sports:

> Is there not a certain defect of gayety in contemporary sport? We Americans seem nowadays to take ours excessively hard. We take some of our soberer matters very easily. We giggle over heresy trials, and have endless patience for the shortcomings of politicians, but we hold our breath over the reports of football games and yacht races, and lose our sleep over intricacies in the management of those events. We worried nearly as much last September over the international yacht races as our fathers did a generation ago over Mason and Slidell and the affair of the Trent.[4]

Many issues are present in sports as ethical, business, and legal issues abound in both professional and amateur sports. Race and ethnicity are at the forefront of social issues in sports. Whether it is the NFL's Rooney Rule or the use of Native American mascots by universities, race and ethnicity are significant topics in any discussion of sports ethics. Other issues such as drug testing, athletic eligibility, gender equity, intellectual property rights, and violence in sports all present serious issues for an intellectual debate on sports ethics. U.S. collegiate sports are fraught with ethical issues ranging from the illegal payment of student-athletes to agent regulation, low student-athlete graduation rates, and violence.[5]

---

[1] *See Forbes.com*; "Analyzing Salaries for Football Bowl Subdivision Coaches," *USA Today*, November 10, 2009.

[2] Matthew Futterman, "Under Pressure," *The Wall Street Journal*, October 4, 2008.

[3] "Bad Sports: A Study Conducted by the University of Missouri-St. Louis," *Pittsburgh Post-Gazette*, November 29, 2005.

[4] "We Take Our Sports Too Seriously: While Soberer Matters Are Treated with Unbecoming Levity," *New York Times*, November 5, 1895.

[5] Rick Telander, *The Hundred Yard Lie: The Corruption of College Football and What We Can Do to Stop It* (Chicago: University of Illinois Press, 1989); Murray Sperber, *Beer and Circus: How Big-Time College Sports Is Crippling Undergraduate Education* (New York: Holt Paperbacks, 2001); Hela Sheth and Kathy M. Babiak, "Beyond the Game: Perceptions and Practices of Corporate Social Responsibility in the Professional Sport Industry," *Journal of Business Ethics*, 91, no. 3 (2010), 433–450.

Why Study Sports Ethics?

Some may ask, "Why study sports ethics?" Is there a specific discipline of sports ethics as there is for business, legal, or medical ethics? Many think so. A good deal of scholarship has been produced on the subject of sports ethics.[6] Several noted scholars have been appointed sports ethics fellows, and universities have created centers for the study of sports ethics.[7] Is there a practical reason for studying sports ethics? Some think not and argue that sports ethicists should stick to what they know best—sports. "If we have to have ethics at all in sports, let's make sure those moral philosophers explore the right issues. Should Pete Rose wear his Phillies or Reds cap to the Hall of Fame? Was O. J. Simpson the greatest running back in history?"[8]

For the sports management professional (SMP), there is a clear advantage to the study of sports ethics coupled with a study of management and law. Sports executives need to have a solid grasp of the ethical decision-making process to perform their duties honestly, professionally, and ethically. Whether that individual is an athletic director, coach, general manager, business owner, agent, or sports executive, all must deal with significant ethical and legal concepts prevalent in sports.

Sports morality and ethics were much debated topics, even in the early years of the 20th century.[9] All-pro defensive end Bill Glass wrote a book in the late 1960s titled *Don't Blame the Game*, with chapter titles including "Win at Any Cost," "Booze Makes It Better, "Trainers Are Junkies," and "Racism Is Everywhere." An excerpt from the book stated: "You know the type, 'Broadway' Joe, Dave Meggyesy, Bernie Parrish, Jim Bouton—a handful of professional athletes whose escapades on and off the field have cast a shadow across the entire sport world." Yet Bill Glass says the "swingers" are really not representative of the majority of professional sport personalities.[10] It does not sound like Glass did himself any favors by naming specific players. One wonders what Glass thinks of today's sports world.

This book contains numerous cases and case studies in which ethics and morality come into play in sports. For a quick overview of some of the issues involved, consider the following scenarios and the types of ethical and moral decision making processes that may be required of the sports management professional.

1. NBA player Gilbert Arenas said he faked an injury in a preseason game to allow a teammate to get more playing time.[11]
2. NFL Houston Texans team owner Bob McNair ordered his team's staff to search the players' locker room to make sure they were not using any banned substances.[12]

---

[6] See Robert L. Simon, *Fair Play: The Ethics of Sport* (Boulder, CO: Westview Press, 2003); Claudio Tamburrini, *Values in Sport: Elitism, Nationalism, Gender Equality and the Scientific Manufacturing of Winners (Ethics and Sport)* (New York: Taylor & Francis, 2000); William J. Morgan, *Ethics in Sport* (Champaign, IL: Human Kinetics, 2007); Tommy Boone, *Basic Issues in Sports Ethics: The Many Ways of Cheating* (Lewiston, NY: Edwin Mellen Press, 2009).

[7] "Institute for International Sport and Positive Coaching Alliance Announce 2010 Sports Ethics Fellows," March 31, 2010; Centers include the *Center for Sports and Citizenship*, The Ohio State University; *Institute for Diversity and Ethics in Sport*, University of Central Florida, Director Richard Lapchick; Also, *Center for Sports, Ethics, and Culture*, Ball State University.

[8] Robert Lipsyte, "The Sports Ethicists Come Out in Force: Let's Ignore Them, O.K.?," *New York Times*, March 19, 2000, SP13.

[9] Sol Metzger, "Sport Ethics Grow Cleaner at 4 Colleges," *Chicago Daily Tribune*, January 2, 1916, B4; Bernie Lincicome, "From Nero Down, Sports Cheaters Are Rife," *Denver Rocky Mountain News*, September 19, 2007.

[10] "Bill Glass Answers the Sport World Swingers in *Don't Blame the Game*," *Chicago Tribune*, January 21, 1973, F6.

[11] "Gilbert Arenas Says He Faked Injury," *ESPN.com*, October 12, 2010.

[12] Associated Press, "Texans Searched Locker Room," *ESPN.com*, October 29, 2010.

3. The University of Mississippi's new mascot, the "Rebel Black Bear," replaced its former mascot, "Colonel Reb."[13]
4. In 2010 the Bahrain national soccer team beat Togo's national team 3–0, or at least they said they were the Togo team. However, Togo fans should not worry because the team that was shut out was a fake team organized by someone to "pocket" money from the event.[14]
5. In November 2008, Grapevine Faith, a small Christian school in Dallas, played a football game against Gatesville, a state school at a maximum-security correctional facility for male teenage felons. The Gatesville players were required to travel in handcuffs. Grapevine's coach, Kris Hogan, split his school's fans and cheerleaders into two groups with one group cheering for Gatesville. One Gatesville player said, "Lord, I don't know how this happened, so I don't know how to say thank you, but I never would've known there was so many people in the world that cared about us."[15]
6. A drunk adult Cleveland Browns fan tackled an 8-year-old New York Jets fan after a game between the two teams.[16]
7. After dropping a sure touchdown pass in an NFL game, wide receiver Stevie Johnson posted on his Twitter account a message wondering how God could allow him to drop the pass:[17] "I PRAISE YOU 24/7!!!!!! AND THIS HOW YOU DO ME!!!!! YOU EXPECT ME TO LEARN FROM THIS??? HOW???!!! ILL NEVER FORGET THIS!! EVER!!! THX THO"
8. In 2010 the LPGA voted to amend its constitution to allow transgendered players to participate.[18]
9. In 2009 Sheffield United sued West Ham, and the two settled a lawsuit for $30 million. West Ham had used ineligible players, thereby cheating during the 2007 season, and Sheffield United claimed they were the victims. West Ham player Carlos Teves scored a goal in the final match of the year against Manchester United, causing Sheffield to drop from England's top division, the Premier League.[19]
10. New York Yankees shortstop Derek Jeter faked that he was hit with a ball to get on base.[20]
11. New York Governor David Paterson was called before an administrative law judge to determine whether he violated ethics laws when he was able to secure tickets to the first game of the 2009 World Series at Yankee Stadium.[21]
12. NBA player Ron Artest announced he would donate "either all or some" of his 2011–2012 salary to charity.[22]

---

[13] Sandra Knispel, "University of Mississippi Introduces New Mascot," www.npr.org, October 15, 2010.
[14] David Gauthier-Villars, "When Togo Played Bahrain, the Whole Match Was a Fake: Taking the Field as African Nation's Team, Impostors Lose Game but Net Fees," *Wall Street Journal*, October 4, 2010.
[15] Joe Lemire, "The Decade in Sportsmanship," *Sports Illustrated*, December 22, 2009.
[16] Rich Cimini, "Report: Young Jets Fan Roughed Up," *ESPN.com*, November 17, 2010.
[17] Associated Press, "Bills Stand Behind WR Stevie Johnson," *Espn.com*, November 29, 2010.
[18] Ryan Ballengee, "LPGA Votes to Amend Constitution to Allow Transgender Players," *NBC Sports*, November 20, 2010.
[19] "Can Rule-Abiding Players Sue Alleged Cheaters? English Soccer Squabble May Hold the Answers," *ctsportslaw.com*, March 18, 2009.
[20] "The Jeter School of Acting," *Sports Illustrated*, September 16, 2009.
[21] "Paterson Won't Attend Ethics Hearing on Yankees Tickets," *Wall Street Journal*, August 16, 2010. The governor was fined $62,125. David M. Halbfinger, "Paterson Fined $62,125 over World Series Tickets," *New York Times*, December 20, 2010.
[22] Dave McMenamin, "Ron Artest to Donate 2011–12 Salary," *ESPN.com*, December 8, 2010.

13. The MCC World Cricket committee contemplates using lie-detector tests to fight corruption.[23]
14. NBA star Kobe Bryant's endorsement deal with Turkish Airlines caused an uproar with the Los Angeles Armenian community.[24]
15. The NFL banned the "Captain Morgan" (producer of rum) end zone celebration after Eagles tight end Brent Celek performed it on a Sunday night telecast after catching a touchdown pass. The Captain Morgan Rum Company had intended to offer charity contributions each time a player was caught on camera striking the "Captain Morgan" pose.[25]
16. A high school wrestler was charged with sexual assault after performing a novel move called the "butt drag" on a teammate during a practice.[26]
17. In 1982 with the game between the NFL Patriots and Dolphins tied at 0–0, the Patriots coach ordered snowplow operator Mark Henderson to clear a spot for the New England kicker. The 33-yard field goal was good and the Patriots won 3–0. Dolphins coach Don Shula called the NFL commissioner and said "it was the most unfair act that had ever happened in a football game."[27] Henderson, a convicted felon, was on a work release program at the time of the game. He received a game ball from the Patriots.
18. In 2010, five student-athletes at Ohio State University violated NCAA rules by selling championship rings, game gear, and personal awards for cash. They were not suspended by the NCAA for the Sugar Bowl but instead were suspended for the first five games of the 2011 season.[28]
19. After a game between the Dallas Cowboys and the Philadelphia Eagles, Cowboys running back Tashard Choice asked Eagles quarterback Michael Vick to sign a glove for a family member who was a big fan of Vick's. Choice said, "I don't want anybody to think I was disrespectful. . . . My teammates, coaches, and Jerry [Jones] know where my heart is. I care about football. I meant no disrespect."[29]
20. Six-year-old Kennedy Tesch was tossed off the flag football cheerleading squad when her parents objected to the cheer "Our backs ache, our skirts are too tight, we shake our booties from left to right." Her parents thought the cheer was inappropriate for 6-year-old girls. After a team meeting, other parents voted to kick Kennedy off the squad because of her parents' objections.[30]

Ethical Reasoning and Ethical Models

Any individual faced with an ethical or moral decision must make that decision based on certain guiding principles.[31] How are ethical decisions to be made? Which guiding principles should be

---

[23] "Cricket Chiefs Consider Lie-Detectors to Fight Corruption," *CNN.com*, December 15, 2010.
[24] "Report: Kobe Endorsement Causes Flap," *FoxSports.com*, December 15, 2010.
[25] Charles Robinson, "NFL Shipwrecks Captain Morgan Campaign," *Yahoo! Sports*, November 12, 2009.
[26] Jesse McKinley, "Wrestler Sees Legal Move; Prosecutor Sees Assault," *New York Times*, December 18, 2010.
[27] Mike Reiss, "'Snowplow Game' Still Stings Shula," *ESPN.com*, January 28, 2010.
[28] "Bowl CEO Wanted Buckeyes Eligible," *FoxSports.com*, December 29, 2010; Pat Forde, "NCAA Ruling Defies Common Sense," *ESPN.com*, December 23, 2010.
[29] Tim MacMahon, "Michael Vick Signs Cowboys RB's Glove," *ESPN.com*, December 12, 2010.
[30] Joshua Rhett Miller, "Girl, 6, Removed from Cheerleading Team After Parents Object to 'Booty' Cheer," *Fox News*, September 15, 2010.
[31] Ronald C. Arnett and Clifford Christians, *Dialogic Confession: Bonheoffer's Rhetoric of Responsibility* (Carbondale, IL: Southern Illinois University Press, 2005); Dietrich Bonheoffer, *Letters & Papers from Prison* (New York: Touchstone, 1997).

employed in the decision making process? Should individuals merely do what they believe is right? Should individuals employ the "Golden Rule"—"Do unto others as you would have them do unto you."—in all decisions and in their conduct when dealing with others? Are there any guiding religious principles that should affect the choices made by the decision maker? Should an ethical decision maker be concerned solely with what is legal and discard all other relevant principles, or should other factors come into play? Can an action be considered legal but be immoral? These are all tough questions that must be addressed.

In this chapter we discuss how ethical standards serve as the basis for sports ethics. This topic is a fundamental introduction for encouraging an environment that highlights the essence of sports: fair play, character development, and excellence. Sports, just as any other endeavor, places much emphasis on rules and regulations.

Ethics is considered to be a branch of philosophy because it is concerned with what is morally right and wrong. The challenge lies in finding the standard by which we determine what is right and wrong. The philosophy of ethics is intimately connected with metaphysics, specifically with ontology, or the study of being. Where do we come from? Why are we here? What is our purpose? How do we determine a standard of right and wrong? What universal ideas do we embrace that help us make sense out of particular situations that we face in life? The following diagram illustrates this idea:

$$\frac{U}{P} = \frac{\text{Universal (or Upper Story)}}{\text{Particular (or Lower Story)}}$$

As we make choices in the day-to-day situations that we face (or particulars), why do we make these choices and not others?[32]

Ethical theories are divided into three general subject areas: metaethics, normative ethics, and applied ethics.[33] Metaethics examines the origins of theoretical concepts and notions and what they mean. Are ethics merely a social invention? Are they more than expressions of our individual emotions? The answers to these types of questions focus on issues of universal truth, God's will, the role reason plays in ethical decision making, and in defining ethical terms themselves.

Normative ethics takes on a more practical task. In normative ethics the inquiry is to determine what moral standards regulate right and wrong conduct and behavior.[34] This search for the ideal litmus test for proper conduct focuses on the duties and rules individuals should follow or the consequences that behavior or conduct has on other individuals. An example of normative ethics is the Golden Rule. What systems or ideas are put forth to guide an individual's conduct and assist him or her in determining right from wrong? Subfields include deontological theories, (duty) consequential theories, evolutionary ethics, and virtue theories.[35]

Applied ethics examines specific, unresolved, controversial issues such as environmental concerns, social inequality, capital punishment, abortion, and racial discrimination.

Distinguishing between metaethics, normative ethics, and applied ethics can be a difficult task. In metaethics it is argued that God or a form of Supreme Being, provides the foundation of all ethical

---

[32] "Five Steps of Principled Reasoning," *An Ethical Decision-Making Model* (Los Angeles, CA: Josephson Institute, 1999).

[33] Steven M. Cahn and Peter Markie, *Ethics: History, Theory, and Contemporary Issues*, 4th ed. (New York: Oxford University Press, 2008).

[34] Tara Smith, *Ayn Rand's Normative Ethics: The Virtuous Egoist* (New York: Cambridge University Press, 2006).

[35] Michael Ruse, "Evolutionary Theory and Christian Ethics: Are They in Harmony?" *Journal of Religion & Science* 29, no. 1 (1994): 5–24.

decision making. In normative ethics it is argued that the foundation for ethical thought and decision making originates from agreements between individuals, from duty or virtue, or from consideration of the consequences of various actions on individuals or groups. In applied ethics controversial issues such as capital punishment, stem cell research, gun ownership, and personal control over end-of-life are addressed.

Normative principles that can be applied uniformly, that are not too narrowly focused, and that take into account varying points of view include the following:

- *Benevolence*: assisting those in need.
- *Honesty*: not deceiving or lying to others.
- *Autonomy*: acknowledging an individual's bodily freedom.
- *Justice*: honoring an individual's right to due process and to live in a fair and just society.
- *Paternalism*: assisting others to achieve what is in their best interests when they are unable to do so.
- *Harm*: do no harm to others.
- *Social benefit*: acknowledging that certain actions are beneficial to society as a whole.
- *Rights*: acknowledging an individual's right to autonomy, privacy, free expression, and personal safety.
- *Lawfulness*: understanding that the rule of law benefits individuals and society as a whole.

These traditional normative principles are derived from several ethical approaches and can be applied to almost every ethical dilemma.

Sports ethics is concerned with what is the right thing to do in sports for all those involved.[36] One aspect of sports ethics addresses how individuals and teams conduct themselves when competing or preparing to compete in sporting events.[37] In this case, the major concern is competing hard, yet doing so in the right way. In youth sports, the goal is character development, and ethical concerns center on working hard, honor, team work, diligence, courage, and self-discipline. In competitive sports, including professional sports, the goal is to win through effort and excellence rather than by cheating. This is more a personal ethical matter, but there can be strong influences from others including coaches, teammates, friends, family, and fans.

The business aspect of sports applies to youth league organizations as well as to professional sports. How do organizations manage their sports programs and sporting events? Is the sports organization as a whole following ethical guidelines and making ethical decisions? This is where sports ethics intersects with business ethics. Corporations face increasing competition in a rapidly changing global economy, and with that change comes more pressure to develop unethical ways to compete. Many times this pressure leads to the notion that "business is business" and an "anything goes" attitude.[38] Unfortunately, this same mind-set can sometimes be found in the sports world. Individuals and teams often face increased competition and, like corporations, the challenges and pressures can come from several entities including government, sports governing organizations, agents, fans, parents, coaches, other athletes, and other clubs.

---

[36] Mike McNamee, "Sports, Ethics and Philosophy; Context, History, Prospects," *Sports, Ethics and Philosophy* 1, no. 1 (2007).

[37] J. Brent Crouch, "Gender, Sports, and the Ethics of Teammates: Toward an Outline of a Philosophy of Sport in the American Grain," *Journal of Speculative Philosophy, New Series* 23, no. 2 (2009): 118–127.

[38] See, generally, Laura Hartman, *Perspectives in Business Ethics*, 3d ed. (New York: McGraw-Hill, 2004).

To change this mind-set, organizations must understand the long-term benefits of ethics to individual, team, and organizational success. It is easy to believe that it is necessary to cut corners ethically to succeed in sports. Everyone connected with sports must realize that this reflects a short-term view of success that often ignores the potential for long-term consequences. Unethical viewpoints and conduct must be replaced by the realization that sound ethical principles are good for sports and for the individuals and clubs participating in sports.

The key to sports is competitive cohesion. The nexus between athletes and fans should be collaborative as opposed to adversarial. There are many examples of both the collaborative model and the adversarial model. In the collaborative model, athletes play with sportsmanship and enthusiasm while at the same time showing respect for fans, management, opposing players, and referees. For example, an outfielder practicing before the game will throw the last ball to a young fan. In the collaborative model, professional athletes visit hospitals and chat with sick children at every opportunity. In the collaborative model, fans respect the athlete's privacy and do not use profane, rude, or disrespectful language. The ethical fan appreciates the time and energy the athlete spends in pursuing goodwill. Conversely, the adversarial model is typified by the spoiled athlete and the obnoxious fan. The athlete will not readily sign autographs—he or she will seek the adversarial motif. The obnoxious fan will taunt the athlete, drink to excess, and "pester" the athlete, not respecting his or her privacy.

The standard between athletes and fans should be one of collaborative ethics. All parties involved in sports should collaborate to maintain the integrity of the sport and the greater glory, pride, and self-esteem of the team, city, or country. The inherent value of a sports contest is its capacity to produce in the participants and the fans a quality of experience that is evaluated as good in itself.

CHEATING

Defining Cheating and Fairness

Cheating would seem to be a rather simple concept to define but that is not always the case. Before a determination can be made whether an individual is a cheater or acting unethically, a definition of cheating must be established. The *American Heritage Dictionary* defines cheating as follows:

> to cheat is to deprive of something valuable by the use of deceit or fraud; to influence or lead by deceit, trick, or artifice; to elude or thwart by or as if by outwitting; to practice fraud or trickery; to violate rules dishonestly; to be sexually unfaithful; or to position oneself defensively near a particular area in anticipation of a play in that area.[39]

Some propositions are universal. For instance, all would agree that stealing is morally wrong, correct? However, what if an individual is stealing food to feed his or her family? Would their actions then be considered unethical or "wrong" even though it is against the law or violating another person's rights? Sometimes it is not easy to define a wrong that has been done or to claim that someone has cheated. Is killing a person always against the law or immoral? What about an individual's right to self-defense or a state that enforces the death penalty? Would everyone agree that cheating on one's spouse is always immoral? Is telling a lie always wrong? Is just a little cheating allowable

---

[39] *American Heritage Dictionary, New College Edition* (Boston, MA: Houghton Mifflin, 1976).

as long as it does not hurt anyone? Can fairness or cheating be objectively defined, or is it left to the subjective perception of each individual?

Some have argued for a universal concept of fairness, that all individuals should recognize and employ. Noted Scholar C. S. Lewis described it as follows:

> [Men appeal] to some kind of standard of behavior which he expects [other men] to know about and [other men] very seldom [reply]: 'To hell with your standard.' It looks, in fact, very much as if [all men have] in mind some kind of Law or Rule of fair play or decent behavior or morality or whatever you like to call it, about which they really agreed. And they have. If they had not, they might, of course, fight like animals, but they could not quarrel in the human sense of the word. Quarreling means trying to show that the other man is in the wrong. And there would be no sense in trying to do that unless you and he had some sort of agreement as to what Right and Wrong are; just as there would be no sense in saying that a footballer had committed a foul unless there was some agreement about the rules of football.[40]

A Cheating Culture

It seems the headlines and the Internet are packed with "serial cheaters" and unethical people engaging in a myriad of acts in a variety of industries; business, education, religion, and, yes, even sports. This is not to say that there are not honest people, for there are many. For example, Jerry Mika returned a check in the amount of $2,245,342 that was sent to him in error by the state of Utah.[41] Notwithstanding Mika's ethical actions, in the last 10 years the United States has been fraught with financial scandals of gigantic proportions. Bernard Madoff defrauded numerous investors for hundreds of millions of dollars through fraudulent investment schemes. His investors included actor Kevin Bacon and Hall of Fame baseball player Sandy Koufax. Enron was the largest corporate scandal in U.S. history, causing thousands of people to lose their jobs and many their entire retirement income. Kenneth L. Lay was the CEO of Enron and went to prison. Prior to his prison career, he donated $1.2 million to the University of Missouri to endow the Kenneth L. Lay Chair in International Economics. Tyco CEO Dennis Kozlowski was sentenced to 30 years in prison for his part in the Tyco financial scandal. John Bogle, founder and former chief executive of the Vanguard Group of Mutual Funds, has argued that to combat unethical behavior, a "fiduciary society" must be established that places the interests of clients above your own interests.[42]

Cheating in colleges and universities is on the rise as well.[43] Many students cheat because they see others doing it and want to "level the playing field." Others do it out of ignorance or just because they are lazy. Plagiarism, for instance, is not always well understood by college students. Students have found creative ways to cheat in the technological age, with text messaging answers and "googling" during exams becoming increasingly common.[44] Some of the nation's top business

[40] C. S. Lewis, *Mere Christianity* (New York: HarperCollins, 1952), 3–4.

[41] Tonya Papanikolas, "Man Mistakenly Given More than $2 Million," *KSL.com*, November 21, 2007.

[42] Laura Sullivan, "Madoff Likely Won't Be Serving Time in 'Club Fed,'" *www.npr.org*, July 2, 2009; "The Kenneth L. Lay Chair in Business Ethics?" *Wall Street Journal*, May 31, 2006; "Ex-Tyco Officers Sentenced," *The Washington Post*, September 20, 2005; Vanessa O'Connell, "Test for Dwindling Retail Jobs Spawns a Culture of Cheating," *Wall Street Journal*, January 7, 2009.

[43] "Cheating in College is Widespread—But Why?" *www.npr.org*, July 19, 2010.

[44] Ellen Gamerman, "Legalized 'Cheating,'" *Wall Street Journal*, January 21, 2006.

schools now require a high-tech identity scan for standardized admissions tests to prevent cheating.[45] In 2007 Duke business students faced discipline charges in the largest undergraduate cheating scandal in the school's history.[46] The list of ethical and criminal violations of politicians is long as well, but a few are worth mentioning: President Richard M. Nixon (R) ("high crimes and misdemeanors"), President William J. Clinton (D) (lying under oath), and Charlie Rangel (D) (censured by U.S. House of Representatives for failure to pay taxes).[47]

Exaggerating one's accomplishments on a resume may be commonplace, but some individuals have been caught in a "bold-face" lie. The president of the United States Olympic Committee (USOC) was forced to resign in 2002 after it was discovered that she lied about her academic credentials.[48] George O'Leary had waited a lifetime to coach the "Fighting Irish" of Notre Dame but was forced to resign 5 days after he was hired when it was discovered that he had lied on his resume. O'Leary claimed to have a master's degree in education and to have played 3 years of college football, both of which were false. O'Leary later explained, "Many years ago, as a young married father, I sought to pursue my dream as a football coach. . . . In seeking employment I prepared a resume that contained inaccuracies regarding my completion of course work for a master's degree and also my level of participation in football at my alma mater. These misstatements were never stricken from my resume or biographical sketch in later years."[49] When looking for a job, experts still think "honesty is the best policy."[50] Why do people lie in such a bold fashion? Each seems to have specific reasons. People even have lied about the most honorable things possible. Actor Brian Dennehy had claimed for years that he had served a 5-year tour in Vietnam. In reality the closest he ever came to Vietnam was playing football in Okinawa in 1962.[51] Ironically, Dennehy starred in *Rambo*, with actor Sylvester Stallone.

Cheating in one's private life can affect other people and business interests as well. Some people have trouble telling the difference between reality and real life and need a "reality check." Such is the case with Ric Hoogestraat, who had an online relationship in a virtual world with a woman of his own choosing, who was, of course, not real. Some people may not consider it technically cheating, but his wife certainly did: "It's really devastating . . . you try to talk to someone or bring them a drink, and they'll be having sex with a cartoon."[52]

Cheating in one's personal life can translate to lost income, and that can certainly occur if you are a world-class athlete. No "cheater" has gotten more play in the headlines in the last few years than

---

[45] John Hechinger, "Business Schools Try Palm Scans to Finger Cheats," *Wall Street Journal*, July 22, 2008.

[46] Alan Finder, "34 Duke Business Students Face Discipline for Cheating," *New York Times*, May 1, 2007; Len Boselovic, "Study Suggests Cheating 101 More Prevalent at Business Schools," *Pittsburgh Post-Gazette*, October 1, 2006. For a list of college cheating scandals, see Ethan Trex, "Seven College Cheating Scandals," *Wall Street Journal*, May 15, 2009.

[47] Also see Brad Parks, "Poison Ivy in the Garden State," *Wall Street Journal*, July 25, 2009.

[48] "U.S. Olympic Chief Resigns in Resume Scandal," *CNN*, May 24, 2002.

[49] "Short Tenure: O'Leary Out at Notre Dame After One Week," *SI.com*, December 14, 2001.

[50] "In Job Hunting, Honesty Is Still the Best Policy," *Wall Street Journal*, April 25, 2010; Associated Press, "Lying on Resume Simply Isn't Worth the Risk: Common Falsehoods Are Overstating Education, Previous Responsibilities," *MSNBC.com*, June 7, 2006.

[51] Nicholas Ehrenberg, "Fake War Stories Exposed: Phony Soldiers Bring Shame to Military Forces," *CBSNews.com*, November 13, 2005.

[52] Alexandra Alter, "Is This Man Cheating on His Wife?" *Wall Street Journal*, August 10, 2007; Naomi Schaefer Riley, "The Young and the Restless: Why Infidelity Is Rising Among 20-Somethings," *Wall Street Journal*, November 28, 2008.

PGA golfer Tiger Woods. Woods's infidelities were splashed across world headlines when his conduct was exposed. It should be noted that Woods is not alone in his cheating confessions, but because he is one of the most famous people in the world, it was considered newsworthy. Woods's personal conduct issues cost him severely. His celebrity endorsements decreased an estimated $22 million in 2010. Most celebrity and athlete endorsement contracts contain moral clauses. After the Woods' scandal, insurers were inundated with inquiries from corporations anxious to protect their corporate name and brands. Dan Trueman, head of the enterprise risk department at R. J. Kiln and Company, the managing agent for Lloyds, said, "Tiger Woods has made people think about their reputations. These days, people don't worry about the office burning down, but about their intellectual property being damaged." The stock price of seven publicly held companies that had dealt with Woods lost approximately $12 billion in market value the months after Woods announced he was taking a break from golf.[53] In 2000, actor Michael Douglas reportedly signed a prenuptial agreement that included a $5 million "straying fee" should he have sexual relations with someone other than his wife, Catherine Zeta Jones.[54] There is no doubt that in some cases personal unethical behavior affects others and also has a direct effect on business.

Consider the following scenarios. Should these people be deemed cheaters, or unethical?

CASE STUDY 1-1 *Hand of God*

Footballer Diego Maradona now admits he struck the ball with his hand when scoring the most controversial goal in the history of soccer in the 1986 World Cup quarterfinals. Football rules prohibit such a move. It appeared that Maradona actually punched the ball into the net. His opponents protested but to no avail. Maradona thought the goal most likely would be waived off but it was not.

Should his admission that he failed to play by the rules produce a forfeit?[55]

CASE STUDY 1-2 *The Spitter and Me*

Gaylord Perry was a good baseball pitcher. He was an expert at "doctoring" a baseball, or was he? Did he just make batters think he was throwing a "spitball"? Over his career Perry was noted for applying a variety of foreign substances to the ball, including Vaseline, baby oil, hair tonic, spit, and a few other substances that were unknown even to Perry. Perry is in the baseball Hall of Fame and has been called baseball's most notorious cheater. He won two Cy Young awards and went to five All-Star games. Perry once stated, "When my wife was having babies the doctor would send over all kinds of stuff and I'd try that too. Once I even used fishing line oil." The title of his biography is *Me and the Spitter.*[56]

---

[53] Reed Albergotti, "How Tiger's Top Man Is Managing the Crisis," *Wall Street Journal*, December 7, 2009; "Tiger's Endorsements Down Estimated $22 Million," *Washington Street Journal*, July 21, 2010; "Sports Players Facing Moral Clauses in Contracts," *Lawyers Weekly*, May 28, 2009; Ken Belson and Richard Sandomir, "Insuring Endorsements Against Athlete's Scandals," *New York Times*, February 1, 2010.

[54] Elise Nersesian, "Sex Addiction Real—Or Excuse for Cheating?" *MSNBC.com*, February 19, 2010.

[55] Associated Press, "Maradona Call Famous Goal 'Bit of Mischief,'" *ESPNsoccernet.com*, August 23, 2005.

[56] Derek Zumstag, "Perry Greased Batters with His Stuff," *ESPN.com*, May 16, 2002; Jack Curry, "In Perry's Book, a Brown Smudge Is Not a Black Mark," *New York Times*, October 24, 2006.

Cheating in sports is generally considered unethical; however, in baseball circles it is tolerated. Why is cheating in baseball accepted to a certain extent whereas other sports draw a very rigid line on cheating? If Perry did cheat (as he admitted), should he be treated any differently than a player who took performance-enhancing drugs?[57]

CASE STUDY 1-3   *"Creative Cheating"*

Mark Schlereth was an offensive lineman for the NFL Denver Broncos. To gain an advantage in a playoff game, he and his fellow linemen coated their arms and the backs of their jerseys with Vaseline. All the linemen were "slimey," and no one could grab onto them. The Broncos won the game 14–12. Schlereth stated, "Did I grease up my jersey, and use sticky substances on my gloves? You're damn right. . . . What you call cheating is a fine line. It's an interesting line. What we did, in the locker room, is called being creative. Certain cheating is snickered at, or applauded."[58]

1. Where should the line be drawn between strategy and blatant cheating?
2. Does the conduct in case study 1-3 rise to the level of unsportsmanlike conduct?

CASE STUDY 1-4   *Lottery Systems and Playing to Lose*

The National Football League Arizona Cardinals have had a horrible season. The Cardinals are 2–13 (post Kurt Warner era) going into the final game with Seattle, who are 9–6 and looking for a wild card spot. The Houston Texans are also 2–13 and are playing the 13–2 Bears, who need to win their final game to gain home field advantage in the playoffs. The Cardinals hold the tiebreaker with the Houston Texans, so if they both lose, the Cardinals will get the first draft pick. The number one draft pick is certainly going to be Joe Savage, a "can't miss" NFL quarterback who by all accounts will be a sure Hall of Famer. Early in the fourth quarter the Cardinals are beating the Seahawks 20–7 when the coach, at the request of the owner, inserts a rookie quarterback into the game who had never played in the NFL. The Cardinals lose 28–20 and get the first draft pick.

1. Should a team ever try to lose a game purposefully?
2. Does it tarnish the integrity of the game if they attempt to do so?
3. How do you view the actions of the Cardinals coaching staff or the owner?
4. Should all leagues adopt a lottery draft system to prevent any season ending shenanigans?[59]

Cheating in Sports

Cheating in sports is not a new phenomenon. Sports have a long and dubious history of cheaters. The first cheater in organized sports may have been Eupolus of Thessaly, a boxer in the Olympics of

---

[57] Derek Zumsteg, *The Cheater's Guide to Baseball* (Boston, MA: Houghton Mifflin, April 2007); Dave Krieger, "Integrity? In Baseball, It No Longer Exists," *Denver Rocky Mountain News*, February 17, 2007.

[58] Lance Pugmire, "Cheating in Sports: The Fine Art of Getting Away with It," *Los Angeles Times*, August 20, 2006.

[59] Associated Press, "Davis Denies Cavs Trying to Lose," *USA Today*, March 3, 2003; Tim Sullivan, "Don't Even Hint at Losing on Purpose," *San Diego Union-Tribune*, December 28, 2003.

388 BC, who allegedly bribed three of his opponents to "take dives."[60] National Public Radio put together a list of the most notorious cheaters in sports history:

- Chicago White Sox (gambling, 1919 World Series)
- City College of New York (point-shaving scandal)
- Paul Hornung and Alex Karras (alleged gambling in the NFL)
- Dancer's Image (drug scandal robbed *Dancer's Image* of 1968 *Kentucky Derby* Title)
- East German Athletes (steroids scandal)
- Pete Rose (gambling in baseball)
- Ben Johnson (steroid use in track and field)
- Danny Almonte (15-year-old playing Little League baseball)
- Floyd Landis (cycling doping scandal)
- Rick Tocchet (NHL gambling scandal)
- Tim Donaghy (NBA referee gambling)
- Bill Belichick (spying and espionage in the NFL)
- Marion Jones (track and field, performance-enhancing drugs)
- Barry Bonds (MLB, alleged use of performance-enhancing drugs)[61]

Can sports withstand the onslaught of cheating that seems to have taken over in the last few years?

Some cheating is quite obvious. For example, former Mexican presidential candidate Roberto Madrazo was declared the winner of a German marathon until it was determined that he took a shortcut.[62] Rosie Ruiz used some form of motorized vehicle in the Boston marathon and won by cheating; however, her title was later taken away.[63] Why do people cheat in sports? What is their motivation? Some of the reasons for the unethical behavior of athletes, owners, and coaches are:

- An overemphasis on winning, which fosters a "winning at all costs" attitude.
- Participants in the sports industry seek prestige or financial wealth.
- Athletes are pressured to perform at a higher level by coaches, universities, parents, and alumni.
- A lack of emphasis on sportsmanship and team work at the amateur levels.
- The lack of role models in sports, although many believe athletes should not serve as role models.
- The "commercialization" of sports participants at the collegiate level.
- A misplaced emphasis on the significance of sports in society in general.

Is too much emphasis placed on winning in sports? The answer to that question would have to be "yes" if you were Mathew Kowald. Kowald was charged with criminal disorderly conduct after

---

[60] Lance Pugmire, "The Fine Art of Getting Away With It," *Los Angeles Times*, August 20, 2006.

[61] Jeffrey Katz, "The Wide World of Sports Cheating," *www.npr.org*, January 15, 2008; Fran Zimniuch, *Crooked: A History of Cheating in Sports* (New York: Taylor Trade Publishing, 2009); Wayne Drehs, "Are Sports Heading Toward 'Major Crash' Because of Cheating?" *ESPN.com*, August 9, 2007.

[62] Associated Press, "Madrazo DQ's from Berlin Marathon for Taking Shortcut," *ESPN.com*, October 9, 2007.

[63] Sam Enriquez, "Marathoner Disqualified for Apparent Shortcut," *Los Angeles Times*, October 10, 2007; Amdur, Neal, "Who Is Rosie Ruiz?" *New York Times*, April 2, 1980.

his wife informed the police that Kowald had restrained his 7-year-old son for more than an hour during a Green Bay Packers playoff victory in 2008 because his son refused to wear a Packers jersey.[64]

With so much money at stake and big contracts available in professional sports, players have more of a "win at all costs attitude" and most owners want nothing less. However, should the same attitude prevail in a 5-year-old's t-ball league? Unfortunately sometimes it does. Is there too much emphasis placed on the significance of sports in society in general? Does this have an effect on the way amateur athletics are conducted? Consider the following scenario dealing with the number of games played in Little League baseball.

CASE STUDY 1-5   *Little League or Big League?*

A 12-year-old little leaguer may play as many as 40 baseball games in a season. How many games should a Little League team play? Should 12-year-olds attempt to play as many games as possible to improve their skill for the "next level"? Many leagues regulate how many "touches" a kid has in a week.[65] What is the rationale for limiting the number of games a little leaguer can play? What restrictions should be placed on Little League participants with regard to participation?

Many parents are beginning to realize that their child may be spending too much time participating in sports. As reported in the *Wall Street Journal*: "[The] escalating time, travel and financial demands of many competitive youth teams are pushing some parents over the edge. Many are pushing back, dropping teams mid-season, barring year-round competition for their children or refusing to make their kids available for holiday or vacation-time play."[66] Do you think youth sports in general place enough emphasis on sportsmanship instead of just focusing on winning?

Hayley Milbourn was a true sportsman in every sense of the word. Hayley was a senior at Poland Park (MD) County High School and was competing in the Maryland Golf Championship. She was a two-time champion of the event. When she completed the tournament, she discovered she had completed the round with someone else's golf ball by accident. No one knew except Hayley. She could have easily claimed another championship, but instead she turned herself in and was disqualified. Hayley said, "I just couldn't accept a trophy for something I didn't deserve."[67] That's true sportsmanship!

CASE STUDY 1-6   *Reggie Bush returns Heisman Trophy*

Reggie Bush was an outstanding football player at the University of Southern California. In September 2010 Bush voluntarily relinquished his 2005 Heisman Trophy, most likely giving the award back before the award was taken from him. The NCAA ruled Bush ineligible for the 2005 season after determining both he and his family had accepted money and gifts from sports agents while Bush was at USC. In the history of the Heisman no winner's trophy has ever been revoked or returned. Bush stated: "The persistent media speculation regarding allegations dating back to my years at USC has been both painful and distracting. In no way should

---

[64] "Father Jailed for Taping Jersey on Son: Boy, 7, Refused to Wear Packers Clothing Before Game," *SI.com*, January 17, 2008.

[65] Jennifer Alsever, "A New Competitive Sport: Grooming the Child Athlete," *New York Times*, June 25, 2006.

[66] Sue Shellenbarger, "Kids Quit the Team for More Family Time," *Wall Street Journal*, July 21, 2010.

[67] Drehs, "Are Sports Heading Toward 'Major Crash' Because of Cheating?", *ESPN.com*, August 9, 2007.

the storm around these allegations reflect in any way on the dignity of this award, nor on any other institutions or individuals."[68]

1. Do you consider Bush's actions honorable?
2. Under what circumstances should an athlete be required to forfeit the Heisman Trophy or any other award?

Should athletes be viewed as societal role models? Consider the following scenario.

CASE STUDY 1-7 *The Cinderella Man: A Real Role Model in Sports*

It is the enduring question: Are athletes role models? Sports has had its share of good and bad characters. Some modern players have exemplified good character, and some have not. The same can be said for past ballplayers. James J. Braddock, The Cinderella Man, was made famous when he was portrayed on Hollywood's big screen by actor Russell Crowe. Braddock led his family through tough times during the Great Depression and was forced to accept government welfare to survive. However, once he was back on his feet, he paid the government back the money he had received as Braddock had promised. Braddock was given a chance, and he capitalized on that chance, eventually beating Max Baer for the world heavyweight championship in 1935. Braddock worked as a longshoreman later in life and joined the Army during WWII. In 1954 he was presented with an award for his longtime service to boxing. It was said of the former champion in the *New York Times*:

> The former heavyweight champion is boxing's most illustrious advertisement, a vivid example of the wonderful things that the sport can do for one of its own. There's nothing new about his story, of course. It's indeed a surprise that Hollywood didn't reach for it long ago. But it would have to be presented in documentary style. As a fiction piece it just wouldn't click. It would be unbelievable.
>   Braddock was back in that same ring but this time he was meeting Baer for the world heavyweight championship. The Big Bad Baer was younger, bigger and more talented. He was favored at 10 to 1 over the dogged, indomitable Braddock. But Jim kept plugging away, left-hooking him to death, and all of a sudden he was the champion. Except for his force of character, Braddock was not a great champion. Judged on his character alone, however, he might have been the greatest. Scrupulously he paid back each debt, including every penny he'd received on relief. He wore his mantle with a natural dignity and his inner nobility glowed through.[69]

Braddock was clearly a role model as an athlete. He was hard working, honest, and fought his way to the top with determination and great skill. What should society expect of its athletes? Should they be role models for the younger generation? There are still role models in sports today. In 2009 former NFL quarterback Kurt Warner was named the NFL's best role model by his fellow players.[70]

Every team likes to have enthusiastic fans and they want these fans to be loud. Consider the effects of crowd noise on player performance in the following scenario.

CASE STUDY 1-8 *Crowd Noise*

The Indianapolis Colts and the New England Patriots are NFL rivals. During a November 2007 game between the two, there was a "conspicuous audio glitch, a repeating crowd-noise crescendo" that occurred on

---

[68] Bill Pennington, "Reggie Bush, Ineligible for '05, Returns Heisman," *The New York Times*, September 14, 2010.
[69] Arthur Daley, "The Cinderella Man," *New York Times, Sports of the Times*, January 14, 1954.
[70] "Which Active Player Is the Best Role Model on and off the Field?" *Sports Illustrated*, December 7, 2009; cf. Tom Weir, "Fans Still Love Their Sports, but Think Twice About Hero Worship," *USA Today*, February 26, 2010.

the first play of the fourth quarter on a 14-yard pass from Tom Brady to Randy Moss. Patriots president Jonathan Kraft asked the NFL Vice President of Security to determine whether the Colts were "piping artificial crowd noise into the dome." Those actions would be illegal under NFL rules. The league investigated the alleged infraction but ultimately attributed the noise to a CBS production problem.[71]

---

1. What is the purpose of the rule?
2. What should be done if a team is found to be in violation of such a rule?

Injuries are a part of every sport. A player must be in peak physical condition to perform at his or her best. Many players will play notwithstanding injuries. Consider the following case study dealing with NFL injury problems.

CASE STUDY 1-9   *Injury Lists*

NFL teams are required to submit to the league office a list of injured players for the next week's game. Under NFL rules, a player is listed as "probable" if he has a better than 50% chance of playing in the next week's game. Players who are listed as "questionable" by the club are 50–50, and "doubtful" means the player has a 75% chance or greater of not playing in the next game. "Out" means exactly that: the player will not play. The NFL has the authority to fine a team who fails to follow the NFL guidelines in reporting injuries. Since 1997 approximately 13 teams have been fined. Former Dallas Cowboys coach Jimmy Johnson stated, "If you want to be real technical about it you could list the majority of your team because in a sport as violent as pro football, nearly all players have something that's not 100%." Former Pittsburgh Steelers coach Bill Cower stated, "Sometimes when a guy had an ankle (injury), I might list it as a knee, just because I didn't want people knowing where to take shots at my players." Jimmy Johnson further stated, "Scanning injury reports rarely had an effect on our preparation, unless it's a key player like a quarterback, and even then, it's iffy." In September 2009 the NFL fined the New York Jets and former coach Eric Mangini $125,000 for violating league rules on reporting injuries for quarterback Brett Favre.[72]

---

1. What is the purpose of the NFL's injury reporting rules?
2. Are coach Cower's actions really protecting his players, or do you consider them a form of cheating?

ETHICAL DECISION MAKING AND THE SPORTS MANAGEMENT PROFESSIONAL

Introduction

A sports management professional faces many difficult situations in the workplace, especially in the employment context. Many times, he or she is required to deal with the human resources department to resolve difficult personnel issues. Disputes will arise in the workplace; that is a given. A part of the job for any SMP is to resolve disputes that may occur in the workplace. No company wants to end up in a lawsuit or in a dispute with an employee. An SMP must be able to bring to the workplace

---

[71] Associated Press, "NFL Blames CBS, not Colts, in Noise Dispute," *NBCSports.com*, November 5, 2007.
[72] Associated Press, "Tannenbaum Also Fined $25,000," *ESPN.com*, September 16, 2009.

a multitude of skills in dealing with employees. One of the most needed skills is that of dispute resolution or conflict management. A skilled professional must be able to resolve disputes fairly, quickly (if possible), and ethically.[73] The old adage "you can't please everyone" may be true, but a good-faith effort must be put forth to satisfy all the parties involved in any dispute. An SMP must be able to understand differing points of view and different cultures in an attempt to resolve any workplace disputes that may arise. Efforts to see another person's viewpoint and not favor one person over another are essential to the fair resolution of any employment dispute. Understanding another person's point of view, even though it may be different from your own, is an important skill the SMP must develop and implement to reflect an ethical decision making process.

One of the most important responsibilities of an SMP is to make the company successful. The SMP must be able to build morale, loyalty, and enthusiasm among employees. "Team loyalty" can be a valuable asset to a company. Making employees feel as though the company is on their side and understands their viewpoint is essential to employee morale. Granting every employee's wish is not realistic, and keeping the employee "happy" cannot always be achieved. However, individuals who enjoy their work will certainly be more productive. Everyone has experienced unfair treatment. Being treated unfairly in the employment context can lead to low employee morale, poor production on the job, "back-biting" between employees, and even lawsuits. Every SMP knows a lawsuit against the company is not a positive step, although some lawsuits cannot be avoided. SMPs must be able to interact with a diverse population of individuals in the workplace and make ethical decisions in the context of that diverse culture.

The sports business has become an extremely lucrative business. It is now clear, more than ever, that sports is a growing business. Major League Baseball's revenues in 2009 were approximately $6.6 billion. Mack Brown, the head football coach at the University of Texas, makes more than the president of the university and, for that matter, the president of the United States. All of those involved in sports— managers, executives, players, agents, sports officials, fans, and owners—face tough ethical decisions.

The discipline of business ethics applies to sports just as it applies to corporate America. The president of an NFL club, the general manager of a baseball team, and club personnel are all faced with ethical decisions in business on a daily basis. Corporate decision makers, including those in the sports industries, are faced with ethical issues relating to employees, fans, clients, and customers. Most SMPs think of themselves as ethical people, and it has been argued that being ethical in business is no different from being ethical in one's private life. Treating people with respect and dignity, being concerned for the welfare of others, and treating people like you want to be treated are all simple propositions that can and have been translated into the corporate culture by many successful companies. On a broader scale, high-level managers have responsibility for the creation and maintenance of an ethical corporate culture that protects against unethical and illegal conduct by employees and customers as well. Each person in a corporation occupies a specific role and has his or her own responsibilities. Whether it is the president of the club or the salesperson at the entrance to the ballpark, each is charged with a specific duty and must discharge that duty in a fair, reasonable, and ethical manner. Some positions may encounter more difficult problems, but ethical decisions must be made just the same, regardless of an individual's status, wage, or position within a company. Everyone at a company must be an ethical example to others.

Business activity takes place within an extensive framework of laws, and some hold the viewpoint that law is the set of rules that should apply in determining whether an activity or conduct is ethical. If it is legal, then it is by definition ethical. However, obtaining approval from a company's legal

---

[73] Lawrence Van Gelder, "On the Job: Conflict Resolution Made Simple," *New York Times*, March 25, 2001.

department does not always translate to the solution of a business problem in an ethical and fair manner. In a more practical sense, SMPs need to consider both the ethical and the legal aspects of a situation when making a decision. Not every immoral act may be considered illegal. For instance, taking credit for someone else's work (unless it constitutes plagiarism) is not necessarily illegal, but most people would agree that it is unethical.

Tough Calls for the Sports Management Professional

Race and Discrimination in the Workplace   Every corporate manager must make difficult decisions, and the same is true for the SMP. Consider the following case in which an employee was extremely offended, and rightly so, by some material distributed by his employer.

📖 CASE 1-1   *Brooks v. CBS Radio, Inc.*

342 Fed.Appx. 771; C.A.3 (Pa. 2009).

In September 2000, Shawn Brooks began working as an account executive for Infinity Broadcasting Corporation ("Infinity"), a corporation which is now named CBS Radio, Inc. ("CBS Radio"). In that position, Brooks sold advertising on radio station WYSP in connection with its broadcast of Philadelphia Eagles football games. Among the approximately twenty-five account executives at WYSP, Brooks was the only African American. Brooks's immediate supervisor was Joseph Zurzolo, the Eagles Radio Network's Sales Manager. Zurzolo was supervised by Peter Kleiner, WYSP's General Sales Manager, who was in turn supervised by Ken Stevens, WYSP's General Manager.

On May 9, 2001, Zurzolo held a sales meeting with the account executives for the Eagles Radio Network. During the meeting, Zurzolo distributed a book entitled *New Dress for Success* and stated, "Per human resources, use it." Zurzolo distributed the book, which was recommended to him by Jeffrey Snodgrass, WYSP's Sports Sales Manager, because he felt one of the account executives, a white female, was dressing too casually at work. Zurzolo did not read the book before distributing it.

After reading *New Dress for Success,* Brooks was offended by a number of the book's passages. On May 10, 2001, Brooks called Sandy Shields, WYSP's Business Manager and Human Resources Director, to complain about the book. Shields told Brooks that he had a right to be upset and that she would look into the matter. Shields contacted Stevens, who instructed her to collect all copies of the book that had been distributed to the station's employees. Shields then contacted Kleiner, and together they collected all copies of the book, except for Brooks's copy. Kleiner also verbally reprimanded Zurzolo for distributing

New Dress for Success without reading it first. One week after the book's distribution, Kleiner attended an Eagles Radio Network sales meeting and told the staff that the book did not represent the views of Infinity, himself, or Zurzolo, who had not read the book prior to its distribution. Brooks, who after the book's distribution returned to the office only once, on May 28, 2001, to submit a resignation letter and collect his personal items, was not present and did not know that Kleiner had addressed the staff regarding the book's distribution.

Specifically, Brooks was offended by . . . the following passages:

(i) "If you are black selling to white Middle America, dress like a white. . . . This clothing conveys that you are a member of the establishment and that you are pushing no radical or other feared ideas."

(ii) "Blacks selling to whites should not wear Afro hairstyles or any clothing that is African in association. If you are selling to corporate America, it's very important that you dress, not as well as the white salesman, but better than them. You have to wear suits, shirts and ties that are expensive and more conservative than your white co-workers."

(iii) "If you are white selling to blacks, you will fare much better if you dress in non-establishment patterns. Black America is essentially divided into two camps, establishment and anti-establishment, and the divisions are not dictated by income alone. . . . Almost all members of Northern ghettos who are in the lower socioeconomic groups are understandably antiestablishment. . . . The black establishment includes all blacks who have made it along with almost all Southern, rural blacks, no matter what their position. Southern blacks do not consider themselves disenfranchised. . . ."

(iv) "When selling to middle class blacks, you cannot dress like a ghetto black. . . ."

(v) "It is an undeniable fact that the typical upper-middle-class American looks white, Anglo-Saxon and Protestant. He is of medium build, fair complexion with almost no pronounced physical characteristics. He is the model of success; that is, if you run a test, most people of all socioeconomic, racial and ethnic backgrounds will identify with him as such."

(vi) "The two groups who have the most problems with their appearances are black men and Hispanic men. It is unfortunate but true that our society has conditioned us to look upon members of both groups as belonging to the lower classes, and no matter how high a minority individual rises in status or achievement, he is going to have some difficulty being identified by his success rather than his background. But clothing can help."

Following two additional telephone conversations with Shields on May 10 and May 11, 2001, Brooks felt Shields was not going to resolve the matter adequately. Although Zurzolo and Kleiner left several phone messages for Brooks asking him to call them, Brooks never communicated with any of his supervisors about the book's distribution because he did not trust them. Zurzolo had offended Brooks on a number of occasions prior to the book's distribution. Specifically, Brooks makes the following additional allegations, which CBS Radio does not dispute . . . . :

 (i) On one occasion, Zurzolo made a comment to Brooks about "having to go with [Brooks's] fiancée," a statement perceived by Brooks to mean that Zurzolo wanted to have sex with his fiancée.

 (ii) On several occasions, Zurzolo "palmed," or put his hand on, the head of an African-American receptionist, a gesture Brooks viewed as racially offensive.

(iii) On several occasions, Zurzolo used ethnic slurs, including "dago," in reference to himself.

 (iv) On one occasion, Zurzolo inappropriately touched an African-American receptionist while on a sales call.

 (v) On one occasion, someone stole a promotional banner relating to Brooks's ING Direct account, an act Brooks perceived as racially motivated.

Although Infinity had adopted a non-discrimination and anti-harassment policy that encouraged employees to report offensive conduct, Brooks did not tell anyone in the office about these incidents because he felt such conduct was tolerated and accepted.

> Infinity's policy stated that the corporation "will not tolerate any form of harassment on account of race" and that "[h]arassing conduct includes, but is not limited to[,] epithets, slurs or negative stereotyping; threatening, intimidating or hostile acts; denigrating jokes and display or circulation in the workplace of written or graphic material that denigrates or shows hostility or aversion toward an individual or group (including through e-mail)." The policy further instructed employees to "report their complaints to their immediate supervisor, their Department Head, their Station Manager, their Station's designated Ombudsperson, or the Human Resources Department *before* the conduct becomes severe or pervasive" and advised that "[i]ndividuals should not feel obligated to file their complaints with their immediate supervisor first before bringing the matter to the attention of one of the other Infinity designated representatives identified above."

On May 16, 2001, Brooks filed a complaint with the Pennsylvania Human Relations Commission ("PHRC") . . . alleging that Infinity had discriminated against him based on his race in violation of the Pennsylvania

```
Human Relations Act by (i) subjecting him to a hostile work environ-
ment and (ii) causing his constructive discharge. Brooks's administra-
tive complaint did not identify any allegation of harassment other
than the book's distribution.
```

Source: Reprinted from Westlaw with permission of Thomson Reuters.

The *Brooks* case started out with a rather innocent proposition. A WYSP sales manager thought a caucasian female account executive was dressing too casually for work, therefore "per human resources" he distributed a book to all account executives for the Eagles Radio Network without first reading the book. Companies are certainly within their right to require their employees to dress appropriately.

In light of the facts of the *Brooks* case, how should the following questions be answered?

1. How could the human resources department have assisted in resolving this problem?
2. What could have been done to prevent this dispute from getting "out of hand"?
3. Did the employer take the appropriate steps after discovering what happened? What else could they have done?
4. Should Zurzolo have been fired for his actions? Should Jeffrey Snodgrass have been fired?
5. If a company wants their employees to improve the way they dress, what is the appropriate and ethical action to take?
6. Should a company-wide memorandum have been issued apologizing for their actions? Is a corporate apology effective?
7. Do you consider the passage from the book racist or offensive? What about the portrayal of white America?
8. Do you find Brooks at fault for failing to report the alleged previous incidents of discrimination and harassment?
9. Should the actions of the company be viewed differently because they are a "sports related" company?

Sometimes even a simple mistake or stray remark, in this case distributing a book to employees without knowing its contents, can prove to be costly to a company. Part of a manager's job is to avoid placing the company at legal risk. An SMP must act ethically toward all its employees and treat each employee with respect and dignity, and that was not done in this situation. Brooks was the only African American among the 25 account executives, but shouldn't the other caucasian employees have been offended as well by the contents of the book? One of the reasons Brooks said he never communicated with any of his supervisors about the distribution of the book was because he did not trust them. Building employee trust is essential to employee morale and can curtail potential employee problems. An SMP must be able to build trust with his or her employees in order to establish an open line of communication to solve problems fairly quickly and ethically.

The Pennsylvania Human Relations Commission (PHRC) found that Brooks had been forced to quit his job (constructive discharge under the law), and that his workplace constituted a "hostile work environment." The commission awarded him $614,262 in economic damages. On appeal, the ruling was reversed in favor of the employer. Infinity eventually prevailed and a court found they did nothing wrong, but the company was forced to fight through an administrative process and two courts to prove their point. The legal fees to defend the case were astronomical. How could a lawsuit have been prevented in this situation? Do you agree that because Infinity did nothing wrong legally that they acted ethically under the circumstances? Do you chalk this situation up to an innocent mistake, negligence or unethical actions on behalf of the company and its employees? However it is viewed, it is certainly a regrettable situation and could easily have been avoided by someone at the company reading or previewing the book before distribution to its sales force.

Sports Participation and Eligibility   No decision in sports is bigger than one of eligibility. Deciding whether an athlete can participate is a tough decision to make. It can be a devastating blow to a student-athlete if they are ruled ineligible. In interscholastic sports (high school or youth sports), resolving a dispute with a sports participant often involves the parents of the participant and many times a lawyer. Consider the following case in which a 13-year-old girl's participation in sports was at issue. The *Baker* case presents some unique issues for the SMP. In this case, the school district was faced with the decision of having to potentially deny a visually impaired 13-year-old student-athlete the right to participate in sports, something she really enjoyed. In fact, when she was denied the opportunity to swim, her grades suffered. Her academic progress was clearly tied to her participation in sports. Needless to say, the decision to allow her to participate was an important one for her and her father.

📖 CASE 1-2 *Baker v. Farmingdale Union Free School District*

887 N.Y.S. 2d 776 (2009)

Joseph M. Baker, father . . . of Amanda Baker, applied to permit his thirteen-year-old daughter Amanda Baker to participate in swim team and track and field athletic activities conducted by the school district. This matter was sent down to determine whether it is in the best interest of Amanda Baker to participate in the respective athletic teams and that it is safe for her to do so.

Amanda Baker is 13 years old and is classified as visually impaired due to blindness caused by neurofibromatosis.

Despite her physical challenges, Amanda retains some degree of visual acuity. She has participated in swimming activities most of her life, including her successful involvement in the swimming activities offered during her seventh grade year. According to Mr. Baker, this is achieved, in part, because Amanda can distinguish color contrasts, such as those present at the bottom of a swimming pool, and can perceive and successfully employ the use of a kickboard positioned at the end of her swimming lane, allowing her to avoid collision with the swimming pool wall and to reverse direction in order to continue swimming. When swimming activities are conducted off school grounds, another individual accompanies her to help her avoid hazards.

Mr. Baker indicated that Amanda thoroughly values her participation in school swimming activities. When she was denied the opportunity to continue swimming, she suffered a strong emotional reaction which, according to Mr. Baker, precipitated a significant drop in her school grades.

Mr. Baker also stated that Amanda would like to participate in track and field programs offered by the school district. However, when questioned about how Amanda would be able to run or jump without hazarding herself or others given the limitations of her sight, Mr. Baker responded that a companion or guide would run with her during training and participation in the specific events. Beyond the presence of this companion or guide, no specific outline or plan was offered to insure Amanda's safety.

Given her nearly life-long experience with swimming and her successful participation in swimming events during her seventh grade academic year, Amanda has demonstrated that she has overcome whatever limitations her blindness may have imposed upon her, in regards to the sport of swimming. Her record of performance coupled with her keen desire to participate in the school district swimming events and the safeguards put in place by the presence of a companion or guide give reasonable assurance that it is in her best interest to participate in such swimming activities and that it is safe for her to do so.

Source: *Reprinted from Westlaw with permission of Thomson Reuters.*

How would you answer the following questions in light of the *Baker* case?

1. If you determine Amanda is not allowed to participate in sports, on what basis would you make that decision?
2. Would you exclude Amanda from both swimming and track and field? If so, on what basis?
3. Would you need an expert medical opinion to assist you in making the decision?
4. At what point would it be necessary to consult the school district lawyer?
5. Do you agree with the suggestion of Mr. Baker that a companion or guide could run with Amanda? What safety issues would that present?
6. How would you handle complaints from parents of other participants? You know they are coming!
7. What if Mr. Baker wanted to have his lawyer present at all meetings? Would you allow that? What if he wanted to tape record all the meetings?
8. Are the legal and ethical issues similar in the *Baker* case?
9. Would you require a medical examination of Amanda Baker before you make a decision regarding her participation? Some parents may find a medical examination intrusive or even abusive and may think their son or daughter is being "singled out."
10. If you are going to deny Amanda's application to participate, how would you inform her of the school's decision? Would you direct the correspondence to her father instead of Amanda?
11. How could you ensure fair and ethical treatment in whatever decision you make?
12. How would your personal beliefs affect your decision? What if you personally believed Amanda should be able to participate, but your boss told you "find a way to keep her out of sports, we can't take the risk"?
13. What legal liability issues does this case present for the school district? For Amanda?

14. If you did choose to allow Amanda to participate, would it be necessary to contact the liability insurer of the school district and inform them of Amanda's participation?
15. Would you make her or her father sign a release in case she was injured or others were injured as a result of her participation?
16. Would it be important to determine if Amanda was disabled as that is defined under disability law?

Telling someone they cannot participate or be part of a team is never an easy decision, especially if it is a 13-year-old visually-impaired girl who is being "singled out" because of her medical condition. The court decided to allow Amanda to participate in swimming but not in track and field because of safety issues. Was their decision fair to Amanda? What other school sports do you believe she could safely participate in?

Disability in Sports   The employment process can be difficult. Hiring managers and executives are faced with tough choices in the interviewing and hiring process. Making the proper ethical decision can ensure that the right employee is hired for the job and will stay and contribute to the company's success. Evaluating potential candidates can be a difficult task. Reviewing résumés, performing background checks, interviewing potential candidates, and chairing a search committee are highly important parts of an SMP's job. There is immense pressure on the SMP to ensure they hire the right person for the job. At the same time, the interviewing and hiring process must be both ethical and legal. Consider the following case scenario dealing with hiring a volleyball coach.

CASE 1-3   *Rickert v. Midland Lutheran College*

2009 WL 2840528 (D. Neb.)

Joan Rickert's employment for Midland began when she was hired as a part-time assistant volleyball coach in August of 1997. She was hired as the part-time head volleyball coach for Midland in 1999.

Steve Schneider ("Schneider") was the Athletic Director and head football coach for Midland when [Rickert] was initially hired, and he was [Rickert's] immediate supervisor throughout her employment as a volleyball coach for Midland. At the time Rickert was first hired, Schneider stated he intended to someday make the head volleyball coach position full-time, and if that happened, the position would be open to all potential applicants and [Rickert] could apply. Rickert knew some of the full-time coaches at Midland not only coached, but taught classes, and she therefore believed any full-time volleyball coaching position would include teaching duties. However, some of Midland's full-time coaches did not have teaching responsibilities.

In 2000, Rickert was hired as Midland's part-time Student Activities Director, which, in combination with her part-time head volleyball coaching position, afforded her full-time employment for Midland.

Rickert was diagnosed with breast cancer in June of 2003 and had a partial mastectomy on July 2, 2003. Although she was hospitalized for three days due to her surgery, she did not miss any work because the surgery occurred in the summer and she was employed by Midland on a ten-month contract. [She] attended a symposium for Midland within fifteen days following her surgery, and by late July, was back on the volleyball court.

Rickert began chemotherapy treatments on August 1, 2003. Four two-hour treatments were administered every third Monday morning, the last one occurring on September 29, 2003. These chemotherapy treatments went "very well," causing only minor nausea, and no emesis or mucositis. Rickert was encouraged to maintain her normal activity throughout her chemotherapy regimen. Rickert's cancer treatment did cause fatigue. She was unable to stand or walk for any length of time, and needed to sit during practices and while at work. It was difficult for her to carry out daily functions, and she was exhausted by night time. She lost her hair, her food occasionally tasted like metal, and she experienced other minor side effects.

Rickert did not, however, miss any work as either the part-time head volleyball coach or the part-time Student Activities Director due to her cancer treatment, in part because her volleyball team changed the practice schedule to accommodate Rickert's medical appointments. From the onset of Rickert's breast cancer and throughout her treatment, Rickert could fully perform her job, and although co-employees asked Rickert if she wanted to go home and rest out of concern for her well-being, no one at Midland criticized her or stated she was unable to perform her job due to her cancer or the treatment side-effects.

Rickert had breast reconstruction surgery on January 4, 2004. Since the surgery was performed during interterm, she missed no work as a Student Activities Director because there were no ongoing activities, and she missed no work as a volleyball coach because it was off-season. By March 2, 2004, Rickert was reportedly "doing well," with no symptoms, her only complaint being the resumption of menses. She was prescribed additional medications to suppress her ovaries and advised to follow up every three months.

On March 23, 2004, Tara Knudson-Carl ("Knudson-Carl") was hired as Vice-President of Student Development at Midland and became Rickert's supervisor in her capacity as part-time Student Activities Director. When Knudson-Carl began the position, she stated that if the budget allowed, she intended to make the Student Activities Director position full-time. However, Knudson-Carl advised Rickert that she would wait a year to see if Rickert could handle both the part-time volleyball head coaching duties and the part-time Student Activities Director duties.

Knudson-Carl knew she had breast cancer and was undergoing breast cancer treatment.

Rickert was seen by her doctor for follow up in May and August 2004. Other than "tolerable" hot flashes, likely caused by medications used to induce menopause, Rickert was "doing well."

Rickert spoke with Schneider in August 2004 and told him she was being treated for her cancer, and would continue receiving injections and medications for the following five years. The expression on Schneider's face indicated he was not happy to hear this news.

In September 2004, less than six months after Knudson-Carl was hired, Knudson-Carl advised Rickert that since there was no Dean of Students at the time, there was money in the budget to make the Student Activities Director a full-time position. Knudson-Carl told Rickert the part-time Student Activities Director position was being terminated and, as such, Rickert's employment in that position was terminated effective September 8, 2004. Rickert's passion and vocation was for volleyball. Knudson-Carl stated Rickert could apply to be the full-time Student Activities Director, but probably would not want to because if hired Rickert could not coach volleyball, and Rickert would probably get a full-time head volleyball coaching position at Midland when that job was created. Rickert did not apply for the full-time position as Student Activities Director because, had she been hired, she would have been required to quit coaching, which would have left her volleyball players without a head coach midway through their season.

Midland hired Tara Mieras ("Mieras"), a woman under the age of thirty, as the full-time Student Activities Director. Rickert agrees Mieras appeared, on paper, to be qualified for the position.

The Midland volleyball season was over in the beginning of November 2004. By the end of 2004, Rickert no longer had an office in Student Development since she was no longer employed as a part-time Student Activities Director. The athletic facilities were under construction, and office space in the athletic department was so scarce that the offices of two assistant football coaches and the golf coach were located in converted closets or storage areas. Schneider could not immediately locate any available office space for [Rickert], so he asked her to work from home by computer while he continued to look. Schneider tried to locate space on campus, but the only option available was in a house three blocks from the field house but close to the residential halls, a location allowing [Rickert] to have access to students. [Rickert] was provided an office in the house. The office was equipped with a single bulb hanging from the ceiling, a desk, two folding chairs, a computer, a file cabinet, a telephone, and a chair. This less than "ideal set-up" made it difficult for [Rickert] to communicate with her athletes and keep connected with the Midland coaching community, but it was the best solution Schneider could find at the time.

Rickert was concerned about losing her full-time benefits, including health care benefits, with the loss of her full-time employment. Schneider and Crume worked with the Human Resources Department and made [Rickert's] part-time head volleyball coaching position a two-thirds time position so she could earn more money and retain her benefits. Schneider and Crume told [Rickert] that if she held some camps and club volleyball tournaments to raise money, then her salary could remain the same and she could retain her benefits.

During the 2003-2004 time frame, the focus of the Midland athletic department began changing. In 2003, Steve Titus became the president of Midland. Before Titus was president, the academic dean was in charge of athletics, but under Titus, Gene Crume became an executive vice president responsible for several departments, including the athletic department. Schneider, the Athletic Director, reported to Crume.

At the outset of the Titus/Crume administration, approximately 35% of Midland's students were involved in athletics. Titus and Crume therefore developed a strategic plan to strengthen the Midland athletic program as a means for recruiting athletically and academically better students. Significant facility upgrades were implemented, and the athletic program was changed from an NAIA coaching model, where coaches both taught and coached, to an NCAA model, where coaches had limited or no teaching responsibilities, and coached and recruited on a full-time basis. As part of the Titus/Crume strategic plan, the head volleyball coaching position was changed from part-time to full-time and a full-time track coach was hired.

Crume's two preferred options for hiring a coach were to either use a search committee or hire an identified candidate with a known record of success. The majority of head coach hires made by Schneider were done through the committee process, including when Jeff Field was hired as the head baseball coach and when Dan Sullivan, who was a part-time soccer coach, was hired as a full-time soccer coach. Schneider also formed a committee to hire an assistant head football coach in preparation for Schneider's possible departure as head football coach to become the full-time Student Activities Director, and the anticipated need to transition the assistant head football coach to head football coach when that occurred. The search committee process was not used when Justin Horner was hired as the head track and field coach, either because the retiring coach had worked with and recommended Horner as his replacement and therefore no search committee was formed, or because the committee was formed but no other qualified applicants applied.

In December 2004, Schneider advised Rickert that the head volleyball coaching position would be made full-time, a five-person search committee would interview the applicants, and Rickert could apply for the position. When [Rickert] asked why the position was being opened for applications, and why she needed to apply if she was already doing the job, Crume stated Midland "wanted to just see if there was something better out there," and Schneider stated "they wanted to move in a different direction."

Volleyball was a revenue-producing sport for Midland, and Crume had concluded [Rickert] was an average coach who had become the part-time head volleyball coach primarily by happenstance. He did not believe [Rickert]'s coaching style was well-organized or focused, and he wanted better results in the area of recruiting and inspiring students to remain engaged in the program. During prior evaluations, [Rickert] was told she was underperforming in the area of recruiting. Midland was investing significant resources in the volleyball program. The arena facilities were being upgraded, and with the change from a part-time to full-time volleyball coach, Crume expected a substantially different commitment and sense of dedication to the program. Crume wanted to select a better than average head volleyball coach from a robust pool of potential applicants.

The application process began. The position was advertised and was different than other coaching positions on the campus in that it consisted of 90 to 95% coaching and recruiting responsibilities with very minimal teaching. A master's degree was preferred, but only a bachelor's degree was required.

The search committee members were Midland coaches, including Keith Kramme, head softball coach and assistant athletic director; Joanne Bracker, head women's basketball coach; Jeff Field, baseball coach; Casey Thiele, football coach; and Becky Wuebben, athletic trainer. Kramme served as the committee chairperson, and the other committee members forwarded their comments to him. From the applications received, the search committee identified five candidates for interviews: Kerry Beidlemann, Kristen Lebeda, Mike Meyer, Pam Wendel, and [Rickert]. The committee interviewed the five candidates and reviewed each candidate's résumé, references, and letter of application. The candidates also met with the volleyball players, who were afforded the opportunity to identify the pros and cons for each applicant. Background checks were performed.

Biedlemann was 26 years old. Field identified Biedlemann's positive traits to include her "youth," experience in the sport, and the fact that she was new to the college and conference. Her youth was considered a positive because "she was vibrant," and likely a "go-getter." However, Field questioned whether Biedlemann would connect to and understand the students, and as negative factors, noted she was engaged to a coach (and therefore would be more likely to move), and did not interview well. Bracker believed Biedlemann's portfolio was extremely impressive, and she was highly articulate and very responsive to questions. Kramme considered Beidlemann a "very strong candidate top to bottom," with a tremendous portfolio and a background of successes with the program at the University of Nebraska at Kearney. Thiele believed Biedlemann's positive traits included being organized, having experience in a successful college volleyball program, and her likely ability to recruit. Thiele further noted, however, that Biedlemann had no contacts with the Fremont, Nebraska, community, lacked familiarity with the Midland program or the NAIA model, and appeared to be looking for more money than Midland could offer.

As to Lebeda, who was 25 years old, Thiele noted as beneficial her experience as a player and her Omaha club connections, both considered helpful for recruiting, but felt she was inexperienced, unfamiliar with running a Junior Varsity program, and did not adequately research Midland before her interview. Field did not believe Lebeda interviewed well, and based on the interview, did not believe she could handle coaching a small college program.

Thiele believed Wendel was a strong candidate, in the top third, whose drawback was a lack of coaching experience at the collegiate level. Bracker, who had previously worked with Wendel, considered Wendel an outstanding candidate, who had experienced success at the high school level, and was intelligent, articulate, and organized.

Meyer, who was in his mid-40s or 50s, was considered a "very strong candidate," who "would be hard to beat."

As to [Rickert], Bracker, who was 60 and a good friend of Rickert at the time of the interviews, was extremely impressed with Rickert's commitment to Midland during her health issues and considered this a positive character trait. Kramme believed Rickert was a successful coach but was concerned she lacked control over her team. Thiele considered, as a positive, that Rickert had gone through a very tough time with her illness and remained very loyal to the school. However, he noted her résumé and cover letter had typographical errors, she acknowledged having conflicts within her team every year, and her first recruiting class was her best, leading him to question whether she would allow recruiting to slip even further in the future. He also believed her practices were disorganized. Like Thiele, Field considered Rickert's positive traits to include her loyalty to Midland, and the fact she knew the current players, and is a good person. However, Field believed Rickert was unorganized and not concerned enough with winning, and while she corrected some problems in the program, she had failed to move the program forward. Wuebben reiterated the positive

traits identified by Thiele and Field, further adding the players
liked her, Rickert believed academics were important, her retention
was good, and she gave a lot to the school during her illness. Wuebben
believed, however, that [Rickert] lacked team control and had two sets
of rules depending on whether the player was on scholarship. Wuebben
noted the search committee process was hard for her, and she was "just
sick about this." Wuebben believed Rickert should have been appointed
to the full-time position rather than having to compete.

> Rickert's declaration contains not only her personal knowledge,
> but also her interpretation of the deposition testimony of other
> witnesses. Some of that deposition testimony was offered as
> evidence; some was not. Rickert's declaration states Wuebben
> testified she ranked Rickert as her first choice for the full-
> time head volleyball coach position. The Wuebben testimony of
> record does not support this statement. Wuebben's email to Kramme,
> which is part of the record, stated Wuebben was "just sick about"
> having to make a decision, and was "still thinking on this."

The players identified Rickert's strengths to include a familiar
coaching style and her willingness to educate herself. Their identified concerns included favoritism, inconsistency, recruiting issues,
and knowledge. Similar issues were identified in a parent letter sent
to Titus on May 15, 2003, but the letter was never discussed with
[Rickert].

Rickert had a "gut feeling" that the selection committee members considered her age as a factor in the hiring process. However, the only
reference to age was Field's positive comment on Beidlemann's "youth."
Field also stated Lebeda may be too young and immature for the job.
Rickert's age was never discussed by the committee. There is no evidence Rickert's breast cancer was identified as an impediment or discussed as limiting Rickert's ability to be the full-time head
volleyball coach.

The interviews were conducted during February of 2005. In the end,
Beidlemann was the committee's first choice, followed by Meyers and
Lebeda. Rickert was the committee's fourth choice. These choices were
forwarded to Schneider. The final decision was left to Crume, who
relied heavily on Schneider's opinion.

Beidlemann withdrew from consideration because she accepted a job
offer from Drake University. Meyer was withdrawn from consideration
following a reference check. Lebeda was offered the position and
accepted it, the job to commence on June 1, 2005. Rickert admits that
on paper, Lebeda appeared to be very qualified for the job. Rickert was

told in March 2005 that her contract for the head volleyball coaching position would not be renewed.

By the time the application process began for the full-time head volleyball coaching position, [Rickert] had no recurrence of breast cancer, and although she remained on medication, she was having no symptoms associated with the disease or its treatment. During the application process, Rickert's stamina was reportedly "excellent" and she was "feeling fine." Rickert continued to be "active with good performance status" when her Midland employment ended on May 31, 2005.

The evidence reveals the search committee considered both objective and subjective factors and traits in comparing the candidates and recommending its choices. Among the traits considered were organizational skills; stability and contacts with the community; loyalty to and knowledge concerning the Midland program and its players; prior experience as a player and coach; community and school contacts, particularly as they related to access to recruiting venues and experience with quality teams; team control; and the ability to interact with the players. Midland offered evidence that on balance and in comparison to Biedlemann, Lebeda, and Meyer, Midland concluded Rickert was not the strongest candidate. No one on the search committee questioned Rickert's loyalty to the school or her knowledge of the program or its players, and they admired her resilience and commitment in continuing to coach throughout her cancer diagnosis and treatment, but they also noted she was unorganized, lacked team control, and was perceived to show favoritism.

Perhaps most important, Midland was changing its program, including upgrading facilities and hiring a full-time head volleyball coach, primarily to recruit better students, yet Rickert had been counseled to improve her recruiting and acknowledged her best recruiting year was her first year as a coach, leading at least one committee member to question whether she was able and willing to improve. The full-time position consisted of 90 to 95% coaching and recruiting, but Rickert was viewed by Crume as only an average coach and Rickert's recruiting skills were in question. Crume wanted more than an average coach, particularly since Midland was investing so much in the program. In contrast to Rickert, the committee, Schneider, and Crume concluded Beidlemann and Lebeda were both able to coach with skills and experience gained from noted and touted outside volleyball programs, and both had connections to volleyball clubs and programs perceived as potentially valuable for future recruiting. Rickert admitted that, on paper, Lebeda appeared very qualified for the position. Although Rickert argues neither Beidlemann nor Lebeda were qualified for the full-time head volleyball coaching position because they lacked a master's degree and could not teach at Midland, both had a bachelor's degree, which was all that was required for the position because teaching was not a significant part of the job.

A search committee composed of Rickert's coworkers, most of whom considered her a friend, interviewed five applicants, compared their qualifications, and decided three of the applicants were better choices for the position than Rickert, two of whom were substantially younger than her, and one who was approximately her age. Rickert may disagree with Midland's decision, but the courts do not "sit as super-personnel departments reviewing wisdom or fairness of employer's judgments unless they were intentionally discriminatory."

> [Rickert] has offered win-loss and retention records to show Lebeda did not perform as well as Rickert had in the volleyball coaching position, in part to show Rickert was more qualified than Lebeda. This challenge to Midland's hiring decision, made with the benefit of hindsight, is irrelevant. The question is whether Midland considered disability or age when it was deciding not to hire Rickert. [Rickert] has presented no evidence that based on the information known by Midland at the time of hiring, [Rickert]'s age or alleged disability were considered, or that Rickert was more qualified than Lebeda to be the full-time head volleyball coach.

The Midland Lutheran College has offered evidence explaining legitimate, nondiscriminatory reasons for hiring Lebeda instead of [Rickert] as the full-time head volleyball coach. [Rickert] has offered no evidence that these reasons are a mere pretext for underlying discriminatory animus.

Source: *Reprinted from Westlaw with permission of Thomson Reuters.*

Coach Rickert sued the university but lost in federal court. Under federal law an individual must be at least 40 years old to state a valid claim for age discrimination. The court's opinion did not list her age but stated that she met the criteria to sue under the law.

Evidently, the fourth best candidate was Rickert. Lebeda was younger than coach Rickert but did not interview well, was unfamiliar with running a junior varsity program, was decidedly "inexperienced," and the committee did not think "she could handle" coaching a small college program. How did this make her a better candidate than coach Rickert? It was not that coach Rickert's commitment to the university was viewed as a "negative character trait" but that she "was not concerned enough with the university."

It would be naïve to say universities always value character development of students over winning, but if character is what they are trying to develop in the student-athlete, how much more character can you show than coach Rickert's battle with cancer? Although there was no evidence that her breast cancer played a role in the committee's decision, do you believe it may have been an "unstated" factor in their decision not to hire her?

After reading the facts of this case, how would you answer the following questions?

1. Was coach Rickert treated fairly during the application process?
2. What part should her loyalty to the university have played in their hiring decision?
3. Was the entire hiring process fair? If not, what should have been done differently?
4. Do you believe her medical condition played any part in Midland's choice to not hire her?
5. Do you believe her age was a factor in Midland not hiring her?
6. Did the university use the correct criteria in evaluating candidates?
7. Does the fact that Schneider was "unhappy" about the news that coach Rickert would have to continue medication for 5 years show he was biased against her during the hiring process?
8. Does any of the written communication of the search committee indicate coach Rickert was treated unfairly or unethically?
9. What part, if any, did the "upgrade" of the athletic program play in their decision not to hire coach Rickert?

Student-Athlete Issues and Team "Chemistry" Team unity and sportsmanship are vital to any team's success at all levels of sports. If a team works together, they are more likely to be successful on the field of play. A team must have the right "chemistry" between the players to win. With that in mind, when is a high school player, allowed to voice his or her opposition to the way a team is being run? This case involves the expulsion of several high school student-athletes from the team after they started a petition attempting to get the coach fired.

📖 CASE 1-4 *Lowery v. Euverard*

497 F.3d 584 (6th Cir. 2007)

Derrick Lowery, Jacob Giles, Joseph Dooley, and Dillan Spurlock were students at Jefferson County High School in Tennessee during the 2005 to 2006 school year. All four were members of the Jefferson County varsity football team. Euverard became the head varsity football coach at Jefferson County in 2004. During the 2005 season, many of the Jefferson County football players . . . became dissatisfied with Euverard's coaching methods. They allege that Euverard struck a player in the helmet, threw away college recruiting letters to disfavored players, humiliated and degraded players, used inappropriate language, and required a year-round conditioning program in violation of high school rules.

In early October of 2005, after discussions with Dooley and Lowery, Giles typed the following statement: "I hate Coach Euvard [sic] and I don't want to play for him." Giles and Dooley asked other players to sign the petition, which would be held until after the football season. Giles and Dooley intended to then give the petition to Schneitman, the principal of Jefferson County, in order to have Euverard replaced as head coach. Eighteen players eventually signed the petition, including Spurlock.

Euverard learned of the petition on October 7, 2005. Darren Whitehead, another player on the team, told Assistant Coach Ricky Upton about the petition, who then told Euverard. Euverard called an all-coaches meeting on October 9. Schneitman was also present at the meeting. At the meeting, the coaches discussed how to deal with the petition. The coaches decided to question the players individually to learn more about the petition.

When the players arrived for practice on October 10 they were told to sit in front of their lockers and remain quiet. Players were then taken one by one into an office in the weight room where they were interviewed by Euverard. Assistant Coach Brimer was also present in the office, taking notes. All the players were asked the same questions: (1) Have you heard about the petition? (2) Did you sign it? (3) Who asked you to sign it? and (4) Do you want to play football with Coach Euverard as coach?

When Wesley Lee, a player who had signed the petition, was called for his interview, Lowery called out, "Are you alright?" Assistant Coach Pippenger then asked Lowery to come over. At first Lowery refused, and then walked over to Pippenger. Lowery told Pippenger "don't put your hands on me," or words to that effect, and refused to go outside with Pippenger. Giles and Dooley then got up and stood by Lowery. Pippenger took the three of them into the weight room, and told Euverard about the situation. Euverard attempted to interview the three boys individually, but they said they would only meet with Euverard as a group. Euverard told them that if they were going to be that way, they could pick up their things and leave. Giles, Dooley, and Lowery gathered their belongings and left. As they were leaving, Dooley said to the other players, "I know how much you hate him, and you guys need to leave with us right now."

Spurlock was not at school on October 10. Euverard interviewed Spurlock on October 11, and Spurlock told Euverard that he signed the petition. Euverard asked Spurlock if he still felt that way, and Spurlock answered that he loved football. Euverard then asked Spurlock if he wanted to play football with Euverard as head coach. Spurlock said no, but that he wanted to play for Jefferson County. Euverard told Spurlock to get his stuff, and that he was no longer on the team. Players who signed the petition but apologized to Euverard and told him they wanted to play for him were allowed to remain on the team.

In the 1986 movie *Hoosiers,* Gene Hackman plays Norman Dale, the new basketball coach at a small Indiana high school. On the first day of practice Dale makes an introductory speech to the players. All of the players attentively listen to Dale except two, who are talking to each other. Dale notices the two players talking, and the following dialogue ensues:

Dale: Basketball is a voluntary activity. It's not a requirement. If any of you feel you don't want to be on the team, feel free to leave right now. Did you hear what I just said?

Player: Me?

Dale: Yes, you.

Player: Sure, I'm just kinda curious to know when we start.

Dale: We start when I say so.

Player: OK, would you kinda let me know, 'cause I'm kinda getting tired of standing.

Dale: Alright. Out. Out of here. Right now.

One of the purposes of education is to train students to fulfill their role in a free society. Thus it is appropriate for students to learn to express and evaluate competing viewpoints. The goal of an athletic team is much narrower. Of course, students may participate in extracurricular sports for any number of reasons: to develop discipline, to experience camaraderie and bonding with other students, for the sheer "love of the game," etc. Athletic programs may also produce long-term benefits by distilling positive character traits in the players. However, the immediate goal of an athletic team is to win the game, and the coach determines how best to obtain that goal. As this Court has recognized:

> Unlike the classroom teacher whose primary role is to guide students through the discussion and debate of various viewpoints in a particular discipline, [the role of a coach] is to train his student athletes how to win on the court. The plays and strategies are seldom up for debate. Execution of the coach's will is paramount.

The success of an athletic team in large part depends on its coach. The coach determines the strategies and plays, and "sets the tone" for the team. The coach, particularly at the high school level, is also responsible for providing "an educational environment conducive to learning team unity and sportsmanship and free from disruptions and distractions that could hurt or stray the cohesiveness of the team." The ability of the coach to lead is inextricably linked to his ability to maintain order and discipline. Thus attacking the authority of the coach necessarily undermines his ability to lead the team. In this case, Spurlock admitted that signing the petition was equivalent to saying he had no respect for Euverard. . . . coaches are entitled to respect from their players. The circulation of a petition stating "I hate Coach Euvard [sic] and I don't want to play for him" was a direct challenge to Euverard's authority, and undermined his ability to lead the team. It could have no other effect.

In addition to challenging Euverard's authority, the petition threatened team unity. In most instances, school officials would be more likely to fire a coach who had a horrible season than one who had a successful season. Thus players advocating the removal of a coach would have a powerful incentive to give less than one hundred percent. The Court is not accusing the [players] of this behavior; they all claim to have played their hardest despite their feelings for Euverard. However, after every missed block, dropped pass, or blown tackle, it would only be natural for other players, knowing the situation, to question the [players] motivation. This would inevitably increase the tension on the team.

The circulation of the petition necessarily divided players into two camps, those who supported Euverard and those who didn't. Although team chemistry is impossible to quantitatively measure, it is instrumental in determining a team's success. Joakim Noah, a player on the University of Florida basketball team that won consecutive NCAA championships in 2006 and 2007, stated that "the difference between winning and losing is so, so small. . . . It's teams that really play together that win. Team chemistry is such a sensitive thing, but we really, really have it." See Paola Boivin, "Gators Bare Their Championship Teeth," *Arizona Republic*, Mar. 19, 2007, 11.

Mutual respect for the coach is an important ingredient of team chemistry. The Detroit Tigers were the talk of the baseball world during the 2006 season, due to their remarkable turnaround and run to the World Series. An opposing player attributed the Tigers' success to "a manager they all trust and respect and that they are behind, and a team chemistry that seems pretty unified." See John Lowe, "Add in Some Hot Bats, and the Tigers Have Found Their Swagger," *Detroit Free Press*, Oct. 16, 2006, 5. See also Mark Gaughan, "Expectations Low in an Uncertain Era," *Buffalo News*, Sep. 7, 2006, C11 ("I truly believe there is team chemistry. I believe the players truly believe and respect Coach Jauron."); David Boyce, "Central Missouri State Working for Series Title," *Kansas City Star*, May 10, 2002, D8 ("We have a deep respect for our coaches. . . . We know they know what they are doing. We have a good team chemistry.").

Conversely, conflict between a player and the coach can shake "the very foundation of team chemistry." See Greg Boeck, "Revolution on Court: Players' Defiance Upsets NBA Leadership Picture," *USA Today*, Dec. 21, 2000, C1.One sportswriter has noted that:

> The feud between [the player and coach] ultimately tore at the fabric of team chemistry and may have contributed to [the team's] postseason failure. At best, the constant discord created an uncomfortable atmosphere on the team. At worst, it forced players

to choose between a coach and a teammate, creating a fissure of
distrust and disunity.

See Glenn Nelson, "Ready to Blow? Enigmatic George Karl Can't Understand Why He's Misunderstood," *Seattle Times*, Nov. 1, 1995, H3.

Conflict between a player and coach has also been described as a
"cancer." See Selena Roberts, "From Sleepless to Selfless," *The New
York Times*, Dec. 10, 1996, B13.

The Court does not have an idealized, pristine view of athletic teams.
Athletic teams are a family of sorts, and, like any family, it is
inevitable that there will be some squabbles. Games are emotional
affairs, and players and coaches may exchange angry words in the heat
of the moment. From time to time, players may also vent their frustra-
tions over play calls, lack of playing time, etc. The petition in this
case, however, cannot be characterized as an isolated expression of
dissatisfaction. The petition, stating "I hate Coach Euvard [sic] and
I don't want to play for him," was part of a concerted effort to have
Euverard fired. Such a petition would necessarily force players to
choose between Euverard and the players that opposed him.

Source: *Reprinted from Westlaw with permission of Thomson Reuters.*

Of course, student-athletes do not completely waive their First Amendment rights when they join
a team. A coach could not dismiss a player simply because the player had religious or political
views that were unpopular with his teammates.

After reviewing the facts of Case 1-4, how would you answer the following questions?

1. Do student-athletes have a right to say whatever they want to a coach?
2. Should student-athletes be dismissed from the team for writing and signing the petition?
3. To what extent can student-athletes at the high school level determine who their coach is
   going to be?
4. How would you handle the allegations against the coach?
5. How would you determine whether the allegations are true?
6. Would you initiate an investigation and if so, how would it be conducted?
7. How much leeway should a coach be given to discipline players?
8. Did the student-athletes act in an unsportsmanlike manner?
9. Do the student-athletes have any free speech rights to be considered?
10. Do you agree with the statement, "Execution of the coach's will is paramount"?
11. Should the coach be disciplined or fired if any of the allegations are proved to be true?

The matter eventually ended up in litigation with a federal court deciding the players had the
right to challenge the coach under these circumstances. Was this the correct decision? How could this
incident have been avoided?

An SMP is required to hear all sides of an issue and make a decision that is fair to all parties
involved. Resolving disputes in any industry is a difficult task. Therefore, every SMP must have the
requisite skills to solve problems and must be able to resolve them within the bounds of ethical

behavior and achieving fairness to all involved. Consider the following case. How is it different from the *Euverard* case?

📖 CASE 1-5 *Wildman v. Marshalltown School District*

249 F.3d 768 (8th Cir. 2001)

In January 1998, Rebecca Wildman was a sophomore student at Marshalltown High School in Marshalltown, Iowa, and a member of the school's basketball team.

Wildman hoped to play on the varsity team and she testified that Coach Rowles, the high school girls' varsity basketball coach, promised in conversations with her before the season that he would promote her to the varsity team. When the promotion never materialized, Wildman testified that she "became frustrated and decided to write a letter to [her] teammates" and that her "purpose was to find out what they thought of the situation and Coach Rowles." She composed a letter on her home computer and distributed it to her teammates in the school's locker room on Saturday, January 24, 1998. The letter stated:

> To all of my teammates:
>   Everyone has done a great job this year and now is the time that we need to make ourselves stronger and pull together. It was a tough loss last night but we will get it back. We have had some bumps in the road to success but every team does and the time is here for us to smoothen it out. Everyone on this team is important whether they think so or not. After watching last nights [sic] Varsity game and seeing their sophomores play up I think and I think [sic] that some of you are think [sic] the same thing. I think that we have to fight for our position. Am I the only one who thinks that some of us should be playing Varsity or even JV? We as a team have to do something about this. I want to say something to Coach Rowles. I will not say anything to him without the whole teams [sic] support. He needs us next year and the year after and what if we aren't there for him? It is time to give him back some of the bullshit that he has given us. We are a really great team and by the time we are seniors and we ALL have worked hard we are going to have an AWESOME season. We deserve better then [sic] what we have gotten. We now need to stand up for what we believe in!

She included below her statement a poem about geese in flight titled "We Makes Me Stronger."

Source: *Reprinted from Westlaw with permission of Thomson Reuters.*

After reviewing Case 1-5, how would you answer the following questions?

1. How would you handle the situation in which a student is disrespectful to a coach on his or her Facebook page? Is that poor sportsmanship or improper conduct that merits discipline?[74] What about a coach who slams players and parents? Royal Oak Michigan varsity soccer coach, Jason Windsor resigned after he used his Facebook page to threaten players and disparage players' parents. Some of his comments included: "3 words my varsity soccer parents will get used to this week. BENCH, JV, CUT. You will all be taught a lesson you sh—stirring pri—!!!!!!!" and "(certain) Parents are the worst part of kid's sports" and finally "great set of results on the field today! shame certain soccer moms make soccer so negative."[75]

2. Should every school have a code of conduct which states student-athletes must respect and abide by all reasonable decisions of the coach?

3. How much credibility do you give to the student-athlete, and her cause, (Case 1-5) considering the numerous typographical and grammatical errors in her letter?

4. Would there be a difference if Rebecca Wildman (Case 1-5) had e-mailed her letter to her teammates instead of distributing the letter to her teammates on school property?

5. Should the use of the word "bullshit" in her letter automatically disqualify her from the team?

College Student-Athletes   An SMP in a collegiate setting is faced with numerous ethical issues on a wide array of topics. One prevalent issue is the student-athlete graduation rate. Shouldn't the graduation rate of student-athletes be a primary concern of the university? After all, it is an educational institution!

📖 CASE 1-6 *Kevin Ross v. Creighton University*

957 F. 2d 410 (7th Cir. 1992)

Kevin Ross filed suit against Creighton University (Creighton) for negligence and breach of contract arising from Creighton's alleged failure to educate him.

In the spring of 1978, Ross was a promising senior basketball player at Wyandotte High School in Kansas City, Kansas. Sometime during his senior year in high school, he accepted an athletic scholarship to attend Creighton and to play on its varsity basketball team.

Creighton is an academically superior university. Ross comes from an academically disadvantaged background. At the time of his enrollment at Creighton, Ross was at an academic level far below that of the average Creighton student. For example, he scored in the bottom fifth percentile of college-bound seniors taking the American College Test, while the average freshman admitted to Creighton with him scored in

---

[74] Andrew Greiner, "Student Suspended for Facebook Teacher Slam," *NVC Chicago*, February 22, 2010.
[75] Marilisa Kinney Sachteleben, "Royal Oak High School Soccer Coach Resigns After Facebook Confrontations," *Associated Content from Yahoo*, October 15, 2010.

the upper twenty-seven percent. According to the complaint, Creighton realized Ross's academic limitations when it admitted him, and, to induce him to attend and play basketball, Creighton assured Ross that he would receive sufficient tutoring so that he "would receive a meaningful education while at Creighton."

Ross attended Creighton from 1978 until 1982. During that time he maintained a D average and acquired 96 of the 128 credits needed to graduate. However, many of these credits were in courses such as Marksmanship and Theory of Basketball and did not count towards a university degree. Ross alleges that he took these courses on the advice of Creighton's Athletic Department, and that the department also employed a secretary to read his assignments and prepare and type his papers. Ross also asserts that Creighton failed to provide him with sufficient and competent tutoring that it had promised.

When he left Creighton, Ross had the overall language skills of a fourth grader and the reading skills of a seventh grader. Consequently, Ross enrolled, at Creighton's expense, for a year of remedial education at the Westside Preparatory School in Chicago. At Westside, Ross attended classes with grade school children. He later entered Roosevelt University in Chicago but was forced to withdraw because of a lack of funds. In July 1987, Ross suffered what he terms a "major depressive episode," during which he barricaded himself in a Chicago motel room and threw furniture out the window. To Ross, this furniture "symbolized" Creighton employees who had wronged him.

Ross's complaint advances three separate theories of how Creighton was negligent towards him. First, he contends that Creighton committed "educational malpractice" by not providing him with a meaningful education and preparing him for employment after college. Second, Ross claims that Creighton negligently inflicted emotional distress upon him by enrolling him in a stressful university environment for which he was not prepared, and then by failing to provide remedial programs that would have helped him survive there. Third, Ross urges the court to adopt a new cause of action for the tort of "negligent admission," which would allow recovery when an institution admits, and then does not adequately assist, a woefully unprepared student. The complaint also sets forth a contract claim, alleging that Creighton contracted to provide Ross "an opportunity . . . to obtain a meaningful college education and degree, and to do what was reasonably necessary . . . to enable [Ross] to obtain a meaningful college education and degree." It goes on to assert that Creighton breached this contract by failing to provide Mr. Ross adequate tutoring; by not requiring Ross to attend tutoring sessions; by not allowing him to "red-shirt," that is, to forgo a year of basketball, in order to work on academics; and by failing to afford Mr. Ross a reasonable opportunity to take advantage

of tutoring services. Ross also alleges that Creighton breached a
promise it had made to him to pay for a college education.

Source: *Reprinted from Westlaw with permission of Thomson Reuters.*

After reviewing the facts of Case 1-6, how would you answer the following questions?

1. What ethical duty does a university have to recruit student-athletes they know will be academically unsuccessful at the university?
2. How did the university fail in its ethical duties to Ross?
3. Is Kevin Ross in any way responsible for his situation?
4. What ethical actions can be taken to prevent this in the future?
5. Should universities ever admit student-athletes who fail to meet the minimum entrance requirements for general students of the university?[76]

NOTES AND DISCUSSION QUESTIONS

Sports in Society

1. How are business ethics and sports ethics interrelated? Are there overlapping principles applicable to both?
2. What are some examples of ethical decisions individuals have to make in the sports industry?[77]
3. What are some examples of ethical decisions corporations are required to make in the sports industry?[78]
4. What ethical choices do professional and amateur athletes have to make?
5. Which principles from business ethics could sports ethics adopt?[79]
6. What is the best way to enforce the idea of sportsmanship in youth sports?
7. In what ways can sports build character?[80]
8. What can be done to further promote the concept of sports ethics?[81]

---

[76] Alison Go, "Athletes Show Huge Gaps in SAT Scores," *U.S. News & World Report*, December 30, 2008. "Football players average 220 points lower on the SAT than their classmates. Men's basketball was 227 points lower. University of Florida won the prize for biggest gap between football players and the student body, with players scoring 346 points lower than their peers. Georgia Tech had the nation's best average SAT score for football players, 1028 of a possible 1600, and best average high school GPA, 3.39 of a possible 4.0, but because its student body is apparently very smart, Tech's football players still scored 315 SAT points lower than their classmates. UCLA, which has won more NCAA championships in all sports than any other school, had the biggest gap between the average SAT scores of athletes in all sports and its overall student body, at 247 points." The schools with the top SAT scores were Georgia Tech, 1028; Oregon State, 997; Michigan, 997; Virginia, 993; and Purdue, 974. The bottom five schools were Oklahoma State, 878; Louisville, 878; Memphis, 890; Florida, 890; and Texas Tech, 901.

[77] See generally, Joy Theresa DeSensi and Danny Rosenberg, *Ethics and Morality in Sport Management* (Morgantown, WV: Fitness Information Technology, 2003).

[78] See D. Stanley Eitzen, "Ethical Problems in American Sport," *Journal of Sport and Social Issues* 12, no. 1 (1988): 17–20.

[79] See Mary A. Hums, Carol A. Barr, and Laurie Gullion, "The Ethical Issues Confronting Managers in the Sports Industry," *Journal of Business Ethics* 20, no. 1 (1999): 51–66.

[80] See Gordon Marino, "Do College Sports Really Strengthen Character?" *Wall Street Journal*, August 31, 2006.

[81] See generally, Robert Simon, *Fair Play: The Ethics of Sport* (Boulder, CO: Westview Press, 2003).

9. How are sports ethics principles applied differently to SMPs, coaches, and participants?
10. Are there any sports ethics principles that can be considered "universal"?
11. How should sports ethics be addressed at the international level? Does sports ethics differ in every culture?[82]
12. What human rights issues are present in sports and sports ethics?[83]

Cheating

13. Do certain sports tolerate cheating, taking the attitude that cheating is tolerated if the player can get away with it?[84]
14. Do you believe there is a universal concept of "fairness" that can be applied to sports?
15. Consider Case Study 1-4, "Lottery Systems and Playing to Lose." Should the league commissioner be allowed to fine a team that loses purposefully? How could you actually prove it? Does it hurt the integrity of the sport if a team or player fails to play its best?
16. Do you believe there is a cheating epidemic in sports? If so, what created the epidemic? Do you believe cheating in sports is just a reflection of cheating in other aspects of society (business, legal, medical, education)?[85]
17. Do large salaries for players at the professional level create an incentive for players to cheat?[86]
18. Do you believe people who are unethical or dishonest in their private life will also engage in unethical behavior in their professional careers? Is there a connection between an individual's personal beliefs and how those beliefs are applied in the corporate culture?
19. How would you prove a violation of the morals clause in the prenuptial agreement for actor Michael Douglas that included a $5 million "straying fee" should he have sexual relations with someone other than his wife, Catherine Zeta Jones?[87]
20. How should cheaters in sports be disciplined? Should they be fined, suspended, or in the worst-case scenario, have their contract terminated?[88]
21. How would you define a good role model in sports? What role does the sports media play in determining the "villains" of sports?[89]
22. How has the increase of sports agents in sports created ethical problems?[90]

---

[82] See Cui Jiang, "China's Traditional Sports Ethics Thought and the Value of Rebuilding Morals of Modern Sports," *CNKI.com.cn*, February 29, 2006; Francois-Xavier Mbopi-Keou, *Health and Sports in Africa: A Challenge for Development* (Esher, Surrey, UK: John Libbey Eurotext, 2008).

[83] See Bruce Kidd and Peter Donnelly, "Human Rights in Sports," *International Review for the Sociology of Sport*, 35, no. 2 (2000): 131–148.

[84] See Fran Zimniuch, *Crooked: A History of Cheating in Sports* (New York: Taylor Trade Publishing, 2009).

[85] See Lance Pugmire, "Cheating in Sports: A Master of Style, and Substance," *Los Angeles Times*, August 20, 2006; Selena Roberts, "The Road to Success Is Paved by Cheating," *New York Times*, April 8, 2007.

[86] See Joshua H. Whitman, "Winning at All Costs: Using Law and Economics to Determine the Proper Role of Government in Regulating the Use of Performance-Enhancing Drugs in Professional Sports," *University of Illinois Law Review* 459 (2008).

[87] See Jonah Goldberg, "Just Like Ozzie and Harriet: When Hollywood Liberals 'Settle Down,'" *National Review*, December 18, 2000.

[88] See "Hitting Sports Cheats in Their Wallets," *New York Times*, August 26, 2009.

[89] See Gill Lines, "Villains, Fools or Heroes? Sports Stars as Role Models for Young People," *Leisure Studies* 20, no. 4 (October 2001): 285–303.

[90] See Mike Celizic, "Are 'Pimp' Agents Any Worse Than Coaches?" *NBCSports.com*, July 22, 2010.

23. Do you agree with the following proposition?

We cannot lament dishonesty in Little League baseball and other sports, and condemn corporate executives and accountants for their second-rate ethics and the loss of their moral compass without taking a careful look at our own profession. Endemic cheating starts when one person after another chooses the cheap advantage, the easy way, often with seemingly reasonable justifications. As more and more people cut ethical corners, the norms of behavior erode exponentially.[91]

Ethical Decision Making and the Sports Management Professional

24. What are the major ethical dilemmas facing the SMP today?[92]

25. What is the best training and education for an SMP to be able to deal with the important issues they will face in the workplace? MBA? Law school? Sports management degree? Military experience? Liberal studies degree? Work experience? A combination of several of the above?

26. What are the essential elements of a corporate ethics program?[93] How would a corporate ethics program in the sports industry differ from an ethics program in another industry such as financial, manufacturing, sales or service?

27. Should every corporation establish an ethics hotline? Would an ethics hotline be a good idea for a professional sports franchise?[94]

28. Because of the many different races involved in the sports world, what type of diversity training should an SMP receive?[95]

29. What are the essential skills an SMP needs to develop an ethical decision-making model?

30. International sports no longer means only the Olympics. The NFL, MLB, NHL, and NBA are all attempting to increase their international influence. What additional training would an SMP need to be successful in the international arena?[96] What additional ethical issues are present on the international stage in sports?[97]

31. A college coach recruits a high school player he is "pretty sure" will not be academically successful at the university. What ethical dilemma does this scenario pose?[98]

32. Rebecca Wildman lost her case in federal district court. She appealed her case to the federal court of appeals, which once again ruled against her in favor of the school. The court stated in part: "Marshalltown had in place a handbook for student conduct in 1997–1998,

---

[91] Bruce Neckers, "Cheating," *Michigan Bar Journal* (September 2002).

[92] See Hums, Barr, and Gullion, "The Ethical Issues Confronting Managers in the Sports Industry."

[93] See Jeanne M. Logsdon and Donna J. Wood, "Global Business Citizenship and Voluntary Codes of Ethical Conduct," *Journal of Business Ethics* 59, nos. 1-2 (2005): 55–67.

[94] www.cces.ca.

[95] See Dana Brooks and Ronald Althouse, *Diversity and Social Justice in College Sports: Sport Management and the Student-Athlete* (Morgantown, WV: Fitness Information Technology, 2007).

[96] See www.ie.edu (Master in Sports Management, an excellent program that focuses on the global aspects of sports management. Director of Program Antonio Martin).

[97] www.internationalsport.com

[98] See generally Peter A. French, *Ethics and College Sports: Ethics, Sports, and the University (Issues in Academic Ethics)* (Lanham, MD: Rowman & Littlefield, 2004).

as well as a Marshalltown Bobcat Basketball Handbook, drafted by Coach Rowles and distributed to Wildman and her teammates at the start of the season. Both handbooks indicated that disrespect and insubordination will result in disciplinary action at the coach's discretion." It also stated, "Wildman's letter, containing the word 'bullshit' in relation to other language in it and motivated by her disappointment at not playing on the varsity team, constitutes insubordinate speech toward her coaches."[99]

33. Woody Hayes, head football coach of The Ohio State University (OSU) from 1951 to 1978, provides another example. He was seen by some as a tough but fair coach who showed compassion by visiting hospitals and taking a personal interest in his students. Yet he exhibited a hot temper that boiled over at a moment's notice. This caused him to lash out at players, other coaches, and even bowl game officials. In addition he destroyed inanimate objects such as telephones, film projectors, water bottles, and tackling dummies. His temper eventually led to his demise as a coach in the 1978 Gator Bowl. OSU trailed Clemson 17–15 late in the game but was driving for what looked to be a game-winning field goal attempt. With less than 2 minutes left, Clemson's Charlie Bauman intercepted an Art Schlichter pass and was tackled out of bounds in front of the OSU bench. Coach Hayes, in front of a national television audience, proceeded to rush over and punch Bauman in the face. When OSU players tried to restrain him, he punched at them. Hayes, though well loved, was fired the next day and never coached again. We might excuse his behavior by saying he was a product of his time, seeing combat in World War II in the Pacific while serving as a Naval Officer. However, a combat mentality does not always apply in an academic and competitive setting. Hayes took a positive quality of excellence and desire to compete hard and twisted it into one that allowed for blowups at any time for any reason.

---

[99] *Wildman v. Marshalltown School Dist.*, 249 F. 3d. 768 (2001).

CHAPTER 2

SPORTSMANSHIP AND GAMESMANSHIP

INTRODUCTION

Everyone likes to win! Adults and children alike enjoy the exuberance of winning. It is also clear that some people like to win more than others. It is *how* people win that is the subject of this chapter. Should we concern ourselves with how people get into the winner's circle or by what means they use to prevail? After all, no one remembers who finished second in the Super Bowl.

Not playing by the rules and hoping to avoid detection is considered cheating. Most everyone in sports would consider this to be ethically or morally wrong. Gamesmanship occupies a gray area between good sportsmanship and outright cheating. Gamesmanship utilizes legal tactics that are morally dubious and are designed to unsettle opponents. These tactics are not technically against the rules. At the professional level, with millions of dollars at stake, gamesmanship can sometimes take precedence over sportsmanship.

Former National Football League player Bob Whitfield said, "Everybody cheats. After that initial handshake, anything goes. The code of honor and respect probably ends when they toss the coin."[1] After all, sports is about competition, with athletes competing on the field or ice to determine a winner. Winning is the most important goal of an athlete at all levels of competition, especially at the professional level. What club owner is going to tolerate a player who does not do everything within his or her power to win? Certainly, sports can be played on a non-competitive basis just for fun; however, even a pickup basketball game among friends can be fiercely competitive.

Competition in most sports is a zero-sum game; there has to be a winner and a loser. Furthermore, competitive sports has a set of rules players must abide by during the game. If a player violates the rules to win, many will say that the player did not legally win because he or she failed to play by the rules. Most fans do not like cheaters, but what about those players who straddle the line between fair play and cheating? Examples of gamesmanship can include trash talking, taking an inordinate

---

[1] George Vecsey, "Sports in the Times; When Gamesmanship Blurs to Cheating," *New York Times*, September 23, 2006.

amount of time between points in a tennis match, or calling an unnecessary time-out to "freeze" an opponent before a crucial foul shot in basketball. Another form of gamesmanship is the strategic foul, which may be committed to prevent an opponent from scoring an easy layup. Unlike outright cheating, these types of fouls are openly committed in the expectation that a penalty will be imposed. What about a manager who intentionally gets himself ejected from a game to motivate his team?[2] Gamesmanship tactics are, at a minimum, a violation of the spirit of the game, but can they all be considered cheating?

Are there certain times in sports when it is acceptable to intentionally break the rules to try to win? Should players try to gain an advantage any way they can even if it means bending the rules just a little? Gamesmanship is not cheating per se, but it cannot really be categorized as sportsmanship either. A fine distinction can be made between sportsmanship and some forms of gamesmanship. Stephen Potter, in his seminal work on golf gamesmanship, states that gamesmanship had its origin in the sport of tennis.[3] There is no doubt that gamesmanship is an art and comes in all forms.[4] Gamesmanship occurs in a variety of industries as well. Certainly gamesmanship is present in the legal profession.[5]

There have been many definitions of sportsmanship, but scholar James Keating has set forth one of the more notable definitions:

> Sportsmanship is not merely an aggregate of moral qualities comprising a code of specialized behavior; it is also an attitude, a posture, a manner of interpreting what would otherwise be only a legal code. Yet the moral qualities believed to comprise the code have almost monopolized consideration and have proliferated to the point of depriving sportsmanship of any distinctiveness. Truthfulness, courage, Spartan endurance, self-control, self-respect, scorn of luxury, consideration for another's opinions and rights, courtesy, fairness, magnanimity, a high sense of honor, cooperation, generosity. The list seems interminable. While the conduct and attitude which are properly designated as sportsmanlike may reflect many of the above-mentioned qualities, they are not all equally basic or fundamental. A man may be law-abiding, a team player, well conditioned, courageous, humane, and the possessor of sangfroid without qualifying as a sportsman. On the other hand, he may certainly be categorized as a sportsman without possessing Spartan endurance or a scorn of luxury. Our concern is not with those virtues which might be found in the sportsman. Nor is it with those virtues which often accompany the sportsman. Our concern is rather with those moral habits or qualities which are essential, which characterize the participant as a sportsman. Examination reveals that there are some that are pivotal and absolutely essential; others peripheral.[6]

---

[2] Michael Bleach, "La Russa Denies Gamesmanship Charge," *Cardinals.com News*, June 30, 2010.

[3] Stephen Potter, *The Theory and Practice of Gamesmanship: Or the Art of Winning Games Without Actually Cheating* (Kingston, RI: Moyer Bell, 1998).

[4] John Paul Newport, "The Art of Gamesmanship," *Wall Street Journal*, January 10, 2009.

[5] See Juha Nasi and Pasi Sajasalo, "Consolidation by Game-Playing: A Gamesmanship Inquiry into Forestry Industry," *The Evolution of Competitive Strategies in Global Forestry Industry, World Forest* 4, no. 3 (2006): 225–256; Daphne Patai, "Gamesmanship and Androcentrism in Orwell's 1984," *PMLA* 97, no. 5 (October 1982): 856–870; Frederick R. Struckmeyer, "God and Gamesmanship," *Religious Studies* 7, no. 3 (September 1971): 233–243; Betty Lehan Harragan, *Games Mother Never Taught You: Corporate Gamesmanship for Women* (New York: Warner Books, 1978).

[6] James W. Keating, "Sportsmanship as a Moral Category," *Ethics* 75, no. 1 (October 1964): 29.

Which "moral habits [and] qualities" is Keating referring to that characterize someone as a true sportsman? Does this definition fit the sports industry in the United States presently?

Alternatively, gamesmanship has been defined as follows:

> The winning-at-all costs mentality; it is the way that sports may be, not how it should be. It includes looking for exceptions to the rules, taunting, fake fouls, illegal head starts, taunting to gain an advantage, intentionally injuring another player and intimidation or espionage.[7]

There is often a fine line between gamesmanship and sportsmanship, but gamesmanship is clearly present in sports, and always has been. The *American Heritage Dictionary* defines gamesmanship as "the method or art of winning a game or contest by means of unsportsmanlike behavior or other conduct that does not actually break the rules."

Most would agree cheating involves breaking the actual rules of the game, with the hope of not getting caught, whereas gamesmanship focuses on the idea of winning at all costs. It embodies the concept "it is only cheating if you get caught." It has been argued by one noted sports writer that American sports is consumed with gamesmanship and that players rarely value sportsmanship.[8] It is the attitude of "show me a good loser and I'll show you a loser." Everyone is looking for an edge in competition, and athletes sometimes do not care how they get it. Many support the concept of gamesmanship, believing it to be a legitimate way to compete in sports.

CASE STUDY 2-1   *Enforcing the Letter of the Law*

As South Pasadena High School's best pole vaulter, Robin Laird stood at the top of the runway preparing for her first vault of the day, a 7 ft 6 in. attempt, Robin was probably not thinking about the friendship bracelet on her left wrist, but someone else was—the coach of the opposing team. She completed her vault, giving her team a 66–61 victory and an apparent league title. However, opposing coach Mike Knowles began pointing at his wrist and gesturing toward Laird. A section of the National Federation of State High School Association rules stated: "Jewelry shall not be worn by contestants," and further stated that competitors, if wearing jewelry, would be disqualified from competition. When Laird found out what happened, she burst into tears, blaming herself for her team's loss of the event and the league championship. Coach Knowles responded, "It's unfortunate for the young lady. But you've got to teach the kids rules are rules." Some questioned the coach's motives for so strictly enforcing the rules.[9]

1. Does the adage "it is not whether you win or lose but how you play the game" still hold true?
2. Does sportsmanship still exist at all levels of sport, or has it become a winning at all costs attitude?
3. Were the coach's actions of strictly enforcing the rules a violation of the spirit of competition?

---

[7] Eugene F. Provenzo, John P. Renaud, and Asterie Baker Provenzo, *Encyclopedia of the Social and Cultural Foundations of Education*, vol. 2 (New York: Sage Publications, 2008): 325.

[8] See "Gamesmanship vs. Sportsmanship," *Sports Illustrated*, September 1, 1999.

[9] Dave Wielenga, "Where's the Sportsmanship? Girl Disqualified for Wearing Bracelet," *Sports Illustrated*, May 11, 2010.

CASE STUDY 2-2   *Ultimate Act of Sportsmanship*

Western Oregon's Sara Tucholsky hit a three-run home run in the second inning of a game against Central Washington. As she rounded first base in her home run trot, she collapsed in the base path when her right knee gave away. Her coach was told by the umpire that a pinch runner could take her place but she would only be credited with a single and two RBIs; the home run would be erased. It was against the rules to allow her teammates to help her around the bases. It was Sara's only home run in four years. Central Washington's first baseman, Mallory Holtman, was her conference's all-time home run leader. She had a solution. Holtman and her teammates would carry Sara around the bases; there was no rule prohibiting that, and that is just what they did. Western Oregon won the game 4–2.[10]

---

1. Were the actions of Holtman and her teammates sportsmanlike?
2. Should you ever assist your opponent to win in a competitive sport?
3. Did the actions of Holtman and her teammates destroy the integrity of the sport?

No one may have been better at gamesmanship than NBA champion Bill Laimbeer of the Detroit Pistons. Oh yeah, and by the way, he was pretty good at basketball too. He was once referred to as the NBA's "consummate actor and psychiatrist." For whatever reason, Laimbeer just had a way of getting under people's skin. Brad Daugherty of the NBA Cleveland Cavaliers said of Laimbeer, "If he is trying to get on people's nerves, he is doing a good job."[11] Laimbeer elbowed, fought, pleaded, annoyed, and cajoled his way to two NBA championships while he had others thinking about how "annoying" he was. One *Sports Illustrated* writer put it succinctly: "As the baddest of the Detroit Pistons' Bad Boys in the late 80s, Laimbeer was as famous for being a crybaby jerk as he was for his contributions to the Pistons' back-to-back championships."[12]

He played the "villain" well and no one was a better actor than Laimbeer, who could "flop" with the best in the league. At 6 ft 11in. and 260 lbs, Laimbeer provoked a long list of NBA Hall of Fame players. Laimbeer's wife once said, "People are always coming up to me and saying how nice I am and how could I be married to such a jackass. . . . You just have to get to know him. Don't take any of his ___ ____, you just can't let him bug you." But many people did, and Laimbeer got two NBA rings while opponents were consumed with Laimbeer's annoying behavior.

Coach Red Auerbach was a master at "head games." Was it just maintenance problems that caused the heaters to come on *only* in the visitor's locker room during May and June NBA playoff games in the Boston Garden?[13] How about all those "dead spots" in the floor at the Boston Garden that only Celtic players knew about? Auerbach turned Boston Garden into a "smoky palace" home court advantage. When the St. Louis Blues were ready to take on the Detroit Red Wings in the 1996 Stanley Cup playoffs, they had a surprise waiting for them at Detroit's Joe Louis Arena. The Red Wings had been thoughtful hosts and had just painted the Blues' locker room. Just painted meaning one hour before the Blues arrived! How thoughtful, you might say. One player remarked: "While the nice, white appearance would have gotten Martha Stewart's seal of approval, the fumes from the paint

---

[10] Graham Hays, "Central Washington Offers the Ultimate Act of Sportsmanship," *ESPN.com*, April 28, 2008.
[11] Clifton Brown, "Gamesmanship or Dirty Play?" *New York Times,* February 7, 1989.
[12] Jeff Pearlman, "Detroit Pistons Center Bill Laimbeer," *Sports Illustrated Vault*, November 10, 1997.
[13] "Auerbach's Gone, but Spirit in Gamesmanship Lives On," *Sports Illustrated*, July 25, 2007.

could have choked a cow." The next year the Red Wings did the same thing again. Blues defenseman Marc Bergevin told reporters, "It looks nice, though."[14] Hockey has had its share of gamesmanship maneuvers. Punch Imlach, general manager for the NHL Buffalo Sabres and a great hockey man, knew how to gain a competitive edge. It was believed he once hired a guy to go to the Montreal Canadiens hotel rooms in the afternoon and "stroll" the hotel hallway playing the bagpipes in an attempt to disturb the Canadiens pregame naps![15]

Tennis player Andy Murray was accused of using gamesmanship tactics to "rattle" his opponent when his opponent claimed Murray had faked an injury. Murray responded:

> That's very disappointing to hear. I never once used any of the rules that certain players have used to try to gain an upper hand in a match or to slow my opponent down. Definitely when I played him at Queen's that was not the case. I didn't know there was a problem but I couldn't grip the racket the following day. There are so many things in matches where guys take toilet breaks, injury time-outs, delay you sometimes when you are trying to serve and take a little bit longer between the points than they are meant to. It happens all the time. It's just part of the sport.[16]

Murray said he never had to resort to gamesmanship, "It's a form of cheating. It's bending the rules to gain advantage. It's a bit like diving in football. It does go on and certain players do it and certain players don't. I'm one of the guys who doesn't do it."[17]

NBA player Danny Ainge was always a "gamer." Was his throwing a towel at the Celtics general manager meant to distract a player or just poor sportsmanship?[18] Is excessively complimenting another team or guaranteeing a win for your team considered gamesmanship?[19] Excessive criticism of referees has also been referred to gamesmanship.[20]

Minnesota Twins first baseman Kent Hrbek was a big man, physically. In a controversial play in the 1991 World Series, Hrbek pulled Atlanta Braves player Ron Gant (172 lbs) off first base and Hrbek (253 lbs) tagged him out. The Braves called it cheating. Hrbek said, smiling, "I didn't get away with anything. . . . I just kept my glove on his leg, and his leg came off the base."[21]

Sports Illustrated listed its five rules of gamesmanship in the NBA:[22]

1. Bench players jump at visiting shooters
2. Coaches wander in the sight line of visiting free-throw shooters

---

[14] Chuck O'Donnell, "Playing Those Mind Games—Gamesmanship in National Hockey League Playoffs," *Hockey Digest*, Summer 2001.

[15] Ibid.

[16] Steve Bierley, "Andy Murray Accused of Using Gamesmanship to Upset Opponent," *Guardian.Co.Uk*, June 24, 2009.

[17] Ibid.

[18] "Celtics' GM Danny Ainge Throws a Towel to Distract a Player: Gamesmanship or Poor Sportsmanship," *Syracuse*, May 5, 2010.

[19] Sam Farmer, "Gamesmanship or Not, Brett Favre Praises Cowboys," *Los Angeles Times*, January 14, 2010; Rich Cimini, "Braylon Edwards Pulls a Joe Namath: Guarantees New York Jets' Playoff Berth," *New York Daily News*, December 31, 2009; "Steelers Defensive Back Smith Guarantees Win vs. Perfect Pats," *ESPN.com*, December 5, 2007.

[20] Mike Bresnahan, "Lakers Coach Phil Jackson on Criticizing Referees: It's Gamesmanship," *Los Angeles Times*, April 24, 2010.

[21] Bill Plaschke, "Hrbek Wins Game of Gamesmanship," *Los Angeles Times*, October 21, 1991.

[22] Jack McCallum, "Breaking the Rules: NBA," *Sports Illustrated Vault*, July 25, 2007.

3. A player who is not in foul trouble quickly raises his hand
4. Defenses steal plays
5. Defenders get grabby

The National Football League is made up of 32 league franchises with 53 players on each team who are earning a large amount of money to play a sport to win games. Should professional players be looking for any advantage they can get over their competitors to prevail? Football has never been categorized as a gentlemanly sport,[23] but the issue becomes a problem when gamesmanship drifts into cheating. Richard Lapchick, director of the Institute for Diversity and Ethics in Sports at the University of Central Florida, has stated: "From my point of view, it is getting worse."[24]

Even in the gentlemanly game of golf, gamesmanship has its place. In the 1947 United States Open, PGA players Sam Snead and Lew Worsham were battling for the title. Just as Snead was about to putt on the 18th green, Worsham stopped him and called for a measurement. The officials brought out a tape measure, and it was discovered that Snead was in fact farther from the hole (30.5 in. to 29.5 in. for Worsham) so Snead did have the honor of putting first. After a delay of five minutes, Snead missed his putt and Worsham subsequently made his putt and won the tournament. Worsham broke no rules in asking for the measurement. Was Worsham a poor sport under the circumstances?[25] In another gamesmanship moment from golf, in the 1971 U.S. Open, on the first tee, PGA golfer Lee Trevino pulled a three foot rubber snake from his golf bag, held it up, wiggled it for the amazed gallery, and then tossed it at Jack Nicklaus's feet. Trevino won the playoff hole and the U.S. Open.

CASE STUDY 2-3 *When Is Enough, Enough?*

Beginning in September 2006, Connecticut high school football teams were subject to a "50 Point Rule." Football coaches who were found to be running up the score when their team was ahead by 50 points or more were subject to sanctions. The first week of the season Bridge Central beat Bassick 56–0. At halftime the score was 49–0. The third touchdown was scored by a third string player. The loss was Bassick's fourth in a row. The Bassick coach noted that Dave Cadelina, coach of the Bridgeport team, had acted in a sportsmanlike manner in coaching the game. A three-member panel examined the actions of the coach, and he was exonerated, finding he did not engage in any unsportsmanlike acts.

1. Do you favor a rule similar to the 50 Point Rule?
2. Would you distinguish between professional and amateur sports?
3. Should different rules apply to different sports? Soccer? Baseball? Football? Hockey?
4. As a coach, should you ever instruct a player not to score or play to the fullest extent of their ability?[26]

---

[23] Jeffri Chadiha, "NFL Players Look for Any Edge They Can Get," *ESPN.com*, August 1, 2007.
[24] George Vecsey, "Sports of the Times; When Gamesmanship Blurs to Cheating," *New York Times*, September 23, 2010.
[25] Al Barkow, "Golf's Gamesmanship Is as Subtle as a Controlled Slice," *New York Times*, June 13, 1993.
[26] Hal Levy, "Connecticut: 50-Point Rule Gets Tested," *MaxPreps High School Sports*, September 28, 2006;
   John Dankosky, "High School Team Tests 50-Point Run-Up Rule," *NPR*, December 14, 2007.

CASE STUDY 2-4   *Poor Taste or Academic Brilliance?*

The Rice University Marching Owl Band (the MOB) has always been a little esoteric, even for the elite. Their "act" is usually received well, even though only a selected few may truly understand their intended purpose. Todd Graham was the head football coach for the second smallest school in Division I-A football, the Rice Owls. He left that job after one year to go to the NCAA's smallest Division I-A football program, Tulsa. The following year Tulsa defeated Rice in the last game of the season at Rice Stadium in Houston. During the halftime show, the MOB's performance became the subject of an investigation by Conference USA. The overriding theme of the performance was a search by the MOB through the nine circles of hell based on Dante's *Divine Comedy*. The band suggested that "Graham's shredded contract was found in the fourth circle of hell with the greedy and the avaricious—also claiming that former Texas A&M coach Dennis Franchione was in that circle." They also claimed that "the coach could be found beyond hell's greatest depths behind a door marked 'Welcome To Tulsa.'"[27] The skit ended with the public address announcer calling Graham a "douche bag." The MOB later apologized, saying the skit was meant to be funny.[28]

1. Should the university or the band be sanctioned for their behavior?
2. How many spectators do you think understood what the performance was actually about anyway?

RULES AND REGULATIONS

The preeminent principle of sportsmanship is to conduct yourself in such a manner as to increase rather than decrease the pleasures found in the sporting activity—both for yourself and your opponent. Sportsmanship involves the values of fair play, which implies adherence to the letter and spirit of equality as indicated in the rules, regulations, and customs that control the play of the sport in question. Many rules and customs regulate sportsmanship. For example, the NCAA attempts to foster sportsmanship in intercollegiate sports with rules on ethical conduct, amateurism, financial aid, academic standards, eligibility, and agents. The amateur athletic association has a myriad of rules dealing with eligibility and personal conduct policies for fans, parents, coaches, and participants. In addition, every sport has customs, which may not necessarily be written rules. Although not officially in the rule book, a baseball player who hits a home run should run at a fairly quick pace around the bases and not at a slow trot. A player who takes his time getting around the bases may be seen as "showing up" the pitcher and could be the subject of retaliation by the opposing club.

The INTEGRITY OF GAME clause (Case Study 2-5), found in the NFL's Standard Player Contract, expresses the idea that it is essential for players to exhibit fair play in playing the game, by assisting in the honest and orderly conduct of games in the National Football League.

CASE STUDY 2-5   *INTEGRITY OF GAME Clause*

INTEGRITY OF GAME. Player recognizes the detriment to the League and professional football that would result from impairment of public confidence in the honest and orderly conduct of NFL games or the

---

[27] Associated Press, "Rice Band's 'Todd Graham's Inferno' Not a Hit at Tulsa," *ESPN.com*, November 27, 2007.
[28] Sarah Rutledge, "MOB Makes National Headlines in Wake of Tulsa Outrage," *The Rice Thresher*, November 30, 2007.

integrity and good character of NFL players. Player therefore acknowledges his awareness that if he accepts a bribe or agrees to throw or fix an NFL game; fails to promptly report a bribe offer or an attempt to throw or fix an NFL game; bets on an NFL game; knowingly associates with gamblers or gambling activity; uses or provides players with stimulants or other drugs for the purpose of attempting to enhance on-field performance; or is guilty of any other form of conduct reasonably judged by the League Commissioner to be detrimental to the League or professional football, the Commissioner will have the right, but only after giving Player the opportunity for a hearing at which he may be represented by counsel of his choice, to fine Player in a reasonable amount; to suspend Player for a period certain or indefinitely; and/or terminate this contract.[29]

Case 2-1 describes what occurs when a soccer player is injured in a recreational soccer match. Would you consider what the player did, unsportsmanlike conduct or an example of gamesmanship? Is the fact that the player violated a rule of the game enough to conclude that he acted in an unethical and unsportsmanlike manner?

📖 CASE 2-1   *Lestina v. West Bend Mutual Insurance Company*

501 N.W.2d 28 (1993)

Robert F. Lestina was injured in a collision with Leopold Jerger . . . during a recreational soccer match organized by the Waukesha County Old Timers League, a recreational league for players over the age of 30.

[Lestina] (45 years of age) was playing an offensive position for his team and [Jerger] (57 years of age) was the goalkeeper for the opposing team on April 20, 1988, when the injury occurred. Shortly before [Lestina] was injured, he had scored the first goal of the game. After his goal [Lestina] regained possession of the ball and was about to attempt a second goal when [Jerger] apparently ran out of the goal area and collided with [him]. [Lestina] asserted that the [goalie] "slide tackled" him in order to prevent him from scoring. Although slide tackles are allowed under some soccer rules, this league's rules prohibit such maneuvers to minimize risk of injury. Jerger claimed that the collision occurred as he and [Lestina] simultaneously attempted to kick the soccer ball.

Source: *Reprinted from Westlaw with permission of Thomson Reuters.*

The safety rule in Lestina that prohibits slide tackles is promulgated to ensure fair play. Although slide tackles are not prohibited in all soccer leagues, they were prohibited in this "Old Timers" league with Lestina, 45 years old, and Jerger, 57 years old. The rule that mandates fair play here takes into consideration the age and skill of the participating athletes.[30]

Consider how the participants acted in the soccer match described in Case 2-2. Were their actions any different from those in the *Lestina* case noted above?

---

[29] NFL Player Contract, Paragraph 15.

[30] For further study, see Hana R. Miura, "*Lestina v. West Bend Mutual Insurance Company*: Widening the Court as a Playing Field for Negligent Participants in Recreational Team Contact Sports," *Wisconsin Law Review*, 1994.

📖 CASE 2-2 *Nabozny v. Barnhill*

334 N.E.2d 258 (Ill. 1975)

A soccer match began between two amateur teams at Duke Child's Field in Winnetka, Illinois. Nabozny was playing the position of goalkeeper for the Hansa team. Barnhill was playing the position of forward for the Winnetka team. Members of both teams were of high-school age. Approximately twenty minutes after play had begun, a Winnetka player kicked the ball over the midfield line. Two players, Jim Gallos (for Hansa) and Barnhill (for Winnetka) chased the free ball. Gallos reached the ball first. Since he was closely pursued by Barnhill, Gallos passed the ball to Nabozny, the Hansa goalkeeper. Gallos then turned away and prepared to receive a pass from Nabozny. Nabozny, in the meantime, went down on his left knee, received the pass, and pulled the ball to his chest. Barnhill did not turn away when Gallos did, but continued to run in the direction of Nabozny and kicked the left side of his head causing him severe injuries.

All of the occurrence witnesses agreed that Barnhill had time to avoid contact with Nabozny and that Nabozny remained at all times within the 'penalty area,' a rectangular area between the eighteenth yard line and the goal. Four witnesses testified that they saw Nabozny in a crouched position on his left knee inside the penalty zone. Nabozny testified that he actually had possession of the ball when he was struck by Barnhill.

[T]he game was played under 'F.I.F.A' rules. . . . [E]xperts agreed that those rules prohibited all players from making contact with the goalkeeper when he is in possession of the ball in the penalty area. Possession is defined in the Chicago area as referring to the goalkeeper having his hands on the ball. Under 'F.I.F.A' rules, any contact with a goalkeeper in possession in the penalty area is an infraction of the rules, even if such contact is unintentional. The goalkeeper is the only member of a team who is allowed to touch a ball in play so long as he remains in the penalty area. The only legal contact permitted in soccer is shoulder to shoulder contact between players going for a ball within playing distance. The contact in question in this case should not have occurred. Additionally, goalkeeper head injuries are extremely rare in soccer. As a result of being struck, [Nabozny] suffered permanent damage to his skull and brain. . . .

Individual sports are advanced and competition enhanced by a comprehensive set of rules. Some rules secure the better playing of the game as a test of skill. Other rules are primarily designed to protect participants from serious injury. The safety rule in *Nabozny* is contained in a recognized set of rules governing the conduct of athletic competition.

This rule mandates the tenets of fair play and ethical behavior. Although, obviously, it is essential to good competition that the athletes try as hard as they can to achieve victory, the most vital aspect of competition is not in victory but in overcoming the challenge presented by a worthy opponent. The glue between opponents is the element of fair play. It is an ethical question, whether to choose to follow the stipulations of fair play between well-matched opponents following established rules and customs, or to allow the behemoth of "winning at all costs" to prevail.

Source: *Reprinted from Westlaw with permission of Thomson Reuters.*

Consider the ethical dilemmas presented for all participants and the sports officials in the following case study.

CASE STUDY 2-6 *Trippin' Coach*

There is no doubt New York Jets strength coach, Sal Alosi, is a competitor both on and off the field. Alosi showed his own strength in a game on Monday Night Football when he tripped Miami Dolphins player Nolan Carroll as Carroll ran by the Jets bench during the game. He was suspended for the remainder of the season and fined $25,000 by the NFL. Alosi said "I accept responsibility for my actions and respect the team's decision . . . You are asking me to give you a logical explanation for an illogical act."

1. Did the league take enough disciplinary action against the coach for his unethical conduct?

2. Was the fine too little, considering the coach could have severely injured the Dolphin player?[31]

Rules and regulations are promulgated by state athletic associations, professional sports, and state laws. Consider Case 2-3, in which a boxer allegedly used a foreign substance in his handwraps in violation of professional boxing rules.

CASE 2-3 *Margarito v. State Athletic Commission*

2010 WL 4010605

1. The Parties

Margarito is a professional boxer who has fought more than 30 times across the United States, including more than half a dozen championship

---

[31] Greg Bishop, "Contrite Jets Suspended Coach After Sideline Trip to Dolphin," *The New York Times*, December 13, 2010. Also see, Kevin Seifert, Dirty Laundry: Trippin' Over Tripping, *ESPN*, October 29, 2009.

fights. Margarito was licensed by the Commission as a professional boxer in California from the mid-1990's until 2009 when his license was revoked.

The Commission is the agency with sole jurisdiction over professional boxing in California and is responsible for adopting and enforcing the professional boxing rules in this state. The Commission has the authority to issue, suspend, and revoke boxing licenses...

2. The Illegal Hand Wraps

Margarito was scheduled to fight Shane Mosley (Mosley) in a welterweight championship boxing contest in Los Angeles on January 24, 2009. Margarito's trainer, Javier Capetillo (Capetillo), was responsible for preparing the hand wraps, bandages, and tape used to protect Margarito's hands during the contest. Capetillo was a professional trainer who had worked with many professional boxers during his 38-year career as a trainer. During his 11 years as Margarito's trainer, Capetillo was the only person who wrapped Margarito's hands before a boxing contest.

Before the contest with Mosley, Capetillo was wrapping Margarito's hands while four Commission inspectors and Mosley's trainer observed the process. After Capetillo finished wrapping Margarito's right hand, Mosley's trainer asked the inspectors to physically inspect a pre-made gauze "knuckle pad" insert that Capetillo was about to wrap over Margarito's left hand. The inspectors found that the inner layers of the pad were discolored and that the pad felt harder than it should have. In a report prepared after the inspection, Commission Inspector Che Guevara (Guevara) described the gauze pad removed from Margarito's left hand as "dirty-looking" and smeared with a white substance that looked like plaster and was hard to the touch. Concluding that the pad violated the rules, the inspectors confiscated the pad and instructed Capetillo to prepare a new one.

Mosley's trainer then asked the inspectors to examine the gauze insert in Margarito's already wrapped right hand. Margarito insisted there was nothing in the right hand wrapping, and held his hand out saying, "Touch it. Feel it. Go ahead. There is nothing in it." The inspectors ordered the wrapping removed and found a similar improperly hardened pad, which they confiscated. After Capetillo prepared two new knuckle pads, the inspectors approved Margarito's hand wraps and allowed Margarito to proceed with the boxing match.

In a letter dated January 27, 2009, the Commission notified Margarito that his boxing license was temporarily suspended pending a final determination of the case. The Commission explained the reason for the suspension as follows:

> "This action is taken because of your recent participation in what appears to be a violation of rule 323. Rule 323 limits the use of gauze and tape on an athlete's hands and requires that both contestants be represented while the gauze and tape are applied. The rule also prescribes the manner in which the gauze and tape is applied to an athlete's hands. Here, it appears that a foreign substance was used in the hand-wraps in violation of Rule 323. Additionally, Commission rule 390 allows the commission to revoke, fine, suspend or otherwise discipline any licensee who 'conducts himself or herself at any time or place in a manner which is determined by the Commission to reflect discredit to boxing.'"

The Commission set a formal hearing on the matter for February 10, 2009.

3. Administrative Hearing

At the February 10, 2009 hearing, Commission Inspectors Guevara, Dean Lohuis (Lohuis), and Mike Bray (Bray) all testified that they felt the knuckle pads Capetillo initially placed in Margarito's hand wraps before the Mosley fight and that the pads felt harder than allowed by the applicable rules and were confiscated. After feeling one of the confiscated pads at the hearing, Margarito admitted that he felt something hard. Capetillo admitted that the confiscated pads violated the applicable rules, and acknowledged that had they been used, they could have seriously injured Margarito's opponent.

The commissioners at the hearing inspected one of the pads that had been confiscated from Margarito's hand wraps and compared it to the soft gauze that is used to wrap a boxer's hand before a contest. The other confiscated pad was sent to the Department of Justice's forensic laboratory for evaluation, where it was photographed under a microscope at six times magnification. The photographs were presented as evidence at the hearing.

At the conclusion of the hearing, all seven commissioners voted unanimously to revoke Margarito's license.

4. The Commission's Decision

In a written decision issued on March 31, 2009, the Commission found that the knuckle pads removed from Margarito's hand wraps before the Mosley fight on January 24, 2009, had been adulterated with a white plaster-like substance. The Commission concluded that the use of adulterated knuckle pads by a boxer seriously endangers the boxer's opponent and gives the boxer an unfair advantage that causes discredit to boxing. The Commission further concluded that "[b]ecause [Margarito] violated Commission Rule 323 there is sufficient cause for revocation of [Margarito's] boxing license...

The Commission rejected Margarito's argument that he could not be held responsible for violating rule 323 because he did not know that Capetillo had inserted the illegal pads into his hand wraps and noted that "[t]he Commission's laws and rules, enacted to protect public health and safety, do not require either knowledge or intent for a violation to occur." The Commission stated: "Because of the serious physical consequences which could have resulted to the other boxer from the use of boxing gloves loaded with illegal knuckle pads, the appropriate penalty is revocation."

. . . the Commission has adopted professional boxing rules. (*Cal.Code Regs., tit. 4, § 201.*) Rule 323 specifies the materials that may be used to wrap a boxer's hands during a contest and prescribes the manner in which those materials may be applied. It states:

"Bandages shall not exceed the following restrictions: One winding of surgeon's adhesive tape, not over one and one-half inches wide, placed directly on the hand to protect that part of the hand near the wrist. Said tape may cross the back of the hand twice but shall not extend within one inch of the knuckles when hand is clenched to make a fist. Contestants shall use soft surgical bandage not over two inches wide, held in place by not more than ten yards of surgeon's adhesive tape for each hand. Not more than twenty yards of bandage may be used to complete the wrappings for each hand. Bandages shall be applied in the dressing room in the presence of a commission representative and both contestants. Either contestant may waive his privilege of witnessing the bandaging of his opponent's hands."

Source: *Reprinted from Westlaw with permission of Thomson Reuters.*

Were the actions of the State Athletic Commission appropriate? Do you think there was an actual violation of the rules by the boxer under these circumstances?

CASE STUDY 2-7 *"Icing" the Kicker*

"Icing" the kicker has become a term of art in American football. Coaches attempt to call a time-out seconds before a field goal kicker lines up to kick an important field goal. If a high school placekicker lines up to kick the winning field goal and just as he begins his kick, the opposing coach calls time-out, is that considered a strategic move or poor sportsmanship? Should time-outs be used in such a fashion? If time-outs are in the discretion of the coach, then it is an ethical move, correct? Does it matter if it occurs in a professional or amateur game?[32]

---

[32] Judy Battista, "New Way to Ice the Kicker: It's Legal, but Is It Sporting?" *New York Times,* October 21, 2007.

Since 2000, placekickers in the NFL have made 77.3% of field goals kicked in the final two minutes or in overtime when no time-out was called. When a time-out was called by the opposing coach, NFL placekickers were successful 79.7% notwithstanding the distance of the kick.[33]

"Butt-ending" is the practice in ice hockey of taking the handle end of the hockey stick and driving it into another player's body. Butt-ending is unexpected and constitutes unsportsmanlike conduct. It can result in a major penalty and subsequent disqualification from the game. The specter and possibility of butt-ending might have been utilized as a sort of gamesmanship to unsettle the opponent in Case 2-4. If the goal of the player was to physically intimidate and bully the opponent, then his decision to butt-end was unethical. Would you say the hockey player cheated or engaged in unsportsmanlike conduct or gamesmanship in the following case?

📖 CASE 2-4 *Gauvin v. Clark*

537 N.E.2d 94 (1989)

On January 30, 1980, the varsity hockey team of Worcester State College played against the team from Nichols College. Gauvin played center position for the Worcester State College team. Clark played center for the Nichols College team. During the second period, Gauvin was involved in a face-off with Clark, in which the referee dropped the puck, and both men vied for possession. Clark won the face-off. As the puck slid down the ice toward the Nichols College team's net, Gauvin felt a stick in his abdomen. Gauvin saw Clark's hockey stick coming away from Gauvin's abdomen, with the back of the hockey stick, called the "butt-end," protruding from Clark's hands. . . . Clark gave Gauvin a shot to the midsection after the puck slid down toward the Nichols goal. The blow to Gauvin's abdomen came after the face-off had been completed. The blow was struck when Gauvin and Clark were no longer competing for the puck.

Source: *Reprinted from Westlaw with permission of Thomson Reuters.*

ETHICAL CHOICES IN THE AMERICAN NATIONAL PASTIME

It is probable that no other sport blurs the thin line between gamesmanship and sportsmanship more than baseball.[34] Stealing signs, pitchers scuffing balls, batters corking bats, phantom tags, ejected managers disguising themselves in the dugout to go undetected by umpires, brushback

---

[33] Michael David Smith, When Icing the Kicker Can Backfire, *Wall Street Journal,* September 22, 2010.
[34] James Wolfe and Mary Ann Presman, *Curse? There Ain't No Stinking Chicago Cubs Curse and Other Stories About Sports and Gamesmanship* (Charleston, SC: BookSurge Publishing, 2009).

pitches, and head games have always been part of the national pastime. Whether before, during, or after the game, baseball has seen its share of gamesmanship and blatant cheating.[35]

Baseball is a game of rules. In some regards it is very strict. It is played on a diamond between two distinct white lines and dominated by statistics and numbers. Notwithstanding this structure, baseball also has its share of unwritten rules that players are encouraged to follow. Baseball's list of unwritten rules has included the following:[36]

1. Don't swing at the first pitch after back-to-back home runs.
2. Don't "work the count" when your team is winning or losing by a wide margin.
3. When a batter is hit by a pitch, the batter should never rub the mark that is made by the baseball.
4. A batter should never stand on the dirt cutout at home plate while a pitcher is warming up.
5. A player should never walk in front of a catcher or umpire when getting into the batter's box.
6. A player should never help the opposition make a play.
7. A reliever pitcher should "take it easy" when pitching to another reliever pitcher.
8. A player should follow the umpire's Code when addressing an umpire on the field.
9. Pitchers should always stay in the dugout until the end of the inning in which they get "pulled."
10. Pitchers should never show up their fielders.

Are players required to abide by these rules even though they are unwritten rules?

An ESPN poll of baseball's unwritten rules asked readers the following questions. In your opinion are these tactics a violation of baseball's unwritten rules? Do they constitute unsportsman-like conduct?

1. A batter calls time-out when the pitcher is in the middle of his wind-up.
2. A batter stands at home plate and admires a home run.
3. A batter flips the bat or takes an excruciatingly slow home run trot.
4. A batter runs across the mound while the pitcher is standing on it.
5. A batter bunts to break up a no-hitter.
6. A batter peeks back at a catcher's setup or gets signs relayed to him from a teammate on second base.
7. A batter intentionally leans over the plate to be hit by a pitch.
8. A batter takes a big cut at a 3–0 pitch when his team is way ahead.[37]

Should players abide by these unwritten codes? Does the amount of money professional athletes earn entice them to break the unwritten codes of a sport? Do you consider breaking an unwritten code unsportsmanlike? After all, it is unwritten! Is it cheating or just gamesmanship to do so? Should a player announce to other players that he will no longer be abiding by the sports' unwritten code? Should amateur players (including youth sports participants) have an unwritten code of rules as well?

---

[35] Jerry Crasnick, "Cheating Done Rather Subtly in Baseball Nowadays," *ESPN.com*, August 9, 2007.

[36] "The 'Code': Ten Unwritten Baseball Rules You Might Not Know," *Yahoo.com*, May 5, 2010.

[37] "Vote: Baseball's Unwritten Rules," *ESPN.com*, May 9, 2010. Also see Jason Turbow and Michael Duca, *The Baseball Codes: Beanballs, Sign Stealing, and Bench-Clearing Brawls: The Unwritten Rules of America's Pastime* (New York: Pantheon Books, 2010); Ross Bernstein, *The Code: Baseball's Unwritten Rules and Its Ignore-at-Your-Own-Risk Code of Conduct* (Chicago, IL: Triumph Books, 2008).

Intentionally throwing a ball at a batter in Major League Baseball is against the rules. Major League rules prohibit it:

8.02 The pitcher shall not—

. . . (d) Intentionally Pitch at the Batter.

If, in the umpire's judgment, such a violation occurs, the umpire may elect either to:

1. Expel the pitcher, or the manager and the pitcher, from the game, or
2. Warn the pitcher and the manager of both teams that another such pitch will result in the immediate expulsion of that pitcher (or a replacement) and the manager.

If, in the umpire's judgment, circumstances warrant, both teams may be officially "warned" prior to the game or at any time during the game.[38]

Elite "fastballers" are able to throw a baseball in excess of 100 miles an hour, which could seriously injure or kill a batter.[39] Baseball is a rather pastoral game—slow, calculating, and deliberate. After all, it is the national pastime. Players wait in anticipation for a ball to be hit their way as fans sit patiently waiting for something exciting to happen. It is a game of anticipation. How could such a slow, calculating game lead to violent behavior?

Enter the "brushback" pitch, also referred to as the "beanball" in baseball circles. The brushback pitch has always been a part of the game of baseball. Some pitchers are well known for guarding the plate with an inside fastball. St. Louis Cardinals pitcher, Bob Gibson, was well known in baseball for intentionally throwing at hitters. After Gibson beaned a batter on opening day of the baseball season, Los Angeles Dodgers pitcher Don Drysdale commented: "Welcome to Bob Gibson's school of what you better do and what you better not do."[40] If anyone dared show him up on the field, Gibson took exception. Former player Dusty Baker once received some good advice from baseball's legitimate home run king, Hank Aaron. Aaron said: "'Don't dig in against Bob Gibson, he'll knock you down. He'd knock down his own grandmother if she dared to challenge him. Don't stare at him, don't smile at him, don't talk to him. He doesn't like it. If you happen to hit a home run, don't run too slow, don't run too fast. If you happen to want to celebrate, get in the tunnel first. And if he hits you, don't charge the mound, because he's a Gold Glove Boxer.' I'm like, 'Damn, what about my 17-game hitting streak?' That was the night it ended."[41]

Is the beanball gamesmanship or unnecessary violence on the part of the pitcher? If intentionally throwing a baseball at a player is in violation of the rules of baseball, should a player try to intentionally break the rules of the game, knowing he or she may only get a warning for the first brushback pitch they throw? Should a pitcher throw this type of pitch knowing that the batter may suffer a serious injury?

The brushback pitch has been around since the early days of baseball and has always been a strategic weapon in the pitchers' arsenal. If a batter "crowds" the plate, a pitcher may see that as an infringement of his territory and send a little "chin music" the batter's way. "Chin music" has been

---

[38] Major League Baseball Official Rules 2010, Rule 8.02(d), p. 142.

[39] David Brown, Scout Clocks Reds' Pitching Prospect Chapman at 105 mph, Yahoo! Sports, August 28, 2010.

[40] Chass Murray, "Drysdale Brushed Back Pitchers and Batters for Beanings," *New York Times*, July 12, 1987. See also Bob Gibson, Reggie Jackson, and Lonnie Wheeler, *Sixty Feet, Six Inches: A Hall of Fame Pitcher & A Hall of Fame Hitter Talk About How the Game Is Played* (Garden City, NY: Doubleday, 2009). Also listen to Jackson and Gibson discuss their baseball career at: "Reggie Jackson, Bob Gibson Slug It Out," *NPR*, October 12, 2009.

[41] Bob Gibson-One of the Greatest MLB Pitchers Ever, *Black Sports: The Magazine*, September 2010, Volume 9.

defined by the *Dickson Baseball Dictionary* as "a brushback or knockdown pitch that passes close to the batter's jaw. Thrown so high and inside that the batter supposedly can hear it 'buzz or sing.' Scott Ostler (*Los Angeles Times*, March 31, 1978). When a pitcher throws inside on a batter causing breeze to whistle on his Adam's apple, baseball folks call it chin music."

The *Dickson Baseball Dictionary's* definition of the brushback pitch is as follows:

> A pitch that comes so close to the batter's body that he is forced to step backward and thereby is unable to dig in at the plate. When a batter crowds the plate, taking away some of the pitcher's target area, a pitcher may throw a pitch close to the batter's body to encourage him to move back. Or, as Jim Brosnan (The Long Season, 1960) put it, "To let the batter know the pitcher may, occasionally, lose control and to keep him from digging in at the plate with confidence." The brushback pitch is not to be confused with a *beanball*, which is intentionally thrown at the batter's head. Red Smith once wrote that the brushback pitch, coming after two strikes, was, "in the classic pattern, as rigidly formalized as the minuet". (Ira Berkow, *Red: A Biography of Red Smith*, 1986). Others are less understanding. Mike Royko (*Houston Chronicle*, August 6, 1987; Charles D. Poe): "Some of the philosophers who broadcast baseball games [say] . . . 'the brushback pitch' is part of baseball. That is what they call a ball thrown 90 miles an hour in the general direction of someone's nose."

> See Paul Dickson, *The Dickson Baseball Dictionary Third Edition*, W.W. Norton & Company, 2009, p. 140.

Consider the following case, involving a college player sending a "message" to an opposing player. The player was injured after being hit by a brushback pitch.[42]

📖 CASE 2-5 *Avila v. Citrus Community College District*

131 P.3d 383 (2006)

Jose Luis Avila, a Rio Hondo Community College (Rio Hondo) student, played baseball for the Rio Hondo Roadrunners. On January 5, 2001, Rio Hondo was playing a preseason road game against the Citrus Community College Owls (Citrus College). During the game, a Roadrunners pitcher hit a Citrus College batter with a pitch; when Avila came to bat in the top of the next inning, the Citrus College pitcher hit him in the head with a pitch, cracking his batting helmet. Avila alleges the pitch was an intentional "beanball" thrown in retaliation for the previous hit batter or, at a minimum, was thrown negligently.

Avila staggered, felt dizzy, and was in pain. The Rio Hondo manager told him to go to first base. Avila did so, and when he complained to the Rio Hondo first base coach, he was told to stay in the game. At second base, he still felt pain, numbness, and dizziness. A Citrus College player yelled to the Rio Hondo dugout that the Roadrunners needed a pinch runner. Avila walked off the field and went to the

---

[42] Also see Timothy Davis, "Avila v. Citrus Community College District; Shaping the Contours of Immunity and Primary Assumption of the Risk," *Marquette Sports Law Review*, 2006–2007.

Rio Hondo bench. No one tended to his injuries. As a result, Avila suffered unspecified serious personal injuries.

Being hit by a pitch is an inherent risk of baseball. The dangers of being hit by a pitch, often thrown at speeds approaching 100 miles per hour, are apparent and well known: being hit can result in serious injury or, on rare tragic occasions, death. Most famously, in August 1920, Cleveland Indians shortstop Roy Chapman was hit by a pitch from New York Yankees' Carl Mays. He died the next day. See Mike Sowell, *The Pitch that Killed*, John Wiley & Sons, 1989, 165-190; Bill James, *The Bill James Baseball Abstract*, Ballantine Books, 1985, 131, 137. At least seven other batters in organized baseball have been killed by pitches. See Bill James, *The Bill James Baseball Abstract*, Ballantine Books, 1985, 131, 137.

Being *intentionally* hit is likewise an inherent risk of the sport, so accepted by custom that a pitch intentionally thrown at a batter has its own terminology: "brushback," "beanball," "*chin music*." In turn, those pitchers notorious for throwing at hitters are "headhunters." Pitchers intentionally throw at batters to disrupt a batter's timing or back him away from home plate, to retaliate after a teammate has been hit, or to punish a batter for having hit a home run. (See Roger Kahn, *The Head Game*, Mariner Books, 2000, 205-239.) Some of the most respected baseball managers and pitchers have openly discussed the fundamental place throwing at batters has in their sport. In George Will's study of the game, *Men at Work*, one-time Oakland Athletics and current St. Louis Cardinals manager Tony La Russa details the strategic importance of ordering selective intentional throwing at opposing batters, principally to retaliate for one's own players being hit. See George Will, *Men at Work*, Harper Publications, 1990, 61-64. As Los Angeles Dodgers Hall of Fame pitcher Don Drysdale and New York Giants All Star pitcher Sal "The Barber" Maglie have explained, intentionally throwing at batters can also be an integral part of pitching tactics, a tool to help get batters out by upsetting their frame of mind. Drysdale and Maglie are not alone; past and future Hall of Famers, from Early Wynn and Bob Gibson to Pedro Martinez and Roger Clemens, have relied on the actual or threatened willingness to throw at batters to aid their pitching. See Roger Kahn, *The Head Game*, Mariner Books, 2000, 223-224; "Yankees Aced by Red Sox," Los Angeles Times, May 31, 2001, D7.

As Maglie explained the strategy: "'You have to make the batter afraid of the ball or, anyway, aware that he can get hurt. . . . A good time is when the count is two [balls] and two [strikes]. He's looking to swing. You knock him down then and he gets up shaking. Now [throw a] curve [to] him and you have your out.'" (*Id.*, 211) Maglie's nickname is attributed to his propensity for shaving batters' chins with his pitches. (*Ibid.*) Similarly for Drysdale: "'[T]he knockdown pitch upsets a hitter's timing, like a change-up. It's not a weapon. It's a tactic.'" (*Id.* 235)

While these examples relate principally to professional baseball, "[t]here is nothing legally significant . . . about the level of play" in this case. See *West v. Sundown Little League of Stockton, Inc.* The laws of physics that make a thrown baseball dangerous and the strategic benefits that arise from disrupting a batter's timing are only minimally dependent on the skill level of the participants, and we see no reason to distinguish between collegiate and professional baseball in applying primary assumption of the risk.

It is true that intentionally throwing at a batter is forbidden by the rules of baseball. See Official Rules of Major League Baseball; 2006 NCAA Baseball Rules. But "even when a participant's conduct violates a rule of the game and may subject the violator to internal sanctions prescribed by the sport itself, imposition of legal liability for such conduct might well alter fundamentally the nature of the sport by deterring participants from vigorously engaging in activity that falls close to, but on the permissible side of, a prescribed rule." It is one thing for an umpire to punish a pitcher who hits a batter by ejecting him from the game, or for a league to suspend the pitcher; it is quite another for tort law to chill any pitcher from throwing inside, i.e., close to the batter's body—a permissible and essential part of the sport—for fear of a suit over an errant pitch. For better or worse, being intentionally thrown at is a fundamental part and inherent risk of the sport of baseball. It is not the function of tort law to police such conduct.

The conclusion that being intentionally hit by a pitch is an inherent risk of baseball extends only to situations such as that alleged here, where the hit batter is at the plate. Allegations that a pitcher intentionally hit a batter who was still in the on-deck circle, or elsewhere, would present an entirely different scenario. See "Dollar Signs on the Muscle ... and the Ligament, Tendon, and Ulnar Nerve: Institutional Liability Arising from Injuries to Student-Athletes," *Virginia Journal of Sports and Law*, 2001, 111-112.

Source: *Reprinted from Westlaw with permission of Thomson Reuters.*

CASE STUDY 2-8   *Alex Rodriguez "Ha!"*

In a game between the Yankees and the Blue Jays in May 2007, Alex Rodriguez, as a base runner for the Yankees yelled "ha!" in an effort to distract Toronto third baseman Howie Clark from catching a fly ball. It worked, and the ball dropped in for a run-scoring single. Baseball has no rules against what Rodriguez did. The Toronto manager commented, "I haven't been in the game that long. Maybe I'm naïve. But, to me, it's bush league. One thing, to everybody in this business, you always look at the Yankees and they do things right.

They play hard, class operation, that's what the Yanks are known for. That's not Yankee baseball." Rodriguez's actions were viewed by many in baseball as a "bush league" tactic. Rodriguez responded, "We're desperate. We haven't won a game in a little bit now. We won the game."[43]

1. Are Rodriguez's actions considered beneath him since he was baseball's highest paid player at the time?[44]
2. How can you criticize Rodriguez's actions?
3. As the most visible and highest paid player on arguably the world's most famous sports club, doesn't he have to give his club every chance to win? Yankees management did not criticize the actions of Rodriguez.

The list of gamesmanship episodes in baseball is long, but a few examples worth noting are presented in the following case studies.

CASE STUDY 2-9   *The "Phantom Tag"*

A "phantom tag" has been defined by *The Dickson Baseball Dictionary* as "a missed tag or a tag from a glove without the ball in it, either one of which is mistakenly credited as a legal tag." Dustin Pedroia is an All-Star second baseman for the Boston Red Sox. Certainly, he knows he needs to tag a base runner with the baseball for that runner to be called out by the umpire. Pedroia supposedly tagged Orioles centerfielder Felix Pie as Pie slid into second base. The only problem was, the baseball was in Pedroia's left hand and he only tagged Pie with his empty glove. With a quick sleight of hand, Pedroia placed the ball in his glove and showed it to the umpire, who immediately declared Pie out. Did Pedroia cheat? He obviously knew what he was doing and even made an attempt to cover up his illegal actions. Could his actions be viewed as a veteran ballplayer doing whatever he needed to do to help his team win a game in a heated pennant race? Pedroia was not being paid to be a "good sport" by his club but was being paid to win. Should Pedroia have come clean, admitted his trick to the umpire, and allowed the umpire to correct his mistake? If Pedroia admitted his intentional breaking of the rules to the umpire, what would Red Sox management have said to Pedroia? Possibly, "Excellent job, Dustin, you have keep the integrity of the national pastime intact"? Most likely not. On the contrary, Pedroia was probably congratulated by his teammates in the clubhouse for his deceptive actions on the diamond.[45]

The Major League Baseball Uniform Player's Contract mentions fair play, sportsmanship, and good citizenship:

In consideration of the facts above recited and of the promises of each to the other, the parties agree as follows:

Loyalty

3.(a) The Player agrees to perform his services hereunder diligently and faithfully, to keep himself in first-class physical condition and to obey the Club's training rules, and pledges himself to the American

---

[43] Tyler Kepner, "Rodriguez Says 'Ha,' but Jays Aren't Laughing," *New York Times*, May 31, 2007. Also see Craig Calcaterra, "A-Rod, Dallas Braden and Baseball Etiquette," *NBC Sports*, April 23, 2010.

[44] "A-Rod's Antics: Bush League or Major Play?" *Associated Press*, May 31, 2007.

[45] Ryan Hogan, "Dustin Pedroia's Prestidigitation: Cheating or Gamesmanship?" *Bombasticsports.com*, July 1, 2009; David W. Rainey, Janet D. Larsen, Alan Stephenson, and Torry Olson, "Normative Rules Among Umpires: The 'Phantom Tag' at Second Base," *Journal of Sport Behavior* 16 (1993).

public and to the Club to conform to high standards of personal conduct, *fair play* and good *sportsmanship*. (emphasis added)

TERMINATION . . .
By Club
7.(b) The Club may terminate this contract upon written notice to the Player (but only after requesting and obtaining waivers of this contract from all other Major League Clubs) if the Player shall at any time: (1) fail, refuse or neglect to conform his personal conduct to the standards of *good citizenship* and good sportsmanship . . . (emphasis added)

A Major League Baseball player is contractually obligated to engage in fair play and sportsmanship and be a good citizen. How does that affect your viewpoint of gamesmanship and sportsmanship if the player is contractually bound to perform such duties?

Jack McDowell was a fierce baseball competitor and gave as much as he got. When he came off the pitching mound in a game in 1995, he heard the boos of 20,000 fans in Yankee stadium, so "Black Jack" gave it right back to them by extending his middle finger and he did it while exiting the mound. The next day, the New York tabloids deemed him the "Yankee Flipper," an obvious play on words with reference to Joe DiMaggio's "Yankee Clipper."[46] How do you view McDowell's actions?

CASE STUDY 2-10 *Mike Scott and "The Right Scuff" (Allegedly!)*

Mike Scott was a great baseball pitcher for the Houston Astros, but he was not so great for the New York Mets. This led some to believe Scott's overnight development of a pitch, called the split finger, was not on the "up and up." Chicago Cubs manager Jim Frey could not understand how Scott went "from being so bad one year to so good the next." In June 1985, Frey mailed a piece of sandpaper to the National League President that Cubs first baseman Leon Durham found near the pitching mound during a game that Scott pitched for the Astros. In that same game, Frey had the umpire check the baseball 10 times to make sure Scott was not scuffing the ball. After examining the baseball the umpire found no signs of foul play by Scott. Scott seemed to be amused by the whole situation, saying "Maybe next time I'll go out there with a portable workbench and power tools." In 1986, Scott drew intense opposition from many teams. Pitching guru Roger Craig said, "I could never tell if he was actually scuffing the ball. I never found any evidence. I was just playing with his mind trying to upset him. What Mike did last year he did on his own." During the 1986 playoffs between the Houston Astros and New York Mets, one New York paper ran a headline, "The Right Scuff." One of the umpires in the series said, "I've checked him 65 times this year, and in my heart all I know is, the man is clean." Mets manager Davey Johnson said of Scott, "I think he could make a cue ball dance." Scott replied, "If scuffing is on the batter's mind, it's to my advantage."[47] Scott pitched for the Mets from 1978 to 1982 and had a win–loss record of 14–27. With Houston, he posted a 110–81 win–loss record and won a Cy Young award. Even though no one ever proved Scott did anything wrong, ESPN unjustly named him the third biggest cheater in baseball history (without any proof whatsoever, we might add). Mike Scott probably got a good chuckle out of that.[48]

If gamesmanship also can be defined as "mind games," did not Mike Scott get the better of his detractors with his laissez faire attitude? After all, Scott was never found guilty of any wrongdoing.

---

[46] "Bird Is the Word," *ESPN.com*, November 27, 2006.
[47] Ron Fimrite, "No Wonder He's Hot," *Sports Illustrated Vault*, January 12, 1987.
[48] *Biggest Cheaters in Baseball*, ESPN.go.com, page 2, 2007.

Isn't part of gamesmanship getting your opponent to think about something else other than winning? If so, Mike Scott was a gamesmanship guru.

CASE STUDY 2-11   *Baseball's Showman*

There is no doubt Bill Veeck was the showman of baseball and proved it over many years in the game with his creative ideas. He used gimmicks and many other strategies to get fans to the ballpark. He also wanted to win.[49] On August 19, 1951, Veeck's last place St. Louis Browns were playing the Detroit Tigers in the second game of a double header in St. Louis. Veeck was looking for something to spice up his clubs last place position. He found it in Eddie Gaedel. Unbeknownst to others, Veeck had signed Gaedel to a major league contract. Veeck instructed Browns' manager, Zack Taylor, to send Gaedel to the plate in the first inning as a pinch hitter. Using a pinch hitter in the first inning may seem odd in baseball circles. However, what was so unique about Gaedel was that he was only 3 ft 7 in. tall. Prior to his baseball career Gaedel had been working in "show business."[50] Tigers pitcher Bob Cain threw four straight balls to Gaedel, who set his bat down and dutifully walked to first base.

There are no height or weight requirements for players in baseball. With that in mind, consider the following:

1. Do you consider Veeck's use of Gaedel as a pinch hitter merely a stunt?
2. Do you consider Veeck's actions demeaning to Gaedel or to the integrity of the game of baseball?
3. Could a club use a player like Gaedel, in today's modern game?
4. If Gaedel had a good chance of getting on base when he batted, would it be acceptable for a club to use him in strategic situations during the game?[51]
5. Are Veeck's actions considered gamesmanship or cheating? Boorish? Discriminatory? Demeaning? Strategic? Poor sportsmanship or merely a marketing ploy by a desperate owner to attract fans to a last place club?

When Veeck owned the Cleveland Indians in the 1940s, he had a movable fence installed in the outfield that could be shifted as much as 15 feet. How much Veeck moved it depended on how the Indians matched up against an opponent. Veeck could find no rule against it, although the American League eventually adopted one in 1947 in response to Veeck's actions, decreeing that outfield fences be kept in a "fixed" position during the season.

How would you categorize the various actions described in the following Case Study 2-12? Are they unethical, cheating, or mere gamesmanship?

---

[49] "Bill Veeck Was No Baseball Midget," *Los Angeles Times*, January 4, 1986.

[50] Richard Goldstein, "Jim Delsing, 80, Pinch-Runner for Midget in Baseball Stunt Dies," *New York Times*, May 9, 2006; Mike Brewster, "Bill Veeck: A Baseball Mastermind," *Bloomberg Business Week*, October 27, 2004.

[51] Jim Tootle, "Bill Veeck and James Thurber: The Literary Origins of the Midget Pinch Hitter," *NINE: A Journal of Baseball History and Culture* 10, no. 2 (Spring 2002). Also see Arthur Daley, "Where's the Strike Zone," *New York Times*, August 19, 1951; Dave Hoekstra, "Valparaiso Outfielder Gaedel Comes from Proud—Albeit Short—Baseball Lineage," *Chicago Sun Tribune*, August 6, 2010.

CASE STUDY 2-12 *National Pastime Ethical Dilemmas*

1. In the 1980s, Chicago White Sox batters were allegedly looking to a flashing bulb on the scoreboard in Comiskey Park that would tell them what the next pitch was going to be from the opposing pitcher.[52]
2. Major league player Sammy Sosa was ejected from a game against the Tampa Bay Devil Rays for using a corked bat.[53]
3. In 1935, marketing genius Bill Veeck was at it again, this time handing out promotional mirrors to fans in the stands who then took the opportunity to reflect sunlight in the opposing batter's face.[54]
4. In the 1980s, there were rumors the Minnesota Twins would turn the air conditioning units off and on to produce tailwinds for Minnesota batters when they came to the plate. Former Metrodome superintendent Dick Ericson confirmed the "vent manipulation" to the *Minneapolis Star-Tribune* in 2003.[55]

CASE STUDY 2-13 *Actor—Derek Jeter*

Major League Baseball official rules allow a batter to take first base if he is struck by a pitched ball. It would seem to be simple to determine if a player has been hit by a ball thrown by the pitcher, but that has not always been the case. New York Yankees shortstop Derek Jeter was undoubtedly *not* hit by a pitched ball, but pretended as if he were. He was so convincing, the umpire awarded him first base.[56]

Former major league catcher Tim McCarver said, "What upset some people, perhaps, is that he was so demonstrative when it hit the bat, but to think that quickly is remarkable . . . You can't say, 'No, the ball didn't hit me.' You're trying to get on base; you're trying to win the game."

"It's gamesmanship," Bob Costas, another veteran baseball commentator, said approvingly of Jeter's actions. "This is completely different from steroids or stealing signs with a pair of binoculars."[57]

THE ETHICS OF SPYING AND ESPIONAGE IN SPORTS

Spying and gaining access to the opponents' strategies is a long-standing issue in sports. The question is, When does it go too far? Should one team try to spy on another team's practice to gain valuable information for the next game? It seems to be acceptable in baseball to steal signs legally, which, of course, is an oxymoron. However, even in baseball there is a line which can be crossed. MLB player Miguel Tejada was accused of "tipping" pitches to friends on opposing teams and also allowing balls his friends hit to get past him at shortstop during games with lopsided scores. No hard

---

[52] Childs Walker, "Many at Home with Cheating: Teams Searching for a Competitive Advantage Have a Long History of Manipulating Conditions," *Baltimore Sun*, December 13, 2005.

[53] "Sammy Sosa Ejected for Corked Bat," *FoxNews.com*, June 4, 2003.

[54] Bill Veeck, *Veeck—As in Wreck: The Autobiography of Bill Veeck* (Chicago: University of Chicago Press, 2001).

[55] See also Derek Zumsteg, *The Cheater's Guide to Baseball* (Boston, MA: Mariner Books, 2007).

[56] Kenneth Plutnicki, Derek Jeter's Emmy—Worth Performance, *The New York Times*, September 16, 2010.

[57] Ben Shpigel, Reviews Are In on Jeter's Role as a Hit Batsman, *The New York Times*, September 16, 2010.

evidence was ever produced, and Tejada vehemently denied the charges. Some A's players had major concerns and called a team meeting over the issue. Pitcher Livan Hernandez said, "If I knew someone was doing that I would fight them there right on the field." The *New York Times* reported:

> What first raised suspicion among the 2001 A's was an early May series in Toronto. Tejada and Blue Jays third baseman Tony Batista, friends from the Dominican Republic, each put up terrific numbers. In the three-game series, Batista went 6 for 13 with a home run and 5 runs batted in, and Tejada was 4 for 10 with 9 R.B.I., including a home run in each game.

More significant in the eyes of some of the players was an incident in the second game of the series. Tejada did not get to an easy ground ball Batista hit off reliever Mark Guthrie with the Athletics leading 8–2. When the inning was over, A's players fumed on the bench. If the charges were proved, what should happen to Tejada? If the score was not close, is it still an issue? Could Tejada's actions have been deemed unethical or cheating? Like other major league players, Tejada has a loyalty clause in his contract. Could the A's terminate Tejada's contract for his disloyalty based on his actions, if it was proved that he was assisting opposing players?[58]

The scenario presented in case study 2-14 deals with the NFL's loyalty clause which states in part: "Club employs player as a skilled football player. Player accepts such employment. He agrees to give his best efforts and loyalty to the club . . ." (NFL Player Contract, paragraph 2.)

CASE STUDY 2-14 *Traitor or Loyal Teammate?*

The Jacksonville Jaguars had an upcoming game against division rival, the Pittsburgh Steelers. In anticipation of the game, the Jags signed linebacker Marquis Cooper from the Steelers practice squad, which they are allowed to do under league rules. They signed him on November 27 and released him December 6, after the game. During the brief time he was on the Jaguars, Cooper said Jacksonville coaches "asked him many questions about the Steelers, with particular interest in some of their players." Everything Jacksonville did was according to NFL rules. Did they do anything that could be deemed unethical? If a team follows the rules, does that mean they were acting ethically?[59] The player has no more legal obligations to his former club. He is now playing under a contract that requires him to give his best effort and loyalty to the new club. If he has information that can help his new club, should he be willing to share that information? For example, the Redskins signed quarterback Andre Woodson away from the New York Giants. Woodson said, "Right now, anything to help the Redskins out, I'm willing to do."[60] Would a quarterback be familiar with all the plays run by the offense including audibles? Do you place this in the "legalized spying" category? How would you view this situation if Woodson had only stayed on the Redskins roster for the game against the Giants and then had his playing contract terminated?

Businesses develop trade secrets and make every effort to protect those secrets from their competitors. Trade secrets are a valuable piece of intellectual property to any business. If a competitor

---

[58] David Waldstein, "Friendship or Betrayal from Inside the Lines," *New York Times*, August 30, 2009.
[59] Ed Bouchette, "The Games Some NFL People Play When You Get Right Down to It, Bill Belichick Not the Only One Working the Shadows Looking for an Edge on Game Day," *Pittsburgh Post-Gazette*, December 16, 2007.
[60] Associated Press, "Giants Think Woodson Spilling Secrets," *ESPN.com*, September 7, 2009.

attempts to misappropriate a trade secret, they can be sued. What should teams do to ensure players value the proprietary and confidential information given to them by the club? A trade secret is defined by the Uniform Trade Secrets Act as follows:

> Information, including a formula, pattern, compilation, program device, method, technique, or process, that: (i) derives independent economic value, actual or potential, from not being generally known to, and not being readily ascertainable by proper means by, other persons who can obtain economic value from its disclosure or use, and (ii) is the subject of efforts that are reasonable under the circumstances to maintain its secrecy.

U.T.S.A. §1(4).

Is there any information in sports that can be protected under trade secret law? In May 2010, the Philadelphia Phillies were accused by the Colorado Rockies of using binoculars from the bullpen to steal signs.[61] MLB issued a warning to the Phillies about their alleged sign stealing even though there is nothing in baseball's rule book about sign stealing. In 2001, MLB Vice President Sandy Aldeson reminded teams that "no club shall use electronic equipment to communicate to or with any on-field personnel."[62] Hall of Famer Christy Mathewson wrote in 1912, "All is fair in love, war, and baseball except stealing signals dishonestly."[63] Former major league pitcher, Bert Blyleven could be classified as an artist. He commented on sign stealing, "Stealing signs, or noticing when a pitcher is unintentionally tipping his pitches is not cheating, that's just baseball. You try to get an advantage over your opponent any way you can."[64]

There is no doubt that the unethical acts of others will affect those around them. Although certain actions may be unethical and even acknowledged as unethical by the parties involved, that does not mean the law necessarily provides a remedy for that unethical behavior. Consider the now infamous NFL "spygate" episode involving the New England Patriots and coach Bill Belichick. Carl Mayer, a New York Jets season ticket holder, argued that the ticket he purchased stated that any game would "be played in accordance with NFL rules and regulations" and furthermore that as a ticket holder he "fully anticipated and contracted for a ticket to observe an honest match that would be played accordingly to NFL rules." He asked the court to award him (and other Jets fans who were in the same situation) $61,600,000, which was the amount paid by New York Jets ticket holders to watch eight "fraudulent games between the New England Patriots and the New York Jets" between 2000 and 2007. In a word, the court said "no" to Mr. Mayer and other Jets fans.

📖 CASE 2-6 *Mayer v. Belichick*

```
605 F.3d 223 (3rd Cir. 2010)

This highly unusual case was filed by a disappointed football fan and
season ticket-holder in response to the so-called "Spygate" scandal.
This scandal arose when it was discovered that the Patriots were sur-
reptitiously videotaping the signals of their opponents.
```

---

[61] Michael S. Schmidt, "Phillies Are Accused of Stealing Signs Illegally," *New York Times*, May 12, 2010; "Phils' Bullpen Coach Caught Spying, Insists He Wasn't Stealing Rockies Signs," *CBSSports.com*, May 12, 2010.

[62] Joshua Prager, "Snoop Dogs," *Sports Illustrated Vault*, December 11. 2006.

[63] Christy Mathewson, *Pitching in a Pinch: Or, Baseball from the Inside* (Lincoln, NE: University of Nebraska Press, 1994).

[64] Bert Blyleven, "Blyleven: The Dos and Dont's of Stealing Signs," *NBC Sports*, October 4, 2009.

[Carl Mayer alleges that] Bill Belichick, during a game with the New York Jets on September 9, 2007, instructed an agent of the New England Patriots to surreptitiously videotape the New York Jets coaches and players on the field with the purpose of illegally recording, capturing and stealing the New York Jets signals and visual coaching instructions. The Patriots were in fact subsequently found by the National Football League (NFL) to have improperly engaged in such conduct. This violated the contractual expectations and rights of New York Jets ticket-holders who fully anticipated and contracted for a ticket to observe an honest match played in compliance with all laws, regulations and NFL rules.

Mayer, a New York Jets season ticket holder, contends that in purchasing tickets to watch the New York Jets that, as a matter of contract, the tickets imply that each game will be played in accordance with NFL rules and regulations as well as all applicable federal and state laws. Mayer [and others] contend that the Patriots tortuously [sic] interfered with their contractual relations with the New York Jets in purchasing the tickets. They further claim that the Patriots violated the New Jersey Consumer Fraud Act and the New Jersey Deceptive Business Practices Act. They also claim that the Patriots violated federal and state racketeering laws by using the NFL as an enterprise to carry out their illegal scheme. Because the Patriots have been found in other games to have illegally used video equipment, Mayer sought damages for New York Jets ticket-holders for all games played in Giants stadium between the New York Jets and the New England Patriots since Bill Belichick became head coach in 2000.

[Court's Decision]

At their most fundamental level, the various claims alleged here arose out of the repeated and surreptitious violations of a specific NFL rule. This rule provides that "'no video recording devices of any kind are permitted to be in use in the coaches' booth, on the field, or in the locker room during the game'" and that "all video for coaching purposes must be shot from locations 'enclosed on all sides with a roof overhead.'" In a September 6, 2007, memorandum, Ray Anderson, the NFL's executive vice president of football operations, stated that "'[v]ideotaping of any type, including but not limited to taping of an opponent's offensive or defensive signals, is prohibited on the sidelines, in the coaches' booth, in the locker room, or at any other locations accessible to club staff members during the game.'"

On September 9, 2007, the Jets and the Patriots played the season opener in Giants Stadium, East Rutherford, New Jersey. Mayer possessed tickets and parking passes to this game, and the Patriots ultimately won, 38-14. ESPN.com then reported that the NFL was investigating accusations that an employee of the Patriots was actually videotaping the signals given by Jets coaches at this game. Specifically, NFL security reportedly confiscated a video camera and videotape from an employee during the course of the game, and this employee was accused of aiming his camera at the Jets' defensive coaches while they were sending signals out to the team's players on the field.

This was not the first time a public accusation of cheating or dishonesty had been made against the Patriots. A man wearing a Patriots credential was found carrying a video camera on the sidelines at the home field of the Green Bay Packers in November 2006. Admittedly, "[t]eams are allowed to have a limited number of their own videographers on the sideline during the game, but they must have a credential that authorizes them to shoot video, and wear a yellow vest." However, this particular individual evidently lacked the proper credential and attire and was accordingly escorted out of the stadium by Packers security.

With respect to the 2007 incident, the Patriots denied that there was any violation of the NFL's rules. A Patriots cornerback named Ellis Hobbs told the press that he was unwilling to believe that his team had cheated and that he was standing by the team and its coaches. However, he also admitted that, "[i]f it's true, obviously, we're in the wrong." Belichick apologized to everyone affected following the confiscation of the videotape. But, at a weekly press conference on September 12, 2007, he refused to take questions from reporters about the NFL investigation and stormed out of the room.

On September 13, 2007, "the NFL found the [Patriots] guilty of violating all applicable NFL rules by engaging in a surreptitious videotaping program." It imposed the following sanctions: (1) the Patriots were fined $250,000.00; (2) Belichick was personally fined $500,000.00; and (3) the Patriots would be stripped of any first-round draft pick for the next year if the team reached the playoffs in the 2007-2008 season and, if not so successful, the team would otherwise lose its second- and third-round picks. Roger Goodell, the commissioner of the NFL, characterized the whole episode as "'a calculated and deliberate attempt to avoid longstanding rules designed to encourage fair play and promote honest competition on the playing field.'" He further justified the penalties imposed on the team on the grounds that "'Coach Belichick not only serves as the head coach but also has substantial control over all aspects of New England's football operations" and therefore "'his actions and decisions are properly attributed to the club.'"

The owner of the Patriots, Robert Kraft, refused to comment on the NFL's sanctions, and the New York Jets issued a statement supporting the commissioner and his findings. On September 13, 2007, Belichick stated the following: "'Once again, I apologize to the Kraft family and every person directly or indirectly associated with the New England Patriots for the embarrassment, distraction and penalty my mistake caused. I also apologize to Patriots fans and would like to thank them for their support during the past few days and throughout my career.'" However, he then "bizarrely . . . attempted to deny responsibility, stating: 'We have never used sideline video to obtain a competitive advantage while the game was in progress . . . [.] With tonight's resolution, I will not be offering any further comments on this matter. We are moving on with our preparations for Sunday's game.' "But, at least according to Mayer, Jets ticket-holders have refused to "move on."

The Patriots and Belichick deployed their surreptitious videotaping program during all eight games played against the Jets in Giants Stadium from 2000 through 2007. Beginning in 2000 when Belichick became head coach, they commenced an ongoing scheme to acquire the signals of their adversaries and then match such signals to the plays on the field, in alleged violation of the "NFL rules that are part of the ticketholders' contractual and/or quasi contractual rights." On the other hand, Jets fans collectively spent more than $61 million on tickets to watch these purportedly honest and competitive games between the two teams.

In 2000, Matt Walsh, an employee in the team's videography department, was hired by the team to videotape the signals of opponents. Relying specifically on statements made by Walsh to the *New York Times* and United States Senator Arlen Specter, Mayer made a series of allegations with respect to this Patriots employee. Walsh claimed that he received his videotaping instructions directly from Ernie Adams, Belichick's own special assistant. The purpose of the videotaping program was to capture signals for use in games against the same opponent later in the season, and the program was later expanded to include teams that the Patriots could encounter in the playoffs. The first instance of taping occurred in a 2000 preseason game against the Tampa Bay Buccaneers. When the two teams played again in the regular season opener, the Patriots appeared to use the acquired signals. Walsh specifically asserted "that this was the first time he had seen quarterback Drew Bledsoe operate a 'no huddle' [offense] 'when not in a two-minute or hurry situation'" and that, when he asked an unnamed quarterback if the taped signals were helpful, the player replied that, "'probably 75 percent of the time, Tampa Bay ran the defense we thought they were going to run.'" Although Walsh left the videotaping program after the 2002 Super Bowl, "he [as a Patriots season ticket-holder] witnessed Patriots employee Steve Scarnecchia continue the same taping practices in multiple games in the 2003, 2004, and 2005 seasons." Walsh was further instructed by the Patriots organization to conceal his actions and misrepresent his activities if challenged on the field by: (1) intentionally breaking the red operating light on the video camera, (2) telling any person questioning "the use of a third video camera on the field" that he was filming tight shots or highlights, and (3) "if asked why he was not filming action on the field, he was to say he was filming the down marker." Finally, at the 2002 American Football Conference championship game against the Pittsburgh Steelers, Walsh was instructed not to wear a team logo while filming.

Walsh's attorney, Michael Levy, likewise released a statement describing the team's method "of securing and tying coaching signals to plays." As reported in the New York Post, the lawyer provided the following description of a videotape made during an October 7, 2001, game against the Miami Dolphins:

> "[It] contains shots of Miami's offensive coaches signaling Miami's offensive players, followed by a shot from the end-zone camera of Miami's offensive play, followed by a shot of Miami's offensive coaches signaling Miami's offensive players for the next play, then edited to be followed by a shot of the subsequent Miami offensive play," Levy told ESPN.com. "And that pattern repeats throughout the entire tape, with occasional cuts to the scoreboard."

Citing again to the *New York Post,* Mayer further alleged that the NFL wrongfully destroyed the illicit videotapes themselves:

> Other tapes produced to the NFL (and later destroyed by order of Commissioner Roger Goodell) include defensive signals from Miami coaches in a game on Sept. 24, 2000, signals from Bills coaches from a Nov. 11, 2001, game, signals from Browns coaches from a game on Dec. 9, 2001, two tapes of signals from Steelers coaches from the 2001 AFC Championship game on Jan. 27, 2002, and signals from Chargers coaches from a game Sept. 29, 2002.

Walsh provided at least eight videotapes to the NFL, while the Patriots likewise furnished at least six tapes to the league. The commissioner claimed that he ordered the destruction of the videotapes to prevent their use by the Patriots, even though the NFL allegedly had a legal duty to preserve these items pursuant, inter alia, to the Sarbanes-Oxley Act and the NFL's own antitrust exemption.

Here, Mayer undeniably saw *football* games played by two *NFL* teams. This therefore is not a case where, for example, the game or games were cancelled, strike replacement players were used, or the professional football teams themselves did something nonsensical or absurd, such as deciding to play basketball.

Nevertheless, there are any number of often complicated rules and standards applicable to a variety of sports, including professional football. It appears uncontested that players often commit intentional rule infractions in order to obtain an advantage over the course of the game. For instance, a football player may purposefully commit pass interference or a "delay of game." Such infractions, if not called by the referees, may even change the outcome of the game itself. There are also rules governing the off-field conduct of the football team, such as salary "caps" and the prohibition against "tampering" with the employer-employee relationships between another team and its players and coaches. A team is apparently free to take advantage of the knowledge that a newly hired player or coach takes with him after leaving his former team, and it may even have personnel on the sidelines who try to pick up the opposing team's signals with the assistance of lip-reading, binoculars, note-taking, and other devices. In addition, even Mayer acknowledge[s] that "[t]eams are allowed to have a limited number of their own videographers on the sideline during the game."

In fact, the NFL's own commissioner did ultimately take action here. He found that the Patriots and Belichick were guilty of violating the applicable NFL rules, imposed sanctions in the form of fines and the loss of draft picks, and rather harshly characterized the whole episode as a calculated attempt to avoid well-established rules designed to encourage fair play and honest competition. At the very least, a ruling in favor of Mayer could lead to other disappointed fans filing lawsuits because of "a blown call" that apparently caused their team to lose or any number of allegedly improper acts committed by teams, coaches, players, referees and umpires, and others.

Professional football, like other professional sports, is a multi-billion dollar business. In turn, ticket-holders and other fans may have legitimate issues with the manner in which they are treated. ("It is common knowledge that professional sports franchisees have a sordid history of arrogant disdain for the consumers of the product.") Fans could speak out against the Patriots, their coach, and the NFL itself. In fact, they could even go so far as to refuse to purchase tickets or NFL-related merchandise. However, the one thing they *cannot* do is bring a legal action in a court of law.

Source: *Reprinted from Westlaw with permission of Thomson Reuters.*

In light of the *Mayer v. Belichick* case, consider the following questions:

1. Do you think the fans who attended the Jets–Patriots games from 2000 through 2007 were defrauded as a result of the unethical and illegal actions of the Patriots team and administration?
2. Do you think the commissioner of the NFL did enough to penalize New England and Coach Belichick for their improper actions?
3. Do you consider the actions of the Patriots team and their coaching staff unethical? Or was it merely gamesmanship at its highest level? Do you think their actions could constitute criminal conduct?[65]
4. The Patriots did break league rules by spying, but is that always translated to be an unethical act?
5. Can Jets' fans still claim that they saw a dishonest match if the Jets won the game? Jets' fans are not done yet, and they intend to appeal their case.[66]
6. Do you consider Mayer and other Jets' fans victims as they argued to the court?
7. Do you believe the alternative remedies suggested by the court, such as never going to another NFL game, are realistic?

THE USE OF PROFANITY AND "TRASH TALKING" IN SPORTS

Profanity in Sports

Generally speaking, most people frown on the use of profanity. That is why children are typically taught not to say "bad words." However, consider the ever-increasing use of foul language on television and the Internet. Parents organize and monitor television programming in hopes of educating all parents about what their children should be watching.[67] In the infamous "clothing malfunction" episode in the 2004 Super Bowl between Justin Timberlake and Janet Jackson, Nielsen estimated 6.6 million kids from ages 2 to 11 were watching as Janet Jackson exposed her right breast to the audience. In the corporate setting, "silk stocking" firm Goldman Sachs cleaned up its act by requiring all Goldman employees to refrain from using "dirty words" commonly used in their industry, when corresponding on e-mail. Clearly, a laudable goal but is it realistic?[68]

Schools and governments are also on board with an anti-cursing campaign.[69] Students at Winthrop High School now abide by the following: "I pledge and support the elimination of the R-word" (or "retarded" or "retard,") referring to people with intellectual disabilities. Should there be limits on speech for athletes, the media, and fans?[70] Some restrictions may bring constitutional law

---

[65] See Samuel J. Horovitz, "If You Ain't Cheating You Ain't Trying: Spygate and the Legal Implications of Trying too Hard," *Texas Intellectual Property Law Journal* (2008–2009).

[66] R.M. Schneiderman, "Jets Fan Will Appeal Spygate Case," *Fox Sports*, May 20, 2010.

[67] See Facts of Statistics, *Parents Television Council*, www.parentstv.org.

[68] Cassell Bryan-Low and Aaron Lucchetti, "George Carlin Never Would've Cut It at the New Goldman: Firm Bans Naughty Words in Emails; An 'Unlearnable Lesson' on Wall Street?" *Wall Street Journal*, July 29, 2010.

[69] Joseph P. Kahn, "Protests Against the R-Word: Anti-Cussing Measures vs. Free Speech, What's Up With all the Profanity?" *Boston Globe*, March 11, 2010.

[70] Mark Conrad, "Fleeting Expletives' and Sports Broadcasts: A Legal Nightmare Needs a Safe Harbor," *Journal of Legal Aspects in Sport* (2008).

issues into play.[71] Professional leagues, youth sports organizations, and media outlets have passed rules and regulations dealing with the use of profanity by participants and employees.

A successful football coach in Louisiana was fired for swearing in the classroom.[72] New York Jets coach Rex Ryan has never been accused of polite behavior. On the HBO presentation of *Hard Knocks* he "dropped more F-Bombs than a script from 'The Sopranos.'"[73] He responded, "I apologize if I offended more people than I usually offend." Tiger Woods has been known to drop a few choice words in the heat of a PGA event. He even promised to clean up his act in a formal apology to the media.[74]

Is cursing merely part of American culture, and more specifically part of American sports culture, and therefore should be tolerated?[75] Should we expect professional athletes who are vying for millions of dollars not to become frustrated and angry during competition and to not swear and curse when competing? Is it different if it happens in an interview after the game rather than in the midst heated competition? Should the use of profanity be treated differently in youth sports?[76]

Trash Talking

The overwhelming majority of high schools as well as the NCAA prohibit trash talking by players and fans. Some people just talk; it's what they do. Some players should take heed of Crash Davis's (played by Kevin Costner) pearls of wisdom to Ebby Calvin "Nuke" LaLoosh (played by Tim Robbins) in the movie *Bull Durham*: "Don't think, you can only hurt the ballclub." Notwithstanding that kernel of wisdom, athletes continue to berate, trash talk, and needle their opponents, hoping to gain an edge. Some remarks are clever, some are not. Some of their statements are offensive or demeaning, others border on the sublime.

Of course, trash talking can go too far, ergo the word "trash." Some people just don't know when to quit. Reggie Parent (a Caucasian) was also a big LSU fan. His co-worker Reggie Drummel (an African American) was an avid Georgia Bulldog fan. Southeastern Conference Football (SEC) fans can be extremely enthusiastic.[77] In a good-natured way, Parent told Drummel that if LSU beat Georgia he would have a "surprise" waiting for him at work. It shocked many people, including Drummel, when he went to work and found the surprise the day after the game. The surprise Parent was talking about was a "hangman's noose." After pointing it out to Parent, he just laughed. Drummel did not laugh but instead called the police. It is a crime in the State of Louisiana to make a public display of a noose.[78]

---

[71] Clay Calvert and Robert D. Richards, "Fans and the First Amendment: Cheering and Jeering in College Sports," *Virginia Sports and Entertainment Law Journal* (2004–2005).

[72] Jere Longman, "South Plaquemines Coach Accused of Profanity Is Fired," *New York Times*, April 28, 2010; Anthony Mague, "Profanity Not Only Way Coaches Motivate," *The Daily Orange*, February 21, 2005.

[73] Rich Cimini, "Rex Ryan Sorry for Profanity Use on TV," *ESPN.com*, August 12, 2010.

[74] Chris Chase, "Tiger Woods' Profanity Aired Live on CBS," *Yahoo Sports*, April 11, 2010.

[75] "Power Players and Profanity: It Can Be Risky," *NPR*, July 10, 2010.

[76] Matt Bartosik, "High School Trash Talk More Like Hate Speech: Facebook Message Made References to Lynching," *NBC Chicago*, April 23, 2010.

[77] Chad Gibbs, *God and Football: Faith and Fanaticism in the Southeastern Conference*, Zondervan, 2010.

[78] Tyana Williams, "LSU v. Georgia Game Noose Leads to Arrest," *WAFB Channel 9*, October 28, 2008; "When SEC Trash Talking Goes Wrong," *The Sporting News*, October 29, 2008.

Parent was arrested for his over-the-top trash talking and criminal activity, as defined by Louisiana law (RE 14:40.5):

> Public display of a noose on property of another or public place; intent to intimidate
>
> A. It shall be unlawful for any person, with the intent to intimidate any person or group of persons, to etch, paint, draw, or otherwise place or display a hangman's noose on the property of another, a highway, or other public place.
> B. As used in this Section, "noose" means a rope tied in a slip knot, which binds closer the more it is drawn, which historically has been used in execution by hanging, and which symbolizes racism and intimidation.
> C. Whoever commits the crime of public display of a noose with the intent to intimidate shall be fined not more than five thousand dollars or imprisoned with or without hard labor for not more than one year, or both.

Do you consider trash talking to be, necessarily, a part of competitive sports? At what level of sports should it be prohibited, if any? Should there be any limitations on what players or fans can say to one another?[79] Trash talking by a player can happen at both the professional and amateur levels. Kevin Garnett was voted the best trash talker in the NBA in 2010.[80]

Could some categories of trash talking be considered hate speech under the law? Mike Basik, a radio jockey in Dallas, was trash talking about the San Antonio Spurs and tweeted, "Congrats to all the dirty Mexicans in San Antonio." It proved to be a controversial statement to say the least. Some people should stay away from all communication devices, and that applies doubly to NFL player Larry Johnson who tweeted a gay slur and also sent derogatory tweets about his head coach. The Kansas City Chiefs banned him for his derogatory tweets.[81]

NOTES AND DISCUSSION QUESTIONS

Introduction

1. The fair play concern in *Lestina* essentially questions whether the goalkeeper exhibited unnecessary roughness. Do you think he did? Is this ethical question even a close call?
2. Should traditional notions of fair play change with the relative ages of the opponents?
3. The player in *Nabozny v. Barnhill* also violated traditional notions of fair play due to his unnecessary roughness. Do you agree with the following statement made in the case, "The glue between opponents is the element of fair play. It is an ethical question, whether to choose to follow the stipulations of fair play between well-matched opponents following established rules and customs, or to allow the behemoth of winning at all costs to prevail."? Is this proposition also applicable to youth sports?

---

[79] Howard M. Wasserman, "Cheers, Profanity, and Free Speech in College Sports," Dissertation, *Florida International University*, August 9, 2004.
[80] J. E. Skeets, "Kevin Garnett Voted NBA's Top Trash Talker," *Yahoo!*, January 13, 2010.
[81] "Johnson Uses Slurs for Harley Reporters," *ESPN.com*, October 26, 2009; "Chief RB Banned Indefinitely for Tweets, Gay Slurs," *Fox Sports*, October 28, 2009.

4. What is the best way to instill sportsmanship and build character in youth sports? For some excellent resources *see*, Josephson Institute, Center for Sports Ethics. www.josephsoninstitute.org.

5. One attribute of sportsmanship has been defined as "not giving into the temptation of cheating in order to pursue your own personal goal of victory." How could this be implemented in youth sports?

6. In 1926, a National Sportsmanship Brotherhood was organized. Its slogan was: "Not that you won or lost—but how you played the game." The purpose of the Brotherhood was to spread the "gospel" of sportsmanship throughout all aspects of life, from childhood games to international events. Its code consisted of eight rules:

    1. Keep the rule.
    2. Keep faith with your comrades.
    3. Keep yourself fit.
    4. Keep your temper.
    5. Keep your play free from brutality.
    6. Keep pride under control in victory.
    7. Keep a stout heart in defeat.
    8. Keep a sound soul and a clean mind in a healthy body.[82]

7. Describe the nuances of sportsmanship and gamesmanship? Do they differ with regard to each sport?

8. Is gamesmanship more acceptable in certain sports? Gamesmanship seems to occur in all sports and is not limited in scope.[83]

9. Should gamesmanship be prohibited in youth sports entirely for all participants? Would you also include coaches?

10. The NCAA invoked a new rule related to trash talking and taunting for 2011.[84] Critics of the rule argue it is too subjective.

Rules and Regulations

11. Is intentionally breaking the rules in a sport always considered poor sportsmanship?

12. Robert Mushtare said he bowled three consecutive perfect games five times in a month (900 series) all before his 18th birthday. The U.S. Bowling Congress sent officials to investigate if he really accomplished the feat. It was such a phenomenal feat, many accused him of cheating. After an investigation, the games were certified as perfect games.[85] What mechanisms should be in place in sport to detect cheating?

---

[82] A sportsmanship brotherhood, Literary Digest, LXXXVIII (27 March 1926).

[83] See "Overheated Locker Rooms, Pregame Stunts Are All Part of the Game," *ESPN.com*, July 31, 2007 (Basketball); Greg Garber, "Gamesmanship Is Name of the Game in Tennis," *ESPN.com*, August 9, 2007 (Tennis); "Socceroos Focused Despite Iraqi Gamesmanship," *Sydney Morning Herald*, June 6, 2008 (Soccer); "Jun Media, Pacquiao Gives Floyd Dose of Gamesmanship," *Manila Times*, March 24, 2010 (Boxing); Thomas Rogers, "Cricket's Controversies and Gamesmanship," *Cricket Suite*, July 11, 2008 (Cricket). Also see "'Puck-Gate' Nothing More Than Playoff Gamesmanship," *nhlhotglove.com*, June 2, 2010. (Hockey)

[84] Chris Low, "NCAA Approves Taunting Rule for 2011," *ESPN.com*, April 15, 2010.

[85] "Bowling Perfection Spurs Accusations of Cheating," *NPR.org*, July 27, 2006; Neil Amdur, "Why a 900 Series Just Isn't What It Used to Be," *New York Times*, July 1, 2007.

13. In *Gauvin v. Clark*, butt-ending an opponent or threatening to use the butt end of the stick can be viewed as another way of unsettling the opponent. The threat of injury when using the butt end as a weapon is real as is the possibility of serious injury. Will this factor move this type of infraction from the realm of gamesmanship into the more serious category of cheating? Should the possibility of a debilitating injury be the deciding factor in how the infraction should be viewed? Should "butt-ending" by definition be determined to be unethical?

14. Is intentionally injuring a player to put him or her out of a game, a strategic move to help the team, or is it cheating?[86] Is intentional injury different from a cheap hit? Consider the hit an opposing player put on Arizona Cardinals quarterback Kurt Warner in the 2009 NFL playoffs. The Saints wanted Kurt Warner out of the game, so Matt Leinart could come in and replace him. Warner was hit by an opposing player on an interception return. Is that "fair game" in the NFL? The Cardinals lost the game to the Saints.[87]

Ethical Choices in the American National Pastime

15. Is watering down the baseball infield to slow down opposing base stealers unsportsmanlike and unethical?

16. Do you believe "head-hunting" in baseball should be outlawed considering the dangerous nature of a ball traveling at someone's head at approximately 100 miles an hour?[88]

17. Do you think cheating in baseball is tolerated more than in other sports? If so, in what ways does baseball lend itself to "people looking the other way"?

18. When an emery board came flying out of Minnesotta Twins pitcher Joe Niekro's back pocket during a 1987 game many accused him of cheating. Niekro said he needed the emery board to file his fingernails. Niekro was suspended by Major League Baseball ten games.[89]

The Ethics of Spying and Espionage in Sports

19. Is spying on another club always wrong? In November 2010 the Denver Broncos and their former coach, Josh McDaniels were both fined $50,000 in what many deemed "spygate 2." McDaniels was an assistant coach for the Patriots when the first spygate incident occurred in 2007. The Broncos team video operations director had filmed a San Francisco's 49ers practice one month before in violation of league rules. After being presented with the film, McDaniels refused to view it. However, the league still fined him for failing to properly report it. McDaniels was fired by the Broncos within a month after the incident.[90]

20. Was former NFL player Brett Favre trying to sabotage his former team, the Green Bay Packers? He said no![91]

---

[86] See Thomas George, "N.F.L. Bounty-Hunting Dispute," *New York Times*, December 6, 1989.

[87] "Cards' Warner returns in 2nd Half," *ESPN.com*, January 16, 2010.

[88] Mike Sowell, *The Pitch That Killed* (Hoboken, NJ: John Wiley & Sons, 1994).

[89] "Joe Niekro 1944–2006," *Sports Illustrated Vault*, November 6, 2006.

[90] Associated Press, Broncos, McDaniels Fined $50K Each, *ESPN.com*, November 28, 2010.

[91] Tom Silverstein, "Favre, Millen Had Talk, but QB Insists He Wasn't Trying to Sabotage Packers," *Journal Sentinel*, October 22, 2008.

21. Should a team's playbook be considered a trade secret?[92] In November 2010 a Connecticut high school football coach was suspended for using an opposing quaterback's missing armband to assist his defense. The opposing player had misplaced the armband during the first half of the game. The principal of the high school suspended the coach after the coach admitted using the list of coded plays.[93]

The Use of Profanity and "Trash Talking" in Sports

22. NFL Tennessee Titans owner Bud Adams gave a "two-bird" salute to opposing fans in 2010.[94] It would most likely be considered the most offensive "bird" display in sports history if it were not so ridiculous. Should the owner of a club be subject to a different code of conduct than the players?

23. Is there ever a reason an owner, player, or fan should make an obscene gesture? Do fans have the right to heckle and boo players without retribution from the player? What about one player making an obscene gesture to another? Is that gamesmanship or just vulgar? Would it matter if it occurred in professional rather than amateur sports?

24. What would a discussion of sports ethics be without boxer Mike Tyson? His infamous trash talking statement was, "When I'm ready I'm going to rip out his heart and feed it to him. . . . My style is impetuous, my defense is impregnable and I'm just ferocious. I want your heart. I want to eat your children. Praise be to Allah."[95] Do you consider his statement a little over the top even for Mike Tyson?

25. Rickey Henderson is clearly one of baseball's all time "hot dogs."[96] Do you think a distinction can be made between a hot dog or a show-off—someone who gives a little extra on the playing field—and a player engaging in gamesmanship?

---

[92] J. Rice Ferreille Jr., "Combating the Lure of Impropriety in Professional Sports Industries: The Desirability of Treating a Playbook as a Legally Enforceable Trade Secret," *Journal of Intellectual Property Law* (2003–2004); Jason Reid and Jason La Canfora, "Photo of Playbook Concerns Coach," *Washington Post*, September 16, 2008.

[93] Associated Press, "Aaron Hernandez' Brother Suspended from H.S. Coaching Gig for Play-Stealing," *Boston Herald*, November 10, 2010.

[94] Matt King, "The Top 10 Middle Finger Moments in Sports," *BleacherReport.com*, November 16, 2009.

[95] Anthony York, "'I Want to Eat Your Children. Praise Be to Allah,'" *Salon.com*, Wednesday, June 28, 2000.

[96] George Vecsey, "Sports of the Times; This Hot Dog's Smothered in Onions, Too," *New York Times*, October 8, 1989. A '"hot dog" in baseball has been defined as: "a player who calls attention to himself with theatrics or plays to the crowd and/or the television camera; a player who grandstands or "exaggerates his place in the mortal scheme of things" (Jim Brosnan, *The Long Season*, 1960). Defenders of hot dog players have puckishly suggested the term came from the fact that they play the game "with Relish." Baseball did not originate this use of "hot dog," which, incidentally, became widespread when surfers began to show off in 1960s. Syn. *Mr. Mustard; mustard man.*" Paul Dickson, *The Dickson Baseball Dictionary, 3rd Edition*, W. W. Norton & Company, 2009, p. 436.

CHAPTER 3

GAMBLING IN SPORTS

GAMBLING IN SPORTS AND SOCIETY

Gambling, whether sports leagues want to admit it or not, has been a part of sports for over a century.[1] A plethora of episodes exist in sports regarding gambling, but no sport seems to despise gambling and the repercussions of gambling more than baseball.

Baseball club owners are sensible business men," Colonel Jacob Ruppert, joint owner of the New York American League Club, once said. "You can bank on the fact that they will conduct their clubs as business men. They must do this to protect their investments. Now, if they permitted gambling to get a hold they would destroy the game and with it their property, their business, would go to ruin. For that reason we have always tried to eliminate any form of gambling. We don't let known gamblers enter the ball park. Instructions are given the gatemen to look out for them.[2]

Gamblers were present at the earliest stages of the American sporting world and baseball has certainly had its share of gambling scandals, with the most notable being the Black Sox Scandal of 1919. ESPN's list of the 25 "hoaxes, cheats, and frauds," names the "Black Sox Scandal" as number one. The 1919 gambling scandal in which Chicago White Sox players allegedly gambled away the World Series is one of the most infamous events in sports history. Ballplayers from the White Sox club allegedly took money from gamblers to "throw" the games. The White Sox lost the 1919 World Series to the Cincinnati Reds, 5 games to 3.[3] Pete Rose, baseball's all time hit leader also was

---

[1] For a historical look at gambling in sports, see Paul Blumenau Lyons, *The Greatest Gambling Stories Ever Told: Thirty-One Unforgettable Tales of Risk and Reward* (Guilford, CT: Lyons Press, 2004); Charley Rosen, *Scandals of '51: How the Gamblers Almost Killed College Basketball* (New York: Holt, Rinehart and Winston, 1978).

[2] William L. Crenery, "Why Gambling and Baseball Are Enemies," *New York Times*, October 3, 1920.

[3] Christopher H. Evans and William R. Herzog II, *The Faith of 50 Million* (Louisville, KY: Westminster John Knox Press, 2002).

involved in a notorious gambling scandal when he was the manager of the Cincinnati Reds and was eventually banned from baseball.[4] Baseball players Pete Rose, Leo Durocher, "Shoeless Joe" Jackson, Ty Cobb, Tris Speaker, and Hal Chase were all involved in gambling scandals.

Gambling in sports is replete with unethical motives and practices. It is an anathema to the continued integrity of sports but has a long history and association with sports. Gambling is a form of cheating, an act through which the conditions for winning in a sports contest have been unfairly changed in favor of one participant over another. As a result, the principle of the equality of chance based on an even matching of skill and strategy is destroyed. Gambling poses major ethical dilemmas for leagues, fans, players, coaches, and society in general. Gambling by players on their own athletic performance is not unusual. Certain sports, such as golf, tennis, horse racing, automobile racing, and rodeo, essentially award participants with prize money. Participants pay entry fees and strive for the sum, either in total or as augmented by tournament sponsors.

Illegal gambling in sports has reached nearly pandemic proportions. The few headlines of suspensions and indictments are the exception rather than the rule, and this is combined with a laissez-faire attitude that is the legal betting fortress of the Las Vegas sports booking empire. The media reports point-spreads, player and team information, injury reports, and a myriad of other statistics and advertising, making gambling more accessible. Like it or not, professional sports and gambling are inherently linked to each other through a relationship between injury reports, bookmakers' and those who like to wager.

Gambling is a big business in the American sports world and in international sports as well.[5] Gambling creates ethical issues at both the professional and amateur ranks of sports. For example, every March, millions of employees across the United States enter "office pools" and wager sums of money hoping to pick the "Final Four" college basketball teams and an eventual winner. Should these "office pools" be considered gambling? Just ask former University of Washington head football coach, Rick Neuheisel, who lost his head coaching job because it was decided he gambled in violation of NCAA rules. Neuheisel won $25,000 in an "office pool" based on the NCAA basketball tournament. Neuheisel, an attorney as well as a coach, later prevailed in court against the university.[6]

Cameron Pettigrew was an account representative at Fidelity Investments; that is, he was, until he was fired for a violation of a company gambling policy, which did not allow employees to play fantasy football during working hours. He said, "Nobody at the entire Westlake site took the policy seriously." He estimates that around 40 people took part in office leagues, with managers and team leaders among the participants, many in his own league. He says a "higher-up" in the company asked him to join a league the year before.[7]

The NFL's Super Bowl creates a frenzy of betting every year. The NFL draws more gamblers than any other sport. In 2010, Super Bowl betters wagered $82.7 million in Nevada's sports books. Of the

---

[4] Aaron Kuriloff, "25 Great Hoaxes, Cheats and Frauds in Sports," *ESPN.com*, April 17, 2005.

[5] Jeff Merron, "Biggest Sports Gambling Scandals," *ESPN.com*, June 2, 2007.

[6] Associated Press, "Neuheisel Said He Feels Vindicated by Settlement," *ESPN.com*, March 8, 2005.

[7] Nando Di Fino, "A Fantasy Player's Worst Nightmare," *Wall Street Journal*, December 18, 2009. See also Bruce Weinstein, "The Ethics of Office Gambling," *Bloomberg Business Week*, January 28, 2008; Chris Good, "The Presidential Bracket: Obama Flashes Pragmatism in NCAA Picks," *The Atlantic*, March 2003; Stephanie Armour, "Anti-Gambling Groups Seek Moratorium on Office Pools," *USA Today*, March 28, 2007; Andrew Zimbalist, "March Madness It Is, Economically," *Wall Street Journal*, March 10, 2009. "Millions of basketball fans, their friends and associates place bracket bets on each game. Experts estimate that more than $7 billion is wagered on the March tournament, surpassing the $6 billion gambled on the Super Bowl."

total amount of money wagered on the Super Bowl every year, only about 1.5% is wagered legally (by a person over 21 years of age who was physically present in the state of Nevada). It seems everyone wants to get on board with Super Bowl betting, including directors of art museums.[8] In one 12-month period in 2009, a total of $1.1 billion was wagered on professional and college football.[9] In 2009 approximately $2.57 billion was legally wagered in Nevada's sports books. Gross revenues for the sports books were $136.4 million in 2009.[10] Of course, everyone likes to win and every gambler seems to have a strategy to be successful, but a good strategy does not always translate to winning.[11]

The top 10 sports betting events are the following:[12]

1. NFL Super Bowl
2. NFL playoffs
3. College football bowl games
4. NCAA "March Madness"
5. NBA playoffs
6. MLB World Series
7. The Masters Golf Tournament and Wimbledon (tie)
8. Indianapolis 500 and the Daytona 500 (tie)
9. Ultimate Fighting Championship (UFC) and professional boxing (championship fights)
10. Triple Crown horse racing (Kentucky Derby, Preakness, Belmont Stakes)

Gambling is an ethical issue on the international level for sports as well.[13] The 2010 World Cup was expected to be the largest gambling event in sports history.[14]

In Pakistan in 2010, some of Pakistan's leading cricket players were alleged to have committed one of the biggest frauds in the game's history. The International Cricket Council (ICC) and its Anti-Corruption Security Unit investigated sports betting allegations. Three Pakistan cricket team members were accused of fixing matches and underperforming in a match between England and Pakistan. ICC Chief Executive Hansie Cronje said, "The integrity of the game is of paramount importance."[15]

Many argue there is too much gambling in sports and in society in general. Is there a valid reason gambling was essentially banned in the United States for many years? Should there be a limit on the amount of money individuals can wager? Losing money is never a good proposition. Terrance Watanabe was a winner and a loser. Anytime one casino (in this case, Harrah's) receives

---

[8] "Art Museums Make Super Bowl Bet," *Wall Street Journal*, January 27, 2010.

[9] Hannah Karp, "The NFL Doesn't Want Your Bets," *Wall Street Journal*, June 19, 2009.

[10] "Sports Wagering Industry Information Fact Sheets: Industry Issues," *American Gaming Association*, February 4, 2009.

[11] "It's Hip to Have the 0-7 Score Square," *Wall Street Journal*, January 30, 2009.

[12] Michael McCarthy, "Gambling Madness can Snag Court Fans," *USA Today*, March 28, 2007, citing to Danny Sheridan, Top 10 Betting Favorites, *USA Today*.

[13] Robin Insley, Lucia Mok, and Tim Swartz, "Issues Related to Sports Gambling," *Australia & New Zealand Journal of Statistics* 46, no. 2 (June 2004): 219–232; Timothy J. Brailsford, Philip K. Gray, Stephen A. Easton, and Stephen F. Gray, "The Efficiency of Australian Football Betting Markets," *Australian Journal of Management* 20, no. 2 (December 1995): 167–197; Warren D. Hill and John E. Clark, "Sports, Gambling, and Government: America's First Social Compact?" *American Anthropologist* 103, no. 2 (June 2001).

[14] William Spain, "The World Cup: Biggest Gambling Event in History?," *MarketWatch*, June 1, 2010; Kate O'Keefe, "Macau Gambling Revenue Jumps," *Wall Street Journal*, August 3, 2010.

[15] Tom Wright and Jonathan Clegg, "Cricket Allegations Deliver Blow to Pakistan," *Wall Street Journal*, August 31, 2010.

5.6% of its gambling revenue from one individual in one year you may have to reconsider your "lucky streak." Watanabe lost $127 million and then sued the casino, saying the casino should have stopped him from losing his money.[16] Do casinos have an ethical duty to individuals who are addicted to gambling to ban them from casinos and further gambling? Do you take the position that people are responsible for their own actions, and if they want to gamble, then so be it? The *Wall Street Journal* also reported on former Philadelphia Eagles owner Leonard Tose stating, "In 1993, former Philadelphia Eagles owner Leonard Tose failed to convince a jury in a civil suit against Hollywood Casino Corp. that employees of the casino had gotten him so drunk that he didn't know what he was doing when he gambled away millions in Atlantic City, N.J. As a result, he had to pay the casino $1.23 million in gambling debts. He died in 2003."[17] Gambling keeps growing, and it seems there is no stopping it. Should state or federal government place limitations on the growth of the gambling industry?[18]

Some scholars argue that gambling produces both a moral and social cost notwithstanding its growth in popularity.[19] Some states have even pushed for legislators to treat gambling as an addiction. Is it ethical to use tax dollars to treat gamblers who are addicted to gambling?[20]

Delaware recently passed a law that allows for gambling on sporting events.[21] Other states are considering a similar move.[22] Is it proper for states to view sports gambling as a "savior" to bail them out when they are having financial difficulties?

The NBA's referee gambling scandal in 2007 was a major news story in sports and provided a wake-up call to all professional leagues. NBA referee Tim Donaghy provided gamblers with picks during the 2006–2007 season. He was sentenced to a 15-month prison term due to his involvement in the betting scandal. He pled guilty to felony charges of wire fraud and transmission of wagering tips through interstate commerce. He admitted to betting on NBA games, but investigators never found that he bet on games he refereed.[23] Does that make a difference? Should a sports official go to federal prison for his or her involvement in a gambling scandal?[24]

One of the most infamous gambling episodes in college sports was the "rigging" of Boston College basketball games in 1978 and1979. Gangster Henry Hill (of *Goodfellas* fame) convinced Boston College players to "shave" points during the season while he ran a gambling ring.[25] The 1951 college basketball betting scandal involved seven schools and 32 players, with 7 being indicted on bribery and conspiracy charges.[26]

---

[16] Alexandra Berzon, "The Gambler Who Blew $127 Million," *Wall Street Journal*, December 5, 2009.

[17] Ibid.

[18] Dale Buss, "Will Gambling Continue to Grow? All Bets Are Off," *Wall Street Journal*, January 2, 2009.

[19] Richard A. McGowan, "Ethics of Gambling," *Boston Globe*, September 21, 2007.

[20] Samara Kalk Derby, "Legislation Pushes for Funding to Treat Gambling Addicts," *Madison State Journal*, November 29, 2009.

[21] Theo Emery, "Delaware Legalizes Wagering on Sporting Events," *New York Times*, May 16, 2009.

[22] Bob Considine, "Could Sports Betting Save New Jersey?" *Star Ledger*, August 9, 2010; Jennifer Jacobs, "Iowa Lawmakers Back Bill for Pro Sports Gambling," *USA Today*, February 4, 2010; Patrick McGreevy, "California May Benefit from Legalizing Sports Betting, State Senator Says," *Los Angeles Times*, August 1, 2010.

[23] Michael S. Schmidt, "League Finds Donaghy Was Sole Referee Culprit," *New York Times*, October 3, 2008.

[24] Jon Saraceno, "Gambling Case Fallout Remains as Donaghy Reports to Prison," *USA Today*, September 23, 2008. For further study, see Lawrence B. Pedowitz, "Report to the Board of Governors of the National Basketball Association," October 1, 2008; Howard Beck, "Lawyer Will Examine N.B.A. Gambling Rules," *New York Times*, August 22, 2007.

[25] Henry Hill, "How I Put The Fix In," *Sports Illustrated*, February 16, 1981.

[26] Joe Goldstein, "Explosion: 1951 Scandals Threaten College Hoops," *ESPN.com*, November 19, 2003.

Art Schlichter was most likely the most infamous gambler to play in the NFL. He was frequently seen on campus with gamblers at Ohio State University. After entering the NFL, he continued his gambling ways. At the end of the 1982 NFL season, he had accrued over $700,000 in gambling debts. The National Football League has always shied away from any association with gamblers, even though the Super Bowl is a heavily bet sports event.[27] The *New York Times* reported in 2003:

> The N.F.L. needs to face the reality of what is going on outside its stadiums. Some form of gambling is now legal in almost every state—and many states, like California, are hoping to balance their budgets by allowing an expansion of gambling. Nevada may be the only state where betting on sporting events is legal, but we have always been honest and consistent about what we are and what we offer.[28]

The National Hockey League has had its own gambling issues as well. Former NHL player Rick Tocchet pled guilty in March 2007 to running a sports gambling ring. The ring handled $1.7 million in wagers that included college football and the Super Bowl.[29] It seems no sport is safe from gamblers, including sumo wrestling.[30]

GAMBLING IN PROFESSIONAL SPORTS

Professional sports leagues have implemented rules and regulations prohibiting gambling and gamblers. All professional sports leagues prohibit players from gambling and from associating with gamblers. Leagues want to ensure the integrity of the sport and provide a sporting event that is based on the skill of the participants rather than produce an outcome that is certain. Every sporting event contains an element of luck, but no fan wants to see a "rigged" or "fixed" match. Fans want to see an athlete vying to be a champion without a gambling element present. The coin toss that starts every NFL game is exactly that, a "flip of the coin," but after that, the skills of the participants should produce the eventual winner and champion, with some luck of course.

Professional sports leagues have taken tough stances against those who engage in or associate with gambling. Leagues will typically suspend, fine, or even ban those who engage in gambling or associate with gamblers. Such was the case of former NBA player Jack Molinas. In *Molinas v. NBA*, professional basketball player Jack Molinas was suspended for life because he gambled on the outcome of a sporting matches. What ethical dilemma did this present for the NBA and Molinas?

📖 CASE 3-1 *Molinas v. National Basketball Association*

190 F. Supp. 241 (S.D.N.Y. 1961)

Jack Molinas is a well-known basketball player. In 1953, upon his graduation from Columbia University, he was 'drafted' by the Fort

[27] Hannah Karp, "The NFL Doesn't Want Your Bets," *Wall Street Journal*, June 16, 2009; Oscar B. Goodman, "The N.F.L.'s Gambling Problem," *New York Times*, January 24, 2003; Jason Kephart, "10 Things the NFL Won't Tell You," *SmartMoney*, January 8, 2010.
[28] Oscar B. Goodman, "The N.F.L.'s Gambling Problem," *The New York Times*, January 24, 2003.
[29] Associated Press, "Tocchet Enters a Guilty Plea," *New York Times*, May 26, 2007.
[30] Lucy Craft, "Sumo Wrestling Grapples with Gambling Scandal," *NPR*, June 28, 2010.

Wayne Pistons, then a member of the National Basketball Association
(now the Detroit Pistons). Subsequently, in the fall of 1953, he signed
a contract to play with the Pistons. In January of 1954, however, he
admitted, in writing, that he placed several bets on his own team, the
Pistons, to win. The procedure he followed was that he contacted a
person in New York by telephone, who informed him of the 'point spread'
on the particular game in question. Molinas would then decide whether
or not to place a bet on the game. He admitted that he received some
four hundred dollars as a result of these wagers, including reimburse-
ment of his telephone calls to New York. After he admitted this wagering, Mr. Podoloff, the president of the league, acting pursuant to a
clause in Molinas' contract and a league rule prohibiting gambling,
indefinitely suspended him from the league. This suspension has continued until the present date. Since the suspension, Molinas [made] several
applications, both oral and written, for reinstatement. All of these
[were] refused, and Mr. Podoloff testified that he [would] never allow
him to re-enter the league. He has characterized [Molinas] as a 'cancer
on the league' which must be excised.

In the meantime, Molinas attended and graduated from the Brooklyn Law
School, and was then admitted to the New York State Bar. He had also
been playing basketball for Williamsport and Hazelton of the Eastern
Basketball League.

In 1954, shortly after the suspension, Molinas brought an action in
the New York State Supreme Court, alleging that he had been denied
notice and hearing prior to the suspension, and that there was no
authority for the indefinite suspension imposed by Mr. Podoloff. The
court, after a trial, found against Molinas, holding that since he had
engaged in reprehensible and morally dishonest conduct, he was not
entitled to seek the aid of an equity court. The court also found that
even if a hearing was required by league rules, it would have been a
futile formality in this case, since Molinas had admitted violations
of his contract and the league rules.

In the action before the court, Molinas allege[d] that the National
Basketball Association had entered into a conspiracy with its member
teams and others in restraint of trade, and thus violated the anti-
trust laws. . . . It is further alleged that the suspension of Molinas
by the league, and its subsequent refusal to reinstate him, is the
result of a conspiracy in violation of these laws. Finally, he
charge[d] that the league has, through this conspiracy, imposed certain collateral restraints upon him, affecting his opportunities to
play in 'exhibition games' against league personnel.

Molinas sought treble damages in the sum of three million dollars . . .
and reinstatement to the league.

With respect to Molinas' suspension from the league in January of 1954, and the subsequent refusal by the league to reinstate him, he . . . failed to establish an unreasonable restraint of trade within the meaning of the anti-trust laws. A rule, and a corresponding contract clause, providing for the suspension of those who place wagers on games in which they are participating, seems not only reasonable, but necessary for the survival of the league. Every league or association must have some reasonable governing rules, and these rules must necessarily include disciplinary provisions. Surely, every disciplinary rule which a league may invoke, although by its nature it may involve some sort of a restraint, does not run afoul of the anti-trust laws. And, a disciplinary rule invoked against gambling seems about as reasonable a rule as could be imagined. Furthermore, the application of the rule to Molinas' conduct is also eminently reasonable. He was wagering on games in which he was to play, and some of these bets were made on the basis of a 'point spread' system. Molinas insists that since he bet only on his own team to win, his conduct, while admittedly improper, was not immoral. But I do not find this distinction to be a meaningful one in the context of the present case. The vice inherent in his conduct is that each time he either placed a bet or refused to place a bet, this operated inevitably to inform bookmakers of an insider's opinion as to the adequacy or inadequacy of the point-spread or his team's ability to win. Thus, for example, when he chose to place a bet, this would indicate to the bookmakers that a member of the Fort Wayne team believed that his team would exceed its expected performance. Similarly, when he chose not to bet, bookmakers thus would be informed of his opinion that the Pistons would not perform according to expectations. It is certainly reasonable for the league and Mr. Podoloff to conclude that this conduct could not be tolerated and must, therefore, be eliminated. The reasonableness of the league's action is apparent in view of the fact that, at that time, the confidence of the public in basketball had been shattered, due to a series of gambling incidents. Thus, it was absolutely necessary for the sport to exhume gambling from its midst for all times in order to survive.

The same factors justifying the suspension also serve to justify the subsequent refusal to reinstate. The league could reasonably conclude that in order to effectuate its important and legitimate policies against gambling, and to restore and maintain the confidence of the public vital to its existence, it was necessary to enforce its rules strictly, and to apply the most stringent sanctions. One can certainly understand the reluctance to permit an admitted gambler to return to the league, and again to participate in championship games, especially in light of the aura and stigma of gambling which has clouded the sports world in the past few years. Viewed in this context, it can be

```
seen that the league was justified in determining that it was
absolutely necessary to avoid even the slightest connection with gam-
bling, gamblers, and those who had done business with gamblers, in the
future. In addition, conduct reasonable in its inception certainly
does not become unreasonable through the mere passage of time, espe-
cially when the same factors making the conduct reasonable in the
first instance, are still present. At any rate, Molinas must show much
more than he has here in order to compel a conclusion that the
[league's] conduct was in fact unreasonable. . . . The proof estab-
lished at most that several league owners, coaches or players may have
felt that it was unwise, possibly because of the likelihood of adverse
publicity, to participate in a game, in which [Molinas], an admitted
gambler, was also involved. This falls far short of the conspiracy
required to establish a violation of the anti-trust laws. [Molinas was
not reinstated.]
```

Source: *Reprinted from Westlaw with permission of Thomson Reuters.*

Jack Molinas was sentenced to 10–15 years in prison and served 5 years. He became the inspiration for the film, *The Longest Yard*, starring Burt Reynolds.[31] Molinas died in 1975 at the age of 43, when he was killed by a gunshot to the head. His murder remains unsolved. Molinas was an interesting fellow. He was a lawyer, outstanding college and professional player, and by all accounts a "crooked" player as well. Unfortunately, his life ended in tragedy.

1. Did the NBA's banishment of Molinas preserve the integrity of the league?
2. Was the league's decision to ban Molinas a correct course of action for the league?
3. Does it make any difference that Molinas said he always bet on his own team to win?
4. Should a player be reinstated into a league if they receive counseling for their gambling addiction?

The current NBA Constitution states the following with regard to gambling:

NBA Const. Art. 35A(g). Article 35(f), which covers players, provides:

Any Player who, directly or indirectly, wagers money or anything of value on the outcome of any game played by a Team in the league operated by the Association shall, on being charged with such wagering, be given an opportunity to answer such charges after due notice, and the decision of the Commissioner shall be final, binding and conclusive and unappealable. The penalty for such offense shall be within the absolute and sole discretion of the Commissioner and may include a fine, suspension, expulsion and/or perpetual disqualification from further association with the Association or any of its Members.[32]

---

[31] Joe Goldstein, "Explosion II: The Molinas Period," *ESPN Classic*, November 19, 2003.
[32] *NBA Legal Compliance Policy and Code of Conduct § II.C.* www.NBA.com.

1. Should all professional leagues adopt gambling rules similar to the NBA's?

2. What is the rule referring to when it says "directly or indirectly"?

Should all states legalize sports betting? What ethical duty do leagues have to their fans to keep the games free from gamblers? Consider Case 3-2 in which the National Football League and other professional sports leagues objected to a Delaware state law that allowed for gambling.

CASE 3-2   *OFC Comm Baseball v. Markell*

579 F.3d 293 (3rd Cir. 2009)

In March 2009, the Governor of Delaware, Jack Markell, proposed legislation authorizing sports betting and table gaming at existing and future facilities in Delaware. On March 19, Governor Markell sought an advisory opinion from the Delaware Supreme Court . . . regarding the constitutionality of his proposal under the Delaware Constitution. In a letter to the Delaware Supreme Court, Governor Markell described three types of proposed sports gambling: (1) point-spread bets on individual games; (2) over/under bets on individual games; and (3) multi-game parlay bets. On May 14, while the request for an advisory opinion from the Delaware Supreme Court was pending, Governor Markell signed the Act into law.

After hearing oral argument, the Delaware Supreme Court issued an opinion on May 29, which found that multi-game betting would not violate state law. In analyzing the legality of the Act and the "lotteries" proposed pursuant to the Act, the Delaware Supreme Court relied heavily on Judge Stapleton's decision in *National Football League v. Governor of the State of Delaware*. That case concerned the NFL's challenge to a sports betting scheme known as "Scoreboard" that Delaware conducted during the 1976 season. *Scoreboard* was comprised of three games: *Football Bonus*, *Touchdown*, and *Touchdown II*. In *Football Bonus*, the State offered two pools of seven NFL games each and betters had to predict the winners, without a point spread, in one or both of the pools. In *Touchdown*, betters selected both the winners and point spreads for either three, four, or five NFL games. Finally, *Touchdown II*, which replaced *Touchdown* midway through the season, required betters to pick the winners, against the point spread, for between four and twelve NFL games. All of the *Scoreboard* games conducted in 1976 were confined to betting on the NFL, and all required that the better wager on more than one game at a time.

In *NFL*, Judge Stapleton held such wagering was permissible under the Delaware Constitution because chance is the "dominant factor" in multi-game (parlay) betting. The Delaware Supreme Court reached the same conclusion in its advisory opinion, *In re Request of Governor*,

2009 WL 1475736, but did not decide the constitutionality of single-game betting, except to recognize that it differs from the parlay games addressed by Judge Stapleton.

Following receipt of the Delaware Supreme Court's advisory opinion, on June 30 the State published its proposed regulations to implement the Act (Regulations). According to the Regulations, Delaware intends to implement a sports betting scheme that would include wagers "in which the winners are determined based on the outcome of any professional or collegiate sporting event, including racing, held within or without the State, but excluding collegiate sporting events that involve a Delaware college or university, and amateur or professional sporting events that involve a Delaware team." Delaware's proposed sports betting scheme includes single-game betting in addition to multi-game (parlay) betting, as the Regulations define the term "maximum wager limit" to include "the maximum amount that can be wagered on a *single sports lottery wager be it head-to-head or parlay. . . .*"

Delaware intends to commence its sports betting scheme on September 1, 2009, in time for the start of the upcoming NFL regular season. Though the NFL is its focus, Delaware intends to conduct—and the Regulations sanction—betting on all major professional and college sports.

On July 24, the Leagues filed a complaint against Governor Markell and Wayne Lemons, the Director of the Delaware State Lottery Office (collectively, Delaware or State), claiming that elements of Delaware's proposed sports betting scheme violate the Professional and Amateur Sports Protection Act (PASPA).

As Judge Stapleton held in *NFL*, and as was not disputed in the proceedings before either the District Court or our Court in this matter, the only sports betting scheme "conducted" by Delaware in 1976 involved the three *Scoreboard* games. That betting scheme was limited to multi-game parlays involving only NFL teams. Thus, any effort by Delaware to allow wagering on athletic contests involving sports beyond the NFL would violate PASPA. It is also undisputed that no single-game betting was "conducted" by Delaware in 1976, or at any other time during the time period that triggers the PASPA exception. ("None of the [1976] games permits head-to-head or single game betting.") Because single-game betting was not "conducted" by Delaware between 1976 and 1990, such betting is beyond the scope of the exception in . . . PASPA and thus prohibited under the statute's plain language.

Under federal law, Delaware may, however, institute multi-game (parlay) betting on at least three NFL games, because such betting is consistent with the scheme to the extent it was conducted in 1976.

Source: *Reprinted from Westlaw with permission of Thomson Reuters.*

CASE STUDY 3-1   *Las Vegas and the NFL*

The city of Las Vegas is a vacation hotspot for many people. Certainly Las Vegas is one of the most popular tourist destination in the world and would be capable of supporting an NFL franchise.[33] Should the NFL place a franchise in Las Vegas? Is it because Las Vegas is considered a "gambling haven" that the NFL has stayed clear of any association with Las Vegas? With the expansion of gambling to other states, would there be any other reason the NFL should not consider placing a team in Las Vegas? Is it because of the image it would create?[34]

Although participants, coaches, and managers determine the game on the field, the decision of the sports official has a much more immediate impact. If sports officials are paid by professional gamblers to affect the outcome and point-spread of the game, then the integrity, honesty, and ethics of the game will forever be in doubt. That was the case of long-time NBA referee Tim Donaghy. The effect of the Tim Donaghy scandal on the integrity of professional basketball was devastating. It is considered by many to be one of the most serious gambling scandals in the history of professional sports.

📖   CASE 3-3   *USA v. James Battista*

575 F.3d 226 (2nd Cir. 2009)

[Tim] Donaghy began his career as an NBA referee in September 1994 and continued in that position for thirteen seasons. He first began placing bets on NBA games, including games he officiated, during the 2003 to 2004 season through his friend Jack Concannon. The conspiracy at issue here, however, began in December 2006 and continued until April 2007. Donaghy provided "picks" on NBA games, again including games he officiated, to co-conspirators Battista and Martino. Battista agreed to pay Donaghy a fee for each game in which Donaghy correctly picked the winner. Donaghy provided the picks to Martino, Martino relayed the information to Battista, and Battista placed the bets. According to the government, Donaghy and Martino devised a code for communicating picks over the telephone using the names of Martino's two brothers. If Donaghy mentioned Martino's older brother, the pick would be the home team; if Donaghy referred to Martino's younger brother, the pick would be the visiting team. In making his picks, Donaghy relied on, among other things, nonpublic information to which he had unique access by virtue of his position as an NBA referee. This information included his knowledge of the officiating crews for upcoming NBA games, the interactions between certain referees, players and team personnel,

---

[33] Daniel Wolf, NFL Expansion: 10 Cities That Could Host an NFL Team in the Future, *Bleacherreport.com*, June 30, 2010.

[34] Selena Roberts, "Las Vegas and Pro Football are Perfect Together," *New York Times*, January 26, 2003.

and the physical condition of players. During the course of the conspiracy, Martino met with Donaghy in several cities for the primary
purpose of paying Donaghy for his correct predictions.

After the government discovered the gambling scheme, Donaghy agreed to
cooperate with its investigation. Thereafter, in August 2007, Donaghy
pleaded guilty to conspiracy to commit wire fraud and conspiracy to
transmit wagering information. In February 2008, Battista and Martino
were both charged with conspiracy to commit wire fraud and conspiracy
to transmit wagering information. As pertinent here, the indictment
alleged that Martino and Battista committed the following overt acts
in furtherance of the conspiracy to transmit wagering information:

A. On or about December 13, 2006, MARTINO spoke with the NBA referee
   [Donaghy] by telephone regarding the NBA referee's pick for an NBA game.
B. On or about December 14, 2006, BATTISTA and MARTINO met with the NBA
   referee in Pennsylvania and gave a cash payment to the NBA referee.
C. On or about December 26, 2006, MARTINO spoke with the NBA referee by
   telephone regarding the NBA referee's pick for an NBA game.
D. On or about March 11, 2007, MARTINO met with the NBA referee in Toronto,
   Canada, and MARTINO gave a cash payment to the NBA referee.

A few months later, Martino pleaded guilty to the wire fraud conspiracy
charge and Battista pleaded guilty to the wagering conspiracy charge.
Battista described his criminal conduct during his plea allocution:

> [F]rom December of 2006 to March 2007, I was engaged in the busi-
> ness of sports betting, and I agreed with Tom Martino and Tim
> Dona[ghy] to use the telephone across state lines to obtain
> information to assist me in wagering on sporting events, on NBA
> basketball games. I received information from Tom Martino, who
> received his information from the NBA referee Tim Donaghy. This
> agreement was formed during a meeting between the three of us, in
> a hotel in December of 2006. During the course of this agreement
> from time to time I directed Mr. Martino to do certain things
> such as having meetings with Mr. Donaghy.

Battista further admitted that he had met with Donaghy in Pennsylvania
for payment.

The NBA, and the United States on its behalf, sought restitution
against all three. . . . The NBA requested restitution for (1) Donaghy's
compensation for the portions of the 2003-04, 2004-05, 2005-06,
and 2006-07 seasons when he officiated games in which he had a financial interest; (2) that portion of the salaries of NBA employees

attributed to reviewing the tapes of the games Donaghy refereed; and (3) attorneys' fees incurred by the NBA in connection with assisting the government in its investigation and prosecution.

After a comprehensive and particularized discussion of each restitution claim asserted by the NBA, the district court ordered the defendants to pay restitution in the total amount of $217,266.94. . . .

Specifically, the government contends that the conduct underlying the wagering conviction was Battista's dealings with Donaghy and Martino as part of a scheme to defraud the NBA of Donaghy's honest services by using NBA insider information to place wagers on NBA games. The district court generally agreed, observing that "the success of Battista's wagering was dependent on Donaghy's fraudulent conduct." In support of its position, the government points to statements made by Battista during his plea allocution and the factual allegations set forth in the indictment, asserting that they demonstrate that Battista's transmittal of wagering information was intertwined with the fraudulent gambling scheme.

The [law] defines [a] "victim" as:

> a person directly and proximately harmed as a result of the commission of an offense for which restitution may be ordered including, in the case of an offense that involves as an element a scheme, conspiracy, or pattern of criminal activity, any person directly harmed by the defendant's criminal conduct in the course of the scheme, conspiracy, or pattern.

On the facts presented in this case, we conclude that the NBA was "directly and proximately harmed" by Battista committing the crime of conspiracy to transmit wagering information and Battista's use of nonpublic information solely belonging to the NBA (conveyed to him by the co-conspirators) to place illegal wagers on its games. Moreover, we must look at Battista's "offense" of conspiracy, in which his criminal conduct encompasses not just his own acts but also those of his co-conspirators. By this standard, Battista's crime plainly harmed the NBA.

Source: *Reprinted from Westlaw with permission of Thomson Reuters.*

1. Do you consider the NBA a victim of Donaghy's gambling scheme?
2. Is restitution a proper remedy under the circumstances?
3. How was the NBA damaged by Donaghy's actions? Do you believe their reputation was harmed?

4. What are the necessary steps the NBA needed to take in order to regain credibility?
5. Should the NBA take measures to keep the name of referees who are going to call a game confidential until just a few minutes before tip-off?

CASE STUDY 3-2 *Leo Durocher, Baseball Manager*

Brooklyn Dodgers manager Leo Durocher was suspended for the entire 1947 season by Baseball Commissioner Happy Chandler for consorting with gamblers. Commissioner Chandler's decision to suspend Leo Durocher from baseball for the 1947 read as follows:

On 15 March 1947, L. S. MacPhall, president of the American League Baseball Club of New York, Inc., placed in the hands of the commissioner a request for a hearing to determine whether: [A] certain statements appearing in the public press, alleged to have been made or issued by Branch Rickey, president, and Leo Durocher, manager of the Brooklyn Baseball club, and [B] articles appearing in the Brooklyn Daily Eagle, under the by-line of Leo Durocher, were authentic, and whether Mr. Rickey and the Brooklyn club might be held responsible, and whether their publication might be considered conduct detrimental to baseball. . . .

The incident in Havana, which brought considerable unfavorable comment to baseball generally, was one of the series of publicity producing affairs in which Manager Durocher has been involved in the last few months.

Managers of baseball teams are responsible for the conduct of players off the field. Good managers are able to insure the good conduct of the players on the field and frequently by their example can influence players to be of good conduct off the field.

Durocher has not measured up to the standards expected or required of [a] manager of our baseball teams. As a result of the accumulations of unpleasant incidences, in which he has been involved, which the commissioner construes as detrimental to baseball, Manager Durocher is hereby suspended from participating in professional baseball for the 1947 season. . . ." "Club owner, manager, players and all others connected with baseball have been heretofore warned that association with known and notorious gamblers will [not] be tolerated and that swift disciplinary action will be taken against any person violating the order."

All parties to this controversy are silenced from the time this order is issued.

Respectfully submitted, A. B. Chandler, commissioner.

The Durocher affair was important because, unlike the Black Sox scandal, a respected coach—the leader of his team—was implicated and associated with gambling. As bad as it is to have athletes who shave points, it is much more damaging to the integrity of the game, to have coaches and managers betting on games. They hold a position of trust and responsibility, and also have a fiduciary relationship with fans to ensure the continued integrity of the game.[35]

Pete Rose, "Charlie Hustle," wowed baseball fans for many years with his exploits on the field. He was also a noted gambler and was suspended by the commissioner for his gambling activities.

📖 CASE 3-4 *Rose v. Giamatti*

721 F. Supp. 906 (S.D. Ohio 1989)

For the last several weeks, the charges against Pete Rose have focused enormous public attention on gambling and the possible corruption of

---

[35] For further study *see*, A. B. (Happy) Chandler, John Underwood, Dunned Down by the Heavies: Durocher's Suspension Triggered Chandler's Downfall. The Owners Didn't Mind Losing Leo- But They Didn't Want a Strong Commissioner, *Sports Illustrated*, May 3, 1971.

the game. Now that Pete Rose has aired these charges by bringing suit, it has become critical for the Commissioner's Office to act promptly to maintain public confidence in the integrity of the game. If every action by the Commissioner to investigate and determine matters affecting the integrity of the game were to be subject to court intervention and delay, the Commissioner's ability to safeguard the integrity of the game would be destroyed. The action of the court below threatens the very reputation of Major League Baseball, and deprives the Commissioner of the power to protect the integrity of the game.

[Rose], field manager of the Cincinnati Reds baseball club, has been under investigation for allegations of gambling on baseball. The Commissioner of Baseball is empowered to investigate and act on such allegations under the Major League Agreement and [Rose's] contract with the Cincinnati Reds.

In this instance the Commissioner enlisted special counsel, John Dowd, to investigate the allegations against [Rose]. Mr. Dowd conducted an extensive investigation and submitted a comprehensive report to the Commissioner consisting of 225 pages and eight volumes of exhibits.

On May 11, 1989, the Commissioner provided a copy of the Report to [Rose] and scheduled a hearing on the matter for May 25, 1989. [Rose] requested from the Commissioner an extension of thirty days in which to prepare for the hearing. This request was granted and the hearing was rescheduled for June 26, 1989.

Rather than prepare for the hearing before the Commissioner, [Rose] filed suit on June 19, 1989, seeking a temporary restraining order, preliminary injunction, and permanent injunction, as well as other relief. After two days of testimony, the trial court granted the temporary restraining order on June 25, 1989, concluding that there is substantial evidence the Commissioner has prejudged [Rose's] case and cannot serve as a fair and impartial decision maker. The trial judge enjoined the Commissioner and the Cincinnati Reds baseball club from taking any disciplinary action whatsoever against [Rose] during the 14-day life of the order. Where a voluntary association has yet to conduct a disciplinary hearing or to render a decision, judicial intervention to enjoin the association's proceeding or to disqualify the decision maker is unprecedented.

The court below has erred on a fundamental matter of law by restraining the Commissioner of Baseball from even holding a hearing with respect to the serious allegations that Pete Rose was gambling on Major League Baseball games.

The sole basis for the court's action was Judge Nadel's finding that Commissioner Giamatti had prejudged the matter of Pete Rose's guilt.

This finding, too, is incorrect. The single item of evidence relied upon by Judge Nadel was a letter, dated April 18, 1989, drafted by the Commissioner's Special Counsel John M. Dowd, signed by Commissioner Giamatti and sent to the Honorable Carl Rubin, who was about to sentence one of Pete Rose's accusers, Ron Peters. The letter recites that "[b]ased upon other information in our possession, I am satisfied Mr. Peters has been candid, forthright and truthful with my special counsel." As discussed in [Giamatti's] Brief, the claim of prejudgment based on this letter is not sustainable as a matter of law or fact.

The unrefuted evidence was that the letter was drafted by Mr. Dowd, reflected only his preliminary assessment of the quality of the testimonial and documentary evidence provided to him by Mr. Peters, represented no independent assessment of evidence by the Commissioner, and did not in any manner constitute a ruling on the ultimate issue which would be before the Commissioner.

Moreover, the type of "prejudgment" about which [Rose] complains forms an insufficient basis as a matter of law for disqualifying decision makers. If the rule were otherwise, judges who made preliminary findings of credibility in preliminary injunction matters, or in connection with warrants in criminal cases would be forever disqualified from subsequent proceedings over the same or related matters. This is plainly not the case.

In supervising the investigation of Pete Rose, the Commissioner was acting pursuant to specific powers given him under the Major League Agreement to investigate conduct not in the best interests of Baseball. The Commissioner will inevitably make certain judgments in the course of his investigations, but there is no reason that his investigatory function should preclude the exercise of his adjudicatory function. The combination of such functions is routine in government agencies, and is certainly not inconsistent with natural justice and fundamental fairness.

Judges repeatedly issue arrest warrants on the basis that there is probable cause to believe that a crime has been committed and that the person named in the warrant has committed it. Judges also preside at preliminary hearings where they must decide whether the evidence is sufficient to hold a defendant for trial. Neither of these pretrial involvements has been thought to raise any constitutional barrier against the judge's presiding over the criminal trial and, if the trial is without a jury, against making the necessary determination of guilt or innocence.

Judge Nadel's suggestion that the hearing of this matter would be futile, given the supposed prejudgment of the Commissioner, is contradicted by the facts before him, and is also inconsistent with the appropriate legal standard. This rule against judicial interference in the decision-making process of a private association cannot be avoided by "[a] mere averment that a remedy is futile or illusory."

The subject of Pete Rose's gambling activities and the extent of gambling on Major League Baseball has been the focus of widespread speculation and intense public concern, putting a cloud over Major League Baseball and its administration. The trial court's issuance of the temporary restraining order has now raised substantial doubt as to baseball's ability to police itself and the Commissioner's power to enforce its rules. The integrity of the game has been damaged by the lower court's ruling and it will continue to suffer as long as the temporary restraining order remains in effect.

It is vital that the Commissioner be allowed to hear the evidence on the allegations against [Rose] and reach a determination as quickly as possible. Indeed, the sport of baseball will be severely damaged if the Commissioner is barred from completing his investigation and taking the actions he sees as appropriate-steps consistent with his mandate to uphold the integrity of the game. The image of a sport no longer capable of policing itself in a matter as serious as a manager betting on his own team's games could only erode public confidence in and respect for the national pastime. The ability of the Commissioner to protect the integrity of baseball, the purpose for which his office was created, is at stake.

Source: *Reprinted from Westlaw with permission of Thomson Reuters.*

The Baseball Commissioner, A. Bartlett Giamatti and Pete Rose settled their dispute by entering into the following agreement:

Pete Rose/A. Bartlett Giamatti Agreement

Office of the Commissioner of Baseball

350 Park Avenue

New York, New York

In the Matter of: Peter Edward Rose, Manager

Cincinnati Reds Baseball Club

Agreement and Resolution

On March 6, 1989, the Commissioner of Baseball instituted an investigation of Peter Edward Rose, the field manager of the Cincinnati Reds Baseball Club, concerning allegations that Peter Edward Rose engaged in conduct not in the best interests of baseball in violation of Major

League Rule 21, including but not limited to betting on Major League Baseball games in connection with which he had a duty to perform.

The Commissioner engaged a special counsel to conduct a full, fair and confidential inquiry of the allegations against Peter Edward Rose. Peter Edward Rose was given notice of the allegations and he and his counsel were generally apprised of the nature and progress of the investigation. During the inquiry, Peter Edward Rose produced documents, gave handwriting exemplars and responded to questions under oath upon oral deposition. During the deposition, the special counsel revealed key evidence gathered in the inquiry to Peter Edward Rose and his counsel.

On May 9, 1989, the special counsel provided a 225-page report, accompanied by seven volumes of exhibits, to the Commissioner. On May 11, 1989, the Commissioner provided a copy of the Report to Peter Edward Rose and his counsel, and scheduled a hearing on May 25, 1989, to give Peter Edward Rose an opportunity to respond formally to the information in the report. Peter Edward Rose received, read and is aware of the contents of the Report. On May 19, 1989, Peter Edward Rose requested, and subsequently received, an extension of the hearing date until June 26, 1989. Peter Edward Rose acknowledges that the Commissioner has treated him fairly in this Agreement and has acted in good faith throughout the course of the investigation and proceedings.

Peter Edward Rose will conclude these proceedings before the Commissioner without a hearing and the Commissioner will not make any formal findings or determinations on any matter including without limitation the allegation that Peter Edward Rose bet on any Major League Baseball game. The Commissioner has determined that the best interests of Baseball are served by a resolution of this matter on the following agreed upon terms and conditions:

1. Peter Edward Rose recognizes, agrees and submits to the sole and exclusive jurisdiction of the Commissioner:
    A. To investigate, either upon complaint or upon his own initiative, any act, transaction or practice charged, alleged or suspected to be not in the best interests of the national game of Baseball; and
    B. To determine, after investigation, what preventive, remedial, or punitive action is appropriate in the premises, and to take such action as the case may be.
2. Counsel for Peter Edward Rose, upon his authority, have executed a stipulation dismissing with prejudice the civil action that was originally filed in the Court of Common Pleas, Hamilton County, Ohio, captioned Peter Edward Rose v. A. Bartlett Giamatti, No. A8905178, and subsequently removed to the United States District Court from the Southern District of Ohio, Eastern Division, Docket No. C-2-89-577.

3. Peter Edward Rose will not avail himself of the opportunity to partic-ipate in a hearing concerning the allegations against him, or otherwise offer any defense to those allegations.

4. Peter Edward Rose acknowledges that the Commissioner has a factual basis to impose the penalty provided herein, and hereby accepts the penalty imposed on him by the Commissioner and agrees not to chal-lenge that penalty in court or otherwise. He also agrees he will not institute any legal proceedings of any nature against the Commis-sioner of any of his representatives, either Major League or any Major League Club.

5. The commissioner recognizes and agrees that it is in the best interests of the national game of Baseball that this matter be resolved pursuant to his sole and exclusive authority under the Major League Agreement.

Therefore, the Commissioner, recognizing the benefits to Baseball from a resolution of this matter, orders and directs that Peter Edward Rose be subject to the following disciplinary sanctions, and Peter Edward Rose, recognizing the sole and exclusive authority of the Commissioner and that it is in his interest to resolve this matter without further proceedings, agrees to accept the following disciplinary sanctions imposed by the Commissioner.

A. Peter Edward Rose is hereby declared permanently ineligible in accor-dance with Major League Rule 21 and placed on the Ineligible List.

B. Nothing in this Agreement shall deprive Peter Edward Rose of the rights under Major League Rule 15(c) to apply for reinstatement. Peter Edward Rose agrees not to challenge, appeal or otherwise contest the decision of, or the procedure employed by, the Commissioner or any future Com-missioner in the evaluation of any application for reinstatement.

C. Nothing in this agreement shall be deemed either an admission or a denial by Peter Edward Rose of the allegation that he bet on any Major League Baseball game.

Neither the Commissioner nor Peter Edward Rose shall be prevented by this agreement from making any public statement relating to this matter so long as no such public statement contradicts the terms of this agreement and resolution.

This document contains the entire agreement of the parties and repre-sents the entire resolution of the matter of Peter Edward Rose before the Commissioner.[36]

---

[36] Rose's Road Back, *CBC Sports*, January 7, 2003.

1. Should Pete Rose be banned from baseball for life because of his gambling activities?
2. Should he be refused admission to Baseball's Hall of Fame because of his admitted gambling on baseball games? If he is banned, is it unethical not to ban other players who engage in misconduct, other than gambling, such as illegal steroid use?
3. Rose said he always bet on his team to win; does that make a difference?
4. Should a coach, manager, or sports official be treated differently than a player for violations of a league gambling policy?

The Black Sox scandal of 1919 is the most famous gambling episode in sports. With pressure building, White Sox players Eddie Cicotte was the first player to step forward and admit his wrongdoing in the series. Cicotte first went to the office of the club's attorney, Alfred Austrian. In the presence of White Sox owner Charles Comisky, White Sox manager Kid Gleason, and attorney Austrian, a destroyed Cicotte admitted he took money to fix the series. Cicotte was then taken to the criminal courts building where assistant state's attorney Hartley Replogle questioned Cicotte in front of Judge McDonald and the grand jury. Cicotte confessed his part in throwing the 1919 World Series saying, "I was a fool," as he exited the jury room.[37] The *New York Times* reported Cicotte's testimony as follows:

> I've lived a thousand years in the last year. . . . In the first game at Cincinnati I was knocked out of the box. I wasn't putting a thing on the ball. You could have read the trademark on it when I lobbed the ball up to the plate. . . . In the fourth game, played at Chicago, which I also lost, I deliberately intercepted a throw from the outfield to the plate which might have cut off a run. I muffed the ball on purpose. . . . At another time in the same game I purposely made a wild throw. All the runs scored against me were due to my own deliberate errors. I did not try to win.
>
> The day before I went to Cincinnati I put it up to them squarely for the last time, that there would be nothing doing unless I had the money.
>
> That night I found the money under my pillow. There was $10,000. I counted it. I don't know who put it there, but it was there. It was my price. I had sold out 'Conny.' I had sold out the other boys, sold them for $10,000 to pay off a mortgage on a farm, and for the wife and kids.
>
> If I had reasoned what that meant to me, the taking of that dirty crooked money—the hours of mental torture, the days and nights of living with an unclean mind, the weeks and months of going along with six of the seven crooked players and holding a guilty secret, and going along with the boys who had stayed straight and clean and honest—boys who had nothing to trouble them—say, it was a hell.
>
> I got the $10,000 cash in advance that's all.

Joe Jackson was next, confessing to his part in the scandal, testifying he was promised $20,000 but only got $5,000. Jackson's story was a confirmation of Cicotte's. He said he was given $5,000 by White Sox pitcher Lefty Williams while the club was in Chicago, and when he threatened to talk about it to the grand jury, White Sox players Chic Gandil, Lefty Williams, and Swede Risberg told him, "You poor simp, go ahead and squawk. Where do you get off if you do? We'll all say you're a liar, and every honest baseball player in the world will say you're a liar. You're out of luck. Some of the boys were promised a lot more than you, and got a lot less." Jackson's story was summarized in the *Chicago Daily Tribune*:

---

[37] "Admit Guilt," *Chicago Daily Tribune*, September 29, 1920, p. 1.

Jackson's Story

Joe Jackson last night described his confession to the grand jury as follows:

"I heard I'd been indicted. I decided that these men couldn't put anything over on me. I called up Judge McDonald and told him I was an honest man, and that he ought to watch this thing. He said to me, 'I know you are not.' He hung up the receiver on me.

I thought it over. I figured somebody had squawked. I got the idea that the place for me was the ground floor. I said 'I'll tell him what I know.'

He said, 'Come on over and tell it to me.' I went over."[38]

At one point the *New York Times* reported that Jackson testified to the grand jury he either struck out or hit easy balls when hits would mean runs. Jackson never testified in front of the grand jury in such a manner.

CASE STUDY 3-3   *Tennis's Slippery Slope*

Bets on tennis pay off for the Australian Open, the only Grand Slam tournament sponsored by a gambling house. A portion of each wager with Betfair Australia placed on Roger Federer, Serena Williams, or any of the hundreds of players at the event goes to Tennis Australia, the nonprofit federation that runs the two-week event. Tennis Australia's Steve Ayles, who oversees Tennis Australia's revenue, said, "We certainly believe that responsible gambling is part of Australian culture. . . . We can also ensure that money goes back into developing the sport."[39]

Simon Chadwick, a professor of sport business strategy and marketing at Coventry University Business School, says, "You're opening yourself up to allegations from the general public that you're condoning online gambling or are complicit in online gambling scandals." Richard Lapchick, Director of the Institute for Diversity and Ethics in Sports at the University of Central Florida deemed the Betfair deal a "slippery slope . . . the argument that it generates little revenue for tennis doesn't help."

1. Whose position is correct?
2. Is allowing just a little betting on professional sports opening up the door for corruption and chipping away at the integrity of the sport?

GAMBLING IN AMATEUR SPORTS

Gambling is very popular in the amateur sports world as well. Over the last 75 years, many point-shaving schemes have been uncovered by the NCAA in both basketball and football. Some have even resulted in criminal prosecutions. In 1945, two Brooklyn College basketball players were arrested in the home of two bookmakers. They had accepted $1,000 in return for intentionally losing a game against Akron University.[40] A 1999 University of Michigan study found that 72% of all Division I athletes had bet on sporting events since entering college. Of course, bookies create point-spreads

---

[38] "Jackson's Story," *Chicago Daily Tribune*, September 29, 1920, p. 2.

[39] Danielle Rossingh and Dan Baynes, "Bets on Federer Pay Australian Open as Tennis Embraces Gambling," *Bloomberg*, January 13, 2010.

[40] Joe Goldstein, "Rumblings: The Brooklyn Five," *ESPN.com*, November 19, 2003.

and establish the odds in college sports as well as in professional sports. However, it is more damaging in amateur sports because of the participants involved, their relative youth and the amateur nature of the match.

The NCAA's official position on gambling states, in part:

- The NCAA opposes all forms of legal and illegal sports wagering on college sports. Sports wagering has become a serious problem that threatens the well-being of the student-athlete and the integrity of college sports.
- The explosive growth of sports wagering has caused a noticeable increase in the number of sports wagering-related cases processed by the Association.
- The Internet has made it easier than ever for student-athletes to place bets, providing easy access, virtual anonymity, and essentially no supervision.
- Student-athletes are viewed by organized crime and organized gambling as easy marks.
- When student-athletes gamble, they break the law and jeopardize their eligibility.
- When student-athletes become indebted to bookies and can't pay off their debts, alternative methods of payment are introduced that threaten the well-being of the student-athlete or undermine an athletic contest—such as point-shaving.

Source: © *National Collegiate Athletic Association. 2010. All Rights Reserved.*

The NCAA has always been concerned about the student-athlete and gambling issues.[41] They want to fend off even the faintest hint of gambling.[42] One of the issues has been the increasing popularity of gambling among college students themselves.[43] Bill Saum was a gambling and agent representative for the NCAA. He testified before the U.S. Congress regarding gambling issues and the NCAA.

Testimony of NCAA Representative Bill Saum

Gambling and Agent Representative

National Collegiate Athletic Association

Before the National Gambling Impact Study Commission

November 10, 1998

Las Vegas, Nevada

Like many other sports organizations, the NCAA has a clear, direct policy regarding sports gambling. The NCAA prohibits the participants in any form of legal or illegal sports gambling because of its potential to undermine the integrity of sports contests while jeopardizing the welfare of the student-athlete and the intercollegiate athletics community. The NCAA membership has adopted specific legislation prohibiting athletics department staff members, conference office staff and student-athletes from engaging in sports gambling activities as

---

[41] Michael McCarthy, "Point-Shaving Remains a Concern in College Athletics," *USA Today*, May 9, 2007.
[42] Eddie Timanus, "NCAA Aims to Avoid NBA's Referee Problem," *USA Today*, July 25, 2007.
[43] Michael McCarthy, "College Kids Caught in Gambling Madness," *USA Today*, March 28, 2007.

they relate to intercollegiate or professional sporting events. These same rules apply to NCAA national staff.

Impact on the Integrity of the Sports Contest

As a sports organization, the NCAA is well aware of the direct threat sports gambling poses to the integrity of each intercollegiate contest. In the late 1940's, the academic community and the public were shocked to learn that the City College of New York basketball team was involved in a point shaving scandal. Sadly, today the scandals appear to be occurring more frequently. Within the last ten months, the public learned of point shaving scandals in the campuses of Arizona State University[44] and Northwestern University.[45] The magnitude of these and similar incidents should not be underestimated. According to federal law enforcement officials, more money was wagered in the Arizona State case than on any point shaving scam in the history of intercollegiate athletics. However, when it comes to sports gambling on college campuses, this is just the tip of the iceberg.

In 1995, four Maryland football players and one men's basketball player were found to have bet on collegiate sporting events. Two years ago, 13 football players at Boston College were involved in sports gambling activities, four admitted to betting against their own team.[46] Just last year, a basketball player at Cal-State Fullerton was approached by a student after a practice and offered $1000 per game to shave points. Earlier this year, law enforcement dismantled a large sports gambling ring that was operating, in part, out of a Columbia University fraternity house.

As you can plainly see, the influence of sports gambling is far reaching, and sports organizations continually live in fear that sports gambling will infiltrate and undermine the contest itself.

Impact on Student-Athletes

As the NCAA staff person responsible for conducting sports gambling investigations at our member institutions, I am acutely aware of the impact that sports gambling can have on the lives of college student-athletes. I have seen students, their families, and institutions publically humiliated. I have watched students be expelled from college, lose scholarships worth thousands of dollars, and jeopardize any hope

---

[44] The Associated Press, "Silman Gets 46 Months for his Part in ASU Point-Shaving Scandal," *Sports Illustrated*, June 20, 1998. (Authors' footnotes added)

[45] The Associated Press, "A Stain on the Game," *Sports Illustrated*, March 27, 1998. (Authors' footnotes added)

[46] Gerry Gallahan, "Dark Days at BC," *Sports Illustrated*, November 18, 1996. (Authors' footnotes added)

of a career in professional athletics. In most cases, the scenario is strikingly familiar. Student-athletes who have begun gambling on sports incur losses beyond their means to repay and, as a result, become vulnerable to point shaving schemes. Sometimes they participate in such schemes voluntarily in a desperate attempt to erase their outstanding debt, other times they are compelled by the threat of personal injury. In the latter cases, often organized crime is involved. In many cases, student bookmaking operations can be traced back to organized crime.

The profile of the typical college student who gambles is someone who believes he can control his own destiny, someone who is willing to take the risks, and someone who believes he possesses the skill to be successful in the endeavor. If you otherwise look at these qualities in a positive light, they are reflected in many college athletes. This may, in part, explain why some student-athletes are drawn to sports gambling.

However, environmental factors may also be playing an influential role. One of the Boston College football players involved in the school's betting scandal stated, "The attitude was: 'It's just part of the college experience.' To tell the truth, it never crossed my mind it was illegal; it was so commonplace." Other statements from student-athletes involved in sports gambling scandals reveal that their gambling habits were developed well before college. One of the athletes involved in the Northwestern University point shaving case admitted that gambling has been a part of his life ever since he was a youngster. He stated that he remembered "guys younger and older saying, 'let's bet $5 to see who is better in one-on-one.' I saw gambling every day in the inner city. People were playing cards and shooting dice. It was normal."

Our NCAA investigations have revealed that there is a very high incidence of gambling among college students. Student bookies are present at every institution. There is certainly no dispute that the impact of sports gambling is being felt on college campuses across the country.

What are the relevant ethical issues of gambling noted in Case 3-5?

📖 CASE 3-5 *Valentine v. National Sports Services (NSS), Smashmouth Sports, Scott Spreitzer, Jim Feist*

No. 3:03CV153(DJS) (D. Conn. 2005)

James Valentine is a Connecticut citizen. Defendant Jim Feist is the President, Secretary, Treasurer, and the Chairman of the Board of Directors for defendant National Sports Services (NSS). Smashmouth Sports and Jim Feist Sports are unincorporated divisions of NSS. Scott Speitzer is a sports gaming consultant retained as an independent contractor by NSS.

NSS provides sports handicapping and information services. NSS advertises its services in certain nationally distributed periodicals. NSS lists toll-free telephone numbers in some of its advertisements and maintains various web sites including *www.JimFeist.com.* Occasionally, NSS advertises on national television networks.

Valentine subscribed to a magazine called *Pro Football Weekly,* in which Jim Feist Sports advertised a free prediction for a college football game. Valentine called the listed toll-free phone number for the free pick, and shortly thereafter, beginning on or about September 24, 2000, representatives of NSS started soliciting him by phone. Valentine purchased services from NSS beginning on or about September 24, 2000 that were worth, in the aggregate, more than $100,000.

Valentine complained to Jim Feist Sports about the accuracy of its picks at various times in October, November, and December of 2000. In response to his complaints, Tom Margoglio, a sales manager at Jim Feist Sports, faxed Valentine the following offer:

> This letter is to confirm our intent to issue a credit in the amount of $5000.00 to your Master Card#. . . . The credit will be issued as soon as we are in receipt of the signed statement below. However, it may take up to one full billing cycle to appear on your credit card statement. December 12, 2000.

Valentine signed the following:

> I hereby authorize all charges made to Jim Feist Sports prior to December 12, 2000. I understand that my Master Card# . . . will be credited as soon as I sign and return the statement below. Once my account has been credited, I agree to take no further action on any charges I may have incurred on Master Card# . . ., Visa Card# . . . and American Express Card# . . . with Jim Feist Sports prior to this date. . . .

After signing this document, Valentine did not purchase services from NSS.

Valentine alleges four causes of action relating to his purchase of sports information and handicapping services from the defendant: (1) violation of CUTPA, (2) fraudulent misrepresentation, (3) negligent misrepresentation, and (4) breach of contract. Defendants move for summary judgment with respect to all counts of the complaint and raise numerous defenses.

Valentine's claims are based upon alleged misrepresentations about the quality of NSS's services. With respect to Jim Feist, Valentine admitted that he never spoke with Jim Feist, and there is no evidence in the record that reflects any other form of direct communication between Jim Feist and Valentine. Although Spreitzer did speak to Valentine over the telephone, Valentine has not provided a sufficient basis for holding Spreitzer liable for any tort alleged in the amended complaint. Therefore, judgment shall enter in favor of the individual defendants on all claims set forth in the amended complaint.

Source: *Reprinted from Westlaw with permission of Thomson Reuters.*

CASE STUDY 3-4 *Rick Neuheisel, Coach and Attorney-at-Law*

Rick Neuheisel was the football coach at the University of Washington. Neuheisel had a 33–16 record in four seasons with the Huskies and had five years remaining on a six-year contract that was to pay him $1.4 million a year. He reportedly won $25,000 in a 2002 office pool when he correctly picked Maryland to win the men's NCAA basketball tournament. Neuheisel eventually entered into a $4.5 million settlement with the NCAA and the university.

Neuheisel argued that NCAA investigators acted improperly because they had not advised him they would ask about his gambling in an auction-style pool on NCAA basketball games. NCAA president Myles Brand said he believed the NCAA acted properly. The NCAA infractions committee had found Neuheisel violated NCAA rules against gambling but did not sanction him. The university had argued that Neuheisel's contract allowed him to be fired for acts of dishonesty. School officials said he was fired for gambling on NCAA basketball, and for lying when first questioned by NCAA investigators.[47]

Review the following article. Discuss the pros and cons of legalized gambling in sports.

Arguments Against Illegalizing Gambling

Those who argue that sports gambling should remain legal argue, among other reasons, that economic benefits can be derived from the conduct, that sports gambling reflects consumer approval of the legality of the activity, and that sports betting has yet to bring the "demise" of any sport.

A. Sports Gambling Brings an Economic Benefit

On-site sports betting has brought unprecedented economic success to Las Vegas, and the popularity of internet sports betting has increased that success. Those who support keeping sports betting legal argue that if the U.S. were to completely ban sports betting, the sports books would move out of the country, or would move "underground," forcing astronomical costs in monitoring that potentially

---

[47] Associated Press, "Neuheisel Said He Feels Vindicated by Settlement," *ESPN.com*, March 7, 2005; Ray Glier, "A Coach Is Ousted, This One for Betting," *New York Times*, June 13, 2003.

new illegal activity. Also, with sports betting being illegal, cities like Las Vegas would not be able to receive the tax benefits that come with the gambling profits. Further, the *Indian Gaming Regulatory Act* limits the use of those profits to fund tribal government operations or programs, provide for the general welfare of Indian tribes, and to promote tribal economic development—all goals that would be much more difficult to achieve without the money from sports books.

This argument parallels those made for years by persons attempting to legalize certain types of drugs and prostitution. For example, drug use, distribution and prostitution occur frequently regardless of their illegality. Additionally, cities do not receive the tax benefits from these activities, and spend millions of dollars enforcing the laws enacted to keep them illegal.

Most states and the federal government have kept drugs and prostitution illegal because they are worried legalization would lead to the exploitation of children and women, as well as increased health problems associated with these activities. Like drugs and prostitution, sports gambling is addictive and leads to exploitation as well. Further, the economic benefit that the country might realize by completely legalizing sports gambling is far outweighed by the potential risks and harm associated with the activity.

B. Sports Gambling Reflects Consumer Approval

Proponents of legalized sports gambling cite the success of sports books and the growth of Las Vegas as consumer approval for the activity. Each year, the number of sports books and off-shore internet sports gambling web sites increases exponentially as revenues rise rapidly. Like the economic benefits argument above, the consumer approval argument is also flawed. Many illegal activities, like drug distribution, make huge profits each year. The profits reflect "consumer approval," yet just because the consumer participates in the activity, it does not mean that the millions of people not involved with sports gambling should be required to pay for the bankruptcies and thefts that occur to feed gambling addictions.

C. Sports Gambling Has Not Led to the Demise of Sports

Although there have been a few well-publicized sports betting scandals, those in favor of keeping sports betting legal contend that a few isolated incidents have not brought about the end of competitive sports. They argue that people go to sporting events to be entertained and that the "purity of sport" is the last thing on most fanatics' minds. They further contend that point-shaving scandals happen so rarely that even sports purists should not worry about sporting events being tainted by athletes not giving their best efforts.

It is true that over the years relatively few reported scandals have arisen compared with the thousands of games played every year. However, it is unclear how many athletes have not been caught for their involvement in point-shaving schemes. For example, how many times have athletes unexpectedly fumbled balls without getting touched, or missed wide-open lay-ups during undecided games? With the ability for people to gamble on sporting events comes the possibility that any athlete could be involved in assisting organized crime or sports bookies. If all sports betting were illegal, it would remove all incentive for athletes to intentionally throw games. The NCAA has made it completely illegal for any athletes to bet on any intercollegiate sports, but the monetary incentive for athletes remains present.[48]

Source: *Reprinted from Westlaw with permission of Thomson Reuters.*

---

[48] Brent J. Goodfellow, "Betting on the Future of Sports: Why Gambling Should Be Left Off the Field of Play," *Willamette Sports Law Journal*, Fall 2005. (Footnotes omitted)

NOTES AND DISCUSSION QUESTIONS

Gambling in Sports and Society

1. Should some sports gambling be legalized? What are the pros and cons of allowing legalized gambling in both professional and amateur sports?
2. Would it tarnish the integrity of a sport if fans could legally bet on a match at the stadium where the games are played?
3. Do you agree that sports gambling provides an "economic benefit" to certain parties?
4. If customers approve of legalized gambling, does that make it ethical? Are you just giving the customers what they want?
5. Does organized crime necessarily follow if legalized gambling is allowed in sports?
6. Should the playing of fantasy sports be considered gambling?[49]
7. Should online gambling be treated differently by sports leagues than other forms of gambling?[50]

Gambling in Professional Sports

8. Should professional players be allowed to bet on sports they do not play? Does it give a professional league a bad image if players go to Las Vegas in the off-season?
9. Why does Major League Baseball seem to treat its violators harsher than other sports when it comes to regulating gambling?[51]
10. Should professional sports betting be allowed in every state?[52]
11. Do you agree with writer Justin Wolfers? He says, "Legalizing wagering on which team wins or loses a particular game, while banning all bets on immaterial outcomes like point spreads, would destroy the market for illegal bookmakers and make sporting events less corruptible by gamblers."[53]
12. What discipline should be assessed against players who have been found betting while playing professional sports?
13. Do you believe the NBA properly handled the Tim Donaghy betting scandal? What else could they have done?[54]

---

[49] See Michael J. Thompson, "Give Me $25 and Derek Jeter for $26: Do Fantasy Sports Leagues Constitute Gambling?" *Sports Lawyers Journal* (Spring 2001); Liz Farmer, "Exempting Fantasy Sports from Gambling Laws," *Maryland Business Daily Record*, February 15, 2010.

[50] See Anthony N. Cabot and Robert D. Faiss, "Sports Gambling in the Cyberspace Era," *Chapman Law Review* (2002); Lori K. Miller and Cathryn L. Claussen, "Online Sports Gambling: Regulation or Prohibition?," *Journal of Legal Aspects in Sport* (2001).

[51] See Thomas J. Ostertag, "From Shoeless Joe to Charley Hustle: Major League Baseball's Continuing Crusade Against Sports Gambling," *Seton Hall Journal of Sport Law* (1992); Rico Longoria, "Baseball's Gambling Scandals," *ESPN Classic*, July 30, 2001; Daniel E. Ginsburg, *The Fix Is In: A History of Baseball Gambling and Game Fixing Scandals* (Jefferson, NC: McFarland and Co., 2004).

[52] See Ari Weinberg, "The Case for Legal Sports Gambling," *Forbes.com*, January 27, 2003.

[53] Justin Wolfers, "Blow the Whistle on Betting Scandals," *New York Times*, July 27, 2007.

[54] See Jonathan Gibbs, "Point Shaving in the NBA: An Economic Analysis of the National Basketball Association's Point Spread Betting Market," *Dissertation*, Stanford University, May 11, 2007; Robert I. Lockwood, "The Best Interests of the League: Referee Betting Scandal Brings Commissioner Authority and Collective Bargaining Back to the Front Court in the NBA," *Sports Lawyers Journal* (Spring 2008).

14. Michael Jordan is a known high-stakes gambler—poker, golf, most everything except basketball. Should the NBA curtail his association with the NBA because of his gambling? Should these concerns be mitigated once we know that he always paid back any of his alleged gambling debts?[55] The NBA cleared Jordan of any wrongdoing.[56]

15. How about Charles Barkley, an admitted gambler who is currently a TNT NBA analyst? Should TNT punish the former "Round Mound of Rebound" for gambling? He claims to have lost $10 million gambling.[57] In 2010, TNT said Barkley would join the network's coverage of the NCAA basketball tournament. In 2008 Barkley was suit by a casino for $400,000. Barkley later paid the gambling debt.

16. *Molinas v. Podoloff* is the seminal case in which the NBA president permanently enjoined a player from continued involvement with the league when the player admitted to gambling. Is this fair? Isn't it the moral and ethical thing to do to admit your transgressions and errors?

17. The Black Sox scandal of 1919 is infamous and immortalized in the films *Eight Men Out* and *Field of Dreams*. Even though the ball players were acquitted, they were still permanently suspended from baseball. Was that fair? Joe Jackson and Eddie Cicotte confessed that they were part of the scheme to "throw" the World Series. Their confessions were later "lost," and their written confessions could not be used against them at the trial.

18. Do you consider the actions of the NBA referee Tim Donaghy more detrimental to the NBA's integrity than issues of domestic violence and gun control that still face the league?

19. If a professional player's contract states that he or she should not gamble, should a team argue that the player is in breach of contract and refuse to pay his or her salary if the player is found to have gambled in violation of league rules?

20. Should professional leagues establish "gambling gurus" to educate and counsel those individuals with gambling addictions?

21. The British Horseracing Authority (BHA) has a position known as "Director of Sporting Integrity." Should all professional leagues establish such a role?[58]

22. Should there be criminal penalties against gambling on sports? If so, what should they be and who should enforce them?[59]

Gambling in Amateur Sports

23. Gambling is the most serious possible infraction in professional sports. Gambling is contrary to the goal of maintaining competitiveness and integrity in sports. Should this apply to amateur sports as well? Illegal gambling in collegiate sports is a billion-dollar business.[60]

---

[55] Daniel Schorn, "Jordan Still Flying High," *CBS News*, August 20, 2006.

[56] Jordan's Gambling Cleared, Sorry for Poor Judgement, *Jet Magazine*, April 20, 1992.

[57] "Barkley Claims Gambling Problem Has Cost Him $10M," *Associated Press*, May 5, 2006.

[58] Bill Wilson, "Sport and Gambling United Against Cheating," *BBC News Business*, May 9, 2010.

[59] See Reuters, "Man Jailed in First Online Gambling Conviction," *New York Times*, August 11, 2000.

[60] See Aaron J. Slavin, "The 'Las Vegas Loophole' and the Current Push in Congress Towards a Blanket Prohibition on Collegiate Sports Gambling," *University of Miami Business Law Review* 715(2002).

24. What should be done about curbing gambling in college sports? Is the NCAA doing enough? Would paying student-athletes curb illegal gambling behavior?[61]

25. The NCAA takes gambling seriously. For further study *see*, "NCAA Study Finds Sports Wagering a Problem Among Student Athletes."[62]

26. Does it send the wrong message when a U.S. President is completing a "final four" bracket while the U.S. Congress is attempting to regulate betting in collegiate sports?

27. Are there different reasons to allow betting in college sports as opposed to professional sports?

28. Amateurs commonly wager on games in which they participate, such as contests in recreational leagues involving softball or bowling. Many collegiate football competitions also sometimes award a prize to the victor, such as the Old Oaken Bucket (Indiana v. Purdue), the Little Brown Jug (Michigan v. Minnesota) and the Commander-in-Chief Trophy (Army, Navy, Air Force).[63] Does awarding a prize to the winner, even if it is an old bucket, constitute a form of gambling?[64]

29. In addition to preserving the integrity of intercollegiate athletics, one of the goals of the NCAA in preventing gambling is to ensure the well-being of student-athletes. Do you agree with this goal?

30. For further study on gambling and ethics in amateur athletics, see "NCAA National Study on Collegiate Sports Wagering and Associated Health-Risk Behaviors," *National Collegiate Athletic Association* (Fall 2003); Michael E. Cross, Jay Basten, Erin Marie Hendrick, Brian Kristofic, and Evan J. Schaffer, "Student-Athletes and Gambling: An Analysis of Attitudes Towards Risk-Taking," *Journal of Gambling Studies* 14, no. 4 (Winter 1998): 431–439; Justin Wolfers, "Point Shaving: Corruption in NCAA Basketball," *American Economic Review* 96, no. 2 (May 2006): 279–283; John Warren Kindt and Thomas Asmar, "College and Amateur Sports Gambling: Gambling Away Our Youth," *Sports and Entertainment Law Journal* (2001–2002). Fish and George Tanber, "As Summer Ends, Heat Is on in Toledo Point-Shaving Case," *ESPN.com*, August, 23, 2007; Rick Hepp, "Indictments Charge 24 in Borgata Sports-Betting Case," *Everything Jersey*, April 10, 2008.

---

[61] See Andrew Metrick, "March Madness? Strategic Behavior in NCAA Basketball Tournament Betting Pools," *Journal of Economic Behavior & Organization* 30, no. 2 (August 1996): 159–172; Dan Bernhardt and Steven Heston, "Point Shaving in College Basketball: A Cautionary Tale for Forensic Economics," *Economic Inquiry* 48, no. 1(January 2010): 14–25; Richard Goldstein, "Irwin Dambrot Dies at 81; Caught in Gambling Scandal," *New York Times*, January 23, 2010; Bill Dedman, "4 Are Indicted in Northwestern Football Scandal," *New York Times*, December 4, 1998; Justin L. Engel, "CMU Betting Expert Says NCAA Tournament Provides 'Perfect Storm' for College Gambling," *MLive.com*, March 4, 2010; "17 Indicted in Alleged Mob-Related Gambling Rings," *Wall Street Journal,* June 28, 2010; Sally Monaghan, Jeffrey Derevensky, and Alyssa Sklar, "Impact of Gambling Advertisements and Marketing on Children and Adolescents: Policy Recommendations to Minimize Harm," *Journal of Gambling Issues* 22 (December 2008).

[62] NCAA News Release, "NCAA Study Finds Sports Wagering a Problem Among Student-Athletes."

[63] Kyle Meadows, The Top Ten College Football Rivalry Trophies, *Bleacher Report,* July 2, 2008.

[64] See Jeffrey Standen, "The Beauty of Bets: Wagers as Compensation for Professional Athletes," *Willamette Law Review* 639 (2006): 640–641.

CHAPTER 4

ETHICS FOR PARTICIPANTS, COACHES, AND SPORTS OFFICIALS

The three essential human components of athletic competition are participants, coaches, and sports officials. The key concern for each party is to make the right ethical decision when the situation arises. When an ethical situation arises, participants should act in a reasonable and sportsmanlike manner without unnecessary violence toward other participants, coaches, or sports officials. Coaches must behave in an ethical manner toward the athletes under their charge. They also must behave ethically in their relationships with superiors, employers, sports officials, media personnel, and security. Ethical behavior includes refraining from committing unnecessary violent acts, properly supervising players, and abiding by all applicable rules and regulations of the relevant governing body (e.g., the National Collegiate Athletic Association) and the university. Sports officials should always conduct themselves in an ethical and sportsmanlike manner. They must adhere to the rules and regulations of their association's bylaws and maintain credibility and integrity while performing their duties. An ethical sports official never provokes a player to violence, gambles on a sporting event, or gives the impression that he or she is biased in any manner.

PARTICIPANT ETHICS

Almost everyone has participated in sports at one time or another. In competitive sports, athletes give it their all, mentally and physically, to achieve success and be declared a champion. Professional athletes are motivated by big contracts, as are fans, coaches, and owners, and must perform at the highest level or possibly lose their position on the club. This may cause some ethical dilemmas for participants.

In individual sports such as golf, tennis, racing, and bowling, there are no guaranteed contracts. The participants must win or not get paid. These athletes certainly have a great incentive to win. They want to stay on the tour or the circuit so they are not forced to go back to a "regular job."

In the midst of competition, sporting participants must make ethical decisions. The list of decisions is endless, but athletes want to gain an advantage and, with so much money at stake, will surely do whatever is required to prevail against their opponent. For example, a football player should never make a "cheap" hit on a quarterback; a coach should never curse at, ridicule, or abuse a player; and a sports official should always remain unbiased. The next section examines whether all participants are abiding by the rules of the game and exercising good sportsmanship in the process.

Standard of Conduct for Participants

The standard for participants in sports was at one time wed to Judge Cardozo's maxim that "the timorous may stay at home."[1] It was acknowledged that the restraints of civilization must accompany every athlete onto the playing field. In *Nabozny*, the court stated:

> When athletes are engaged in an athletic competition; all teams involved are trained and coached by knowledgeable personnel; a recognized set of rules governs the conduct of the competition; and a safety rule is contained therein which is primarily designed to protect players from serious injury, a player is then charged with a . . . duty to every other player on the field to refrain from conduct prescribed by a safety rule.[2]

Unsportsmanlike Conduct

Every participant should refrain from engaging in unsportsmanlike conduct. It is considered unsportsmanlike to act with a reckless lack of concern for the safety and well-being of other participants in an athletic contest. Numerous examples exist of participants who have veered from the path of being a true sportsman. Running the bases in the sport of baseball can be fun, just ask any t-ball player. Running around in a circle to go "home" has a rather pastoral feeling. The great Ty Cobb always considered the bases his territory. His base-running skills were described as "wonderful."[3] Stealing a base in baseball is exactly that, "stealing," and most people do not like stealing! So how should baseball players run the bases?

Case 4-1, *Bourque v. Duplechin*, explores this question. Duplechin, an aggressive base runner, was under an ethical obligation to play softball in a sportsmanlike manner and not cause injuries to other participants. Duplechin breached this duty when he made a conscious decision to recklessly endanger Bourque by choosing not to slide and by taking a path 5 feet away from the base path. He put himself on a collision course with the second baseman, who was unable to protect himself. Duplechin's choice was clearly an unethical decision for a participant.

📖 CASE 4-1 *Bourque v. Duplechin*

331 So.2d 40 (La. Ct. App. 1976)

On June 9, 1974, Bourque was playing second base on a softball team fielded by Boo Boo's Lounge. Duplechin, a member of the opposing team sponsored by Murray's Steak House and Lounge, had hit the ball and

---

[1] *Murphy v. Steeplechase Amusement Co.*, 250 N.Y. 479 (1929).

[2] *Nabozny v. Barnhill*, 334 N.E.2d 258 (Ill. App. 1975), pp. 260–261.

[3] "Ty Cobb's Sensational Base Running Helps Detroit Beat Cleveland in Thirteenth Inning," *New York Times*, September 11, 1911.

advanced to first base. A teammate of Duplechin's, Steve Pressler, hit
a ground ball and Duplechin started to second. The shortstop caught
the ground ball and threw it to Bourque who tagged second base and
then stepped away from second base to throw the ball to first and
execute a double play. After Bourque had thrown the ball to first
base, Duplechin ran at full speed into Bourque. As Duplechin ran into
Bourque, he brought his left arm up under Bourque's chin. The evidence
supports the...factual conclusion that the collision occurred four or
five feet away from the second base position in the direction of the
pitcher's mound. Duplechin was thrown out of the game by the umpire
because of the incident.

. . . Bourque, age 22 at the time of trial, testified that he is
5'7'' tall. He was well out of the way when he was hit, standing four
or five feet from second base and outside the base line. He knew there
was a possiblity of a runner sliding into him but had never imagined
what actually happened, which he regarded as unbelievable under the
circumstances.

Gregory John Laborde, a student at Tulane Law School, testified that
he witnessed the incident from the dugout along the first base line
and saw Duplechin turn and run directly toward Bourque who was standing
four or five feet from second base toward home plate. Duplechin did
not attempt to slide or decrease his speed and his left arm came up
under Bourque's chin as they collided. Duplechin had to veer from the
base path in order to strike Bourque.

Donald Frank Lockwood, baseball coach at USL, testified as an expert
witness that: softball is a noncontact sport; in a forced play to second
such as this, the accepted way to break up a double play is by sliding.

Steve Pressler, who hit the ground ball that precipitated the incident, testified that the sides were retired as a result, because the
collision was a flagrant violation of the rules of the game.

Duplechin admitted that he ran into Bourque while standing up in an
attempt to block Bourque's view of first base and keep him from exe-
cuting a double play. Duplechin also admitted that he was running at
full speed when he collided with Bourque, a much smaller man. Duplechin
attributed the accident to Bourque's failure to get out of the way.

Oral surgeon John R. Wallace saw Bourque following the accident and
said the nature of the injury and the x-rays indicated that it was
caused by a blow from underneath the jaw. Dr. Wallace characterized
the injury as one that may have been common in football before the use
of mouthpieces and faceguards.

There is no question that. . .Duplechin's conduct was the cause in fact
of the harm to. . .Bourque. Duplechin was under a duty to play softball

in the ordinary fashion without unsportsmanlike conduct or wanton injury to his fellow players. This duty was breached by Duplechin, whose behavior was, according to the evidence, substandard and negligent. Bourque assumed the risk of being hit by a bat or a ball. Bourque may also have assumed the risk of an injury resulting from standing in the base path and being spiked by someone sliding into second base, a common incident of softball and baseball. However, Bourque did not assume the risk of Duplechin going out of his way to run into him at full speed when Bourque was five feet away from the base. A participant in a game or sport assumes all of the risks incidental to that particular activity which are obvious and foreseeable. A participant does not assume the risk of injury from fellow players acting in an unexpected or unsportsmanlike way with a reckless lack of concern for others participating.

The trial court awarded . . . Bourque $12,000 for his pain and suffering and $1,496.00 for his special damages. There is no dispute about the amount awarded. Bourque's jaw was fractured; his chin required plastic surgery; seven teeth were broken and had to be crowned; and one tooth was replaced by a bridge.

. . . Bourque's injuries resulted from the negligence of . . . Duplechin; Bourque was not guilty of contributory negligence and did not assume the risk of this particular accident. . .

CUTRER, Judge (dissenting):

As correctly stated in the majority opinion, Duplechin admitted that he ran into the [Bourque] in an attempt to prevent a double play. In essence the [Duplechin] testified that if the [Bourque] did not get out of the way he would run into him in order to prevent the double play. [Bourque] did not get out of the way and Duplechin did run into him. As a result [Bourque] received rather severe facial injuries, principally because of the difference in size between the two players; Duplechin was five feet, eleven inches tall and weighed two hundred ten pounds, while [Bourque] was five feet, seven inches tall and weighed one hundred forty pounds.

In the present case the danger of Duplechin colliding with [Bourque] and causing him injury was more than a foreseeable risk which a reasonable man would avoid. The collision and resulting injury were a substantial certainty, particularly in view of the fact that Duplechin was larger than [Bourque], was running in an upright position at full speed directly at [Bourque], and knew he would run over [Bourque] if the latter did not get out of his way.

Source: *Reprinted from Westlaw with permission of Thomson Reuters.*

It is a participant's ethical duty to act in a sportsmanlike manner. Clearly, Duplechin was not acting in a sportsmanlike manner when he veered 5 feet out of the correct and ethical path to deliberately strike Bourque. Bourque assumed the risk of being hit by a bat or a ball. He also may have assumed the risk of an injury resulting from standing in the base path and being "spiked" by someone sliding into second base. However, he did not assume the risk of Duplechin going out of his way to run into him at full speed when Bourque was 5 feet away from the base. A participant in a sport assumes all of the risks incidental to that sport that are obvious and foreseeable. A participant does not assume the risk of injury from fellow players acting in unexpected or unsportsmanlike ways with a reckless lack of concern for other participants.

What action should be taken when a participant becomes unruly and engages in unsportsmanlike conduct? Should the player be banned from further participation? Should the participant be warned or fined? In Case 4-2 the Special Olympics Organization was forced to deal with a participant who was not playing by the rules.

📖 CASE 4-2 *Thomas v. Special Olympics Missouri, Inc.*

31 S.W.3d 442 (W.D. Mo. 2000)

Mr. Thomas is a person with some degree of mental retardation. For some time prior to July 1, 1993, he participated in a variety of athletic events sponsored by Special Olympics. During that period, various other Special Olympics participants lodged complaints with the organization concerning Mr. Thomas' behavior at Special Olympics' events. The complaints ranged from claims that he exhibited poor sportsmanship, lacked social skills, and showed disrespect for coaches and other personnel, to claims that he harassed other athletes, yelled at members and participants, and placed telephone calls to family members of employees. Special Olympics Missouri, Inc. is a not-for-profit organization that sponsors and organizes sporting events in the Olympic tradition for mentally retarded children and adults.

In response to these complaints, officials at Special Olympics issued written warnings to Mr. Thomas on a number of occasions in 1991 to 1992. In those warnings it advised him that, while he was welcome to continue participating in Special Olympics so long as his behavior was acceptable, he would no longer be permitted to participate if he failed to control his behavior. Eventually, Special Olympics officials decided that Mr. Thomas should not be permitted to remain in the program if his behavior was as suggested in the complaints made about him, and they informed him that they would be conducting an investigation into these allegations.

Source: *Reprinted from Westlaw with permission of Thomson Reuters.*

The *Thomas* case presents a difficult situation for any sports management professional (SMP).

1. What responsibility does an organization have under these circumstances?
2. What unique considerations are present because the Special Olympics are involved?
3. As an SMP, how would you handle this situation?
4. Would an SMP need to obtain a medical opinion to make a fair and ethical decision?
5. How would an SMP conduct a fair and ethical investigation into the allegations against Mr. Thomas?
6. What is the best way to continue to allow Mr. Thomas to participate but not create problems for other participants?

Fans as Participants

Any fan who goes to a baseball game wants to go home with a souvenir ball. Catching a foul ball at a baseball game is a highlight for any fan and certainly for a kid. In Case 4-3, a young fan became a participant when the league enticed young spectators with free tickets for the return of a foul ball.

📖 CASE 4-3   *Haymon v. Auburn Community Non-Profit Baseball Association, Inc.*

2007 NY Slip Op 09071

Joan Haymon's then 14-year-old son, Leonard, was injured when he was struck by an automobile driven by Donald Pettit. Specifically, Leonard chased a foul ball into traffic. The record indicates that he was wearing headphones while chasing the ball and failed to look both ways before crossing the street. Leonard apparently neither saw nor heard the oncoming vehicle. Pettit was operating his vehicle with a blood alcohol level of .11%. At the time, Leonard had congregated with friends outside of Falcon Park, a baseball stadium owned by the City of Auburn and operated by Auburn Community Non-Profit Baseball Association, Inc. (Ball Club). Adjoining the stadium on the third base side is a two-way public street across from which is a parking lot owned by the City of Auburn and utilized by fans during games. At the time of the incident, the Ball Club offered free baseball tickets to non-patrons outside of the park who retrieved foul balls and returned them to the ticket window. Further, the record indicates that Leonard visited the stadium regularly to retrieve and collect foul balls hit out of the stadium.

Haymon argued that the Ball Club's foul ball promotion gave rise to a duty to warn or protect its participants. Specifically, she posited that a duty arose because the Ball Club provided an incentive to fans outside of the stadium to retrieve errant foul balls—namely, the prospect of free tickets. In short, [she] argues that the foreseeability of children chasing balls into the street, coupled with [the league's] incentive for them to do so, required the Ball Club to provide some measure of protection or warning.

Leonard's sister testified that when he left the house to go to the stadium, that he had money but "didn't want to spend it," and that he did not have a ticket but that "he had his glove with him" to try "to catch a [foul] ball." The sister added that Leonard "saved baseballs."

Source: *Reprinted from Westlaw with permission of Thomson Reuters.*

1. Do you agree with the league policy?
2. Do you consider the policy dangerous or criminal?
3. How should the policy be revised?

Participant Violence

Most people would not consider bowling to be a violent sport. However, participants are competitive, that is the simple truth. *Gustaveson v. Gregg* is a case of "bowlers gone wild," in which an assault took place at the local bowling alley between participants.

CASE 4-4 *Gustaveson v. Gregg*

655 P.2d 693 (1982)

Gustaveson and his wife belonged to a mixed league of married, middle aged and retired couples with a non-drinking, church oriented lifestyle. They bowled on Tuesday nights immediately following a men's league, some of whose members drank and used profanity. Shortly before the date on which the assault on Gustaveson occurred, Wasatch Bowling Alley changed its policy and prohibited bowlers from bringing beer and alcoholic beverage mixers into its premises, but required that they be purchased only from its coffee shop. The men's league was accommodated with a new lane assignment closer to the coffee shop, and the mixed league was assigned to bowl in those same lanes immediately following it. The men's league was consistently tardy in clearing the alleys and repeatedly delayed the start of play of the mixed league. The management of Wasatch had met only one week prior to the assault on [Gustaveson] with representatives of the men's league in an effort to solve the problem. Management had made various efforts to get the men's league bowlers off the lanes timely and to restrain their language. Gregg, secretary of the men's league, and other members of the men's league, felt harassed by these complaints to the management. Consequently, tension developed between the two leagues.

On the night of the assault a member of the men's league directed some disparaging comments toward two women from the mixed league. Gustaveson told him that the women did not have to be subjected to such remarks and that he should leave if he had finished bowling. When he responded with a sarcastic remark to Gustaveson, the latter told him that he should gather his belongings and leave. Gustaveson then asked for his name in order to register a complaint with the front desk. The bowler gave his name and went to another area of the building.

Gustaveson reported the incident to a new deskman who had been hired because of the increased number of leagues on Tuesday nights. (He and a manager were taking money and handling the activity associated with the leagues getting off and on the lanes.) The deskman assured him that the problem would be taken care of. However, even though he testified that he could have taken the time to then mediate the conflict, he took no immediate action because he did not consider the problem sufficiently serious to do so.

After he returned from reporting the incident, Gustaveson, who wore a leg brace in order to bowl because of an operation, was preparing to practice bowl when Gregg (not the bowler who had made the remarks) beckoned to him. Because he believed (correctly) that Gregg was the secretary of the men's league, Gustaveson thought he and Gregg would only talk about his interaction with the other bowler. Gustaveson began to go over to Gregg even though his wife, having heard members of the men's league express animosity toward him (and having told her husband that she had heard them) tried to discourage her husband from going. While Gustaveson was looking down at the steps which he was climbing in order to negotiate them successfully, Gregg, who had drunk a couple of beers that night, struck him in the jaw. He was thrown backward from the impact of the blow and he suffered multiple fractures of the jaw, broken dentures and nerve damage.

There is no doubt that Wasatch knew this. Its management personnel had received complaints, had met with the men's league, and had made efforts to curtail the tardiness and other objectionable behavior of men's league bowlers without unduly restricting them.

However, no evidence in the record suggests that Wasatch knew or should have reasonably foreseen that a bowler in one league would assault a member of the other league. Gregg and Gustaveson belonged to separate leagues whose association was minimal. Even though tension existed, there was no evidence that the two leagues, prior to the assault, had exhibited direct confrontations, threats or other behavior which should have reasonably alerted Wasatch that an assault might occur.

In this case, Gregg gave no forewarning or indication that he would strike Gustaveson until moments before he did so. He was not the bowler who had exchanged remarks with Gustaveson. He had not previously assaulted or threatened to assault anyone. In fact, he had displayed no tendency for potentially physically abusive behavior prior to his assault on Gustaveson. There was no history of any exchange between Gregg and Gustaveson, nor Gregg and anyone else. Gustaveson, himself, who was told by his wife about hostile remarks from men's league members against him apparently did not foresee any risk of violence but only thought that Gregg motioned him over to talk. In any event, Wasatch neither was advised nor had any independent knowledge of the remarks. The fact that tension existed between the two leagues, by itself, is simply insufficient from which to find that an ordinarily prudent person in the position of Wasatch's personnel would have foreseen that violence would erupt and one bowler would assault another bowler.

The remarks overheard by Gustaveson's wife were "That's the guy in the blue shirt." "Yes, that is the son-of-a-bitch." "Yes, I would like to kill the son-of-a-bitch." The wife testified that the secretary and president of the men's league made the remarks among a group that included two additional men. She responded by turning to look at them and then proceeding to tell her husband what she had heard.

Source: *Reprinted from Westlaw with permission of Thomson Reuters.*

1. How can violence such as this be curbed in the future?
2. What steps should the owner of the alley take to ensure this never occurs again?

In the classic case of *Atlanta Baseball Co. v. Lawrence*, a baseball pitcher who was being "ragged" on by a fan, made the decision to ignore his ethical, good-decision-making sense, and charged the grandstands, attacking his heckler.

📖 CASE 4-5 *Atlanta Baseball Co. v. Lawrence*

144 S.E. 351(1928)

Where a baseball player employed by the proprietor of a baseball park left his position upon the grounds and entered the grandstand, and there assaulted a spectator because the latter had "ragged" him or criticized his playing, the assault was not committed within the scope of his employment nor in the prosecution of his master's business, but was his personal act in resenting a real or fancied insult.

There being nothing in the petition to show that the assault complained of, or anything of such character, could or should have been anticipated by the defendant, or that the defendant failed to do anything that it should have done for the safety or protection of the plaintiff as its invitee, the petition fails to show negligence...

W. J. Lawrence filed suit against the Atlanta Baseball Company to recover damages for personal injuries alleged to have been inflicted upon him by one of the defendant's employees under the following circumstances:

The defendant was the owner of a baseball park in the city of Atlanta, and had in its employ professional baseball players engaged to play baseball with visiting teams from other cities; the defendant being in control of inclosed grounds where such games were played for the entertainment of the public, the public being invited to enter and witness the games upon the payment of certain charges. On August 3, 1926, a game was being played by the paid employees of the defendant against the baseball team from another city, and "to said game the public were invited upon payment of the admission fee as aforesaid." The petition alleges:

"To the public paying said admission fee and witnessing said game defendant owed the duty of exercising ordinary care to keep its said premises in a safe condition and to protect the persons of said paying public against injury and unlawful assault. *** On said date one of the employees of defendant, engaged in playing said game for hire for defendant, was one Hollis McLaughlin, who was a pitcher in said game. *** A portion of the seats provided by defendant on said date for the occupancy of spectators of said game were located in what is known as the grandstand, a covered inclosure." The plaintiff, accompanied by his little grandson and certain friends, was in attendance upon the game on the occasion named, on paid admission. "Plaintiff and said party were seated in said grandstand while said game was progressing, and the game began to go against the team of defendant. A number of spectators at said game, under the impression that the pitching of said McLaughlin was responsible for a large part of the poor showing made by the team of defendant, began to 'rag' said McLaughlin, as it is called; that is to say, began to make audible remarks that were not particularly complimentary to the pitching ability of said McLaughlin as displayed on said occasion. *** Said custom or 'ragging,' particularly if it is good-natured, consisting of criticisms upon the manner in which the game is being played, is a common custom at practically all the games played by defendant. Plaintiff joined in said 'ragging' only to the extent of saying, good naturedly, 'Give us another pitcher.' In so doing, plaintiff was really following the common custom indulged in by the patrons of defendant at the baseball games played by defendant's employees on said grounds. *** In making said remark plaintiff had no expectation and no ground for expectation that any offensive action would be indulged in by defendant or any of its employees on account thereof. *** So free was plaintiff from an anticipation of any consequences flowing from his good-natured 'ragging' that he was engaged in showing and explaining to his visiting friends a score card of said game which he had bought from defendant, and was sitting down in his seat when, to his astonishment, on looking up he saw standing over him in a threatening attitude said McLaughlin, who had just come in from his position as pitcher on the baseball diamond. Said McLaughlin was accompanied by several other employees of defendant, members of defendant's hired baseball team, and the attitude of said McLaughlin was insulting and threatening.*** Without any provocation on the part of plaintiff, said McLaughlin proceeded to attack, beat, bruise, and wound plaintiff, inflicting several blows upon plaintiff, and battering and bruising plaintiff's face and person."

The petition described the injuries alleged to have been sustained by the plaintiff as the result of such assault, and prayed for the recovery of damages in the sum of $20,000.

1. The conduct of McLaughlin, the pitcher, in leaving his place upon the grounds and coming into the grandstand, and assaulting the plaintiff, was not within the scope of his employment, nor in the prosecution of his master's business, but was his own personal affair in resenting a real or fancied insult. "If a servant steps aside from his master's business, for however short a time, to do an act entirely disconnected from it, and injury results to another from such independent voluntary act, the servant may be liable, but the master is not liable."

2. Is the defendant liable as for a breach of duty to the plaintiff as an invitee? The proprietor of an amusement park is not an insurer of the safety of his patrons, but must use ordinary care to protect them from injury. The rule of liability is expressed in the Civil Code of 1910, §4420:

"Where the owner or occupier of land, by express or implied invitation, induces or leads others to come upon his premises for any lawful purpose, he is liable in damages to such persons for injuries occasioned by his failure to exercise ordinary care in keeping the premises and approaches safe."

Undoubtedly the defendant owed to the plaintiff the general duty of exercising ordinary care for his safety, but the petition wholly fails to show any breach of that duty. There is nothing to indicate that the assault, or anything of such character, could or should have been foreseen or anticipated by the defendant; but the attack appears to have been the result of a sudden outburst of temper on the part of McLaughlin, a manifestation quite unusual with players in general, and one which does not appear to have been of the habit or disposition of McLaughlin in particular, either within or without the knowledge of the defendant. If the defendant had had good reason to apprehend that such a thing would probably happen, then it should have exercised reasonable care to prevent the occurrence, but it was not required to

anticipate the improbable, nor to take measures to prevent a happening
which no reasonable person would have expected. The assault of which
the plaintiff complains appears to have been a happening of that character. Under the facts appearing, the plaintiff's case is not stronger
than if he had been assaulted by some other spectator or invitee upon
the defendant's premises. The petition discloses no breach of duty
on the part of the defendant, and, hence, fails to show negligence.

Source: *Reprinted from Westlaw with permission of Thomson Reuters.*

Golfing Ethics and Etiquette

Millions of people play golf around the world. There is no question that golf is a global sport. Golf is a gentlemanly sport or at least it is the majority of the time. Unlike many sports, golf requires a certain etiquette and golfers are required to keep their own score. The 1951 Professional Golfers Association (PGA) code of ethics stated:

> The name "Professional Golfer" must be and remain a synonym and pledge of honor, service, and fair dealing. His professional integrity, fidelity to the game of golf, and a sense of his great responsibility to employers and employees, manufacturers, and clients, and to his brother professionals, transcends thought of material gain in the motives of the true professional golfer. . . . The underlying purpose of the PGA membership requirement of five years' golf experience in some essential capacity is to uphold the high standards as a protection to the public and the game.[4]

Some people understand and appreciate golf etiquette while others do not. For instance, the majority of golf clubs do not allow players to play without shirts, a message that many have not yet received. Is failing to follow proper golf etiquette unethical or merely boorish behavior? PGA golfer Rory Sabbatini would agree that golf etiquette should be followed. However, he disregarded golf etiquette when playing against and with fellow PGA member Ben Crane. He claims Crane was just playing too darn slow. While playing alongside Crane, Sabbatini left him behind, storming on to the next hole.[5] It is a given that most people (including the authors of this textbook) cannot play golf well. Hitting a small white ball in excess of 300 yards in a straight line is a skill few possess. That is why professional golfers can earn large sums of money if they can do it. Because golf is such a difficult sport, certain golfers (amateur and weekend "duffers" alike) have found various ways to get around the rules.[6] Even some U.S. presidents have cheated at golf![7] Some have even argued that if you cheat in golf, you will cheat in the business world.[8]

---

[4] Horton Smith, "What the PGA Is," *USGA Journal and Turf Management* (April 1951).

[5] Gene Wang, "Crane's Slow Play Bothers Sabbatini," *Washington Post*, June 13, 2005.

[6] Jim Becker, Andy Mayer, Rick Wolff, and Barrie Maguire, *Golf Dirty Tricks: 50 Ways to Lie, Cheat, and Steal Your Way to Victory* (Becker & Mayer, Ltd., 1994); Arnold Palmer and Steve Eubanks, *Playing By the Rules* (New York: Atria Books, 2002).

[7] Don Van Natta, *First Off the Tee: Presidential Hackers, Duffers, and Cheaters from Taft to Bush* (Boston, MA: Little, Brown, & Co., 2003).

[8] See S. Marino, "People Who Cheat at Golf Cheat in Business," *Industry Week* (1998).

It is common fare in golf to give a verbal warning to other golfers if your shot is off the mark. "Fore" is the appropriate phrase to use by the wayward golfer. The golfer in Case 4-6 certainly wished the other participant had yelled "Fore" a little sooner so she could have avoided the ball striking her in the forehead.

📖 CASE 4-6 *Carrigan v. Roussell*

426 A.2d 517 (1980)

On May 12, 1975, Sally Carrigan, a novice golfer, was taking a lesson at the Fort Monmouth Golf Club from the club professional, John Welsh. The lesson was being given in the practice area located along the left side of the first fairway. The practice area was protected by a twenty-foot high nylon net fence commencing about 180 yards from the first tee and extending for about 75 yards. The lesson was taking place in the practice area about 200 to 220 yards from the first tee and 40 to 50 yards to the left of the first fairway. Welsh claimed that the practice area was "not located in the best area" and that it was "a very common situation" for balls hit on the first tee to land in the practice area.

As Carrigan was taking her lesson, Maurice Roussell and three companions were beginning a round of golf. Roussell, an experienced ten or twelve handicap golfer, hit a ball with his driver from the first tee. The first hole was a "perfectly straight" 388-yard par four. The ball began to "hook" to the left, away from the intended line of flight, over the fence and toward the practice area. Roussell testified that he had been aware that Welsh was giving a lesson to a woman in the practice area before he hit the ball, and that when he saw it hooking in that direction he "immediate(ly)" yelled "fore" and the other three members of his foursome also yelled "fore." According to Roussell:

> My observations, once I yelled, Fore, it appears to me that the female receiving the lessons turned toward the yell[,] rather than[,] this is my opinion[,] rather than just ducking and I also saw Mr. Welsh attempting to grab her.

The golf ball struck Carrigan in the forehead. Welsh claimed that when he heard the word "fore" and realized that the ball was coming in his direction he reached for Carrigan and tried to get in front of her. However, she turned away from him and he heard the ball strike her forehead. Carrigan said she heard the cry "fore" at the same time that she was struck in the forehead and that she did not recall Welsh grabbing her or attempting to assist her until after she had been hit.

Roussell claimed that, as an experienced golfer, it was his practice to yell "fore" when he or another member of his party hit an errant shot in the direction of other people. Welsh, who testified as an expert, was asked when it was mandatory to yell "fore." He answered that such a warning should be given when a golfer sees that a ball is going off course and is heading toward people in danger. Welsh added that 300 to 350 people per day played the course. If they all yelled "fore" before striking the ball on the first tee "they would be hollering fore all day on that first tee. That just doesn't happen."

A golfer has a duty to give a timely warning to other persons within the foreseeable ambit of danger. The mere fact that a ball does not travel the intended course does not establish negligence. "(E)ven the best professional golfers cannot avoid an occasional 'hook' or 'slice.'"

The court noted that "(t)here is testimony by a number of witnesses that it was not customary for a player in [Russell's] situation in such circumstances to shout 'fore' before driving his ball, but only to do so when it could be observed that the ball was slicing so as to carry it to the right in the direction of the No. 4 tee."

Source: *Reprinted from Westlaw with permission of Thomson Reuters.*

1. Should every golfer be required to provide timely notice of an errant shot? Do you consider it unethical if they do not?[9]
2. Does the fact that Roussell was an experienced golfer make a difference? If there is no legal duty to warn of an errant golf ball, does it follow there is no ethical duty to warn of an errant shot?

CASE STUDY 4-1 *Furyk Sleeps In*

Jim Furyk is one of the good guys in sports and has always been considered a gentleman in a gentleman's game. As he was preparing for the Barclays Tournament in 2010, he set his alarm on his phone, as he always did. However, the battery went dead and his alarm did not ring as he had planned. When he woke up, he ran to the tee box for his scheduled tee-time in the pro-am event but was late, so the PGA disqualified him from the entire tournament. Furyk said it was his fault. However, because it was the pro-am (before the tournament started), some thought the rule had been "overapplied." Phil Mickelson said that because the rule did not apply to everyone, it should not apply to anyone. It should not have been enforced:

---

[9] Gene Wojciechowski, "Nothing Went Right in Woods' Worst Pro Major," *ESPN.com*, June 17, 2006. Also see Louis J. DeVoto, "Injury on the Golf Course: Regardless of Your Handicap, Escaping Liability Is Par for the Course," *University of Toledo Law Review* (1992–1993); Daniel E. Lazaroff, "Golfers' Tort Liability: A Critique of an Emerging Standard," *Hastings Commercial and Entertainment Law Journal* (2001–2002).

"The rule itself applies to only half the field" (noting that only 54 of the 122 players were in the pro-am). "So if you're going to have a rule that does not apply to everybody, you cannot have it affect the competition. . . . I cannot disagree with it more. I have no idea how the commissioner let this rule go through. It's ridiculous."[10]

Was this an overapplication of the rules? As a result of Furyk's disqualification the PGA revised its rules and adopted the "Furyk rule," which PGA commissioner Tim Finchem admits is somewhat vague but allows for flexibility. The commissioner stated, "If you're negligent with respect to a tee time in the pro-am—negligent, meaning, you made a mistake for whatever reason—it's not a disqualification. If you blow it off, then you're not going to be able to play in that tournament."[11]

COACHES' ETHICS

Like participants, coaches must make the correct ethical choices. There are unique ethical problems in the administration and organization of sports that coaches must face. The goal is to grasp the meaning of ethical conduct and what constitutes misconduct for coaches. The main task of ethics is to evaluate the standards of right or wrong that people assign to behavior, motives, and intentions.[12] There is always the question of ethics versus morals, ethics being the set of theories or principles that determine right and wrong.[13] Morals, on the other hand, involve the practice of ethical theories or principles. Some coaches must also double as teachers and employ all the characteristics and virtues of a good teacher. The ethical coach insists on discipline, hard work, and proper behavior from student-athletes similar to a teacher because any misstep in the process of instruction might result in serious injury or even death.[14]

A college coach must "be an instructor, fundraiser, recruiter, academic coordinator, public figure, budget director, television and radio personality, alumni 'glad-hander,' and whatever else the university's athletic director or president may direct the coach to do in the best interests of the university's athletic program."[15] Professional coaches, and some collegiate football and basketball coaches at nationally known institutions will receive large salaries and extensive benefits. But coaches do not have job security or unions, and rarely have contract protection similar to that of professional athletes.[16]

Ethical Duty of Safety

A coach has a duty to provide for the safety of those under his or her charge and even more so in youth sports. At the professional level, players have access to doctors, agents, teams, unions, and leagues that monitor safety issues. It is essential at the youth sports level that coaches provide for the safety of the players under their tutelage. They have an ethical duty to do so.

---

[10] Doug Ferguson, "Furyk Oversleeps, Disqualified from Barclays," *Associated Press NBC Sports*, August 25, 2010.

[11] Ryan Ballangee, "Tour Creates the Furyk Rule for Missing Pro-AM Tee Times," *NBC Sports*, December 9, 2010.

[12] Sheryle Bergmann Drewe, "Coaches, Ethics, and Autonomy," *Sport, Education, and Society* 5, no. 2 (October 2000): 147–162.

[13] Moisekapenda Bower, "Fleeing Coaches Leave Many Feeling Empty," *Houston Chronicle*, December 5, 2007, C1.

[14] *See generally*, Robert Simon, *Fair Play: The Ethics of Sport* (Boulder, CO: Westview Press, 2004).

[15] Martin Greenberg, *Sports Law Practice* (Charlottesville, VA: Lexis Law Publishing, 1993).

[16] Walter Champion, *Fundamentals of Sports Law* (Belmont, CA: Thomson West, 2004).

The following safety tips for coaches should be employed:

1. Inspect the field or ice prior to the game.
2. Inspect the playing equipment.
3. Have first aid available at all times.
4. Beware of players who are struggling physically.
5. Assign coaches certain key players to watch, if a player is struggling physically or mentally.
6. Observe the weather at all times for extreme heat, lightning, and other adverse weather conditions.
7. Ensure all participants are accounted for when traveling.
8. Ensure all participants know how to use the equipment properly and safely.
9. Address all safety issues immediately and notify all safety personnel when appropriate.
10. In youth sports, beware of individuals who are uninvited to practice or loitering around the playing field.
11. Be aware of any serious medical conditions of athletes.

Coaches have an absolute duty to care for the players under their charge.[17] In August 2008, 15-year-old Max Gilpin collapsed at football practice and died the next day. His coach, Jason Stinson, was charged with "wanton endangerment and reckless homicide" for Max's heat-related death. In 2009, coach Gilpin was found not guilty in the first case of its kind in which a coach had been charged with criminal conduct for failure to remove a player from the field for safety reasons.[18] In 2010 Declan Sullivan, a 20-year-old student manager for the University of Notre Dame football team was killed during a Notre Dame football practice after an "extraordinary burst of wind" toppled a video tower that Sullivan was working in. In an amazing statement, Notre Dame President, the Rev. John Jenkins, sent an e-mail to students, faculty, staff and alumni saying the university was responsible for the student's death. He stated, "Declan Sullivan was entrusted to our care, and we failed to keep him safe . . . We at Notre Dame and ultimately I, as President are responsible. Words cannot express our sorrow to the Sullivan family and to all involved."[19] Regulators began investigating whether the University of Notre Dame violated safety rules. Should the Notre Dame football coach ultimately be held responsible for this situation?

Strock v. USA Cycling, Inc. shows the extent to which some coaches will go in order to win. In this case, a cycling coach lied to his athletes about drugs he gave to them, saying they were legal when they were not. In doing so, he failed to act in the best interests of the athletes he was responsible for coaching.

📖 CASE 4-7 *Strock v. USA Cycling, Inc.*

2006 WL 1223151 (D.Colo.,2006.)

Facts

Greg Strock and Erich Kaiter were both members of the United States' junior cycling team in early 1990. The United States' cycling program

---

[17] "Athlete Death Blamed on Excessive Coaching," *United Press International*, August 27, 2008; "Parent, Player Blame Coach for High School Football Injuries," *KTVB.com*, August 20, 2010.

[18] Lindsay English, "Former PRP Football Coach Found Not Guilty on All Charges," *Wave 3*, September 17, 2009; "After Player's Death, High School Football Coach Charged with Homicide," *Wall Street Journal*, January 23, 2009.

[19] Associated Press, "Notre Dame President: School Responsible in Student Death," *Sports Illustrated*, November 5, 2010.

is operated by USA Cycling, Inc. That organization hired Rene Wenzel to be head coach of the junior national team (Junior National Team). Wenzel served in this capacity for all relevant times in this lawsuit.

In April 1990, the Junior National Team traveled to Europe to train and compete. Strock rendezvoused with the team shortly thereafter upon his return from racing in Spain. While in Spain, a local physician prescribed antibiotics to Strock to treat an illness. When he convened with the Junior National Team, however, Wenzel allegedly gave Strock a substance to be taken in lieu of the antibiotics. Strock maintains that he inquired of Wenzel about the substance, and Wenzel indicated it was a mixture of extract of cortisone and vitamins. Strock further asserts Wenzel represented the mixture as safe and legal, and that Wenzel informed Strock he should not question the good judgment of the coaching staff.

Strock's health appeared to improve, and that July he competed in the world championship in Cleveland, England. There, both Strock and Kaiter allege they were injected up to three times per day with unknown liquids by USAC staff under Wenzel's supervision. In all, Kaiter maintains he received forty-two to forty-eight injections during the world championship period. When Strock and Kaiter inquired as to the substance in the injections, Wenzel purportedly told them it was the safe and legal extract of cortisone/vitamin mixture. Kaiter also claims he followed instructions from Wenzel to take several non-steroidal anti-inflammatory drugs (NSAIDs) such as Motrin each day.

Following the world championship, in August 1990 Wenzel allegedly gave Strock and Kaiter each a box of twenty ampules of liquid to help them prepare for the upcoming Washington Trust race in Spokane, Washington. Strock maintains he was injected with the liquid in a hotel room there by USAC coaching staff. According to Strock, Wenzel implied the liquid was the same extract of cortisone/vitamin mixture Strock had consumed in April and during the world championship.

Around this time, Kaiter began to notice blood in his stool. He was diagnosed with Crohn's disease several months later in July 1991. Strock claims he was overwhelmed by illness in March 1991. After initially suspecting he had HIV or lymphatic cancer, doctors that summer diagnosed him with human parvovirus. Although Strock subsequently raced with the Amateur Banesto Team, both Strock and Kaiter attribute the end of their elite cycling careers to parvovirus and Crohn's disease, respectively. In 1993 Wenzel informed Strock about a rumor Wenzel had doped Junior National Team riders.

Following a bout with depression, Strock matriculated at Indiana University's medical school. While taking a pharmacology class there in November 1998, Strock claims he learned there was no such thing as "extract of cortisone" that Wenzel had allegedly given him in 1990. Strock insists this was the first time he had reason to believe he had been administered steroids by USAC coaching staff. Strock discussed the alleged doping in a nationally televised interview in September 2000. Kaiter contends this was the first time he learned that he, too, may unwittingly have been administered steroids.

Source: *Reprinted from Westlaw with permission of Thomson Reuters.*

In *Strock*, what unethical actions were taken by the coach? What disciplinary measures should be taken against him for his improper actions?

In Case 4-8, a coach "participated" with one of his middle school students in a wrestling match which some may have deemed an attack by the coach.

CASE 4-8 *Reaume v. Jefferson Middle School*

2006 WL 2355497 (Mich. App.,2006)

On January 7, 2003, Matthew Reaume, a middle school student, went to the Jefferson Middle School gym for wrestling practice. As Reaume waited in the gym for the rest of the team and the coaches to arrive, he talked to his friends with his back to the entrance. Nadeau, an assistant wrestling coach, entered the gym, came up behind Reaume and, allegedly without alerting or informing Reaume, wrapped his arms around Reaume's chest and took Reaume to the ground. Once on the ground, Nadeau performed a wrestling roll. As the roll ended, Reaume posted his arm on the floor to right himself. However, Nadeau performed a second roll. During the second roll, Reaume's elbow was fractured and required surgery to repair it. During Reaume's recuperation, he developed osteomyelitis. Although Reaume was a middle school student, he was an experienced wrestler. He had wrestled since he was six-years-old in both school and non-school athletic programs using freestyle, folk-style, and modified folk-style wrestling techniques. Nadeau had been Reaume's coach since Reaume was in the third grade. Nadeau was a qualified coach. . . .

Source: *Reprinted from Westlaw with permission of Thomson Reuters.*

Ethical Duty to Supervise and Instruct

Coaches have the responsibility to properly supervise and instruct their charges with special consideration to the danger of the activity, age, and maturity of the participant. A properly coached, trained, and equipped athlete consents to the blows and bodily contact that are an integral part of the sport. In contrast, inadequate instruction and improper training could cause serious injury and, in extreme cases, death. Coaches should not ignore any technical aspects of instruction, fail to emphasize proper training methods, or fail to implement any necessary safety measures to prepare athletes physically and mentally for their sport. Coaches should inspect all equipment before the sporting contest begins and ensure the equipment is state-of-the-art and presents no safety issues to the participants.[20]

The failure of a duty to supervise and instruct can be fatal to a youth participant, as can be seen in Case 4-9. In *Brahatcek v. Millard School District*, during a mandatory physical education class, a ninth-grade student was killed when he was struck in the head with a golf club by another student. Did the coaches fail to properly supervise the class? Do you consider the conduct of the coaches or the school district criminal? Would you consider it gross negligence?

CASE 4-9 *Brahatcek v. Millard School District*

273 N.W.2d 680 (Neb. 1979)

David Brahatcek, who was a ninth grade student 14 years of age, was injured on April 3, 1974, during a physical education class conducted in the gymnasium of Millard Central Junior High School. He was struck by a golf club swung by a fellow student, Mark Kreie. He was rendered unconscious and died two days later without regaining consciousness. Mandatory golf instruction during physical education classes at the school began on Monday, April 1, 1974. Because he was absent from school on that day, his first exposure to the program was when his class next met on Wednesday, the day of the accident. Classes on both dates were conducted in the school gymnasium because of inclement weather. Instruction was coeducational. Brahatcek's class of 34 boys combined with a girls' physical education class having an enrollment of 23. Two teachers, one male and one female, were responsible for providing supervision and instruction. The faculty members present on Monday were Max Kurtz and Vickie Beveridge, at that time Vickie Lindgren.

On Monday, after attendance was taken, the students were gathered around in a semicircle and received instruction on the golf grip, stance, swing, etiquette, and safety. Mr. Kurtz then explained to them the procedure that would be followed in the gym.

With the bleachers folded up, the gym was nearly as wide as it was long. Approximately 12 mats were placed across the width of the gym, in two rows of six each. One row of mats was located in the south half of the gym about even with the free throw line on the basketball court. The other row was placed along the free throw line in the north half of the gym. The mats measured about 2 feet square and were spaced

---

[20] Allan Korpela, "Tort Liability of Public Schools and Institutions of Higher Learning for Injuries Resulting from Lack or Insufficiency of Supervision," *American Law Reports* (1971); Andrew McCasky and Kenneth Biedzynski, "A Guide to the Legal Liability of Coaches for a Sports Participant's Injuries," *Seton Hall Journal Sport Law* (1996).

10 to 12 feet apart. Each row contained approximately six mats. A golf club and three or four plastic "wiffle" balls were placed by each mat.

The students were divided into groups of four or five students and each group was assigned to the use of one of the mats. The boys used the mats on the south side of the gym and hit in a southerly direction. The girls used the mats on the north, and hit the golf balls in a northerly direction. At the start of the class all of the students were to sit along the center line of the basketball court between the two rows of mats. On the signal of one of the instructors one student from each group would go up to the assigned mat, tee up a ball, and wait for the signal to begin. After the student had hit all of the balls on the mat he was to lay the club down and return to the center of the gym. When all of the students were back at the center line, the next student in each group was directed to retrieve the balls and the procedure was repeated.

Mr. Kurtz was not present for class on Wednesday, the day of the accident, because his wife had just given birth to a baby. His place was taken by a student teacher, Tim Haley, who had been at the school for approximately 5 weeks and had assisted with four to six golf classes on Monday and Tuesday. At the beginning of the class on Wednesday, Mrs. Beveridge repeated the instructions which had been given by Mr. Kurtz on Monday. The groups were again divided. One student went up to each mat and Mrs. Beveridge testified she gave the signal for the first balls to be hit.

Brahatcek, who prior to the date of his death had never had a golf club in his hands, was either the second or third student to go up to the easternmost mat on the boys' side of the gym. He had difficulty and asked his group if anyone could help him. Mark Kreie, who had been the last to use the club, came forward and showed him how to grip the club and told him that he (Kreie) would take two practice swings then hit the ball. Brahatcek moved to the east and stood against the folded up bleachers about 10 feet to the rear of Kreie. Kreie looked over his shoulder to observe him before taking two practice swings. He then stepped up to the ball and took a full swing at it. Unaware that Brahatcek had moved closer, he hit him with the club on the follow-through. During all of this time, Mr. Haley was helping another boy a few mats away. Mark did not know whether Mr. Haley saw Brahatcek and him standing together at the mat. Mrs. Beveridge was positioned along the west end of the girls' line.

Mark Kreie testified Mrs. Beveridge gave instructions to the students as to the proper use of the clubs. They were also told to remain behind a certain line on the gym floor when they were not up at the mats. He also testified on Wednesday Mrs. Beveridge told them they were to help any of the students who didn't understand. Mrs. Beveridge denied making this statement. The fact that the deceased asked for help of the students might support Kreie's statement.

Mrs. Beveridge testified she was in charge of the entire class on Wednesday but after telling the students when they could hit the ball, she concentrated on the girls. At the time of the accident she was standing on the west side of the gym, between the center line and the row of girls' mats. She testified that had she seen Mr. Haley devoting all of his attention to one boy she would have watched the entire class. She did not instruct Mr. Haley prior to class that he should not spend too much time with one student. Neither did she see Brahatcek get hit.

Mr. Haley, who was a second semester senior at Wayne State Teachers College, had been student teaching at Millard Central Junior High School for approximately 5 weeks. He testified he told the boys when to start and Mrs. Beveridge told the girls. He testified during the class he walked up and down between the boys standing at the mats and those seated at the center of the gym. A short time after the first student went up to the mats a few boys in [Brahatcek]'s group stood up, although not close to the mats. He told them to sit down and they complied. At the time of the accident Mr. Haley was giving individualized instructions to a boy near the middle of the gym. He did not see [Brahatcek] get hit.

David Thompson, who was in the group with Brahatcek and Mark Kreie, testified he was in the class on both Monday and Wednesday, although the attendance records indicate he was absent on Monday. He stated instructions were given on Monday but not on Wednesday. On Wednesday, the students were standing and talking between groups. From the beginning of class until the time of the accident, Mr. Haley and Mrs. Beveridge were holding a discussion in the southwest portion of the gym in front of the door to the girls' locker room. Kreie points out that standing in this location would have placed them in the line of flight of golf balls being hit by the boys.

Thompson testified Brahatcek was the fourth or fifth in the group to go to the mat. He was having some trouble so Mark Kreie, who had just finished hitting, returned to the mat and took the club to show him the grip and stance. Brahatcek then moved a couple of feet behind Mark and to his right while Mark took two practice swings. Mark then attempted to take a full swing but he hit Brahatcek while bringing the club back. This testimony, that Brahatcek was hit during the back swing, is contrary to the testimony of Mark Kreie, and inconsistent with the physical evidence that Brahatcek was struck on the left side of the back of his head. There are other inconsistencies between his deposition and trial testimony. He admitted his recollection was hazy. The trial was held 3 years after the accident.

Mark Kreie stated he was simply doing what Mrs. Beveridge instructed, namely to assist a student in need. During his instruction of Brahatcek he did not receive any warning or admonition from either teacher. During the class various students from each group were intermingling around the court, visiting with each other. Mrs. Beveridge did not hear what instructions, if any, student teacher Haley gave his charges and did not see the incident which led up to the fatal injury of Brahatcek.

Ike F. Pane, principal of Millard Central Junior High School, testified golf was a mandatory course of instruction. Golf instruction was provided to ninth grade students in April of 1974, with the first class on Monday, April 1, 1974. Pane identified exhibit 9 as his school's written rules of instruction which stated the objectives to be achieved in teaching golf to the ninth grade class, and specifically setting forth in what manner or procedure the instruction was to be undertaken and achieved. The objectives were to develop the skills and appreciation for the sport of golf, with the coequal consideration that the instruction be accomplished with safety. On page 2 of exhibit 9, the following appears: "Safety should be stressed at all times, especially when you are rained out. If in the gym, one can set up stations on the floor along one side of the bleachers, divide all students into that many stations and have them sit on the outstretched bleachers on the opposite side. Have the first person hit four or five balls, (sic) to the second person across the gym. When the first is done hitting, he will go to the end of his group and the second person hits and the third retrieves the ball and so on."

On the next page of exhibit 9, the following appears under "Safety Hints:" "1. Never hit a shot until you are sure those in front of you are out of your range. If you hit another player, you may be liable for damages. 2. Never swing a club, especially on the tees, unless you are sure no one is standing close to you."

Pane testified he approved of exhibit 9 and the procedure set forth therein, and that it was his understanding the instruction was undertaken in conformity with exhibit 9. However, after Brahatcek's fatal injury he discovered that the physical arrangements for instruction were quite different than that specified.

Pane acknowledged that if the instructions had been followed it would have been difficult to have two people on a mat at the same time. It was not until after the accident that he realized the arrangement was different from what was recommended. He recognized that in any of the areas where there might be danger there is a potential for harm if the students were not properly supervised. If the procedure recommended had been followed, it would have made it more difficult for another student from the group to walk across the width of the gymnasium. It was Mr. Kurtz and Mrs. Beveridge who decided to vary the placement of the mats from that recommended in exhibit 9.

Mr. Kurtz testified that on Monday when he was giving the instruction, one from each group would go up all at the same time to the respective mats. Both he and Mrs. Beveridge would see that only one individual was at each mat when the students were to commence their swings. While the students were shooting their two or three balls, he would walk up and down in the back of them, more or less patrolling to make sure everything was okay. They walked the students through the hitting of the first ball. The second ball the students would hit on their own. In the instruction, he followed the curriculum guide, which is exhibit 9.

After each person had hit his three balls, he was supposed to lay his club down on the carpet and go back to his group and sit down. After all the stations had been cleared and no one else was standing, the next golfer would be told to go out and gather the wiffle balls, bring them back, and set them on the carpet, standing there by the proper mat. Then when that group had gathered all the balls and the designated students were standing at their respective mats, they would go through the same procedure again.

It is evident the instruction procedure used Monday was not followed on Wednesday. If it had been, the instructor would have observed the dilemma of [Brahatcek] and given him the instruction he had missed. Also, the students would not have been assisting one another.

Mr. Haley testified he had received no instruction from any of the regular teachers or faculty prior to the commencement of the class, nor did he have a lesson plan because Mrs. Beveridge was going to handle that. He further stated he gave no oral instruction to any of the students as a whole. He recognized he was teaching unskilled young people in a game dealing with potentially dangerous instruments. At the time Brahatcek was injured, Haley was at the fifth mat, giving some individual instruction. Haley testified that if he had seen another student approach the mat, he would have directed him to sit down. At the time in question his attention was diverted from those students who were supposed to be observing rather than using the clubs. When he was giving specialized instruction the only persons he was seeing were the individuals who were using that particular mat he was working with. Haley was asked the following question: "'Who told you after—instructed you, if anybody, that once the instructions started on the mat that you were to lead the group from center court and go down and pass in review, more or less, in front of the mats, and if the students needed

help to give them help. A. Who told me personally to do that? Q. Yes.
A. No one.'"

Millard called a retired school gym teacher who had a B.A. degree in
physical education. He had been an instructor in golf until he entered
the naval service. He played golf regularly, besides teaching and
supervising the instruction of the sport. He knew, understood, and
appreciated the basic techniques used in pursuing the sport of golf.
He would have used the procedure outlined in exhibit 9 rather than
that used on the occasion of the accident. He testified the teacher
should be supervising and keeping an eye on all the students using the
mats; that if he noticed a boy or girl having difficulty or needing
specialized instruction, the appropriate way would be to blow the
whistle, call the class to a halt, and stop the children from talking
or engaging in conversation, if any, on the bleachers, so as to gain
their control and attention. Then he would demonstrate to the one student in need while all students, those seated and those standing by
the mats, would watch and listen, and thereby, in effect, give a
public lesson to all in attendance.

Mr. Kurtz and Mrs. Beveridge testified they did not use the procedure
outlined in exhibit 9 because they did not want the wiffle balls hit
toward other students. They also felt there was a danger of a golf
club flying loose. Mrs. Beveridge also envisioned a problem with
wiffle balls going underneath the bleachers if they were hit across
the width of the gym.

In the instant case, we are dealing with a ninth grader who had never
before swung a golf club. The instruction was conducted indoors, in
close quarters. There is a question as to whether there was adequate
safety instruction regarding the use of a golf club prior to the commencement of the class at which the fatal injury occurred. There is
evidence, which the court could have accepted, that on the day the
accident occurred the teaching procedure outlined by the regular
instructor was not followed by the student teacher. The record would
also indicate the student teacher may not have been properly informed
as to the procedure to be followed. The risk reasonably to be perceived
defines the duty to be obeyed; it is the risk reasonably within the
range of apprehension, of injury to another person, that is taken into
account in determining the existence of the duty to exercise care.

David Wayne Brahatcek was a normal, healthy, responsible 14-year-old
boy who had a part-time job with Samson Construction Co., Omaha,
Nebraska. On the day of the fatal accident he attended the golf class
instruction, which included the subject of safety. He followed instructions given concerning his waiting to take his turn and then advancing
alone to the mat where he held the club and attempted to use it. He had
the opportunity to examine the golf club and become aware of its size

and weight. After fellow student Kreie briefly explained the fundamentals, Brahatcek retreated to the side and rear from Kreie about
10 feet, and Kreie informed him that he would take two practice swings
with the club and then hit the ball. After two practice swings, Kreie
advanced further away from Brahatcek towards the ball and hit it.
Thereafter, in some unexplained circumstance, Brahatcek came into the
area of the golf swing arc and he was struck, causing his tragic death.

Source: *Reprinted from Westlaw with permission of Thomson Reuters.*

1. What ethical duties did the coaches have under the circumstances to provide for student safety?
2. What policies could have been in place to prevent this tragic death?
3. What unethical decisions led to this tragedy?
4. Should anyone be legally responsible for the death of the student?
5. Did any of the coaches breach their ethical duty to supervise and instruct?

One aspect of a coach's duty to supervise is to properly remove injured athletes from further participation. This concept is explored fully in the following case.

CASE 4-10 *Welch v. Dunsmuir Joint Union High School District*

326 P.2d 633 (Cal. App. 1958)

Prior to the opening of school on August 29, Welch was given a physical examination by a Doctor Reynolds and found to be physically fit.
The coaches were on the field directing or supervising the play and
there were no "game officials" there. The teams alternated in carrying
the ball, and after each sequence of plays the coaches stopped the
activity and instructed the players. Welch took the ball on a "quarterback sneak" and was tackled shortly after he went through the line.
As he was falling forward another player was coming in to make the
tackle and fell on top of him. After this play Welch was lying on his
back on the field and unable to get to this feet. [Welch] was moved by
eight boys, four on each side; with no one directing the moving...
[Welch] is [now] a permanent quadriplegic caused by damage to the
spinal cord at the level of the fifth cervical vertebra. . . . The
removal of Welch from the field without the use of a stretcher was an
improper medical practice in view of the symptoms.

Source: *Reprinted from Westlaw with permission of Thomson Reuters.*

1. How should coaches respond to an injured player?
2. What procedures and policies should be put in place regarding injured athletes?

In Case 4-11, coaches satisfied their ethical duty to supervise and instruct when they provided the players with adequate instruction in the game of football.

📖 CASE 4-11   *Vendrell v. School District No. 26C, Malheur County*

376 P.2d 406 (Cal. 1962)

August 24, 1953, a week before classes assembled in the high school, Louis Vendrell registered for football practice and play. He shortly enrolled in the school as a freshman. October 9, about six weeks after he had turned out for football and while playing as a member of the Nyssa High School team against the Vale High School team, he was injured. At the time of his injury [Vendrell claimed] (1) he was "an inexperienced football player"; (2) . . . weighed 140 pounds; (3) . . . was "not physically coordinated"; (4) his injury befell him when he was "tackled hard by two Vale boys"; (5) . . . had not received "proper or sufficient instructions"; and (6) . . . had not been furnished with "the necessary and proper protective equipment" for his person. . . .

[A] coach or physical education instructor is required to exercise reasonable care for the protection of the students under his supervision. Before entering Nyssa High School Vendrell had completed the course of study offered by Nyssa Junior High School. The latter maintains a football team, two coaches and scheduled games. While a student in that school Vendrell had constantly been a member of its football team. He played the position of left half-back, the same position that he was playing at the time of his injury. Nyssa High School has about 300 students, two football coaches and a manager for the team. It played scheduled games with other high schools. Vendrell was 15 years of age when he entered the high school—one year older than most pupils. He sustained his injury during the close of the fourth quarter of a game in which Nyssa's opponent was the Vale High School team. He was injured when he was tackled by two Vale players while he was carrying the ball.

As a witness Vendrell described as follows what happened: "And I saw the Vale players in front of me and I knew I couldn't go any further so I put my head down and just ran into em and that is when I heard my neck snap." At that moment he suffered the injury for which he seeks redress in damages. It consists of a fracture of the fifth cervical vertebra of the neck.

Thomas D. Winbigler, football coach of the Bend High School, saw the Nyssa-Vale game and the play in which Vendrell sustained his injury.

Referring to that play and Vendrell's handling of it, he testified:
"It was a well-executed play. I will say that. Any play that will go
for that much yardage is a well-executed play."

Before Vendrell had turned out on August 24, 1953, for football practice he had played for two years as a member of the football team of
Nyssa Junior High School. Evidently, the training given to the football squad in the junior high school is substantial, for Vendrell mentioned that the squad was taught how to tackle, block, stiff-arm,
carry the ball and keep the ball from the opponent. While a member of
the junior high school football team Vendrell played in games against
Adrian, Vale, Payette, and Parma.

Before any student was accepted as a member of the Nyssa High School
football squad it was necessary for him to be pronounced physically
fit by a physician and for his parents to give their written consent.
Vendrell met both requirements. He had worked in the preceding summer
upon farms and deemed himself in good condition. More than one of the
witnesses spoke of him as a promising football player, and none
referred to him in any other way. He concedes that he was generally
the first member of the squad present for football practice and the
last to leave the training field.

Football practice was conducted every afternoon, Monday through
Thursday, for about two hours. No practice was maintained on Fridays
because that was the day upon which the team played its games. The
training for football play which [Vendrell], as a member of the Nyssa
High School football squad, underwent was, of course, dependent somewhat upon the competency of the school's coach. All other coaches who
mentioned the subject described Nyssa's head coach, Howard Lovelace,
as competent and well regarded. Thomas D. Winbigler, aforementioned,
was the football coach of Weiser High School in 1953 but at the time
of the trial was the football coach of Bend High School. He testified:
"I have a high regard for Howard in his ability to coach and his teams
were well coached."

The training of the squad consisted of a program of calisthenics,
classes on physical conditioning and training rules. The calisthenics
were intended to strengthen the body. One of them was called bull-neck
exercise. It was engaged in for several minutes each day and was
designed to strengthen the neck. Vendrell described it as hard. The
training program was also intended, Vendrell said, to enable the players to learn the plays and the fundamentals of football such as tackling, running, blocking and the proper position of the head and body
while in play. We observe that the players engaged in scrimmage, line
play, dummy tackling, and backfield movements. Vendrell conceded that
the coaches stressed the necessity for each player to learn "the

fundamentals of football" and told them that otherwise they could not enjoy the game or play it successfully. The coaches stated that calisthenics, training and hard work were essential for self-protection. The players were instructed in the manner of gaining protection from blows and taking them on their protective equipment. Mr. Winbigler testified that the school's program of drills, practice and exercises was proper and adequate. He also expressed the belief that the Nyssa High School team was well coached.

Vendrell practiced, so he testified, "most of the time" with what he termed the "varsity" team. He attended every practice session. Since in junior high school he played the position of left half-back, the same as in the senior high school, he conceded that when he was injured he was playing that position for the third year. His testimony upon that subject was:

Question: "So this was your third year in that particular position?"

Answer: "Yes."

Before Vendrell played in the game against Vale he had played (1) in the preceding two year period in several games as a member of the football team of Nyssa Junior High School, (2) as a member of the Nyssa High School's "A" team for a few plays against the John Day High School team, and (3) as a member of Nyssa High School's "B" team in games against Ontario, Parma, and Vale. Vendrell claims that the Vale team was powerful and that it contained many players of outstanding skill. Before Vendrell entered the game in the fourth quarter the score was 48 to 0 in Vale's favor. The Vale team believed that with that score it could not lose the game, and, accordingly replaced virtually all of its best players with substitutes. One of its players, Kay Smith, who was a sophomore and left half-back, testified that at the time of Vendrell's injury, "we had most of our freshmen and sophomore players in the ballgame." He added, "They were pretty close evenly matched," that is, the two teams that were then in the field. Smith was one of the players who tackled him.

Vendrell weighed 140 pounds. Smith, Vale's half-back who tackled him, weighed 130 to 135 pounds. Don Savage was a junior in Nyssa High School and, like Vendrell, was a left half-back upon its team. He played in the Vale-Nyssa game. When he was taken out of the game Vendrell replaced him. He weighed, so he swore, "125 to 130 pounds" at that time. Dirk Rhinehart, another backfield player upon the Nyssa team, weighed 120 pounds. Mr. Winbigler testified:

Question: "And I believe you said that on a man-to-man basis, the Vale and Nyssa teams were pretty much equal—about the same?"

Answer: "That's right."

The following was given by Don Savage who was a member of the Nyssa football team at the time of Vendrell's injury.

Question: "Will you describe his physical co-ordination and how he handled himself, generally?"

Answer: "Well, he was a pretty fast boy. He was—ah—not too awkward, but he certainly wasn't as well co-ordinated as some of the other members of the team—the older ones."

Question: "What do you mean in 'co-ordinating'? Will you describe it?"

Answer: "Well, I mean the way that he would run with the ball and things of that nature."

Vendrell made the outstanding gain of the game for Nyssa and Mr. Winbigler swore that the run in which he made the gain was a well executed play. Vendrell saw the tacklers charging upon him and realized that he could not escape them. One of the tacklers (Smith) was to the side and rear of him. The other tackler (Carl Gustafson) came from the front. He came into contact with Vendrell before Smith did.

A day after August 24 when Vendrell enlisted for football practice, the protective equipment was distributed to the players. The manager supervised its allotment and the coaches were present. The equipment consisted of helmets, shoulder pads, rib pads, and hip pads together with the uniforms. The quantity was larger in amount than the number of players. The gear was placed upon tables and the lettermen were given first choice. Next came the seniors and finally the freshmen. Vendrell testified that after he had chosen the equipment he wanted, "I just took it to my locker and put it on." He added, "Whatever didn't fit, I'd bring it back and try—until I'd get the right deals and the right equipment." Although the coaches in some other schools helped their players fit their equipment, Nyssa's coaches did not. The Nyssa coaches were present, however, when the players made their selections and tried on their equipment. Vendrell did not testify that he needed help in order to determine whether the gear which he chose fitted him. The helmet which he selected in August was discarded several weeks later when he split it in a game by running head-on into an opposing player. He then returned to the equipment room and selected another helmet. Concerning it he said, "It was just a little bit loose." He admitted that he did not try on all of the available helmets before he took the one that "was just a little bit loose," but described as "old" the helmets which he did not try on. He also testified that one of his shoulder pads was loose because the string which was intended to draw it into a snug position was broken and therefore too short. Other strings were readily available. The two complaints

just mentioned are the only ones that [Vendrell] voiced concerning
his equipment. He made no claim that his equipment was defective nor
did he find any fault with his uniform. All of the equipment was regularly inspected; defective parts were discarded and replaced with
new. Vendrell conceded that he did not mention to the manager, the
coaches, or any other school representative the fault that he found
with his gear. He also conceded that he had the privilege of returning any of his equipment and of selecting a substitute. He testified
that when he played in a game, such as the Nyssa-Vale game, he wore a
jersey and that since it fitted tight it held the shoulder pad well
in place...the complaint did not aver any shortcoming in the protective equipment. If it was in any way unsuitable to [Ventrell's] needs
he was intimately familiar with that fact and voluntarily decided to
proceed.

The playing of football is a body-contact sport. The game demands that
the players come into physical contact with each other constantly,
frequently with great force. The linemen charge the opposing line vigorously, shoulder to shoulder. The tackler faces the risk of leaping
at the swiftly moving legs of the ball-carrier and the latter must be
prepared to strike the ground violently. Body contacts, bruises, and
clashes are inherent in the game. There is no other way to play it. No
prospective player need be told that a participant in the game of
football may sustain injury. It draws to the game the manly; they
accept its risks, blows, clashes and injuries without whimper.

No one expects a football coach to extract from the game the body
clashes that cause bruises, jolts and hard falls. To remove them would
end the sport. The coach's function is to minimize the possibility
that the body contacts may result in something more than slight
injury. The extensive calisthenics, running and other forms of muscular exercise to which the coaches subjected the squad [to] were
intended to place the players in sound physical condition so that they
could withstand the shocks, blows and other rough treatment with which
they would meet in actual play. As a further safeguard for the players' protection the [school district] provided all of the players with
protective equipment. Each player was taught and shown how to handle
himself while in play so that a blow would fall upon his protective
equipment and not directly upon his body. We have also noticed the
fact that every player was instructed in the manner of (1) running
while carrying the ball, (2) tackling an opposing player, and (3) handling himself properly when about to be tackled. For example, Vendrell
testified:

Question: "Now, if you would stiff-arm properly, or run properly,
with your tail down and your legs underneath you, with your
head up and your back straight, wouldn't the coach point

this out to you? Wouldn't he work with you and discuss
these matters with the various backs?"

Answer: "Yes, he did."

Question: "At any time, in your coaching by Mr. Lovejoy or Mr. McGinley,
were you ever told that you should either strike a dummy or
an opposing player with your head?"

Answer: "No, but, see I had done it in practice. In actual scrimmage. I had done that very same thing in practice-in scrimmage and nobody had ever told me any different."

The purpose of the extensive instructions and arduous practice was to
enable the player not only to make for his team the maximum yardage
but also to reduce to the minimum the possibility that an injury would
befall him. All of the football coaches who testified upon the subject
swore that the instructions and practice which were given to the
school's football squad were adequate and were similar to that which
they gave to their own players. No criticism was offered of the
instructions and practice. Had Vendrell followed the instructions that
were given to him about holding his head up, his injury would not have
occurred, assuming, of course, that the failure to hold up his head
was the cause of his injury.

But Vendrell says that the school's coaches had not told him that if he
used his head as a battering ram an injury might befall him. One of the
first lessons that an infant learns when he begins to toddle about on
his feet is not to permit his head to collide with anything. Not only
do his parents, playmates and teachers unite in teaching him that
lesson, but every door, chair and other protruding object that is in
the child's presence becomes a harsh but effective teacher that injury
occurs if he bumps his head upon something. Less than two weeks before
his lamentable injury befell him, Vendrell was taught the lesson again
that he had learned in his infancy. This time it was taught to him when
he ran head-on into a player in the Parma game and split his head gear.
When he discarded his ruined helmet and borrowed one from a teammate he
saw from the split helmet in his own hands what could have happened to
his head. No coach could have spoken to him more effectively.

The school's coaches were Vendrell's teachers. He had the right—in
fact, the duty—to ask the coaches questions concerning any matter
which was not clear. In turn, the coaches had the right to assume that
he possessed the intelligence and stock of information of a normal
young man. Thus, they had the right to assume that he knew of the possibility of injury that comes to an individual who uses his head as a
battering ram. Vendrell swore that he lowered his head when he saw
that he was about to be tackled.

Vendrell assumed the risk attendant upon being tackled. The risk of injury that was inherent in being tackled was obvious. He was thoroughly familiar with it. He had been tackled scores of times and had been the tackler many many times. The tackle in question was made fairly and according to the rules.

The school's coaches gave to the football squad adequate, standard instruction and practice. The school's coaches did not negligently omit any detail; certainly the school's coaches did not omit to perform any expected duty. Vendrell assumed all of the obvious risks of which tackling was one.

Source: *Reprinted from Westlaw with permission of Thomson Reuters.*

1. What duty of instruction does a football coach owe to his players?
2. Does the duty of instruction owed, differ with regard to the age of the participants?
3. As an SMP (athletic director), how would you determine if a coach has met the standard required for the duty of supervision and instruction?

Coach Violence

There are numerous examples of coach violence, and many of these are seen in Chapter 6.[21] *Hills v. Bridgeview Little League Association* is one of the worst cases of violent behavior as exhibited by youth sports coaches.

📖 **CASE 4-12   *Hills v. Bridgeview Little League Association***

---

745 N.E.2d 1166 (Ill. 2000)

On July 30, 1990, John Hills was attacked and beaten while coaching first base for a Little League baseball team. His attackers, Ted Loy, George Loy, Sr., and George Loy, Jr., were, respectively, the manager and assistant coaches for the opposing team, which was sponsored by Bridgeview Little League Association (Bridgeview). The attack occurred during a Little League baseball tournament hosted by Justice Willow Springs Little League. . . . [I]n the summer of 1990, [Hills] was the first base coach on an all-star Little League baseball team sponsored by the Lemont Little League Association. The players on the team were 14-year- olds. In July 1990, the Lemont team entered a Little League baseball tournament sponsored by Justice.

---

[21] See also "Youth Football Coach Charged with Assaulting Referee," WKRN.com, August 9, 2010; Jeff Merron, "The List: Coaches Gone Wild," *ESPN.com*, October 23, 2003.

On July 30, 1990, as part of the regular tournament schedule, the Lemont team played a game against an all-star Little League team sponsored by Bridgeview. Accordingly to Hills, approximately 40 people were in attendance at the game. Hills stated that the Lemont and Bridgeview teams had played each other earlier in the tournament without incident and that, prior to July 30, he had never heard anything negative about the Bridgeview coaches or manager. Hills exchanged "hellos" in the parking lot with the manager of the Bridgeview team, Ted Loy, before the game began. As the teams took the field, Hills sensed no problems with anyone's behavior and had no indication that anything was out of the ordinary.

During the game, the Bridgeview team occupied the first base dugout and the Lemont team occupied the dugout near third base. While their respective teams were batting, the first base coaches from each team stood in a designated area between first base and the Bridgeview dugout known as the coach's box and directed the players who safely reached first base to stop or to keep running. Bridgeview's first base coach was Ted Loy's nephew, 16-year-old George Loy, Jr.

Hills testified that, during the first inning, in an attempt to influence the first base umpire's calls, George Loy, Jr., began gesturing and yelling "safe, safe safe" as the Bridgeview players crossed first base. The Lemont team called time-out. A conference was held . . . [d]uring the conference, [umpire] Van Wagner told the Bridgeview coaches to stop trying to influence the first umpire's calls. Play resumed. . . . Bridgeview assistant coach George Loy, Sr., began shouting [obscenities] at Hills from the Bridgeview dugout.

During the fifth inning, George Loy, Sr., again swore at Hills. During the sixth inning, Hills' team scored several runs and took the lead in the game. Loy continued swearing, but he was now angrier and his voice was louder.

At the end of the sixth inning, Hills bent down to pick up a scorebook that he had set on the ground near first base. . . . [H]e was suddenly hit in the back of the head and knocked to the ground on his hands and knees. . . . Hills was then punched in the face and hit several times in the side and back. Hills struggled to get up to his feet, he was punched again. . . . George Loy, Jr., then dug his thumb into Hills' eye and tried to rip it out. After Hills was punched again in the body and face, there was a "lull" in the attack. [After] the "lull," . . . [Loy punched and broke his nose].

Hills was in a daze when he heard someone yell, "Oh, my God, look out, he's got a bat." Hills then saw, out of the corner of his eye, George Loy, Jr., swinging a baseball bat at his knees . . . [and was] struck . . . on the inner side of the left knee. Hills then fell to

the ground. Hills stated that the next thing he remembered was John
O'Neill, a parent of one of the Lemont players, telling him to stay
down and not to move. Hills could not recall being taken to the hospital or being treated in the emergency room. As a result of the attack,
Hills suffered serious injuries and was hospitalized for five days.

Source: *Reprinted from Westlaw with permission of Thomson Reuters.*

1. What actions should be taken against the violent coaches in this case?
2. Should criminal charges be brought against coaches who engage in violence?

CASE STUDY 4-2   *Coach Interview*

One of the most controversial remarks ever made in sports was made by former basketball coach Bobby
Knight. In April 1988, Knight was being interviewed by newswoman Connie Chung during an NBC-TV special and was asked by Chung, "There are times Bobby Knight can't do it his way—and what does he do then?"
Knight responded, "I think that if rape is inevitable, relax and enjoy it."[22] Knight quickly added that his remarks
should not be misinterpreted. Indiana University president Thomas Ehrlich stated, "Coach Knight was not
speaking for the university. His reference to rape and his coarse language were in very poor taste. Period. That's
all I really want to say." Many women's groups protested Knight's statement.[23]

---

1. Should Knight have been fired from his coaching position for his statement?
2. How do you categorize Knight's statement? Do you consider it merely insensitive and vulgar
or something more serious?
3. Knight made his controversial statements in 1988. Assume coach Knight had a clause on his
contract that required him to conduct himself in accordance with "good citizenship." Could the
university have terminated his contract under that provision based on the statements he made?

Coach Abuse

Sexual abuse by coaches is covered extensively in Chapter 10. Sexual abuse and sexual harassment by coaches must yield a zero-tolerance policy and must be reported to the appropriate officials
and law enforcement as soon as reported or discovered. Society is unfortunately replete with horrific
examples of sexual abuse and harassment by coaches.[24] In the following case, what coaches thought
was a joke constituted abuse.

---

[22] Rick Telander, "Not a Shining Knight," *Sports Illustrated Vault*, May 9, 1988.
[23] See "Bob Knight's Outburst Timeline," *USA Today*, November 14, 2006. Also see "300 Protesters Demand
Knight Apologize for Reprimand,"*Associated Press* via the *Washington Post*, (1974-Current file).
[24] See "Gymnastics Coach Charged with Sex Assault of Teen," SFGate.com, August 20, 2010; Kristi E. Swartz,
"Former Middle School Swim Coach Charged with Rape," *Atlanta Journal-Constitution*, February 16, 2010. See
also "Abuse Drives Away Hockey Umpires," *The Daily Examiner*, May 27, 2010. In 2010, a former NHL player
and now a coach with the NHL Los Angeles Kings was charged with sexually assaulting his own daughter. See
Keith Alexander, "Hockey Coach Charged in Hotel Sex Assault," *Washington Post*, May 21, 2010.

CASE 4-13   *Spacek v. Charles*

928 SW 2d 88 (Tex.App.-Houston [14 Dist.] 1996)

Spacek and Ramsey, athletic coaches at New Waverly High School (the coaches), called Joshua Maxey, a fourteen-year-old junior high school student, into Spacek's office during school hours to talk to Maxey about improving his grades so that when he entered high school he could participate in sports. Spacek allegedly threatened to hang Maxey if he did not improve his grades. Maxey also claims that Spacek reached for a white extension cord, told him to look at the ceiling, and attempted to grab him. Ramsey allegedly retrieved what Maxey believed to be a hand-gun, placed Maxey in a headlock, put the weapon against Maxey's head, and threatened to kill him if his grades did not improve.

The coaches maintain that, as teachers, they were acting within the scope of their employment and exercising their discretion and judgment in encouraging Maxey to improve his grades.

[Coach Spacek said,] "I never threatened to hang him and Ramsey, who was present during most of this encounter, which lasted a few min-utes, never threatened to shoot him. . . . I did not discipline Maxey. I used no force upon him. He suffered no bodily injury in my presence." Likewise, Ramsey stated, "I never threatened Maxey and I did not hear Spacek threaten him. . . . I observed no discipline of any kind of Maxey during this incident. He was not physically harmed in any way."

Superintendent Davis said Spacek admitted reaching for the extension cord, but claimed that he was "just playing" with Maxey and trying to establish a rapport with him. An excerpt from Spacek's testimony reflects that Spacek portrayed he and Maxey as "laughing it up" while in his office. In testifying before the school board, Spacek said he playfully responded to Maxey's dare that he couldn't catch him by picking up the extension cord and saying, "[Y]es, I will catch you and I will tie you up and we will whip you."

"In determining whether force or confinement is reasonable for the control, training, or education of a child, the following facts are to be considered:

(a) whether the actor is a parent; (b) the age, sex, and physical and mental condition of the child; (c) the nature of his offense and his motive; (d) the influence of his example upon other children of the same family or group; (e) whether the force or confinement is reason-ably necessary and appropriate to compel obedience to a proper com-mand; (f) whether it is disproportionate to the offence, unnecessarily degrading, or is likely to cause serious or permanent harm."

Consistent with the public policy of Texas to give teachers the necessary support to enable them to efficiently discharge their responsibilities, teachers may use reasonable force not only to punish
wrongful behavior, but also to enforce compliance with instructional
commands. However, "a teacher may not use physical violence against a
child merely because the child is unable or fails to perform, either
academically or athletically, at a desired level of ability, even
though the teacher considers such violence to be 'instruction and
encouragement.'"

Although the facts of this case do not involve paddling or spanking or
other physical force typically associated with corporal punishment,
allegations that a teacher restrained a child in a headlock and placed
a weapon against his head, and that another teacher attempted to grab
the student to hang him with an extension cord, undoubtedly raise a
question of excessive force.

Source: *Reprinted from Westlaw with permission of Thomson Reuters.*

1. Do you believe the coaches in *Spacek* used excessive force which constituted physical and
   mental abuse?
2. As an SMP what acts would you have taken to ensure this conduct never occurs again?
3. Should the coaches have been fired for their conduct?

In the following case, a coach disciplined a student because the student was talking in class.

📖 CASE 4-14 *Moore v. Willis Independent School Dist.*

233 F.3d 871 (5th Cir. 2000)

In February 1997, fourteen-year-old Aaron Moore was an eighth-grade
student at Lynn Lucas Middle School in the Willis (Texas) Independent
School District. Aaron was a student athlete who had just finished the
season playing on the school's basketball team and was looking forward
to trying out for the track team. He and approximately eighty other
boys were enrolled in an elective gym class of which Allen Beene was
one of the teachers. On the day in question, Beene observed Aaron
talking to a classmate during roll call, a violation of a class rule.
As punishment, Beene told Aaron to do 100 "ups and downs," also known
as squat-thrusts. Aaron had not been subjected to similar punishment
before, but he understood that if he stopped during this punishment,
he either would be made to start over or would be sent to the
principal's office. A classmate counted the 100 repetitions.

Aaron then participated in approximately twenty to twenty-five minutes of
weight lifting required of the gym class that day. He did not complain
to Beene of pain or fatigue, fearing that would make matters worse.

In the following days, however, Aaron was diagnosed with rhabdomyolysis and renal failure; he also developed esophagitis/gastritis. Aaron was hospitalized and missed three weeks of school. He continues to experience fatigue, and has been unable to participate in school sports or physical education class.

Nancy Moore, Aaron's mother, states that Beene told her the "ups and downs" were a means of punishment necessary to control middle school students. Mrs. Moore also states that Beene told her that he had intentionally inflicted pain on her son, explaining: "With high school kids you can have them do two ups and downs and they remember the next time. With junior high kids, you have to inflict pain or they don't remember." Mrs. Moore further states that the school district's athletic director, Ron Eikenberg, told her that "the coaches at the junior high were out of control and they did their own thing." By now, every school teacher and coach must know that inflicting pain on a student through unreasonably excessive exercise poses a risk of significant injury.

Source: *Reprinted from Westlaw with permission of Thomson Reuters.*

1. Were the actions of the coach in *Moore* physically and mentally abusive?
2. Is it ever appropriate to discipline a student with excessive physical exercise?

CASE 4-15 *Hagan v. Houston Independent School District*

51 F.3d 48 (5th Cir. 1995)

Plaintiffs . . . in this case are three former students of Wheatley High School (WHS) in Houston, Texas, and their mothers. These students allege that they were sexually molested by their former high school coach, Tommy Reaux. The students and their mothers filed suit against several defendants, including the principal of WHS, Eddie Orum, III, for failing to prevent Reaux's abuse.

On September 12, 1989, . . . Roland Major [student at WSH] informed several WHS teachers that Reaux had pinched and patted him on the buttocks. One of these teachers sent Major to [principal] Orum, who interviewed Major and had him make a written statement. Orum then met with Reaux, who admitted that he had patted Major on the behind. Reaux told Orum that he had been trying to persuade Major to rejoin the football team and that the pat had simply been a "coach's gesture." At this meeting, Orum told Major that because there were no witnesses to the incident, nothing further could be done.

Orum did not personally contact Major's mother to tell her of the incident. Later that afternoon, Reaux approached Major and asked if he could give Major a ride home after school so that Reaux could talk to

Major's mother. Accompanied by another teacher, Reaux and Major went to Major's home. Reaux told Major's mother that he had patted her son on the buttocks and that Reaux, Major and Orum had already met and discussed it. At some later time, Orum warned Reaux that he should be careful in his gestures with students. Aside from this warning Orum did nothing further about Major's complaint.

On October 25, 1989, . . . Cleveland McCord [student at WSH] reported to several teachers that he had been having sexual relations with Reaux. One of these teachers took him to speak to Orum. Orum met separately with McCord and with Reaux, then met with them together. In Reaux's presence, Orum had McCord make a written statement. Orum also separately questioned Reaux, who denied McCord's allegations. Later that day, Orum tried to telephone McCord's mother, but could not reach her because the telephone number was either disconnected or incorrect. Orum contacted an official with the Houston Independent School District (HISD) and relayed the information McCord had given him. The HISD instructed Orum to get statements from McCord and Reaux and to prepare a written report. The HISD also told Orum that William Morgan, the HISD District IX Superintendent, would begin an investigation. Orum sent a written report to the HISD that day.

Shortly afterward, Reaux approached McCord and offered him fifty dollars to say that nothing had happened. McCord took the money and on October 26 made a new written statement withdrawing his allegations. When Orum questioned McCord about the reason for his change of heart, McCord told Orum that he just wanted to drop it. Orum again contacted the HISD and informed them of McCord's new statement. Orum told the HISD that he still considered the situation serious and stated that he had warned Reaux that, in spite of McCord's retraction, Orum would recommend that Reaux be fired if there was reason to believe the original charges. At that point, Orum intended to discontinue his active investigation but to monitor the situation by "keep[ing] [his] eyes open."

Several days later, McCord told Orum that he wanted to revive his complaint. On November 1, Orum went to McCord's home to speak to his mother. Orum informed McCord's mother of McCord's allegations and told her that he had spoken with both McCord and Reaux. Orum also told McCord's mother that Reaux would no longer be allowed to be alone with students. This was apparently the first that McCord's mother had heard of this matter and she told Orum to hold off his investigation because she wanted to speak to her son first. The next morning, McCord's mother visited Orum's office, informed Orum that the relationship between Reaux and her son had been consensual and asked Orum to stop investigating. On that day, Orum wrote to Morgan and informed him that his investigation had been inconclusive and that he planned to end his inquiry unless he was instructed otherwise.

Some time in 1990, Orum was approached by Daphne Chappell, the band teacher at WHS, who suggested that he speak with a student named Earl Armstrong to see if Armstrong had been having problems with Reaux. Chappell told Orum that Armstrong's youngest brother had said that Reaux and Armstrong were having sexual relations. Orum spoke to Armstrong and to Reaux, both of whom denied the allegations. Orum also spoke to Armstrong's mother, who told him only that she was concerned that the WHS football and band departments were too aggressively vying for Armstrong's exclusive participation. At this time, Orum believed that some of the past allegations against Reaux might have been true, but because of the outcome of his interviews with Armstrong, Armstrong's mother and Reaux, Orum concluded that he should take no further action.

Source: *Reprinted from Westlaw with permission of Thomson Reuters.*

1. What actions need to be taken to stop sexual abuse by coaches?[25]
2. As an SMP, what training do you believe should be given to coaches concerning sexual harassment and abuse?
3. How often and when should criminal background checks be performed on coaches?
4. Should men coach women's athletic teams? If so, is there an age limit that is ethically advisable to do so?
5. Did the principal in Case 4-15 investigate the matter properly?
6. What procedures should be in place for school officials to report sexual abuse of students by teachers?

The Coach as a Role Model

Coaches function as role models to players and student-athletes at both the professional and amateur levels. At the professional ranks, coaches must exhibit characteristics of fair play, discipline, and hard work. At the collegiate and high school levels, coaches have a major influence over student-athletes. Coaches must understand that they function as a role model for students and conduct themselves accordingly.

Review the following model code of ethics for coaches. What are your impressions of the code of ethics? Is there anything missing? What would you add or delete from the code?

Model Code of Ethics for Coaches

The function of a coach is to educate students through participation in competition. An athletic program should be designed to enhance academic achievement and should never interfere with opportunities for academic success. Each student-athlete should be treated with respect and dignity, and his or her welfare should be the utmost concern of the coach at all times.

---

[25] See Danielle Deak, "Out of Bounds: How Sexual Abuse of Athletes at the Hands of Their Coaches Is Costing the World of Sports Millions," *Seton Hall Journal of Sport Law* (1999); Joy D. Bringer, Celia H. Brackenridge, and Lynne H. Johnston, "Defining Appropriateness in Coach-Athlete Sexual Relationships: The Voice of Coaches," *Journal of Sexual Aggression* 8, no. 2 (July 2002); Michael Gibbons and Dana Campbell, "Liability of Recreation and Competitive Sport Organizations for Sexual Assaults on Children by Administrators, Coaches, and Volunteers," *Journal of Legal Aspects in Sport* (2002–2003); Trisha Leahy, Grace Pretty, and Gershon Tenenbaum, "Prevalence of Sexual Abuse in Organised Competitive Sport in Australia," *Journal of Sexual Aggression* 8, no. 2 (July 2002).

The coach shall be aware that they have a tremendous influence (good or bad) on the education of the student-athlete and should never place the value of winning above the value of instilling the highest ideals of character in the student-athlete.

The coach shall uphold the honor and dignity of the profession. The coach shall strive to set an example of the highest ethical and moral conduct for all.

The coach shall take an active role in the prevention of drug, alcohol and tobacco abuse by student-athletes.

The coach shall avoid the use of alcohol and tobacco products when in contact with players.

The coach shall promote the entire academic program of the school and direct his or her program in harmony with the total school academic program.

The coach shall master the contest rules and shall teach them to his or her team members. The coach shall not seek an advantage by circumvention of the spirit or letter of the rules.

The coach shall exert his or her influence to enhance sportsmanship by spectators.

The coach shall respect and support contest officials. The coach shall not indulge in conduct which would incite players or spectators against the officials. Public criticism of officials or players is unethical.

Before and after contests, coaches for the competing teams should meet and exchange cordial greetings to set the correct tone for the event.

A coach shall not scout opponents by any means other than those adopted by the league and/or state high school athletic association.

What about having the coach sign a "Coaches' Ethics Code" like the one listed below?

Coaches' Ethics Code Agreement

I, the undersigned coach, have read and agree to abide by the Coaches Ethics Code.

I understand that violations of the Coaches Ethics Code may result in full or partial forfeiture of my coaching privileges.

I further understand that lack of awareness or a misunderstanding of an ethical standard on my part is not a defense to a charge of unethical conduct.

CASE STUDY 4-3   *Regulating Coach Conduct*

There is no doubt Rick Pitino can coach basketball. He had been a successful college basketball coach for many years. However, some of his conduct became an issue at a criminal trial of a woman who was convicted of attempting to extort money from Pitino after he admitted having an affair with her in 2003. Pitino apologized for his indiscretions. Pitino had given the woman $3,000 to help her get medical care. The woman later had an abortion. Pitino's coaching contract with the University of Louisville contained a moral clause for acts of "moral depravity."

1. Should the university have terminated coach Pitino's contract for his actions?

2. Should a coach's "off the field" conduct ever be subject to regulation by the university?[26]

---

[26] Eamonn Brennan, "Uh Oh, Rick Pitino's Contract Contains a Morality Clause," *Yahoo! Sports*, August 12, 2010.

SPORTS OFFICIALS' ETHICS

Introduction

It can be argued that sports officials are the most significant individuals involved in the sporting contest. There is no doubt that the sports official has a tough job. Being a sports official is not an easy job by any measure. The official may be subjected to taunts, heckling, physical abuse, emotional abuse, and even extreme violence sometimes tragically resulting in death.[27]

The question is how the sports official discharges his or her ethical duty in the midst of the chaos that takes place on the playing field. The players give it their all and the coaches instruct them on how to play, but it is the sports official who eventually decides the outcome of a play, who can participate, and sometimes who wins a match or game. The final outcome of a sporting event can sometimes be determined by an official's call. That is why the sports official must make the correct call; however, because they are human, that is not always the case. It is just as difficult to become an NHL referee or an MLB umpire as it is to become a professional player. The "weeding out" process is fierce, and only the elite will have the opportunity to call themselves an official, referee, or umpire. With that opportunity comes the obligations of making the right call on the field or ice. A sports official must be physically and mentally ready for a sporting event just as players are. The sports official must be able to move up and down the field, ice, or court with ease; weave between players; break up scrums, fights, and shoving matches; and at the same time watch the action to ensure compliance with the rules. One of the toughest jobs the sports official has is to call a foul or unsportsmanlike play on an athlete who is much larger than the official, informing that player he has broken the rules and now must suffer the consequences. The official also has the ultimate power of ejecting a player from a game, which prevents the player's further participation in the match. Most professional athletes, and amateur athletes as well, are not happy about being ejected from a sporting match and more than a few have shown their displeasure over an ejection by the sports official.

There are numerous cases in which sports officials have been subjected to violence. Unfortunately in youth sports, many parents of participants have attacked officials (see Chapter 5). Officials are in a tough position. Whether it be a Little League baseball game or a professional sports league, the sports official is under pressure from fans, players, leagues, agents (in the case of professional officials), and others to get the call right on the field. *Kill the Umpire* was a 1950 movie starring William Bendix and "Kill the Umpire" has been a phrase associated with early baseball. The following poem was published in the *Chicago Tribune* in 1888.

> Mother, may I slug the umpire
> May I slug him right away?
> So he cannot be here, mother
> When the clubs begin to play?
>
> Let me clasp his throat, dear mother,
> In a dear, delightful grip

---

[27] See Associated Press, "Player Banned 27 Games for Attack," *ESPN.com*, July 21, 2010. Also see Ali Bracken, "Up to Six Face Charges for Assault on GAA Referee," *TribuneSport*, August 8, 2010; "Colombian Soccer Referee Murdered," *CBC Sports*, May 6, 2000; "Referee Killed on Duty," *Kenya Football*, August 31, 2009.

With one hand and with the other
Bat him several in the lip.

Let me climb his frame, dear mother,
While the happy people shout;
I'll not kill him, dearest mother
I will only knock him out.

Let me mop the ground up, mother,
With his person, dearest do;
If the ground can stand it, mother
I don't see why you can't, too.

Mother may I slug the umpire,
Slug him right between the eyes?
If you let me do it, mother
You shall have the champion prize.[28]

In today's sporting world, with large amounts of money at stake, players can become very angry with an official's ruling. Tennis star Serena Williams created a huge controversy in the 2009 U.S. Open with her actions toward an official. Williams told a line judge, "I swear to God I'm f——going to take this f—— ball and shove it down your f—— throat, you hear that. I swear to God!!"[29] After the match Williams said, "I wanted to offer my sincere apologies to anyone that I may have offended . . . I need to make it clear to all young people that I handled myself inappropriately and it's not the way to act." There was then a dispute about whether Williams had said she was going to kill the line judge. Whatever she said, it was clearly inappropriate, unsportsmanship, and was unethical.

Ethical Duty of a Reasonably Prudent Sports Official

Sports officials must ensure that they are physically and mentally ready for a game or match. If they are not, then they have the ethical duty to disqualify themselves from participation. Sports officials, similar to players, must give their best effort on the field to ensure the integrity of a match. Notwithstanding, officials make mistakes.[30] If a sports official misses a call but has done everything possible to get the call correct, then the official has discharged his or her ethical duty even though a mistake was made in the call. If a sports official blows a call or makes a mistake in the interpretation of the rules, is that considered unethical conduct or just the breaks of the game? Bad calls have always been a part of sports and will continue to be as long as the human factor is present in sports.[31] Boxing's top referee, Howard Foster, described his method and style of refereeing as follows: "The secret is just keeping your nose clean, don't get too friendly and just get in there and apply the

---

[28] Also see, Harold Seymour, *Baseball: The Early Years*, Oxford University Press, 1960.

[29] "Clijsters Wins After Controversial Ending," *ESPN.com*, September 12, 2009.

[30] Graham Houston, "Cortez Not the First Referee to Drop the Ball in a Big Fight," *ESPN.com*, July 1, 2008.

[31] Jonah Keri, "Does Baseball Need Umpires? Recent Bad Calls Have Critics Howling for Better Umps, but Maybe It's a Job for Machines," *Wall Street Journal*, October 14, 2009.

rules. If the crowd don't like it, there's nothing you can do because you've just got to get on with it. As long as your decision is honest it doesn't matter if the commentators on TV don't agree with you."[32]

Sports officials have a conscience and want to perform their job flawlessly, but should they be required to apologize for their errors?[33]

CASE STUDY 4-4   *Is Honesty Always the Best Policy?*

Most people would agree, honesty is always the best policy. NFL referee Bill Leavy certainly believes so. In 2010 he admitted that in the 2006 NFL Super Bowl he made two calls in the fourth quarter of the game that were both wrong and affected the outcome of the game.

1. Why was it necessary for him to admit his mistakes four years later?
2. What personal motivation could have led him to issue a statement that said he had made two bad calls?[34]

CASE STUDY 4-5   *The "28-Out" Perfect Game*

As Armando Galarraga caught the ball at first base, he jumped for joy, as he had just joined baseball's elite and had a perfect game. After all, in more than 130 years of baseball history, there had only been 20 perfect games.[35] But wait, umpire Jim Joyce calls the runner "safe!" A chorus of boos rained down on Joyce. A replay clearly showed the runner was out. He had blown the call. Joyce later admitted he "kicked the shit out of it." The cries went out to the commissioner to rule it a perfect game, but he refused. Galarraga was awarded a $53,000 Corvette the next day by his club. The U.S. State Department hailed Galarraga's sportsmanship; they deemed it a "28-out perfect game." The next night Joyce admitted his mistake to Galarraga in person and hugged him. The episode has been called a "shining moment of sportsmanship."[36]

The following are the instructions given to umpires by Major League Baseball:

General Instructions to Umpires

- Umpires, on the field, should not indulge in conversation with players. Keep out of the coaching box, and do not talk to the coach on duty.
- Keep your uniform in good condition. Be active and alert on the field.
- Be courteous, always, to club officials; avoid visiting in club offices and thoughtless familiarity with officers or employees of contesting clubs.

---

[32] "Doncaster's Top Boxing Referee," *Doncaster Today*, August 22, 2010.
[33] Associated Press, "Referee Remains 'Devastated' over Blown Call," *NBC Sports*, September 18, 2008.
[34] Rap Admits Errors in 2006 Super Bowl in Detroit," *Freep.com*, August 7, 2010.
[35] www.MLB.com
[36] Jason Beck, "Galarraga Brings Lineup to Tearful Joyce," *MLB.com*, June 3, 2010; Associated Press, "U.S. State Department Hails Armando Galarraga's Sportsmanship," *MLB.com*, June 4, 2010; Michele Maynard, "Good Sportsmanship and a Lot of Good Will," *New York Times*, June 3, 2010. See also Bruce Weber, "Perfect Asterisk," *New York Times*, June 5, 2010.

- When you enter a ball park, your sole duty is to umpire a ball game as the representative of baseball.
- Do not allow criticism to keep you from studying out bad situations that may lead to protested games.
- Carry your rule book. It is better to consult the rules and hold up the game 10 minutes to decide a knotty problem than to have a game thrown out on protest and replayed.
- Keep the game moving. A ball game is often helped by energetic and earnest work of the umpires.
- You are the only official representative of baseball on the ball field. It is often a trying position which requires the exercise of much patience and good judgment, but do not forget that the first essential in working out of a bad situation is to keep your own temper and self-control.
- You no doubt are going to make mistakes, but never attempt to "even up" after having made one. Make all decisions as you see them, and forget which is the home or visiting club.
- Keep your eye everlastingly on the ball while it is in play. It is more vital to know just where a fly ball fell, or a thrown ball finished up, than whether or not a runner missed a base. Do not call the plays too quickly, or turn away too fast when a fielder is throwing to complete a double play. Watch out for dropped balls after you have called a man out.
- Do not come running with your arm up or down, denoting "out" or "safe." Wait until the play is completed before making any arm motion.
- Each umpire team should work out a simple set of signals, so the proper umpire can always right a manifestly wrong decision when convinced he has made an error. If you [are] sure you got the play correctly, do not be stampeded by players' appeals to "ask the other man." If not sure, ask one of your associates. Do not carry this to extremes, be alert, and get your own plays. But remember! The first requisite is to get decisions correctly. If in doubt, don't hesitate to consult your associate. Umpire dignity is important, but never as important as "being right."
- A most important rule for umpires is always *"Be in Position to See Every Play."* Even though your decision may be 100% right, players still question it if they feel you were not in a spot to see the play clearly and definitely.
- Finally, be courteous, impartial, and firm, and so compel respect from all.[37]

Case Study 4-6 is the National Association of Sports Officials Code of Ethics. Is it apparent that NASO implies a fiduciary relationship between sports officials and fans? What indices of trust must a sports official exhibit on the playing field?

CASE STUDY 4-6 *NASO Code of Ethics*

Sports Officials Code of Ethics

Introduction

The National Association of Sports Officials believes the duty of sports officials is to act as impartial judges of sports competitions.

---

[37] www.MLB.com

We believe this duty carries with it an obligation to perform with accuracy, fairness and objectivity through an overriding sense of integrity.

Although the vast majority of sports officials work contests played by amateur athletes, it is vital every official approach each assignment in a professional manner. Because of their authority and autonomy, officials must have a high degree of commitment and expertise. NASO believes these facts impose on sports officials the higher ethical standard by which true professionals are judged.

Officials who are "professionals" voluntarily observe a high level of conduct, not because of fear of penalty, but rather out of personal character. They accept responsibility for their actions. This conduct has as its foundation a deep sense of moral values and use of reason which substantiate the belief a given conduct is proper simply because it is.

The Code

The purpose of the National Association of Sports Officials Code of Ethics is briefly summarized through the following three provisions:

First, to provide our members a meaningful set of guidelines for their professional conduct and to provide them with agreed-upon standards of practice;

Second, to provide to other sports officials these same guidelines and standards of practice for their consideration;

Third, to provide to others (i.e., players, coaches, administrators, fans, media) criteria by which to judge our actions as "professionals."

NASO has adopted this Code and strongly urges its members and officials in general to adhere to its principles. By doing so, notice is given that we recognize the need to preserve and encourage confidence in the professionalism of officiating. This confidence must first be fostered within the "community" of officials and then within the public generally.

NASO believes the integrity of officiating rests on the integrity and ethical conduct of each individual official. This integrity and conduct are the very basis of the future and well-being of organized sports and the effectiveness of this Association. The Association shall, by programs of education and other means, encourage acceptance and implementation of these Articles.

To these ends NASO declares acceptance of this Code:

Article I

Sports officials must be free of obligation to any interest other than the impartial and fair judging of sports competitions. Without equivocation, game decisions which are slanted by personal bias are dishonest and unacceptable.

Article II

Sports officials recognize that anything which may lead to a conflict of interest, either real or apparent, must be avoided. Gifts, favors, special treatment, privileges, employment or a personal relationship with a school or team which can compromise the perceived impartiality of officiating must be avoided.

Article III

Sports officials have an obligation to treat other officials with professional dignity and courtesy and recognize that it is inappropriate to criticize other officials publicly.

Article IV

Sports officials have a responsibility to continuously seek self-improvement through study of the game, rules, mechanics and the techniques of game management. They have a responsibility to accurately represent their qualifications and abilities when requesting or accepting officiating assignments.

Article V

Sports officials shall protect the public (fans, administrators, coaches, players, et al.) from inappropriate conduct and shall attempt to eliminate from the officiating avocation/profession all practices which bring discredit to it.

Article VI

Sports officials shall not be party to actions designed to unfairly limit or restrain access to officiating, officiating assignments or association membership. This includes selection for positions of leadership based upon economic factors, race, creed, color, age, sex, physical handicap, country, or national origin.

Source: *Courtesy of the National Association of Sports Officials.*

NASO believes that there should be a higher standard for sports officials because of their fiduciary relationship with both the participants and the spectators. An ethics code, such as NASO's, is one standard to which all ethical sports officials must strive. Other rules and standards for sports officials could be enunciated by cases, contracts, or league rules.

Bias

Nothing is more important to a sports official than to be unbiased. Sports officials must show no favoritism in their rulings. The official must stay objective at all times. It is the duty of the sports official to act as an impartial judge. This duty is accompanied by an obligation to perform his or her duties with accuracy, fairness, and objectivity, and with an overriding sense of integrity.[38] If a sports official appears to favor one club over another, then the integrity of the match becomes suspect and loses its sporting value. No sports official wants his or her call to decide a winner, even if it is a correct call. The official desires the skills of the competitors to determine a champion.

There has been much written about the idea that an umpire is like a courtroom judge. U.S. Chief Justice John Roberts declared in the opening remarks of his confirmation hearings to the United States Supreme Court that "judges are like umpires . . . umpires don't make the rules, they apply them." The role of an umpire or a judge is critical. They make sure everybody plays by the rules. But it is a limited role.[39]

An umpire must be objective and fair. Sports officials must be unbiased and free from conflicts of interest to protect the integrity of the sport.[40] An official is called upon to make a split-second decision in front of thousands of fans at the stadium, and millions of fans on TV, and apply the rules of the game to make the right call.[41] Everyone, regardless of how objective he or she claims to be, brings his or her own experience and perspective to an issue. The same can be said for the sports official. Many have argued that sports officials are biased regardless of their efforts to try to remain objective. Some have argued that the race of a player determines whether an official is biased.[42] Does the home team have an advantage in a sports match? Many have argued there is definitely a home field advantage.[43] Does a bias exist against tall players?[44] Do sports officials unconsciously favor players who wear red?[45] Are sports officials biased without even trying? Do certain countries in the Olympic Games get more favorable treatment than others?

---

[38] Michael Mayer, "Stepping In to Step Out of Liability: The Proper Standard of Liability for Referees in Foreseeable Judgment-Call Situations," *DePaul Journal of Sports Law and Contemporary Problems* (Summer 2005).

[39] Bruce Weber, "Umpires v. Judges," *New York Times*, July 11, 2009. Also see Neil S. Siegel, "Umpires at Bat: On Integration and Legitimation," *Constitutional Commentary* (2007); Aaron S. J. Zelinsky, "The Justice as Commissioner: Benching the Judge-Umpire Analogy," *Yale Law Journal* (March 4, 2010); George F. Will, "Baseball's Judicial Branch," *Washington Post*, April 9, 2009.

[40] See Brian Soebbing and Daniel Mason, "Protecting Integrity in Professional Sports Leagues: Preserving Uncertainty of Outcome," *2008 North American Society for Sport Management Conference* (May 29, 2008); Gary Parrish, "Time to Blow Whistle on Risky Referee Business?" *CBS Sports*, July 18, 2008; David Haugh, "NU Questions Lacrosse Ref's Conflict of Interest," *Chicago Tribune*, June 5, 2010.

[41] Bruce Weber, "'As They See 'Em," *New York Times*, March 13, 2009.

[42] "Collegiate Study Finds Racial Bias Among MLB Umpire Crews," *Street & Smith's Sports Business Daily*, August 14, 2007; "Study Suggests Referee Bias," *Seattle Times*, May 2, 2007; Joseph Price and Justin Wolfers, "Racial Discrimination Among NBA Referees," *National Bureau of Economic Research* (May 2, 2007); "Are Baseball Umpires Racist?" *Time Magazine*, August 13, 2007.

[43] Associated Press, "Fewer Fouls Called on Home Team," *ESPN.com*, November 23, 2009; "Is Home-Country Bias Inevitable for Figure-Skating Judges?" *New York Times*, February 24, 2010; Matthias Sutter and Martin G. Kocher, "Favoritism of Agents: The Case of Referees' Home Bias," *Journal of Economic Psychology* 25, no. 4 (August 2004); N. J. Balmer, A. M. Nevill, and A. M. Lane, "Do Judges Enhance Home Advantage in European Championship Boxing?" *Journal of Sports Sciences* 23, no. 4 (April 2005); Nick Harris, "Revealed: Biased Rugby Referees in Both Codes Hand Big Advantage to Own Countries," *Sporting Intelligence*, July 29, 2010; Andrew M. Lane, Alan M. Nevill, Nahid S. Ahmad, and Nigel Balmer, "Soccer Referee Decision-Making: 'Shall I Blow the Whistle?'" *Journal of Sports Science and Medicine* 5 (June 1, 2006).

[44] "Soccer Referees Hate the Tall Guys," *Wall Street Journal*, February 8, 2010.

[45] Matt Kaplan, "Referees Award More Points When They See Red," *ABC News*, July 12, 2008.

Noted scholar George Will put it succinctly, "Umpires are islands of exemption from America's obsessive lawyering: As has been said, three strikes and you're out—the best lawyer can't help you. But because it is the national pastime of a litigious nation, baseball is the only sport in which a non-player is allowed onto the field to argue against rulings."[46]

Ethics and Safety for the Sports Official

Does the sports official have an ethical duty to provide for the safety of the participants? In the professional arena, players typically assume the risk of injury, but what about youth sports? What happens when an injury occurs as a result of a referee not doing his or her job properly, as in the following cases?

Carabba v. The Anacortes School District gives an example of a referee's conduct which violated the duty to provide for the safety of the participants.

CASE 4-16   *Carabba v. The Anacortes School District*

435 P.2d 936 (Wash. 1967)

On January 31, 1963, a wrestling meet was held at Anacortes High School between the wrestling teams of Anacortes High School and Oak Harbor High School.

The referee for this meet was Mr. Robert L. Erhart, a state trooper, and a member of the Northwest Wrestling Officials Association.

In one of the matches held during that wrestling meet, Stephen Carabba, a senior at Anacortes High School and a member of that school's varsity wrestling squad, was opposed by Roger Anderson, a senior at Oak Harbor High School. Both boys wrestled in the 145-pound-weight division.

Near the end of the third round of the match between these two boys, Anderson, who was well ahead on points, was attempting to pin Stephen Carabba's shoulders to the mat and thus score additional points for his team. In the course of this attempt, he was alternating half nelsons, first to one side and then to the other, trying to roll Carabba into a pin position. This process had taken the boys to the northwest corner of the main mat near where small side mats were placed against the main mat. The referee, Mr. Erhart, noticed a separation between the main mat and side mat, and moved to close the gap to protect the contestants should they roll in that direction and off the main mat onto the bare floor. In so doing, his attention was diverted from the boys momentarily.

---

[46] George F. Will, "Baseball's Judicial Branch," *Washington Post*, April 9, 2009.

While the referee's attention was so diverted, Anderson applied what appeared to many of the eyewitnesses to be a full nelson. The estimates made by the witnesses of the length of time during which the full nelson was applied varied from 1 to 10 or more seconds.

Almost simultaneously the buzzer sounded the end of the round, the referee blew his whistle, and Anderson broke the hold on Carabba after a final lunge. Carabba slumped to the mat, unable to move due to the severance of a major portion of his spinal cord resulting in permanent paralysis of all voluntary functions below the level of his neck. . . .

Source: *Reprinted from Westlaw with permission of Thomson Reuters.*

The case of *Brown v. National Football League* involved the maiming of a player when a NFL referee threw a penalty flag weighted with BB pellets that struck Orlando Brown in the eye, causing him to sustain injuries that ended his professional football career.

CASE 4-17 *Brown v. National Football League*

219 F.Supp.2d 372 (S.D.N.Y. 2002)

On December 19, 1999, during the second quarter of a football game in Cleveland in which Brown was playing, NFL referee Jeff Triplette ("Triplette") called a "false start" penalty and released a penalty flag to signal the infraction. Brown alleges that instead of properly dropping the penalty flag in accordance with NFL rules, regulations, and guidelines, Triplette negligently threw the weighted penalty flag into the air in Brown's direction. The flag flew through an opening in Brown's protective helmet and struck him in the eye. The incident caused serious injury to Brown's eye, such that "[h]e can no longer play football without significant risk of sustaining further damage to his eye, including blindness." As a result, Brown's previously successful and potentially lucrative career as a professional football player came to an end.

Source: *Reprinted from Westlaw with permission of Thomson Reuters.*

1. What duty of safety did the referee breach in the *Brown* case, if any?
2. Do you consider the official's actions merely an accident?

In Case 4-18, some softball players got out of control and the umpires were forced to deal with their boorish and unsportsmanlike behavior.

📖 CASE 4-18 *Santopietro v. City of New Haven*

682 A.2d 106 (1996)

On October 16, 1988, Raymond Santopietro, Jr. attended a softball game played at East Shore Park in New Haven by teams belonging to an organized league. David Brennan and Bruce Shepard served as the umpires for that game. Mark Piombino was a participant in the game.

Santopietro, Jr. observed the softball game from a position behind the backstop and was not on the field of play. Santopietro, Jr. was approximately ten to fifteen feet from his son watching another game being played on an adjacent field.

In the sixth inning, Piombino came to bat in the game that Santopietro, Jr., was watching and hit a fly ball. In frustration, he intentionally flung his bat toward the backstop. Somehow the bat passed through the backstop and struck Santopietro, Jr., in the head. As a result, Santopietro, Jr., suffered a fractured skull and other serious injuries.

During the course of the game that Santopietro, Jr., was watching when he was injured, there occurred several incidents of unruly behavior by players who were on the same team as Piombino. Some players used vulgar language in a loud and angry manner. Players taunted members of the other team in an attempt to intimidate them. Players threw their gloves and kicked the dirt, and one player kicked a garbage can, upsetting its contents and creating a loud noise. After his turn at bat resulted in an out, another player angrily threw a bat along the ground in the direction of the bats not in use. Another player threw his glove from the pitcher's mound into the dugout. A player inside the dugout repeatedly banged a bat against the dugout, producing a loud noise. . . .

After passing a written examination, Brennan and Shepard were both trained and approved to be softball [umpires] by the Amateur Softball Association (association), a national organization that regulates the conduct of organized amateur softball in the United States. Both Brennan and Shepard possessed years of experience and had umpired hundreds of games. Shepard had received an award honoring him for being the best umpire in New Haven. Brennan testified that, as an umpire, he possesses specialized knowledge about softball and softball rules that is greater than the average person's knowledge. Both Brennan and Shepard were familiar with the association's rules governing the conduct of umpires.

Brennan and Shepard testified that when they observed unsportsmanlike conduct, they would issue a warning and, if the warning was disregarded,

they would eject the player from the game. Specifically, they testified that they would have taken such action if they had observed the
disruptive behavior described by several witnesses, including taunting, loud swearing, kicking a garbage can, hitting the inside of the
dugout with a bat, or throwing a glove from the pitcher's mound into
the dugout.

Brennan and Shepard further testified that when they give a warning,
it usually has the effect of stopping the disruptive behavior and preventing future improper acts. They testified that any player who
tosses a bat should be ejected immediately, and Brennan testified that
if he had seen a player toss a bat as described by the witnesses, he
would have ejected that player without warning. They testified that
such disciplinary action is an effective means by which to control the
actions of players.

Shepard testified that, as an umpire, he had the duty to maintain control of the game to prevent harm to spectators, and that warnings constitute the primary means by which to maintain that control. Moreover,
Brennan testified that umpires have the authority to suspend the game
if necessary to keep order or to prevent harm to spectators.

Brennan and Shepard also testified that the decision of whether to
impose discipline in any given instance of unruly behavior is a discretionary matter for the umpire. Brennan testified that the rule
against unsportsmanlike conduct gives the umpire authority "at his
discretion, to disqualify any player who exhibits unsportsmanlike conduct in the judgment of the umpire." He further testified that decisions whether to take disciplinary action in response to loud
swearing, throwing a glove or kicking dirt "are umpire judgment or
umpire discretion calls." Shepard testified that the question of
whether unruly behavior, such as using loud and abusive language,
throwing a glove or kicking a garbage can, constitutes unsportsmanlike
conduct will depend on the particular situation. Shepard further testified that the determination of whether unsportsmanlike conduct has
occurred sometimes depends upon "the whole tenor of what is going on,
the language, plus the gloves, plus whether it's considered taunting
or not." Similarly, Brennan testified that "[t]here are a lot of vari-
ables that go into" determining whether unsportsmanlike conduct has
occurred. Brennan further testified concerning the subjective nature
of the decision whether to discipline a player for unsportsmanlike
conduct. Specifically, he stated that "the majority of the time you'll
find that umpires are former players, and umpires will use the term
unsportsmanlike conduct as some type of action which, had I been a
player, I wouldn't like done to me, I wouldn't let another group do it
to another player."

In the absence of exceptional circumstances, a softball umpire, when confronted with unruly behavior by a player that arguably constitutes unsportsmanlike conduct, faces a spectrum of discretionary options. At one end of the spectrum is taking no action; at the other end is ejection of the player or suspension of the game. In between are warnings and other appropriate disciplinary action. The umpire has discretion, within the spectrum, to respond to the offensive behavior in the manner that the umpire finds to be most appropriate in the given circumstances.

An umpire obtains, through formal training and experience, a familiarity with the rules of the sport, a technical expertise in their application, and an understanding of the likely consequences of officiating decisions. As a result, the umpire possesses knowledge of the standard of care to which an umpire reasonably may be held, and of what constitutes a violation of that standard.

Umpires such as Brennan and Shepard have a duty to exercise reasonable judgment as umpires in order to maintain control of a game so as to prevent an unreasonable risk of injury to others. Brennan and Shepard testified that unsportsmanlike conduct is prohibited and that it is appropriate for an umpire to take action to prevent or stop such conduct. They further testified that the umpire possesses the authority to warn players, eject them or suspend the game if necessary to deter unsportsmanlike conduct or to maintain control of a game. Moreover, when questioned about specific incidents that allegedly had occurred during the game at which Santopietro, Jr., was injured, Brennan and Shepard testified that if they had seen the incidents described by the witnesses, they would have taken some disciplinary action. They also testified, however, that the umpire possesses discretion in the application of the rule prohibiting unsportsmanlike conduct and that the decision whether to take some action against a player is made according to the judgment of the umpire based on the specific circumstances. Neither Brennan nor Shepard testified that, in the specific circumstances of that game, a reasonable umpire would have been required to take action in response to those incidents, or that it would have been unreasonable for an umpire not to have taken such action.

Brennan and Shepard improperly failed to act in response to two incidents. First, witnesses testified that a player tossed a bat toward other bats after an unsuccessful plate appearance. Brennan and Shepard testified that the local rule required them to eject immediately any player who throws a bat. Brennan further testified that the incident described by the witnesses would "merit an ejection." If we were to interpret this testimony to constitute an expert opinion that a reasonable umpire must have ejected the player in those circumstances, then this evidence would support the conclusion that Brennan and

Shepard improperly failed to act with respect to that particular incident. Second, a witness testified that some players taunted members of the other team. Shepard testified that an umpire should take immediate action in response to taunting.

Source: *Reprinted from Westlaw with permission of Thomson Reuters.*

In the following Case 4-19, more violent play erupted at a softball game resulting in injuries. What could the sports officials have done in this case to prevent violence from breaking out?

CASE 4-19 *Donnell v. Spring Sports, Inc.*

920 S.W.2d 378 (Tex. App.—Houston [1st Dist.] 1996)

On the evening of August 18, 1991, Donnell was pitching for the softball team "Ground Zero" against the team "Ten White Guys and a Mexican." The game was played at Softball Plus, a softball park owned by Spring Sports. During the game, Donnell got into a fight with members of the opposing team and sustained the following injuries: (1) a bruised kidney that had to be removed; (2) a torn intestine; (3) a bruised liver; (4) internal bleeding; (5) two black eyes; and (6) lacerations to the head. Donnell sued "Ten White Guys and a Mexican" and Wammack [manager, "Ten White Guys and a Mexican"] for negligence and gross negligence based on the use of force and profane language against Donnell. He sued Spring Sports for negligence and gross negligence based on failure to maintain proper security on the premises.

In his deposition, Donnell testified he paid $1 to enter the park and received a ticket that was redeemable at the concession stand for a small beer or soda. He redeemed his ticket for a beer before the first game.

Donnell said "Ground Zero" played games at Softball Plus for at least a year before this incident without getting into any fights. The fight happened during the middle of the second game of the evening when "Ground Zero" was losing by seven or eight runs. "Ten White Guys and a Mexican" was at bat and Donnell was pitching for "Ground Zero." There was a runner on third base. As Donnell went to catch an infield fly, the ball spun out of his glove and onto the ground. The runner on third base advanced toward home plate. Donnell picked up the ball and, after realizing he could not make a play at first base, looked toward home to make a play. As he turned to throw the ball, Donnell saw that the catcher was not behind home plate. The runner advancing toward home stopped several feet short of the plate and began to "dance" and taunt Donnell. In frustration, Donnell threw the ball at the runner and hit him in the side or somewhere in his midsection.

Donnell then turned and walked toward the dugout. As he crossed the third base line into foul territory, Donnell was hit in the back and knocked to the ground. Several members from the other team hit and kicked him. Although he tried to protect his head with his arms, Donnell remembered getting beaten around the head and midsection. After he stood up, he sustained a final blow to the face that nearly knocked him unconscious. Donnell did not remember how the fight ended, but he returned to finish the game.

Evette Donnell, [Donnell]'s wife, stated in an affidavit she attended several of her husband's games and was there the night of the fight. She testified: (1) her husband paid to gain admittance to the park and to play on the team; (2) Softball Plus had been the site of a number of past disorderly occurrences; (3) alcohol was served at the games and consumed by the players and spectators; (4) "Ten White Guys and a Mexican" were using profanity and appeared intoxicated before the game in which her husband was injured; (5) "Ten White Guys and a Mexican" had a reputation for aggressiveness and intimidation and had been involved in confrontations with other teams when profanity had been used and scuffles had occurred; and (6) she did not see any security guards monitoring the field on the night of the fight or at any other games.

R.C. Sanchez, an umpire of the game in which Donnell was injured, stated in deposition he had served as an umpire for "Ten White Guys and a Mexican" at other games and the players had always conducted themselves in a sportsmanlike manner. Sanchez testified that the incident in question occurred in the following manner: A batter from "Ten White Guys and a Mexican" hit an infield fly that touched the ground before Donnell had a chance to catch it. The runner from third base, before scoring, stopped to taunt his opponents. After the play was over and the base runner was walking to his dugout, Donnell picked up the ball and threw a line drive that hit the runner in the back. Sanchez testified that, in his opinion, Donnell threw the ball with the intent to hurt the base runner. As the base runner turned around, Donnell said something to him. The base runner and Donnell ran toward each other and met in front of the mound, where they began fighting. Although both teams immediately joined the fight, Sanchez testified the fight lasted no longer than one-and-a-half minutes. Both teams returned to complete the game.

Sanchez said he would have ejected Donnell from the game for hitting another player with the ball, but the fight started too quickly for him to do so. He noted that park rules prohibited umpires from breaking up fights, and said he did not know who was supposed to break up fights. Finally, Sanchez stated that he had observed 10 to 12 small fights while umpiring games at *other* ball parks, but none as serious as this incident.

Wammack, the manager for "Ten White Guys," stated in deposition his team had played "Ground Zero" before without any problems. Wammack testified that although both teams entered the field when the fight began, Donnell and the base runner were the only two individuals actually involved in the fight. Wammack said the fight occurred so quickly that there was nothing the umpires could have done to prevent it from happening. Further, he said the confrontation between the two teams lasted no longer than a minute before it was broken up by the umpires.

Donald R. Millik testified in deposition that Softball Plus employed a night manager to take phone calls and deal with customers, four concessionaires to serve food and beverages at the games, a ticket booth employee to take the entry fee at the park's entrance, and daytime maintenance crews. Millik also stated that the park's umpires were independent contractors hired by the teams and Spring Sports did not hire an independent security firm to monitor games. Softball Plus did not post any park rules before this incident in which Donnell was injured.

1. Donnell testified in deposition that "Ground Zero" played games at Softball Plus for at least a year before the incident in question without engaging in any fights.
2. Sanchez testified in deposition that he had umpired previous games for "Ten White Guys," and they conducted themselves in a sportsmanlike manner.
3. Sanchez also testified he had seen 10 to 12 small fights while umpiring games at other ball parks but had never witnessed a fight "like this one" before.
4. Wammack testified in deposition that "Ten White Guys and a Mexican" had played "Ground Zero" before without fighting.
5. Donnell, Sanchez, and Wammack testified the fight occurred after Donnell threw a ball that hit a base runner for "Ten White Guys."
6. Sanchez and Wammack both testified the fight started very quickly and was broken up very quickly—it lasted only 45 to 90 seconds.
7. Sanchez testified he would have ejected Donnell from the game for having hit an opposing player with the softball, but the fight erupted within seconds of that act.
8. Donald Millik testified in deposition that before this incident, no rules were posted at the ball park prohibiting alcohol, profanity, or physical abuse, and Spring Sports did not employ security guards.
9. Evette Donnell submitted an affidavit in which she testified:
     A. Softball Plus had been the site of a number of past disorderly occurrences.
     B. Alcohol was served at the games and consumed by the players and spectators.
     C. "Ten White Guys and a Mexican" appeared intoxicated before the game in which her husband was injured.

D. "Ten White Guys and a Mexican" had a reputation for aggressiveness and intimidation and had been involved in confrontations
   with other teams when profanity had been used and scuffles had
   occurred.

E. She saw no security guards at the game on the night of the fight
   or at any other game.

Source: *Reprinted from Westlaw with permission of Thomson Reuters.*

NOTES AND DISCUSSION QUESTIONS

Participant Ethics

1. *Bourque v. Duplechin* discussed the concept of sportsmanship as a good ethical decision. In that case, Duplechin made a bad ethical decision by acting in an unsportsmanlike manner. Duplechin was purported to have purposefully moved 5 feet off his intended route to strike Bourque. If he only veered 2 feet from his path, would that have been unsportsmanlike behavior? What other facts might also suggest unsportsmanlike behavior?

2. Is it ethical to allow a sport to continue to be played in such a fashion that concussions are a part of "doing business"? What mandatory safeguards should be in place to prevent concussions?

Coaches' Ethics

3. Los Angeles Lakers coach Phil Jackson was reprimanded by the NBA for making a sexual reference in his postgame remarks following a 107–92 loss to the Spurs in San Antonio. "We call this a Brokeback Mountain game, because there's so much penetration and kick-outs. . . . It was one of those games."[47]

4. In *Nydegger v. Don Bosco Preparatory High School,* 495 A.2d 485 (1985), a high school soccer coach urged his athletes to compete in an "aggressive and intense manner," which allegedly led to an injury when one of the players in the opposing team was injured. If the coach urged the players to play aggressively while inferring that they should ignore the risk of injury or that they should intentionally cause injury, then the coach's behavior would be unethical. An ethical coach would require his athletes to play fairly and according to the rules.

5. In *Nganga v. College of Wooster,* 557 N.E. 2d 152 (Ohio 1989), an intramural soccer player sued the opposing team, who were allegedly known for their rough play, for his injury as a result of a slide tackle.

6. In *City of Miami v. Cisneros,* 662 So.2d 1272 (Fla. 1995), a 78-lb 11-year-old broke his leg tackling another player who weighed 128 lbs. Did the coach violate an ethical duty by allowing two players with such disparate weight to compete against each other?

7. In *Koffman v. Garnett,* 574 S.E.2d 258 (Va. 2003), a middle school football player was injured when a coach thrust his arm around the player's body, lifted him off his feet, and slammed him to the ground while explaining proper tackling technique. How should this coach be disciplined for his actions?

---

[47] Associated Press, "Phil Jackson Under Fire for 'Brokeback Mountain' Remark," *USA Today,* November 15, 2007.

8. In *Kelly v. North Highlands Recreation and Park District*, 2006 WL 1652667 (E.D.Cal.), . . . Adam G. Kelly was thirteen years old at the time of the events in question. . . . Ralphelia B. Grandinetti is Adam's foster mother and legal guardian. Adam is a "special needs" foster child who has the mentality of a child of six to eight years of age and who also has epilepsy and some physical abnormalities. Adam was a member of [the] North Highlands Recreation & Park District's ("District") swim team, the "Highlander Dolphins Swim Team."

On June 14, 2004, Adam was participating in his scheduled swimming practice . . . Christine Bagley ("Bagley"), a swim coach for the team, placed or forced Adam to sit on a hot metal folding chair in direct sun in approximately 100 degree weather as some sort of discipline. Adam was forced to remain on the hot metal chair for approximately 35–45 minutes while Bagley yelled at Adam only inches from his face. When Adam complained that the hot metal chair was hurting him and got up from the chair, Bagley yelled at Adam that he had to remain in the chair and physically forced Adam back into the chair . . . as a result of these events, Adam became seriously ill and was treated at the Mercy San Juan Hospital Emergency Room that evening and into the next morning. How should this coach be disciplined?

9. In *O'Brien v. Ohio State University*, 2007 Ohio 4833, 2007 Ohio App. LEXIS 4316, former basketball coach James O'Brien gave $6,000 to the mother of a basketball recruit who had just lost her husband in a war-torn region of the former Yugoslavia. The coach's conduct in making the loan to the family of the recruiting prospect and then failing to report it to the university's athletic director constituted a breach of employment agreement because his actions were contrary to NCAA's rules and regulations. Would the additional facts that it was O'Brien's own money and that the prospect, Alex Radojevic, never played for Ohio State, change your opinion regarding the ethical choices that coach O'Brien made?

10. How important is it for the coach to be a role model at the collegiate level? What about at the high school level?

11. Is it ethical for college football coaches to make more money than professors at an institution of higher learning? More than the president of the university?

12. In *Mogabgab v. New Orleans Parish School Board*, 239 So. 2d 456 (La.App., 1970), coaches were negligent by actively denying players access to treatment for some 2 hours after symptoms of heat stroke and shock appeared.

13. Coaches should be trained to properly instruct students. In *Stehn v. Bernarr MacFadden Foundations, Inc.*, 434 F. 2d 811 (C.A.Tenn. 1970), a wrestling coach instructed other wrestlers to use the "agura" maneuver, but failed to explain a method of escape or a defense to the hold.

14. It is both ethically and legally consistent that coaches must refrain from sexually harassing employees.[48]

15. Coaches should remain in control at all times and not give obscene gestures (flipping the bird) to the opposing team.[49]

16. Coaches should be careful not to overemphasize the importance of a win or loss by keeping in mind that it is just a game.[50]

---

[48] See Richard Sandomir, "Jury Finds Knicks and Coach Harassed a Former Executive," *New York Times*, October 3, 2007, A1.

[49] See Associated Press, "Wyoming Coach Apologizes for Gesture," *Denver Post*, November 12, 2007.

[50] Associated Press, "Saban References 9/11, Pearl Harbor as Examples," *College Football*, November 20, 2007.

17. Coaches should refrain from ordering intentional "hits"[51] like John Chaney did.
18. How do you place the remarks from former Texas Tech football coach, Mike Leach, who blamed his team's loss on the players' "fat little girlfriends"? Should he apologize? He refused to do so.[52]
19. For further study, see Earl F. Hoerner, *Safety in American Football*, ASTM International, 1997; Thomas R. Hurst and James N. Knight, "Coaches' Liability for Athletes' Injuries and Deaths," *Seton Hall Journal of Sports Law* (2003); Hee-Joon Shin and Joeng-Woong Baik, "Vicarious Liability Against University and Coach," *Journal of Physical Education, Recreation, and Dance* 75 (2004); Anthony C. Luke and Michael F. Bergeron, "Heat Injury Prevention Practices in High School Football," *Clinical Journal of Sport Medicine* 17, no. 6 (November 2007).

Sports Officials' Ethics

20. A gambling referee lacks integrity. If there is a possibility that gambling exists in a sport, it will no longer be viewed as a fair contest. What should be done to prevent a recurrence of this type of unethical behavior?
21. Should sports officials be required to disclose all potential conflicts of interest similar to a judge? Should a referee be disqualified from officiating a game, a relative is playing in?
22. What ethical duties do sports officials owe to a crowd at a sporting event?[53]
23. A sports official should never threaten or inappropriately touch a player.[54]
24. The baseball umpire has been the subject of much debate.[55]
25. For further comparisons of umpires and judges, consider the following:

> "It's like the Constitution," . . . "The strike zone is a living, breathing document." Last week, the umpire Marty Foster called the Yankees' Derek Jeter out on a steal of third and though it appeared he was never tagged, Mr. Jeter said Mr. Foster explained that he didn't need to be tagged to be called out because the ball beat him to the bag. Talk about judicial activism. An uproar arose over this, but in fact, if that's what Mr. Foster said, he was simply—if unwisely—expressing aloud a generally unspoken umpire tenet that allows for some discretion on close plays to keep managers and fans, who can clearly see throws but not tags from the dugout or the stands, from causing a ruckus.[56]

---

[51] See Jere Longman, "Temple Increases Suspension for Chaney," *New York Times*, February 26, 2005.
[52] See James Gilbert, "Texas Tech Coach Blames Loss on 'Fat Little Girlfriends,'" *WLTX*, October 29, 2009.
[53] See "Chile Officials Blame T.O. Police for Soccer Brawl," *CTV News*, August 22, 2010.
[54] See "NFL Fines Official for Physical Contact with Players," *Fort Worth Star Telegram*, December 29, 2007, D4.
[55] See David Q. Voigt, "America's Manufactured Villain: The Baseball Umpire," *Journal of Popular Culture* 4, no. 1 (Summer 1970): 1–21; J. D. Larsen and D. W. Rainey, "Judgment Bias in Baseball Umpires' First Base Calls: A Computer Simulation," *Journal of Sport and Exercise Psychology* 13, no. 1 (1991): 75–79; William Blake, "Umpires as Legal Realists," *Social Science Research Network*, July 23, 2010; Richard Lempert, "Error Behind the Plate and in the Law," *Southern California Law Review* (1985–1986); D. Rainey and G. Schweickert, "Fans' Evaluations of Major League Baseball Umpires' Performances and Perceptions of Appropriate Behavior," *Journal of Sport Behavior* 13, no. 2 (1990): 122–129; Kirkley L. Russell, "A Qualitative Investigation of Confidence of Novice and Experienced American Legion Baseball Umpires," Dissertation, 2007; Ge Weizhuo, "Study on Baseball Umpire Selection from Psychological Characteristics," *Journal of Tianjin Institute of Physical Education* (1995).
[56] Bruce Weber, "Umpires v. Judges," *New York Times*, July 12, 2009.

26. When does sports officials' conduct on the field cross the line?[57]
27. Do you agree with the proposition that sports officials are supposed to be seen and not heard?[58]
28. The quintessential sports official will be a model of trust and integrity.[59]
29. Be careful as a participant, if you criticize an umpire too much, he or she may sue you![60]
30. An sports official should never get involved or give the impression he or she is involved in a play on the field.[61]
31. For further study on bias, see Matt Sussman, "Proof of Umpire Conspiracy Against Detroit Tigers Surfaces," *Michigan Live*, June 28, 2010; Tony D. Myers, Nigel J. Balmer, Alan M. Nevill, and Yahya Al-Nakeeb, "Evidence of Nationalistic Bias in Muay-Thai," *Journal of Sports Science and Medicine* (July 2006); "David Stern Fires Back at Referee Bias Study," *New York Times*, May 7, 2007; Babatunde Buraimo, David Forrest, and Robert Simmons, "The 12th Man?: Refereeing Bias in English and German Soccer," *Journal of the Royal Statistical Society* 173, no. 2 (April 2010); Kyle J. Anderson and David A. Pierce, "Officiating Bias: The Effect of Foul Differential on Foul Calls in NCAA Basketball," *Journal of Sports Sciences* 27, no. 7 (May 2009); Alan Schwarz, "A Finding of Umpire Bias Is Small but Still Striking," *New York Times*, August 19, 2007; Per Pettersson-Lidbom and Mikael Priks, "Behavior Under Social Pressure: Empty Italian Stadiums and Referee Bias," *Economic Letters,* February 17, 2009; "Is Home-Country Bias Inevitable for Figure-Skating Judges?" *New York Times*, February 24, 2010; John W. Emerson, Miki Seltzer, and David Lin, "Assessing Judging Bias: An Example From the 2000 Olympic Games," *The American Statistician* 63, no. 2 (May 1, 2009).

---

[57] See Joshua Robinson, "Did an Umpire Cross the Line at Shea?" *New York Times*, June 25, 2008.

[58] See Wallace Matthews, "Ump Should Be Praised, Not Punished," *ESPN.com*, April 8, 2010.

[59] See Andy Katz, "Referees Desperate to Avoid Credibility Issues," *ESPN.com,* July 23, 2007; Tony Massarotti, "Public Trust Has Officially Been Lost," *Boston Globe*, June 4, 2010.

[60] See Muray Chass, "Umpire's Suit Against Piniella Is Settled Out of Court," *New York Times*, December 19, 1991.

[61] See "Spurrier, SEC Clear Official in Collision with South Carolina QB Garcia," *ESPN.com*, October 20, 2008.

ETHICAL CONSIDERATIONS
FOR PARENTS AND FANS

Parents and fans are essential to any successful sports program or franchise. Ethical concerns abound, however, with abusive parents injuring coaches and children, and out-of-control fans engaging in unethical conduct.[1] Parents are a significant part of any youth sports organization. Many serve as volunteers and are necessary for the administration and the eventual success of the league. Ethical parents are supportive of coaches, participants, and other parents. They teach young athletes respect for coaches, other participants, and sports officials. Parents set the tone for their young athlete by setting an example of a true sportsman. Fans are essential to professional sports; after all, they buy tickets! Ethical fans are not obsessed with their hero as was Wesley Snipes in the movie *The Fan* with Robert De Niro. Good fans are polite and not abusive: they are, in essence, good sports.

Negative comments or acts of displeasure from parents or fans toward the coach, visiting team, or officials undermine the sporting efforts of all involved. Ethical standards attempt to mold good behavior on the part of parents and fans. These standards usually come into play as punishment for unacceptable behavior, with the hope that these penalties will act as a deterrent of future acts of bad behavior or poor sportsmanship by both parents and fans.

PARENTAL ETHICS

The joy of being a parent of a young athlete comes from watching your child compete in athletic events and, of course, winning. No one likes to lose, but for a young athlete it is inevitable; the athlete must learn to lose and be a good sport in the process. That is a tough task for a 9-year-old but sometimes an even tougher task for the parents of that child. Young athletes are encouraged and are excited when they look into the stands and see their parents cheering for them.[2]

---

[1] Michael Crowley, "Outrageous! Field of Screams," *Reader's Digest*, October 2007.
[2] "Soccer Moms Gone Wild: When Parents Need to Be Refereed at Youth Sports Games," *Wall Street Journal*, April 28, 2009.

Amateur sports leagues and associations sometimes have a difficult job ensuring that parents set good examples for their children, play within the rules, act ethically, and conduct themselves properly at sporting events. Many parents are enthralled with the idea of their child hitting the winning home run, scoring the winning touchdown, or making the winning goal. There is certainly nothing wrong with that, but when a parent loses his or her focus or perspective, then trouble looms on the horizon.[3]

The Standard of Appropriate Behavior for Parents

The standard of appropriate behavior for parents is the reasonably prudent parent. Ethical parents view the participation of their child in sports as a part of the educational process. Participation in interscholastic or youth sports is a learning experience for students; kids will make mistakes and parents must understand that. Ethical parents praise their children's attempts to improve as dedicated students, athletes, and citizens. Parents must operate as role models for their children in all areas of life, and that includes sports participation. Parents should encourage good sportsmanship by demonstrating positive support for all players, coaches, and officials at every game or practice. Parents' conduct is considered unethical if they "misbehave." Parents would do well to follow these suggestions:

1. Stress good sportsmanship. Talk to youth participants about what it means to be a good sport. Stress that "winning isn't everything," especially at the early stages of youth involvement in sport.
2. Watch for "teachable" moments. If a scenario arises where youth sports participants can learn a lesson, step in and instruct.
3. Teach how to lose gracefully. Shaking hands with the opposing team and teaching youth participants how to accept defeat is a giant step toward good sportsmanship.
4. "Check yourself." If emotions are getting out of control, step away from the field and perform a self-evaluation of your own conduct.

Hostile and abusive parents at youth sporting events are a far too common occurrence in recent years.[4] For whatever reason, Little League baseball and youth sports in general, seem to bring out the worst in some parents. Whether it is the dad who sends "nasty" e-mails to his son's t-ball coach, or the mom who complains about how everything is organized but does nothing to support the team, irate and negative parents come in all forms. The majority of parents are well-behaved, but a few disruptive parents can sour youth sports for the good people. Everyone cannot be Chrissy Lisle, Little League Mom of the Year (although we wish they could be). Stephen D. Keener, President and Chief Executive Officer of Little League Baseball and Softball, said of Ms. Lisle:

> This year's Mom of the Year truly represents the majority of Little League Moms. Growing up with baseball as part of her life, Chrissy Lisle has a special appreciation for the game and what Little League is about. As a parent, she has embraced the role of Little League volunteer by simply enjoying the experience. Serving as a team mom, while supporting her children and husband during this special time in all their lives, has shown her to be an impactful role model. Little League International is pleased to honor her with this special award.[5]

---

[3] Michelle Koidin, "'Cheerleader Mom' Freed After Serving Six Months," *Associated Press*, March 1, 1997.
[4] William Wilcoxen, "Out-of-Control Parents Threaten Youth Sports," *Minnesota Public Radio*, July 19, 2001.
[5] "Chrissy Lisle Recognized as 2009 Little League Mom of the Year," *LittleLeague.org*, July 31, 2009.

In contrast to Ms. Lisle is Matthew Collins, an out-of-control parent, who assaulted a coach after a Little League baseball game.[6] Criminal acts have even occurred at youth sports. Unbelievably, in a Little League game in Vallejo, California, a parent was stabbed.[7] With tight family schedules and kids playing 40-plus games in a short season, taking music lessons, playing Wii, and sometimes even doing homework, parents, kids, and coaches are under extreme pressure.[8]

Former MLB Most Valuable Player Dale Murphy knows a thing or two about playing baseball and being a good sport. His "I Won't Cheat Foundation" is "on a mission to encourage young players to avoid shortcuts":

> It takes courage, and we encourage kids to speak up. One of the more challenging things in life is not being the guy who does the cheating, but not saying anything about it and going along with it. . . . Kids especially, they need as many people as possible to say: You don't want to do that. You want to do it the right way to be successful. Kids see the short-term gain, that's kind of the challenge with all of us at any age—you see the short-term gain, you don't see the long-term consequences.[9]

What parents say to their children can have a major affect on their sports experience. Six-year-olds do not need to be told they are showing "lack of effort," are "dogging it," or are not giving it "110 percent." After all, sports are supposed to be fun (at least to a certain point). Little League parents would be wise to consider how the sport of baseball is played and the pace of the game. Nine players waiting in a field to hopefully get a chance to "muff" a "soft" ball is not exactly an activity the average 5-year-old considers enticing. Parents should keep in mind the nature of the sport when "encouraging" their child to be successful. What about penalizing disruptive parents and keeping them a certain distance from the field? About a hundred yards to be exact! That is what happened to a parent in one Maryland soccer league. The league president said:

> The league's disciplinary board has had better luck barring individual parents from attending games in the past three years rather than fining them, because the parents would pay the money and continue the bad behavior. We have taken a strong stance. It's important. This isn't the World Cup . . . and for the parents to be shrieking on the sidelines and belittling people goes against everything we're trying to do . . . it's not acceptable behavior.[10]

Little League Baseball has set forth the following parent code of conduct for all participating parents:

Sport Parent Code of Conduct

```
We, the _____ Little League, have implemented the following
Sport Parent Code of Conduct for the important message it holds about
```

[6] Jason Lea, "Court Date Delayed Again for Man Accused of Attacking Little League Coach," *The News-Herald*, June 15, 2010. See also Skip Bayless, "Little League Is Out of Control," *ESPN.com*, August 31, 2006.
[7] Joe Vazquez, "Parent Stabbed at Vallejo Little League Game Fight," *CBS.com*, May 19, 2010.
[8] Bernie Augustine, "Big Demands on Little League Parents," *SILive.com*, August 26, 2009. Also see Les Edgerton, *Surviving Little League: For Players, Parents, and Coaches* (New York: Taylor Trade Publishing, 2004).
[9] Associated Press, "Former MVP Takes a Stand Against Cheating," *New York Times*, August 14, 2010.
[10] Annie Gowen, "100-Yard Penalty on Players' Parents: Fans of Md. Soccer Team Banned After a Few Berate the Referee," *Washington Post*, April 21, 2009.

the proper role of parents in supporting their child in sports. Parents should read, understand, and sign this form prior to their children participating in our league.

Any parent guilty of improper conduct at any game or practice will be asked to leave the sports facility and be suspended from the following game. Repeat violations may cause a multiple game suspension, or the season forfeiture of the privilege of attending all games.

Preamble

The essential elements of character-building and ethics in sports are embodied in the concept of sportsmanship and six core principles:

- Trustworthiness,
- Respect,
- Responsibility,
- Fairness,
- Caring, and
- Good Citizenship.

The highest potential of sports is achieved when competition reflects these "six pillars of character."

I therefore agree:

1. I will not force my child to participate in sports.
2. I will remember that children participate to have fun and that the game is for youth, not adults.
3. I will inform the coach of any physical disability or ailment that may affect the safety of my child or the safety of others.
4. I will learn the rules of the game and the policies of the league.
5. I (and my guests) will be a positive role model for my child and encourage sportsmanship by showing respect and courtesy, and by demonstrating positive support for all players, coaches, officials, and spectators at every game, practice or other sporting event.
6. I (and my guests) will not engage in any kind of unsportsmanlike conduct with any official, coach, player, or parent such as booing and taunting; refusing to shake hands; or using profane language or gestures.
7. I will not encourage any behaviors or practices that would endanger the health and well being of the athletes.
8. I will teach my child to play by the rules and to resolve conflicts without resorting to hostility or violence.
9. I will demand that my child treat other players, coaches, officials, and spectators with respect regardless of race, creed, color, sex or ability.
10. I will teach my child that doing one's best is more important than winning, so that my child will never feel defeat by the outcome of a game or his/her performance.

11. I will praise my child for competing fairly and trying hard, and make my child feel like a winner every time.

12. I will never ridicule or yell at my child or other participants for making a mistake or losing a competition.

13. I will emphasize skill development and practices and how they benefit my child over winning. I will also de-emphasize games and competition in the lower age groups.

14. I will promote the emotional and physical well-being of the athletes ahead of any personal desire I may have for my child to win.

15. I will respect the officials and their authority during games and will never question, discuss, or confront coaches at the game field, and will take time to speak with coaches at an agreed upon time and place.

16. I will demand a sports environment for my child that is free from drugs, tobacco, and alcohol and I will refrain from their use at all sports events.

17. I will refrain from coaching my child or other players during games and practices, unless I am one of the official coaches of the team.

Parent/Guardian Signature

Source: © 2011 *Little League Baseball, Incorporated. All Rights Reserved.*

What are your thoughts on the parent code of conduct? Should each parent be required to sign a pledge that he or she will promote sportsmanship as well as following a code of conduct?[11]

Parental Choices

There are many ethical issues in youth sports, and none are more difficult to deal with than religion and gender. Examine the following two case studies dealing with girl participants in a boys' league and prayer before a youth sports game.

CASE STUDY 5-1 *Co-Ed Participation*

At what levels should girls no longer be allowed to participate in a boys' league, if ever? If a high school girl is capable of playing football, can she participate on the boys' team? If not, why not?[12] Should girls be allowed to play youth baseball? The Little League believes so.[13]

---

[11] For further study, see Lynn Kidman, Alex McKenzie, and Bridig McKenzie, "The Nature and Target of Parents' Comments During Youth Sport Competitions," *Journal of Sport Behavior* 22 (1999); Margaret Gatz, Michael A. Messner, and Sandra J. Ball-Rokeach, *Paradoxes of Youth and Sport* (New York: State University of New York Press, 2002).

[12] Jessica Rudis and Rich Schapiro, "Queens High Schooler Tackles Her Football Dream," *New York Daily News*, October 4, 2008.

[13] Dave Merchant, "Local Woman Changes Face of Little League Baseball," *Heritage Newspapers*, August 17, 2010; Bruce Weber, "Judge Sylvia Pressler, Who Opened Little League to Girls, Dies at 75," *New York Times*, February 17, 2010.

Check out one response to 12-year-old Jaime, a girl who was "dominating" a boys' basketball league:

They were great . . . until she blocked the first shot. Then they were like, "Hey, we don't want this big kid coming out and making us look bad," said Michael Abraham, Jaime's coach. After parents complained, The Hoop, a private league that organizes the games, told Jaime she could no longer play with the boys, citing a rule that bars mixed-gender teams.[14]

Consider the following questions regarding Jaime's participation on the boys' basketball team.

1. What actions, if any, should be taken?
2. What reasons can you provide that Jaime should not be able to play basketball with the boys? What reasons can you give in support of her participation?
3. What would you do about the parents who do not want her making their sons look bad on the court?
4. Is there an age limit at which girls should no longer participate in a boys' league?

CASE STUDY 5-2   *"There's No Religion in Baseball"*

Youth sports can present multiple problems that need to be resolved fairly and ethically. Consider the one faced by the Medford Little League in Oregon. A parent pulled his son from coach Chris Palmer's Indians baseball team (the name of which presents another ethical issue) because the parent said Palmer "forced" religion on the kids by leading them in prayer and quoting Bible verses. "All I wanted was for my daughter to sign up and play baseball this spring. Not to have religion or prayer shoved down her throat. There's a time and place for prayer—and baseball isn't it," said Mike, a former assistant coach for Palmer. Coach Palmer said, "I just pray that the Lord will watch over us. . . . I've never had anyone raise a stink about it."[15]

Consider the following questions as they relate to the place of prayer in youth sports.

1. What is wrong with a short solemn prayer for the safety of children nothwithstanding which higher power you choose to worship?[16]
2. Would a prayer at a youth sporting event be more acceptable if it uses neutral language, specifying no particular religion, during the prayer?[17]
3. Should prayer be allowed under any circumstances? What if a child is severely injured? Is prayer still prohibited under those circumstances?[18]

---

[14] Kari Pricher, Lisa Fletcher, Nicole Young, and Stephanie Dahle, "Banned from Playing Basketball with the Boys," *ABC News*, May 24, 2008.

[15] Associated Press, "Little League Calls Coach's Pre-Game Prayer Fair, Not Foul," *KCBY News*, May 3, 2010.

[16] See Dennis Collins, "Nearer My God to the Goal Line: 'Suppose I Pray to Win, and the Other Guy, He Prays to Win, What's God Gonna Do?'" *Washington Post*, November 19, 1978.

[17] See Charles S. Prebish, "'Heavenly Father, Divine Goalie': Sport and Religion," *The Antioch Review* 42, no. 3 (Summer 1984): 306–318.

[18] See Pat McManamon, "Major Gains for Boy Hit by Ball at Minor League Game," *Fanhouse.com*, July 26, 2010; Sara Pulliam Bailey, "Where God Talk Gets Sidelined: Sports Journalists Are Reluctant to Tackle Faith on the Field," *Wall Street Journal*, February 4, 2010.

4. What consideration should people of different faiths be given in this scenario?[19]

5. What role should religion play in youth sports, if any? Consider the debate over whether cheerleaders could use Bible verses on the banner a football team runs through when they enter the playing field. The principal of the school stated:

> As a Christian I would not have liked it if they had used verses from the Quran, and if I had known about it, I probably would not have approved of them doing so . . . that's the basis of the court's ruling . . . if you allow Christian verses then you have to allow Buddhist, or Jewish and everything else. And to be perfectly honest with you, that would have been a problem here.[20]

Parental Rage

People, and especially parents, can become angry, and sometimes at the smallest things. The issue becomes urgent when parents or fans fail to control their anger, and it boils over to rage with negative consequences. "Rage" has become a term of art.[21] Sports rage has been defined as "within the context of an organized athletic activity, any physical attack upon another person such as striking, wounding, or otherwise touching in an offensive manner, and/or any malicious, verbal abuse, or sustained harassment which threatens subsequent violence or bodily harm."[22] Parental rage can cause major ethical dilemmas for youth sports organizations and even present serious legal concerns.[23]

Parental rage has taken youth sports to a new level. Anyone who has ever coached a youth sports team knows it can be tainted by one "raging" parent. It would be naïve to think youth sports coaches and officials, which consists primarily of volunteers (the key word being "volunteer"), will not be subject to criticism; they will. However, violent acts and parental are different acts than verbal criticism.[24] Parental abuse or rage can include any of the following:

- Profanity
- Improper touching of a participant, referee, coach, or other parent
- Abusive language (including profanity) that demeans, ridicules, or belittles a participant's physical makeup, sex, national origin, gender, religion, skin color, skill level, sexual orientation, or parental heritage
- Entering the playing field uninvited
- Making derogatory comments to coaches, parents, officials, league officials, or other participants
- Failing to follow the rules and regulations of the league[25]

---

[19] See "Kurt Warner: Jesus Brought Me Here," *Christian Post*, January 30, 2010; Hannah Karp, "Can Buddha Help Your Short Game?" *Wall Street Journal*, April 27, 2010.

[20] L. Z. Granderson, "The Debate at Lakeview-Fort Oglethorpe," *ESPN.com*, October 6, 2009.

[21] Sophronia Scott Gregory and Adam Cohen, "Black Rage: In Defense of a Mass Murderer," *Time Magazine*, June 6, 1994.

[22] Gregg S. Heinzmann, "Parental Violence in Youth Sports: Facts, Myths, and Violence," *Youthsports.Rutgers.edu*.

[23] See Howard P. Benard, "Little League Fun, Big League Liability," *Marquette Sports Law Journal* (1997–1998).

[24] Paulo David, "Young Athletes and Competitive Sports: Exploit and Exploitation," *International Journal of Children's Rights* 7 (1999): 53–81.

[25] For further study, see G. S. Heinzmann, "Parental Violence in Youth Sports: Facts, Myths and Videotape," *National Recreation and Parks Association*; Joel Fish and Susan Magee, *101 Ways to Be a Terrific Sports Parent* (New York: Fireside, 2003).

As an SMP, what should be done to control a "raging" parent? What steps would you recommend?[26] In the following case, an out-of-control parent threatened violence against a young player. When is that ever appropriate? The simple answer: never.

📖 CASE 5-1   *Hale v. Antoniou*

2004 WL 1925551

Jordan Hale was thirteen at the time of the incident. When Jordan was in the seventh grade, he signed up to play in the Casco Bay hockey league. On December 10, 2001, Jordan's team played another team on which Michael Antoniou was a player. Jordan knew Michael and they were friends. Jordan also knew Michael's father, Demetri Antoniou.

Towards the end of the hockey game, Jordan and Michael collided. Jordan had lowered his shoulder and checked Michael. Michael went down onto the ice. Michael took a while to get up, and Jordan could tell Michael had been jarred by the hit. Michael returned to his team bench, and the game ended about ten seconds later. No penalty was called against Jordan.

From Demetri's perspective, it appeared as if Jordan drove his hockey stick onto Michael's "right jaw and right neck." Demetri testified that he thought his son might have suffered a concussion. In fact, Michael was injured as a result of the hit.

After the game, the teams went to their respective locker rooms. Jordan was in the locker room for about five minutes and had already started getting out of his hockey equipment when he saw Demetri at the doorway of his team's locker room. . . .

Scalia [Jordan's coach] testified that Demetri asked him where Jordan was, came into the locker room with a "hockey stick under—a bag on his shoulder, a hockey stick under his arm."

In his affidavit, Jordan testified that after the incident, when he tried to stand up, his knees buckled and he had to sit back down.

The court denied Demetri's motion for summary judgment, because Jordan's claims for civil assault and intentional infliction of emotional distress are allowed to go forward, their punitive damages claim were not barred by the absence of an underlying tort.

---

[26] For further study on parents and youth sports, see Dianna K. Fiore, "Parental Rage and Violence in Youth Sports: How Can We Prevent Soccer Moms and Hockey Dads from Interfering in Youth Sports and Causing Games to End in Fistfights Rather Than Handshakes," *Villanova Sports and Entertainment Law Journal* (2003); Geoffrey G. Watson, "Games, Socialization and Parental Values: Social Class Differences in Parental Evaluation of Little League Baseball," *International Review for the Sociology of Sport* (1977).

Jordan showed that there is a dispute regarding whether Demetri's alleged actions were motivated by ill will toward Jordan or so outrageous that malice towards Jordan as a result of that conduct can be implied. The court cites Scalia's testimony that Demetri asked him where Jordan was, came into the locker room with a "hockey stick under a bag on his shoulder, a hockey stick under his arm," and said, "Jordan Hale is an asshole."

Express malice exists when the defendant's tortuous conduct is motivated by ill will toward the plaintiff and that implied malice exists when deliberate conduct by the defendant, although motivated by something other than ill will toward any particular party, is so outrageous that malice toward a person injured as a result of that conduct can be implied.

Source: *Reprinted from Westlaw with permission of Thomson Reuters.*

Consider the following questions regarding Case 5-1.

1. It is clear this parent was "enraged." What discipline measures should be assessed against the parent?
2. Should a police report have been made in this case?
3. Should the parent be made to apologize to all involved?
4. Should the parent be forced to take anger management classes before he can come back to the league?

The "hockey dad" case study that follows, involves the tragic death of a parent.

CASE STUDY 5-3 *Thomas Junta, Hockey Dad*

The most notable occurrence of parental rage resulted in the death of a young hockey player's father at a Massachusetts hockey rink. The encounter between Thomas Junta, known as the "Hockey Dad," and Michael Costin occurred on July 5, 2000. Costin was supervising a hockey practice for 10-year-old boys, including his three sons and Junta's son. Junta was in the stands observing his son in a non-contact scrimmage.

During the scrimmage, Junta became upset when he saw players acting rough and engaging in what he thought was unnecessary "body-checking." Junta then left the stands and went onto the ice, yelling at Costin for allowing the rough play between the boys. Costin was in his protective hockey gear and attacked Junta by choking him with Junta's necklace and then kicking Junta's shins and feet with the 3-inch blades of his ice skates. After the physical altercation, a rink employee separated Junta and Costin and requested that Junta leave the rink. Junta left the rink with his son and later returned to pick up his son's two friends.

When Junta returned to the rink, he once again ran into Costin. A second argument ensued, and both men "squared off" and began punching each other. Junta threw Costin to the floor and repeatedly beat Costin in the head and the neck. Upon their arrival at the rink, paramedics found Costin without a pulse. At the hospital, he fell into a coma and was placed on a ventilator. A day after the incident, Michael Costin was declared brain dead, was removed from the ventilator, and died. Junta surrendered to the police and was arrested for manslaughter.

In January 2002, Junta's trial began with jury selection, which consisted of asking potential jurors if they had children, if their children played on sports teams, and if they ever had witnessed an incident of parental rage at a youth sports game. Junta was found guilty and sentenced to 6 to 10 years in prison.[27] He was found guilty of involuntary manslaughter. The jury refused to find him guilty of the more serious charge of manslaughter, which would have sentenced Junta to 20 years in prison.[28]

Parents should be supportive of their student-athlete. Any violence or abusive language is anathema to the desired goal of the ethical parent. When the stakes appear to be higher for the parents than for the children, parents have an obligation to examine their own behavior and to refrain from unethical conduct.

📖 CASE 5-2   *Bill Brantley v. Bowling Green School*

2003 WL22533643 (E.D. Louisiana)

Bill Brantley was injured while working as a referee at a high school boys' basketball game at Bowling Green School. Frank Glenn came onto the court and began assaulting Brantley's referee partner, Charlie Ackerman. Apparently, this occurred when Glenn's minor son was ejected from the game because of a technical foul. Glenn allegedly was joined in his assault of Ackerman by Donald McGehee. When Brantley tried to stop the assault, McGehee allegedly punched, clawed, and battered him. In the melee that ensued, McGehee was soon joined by two other McGehees, who allegedly punched, kicked, and beat Brantley until he was unconscious. Brantley alleges that his injuries were caused by the intentional acts of Glenn, Bowling Green School, and the three McGehees. Here, Glenn's alleged acts occurred at a high school sports event where Brantley and his fellow referee were charged with officiating and keeping order.

Source: *Reprinted from Westlaw with permission of Thomson Reuters.*

Consider the following questions with regard to Case 5-2.

1. Should there be a harsher penalty for the parent who assaults a sports official?
2. Should criminal charges be brought in this case?
3. What ethical and legal decisions would the school's athletic department be faced with in this case?

Preventing Parental Rage

What can be done to ensure parents are kept under control? If they are not held in check, it could lead to dire consequences and possible legal action.

---

[27] "Hockey Dad, Gets 6 to 10 Years for Fatal Beating," *CNN.com*, January 25, 2002.
[28] Fox Butterfield, "Fatal Fight at Rink Nearly Severed Head, Doctor Testifies," *New York Times*, January 15, 2002, A9.

CASE STUDY 5-4   *Parents' Ethics Course*

A youth athletic league in Florida is adding a requirement for kids who want to be sports participants. Their parents must learn how to behave on the sidelines as well.

The Jupiter-Tequesta Athletic Association is requiring parents to take an hour-long mandatory ethics course. Jeff Leslie, the volunteer president of the association and father of four, stated: "We just want to try to de-escalate the intensity that's being shown by the parents at these games." The program, Parents Alliance for Youth Sports (PAYS) of the National Alliance for Youth Sports, costs $5 and will be required for at least one parent or guardian for each family. It states the roles and responsibilities of a parent of a youth athlete in a 19-minute video and a handbook. The first season had many parents enrolled in the class.

It is always good to ask an expert. Joey Scherperborg, an 8-year-old who plays in the White Oak League, puts it succinctly when discussing parental misconduct: "It makes it not as fun. . . . I wish parents wouldn't do that."[29]

CASE STUDY 5-5   *Mark Downs*

Youth baseball coach, Mark R. Downs Jr. was charged with offering one of his players $25 to hit a boy in the head with a baseball. The boy was hit in the head and in the groin with a baseball just before a game and was not able to play in the game. The boy who was hit with the ball was an 8-year-old teammate with a mental disability. Witnesses told police that Downs, who was a t-ball coach, did not want the boy to play in the game because of his disability.

In a previous game, another coach said that Downs had been cautioned by an umpire about venturing onto the field and had remarked to the entire team in jest, "Anybody who can line drive the ref with a ball, I'll give you $25." The boy's mother called state police after the boy was struck. She said she suspected the coach wanted to keep the boy off the field, despite a league rule that required every player to participate in three innings a game. Downs was arrested and arraigned on charges of criminal solicitation to commit aggravated assault, corruption of minors, criminal conspiracy to commit simple assault, and recklessly endangering another person.[30] He was convicted on corruption charges of a minor and criminal solicitation to commit assault.

CASE STUDY 5-6   *Parental Rage and Violence in Youth Sports*

How Can We Prevent "Soccer Moms" and "Hockey Dads" from Interfering in Youth Sports and Causing Games to End in Fistfights Rather Than Handshakes?

By: Dianna K. Fiore

Villanova Sports and Entertainment Law Journal, 2003

---

[29] Richelle Thompson, "Youth Leagues Make Parents Play by the Rules," *Cincinnati Enquirer*, March 22, 2000.
[30] "Coach Denies Targeting Child," *CBSNews.com*, July 18, 2005.

Excitement suddenly turned to fear for the 49ers youth football team
. . . as players ran off the field holding their stomachs and began vomiting violently on the sideline. Parents and coaches helped the eight
boys, ages 12 to 14, into cars and headed to the hospital, ending the
practice for a championship game a few days later. No one knew it at
the time, but the sick 49ers had been poisoned, casualties in an epidemic of parental rage sweeping through youth sports. . . .

Youth sports have been a part of American culture for a long time. For
many years, sports have provided positive experiences for children.
When children play sports, they may experience the joy of learning a
new athletic skill or even scoring the winning point in a game. Playing sports should not only be a positive experience for children, but
should also be an enjoyable experience for parents who proudly watch
their children play from the sidelines or the stands.

Occasionally, parents are not involved in their children's sporting
interests. Before being introduced to the world of organized youth
sports, children often gather in streets to play stickball, shoot
hoops, or play touch football with family and friends in a backyard.
Overall, children participate in sports for exercise, fun, and
camaraderie.

Today, the games that carefree children played in the backyard with
friends are replaced by more structured activities such as organized
youth sports programs. Sadly, parents and other adults have become too
involved in youth sports, making them more structured, competitive,
and violent, rather than carefree, recreational, and fun. As a result
of this invasiveness, tragedies have occurred . . . this rage is
taking the fun out of sports and creating a negative learning environment for children.

With an estimated thirty to thirty-five million children between ages
five and eighteen participating in youth sports, it is clear that
youth sports are integrated significantly in modern American culture.
Children play to have fun with their friends and to practice and
improve their athletic skills. Moreover, parents want their children
to be involved in sports to build character and to manage the children's free time with a healthy, positive activity. Participating in
youth sports programs . . . can fulfill the needs and desires of both
children and their parents. . . .

In the late 1800s and early 1900s, organized youth sports emerged in
urban America because parents sought to occupy their children's free
time while they worked in factories and mills. Parents organized
sports activities for their children to compensate for a non-rural

upbringing and to fill the void caused by parents' working
long hours.

With this increased interest in engaging their children in sports
activities with friends, parents had to organize and implement a more
structured sporting experience for their children. . . . Little League
Baseball is highly structured, organizing programs within local communities around the world. . . . Little League has brought young girls
and boys together on ball fields around the world and currently claims
to have almost 3,000,000 baseball and softball participants worldwide.

. . . American Youth Soccer Organization ("AYSO") offers children from
ages five to nineteen an opportunity to participate in an organized
soccer league. AYSO modernized youth sports by implementing philosophies such as "Everyone Plays" and "Balanced Team," which have become
part of AYSO's trademark. Parents found soccer and AYSO's ideology
appealing because soccer is not as dangerous as football and does not
place the same kind of focalized pressure on children as baseball does
when a child is alone at bat. . . .

Although youth sports leagues were created with the best intentions
for children, they were motivated by the ideal of "winning." Over
time, these youth sports leagues progressed into intensely competitive
programs, creating a competitive athletic environment for young children and shaping today's youth sports model. Now more than ever,
adults structure youth sports programs to represent "miniaturized"
versions of professional sports.

Due to the highly structured organization of youth sports programs,
they may appear to have been modeled after professional sports
leagues. In fact, however, youth sports programs were never intended
to replicate professional sports leagues. Carl Stotz, Bill Hughes, and
Glen "Pop" Warner, the founders of the oldest youth sports organizations, intended youth sports to be fun, recreational, and social.
Despite their intentions, youth sports eventually became so structured
that they began to emulate their professional counterparts. Over time,
parents became more involved in making youth sports just as intense
and competitive as professional sports. Due to the combination of
adults' over-structuring of youth sports programs and parents' over-
involvement in their children's sports, youth sports comprise almost
all of the same characteristics as professional sports. From scheduled
practices and games, leagues, officials, umpires, referees, championships, tournaments, professional team names, trophies, team meals,
travel, and even corporate sponsorship, children experience what it is
like to be a professional athlete.

Unfortunately, some adults overlook the reality that exposure to the rigorous schedules and fierce competition that professional athletes face may be overwhelming for children who simply want to play sports to have fun with friends. Parents often neglect that the primary goal of youth sports is for children to have fun. Therefore, if the players are not enjoying themselves, the whole purpose of participation in youth sports is averted. . . .

Although most violence in sports occurs at the professional level, particularly in football and hockey, there is an inherent degree of violence at all levels. As a result, sports involve a serious risk of physical injury. . . .

Unnecessary violence now plagues youth sports across the country and has escalated to the point where parents, coaches, umpires, and referees are fighting and beating each other to death. The labels "sports rage" and "parental rage" refer specifically to parents who lose control and take their "rage" out on other adults. Sports rage and parental rage are not new developments. Yet, the number of violent incidents in youth sports has increased at an alarming rate in the past five years. "From Little League to the big leagues, violence at sporting events is no longer startling." Organized youth sports programs are earning a reputation for producing a generation of unhappy child athletes. Children either must drop out of youth sports programs because they are too competitive and no longer fun, or be exposed to the violence that increasingly erupts.

In addition, the trend of violence in youth sports is exposing young athletes to the judicial system. . . . Given the extreme nature of this growing problem, parents, children, coaches, and youth sports organizations have sounded the alarm for youth sports league administrators and legislators to take action: first, to find out what is causing the unfortunate trend of parental rage and unnecessary violence in youth sports; and then to find a way to address the problem before it is exacerbated. . . .

There are several factors that contribute to the alarming increase in unnecessary violence in today's youth sports. The "win-at-all-cost coaches, violent parents and poor role models in professional sports" are primary causes. . . . This mentality in professional sports has been integrated in youth sports. The ideal of winning in youth sports has become much more important than mere participation as a team player. Because there is so much emphasis on winning, the physical and emotional nature of youth sporting events continues to change for the worse.

Unfortunately, the intense competition in youth sports has caused young athletes to play more aggressively on the field and has led to more violent outbursts by parents on the sidelines. Everyone involved in youth sports, including the athletes, coaches, referees, umpires, spectators, and parents, are at unnecessary risk of injury due to this win-at-all-costs mentality. . . .

An early 1990s survey revealed that out of the 20,000,000 American children who participate in youth sports programs, approximately 14,000,000 will quit before they reach the age of thirteen. According to the survey, these children drop out "mostly because adults—particularly their own parents—have turned playing sports into a joyless, negative experience."

Parents have contributed largely to the "winning is the only thing" attitude in youth sports. Child athletes now struggle to succeed to please their parents, not to achieve personal goals. This struggle for perfection is causing anxiety among young athletes and their parents.

Parents traditionally attend their children's sporting events to avoid missing an opportunity to interact with their children. Today, however, parents are more involved in structuring their children's lives to ensure that their children become successful athletes. Thus, putting pressure on a child to make a high school varsity team to increase his or her chance of procuring a college athletic scholarship has become the new motivation for parents. Consequently, because of all they have invested in their children's success, parents become emotionally involved.

It is very easy for parents to participate excessively in sports competition when their own children are the players. The parental instinct to protect their children when hurt during a game compels parents to lose control of their emotions and temper.

Today's youth sports coaches should . . . act as role models to exert positive influences for children. In youth sports, the most successful coaches are concerned more about treating each child as an individual and displaying concern, respect, understanding, and patience with each child as he or she develops skills. Unfortunately, some youth sports coaches have become fanatical about winning and have resorted either to instructing young players to play violently, or to coaching violently to ensure victory.

Child athletes strive to be professional athletes and struggle to be the best in their sports. To be recognized by scouts as especially gifted and to succeed in competition, young athletes push themselves to their limits of talent and skill. When these athletes can no longer rely on their talents and skills, they panic over the possibility of losing, and consequently resort to aggressive, intimidating, and "unsportsmanlike" conduct on and off the field.

Each instance of unnecessary violence in youth leagues contributes to the erosion of constructive values gleaned from participation in sports. Parents who seek to prevent their children from becoming violent and overly aggressive should be proactive and set an appropriate example. Coaches and youth sports league administrators who aim to prevent incidents of parental rage at youth sports games should communicate with parents and set guidelines for acceptable and unacceptable behavior. With so many notable violent events in youth sports, parents, coaches, youth sports administrators, and even lawmakers are acknowledging finally that a problem exists and are making reasonable efforts to prevent future incidents of unnecessary violence.

League self-control and self-regulation have emerged as effective ways to curb violence in sports. Youth sports leagues are establishing more training programs for administrators in managing youth sports programs. To be fully effective, however, more youth sports supervisors are needed to train volunteer coaches, sports administrators, and parents.

Some youth sports leagues require that coaches undergo criminal background checks to obtain a coaching position. The background checks are intended to minimize children's exposure to violent offenders. . . .

NAYS president Fred Engh commented that "[n]o organization that runs sports for children should allow parents to register their child without the parent going through an orientation and training program on ethics and sportsmanship."

. . . It is imperative that adults and children involved in youth sports control their violent behaviors because rage has no place in recreational sporting activities for children. Unfortunately, parents and other adults have committed senseless violent acts with little or no consequence, inadvertently transmitting an example to children that violence wins. Their inappropriate actions have created a cycle of uncontrollable behavior both on and off the field. Lawmakers, youth sports leagues, coaches, parents, and children nationwide should . . . find a way to stop sports rage and put the fun back into sports.

Implementing a national standard for behavior at youth sports games will reduce the number of tragic incidents resulting from violence in youth sports. . . . "The bottom line is we want players to play the game, the coaches to coach the game and the parents to be able to enjoy watching their children play the game."

Source: *Reprinted from Westlaw with permission of Thomson Reuters.*

Consider the following questions as they relate to the Fiore article on parental behavior at sporting events.

1. Are there portions of the Fiore article you disagree with?
2. Do you think a national standard of behavior for youth sports is feasible?
3. Should youth sports leagues be less organized with less parental involvement? What about allowing the youth participants to pick their own team captains and their own teams? What an original idea!
4. Are umpires essential for every youth sporting event? Should the kids just be left to resolve their own disputes?

FAN ETHICS

Fans can be adamant about supporting a team. They like to go to the stadium or park and have a good time; however, sometimes a "good time" can get out of hand. Just as any other participant in a sporting contest, fans must regulate their conduct to conform to societal expectations. Although fans should have a good time at the ballpark, there is a line that cannot be crossed. Getting 100,000 fans or more together in a large stadium with alcohol present and enthusiasm running high can create a lot of excitement. Teams and stadium owners have both a legal and an ethical duty to their fans to ensure that spectators conduct themselves in a proper manner so as not to offend others. Some conduct inappropriate in a restaurant may be perfectly acceptable at an outdoor sporting event. The key is knowing when a spectator has crossed the line into inappropriate or unethical conduct. What should happen if a fan crosses the line? Should stadium officials taser them?[31] How about an out-of-control, intoxicated heckler at a golf match? Is a taser appropriate under these circumstances?[32] Should there be an age limit defining which fans are subject to taser or assault?

Fans can become overly boisterous and rowdy, even violent.[33] Fans have a responsibility to act in accordance with the rules and to control their behavior at sporting events.[34] Unnecessarily violent behavior is anathema to the proper conduct that ethical fans should follow. Fans, like participants, must make ethical decisions. They can choose the ethical course or allow themselves to lose their sense of perspective by abusive heckling or even violently interacting with participants, coaches, referees, or other sports officials.

The Appropriate Standard for Fan Behavior

Enthusiastic hockey fans banging on the glass during a game is generally considered part of the game. Good natured "ragging" of a player by a fan is generally accepted, but cursing, profane or abusive language is not. Stadium owners want fans to come back to the ballpark. They have an investment in ensuring fans behave themselves. The fan has a responsibility for behaving ethically during a sporting contest. Spectators at sporting events are encouraged to (in a reasonable manner)

---

[31] See Jason Gay, "Would Taser Boy Electrify Broadway?" *Wall Street Journal*, May 5, 2010.
[32] See Samuel Goldsmith, "Drunk Golf Fan Tasered for Heckling Tiger Woods at The Players Championship," *New York Daily News*, May 8, 2010.
[33] For a good chuckle, see Bill Simmons's list of "20 Most Annoying Fans at a Baseball Game." Bill Simmons, "Bane of the Ballpark," *ESPN.com*, August 8, 2001.
[34] Matt Mosley, "NFL's Best Fans? We Gotta Hand It to Steelers (Barely)," *ESPN.com*, August 29, 2008.

yell, scream, and cheer in an effort to provide support to their team and express their opinion to sports officials. (Again, only if done reasonably.) This behavior is done to encourage and motivate the players.

The spectator and fan should be enthusiastic, but fair, and adhere to the tenets of good sportsmanship. Committing a violent, drunken, or criminal act will not be tolerated and is considered inappropriate fan conduct. This behavior can be punished by expulsion from the stadium as well as the fan suffering the legal consequences of his or her actions. Owners want fans excited about their team, but only if fans do so ethically and follow the conduct rules set down by the owner and society in general. Professional leagues and teams have recently begun to publish codes of conduct for fans. The following is a model code of fan conduct:

Fan Code of Conduct

The club expects all who enter the stadium and surrounding parking lots to adhere to the fan code of conduct. Failure to follow this Code will result in possible ejection from the stadium, revocation of ticket privileges, and arrest. Although Season Ticket Holders may give their tickets to others, the account holder is responsible for the actions of those using their tickets.

The following actions are prohibited at the stadium and in surrounding parking lots:

- Fighting, taunting, or engaging in any action that may harm, threaten, or bring discomfort to anyone in the stadium
- Sitting in a seat other than one's ticketed seat location or refusing to produce one's game ticket upon request by stadium personnel
- Possession or use of any illegal drugs or irresponsible use of alcohol
- Loitering in concourses, aisles, tunnels or stairs
- Smoking in the stadium
- Use of foul, abusive, or obscene language or gestures
- Damage, destruction, vandalism, or theft of any property of other fans or the club
- Failure to follow the directions of law enforcement, security, ushers, ticket takers, or any other stadium personnel
- Unauthorized use of any seating designed for persons with a disability
- Engaging in any action that causes a disruption, creates an unsafe environment, interferes with the game, or hinders the enjoyment of the game for other fans
- Mistreatment of visiting team fans, including verbal abuse, harassment, profanity, confrontations, intimidation, or threatening behavior
- Refusal to remove or turn inside-out clothing deemed offensive or obscene upon request by stadium personnel

Consider the following with regard to the model code of fan conduct:

1. Is the code of conduct complete? If not, what would you add?
2. Under what circumstances should club officials remove a fan?
3. How do you define "irresponsible use of alcohol"?

The NFL's code of conduct prohibits the following:

- Behavior that is unruly, disruptive, or illegal in nature
- Intoxication or other signs of alcohol impairment that result in irresponsible behavior

- Foul or abusive language or obscene gestures
- Interference with the progress of the game (including throwing objects onto the field)
- Failing to follow instructions of stadium personnel
- Verbal or physical harassment of opposing team fans[35]

Fan Heckling

"Heckling" is very common in baseball, and in other sports as well. As long as it does not get out of hand, it is considered acceptable behavior. Is it a "fair comment" when fans heckle a player when the player is not playing well? Should athletes be subject to heckling in a public place? LeBron James was heckled at a wedding reception and also heckled at an amusement park.[36] There is evidently an art form to heckling.[37] The question is, when does a heckler go too far? One expert has stated it well:

Heckling players is not an act of sportsmanship and should be avoided. While many players will ignore most verbal heckling, it is a little more difficult to avoid items that are being thrown. Noise is acceptable at certain spectator events and taboo at others. Dealing with noise is a challenge for many athletes. Although at times it may be distracting, noise is considered a big advantage by a home team's athletes and coaches. At spectator events such as football, baseball, and basketball, it is considered appropriate to yell and cheer for your team. It is not considered appropriate to yell comments about a player's family, race, or any other disparaging remark. In the game of golf, however, noise is disrespectful. One golfer, following a noisy tournament, commented: "I'm certainly not going to go out and disrupt a business person in their business life, and they shouldn't disrupt our game."

Another inappropriate behavior by spectators is running out on fields and floors after their teams win. While this was previously done only when a team was ranked and played a ranked team, it now happens for no apparent reason. Fans should consider taking this bit of advice: "Try winning like you've done it before" (Hummer, 2004, p. C2).[38]

How a player reacts to a heckler may dictate whether a heckler will continue his or her verbal barrage. Charles Albert "Chief" Bender was a great Native American baseball player during the first two decades of the 20th century and is in Baseball's Hall of Fame. At the time he was playing, African American players were prohibited from playing. Bender was subject to racial prejudice when he played the game. He was known for handling racial taunts gracefully and with a little wit. When fans heckled him or greeted him with "war whoops" when he came onto the field, he responded with his own style, yelling back, "Foreigners, Foreigners."[39]

---

[35] Michael McCarthy, "NFL Unveils New Code of Conduct for Its Fans," *USA Today*, August 6, 2008.

[36] Chris Sheridan, "LeBron James Heckled at Carmelo's Wedding Reception," *ESPN.com*, July 12, 2010; Rick Chandler, "LeBron James Heckled at Amusement Park, Beaten by This Guy in 3-Point Shootout," *NBC Sports*, August 10, 2010.

[37] Katlin Stinespring, "The Art of Sports Heckling," *The Charleston Gazette*, June 11, 2010.

[38] Jeanette S. Martin and Lillian H. Chaney, "Sports Etiquette," *Proceedings of the 2007 Association for Business Communication Annual Convention. Citations are omitted on quote.*

[39] Frederick E. Hoxie, *Encyclopedia of North American Indians* (Boston, MA: Houghton Mifflin Harcourt, 1996), p. 66. Also see Tom Swift, *Chief Bender's Burden: The Silent Struggle of a Baseball Star* (Lincoln, NE: Bison Books, 2010).

Are certain subjects off-limits for fans and hecklers? How much should a fan be able to say about an athlete's personal life? There was much debate about this issue when Tiger Woods returned to the golf course in 2010. Some fans made comments about Woods's off-course activities.[40] There are ethical guidelines for hecklers.[41] Legal constraints impose obligations on fans that mandate appropriate behavior and fans can also be ejected for poor sportsmanship and conduct.

CASE STUDY 5-7   *Ultra Spectator Michael Katz*

Michael Katz, a spectator who heckled coach Isiah Thomas of the New York Knicks, received a warning card from a security guard to stop what he was doing or he would be ejected from Madison Square Garden. Katz, an accountant, said he was not cursing or swearing but merely yelling critical remarks at Thomas. Katz said his comments were within the boundaries of "fair comment." Representatives of the Knicks and the NBA said the warning was "routine" and part of a leaguewide effort to control fan behavior that was instituted after a brawl in 2004 involving the Detroit Pistons, the Indiana Pacers, and some spectators. Verbal criticism of Thomas had been common in 2004, with some Knicks fans sometimes chanting "Fire Isiah!"

The card given to Katz featured blue letters on a white background and read: "You are being issued a warning that the comments, gestures and/or behaviors that you have directed at players, coaches, game officials, and/or other spectators constitute excessive verbal abuse and are in violation of the NBA Fan Code of Conduct. This is the first and only warning that you will receive. If, after receiving this warning, you verbally abuse any player, coach, game official or spectator, you will be immediately ejected from the arena without refund."[42]

After receiving the warning, Katz said he moved to a different seat and was not ejected from the Garden.

Consider the following questions related to Katz's behavior.

1. Is giving a fan a warning card if they engage in improper conduct a good idea?
2. Should there be different levels of warning to fans before they are ejected?
3. What conduct should a fan be ejected for?
4. Would a fan commenting on the sexual harassment lawsuit against Isiah Thomas while he was the general manager of the New York Knicks be considered "fair comment"? It is, after all, a public record.

The national pastime can sometimes bring out the worst in baseball fans.[43] Baseball fans can be very loyal to their team and hostile to visitors. According to an algorithm designed by Nielsen, the most hated team in Major League Baseball is actually the Cleveland Indians, not the New York Yankees, who finished a distant fifth.[44] Consider the following case in which a heckler provoked a player.

---

[40] Larry Dorman, "Woods Is Getting Ready; So Are the Hecklers," *New York Times*, March 24, 2010.

[41] Robin Ficker, "The Heckler's Code," *New York Times*, November 22, 2004.

[42] Joe Lapointe, "NBA Gives Etiquette Warning to Fans," *International Herald Tribune*, December 14, 2007.

[43] Ashby Jones, "The Happy Heckler Can't Be Heard Now in the Din at Tropicana Field," *Wall Street Journal*, October 25, 2008.

[44] David Biderman, "Are the Yankees Truly the Most-Despised Ballclub?" *Wall Street Journal*, April 28, 2010.

📖 CASE 5-3 *Manning v. Grimsley and The Baltimore Baseball Club*

643 F.2d 20 (1st Cir. 1981)

On September 16, 1975, David Manning, Jr., was a spectator at Fenway Park in Boston for a baseball game between the Baltimore Orioles and the Boston Red Sox. Ross Grimsley was a pitcher for Baltimore. During the first three innings, Grimsley was warming up by throwing a ball from a pitcher's mound to a plate in the bullpen located near the right field bleachers. The spectators in the bleachers continuously heckled Grimsley. On several occasions immediately following the heckling, Grimsley looked directly at the hecklers, not just into the stands. At the end of the third inning, Grimsley, after his catcher had left his catching position and was walking over to the bench, faced the bleachers and wound up or stretched as though to pitch in the direction of the plate. Instead, the ball traveled from Grimsley's hand at more than 80 miles per hour at an angle of 90 degrees to the path from the pitcher's mound to the plate and directly toward the hecklers in the bleachers. The ball passed through the wire mesh fence in front of the bleachers and struck Manning.

Source: *Reprinted from Westlaw with permission of Thomson Reuters.*

It might be illegal for hecklers to heckle temperamental relievers; however, it was certainly illegal for Grimsley to intentionally throw a "pitch" into the grandstands where the hecklers were situated. What ethical and legal duties does this case present?

In the following case, a minor league baseball player decided to take matters into his own hands with a heckler. Not only was he sued for his actions in civil court, he was also charged with a felony.

📖 CASE 5-4 *Simmons v. Baltimore Orioles, Inc.*

712 F. Supp 79 (W.D. Va. 1989)

Simmons, along with a friend, attended the Fourth of July, 1988 game between the Martinsville Phillies and the Bluefield Orioles, a Baltimore farm team, at Bluefield, Virginia. Bluefield was not having a good year, and whether for this or some other reason Simmons moved down to the third baseline along about the eighth inning, and started to heckle the Oriole players sitting in the bullpen. Champ [Orioles player] stated in his deposition that Simmons was accusing the ballplayers of stealing the local women, and that he (Simmons) would show the Orioles what West Virginia manhood was like by blowing the players' heads off. Whatever was precisely said, the pitching coach [of the Orioles] then asked Simmons to leave. After the game (Bluefield lost, 9-8, stranding

```
three runners in the bottom of the ninth), Champ encountered Simmons in
the parking lot. Simmons . . . offers no details of what ensued other
than that he was punched and kicked by Champ and then hit in the jaw
by a baseball bat wielded by Hicks [Orioles player], causing his jaw to
be broken in two places. Champ's version was that Simmons saw him car-
rying a bat, made a gesture as if he were shooting Champ with his
finger, and said "Oh, so you need a bat, huh?" Champ said "No, I
don't," and threw his bat down. Simmons gestured toward his car and
said, "Let's go over to my car, and I'll blow your head off." Another
player tried to intervene, and Champ said, "Just get out of here."
Simmons then advanced threateningly upon him, and Champ hit Simmons in
the face. Simmons was unfazed, and Champ kicked him in the chest,
causing Simmons to stagger back. According to Champ he then smiled and
said "I'm drunk. I didn't feel that." Champ turned to walk away, and
at that point . . . Hicks hit Simmons. Simmons says Hicks hit him with
a bat, but Hicks says that he used only his fist. Hicks had not been
near any of the heckling and says he intervened because he was afraid
Simmons was about to pull a gun on Champ.

Source: Reprinted from Westlaw with permission of Thomson Reuters.
```

1. What actions should be taken against players who enter the stands and assault hecklers?
2. If a fan merely has a license to be on the premises, under what circumstances could the license be revoked?

Fan Rage

Fan rage is much like parental rage; it should never be tolerated and stadium personnel should take immediate action to remove abusive fans from the premises. In the fourth quarter of a 1995 NFL game between the Giants and the Chargers, fans began throwing snowballs from their seats and one struck Chargers equipment manager Sid Brooks in the face, rendering him unconscious for 30 seconds. A melee ensued with fourteen fans being arrested, 175 ejections, and 15 injuries. It was reported, "Early in the fourth quarter, an ice ball sent in the direction of the San Diego bench hit Brooks in the left eye. 'He went down like a ton of bricks,' said the Chargers' doctor, Paul Black, rendering him unconscious. As the teams were called off the field and the crowd was warned a cancellation was imminent, ugly got uglier: more snowballs were hurled at the circle of trainers and players surrounding Brooks, out for thirty frightening seconds, down for two frightening minutes."[45]

A Bowie hunting knife with a 5-inch blade was thrown at California Angels rookie Wally Joyner after his team's 2–0 defeat of the Yankees. "Joyner was grazed on the left arm by the butt end of the weapon, escaping injury. Said Joyner, 'I picked it up and gave it to [Angels' manager] Gene Mauch.'"[46]

A local disc jockey set up an anti-disco promotion to be held between games of a White Sox/Tigers doubleheader. Fans bringing a disco record were charged only 98 cents for admission.

---

[45] Ian O'Connor, "Giants Get Snowballed: Fans Show Disgusting Lack of Class," *New York Daily News*, December 24, 1995.
[46] "Previous Examples of Fan Violence," *SI.com*, September 19, 2002.

The thousands of records were then jammed into a large wooden box in center field and blown to pieces. A riot ensued on the field as about 7000 fans brawled and set off bonfires with the debris, forcing the postponement of the second game. Former major league player Rusty Staub said, "They would slice around you and stick in the ground. It wasn't just one, it was many. Oh, God almighty, I've never seen anything so dangerous in my life. I begged the guys to put on their batting helmets."[47]

Even coaches are not immune to fan violence. The attack against Kansas City Royals first base coach Tom Gamboa was unprecedented. The "fan," William Ligue, Jr. and his 15-year-old son ran onto the field and attacked Gamboa from behind. Ligue had telephoned his sister before Thursday night's attack and told her to watch the White Sox game. Ligue was charged with aggravated battery—he told the police that he charged the field because he was angry that the White Sox were losing. However, the evidence strongly supports the fact that the attack was premeditated—shortly before he ran onto the field, he handed his keys, cell phone, and jewelry to another of his sons; he was wearing a pocketknife on his waistband when he ran on the field. His 15-year-old son was charged with two juvenile counts of aggravated battery; one for attacking Gamboa and the other for hitting a White Sox security guard, who was an off-duty police officer. Gamboa was pummeled and received several cuts and a large bruise on his forehead.[48] These episodes are emblematic of improper conduct by fans.

Fan Stalking

Stalking is a serious societal crime and should be treated as such. Unfortunately, many women have been the victims of stalking, including entertainers and sports stars.[49]

A man was found to be stalking Olympic gold medalist Shawn Johnson.[50] Fans stalking sports stars has become a major problem in sports.[51] The *New York Times* reported:

Whether they are obsessed fans fixating on celebrities or former romantic partners, stalkers . . . typically invoke spurned love—real or imagined—to defend their actions. But stalkers seldom have to justify their behavior in the legal system because only one in three cases is ever reported to the authorities.[52]

In Case 5-5, Bob Uecker, "Mr. Baseball," had been stalked and procured a restraining order against his stalker.[53] She subsequently sued her for defamation.

---

[47] Joe LaPointe, "The Night Disco Went Up in Smoke," *New York Times*, July 5, 2009.

[48] Phil Rogers, "Two Fans Attack Coach During White Sox Game," *Chicago Tribune*, September 20, 2002.

[49] Elizabeth Olson, "Though Many Are Stalked, Few Report It," *New York Times*, February 15, 2009.

[50] Anthony McCartney, "Trial Begins for Accused Shawn Johnson Stalker," *USA Today*, June 8, 2010. Also see Justin Scheck, "Stalkers Exploit Cellphone GPS," *Wall Street Journal*, August 3, 2010; Subhajit Basu and Richard Jones, "Regulating Cyberstalking," *Journal of Information, Law, and Technology* (February 2007).

[51] Kimberly S. Schimmel, C. Lee Harrington, and Denise D. Bielby, "Keep Your Fans to Yourself: The Disjuncture Between Sport Studies' and Pop Culture Studies' Perspectives on Fandom," *Sport in Society* 10, no. 4 (July 2007): 580–600; J. Reid Meloy, Lorraine Sheridan, and Jens Hoffmann, *Stalking, Threatening, and Attacking Public Figures: A Psychological and Behavioral Analysis* (New York: Oxford University Press, 2008).

[52] Barbara De Lollis, "ESPN's Erin Andrews to Fight for Stronger Federal Anti-Stalking Laws," *USA Today*, July 2010.

[53] "Accused Bob Uecker Stalker Gets Restraining Order," *CBS Sports*, September 7, 2006.

CASE 5-5   *Ladd v. Uecker and Milwaukee Brewers Baseball Club*

780 N.W.2d 216 (2010)

Uecker is the radio broadcaster for the Brewers. In June 2006, Uecker petitioned the Milwaukee County Circuit Court for an injunction against Ladd, alleging a six- or seven-year pattern of harassment. Around the same time, Ladd, a self-described "devoted fan," was charged with felony stalking. The injunction petition hearing was held on July 3 and September 7, 2006. The court commissioner found probable cause and issued an injunction charge.

On September 8, 2008, Ladd filed a sprawling pro se complaint alleging that between June 1 and September 7, 2006, Uecker defamed her in the affidavit supporting the injunction petition; he and/or the Brewers published the allegedly defamatory affidavit to a website called thesmokinggun.com; the Brewers posted on their website a defamatory article regarding her removal from a spring training game in Maryvale, Arizona; and a claim for "false light invasion of privacy" for, among other things, making and republishing false, defamatory statements and photographing her in the stands at various baseball stadiums.

Ladd's September 8, 2008, complaint alleges that Uecker defamed her: (1) in the affidavit in support of his petition for the harassment injunction; (2) by publishing the affidavit to thesmokinggun.com; (3) during the two-day injunction hearing; and (4) in a media interview after the first day of the hearing. Distilled to its essence, Ladd's claim is that the false depiction of her as a stalker has damaged her personal and professional reputations. Except for the continued injunction hearing on September 7, 2006, however, all of these incidents occurred more than two years before Ladd filed her complaint.

Ladd also argues that, although Uecker and/or the Brewers allegedly posted his affidavit to thesmokinggun.com on June 2, 2006, the purportedly defamatory statements still can be accessed on the Internet today. She contends that the information therefore is republished each time someone visits that website or others to which the material has found its way, thus renewing her cause of action.

Ladd asserts, however, that Uecker's statements lost their absolute privilege through "excessive publication" on the Internet, because the "stalker label" "defame[ed][her] as a criminal" and because Uecker defamed her to law enforcement officials.

Ladd's complaints that the Brewers defamed her likewise fail. The Brewers advised Ladd in December 2006 that, in light of the harassment injunction, they would deny her entrance to the spring training facility in

March 2007 should she purchase a ticket. Upon finding her in the stands, they were entitled to have her removed. As Ladd's ticket indicates, a ticket of admission to a place of amusement is simply a license to view a performance that the owner or proprietor may revoke at will.

Ladd included a photocopy of her ticket as an exhibit, evidently to show she had a right to be at the game. The ticket reads: "The license granted by this ticket to enter the Club baseball game is revocable."

Ladd then directs us to an allegedly defamatory March 20, 2007, article in the Brewers' online news archive about the Maryvale incident. Assuming, as Ladd contends, that the Brewers posted the story there, and accepting simply for argument's sake that the article is defamatory, this claim also fails. Before filing suit, Ladd did not give written notice to the Brewers providing them "a reasonable opportunity to correct the libelous matter."

Ladd alleges that the Brewers took photographs of her in the stands at baseball parks and disseminated her "mug shot" and information about the injunction and the spring training incident. None of these involved private places, using her likeness for advertising or trade, or depictions of nudity. Further, they are matters of public record.

Source: *Reprinted from Westlaw with permission of Thomson Reuters.*

Ladd had been hounding Uecker for six or seven years, sending him unusual gifts, seeking his autograph, and appearing at ball parks and hotels where he was staying.

Consider the following questions in light of the Uecker case.

1. What can be done to prevent crazy fans from stalking players?
2. What actions should stadium officials take to prevent such conduct? How could the stadium owners keep stalkers from entering the ball park?
3. Where is the ethical line drawn between an enthusiastic fan and a stalker?
4. The fan was banned from Brewers' home and road games. How can that be enforced?[54]

Other Inappropriate Fan Conduct

Going onto a playing field without permission constitutes criminal trespass and the fan can be arrested. However, that does not stop many fans from doing just that. Running on a sports field without permission is a crime and also creates multiple safety issues for fans, security personnel, and participants. Erica Eneman and Amy Nadler alleged to have suffered personal injuries when they were crushed by persons attempting to come onto the playing field at Camp Randall Stadium after the 1993 Wisconsin/Michigan football game. They assert their injuries would not have occurred if certain gates had not been closed by security personnel at the conclusion of the game. Consider what happened in Case 5-6 when fans ran onto the field at the University of Wisconsin.

---

[54] See Andrew Greiner, "Bob Uecker's Stalker Banned from Road Games," *NBC Chicago*, December 8, 2009.

📖 CASE 5-6 *Erica Eneman and Amy Nadler v. Pat Richter*

577 N.W.2d 386 (1998)

Camp Randall Stadium is the site used for football games and other outdoor events at the University of Wisconsin at Madison. The football field is encircled by a chain-link fence with a walkway between the fence and the bottom row of bleachers. Ingress and egress of the bleachers varies, depending on the section of the stadium. Sections O and P were at issue in this lawsuit. The lower rows of sections O and P exit to the walkway and then through the home team tunnel. It was also possible for those rows to exit to the field itself, even though security personnel directed spectators not to do so.

Prior to the 1993 football season, access to the field was limited by handheld ropes, which provided no real barrier to a spectator determined to enter the field. In anticipation of the 1993 football season, the University installed metal gates that could be positioned to close off the walkway at the bottom of the bleachers in order to permit the team to exit the field into the tunnel without interference from the spectators. When the walkway was closed off by the gates, sections O and P spectators' means of egress was restricted, until the team had made its way through the tunnel and the gates were opened again.

On October 30, 1993, after the University of Wisconsin's football team defeated the University of Michigan's team at Camp Randall, many of the students in sections O and P attempted to come onto the playing field. However, a few minutes before the game's end, the gates had been closed and latched by security personnel. This provided a significant barrier to the spectators' egress onto the field, and it also created a dead end for tunnel egress from sections O and P, at a time when spectators were moving down the bleachers to exit the stadium or to push onto the field. The plaintiffs were crushed against a metal railing and the gates when security personnel were unable to quickly unlatch the gates to open them.

Ward and Richter had no personal responsibility to manage the crowd at the Camp Randall games. On the other hand, Riseling's, Green's and Williams's activities at Camp Randall were arguably within the scope of the Standard Operating Procedures for Camp Randall relating to crowd control. Additionally, prior to the Michigan game, and subsequent to the installation of the gates, Riseling knew that it was possible that the students might try to rush onto the field at the game's end. In response to this potential for congestion in the student sections, she formulated and issued a directive entitled, *"Post Game Crowd Tactics,"* whose goal was "to prevent injury to people—officers, band members and fans." The plan outlined a general strategy to follow which, in her judgment, would have prevented injury. Although her plan was implemented by security personnel, it was not successful.

Riseling, as Chief of Police and Security did not ignore the potential danger. She, with the assistance of others, formulated a plan, the "POST GAME CROWD TACTICS," the goal of which was "to prevent injury to people—officers, band and fans."

The plan established no specific tasks that were to be performed at a certain time; rather, it made general statements and set general guidelines such as,

> We expect that if Wisconsin wins today, especially if it is a close game, there will be an attempt by fans to come onto the field.
>
>   . . . .
>
> If there is a crowd surge, officers at that point will make the initial decision to move aside and begin pulling back to the goalpost assignment. Lt. Johnson will be observing from the press box and will make decisions on giving the command for all offi- cers to pull back.
>
>   . . . .
>
> There may be times during and after the game when people crowd the fence and put pressure against it. Actively encourage them to move back. If it seems there is danger of the fence breaking (it has in the past) move back to a safe position.

Here, the formation of the post-game crowd control plan represented Riseling's judgment about how best to reduce the potential for injury to persons at the game. Additionally, the implementation of the plan required Riseling, Green and Williams to respond to their assessment of what the crowd's actions required. By its very nature, the way the plan was effected had to change from moment to moment because the plan was responsive to the crowd. Reacting to the crowd also constituted the exercise of discretion. Furthermore, neither the documents nor the testimony contained in any of the portions of the depositions submit- ted in opposition to respondents' motion for summary judgment estab- lished a factual dispute about whether any specific acts were required of any of the respondents.

Here, documents provided establish no inconsistency between the actions of those respondents whose job duties took them personally into crowd control management activities, and the University's policy of safe management of the crowd at football games. Rather, they acted in accord with the General Operating Procedures for Camp Randall

```
Stadium. Neither the formulation of the plan nor the implementation
of it required highly technical, professional skills, such as a
physician's.
```

```
Source: Reprinted from Westlaw with permission of Thomson Reuters.
```

Consider the following questions as they apply to the Camp Randall incident.

1. What ethical duties do stadium owners owe to fans? Were the fans at Camp Randall engaging in poor sportsmanship, criminal activity, or unethical conduct?
2. Did the university violate any ethical duty they had to the fans?
3. How could stadium owners prevent these tragic events in the future?

NOTES AND DISCUSSION QUESTIONS

Parental Ethics

1. A Sport Parent Code of Conduct consists of trustworthiness, respect, responsibility, fairness, caring, and good citizenship. Should there be penalties, either civilly or criminally, for those parents who fail to act properly?
2. Should states enact laws specifically to police the behavior of parents at sporting events?
3. Youth sports are for children; therefore, by definition, they should be fun. It has been stated, "but maybe it's inevitable that kids' priorities change as they mature. They have more homework, new social lives and don't always love baseball enough to put in long hours of practice and play. If they also play basketball, soccer or football, they often start specializing in one sport by middle school, rather than alternating with the seasons."[55] Do you agree with this statement?
4. Some sports organizations insist that parents sign a pledge before enlisting their child in sports program. A sample pledge consists of the following: "I hereby pledge to provide positive support, care, and encouragement for my child participating in youth sports. I will encourage good sportsmanship by demonstrating positive support for all players, coaches, and officials at every game, practice, or other youth sports event." Do you consider this pledge an effective tool to curb potential parental rage?
5. One sportsmanship parents' guide included tips for parents such as "be supportive of coaches," "teach respect for authority," "focus on your child as an individual," and "be mindful of your role as a role model." Which of these tips is the most important? Is it the role of youth sports to teach respect for authority or is it the job of teachers and parents?[56]
6. Leonard Zaichowsky, a professor of sports psychology at Boston University, grew up playing hockey in Alberta, Canada, and notes that one important development in youth sports has been the sheer increase of parental involvement in sports. "When I was growing up, parents were minimally involved," he said. "Kids rode their bikes or walked to games, and

---

[55] Associated Press, "Youth Baseball Loses Kids When Playing the Game Isn't Fun Anymore," *Texarkana Gazette*, April 9, 2009.
[56] See "Must Parents Attend All Sports Events," *Wall Street Journal*, April 19, 2007.

they settled things themselves. Now parents drive the kids to practice and games, and as things have gotten more organized, the stakes are higher."[57]

7. What factors cause parents to get out of control at sporting events?

8. Is a mandatory ethics course for parents who want to participate in sports a good idea? What would be on the test? Could a league ever revoke a parent's license?

9. How should a youth sports league penalize parents who exhibit unethical behavior? What about fines, or an expulsion or banishment from the league?

10. Should parents be required to recite the parent code of conduct before they can participate? Is it a good idea to require a criminal background check for participating parents, similar to a service provided by Protect Youth Sports (protectyouthsports.com)?

Fan Ethics

11. What conduct do you consider "crossing the line" for a fan?

12. What are your thoughts on the Philadelphia Phillies fan described below? Should he be banned for life from all future Philadelphia sporting events?

> Matthew Clemmens, of Cherry Hill, New Jersey, pleaded guilty in May to charges of assault, harassment, and disorderly conduct. Clemmens admitted he stuck his fingers down his throat and vomited on Michael Vangelo, an off-duty Easton, Pennsylvania, police captain, and Vangelo's daughter, after they began arguing at the Phillies-Washington National game on April 14 at Citizens Bank Park.[58]

13. Should youth sport leagues ban "negative cheering," as some have already done?[59] Should parents and fans be allowed to cheer "against" an eight-year-old ball player, for instance when he makes an error? At what age do opponents become "fair game" for "running commentary" from opposing players?

14. The NBA gives written warnings to fans who heckle participants and coaches. This practice was intended to control unruly behavior. The heckler in one case said the words "Fire Isiah!" Is this "over-the-top"? Should warning systems for abusive fans be put in youth sports similar to that of the NBA? In youth sports, what should the warnings consist of?

15. Heckling and violent behavior is a serious problem in sports.[60]

16. Stalking is an issue as well unless, of course, you marry your stalker![61]

17. Should there be a higher standard to protect coaches? Participants? Referees?

18. What part does the media play in creating or encouraging fan rage? Here is a question that should never be posed![62] "Are New York Fans Getting Too Tame?"

---

[57] Fox Butterfield, "A Fatality, Parental Violence and Youth Sports," *New York Times*, July 11, 2000.

[58] Barry Leibowitz, "Matthew Clemmens, Vomiting Phillies Fan, Will Do Time for Nauseating Crime," *CBS News*, July 30, 2010.

[59] Kelley Tiffany, "Cheering Speech at State University Athletic Events: How Do You Regulate Spectator Sportsmanship?" *Sports Law Journal* (2007).

[60] See Jonathan Singer, "Keep It Clean: How Public Universities May Constitutionally Enforce Policies Limiting Student Speech at College Basketball Games," *University of Baltimore Law Review* (Winter 2010). See Associated Press, "Player Who Shot Heckler Is Back on the Field," *New York Times*, January 21, 2010.

[61] See "Chris Chambers Gets Married to His Stalker," *The National Football Post*, August 11, 2010.

[62] Jason Gay, "Are New York Fans Getting Too Tame?" *Wall Street Journal*, June 9, 2010.

CHAPTER 6

VIOLENCE IN SPORTS

INTRODUCTION

Violence is prevalent throughout sports. Many sports are violent by nature, but instances of extreme violence in sports are becoming more of a common occurrence, both on and off the field. Whether it be an NFL linebacker making a tackle on a quarter back, an NHL enforcer protecting his star player, or a major league pitcher throwing a "beanball" at a batter, violence is a major part of the landscape of both professional and amateur sports. Bench clearing brawls in baseball, sticks to the head in hockey, and "helmet-to-helmet" contact in the NFL have become commonplace in the sports world. NHL commissioner Gary Bettman has even said fighting is a part of the game, and the NHL tolerates fighting to a certain extent.

The news is filled with stories of athletes committing violent acts both on and off the field, with many commentators calling for stricter punishments for bad behavior by athletes. Leagues and clubs impose fines and suspensions in an attempt to stop violent and inappropriate behavior by athletes. The NFL has instituted a personal conduct policy as well as a gun policy in an attempt to ensure better behavior from players both on and off the field.[1]

When determining what is "normal" in society, boxer Mike Tyson does not usually come to mind. Tyson may be the poster child for senseless acts of violence in sports, notwithstanding his profession. His act of biting off a part of Evander Holyfield's ear in a 1997 boxing match is infamous and may be one of the "lowest blows" ever dealt in the boxing world.[2] Tyson was disqualified from the match for his actions. He said he did it in response to Holyfield's constant head butts during the match that went unchecked. He said, "He butted me in the second round and he looked at me and butted me again. . . . No one deducted points. This is my career. What am I supposed to do? I've got children to raise."[3]

---

[1] "NFL Personal Conduct Policy," *ESPN.com*, March 13, 2007.
[2] Rick Weinberg, "30: Tyson Bites Holyfield's Ear in Rematch," *ESPN.com*, June 28, 1997.
[3] Tom Friend, "Tyson Disqualified for Biting Holyfield's Ears," *New York Times*, June 29, 1997.

One of the more infamous violent incidents in NBA history occurred in November 2004 in a major brawl between the Detroit Pistons and the Indiana Pacers. Ron Artest of the Pacers fouled Ben Wallace of the Pistons. After the foul Wallace said something Artest did not like, so he pushed Wallace who then grabbed Artest by the neck. When the fight had almost stopped, Artest, who was lying on the scorer's table with headphones on to "calm himself," was hit in the face by a paper cup thrown by a Detroit fan. Artest became enraged and stormed into the crowd, throwing punches and assaulting fans. The police were forced to use pepper spray to break up the melee.[4] The Oakland county prosecutor charged four Pacers' players with assault and battery. In 2005 Artest and other Pacer players pleaded no contest to criminal charges and were sentenced to one year of probation and a $250 fine. NBA league commissioner David Stern issued suspensions to nine players totaling 143 games as a result of the fight.

There have been numerous instances of violence at the amateur level in recent years as well. An excessive display of violence occurred when a brawl broke out in a college football game between the University of Miami and Florida International University in 2006. Both benches were cleared, with players swinging helmets at one another. The respective universities reviewed the film, and 31 players were suspended from Florida International University, with 2 dismissed from the team permanently.[5]

CASE STUDY 6-1   *1970 Major League Baseball All-Star Game*

Pete Rose, "Charlie Hustle," was one of baseball's all-time greats and played the game at full speed no matter what he did. In the 1970 Major League Baseball All-Star Game, Rose ran over Ray Fosse of the Cleveland Indians at home to score the winning run for the National League. Fosse was injured in the play. Rose's actions were questioned by some as unnecessary considering it was an all-star game, which had no impact on a club's record in the standings. Rose later commented about the incident, saying he did not know they changed the game to girls' softball between third base and home plate.[6]

Was Rose's aggressive and violent play inappropriate for All-Star contest? Baseball now awards home field advantage in the World Series to the league that wins the All-Star Game.

RULES AND REGULATIONS

The purpose of rules and regulations in sports is to allow the participants to fairly compete with some assurance that it is safe to do so. The rules are in place to regulate competition, but all participants agree to a certain measure of contact during the competition, depending on the sport. The rules are in place to standardize play and to protect participants, and sometimes to directly regulate participant violence. Some rules are made to be broken, however. For instance, in hockey, fighting is prohibited by the rules, and players are penalized when they engage in such conduct, but players still fight for various strategic reasons. There are even different categories of fighting in hockey, major and minor. The NHL accepts fighting as part of the game itself. In baseball, a player will try to break up a double play by intentionally sliding into another player, even though it is against the rules and injuries can result from the play. In the NBA a player may commit a "hard foul" to prevent a score, but all players understand it as a strategic play essential to the game.

---

[4] "Carlisle: 'I Was Fighting for My Life Out There,'" *ESPN.com*, November 19, 2004.
[5] Charles Nocles, "31 Players Suspended for Miami-F.I.U. Brawl," *New York Times*, October 16, 2006.
[6] Joel Sherman, "The Man Who Caught Rose's Shoulder—Fosse Isn't Bitter 18 Years After All-Star Game," *Los Angeles Times*, July 12, 1988.

Prospective Rules

Prospective rules prohibit particular types of actions during the game. "Spearing" in football, "cleating" another player in baseball while sliding, "high sticking" in hockey, or using a "chop block" in the NFL are all prohibited, but all are still occasionally performed by participants trying to gain a competitive edge. These rules are in place for the safety of the participants and to prevent athletes from intentionally harming one another. Professional and amateur leagues and associations alike have instituted such rules.

Sportsmanship Rules

Sportsmanship rules are instituted to encourage participants to play within the rules in a sportsmanlike manner. These kinds of rules are put into place to promote ethical conduct and to prevent violent behavior. In golf, players must self-report if they touch or move a golf ball in play. They also keep their own score and must report themselves if they make a mistake in calculating their score. In baseball, players can be ejected from the game by the umpire for arguing a call too intensely. Some comments are tolerated by the umpire, but there is definitely a line that a player should not cross. The rule exists to allow a player to "blow off some steam" if he thinks he has been the subject of a bad call, as well as to control violence within the game. In college football, teams can be penalized for "excessive celebration" if they celebrate too much after scoring. This rule is in place to promote sportsmanship, to prevent trash talking, and to curb violent behavior.

Both professional and amateur athletic associations have instituted rules and regulations to establish fair play, encourage sportsmanship, prevent injuries, and establish proper decorum by participants on and off the field.

CASE STUDY 6-2   *Andy Roddick, True Sportsman*

Andy Roddick saves people from fires, does the job of an umpire on the court, and also happens to be a fairly good tennis player. At the Rome Masters in May 2005, Roddick "overturned" a call by the umpire. He was leading 5–3 in the second set when his opponent, Fernando Verdasco, hit an apparent double fault. The line judge called the ball out, but Roddick checked the mark left by the ball in the clay, which gave Verdasco an ace. Verdasco then rallied, beating Roddick. Roddick stated afterward, "I didn't think it was anything extraordinary. The umpire would have done the same thing if he came down and looked. I just saved him the trip. He's working hard up there."[7]

1. Should a participant ever attempt to reverse an umpire or referee's call?
2. What if a baseball player knew he failed to touch first base on his way to second? Should he call himself out?
3. Should an NFL wide receiver who only got one foot down on a touchdown catch tell the referee or merely act as if he scored the touchdown?
4. Isn't the honest and ethical thing to do to report your "misdeeds" to the official?
5. Was Roddick's conduct required under the circumstances, or does it merely display his penchant for engaging in ethical play and show what a great sportsman he really is?

---

[7] Associated Press, "Good Sport, Bad Finish: Roddick's Sportsmanship Backfires in Rome Masters," *SI.com*, May 5, 2005.

Incidentally, before the 2004 Rome Masters a fire broke out in a hotel killing three people. Roddick waited on his sixth-floor balcony during the fire, assisting people as they jumped to safety nets below. Tragically three people died in the fire.[8]

CASE STUDY 6-3 *Spitting in the Face of the Umpire*

In September 1996, Roberto Alomar made national headlines when he spit in the face of MLB umpire John Hirshbeck during a very heated argument over a called third strike. Alomar was suspended for five games by the league. Many thought his conduct crossed the line and that his five-game penalty was not enough punishment.[9]

Does it make any difference if the umpire initially cursed at Alomar, a charge Hirshbeck has vehemently denied?

CASE STUDY 6-4 *Taunting*

Taunting is considered by many to include actions or comments by a coach, player, or spectator that are intended to bait, embarrass, ridicule, or demean others. This would include actions or words that are vulgar or racist. Penalties under these rules may include ejection or point deduction for flagrant unsportsmanlike offenses.

1. Should a touchdown be taken away if a player taunts an opposing player on his way into the end zone or after a score?[10]
2. Should different rules apply at the professional, collegiate, and high school levels for taunting violations?
3. How should taunting be defined?

CASE STUDY 6-5 *Handshake Requirement*

Beginning in January 2007, Italian soccer league players were required to shake hands with their opponents after a game. As Roma captain Franceso Totti stated, "It's something that should be extended to the entire world of soccer. Being sporting enemies on the field but then greeting as friends after the final whistle."[11]

1. Should professional athletes be required to shake hands with opposing players?
2. Should it be required for all amateur sports leagues as well?

CIVIL AND CRIMINAL SANCTIONS

Civil Sanctions

Holding a violent athlete civilly liable is one way to deter violent behavior in sports. If violent offenders know they can be held responsible for any damages they might cause, they may think twice

---

[8] Alix Ramsay, "Tennis Star Roddick Saves Lives in Rome Fire," *Telegraph.co.uk*, May 2, 2004.
[9] Jay LeBlanc, "Cooperstown Bound?" *Washington Times*, May 28. 2008.
[10] Dennis Dodd, "Rules Committee: Taunting on Scoring Plays Might Wipe Out TDs," *CBS Sports*, February 11, 2009.
[11] "More Sportsmanship in Italian League," *Houston Chronicle*, December 4, 2007.

about engaging in violent behavior with an opponent on the court or ice. When Kermit Washington punched Rudy Tomjanovich in the face in an NBA game on December 9, 1977, Rudy T suffered fractures of the nose, jaw, and skull. He further sustained facial lacerations, a brain concussion and leakage of spinal fluid from his brain cavity. It may have been the most devastating punch ever thrown in a sporting event by a participant. Tomjanovich missed the remainder of the season due to the injury. Noted sports lawyer Nick Nichols[12] handled the case on behalf of Rudy T against the Lakers and won a multimillion-dollar lawsuit on behalf of his client, the first of its kind. The case was eventually settled for $1.8 million.[13] The case became the subject of a book, *The Punch*, by John Feinstein.

Criminal Sanctions

Criminal charges also can be used to punish an athlete's violent actions. The state has the authority to charge and hold athletes accountable for their criminal actions just as they do for any other individual.[14] There are numerous cases in which the state has prosecuted criminal behavior that occurred in a sporting event.[15]

CASE STUDY 6-6   *Gun Control in Sports and League Gun Policies*

Professional sports has seen its share of violence in recent years. NFL player Sean Taylor was murdered in a 2007 home invasion. Houston Texans player Dunta Robinson was robbed at gunpoint in his house. Denver Broncos player Darrent Williams was killed in a drive-by shooting in 2007. NFL player Plaxico Burress suffered a self-inflicted gunshot wound at a nightclub in 2008. In 2009 two NBA players drew guns on each other in the team's locker room over a gambling debt.[16] Many athletes claim they need firearms for their own protection. The NFL instituted a gun policy in 1994.[17] The current NFL gun policy states, in part:

Prohibitions. Whether possessed legally or illegally, guns and other weapons of any kind are dangerous. You and your family can easily be the losers if you carry or keep these items in your home. You must not possess these weapons while traveling on League-related business or whenever you are on the premises of the following:

- A facility owned, operated or being used by an NFL club (for example, training camp, dormitory, locker room, workout site, parking area, team bus, team plane, team hotel/motel);
- A stadium or any other venue being used for an NFL event (for example, a game, practice or promotion);
- A facility owned or operated by the NFL or any League company.

Put simply, the League, the Players Association and law enforcement authorities urge you to recognize that you must not possess a gun or other weapon at any time you are performing any service for your team or the NFL.[18]

---

[12] www.abrahamwatkins.com (Mr. Nichols not only knew his way around the courtroom but the basketball court as well. He attended Rice University on a basketball scholarship).

[13] "Lakers, Rockets Settle Suit," *New York Times*, August 29, 1979; "Basketball as Combat Sport," *New York Times*, December 16, 1977.

[14] Michael McCarthy and Jodi Upton, "Athletes Lightly Punished After Their Day in Court," *USA Today*, May 4, 2006.

[15] Jeff Yates, "The Problem of Sports Violence and the Criminal Prosecution Solution," *Cornell Journal of Law and Public Policy* (Fall 2002).

[16] Peter Vecsey and David K. Li, "Wizards Gilbert Arenas and Javaris Crittenton Pull Pistols on Each Other," *New York Post*, January 2, 2010.

[17] Mike Freeman, "For Athletes with Guns, There Are Few Controls," *New York Times*, August 11, 1997; David Barron, "Can There Be Gun Control in Pro Sports?" *Houston Chronicle*, December 7, 2008.

[18] NFL Gun Policy, *ESPN.com*, May 2, 2008.

1. Do you find the NFL gun policy complete?

2. What actions should be taken against those who violate a league's gun policy?

In the following case, participants in a basketball game at the YMCA engaged in a brawl ending in severe injuries for multiple individuals. Criminal charges were filed against the wrongdoers, holding them criminally responsible for their violent actions.

📖 CASE 6-1 *State of Iowa v. William Maurice Floyd*

466 N.W.2d 919 (Iowa 1990)

On August 15, 1988, William Maurice Floyd had been participating in a four-on-four basketball game for the Council Bluffs YMCA recreational summer league championship. By all accounts, the half-court game was rough, though not necessarily dirty, and tempers were as hot as the action on the court. Play was very physical, and the fouls were hard; there was considerable "hacking" and a lot of shoving for rebounds. Each team was aggressive and sought to intimidate its opponent with deed and word.

The opposing team had not lost a game during the regular season and had beaten Floyd's team twice. During the first half of play, passions were aroused when a member of Floyd's team, Andre Brown, struck Scott Rogers, a member of the opposing team, in the face as Rogers attempted to inbound the basketball. Brown was ejected from the game but remained in the gymnasium to watch the game. The game score remained fairly even until the second half of play, when [Floyd's] team pulled ahead by eight to ten points.

With three to five minutes left to play in the game and with his team lagging behind on the scoreboard, Rogers was aggressively guarding John Floyd, Floyd's cousin. John Floyd was dribbling the basketball beyond the free-throw line when Rogers fouled him in an attempt to steal the ball. The foul was a "reach-in" type that caught John Floyd either in the face or on the arm. The referee stopped play to report Rogers' foul to the scorer. The ensuing events developed quickly. With play still stopped, Rogers and John Floyd exchanged words. The evidence conflicts as to precisely what was said. It appears John Floyd told Rogers to stop fouling. According to John Floyd, who is black, Rogers, who is white, used a racial slur in response. John Floyd shoved Rogers, and the referee called a technical foul on John Floyd. As Rogers stepped back and raised his unclenched hands, John Floyd hit Rogers in the face with a fist, knocking Rogers to the floor. Michael Kenealy, Rogers' teammate, had attempted to intervene, but failed and pushed John Floyd away from the downed Rogers. Two or three members of [Floyd's] team then attacked Kenealy, hitting him from behind in the head and ribs. As these incidents unfolded, Gregg Barrier and John

McHale (Rogers' teammates) and [William Floyd] and the ejected player, Brown, were on the sidelines. They were not involved in the play immediately prior to happenings described above. Although the order of [William] Floyd's actions is not entirely clear, it is clear that [William] Floyd left his team's bench area after play had been stopped and punches had been thrown. Floyd then assaulted McHale and Gregg Barrier on the sidelines and Duane Barrier on the basketball court.

McHale, who was simply standing on the sidelines when disturbances began to occur on the court, suffered the worst from blows by [William Floyd]. Floyd hit McHale and knocked him to the floor. McHale suffered a concussion, severe hemorrhaging, and loss of brain tissue. He spent the next two days in intensive care. He has permanently lost the sense of smell, has some amnesia, and is at risk of epileptic seizures.

Leaving McHale unconscious on the floor and bleeding profusely, [William] Floyd attacked Gregg Barrier and Duane Barrier. Like McHale, Gregg Barrier was on the sidelines, but was returning from a water fountain. Gregg Barrier was able to cover up against Floyd's punches to the back of his head and shoulders, and Floyd did not seriously injure him.

Duane Barrier had been in the game when play had been halted. As Duane Barrier watched the incidents on the court, [William] Floyd approached and punched him in the side of the head. When Duane Barrier turned to see what had hit him, [Floyd] hit him squarely on the nose. Duane Barrier suffered a severely deviated septum and required reconstructive surgery.

The record includes descriptions of various attacks by different members of Floyd's team. These cowardly antics seem primarily to have involved John Floyd and Andre Brown. The disturbance lasted a few minutes and even spread to the YMCA staff offices, where members of Floyd's team beat Rogers as he attempted to call an ambulance for McHale. The State filed two charges of willful injury against [William] Floyd. He was convicted by a jury on two counts of assault causing bodily injury. The trial court sentenced Floyd to serve the maximum sentence of one year for each conviction, and to serve these terms consecutively.

Source: *Reprinted from Westlaw with permission of Thomson Reuters.*

Boxing champ Muhammad Ali refused to accept his induction into the U.S. Army to serve in the Vietnam War. Ali said, "I ain't got no quarrel with them Viet Cong."[19] As a result, the World Boxing Association stripped him of his title. Several American athletes talked to him about his decision in view of his position in the American sport world. These athletes included Lew Alcindor (Kareem Abdul-Jabbar), NBA champion, Bill Russell and NFL star, Gayle Sayers.[20] Ali was arrested and

---

[19] George Plimpton, "Muhammad Ali: The Greatest," *Time*, June 14, 1999.

[20] "Negro Athletes Will Try to Make Ali See Light," *Washington Post*, June 3, 1967.

found guilty on draft evasion charges. He was sentenced to five years in prison but never served a day in jail. He did not box for four years as a result of his suspension.[21]

📖 CASE 6-2   *Muhammad Ali v. The State Athletic Commission*

308 F.Supp. 11 (D.C.N.Y. 1969)

On April 28, 1967, Muhammad Ali (also known as Cassius Clay) refused to submit to induction into the armed forces. He was at the time "recognized" in New York and elsewhere as the world's heavyweight champion prize fighter. His resistance to the draft was predicated, upon a claimed ministerial exemption, a conscientious objector claim, and hardship grounds. On June 20, 1967, after rejection of his attacks upon the denial of an exemption for religious reasons, a jury found him guilty of criminally refusing induction, and he was sentenced to a term of five years in prison (subject, the District Judge said, to consideration of "clemency" if and when the conviction was affirmed).

"Cassius Marsellus Clay, Jr., also known as Muhammad Ali, heavyweight professional boxing champion of the world, was convicted after trial by jury on an indictment for knowingly and willfully refusing to report for and submit to induction into the armed forces of the United States. Clay's draft case has been through practically every phase of selective service procedure, beginning with the date he registered on April 18, 1960, until he was ordered to report but declined to submit to induction on April 28, 1967, and was thereafter convicted by jury trial held on June 19, 20, 1967. On four different occasions he was classified 1-A (available for military service) by his local board, twice by two different appeal boards (in Kentucky and Texas) and once by the National Selective Service Appeal Board (the Presidential Appeal Board). In every instance the vote of the boards was unanimous.

"There has been no administrative process which Clay (Ali) has not sought within the Selective Service System, its local and appeal boards, the Presidential Appeal Board and finally the federal courts, in an unsuccessful attempt to evade and escape from military service of his country. Being entirely satisfied that he has been fairly accorded due process of law, and without discrimination, we affirm his conviction."

Reviewing the claimed right to a ministerial exemption, the appellate court noted the long course of Muhammad Ali's self-description, to the draft board and elsewhere, as a "professional fighter" and "boxer," observing that the claim to a minister's exemption followed only after

---

[21] Thomas Johnson, "Muhammad Ali Loses His Title to the Muslims," *New York Times*, April 20, 1969.

the "eventful and important" change of his classification from 1-Y to
1-A and that "Clay (Ali) had never stated to his board or claimed to
be a minister or a conscientious objector prior to that time." The
Court concluded that the board had correctly denied the exemption.
"His vocation is clearly that of a professional boxer."

Source: *Reprinted from Westlaw with permission of Thomson Reuters.*

At the time of Muhammad Ali's conviction, the law required Ali to perform military service on
behalf of his country unless he was exempted. Did the state athletic commission make the ethical
choice in denying Ali the boxing title?

Everyone likes to ski down the side of a mountain fast. But just like golf, some can do it and
some cannot. Should you be aware of your skill level before you engage in a sport? Consider the following case in which an out-of-control skier killed another skier. Snow skiing has never really been
thought of as a contact sport, except in some extenuating circumstances for the novice who has not
yet learned the control necessary to be successful on the snow and ice. In the following case, a snow
skier was criminally charged for his actions on the slopes.[22]

📖 CASE 6-3 *State of Colorado v. Nathan Hall*

999 P.2d 207 (Col. 2000)

While skiing on Vail Mountain, Nathan Hall flew off of a knoll and
collided with Allen Cobb, who was traversing the slope below Hall.
Cobb sustained traumatic brain injuries and died as a result of the
collision. On April 20, 1997, the last day of the ski season, Hall
worked as a ski lift operator on Vail Mountain. When he finished his
shift and after the lifts closed, Hall skied down toward the base of
the mountain. The slopes were not crowded. On the lower part of a run
called "Riva Ridge," just below where the trail intersects with
another called "North Face Catwalk," Hall was skiing very fast, ski
tips in the air, his weight back on his skis, with his arms out to his
sides to maintain balance. He flew off of a knoll and saw people below
him, but he was unable to stop or gain control because of the moguls.
Hall then collided with Cobb, who had been traversing the slope below
Hall. The collision caused major head and brain injuries to Cobb,
killing him. Cobb was taken to Vail Valley Medical Center, where
efforts to resuscitate him failed. Hall's blood alcohol level was
.009, which is less than the limit for driving while ability impaired.
A test of Hall's blood for illegal drugs was negative.

---

[22] Associated Press, "Skier's Manslaughter Trial to Start," *ABC News*, November 13, 2009.

Hall was charged with manslaughter (a class 4 felony) and misdemeanor charges. At the close of the prosecution's case at the preliminary hearing, the state requested that, with respect to the manslaughter count, the court consider the lesser-included charge of criminally negligent homicide (a class 5 felony).

Judge Buck Allen, who serves as a judge for several mountain towns and lives in Vail, testified that he is an expert skier and familiar with Vail's slopes. He was making a final run for the day when he first noticed Hall on the slope. Allen was on part of the run called "Lower Riva," which is just below the "North Face Catwalk." From that part of the slope, Allen had a direct line of sight to the bottom of the run. Allen said that he could see other skiers traversing the slope below him at least from their waists up and that there were no blind spots on that part of the run.

Hall passed Allen skiing "at a fairly high rate of speed." Allen estimated that Hall was skiing about three times as fast as he was. Allen stated that Hall was "sitting back" on his skis, tips in the air, with his arms out to his sides in an effort to maintain his balance. Hall was skiing straight down the fall line; that is, he was skiing straight down the slope of the mountain without turning from side-to-side or traversing the slope. Hall "bounded off the bumps as he went," and "[t]he terrain was controlling [Hall]" rather than the other way around. In Allen's opinion, Hall was skiing too fast for the skill level he demonstrated, and Hall was out of control "if you define 'out of control' as [not] being able to stop or avoid someone." Although he watched Hall long enough to note Hall's unsafe skiing—approximately two or three seconds—Allen did not see the collision.

Source: *Reprinted from Westlaw with permission of Thomson Reuters.*

1. Do you consider Hall's actions criminal?
2. What is the appropriate punishment for Hall?
3. As an SMP how do you prevent this kind of accident in the future?

Violence in Ice Hockey

Ice hockey distributes its own brand of justice. No other sport integrates fighting into the actual playing of the game the way ice hockey does. Because hockey is a sport where fighting is part of the game and tolerated, special considerations must be given to violence within the sport.[23]

---

[23] For further study, see Tracey Oh, "From Hockey Gloves to Handcuffs: The Need for Criminal Sanction in Professional Ice Hockey," *Hasting Communications and Entertainment Law Journal* (Winter 2006); "Britain Targets 'Hooligans' Ahead of Cup," *Wall Street Journal*, June 11, 2010.

CASE STUDY 6-7   *Assault on Ice*

The term "enforcer" does not appear in the NHL rulebook. However, every player, coach, and manager knows what that term means. Steve Moore, former Harvard captain and a player for the Vancouver Canucks, and Moore's parents sued NHL tough man Todd Bertuzzi, the Vancouver Canucks, and the partnership that owned the Canucks, for an on-ice incident that occurred between Moore and Bertuzzi on March 8, 2004.

The dispute between Moore and Bertuzzi actually began on February 16, 2004, when Moore checked the Canucks' captain, Markus Naslund, in a regular season game between the two clubs. As a result of the check, Naslund received a concussion, facial lacerations, and suffered soreness to his wrist. No penalty was called on Moore, and after a review by the NHL, the hit was ruled a "clean" hit.

The next game scheduled between the two teams was March 3, 2004. Leading up to the March 3, 2004, game, Todd Bertuzzi made several statements to the effect that he or his teammates would retaliate against Moore. In fact, the threat became so publicized that NHL Commissioner Gary Bettman and Executive Vice President and Director of Hockey Operations, Colin Campbell, attended the March 3, 2004, match. However, no retaliation took place in that game. Bertuzzi was questioned after the game about why nothing occurred, and he said that the game was too close but added that other situations would present themselves.

The final regular season game between the two clubs was played just five days later. Moore's parents were watching the game from their home in Ontario. The NHL Director of Officiating contacted the game officials and warned them about possible retaliation against Moore. In the final period, the Canucks were in the middle of a line change when Bertuzzi confronted Moore. When Bertuzzi tried to get him to fight, Moore merely skated away. Bertuzzi continued to follow Moore the length of the ice and halfway back up the ice in the opposite direction. Bertuzzi finally struck Moore from behind, dropping him to the ice face first. Moore remained unconscious on the ice for some time and was taken to the hospital. He sustained massive injuries as a result of the assault, including a broken neck with fractures to the C3 and C4 vertebrae and a T1 avulsion fracture. Bertuzzi was suspended for the rest of the season. The Canucks were fined $250,000 by the league. The NHL eventually reinstated Bertuzzi after a 17-month suspension. The suspension cost Bertuzzi more than $500,000 in salary and $350,000 in endorsements. Bertuzzi was charged with assault by Canadian authorities and eventually pleaded guilty to "assault causing bodily harm" on December 22, 2004, in British Columbia.[24]

Hockey is clearly a rough sport. The league cannot and does not penalize or discipline players every time they cause injury to another player and neither do the courts. In the following situation, a court said a "body check" is merely a part of the game of hockey.

📖 CASE 6-4   *McKichan v. St. Louis Hockey Club*

967 S.W.2d 209 (1998)

In 1988, Steve McKichan signed a contract with the Vancouver Canucks, a professional National Hockey League team. The team assigned him to its professional "minor league" International Hockey League (IHL) team, the Milwaukee Admirals. On December 15, 1990, the Milwaukee Admirals played the Peoria Rivermen in a regulation IHL game in

---

[24] Patrick Thornton, "*Moore v. Bertuzzi*: Rewriting Hockey's Unwritten Rules," *Maine Law Review*, 61, no. 1 (2009).

Peoria, Illinois. The Peoria Rivermen is an IHL team affiliated with the St. Louis Hockey Club. IHL hockey is played on an ice rink measuring at least 200 feet by 85 feet with goals on opposing ends of the ice. The rink is surrounded by a wall made partially of clear Plexiglass, customarily referred to as the "boards." The rink is divided in two by a center line. On each side of the center line is a line called the "blue line." The blue lines are parallel to the center line and have to be at least 60 feet from the boards behind the goals. A game consists of three twenty-minute periods.

In the second period, an incident took place between McKichan and a Rivermen player. McKichan was penalized as a result of that incident. During the third period, McKichan and the Rivermen player were both playing and "on the ice." A videotape of the incident discloses that the Rivermen player was skating near center ice and McKichan was positioned in front of his goal. The hockey puck was shot in the general direction of McKichan's goal by a teammate of the Rivermen player. However, it traveled over the goal and the boards and out of play. As the puck was traveling, McKichan skated several yards to the side of the goal. A linesman blew his whistle stopping play. About this time, McKichan began turning his body toward the boards and moved closer to them. As he was moving away from the goal, the Rivermen player was skating from the near blue line toward McKichan. The Rivermen player continued skating toward McKichan after a second whistle. Holding his stick, the Rivermen player partially extended both arms and hit McKichan with his body and the stick, knocking him into the boards. He fell to the ice and was knocked unconscious. The Rivermen player received a "match penalty" from the referee and was suspended for a period of games by the IHL.

Rough play is commonplace in professional hockey. Anyone who has attended a professional hockey game or seen one on television recognizes the violent nature of the sport. In order to gain possession of the puck or to slow down the progress of opponents, players frequently hit each other with body checks. They trip opposing players, slash at them with their hockey sticks, and fight on a regular basis, often long after the referee blows the whistle. Players regularly commit contact beyond what is permitted by the rules, and, we are confident, intentionally. They wear pads, helmets, and other protective equipment because of the rough nature of the sport.

Professional hockey is played at a high skill level with well conditioned athletes, who are financially compensated for their participation. They are professional players with knowledge of its rules and customs, including the violence of the sport. In part, the game is played with great intensity because its players can reap substantial

financial rewards. We also recognize that the professional leagues
have internal mechanisms for penalizing players and teams for violating league rules and for compensating persons who are injured.

In summary, a severe body check is a part of professional hockey. This
body check, even several seconds after the whistle and in violation of
several rules of the game, was not outside the realm of reasonable
anticipation. For better or for worse, it is "part of the game" of
professional hockey.

Source: *Reprinted from Westlaw with permission of Thomson Reuters.*

Is it unethical or unsportsmanlike to intentionally injure a player? If you know you will only
spend 2 minutes in the penalty box while putting the other team's star player out for the game or possibly the season, is it then deemed a good strategy?[25] Is intentional injury by a player for "strategic
reasons" to be considered gamesmanship, unsportsmanlike conduct, criminal behavior, or just unethical? Is "retaliatory" violence ever ethical, even if it is allowed within the rules of the game? Consider
such ethical dilemmas in light of the following case.

📖 CASE 6-5 *Babych v. McRae*

567 A.2d 1269 (1989)

[O]n September 24, 1986, while employed as a professional hockey
player for the Hartford Whalers, Dave Babych participated in a hockey
game at the Hartford Civic Center against Ken McRae and the Quebec
Nordiques hockey team of Quebec, Canada. On that date, he was struck
across his right knee causing personal injury and financial losses.
Babych contends that the injuries and losses were caused by McRae's
negligence in one or more of the following ways: (1) that McRae swung
his stick when he knew or should have known that such action could
cause serious injury; (2) that such action was unnecessary; (3) that
the action violated Rule 77 of the National Hockey League Rules; and
(4) that the action was retaliatory.

Source: *Reprinted from Westlaw with permission of Thomson Reuters.*

1. Is hockey violence out of control? Is it good for the game of hockey?
2. Should hockey fighting be prohibited, or is it too much a part of the history of the game to
   remove it from the game?
3. Why don't other sports have a "tradition" of fighting?

---

[25] "H.S. Football Player Charged for Game Hit," *ABC News*, December 5, 2009. (High school football player is
charged with third degree assault for breaking and dislocating an opponent's elbow during a game.)

4. Do you consider hockey violence necessary to the continued success of the sport?
5. Does the NHL encourage players to fight? Is that an ethical stance to take for the league? Is allowing players to fight just giving the fans what they want to see? Is it really a marketing ploy on behalf of the NHL?

The Canadian Approach to Hockey Violence

Different cultures have varying views on sports violence. Canadians tend to take a more aggressive posture, criminally prosecute those who commit violent acts in their national sport of ice hockey. American courts have been less willing to criminally charge those who engage in violent behavior on the ice, but Canadian criminal prosecutors have used criminal laws to place violent offenders behind bars. In 1988, Dino Ciccarelli became the first NHL player to receive a jail term for an on-ice assault of another player.[26]

The following case is an example of how Canadians have dealt with on-ice violence in their national sport.

📖 CASE 6-6 *Regina v. Edward Joseph Green*

2 C.C.C.2d 442 (1970)

Edward Joseph Green was charged on September 21, 1969, at the City of Ottawa in the Regional Municipality of Ottawa-Carleton, he unlawfully assaulted one Wayne Maki. The incident occurred on the evening of September 21, 1969, when an exhibition game involving two National Hockey League teams, the Boston Bruins and the St. Louis Blues, was being played at the Ottawa Civic Centre. Green was a member of the Boston Bruins and had for some time played for that team and was a defenseman. Maki was at that time a member of the St. Louis Blues. The game was being refereed by Mr. Bodendistel, and the other officials employed were Ronald Finn and Robert John Waddel. All were relatively inexperienced in officiating at the National Hockey League level, but nevertheless they impressed me as alert and competent officials. . . . At approximately the 13-minute mark of the first period at the exhibition game (which time was established by the referee, Bodendistel), the puck came into the end that was being defended at that time by the Boston Bruins. Both Green and Maki were on the ice at that time. The puck went round behind the Boston net. Mr. Maki went in to attempt to get it out in front, and of course Green was there in his capacity as defenseman for the Boston Bruins in order to clear the puck out of his own zone if at all possible. A skirmish developed along the boards behind the Boston net, to the left of it, that is the goalie's left—a skirmish such as any one of a thousand skirmishes that occur during the course of the National Hockey League season. Somewhere in the

---

[26] Associated Press, "Ciccarelli Cited for Assault," *New York Times*, August 25, 1988.

skirmish, Green struck or pushed Maki in the face with his glove. A penalty was signaled at that point, a delayed penalty which would be finally called when the whistle had blown when Boston had control of the puck. Shortly thereafter the players came off the boards and the sticks of both players were raised on high. There appeared to be a blow struck by Maki at Green, as a result of which Green was very seriously injured.

Neither the referee nor either of the linesmen made any reference to any spearing that may have been taking place on the boards; but there are competent witnesses—Larkin, Kealey, and Schmidt—who were there who stated that, while the two players were scuffling along the boards, Maki made a spearing motion, jabbed at Green, with the blade of his stick in the lower abdomen. Kealey, who was himself a hockey player, as far as at any rate A level, and a very competent witness, saw this. Larkin, who was stationed immediately behind the Boston Bruins' net, and who has been a sports observer for many years, saw this. And Green in his own testimony stated that this in fact occurred.

Maki has no memory of this having happened; he does not remember spearing Green. But he was quite careful to say that he does not say that he did not spear him; he just does not remember whether he speared him or not. In any event, on that evening around that time, the 13-minute mark, in the scuffle that took place Green was in fact speared in the lower abdomen in the genital region by Maki.

There is probably no more serious attack that can be made by one hockey player on another, in the view of the hockey players themselves than the action of spearing. Kealey was asked in examination or cross-examination what he thought of spearing and he used the expression that in his opinion it was "dirty pool," and that pretty well defines the hockey players' attitude towards spearing. It is an extremely dangerous type of attack, directed as it very often is at the abdomen, which is relatively unprotected, and at the lower abdomen, and normally speaking it results in instant retribution, if the player who has been speared has not been hurt in the process and is unable to defend himself.

Green was at that time, and had been for a good many years, a member of the Boston Bruins. His reputation was well established. He was a star in the hockey league. He had nothing to prove. He was merely, as he said himself in his own evidence, getting into shape for the season; he was using the exhibition game for that purpose. So [he is not] a young man who had to make his mark in the league and who had to prove something in order to obtain a place on the team once the season started.

These events took no considerable time. In fact, the whole incident probably did not consume more than 10 seconds. Hockey is a game that is played at great speed, and we are here dealing with players from the

National Hockey League, who are the best trained and probably the best hockey players anywhere. [They are] men wearing the very best equipment, with one notable and totally incomprehensible omission, and that is the fact that most players do not wear helmets. But apart from that they are very well equipped, they are very well trained, and they are playing in the best surroundings and on the best possible ice surface. They also in the very nature of the game assume certain risks. . . .

Since it is assumed and understood that there are numerous what would normally be called assaults in the course of a hockey game, but which are really not assaults because of the consent of the players in the type of game being played, where do you draw the line? It is very difficult for a player who is playing hockey with all the force, vigor and strength at his command, who is engaged in the rough and tumble of the game, very often in a rough situation in the corner of the rink, suddenly to stop and say, "I must not do that. I must not follow up on this because maybe it is an assault; maybe I am committing an assault." Any of the actions that would normally be considered assaults in ordinary walks of life can possibly be considered assaults at all.

The two most serious, grievous assaults that were committed that night—blows that caused most of the trouble, the blows that almost cost Green his life—were (a) the spearing of Green by Maki and (b) the hitting of Green over the head by Maki.

If that second blow had not been struck, if Maki had not struck Green, it is difficult for me to imagine that any charge would have been laid against Green. In other words, after the blow that was struck by Green on Maki, if that had been the end of the matter, if nothing else had happened, it would appear the necessary penalties would have been called (as they were in the process of being called) and that incident might have merited a line or two in the sporting pages the next day, and perhaps a comment or two in the sports telecasts and the radio sports broadcasts that evening. But that would have been the end of it and no more would have happened.

Source: *Reprinted from Westlaw with permission of Thomson Reuters.*

Should there be differing international standards for dealing with hockey violence? Do you agree with the Canadian approach to hockey violence?

VIOLENCE IN PROFESSIONAL AND AMATEUR SPORTS

Professional Sports

It is natural that everyone likes to be on the winning team. No one wants to be deemed a loser. The cultural imperative of winning influences the sports world, starting at the lowest level of competition, and seems to affect all sports. This can sometimes lead to a "win at all costs" attitude, regardless of the sport or the age of the participants. Certainly, in the professional ranks competition increases and winning becomes more important as a result of the rewards of bigger contracts, larger paychecks, and awards. High school competition has increased due to chances of getting a sports scholarship to a university as well as intense parental involvement. The ethics of fair competition have seemed to erode in recent years as participants, coaches, players, and parents become more competitive the more they perceive to be at stake.

Wanda Holloway, the "Texas Cheerleader Mom," needless to say was an avid cheerleading fan. After an 8-day trial, Holloway was convicted and given a 15-year sentence for solicitation of capital murder. Holloway tried to arrange for the murder of her daughter's rival mother and was heard saying "I want her gone."[27] Holloway was not the only individual who took cheerleading too seriously. Although the following mom didn't try to kill anybody she was still charged with identity theft for her actions. Wendy Brown always wanted to be a cheerleader. Evidently she wanted it so bad she enrolled in a local high school as her 15-year-old daughter (she was actually 33) and tried out for the cheerleading squad. She went to practices, received a locker, and went to a pool party at the coach's house before she was "busted." The school became suspicious when Brown's check for $134.50 for the cheerleading uniform was returned for insufficient funds.[28]

NBA player Latrell Sprewell may be tied with Mike Tyson for the "overzealous athlete" award. Sprewell became enraged at a team practice and choked his coach P. J. Carlesimo. Sprewell hired super lawyer Johnnie Cochran as his legal advisor, and he would need him. Sprewell said he didn't choke his coach but did admit he attacked him because he "couldn't take it anymore."[29]

📖 CASE 6-7   *Sprewell v. Golden State Warriors*

266 F.3d 979 (9th Cir. 2001)

Latrell Sprewell joined the NBA in 1992 as a guard for the Golden State Warriors. During Sprewell's tenure with the Warriors, he played under four different head coaches, the last of whom was P. J. Carlesimo. Sprewell's star-crossed relationship with Carlesimo, while amicable upon its inception in June of 1997, quickly deteriorated over the ensuing six months to the point that both Sprewell and the Warriors openly entertained the possibility of trading Sprewell to another team.

Tensions between Sprewell and Carlesimo climaxed during a closed-door practice on December 1, 1997, during which Carlesimo told Sprewell to

---

[27] Sonja Steptoe, "The Pom-Pom Chronicles," *Sports Illustrated*, December 30, 1991. Also see Anne McDonald Maier, *Mother Love, Deadly Love: The Texas Cheerleader Murder Plot* (New York: Carol Publishing Corporation, 1992).

[28] Associated Press, "Mom, That's My Cheerleading Outfit! Wisconsin Woman Steals Daughter's Identity to Join Pom-Pom Squad," *New York Daily News*, September 13, 2008.

[29] Richard Sandomir, "Students Take Side in the Sprewell Debate," *New York Times*, December 11, 1997; Corky Siemaszko, "Sprewell Says He Didn't Choke Coach," *New York Daily News*, March 9, 1998.

pass the ball to a teammate for a quick shot. Despite Sprewell's contention that he passed the ball "admirably, as one would expect of an All-Star," Carlesimo rebuked Sprewell for not putting more speed on his pass. When Carlesimo subsequently repeated his criticism, Sprewell slammed the ball down and directed several expletives at Carlesimo. Carlesimo responded with a similar showing of sophistication. Sprewell immediately either walked or lunged at Carlesimo and wrapped his hands around Carlesimo's neck. With his arms fully extended, Sprewell moved Carlesimo backwards, saying "I will kill you." Carlesimo offered no resistance. Sprewell grasped Carlesimo's neck for approximately seven to ten seconds—the time it took for other players and coaches to restrain Sprewell. Sprewell then left the practice floor, saying "trade me, get me out of here, I will kill you," to which Carlesimo countered, "I am here."

After showering and changing, Sprewell returned to the practice facility to again confront Carlesimo. Despite the efforts of two assistant coaches to restrain him, Sprewell was able to approach Carlesimo and throw an overhand punch that grazed Carlesimo's right cheek. Sprewell landed a subsequent blow to Carlesimo's shoulder, but it is uncertain whether it was intentional or the product of Sprewell's attempt to free himself from those restraining him. As Sprewell left the facility, he again told Carlesimo, "I will kill you."

That evening the Warriors suspended Sprewell for a minimum of ten games and expressly reserved its right to terminate Sprewell's contract. Two days later, the Warriors exercised that right and ended Sprewell's reign as a Warrior. The NBA subsequently issued its own one-year suspension of Sprewell after conducting an independent investigation of the matter.

On December 4, 1997, Sprewell invoked the arbitration provisions of his collective bargaining agreement ("CBA") by filing a grievance challenging both his suspension by the NBA and the Warriors' termination of his contract. The arbitrator held nine days of hearings, received testimony from twenty-one witnesses, accepted over fifty exhibits, and was presented with over 300 pages of pre and post-hearing briefs. The arbitrator found that the dual punishments issued by the NBA and the Warriors were permissible under the CBA, but found that: (1) the Warriors' termination of Sprewell's contract was not supported by just cause because after the Warriors' initial suspension of Sprewell, any residual interest of the Warriors was absorbed by the NBA's investigation of the matter; and (2) the NBA's suspension should be limited to the 1997-98 season.

Source: Reprinted from Westlaw with permission of Thomson Reuters.

CASE STUDY 6-8   *Tailgater Rights*

NFL Commissioner Roger Goodell is known to be a heavy-handed commissioner regarding player discipline. However, he took fans to task with a fan code of conduct and followed that up with recommendations to teams about maximum serving sizes for beers and the number of alcoholic drinks a fan can purchase at one time at the stadium. Every beer cup would also have the message: "Fans don't let fans drive drunk."[30] The league also recommended that teams restrict tailgaters' entrance to the parking lot of NFL games to only three and a half hours before a game.

Why would the NFL restrict fans from entering the parking lot of the stadium to only three and a half hours before the game? Are there safety reasons for doing so?

NFL Hall of Famer Dick Butkus once joked, "I never set out to hurt anybody deliberately unless, it was, you know, important . . . like a league game or something."[31] Player injuries are assumed in professional football. There are certain rules in place that attempt to curb the violent behavior of NFL participants. For instance, the "chop block," or hitting below the knees within 15 yards of the line of scrimmage, is prohibited. The NFL does protect its quarterbacks very closely and prohibits certain kinds of contact with the quarterback. Is that a good rule, or should everyone on the field be "fair game"? Helmet-to-helmet contact is prohibited as well, for safety reasons. With that said, players in the NFL essentially assault one another in every play, with consent, of course.

Players must abide by certain rules and guidelines or suffer the consequences, which can include fines, penalties, and possible expulsion from the league. Should there be any limits to violent behavior between NFL players? In Case 6-8 one NFL player violently attacked another player.

CASE 6-8   *Hackbart v. Cincinnati Bengals*

601 F.2d 516 (10th Cir. 1979)

An injury occurred in the course of a game between the Denver Broncos and the Cincinnati Bengals, which was played in Denver in 1973. The Broncos' defensive back, Dale Hackbart, was injured by the Bengals' offensive back, Charles "Booby" Clark. . . . Clark had run a pass pattern to the right side of the Denver Broncos' end zone. The pass was intercepted by Billy Thompson, a Denver free safety, who returned it to mid-field. As a consequence of the interception, the roles of Hackbart and Clark suddenly changed. Hackbart, who had been defending, instantaneously became an offensive player. Clark, on the other hand, became a defensive player. Acting as an offensive player, Hackbart attempted to block Clark by throwing his body in front of him. He thereafter remained on the ground. He turned, and with one knee on the ground, watched the play following the interception.

---

[30] Michael McCarthy, "NFL Targeting Binge Drinking Among Fans in New Season," *USA Today*, August 22, 2009.
[31] Jonathan Rand, *300 Pounds of Attitude: The Wildest Stories and Craziest Characters the NFL Has Ever Seen* (Guilford, CT: Lyons Press, 2006).

Clark, "acting out of anger and frustration, but without a specific intent to injure . . . stepped forward and struck a blow with his right forearm to the back of the kneeling [Hackbart's] head and neck with sufficient force to cause both players to fall forward to the ground." Both players, without complaining to the officials or to one another, returned to their respective sidelines since the ball had changed hands and the offensive and defensive teams of each had been substituted. Clark testified at trial that his frustration was brought about by the fact that his team was losing the game. Due to the failure of the officials to view the incident, a foul was not called. However, the game film showed very clearly what had occurred. Hackbart did not, at the time, report the happening to his coaches or to anyone else during the game. However, because of the pain he experienced, he was unable to play golf the next day. He did not seek medical attention, but the continued pain caused him to report the incident to the Bronco trainer, who gave him treatment. Apparently, he played on the specialty teams for two successive Sundays, but after that, the Broncos released him on waivers. (He was in his thirteenth year as a player.) He sought medical help and it was then that it was discovered by the physician that he had a serious neck fracture injury.

Despite the fact that Clark admitted that the blow which had been struck was not accidental, that it was intentionally administered, the court ruled as a matter of law that the game of professional football is basically a business which is violent in nature, and that the available sanctions are imposition of penalties and expulsion from the game. Many fouls are overlooked, the game is played in an emotional and noisy environment, and [these kinds of] incidents are not unusual.

Applying the laws and rules which are a part of injury law to the game of professional football can be unreasonable, holding that one player has a duty of care for the safety of others. Hackbart had to recognize that he accepted the risk that he would be injured by such an act.

Source: *Reprinted from Westlaw with permission of Thomson Reuters.*

1. Was the player violence in *Hackbart* excessive, even for the NFL?
2. What limits should there be on violence in the NFL?
3. Was there any unethical conduct or violations of fair play by any of the parties in *Hackbart*?

Amateur Sports

American society seems to worship their athletes and entertainers. From an early age, athletes in the United States are treated like superstars and coddled because they can shoot a ball, pass a puck, or jump higher than anyone else. Some athletes develop a sense of entitlement as a result of this extravagant treatment. More youth are now involved in organized sports than ever before, and youth sports have become extremely competitive. There are Little League baseball drafts for 5- and

6-year-olds. Special players are on selected teams that promote all-star competition and some teams play 50 games or more in a little league season. This overemphasis on sports at such an early age has led some to argue that it has created too much of a competitive atmosphere for kids at too young an age.[32] Consider the following case involving an assault in a basketball game.

📖 CASE 6-9 *Baker v. Trinity-Pawling School*

21 A.D.3d 272 (2005)

Rayon Baker, a student basketball player at Hotchkiss, was injured as the result of an assault by Carl Elliott, a student basketball player at Trinity. The assault followed a basketball game between the two schools at Hotchkiss on February 12, 2000. Baker was unaware of any rivalry between the schools and he had never been cited for any disciplinary problems while at Hotchkiss. During the course of the game, he was punched in the eye and elbowed in the mouth, although he was unaware which of the Trinity players hit him. He [stated] that Elliott threatened him at the postgame handshake and, as he was leaving the building, he was hit from behind and fell down, at which point Elliott jumped on top of him and began striking him. The Trinity coach also testified that there was no special rivalry between the schools, that Baker was hit with an inadvertent elbow by a player named Billy Allen, and that there had been a commotion in the handshake line. The coach stated that Baker and Elliott had words, and the assault by Elliott, according to some of his other players, was provoked by Baker, who had spit on Elliott. Elliott, the coach noted, also had no prior history of violent behavior. The Hotchkiss coach echoed Baker's claim that Baker had no history of behavior problems, and stated that Baker was not violent or aggressive, and that although the game was loud and intense, there was no excessive jeering or fouling. The coach maintained that there was a disruption in the handshake line between Elliott and Baker, but nothing physical occurred, although the coach later saw Baker upset and holding his face, while other players explained that Baker had been jumped.

Schools are under a duty to provide adequate supervision to ensure the safety of the students in their charge and are liable for foreseeable injuries which are proximately caused by the absence of adequate supervision...

. . . [t]here was no prior history of violent conduct or behavioral problems on the part of Baker or Elliott, or between the two teams, so

---

[32] Jacqueline Stenson, "Pushing Too Hard Too Young: Take Away the Fun Factor in Sports and Kids Can Burn Out," *MSNBC.com*, April 29, 2004.

as to have placed Trinity on notice of the conduct which caused Baker's injuries. In addition, there was no violent history between Baker and Elliott, and Elliott was concededly not part of either the elbowing or eye-punching incidents, which themselves were not shown to be outside the bounds of normal play. In sum, Trinity and Hotchkiss demonstrated they had no actual or constructive knowledge of dangerous conduct on the part of Baker's attacker, and, accordingly could not have reasonably foreseen the attack on Baker.

Source: *Reprinted from Westlaw with permission of Thomson Reuters.*

What responsibilities should the school have with regard to violence in the *Baker* case?

CASE STUDY 6-9   *Violence in Ice Skating*

Women's amateur ice skating would seem to be a sport free of violence but that was not the case leading up to the 1994 Olympics. Tonya Harding and Nancy Kerrigan were both outstanding ice skaters and fierce competitors. Harding, however, would take the competition just a bit too far. She conspired with her ex-husband Jeff Gillooly to attack her competitor, Nancy Kerrigan, at a practice session during the 1994 U.S. figure skating championships. After she admitted to covering up the attack, the USOC initiated proceedings against her to remove her from the 1994 U.S. Olympic team. She pled guilty to hindering the investigation of the attack and received three years probation. The United States Figure Skating Association met to determine whether Harding had violated their code of ethics. The association code of ethics stated, in part: "Any person whose acts, statements or conduct is considered detrimental to the welfare of figure skating is subject to the loss of the privilege of registration by the U.S.F.S.A."[33] Harding later became a boxer.[34]

What rules should be in place regarding the physical contact of a student by a coach? Should a coach be required to always seek permission before he or she touches a player? In Case 6-10, the coach did more than merely touch a player during a football scrimmage.

CASE 6-10   *Koffman v. Garnett*

574 S.E.2d 258 (2003)

In the fall of 2000, Andrew W. Koffman, a 13-year-old middle school student at a public school in Botetourt County, began participating on the school's football team. It was Andy's first season playing organized football, and he was positioned as a third-string defensive player. James Garnett was employed by the Botetourt County School Board as an assistant coach for the football team and was responsible for the supervision, training, and instruction of the team's defensive players.

[33] Richard Sandomir, "Harding Faces New Threat on Ethics," *New York Times*, February 4, 1994; Jere Longman, "Kerrigan Attacked After Practice, Assailant Flees," *New York Times*, January 7, 1994.
[34] Stan Grossfel, "From the Rink, to the Rink," *The Boston Glove*, January 26, 2005.

The team lost its first game of the season. Garnett was upset by the defensive players' inadequate tackling in that game and became further displeased by what he perceived as inadequate tackling during the first practice following the loss. Garnett ordered Andy to hold a football and "stand upright and motionless" so that Garnett could explain the proper tackling technique to the defensive players. Then Garnett, without further warning, thrust his arms around Andy's body, lifted him "off his feet by two feet or more," and "slamm [ed]" him to the ground. Andy weighed 144 pounds, while Garnett weighed approximately 260 pounds. The force of the tackle broke the humerus bone in Andy's left arm. During prior practices, no coach had used physical force to instruct players on rules or techniques of playing football. . . .

The disparity in size between Garnett and Andy was obvious to Garnett. Because of his authority as a coach, Garnett must have anticipated that Andy would comply with his instructions to stand in a non-defensive, upright, and motionless position. Under these circumstances, Garnett proceeded to aggressively tackle the much smaller, inexperienced student football player, by lifting him more than two feet from the ground and slamming him into the turf. According to the Koffmans' allegations, no coach had tackled any player previously so there was no reason for Andy to expect to be tackled by Garnett, nor was Andy warned of the impending tackle or of the force Garnett would use.

Receiving an injury while participating in a tackling demonstration may be part of the sport. Andy's injury, however, goes beyond the circumstances of simply being tackled in the course of participating in organized football. Here Garnett's knowledge of his greater size and experience, his instruction implying that Andy was not to take any action to defend himself from the force of a tackle, the force he used during the tackle, and Garnett's previous practice of not personally using force to demonstrate or teach football technique signify that his actions were imprudent and taken in utter disregard for the safety of the player involved.

Source: *Reprinted from Westlaw with permission of Thomson Reuters.*

OFF-THE-FIELD VIOLENCE

The news is replete with stories of athletes allegedly engaging in improper conduct off the field.[35] Whether in professional or collegiate athletics, off-the-field conduct of athletes has become a concern for both professional leagues and universities. Drunk driving, drugs, domestic violence, assault, theft, and identity theft have all become issues. At the collegiate level, universities are forced to step in and take action against student-athletes who behave badly. Many student-athletes are on a

---

[35] "Are NBA Stars Out of Bounds Off the Court?" *ABC News*, July 2, 2004.

scholarship at the university, and when they act poorly, it makes the news. However, sometimes a university seems to overlook problems a star player may have just to keep him on the field of play. Many have argued that the penalties are not severe enough for professional athletes for their off-the-field misdeeds.[36] However, there are some lines that cannot be crossed.[37]

New York Mets pitcher Francisco Rodriguez, a four-time all-star, was arrested and charged with third-degree assault and second-degree harassment after assaulting his girlfriend's father at Citi Field. As a result of the assault on his girlfriend's father, Rodriguez tore a ligament in his hand. He had surgery on his hand and missed the remainder of the 2010 season. As a result, the Mets converted his guaranteed contract to a non-guaranteed contract as permitted to do under the terms of the contract and announced the club would not pay him until he was able to play again. The players' union filed a grievance on Rodriguez's behalf, which was eventually settled between the parties.[38]

Domestic Violence

No other issue seems to be in the news more than athletes beating up women. ". . . [d]omestic violence has been largely ignored by professional sports leagues. This inaction persists despite the fact that a survey revealed seventy six percent of U.S. adults and eighty two percent of teens think it is "bad for society" to allow athletes to continue their sports careers when convicted of a violent crime."[39] Even sportscasters are sometimes involved in domestic violence.[40]

In an attempt to curb domestic violence in the NFL, the league has instituted a personal conduct policy that covers domestic violence, among other issues:

> Examples of such prohibited conduct include, without limitation: any crime involving the use or threat of physical violence to a person or persons; the use of a deadly weapon in the commission of a crime; possession or distribution of a weapon in violation of state or federal law; involvement in "hate crimes" or crimes of domestic violence; theft, larceny or other property crimes; sex offenses; racketeering; money laundering; obstruction of justice.[41]

The episodes of domestic violence in sports are too numerous to list, but a few examples are noteworthy. Former NFL player Mark Fields was arrested after he allegedly beat the mother of his 6-year-old daughter outside the child's day care center.[42] A. J. Nicholson was one of nine Bengals players arrested during a 9-month span, turning the team into a prime example of player misconduct.[43] Corey Dillon, a former Cincinnati Bengal denied touching his wife, but the two were engaged in an argument when they allegedly began "throwing water and soy sauce" in each other's direction.[44]

Some scholars argue that professional athletes are treated more leniently when dealing with domestic violence issues:

---

[36] John Levesque, "Violence Part of NBA's History," *SeattlePI.com*, November 23, 2004.

[37] "NFL Players Arrested This Year," *Washington Post*, December 16, 2006.

[38] "Union Files Grievance over Mets' Stance on K-Rod," *SI.com*, August 18, 2010; Adam Rubin, "Union Grievance on Francisco Rodriguez," *ESPN.com*, August 18, 2010.

[39] Bethany P. Withers, "The Integrity of the Game: Professional Athletes and Domestic Violence," *Journal of Sports and Entertainment Law, Harvard Law School,* 1, no. 1 (Spring 2010).

[40] "ESPN's Jay Mariotti Released from Jail on $50,000 Bail," *Los Angeles Times*, August 21, 2010.

[41] "NFL Personal Conduct Policy," *ESPN.com*, March 13, 2007.

[42] Caroline Black, "Mark Fields, Ex-NFL Player, Arrested for Alleged Domestic Violence," *CBS News*, August 13, 2010.

[43] Associated Press, "Bengals' Nicholson Arrested on Domestic Violence Charge," *ESPN.com*, May 18, 2007.

[44] "Corey Dillon Domestic Violence? Ex-NFL RB Arrested," *Huffington Post*, May 3, 2010.

It's pretty sobering to visualize a big muscular athlete knocking down a woman or pummeling a grandfather. Against the sheer violence involved in each of these cases, it's easy to overlook the fact that each of these incidents played out in front of plenty of witnesses. Typically, domestic violence is the kind of crime that goes on behind closed doors, where bullies carry out threats and violence without fear of being seen or caught.

But athletes are less prone to fear consequences, especially when it comes to their off-the-field behavior. [Mark] Fields confronted his ex-girlfriend outside a child care facility at five o'clock on a Monday afternoon. Rodriguez couldn't have picked a more public place to berate his girlfriend and strike her father than at a ballpark, never mind the fact that there were security guards on hand.[45]

1. Are the NFL and other professional sports leagues doing enough to curb domestic violence by players?[46]
2. Should fans boycott the NFL until the issue of domestic violence in the league is addressed by the league sufficiently?
3. Do you believe it is just a few criminals in sports that are giving the majority of players a bad name?[47]
4. What ethical duties do professional leagues owe to their fans to produce a criminal-free product?
5. Does a double standard exist for professional players when it comes to off-the-field conduct, and specifically with regard to domestic violence?

Other Types of Violence

In the following case study, an NFL player was charged with DWI manslaughter after he killed a pedestrian.

CASE STUDY 6-10 *NFL Player Conduct*

Donté Stallworth was a standout wide receiver in the NFL for the Cleveland Browns. On March 14, 2009, he struck and killed a 59-year-old man while driving his 2005 Bentley. Stallworth had been at a bar celebrating a $4.5 million roster signing bonus the night of the crash. His blood alcohol level of .126 was well above the .08 legal limit of the state of Florida. He pled guilty to DWI manslaughter, a second degree felony, and served 24 days in jail. He was placed on two years probation and performed 1,000 hours of community service. Stallworth was suspended for the entire 2009 season by the NFL commissioner for his actions.[48]

1. Were the actions of the NFL commissioner proper and just?
2. Do you think Stallworth received preferential treatment by the justice system because he was a professional athlete? Compare Stallworth's sentence to that of Andrew Gallo. Gallo was a

---

[45] Jeff Benedict, "A Double Standard When It Comes to Athletes and Domestic Violence," *SI.com*, August 18, 2010. Also see Jeff Benedict, *Public Heroes, Private Felons: Athletes and Crimes Against Women* (Lebanon, NH: Northeastern University Press, 1997).

[46] See Anna L. Jefferson, "The NFL and Domestic Violence: The Commissioner's Power to Punish Domestic Abusers," *Seton Hall Journal of Sports Law* (1997).

[47] See Gerry Dulac, "NFL Finds Domestic Violence Difficult to Gauge," *Post Gazette*, March 12, 2008.

[48] Associated Press, "Donté Stallworth Suspended Without Pay for Season," *New York Times*, August 13, 2009.

24-year-old construction worker who killed three people while driving drunk. One of the individuals he killed was Los Angeles Angels pitcher Nick Adenhart. Gallo was sentenced to "51 years to life" by a California judge. Gallo's blood alcohol level was three times the legal limit when he ran a red light at 65 miles per hour. At the time of the crash, Gallo was on parole for a felony DUI conviction.[49]

HAZING

Hazing exists at all levels of sports. Some sports initiations are simple and just poke a little fun at rookies. When NFL player Tim Tebow joined the Denver Broncos, they gave him a new, rather unattractive haircut. That is not the kind of hazing discussed in this chapter. Multiple episodes of illegal behavior, abuse, and horrific acts that have ended in death and injuries have occurred on both college and high school campuses across the United States in the last few years, bringing this issue to prominence.[50] Many of these episodes go unreported, but hazing incidents can result in a criminal indictment in many jurisdictions.[51] Many times the hazed individual sues the school district and the individuals who performed the hazing.[52] Many student-athletes who were involved in hazing are suspended by the school for their participation in hazing.[53]

In the following case, members of a sports team were criminally charged with hazing.

📖 CASE 6-11 *Haben v. Anderson*

597 N.E. 2d 655 (1992)

Nicholas E. Haben was an 18-year-old freshman at Western Illinois University in the fall of 1990. On October 18, 1990, Haben was a "rookie" in the Lacrosse Club, a recognized and sanctioned student activity at the University. Club membership was "a valued status." On October 18, 1990, between 3:00 p.m. and 10:30 p.m., the defendants participated in the "initiation" of new recruits of the Club known as "rookies," which included Haben.

It was alleged that during the initiation ceremony, the defendants caused or participated in causing various types and quantities of intoxicating beverages to be given and ingested by the rookie initiates of the Club. The rookies, including Haben, were required to engage in various strenuous physical activities, and submit to acts intended to

---

[49] Associated Press, "Nick Adenhart's Killer Sentenced," *ESPN*, December 22, 2010.

[50] "Sports Hazing Incidents," *ESPN.com*, June 3, 2000.

[51] "Judge Adds Charges in Hazing Case," *CNN.com*, June 11, 2003; Associated Press, "Hazing Case Ends in Some Jail Time for Ball Players," *KATU.com*, May 13, 2008.

[52] "Coopersville School District Settles Hazing Case for Undisclosed Sum," *Grand Rapids Press*, July 15, 2009.

[53] Maria Newman, "14 Girls Tied to Hazing Case Are Suspended from Team," *New York Times*, September 5, 2001. Also see Michael S. Carroll, Daniel P. Connaughton, John O. Spengler, and James J. Zhang, "Case Law Analysis Regarding High School and Collegiate Liability for Hazing," *European Sports Management Quarterly* 9, no. 4 (December 2009): 389–410. Also see Marc Edelman, "How to Prevent High School Hazing: A Legal, Social, and Ethical Primer," *North Dakota Law Review* 81 (2005).

ridicule and degrade them, including smearing their bodies, faces, and hair with various food and other materials. These activities allegedly violated the Hazing Act and University regulations. It was alleged that the hazing and drinking activities had been conducted by the Club members for a number of years and had become a "tradition of, and a *de facto* requirement for, membership in the Club," and that the pressure to consume dangerous quantities of alcohol created a hazardous condition threatening the initiate's physical welfare.

Haben became highly intoxicated and lost consciousness. He was carried to defendant Kolovitz's dorm room, where, in Kolovitz's presence, he was laid on the floor and then left alone. Kolovitz returned to the room on more than one occasion to check on Haben and heard him "gurgling." Haben was discovered dead about 9:00 a.m., on October 19, 1990. He died from acute ethanol intoxication, possessing a blood ethanol level in excess of .34.

Source: *Reprinted from Westlaw with permission of Thomson Reuters.*

As an SMP what measures should be taken to limit hazing by athletes? What should be contained in a school district anti-hazing policy? How would you define hazing? Consider the following Connecticut state law on hazing. Is it complete or are there other measures that needed to be added?

Sec. 53-23a. HAZING

1. "Hazing" means any action which recklessly or intentionally endangers the health or safety of a person for the purpose of initiation, admission into or affiliation with, or as a condition for continued membership in a student organization. The term shall include, but not be limited to:
   a. Requiring indecent exposure of the body;
   b. Requiring any activity that would subject the person to extreme mental stress, such as sleep deprivation or extended isolation from social contact;
   c. Confinement of the person to unreasonably small, unventilated, unsanitary or unlighted areas;
   d. Any assault upon the person; or
   e. Requiring the ingestion of any substance or any other physical activity which could adversely affect the health or safety of the individual. The term shall not include an action sponsored by an institution of higher education which requires any athletic practice, conditioning, or competition or curricular activity.

NOTES AND DISCUSSION QUESTIONS

Introduction

1. What are some of the primary causes of violence in sports?[54]
2. What measures can be taken to stem the rising tide of violence in sports?
3. How should violence against spectators be dealt with on the professional level?
4. Should violent fans be banned from further events?

---

[54] See "Geauga Dad Sues Baseball Coach After Son Hit by Pitch," *The News-Herald*, July 16, 2010.

5. What steps should professional leagues take to curb violence? What should they do to ensure that fans do not incite players to violent acts?

6. What rules and procedures should be in place to prevent violent acts from occurring in amateur sports?

7. What can be done to curtail the "win at all costs" attitude in youth sports?

8. How can a balance be achieved between the competitive spirit and allowing the participants to have fun?

9. Sports violence is not new. Former Heavyweight Champion John Sullivan once beat up a one-armed lawyer on a train and choked him. He was charged criminally for his actions.[55]

10. Detroit Tiger great Ty Cobb once entered the stands to "thrash profane commentators." *The New York Times* reported:

> Everything was very pleasant at the Detroit-Yankee game on the Hilltop yesterday until Ty Cobb Johnny-Kilbaned a spectator right on the place where he talks, started the claret, and stopped the flow of profane and vulgar words. Cobb led with a left jab and countered with a right kick to Mr. Spectator's left Welsbach, which made his peeper look as if someone had drawn a curtain over it. Silk O'Loughlin, without a license from the boxing commission, refereed the go. He gave the decision to Cobb and then put him out of the ring. The spectator went to a lawyer's office to make out his will.
>
> The scrap broke up the game for a while. Umpire O'Loughlin and several Detroit players subtracted Cobb from his victim. Cobb's execution was rapid and effective. Ty used a change of pace and nice control. Jabs bounced off the spectator's face like a golf ball from a rock. Cobb was dragged back to the clubhouse. The spectator got the gate.[56]

Should a player who enters the stands from the playing field be subject to special discipline by the league commissioner or the team?

11. Is the sport of boxing too violent? Many boxers have died after bouts in the ring.[57] What regulations should be in place to ensure the integrity of boxing?[58]

12. The National Collegiate Athletic Association discontinued boxing championships after 1960. At the 1960 NCAA championships, Charlie Mohr from the University of Wisconsin Madison collapsed with a brain hemorrhage and passed away a week later. Should the NCAA allow boxing if they also allow wrestling, football, and ice hockey? Is football any less violent than boxing or hockey?[59]

13. Should rules differ for a "brush-back" pitch at the amateur and professional levels? In April 2009, Patrick Clegg, a high school player, tragically died after he was struck in the head by a pitched ball.[60]

14. Ultimate Championship Fighting (UCF) has become a very popular sport. At what age should kids be allowed to participate in such a sport? These bare knuckle fighting events

---

[55] See "Sullivan at It Again," *New York Times*, May 16, 1893.

[56] "Cobb Whips Hilltop Fan For Insults," *New York Times*, May 16, 1912.

[57] See Geoffrey Gray, "In Debate over Safety, No Neutral Corner," *New York Times*, December 3, 2005.

[58] See Antoinette Vacca, "Boxing: Why It Should Be Down for the Count," *Sports Lawyers Journal* (Spring 2006); Dave Anderson, "Finally! Federal Law for Boxing," *New York Times*, June 29, 1997.

[59] See "Boxing's Final Round," *The Badger Herald*, April 29, 2004.

[60] Associated Press, "High School Baseball Player Killed by Wild Pitch," *Fox News*, April 25, 2009. Also see Mike Sowell, *The Pitch That Killed* (Hoboken, NJ: John Wiley & Sons, 1991).

are now drawing kids as young as 6 years old as participants. It is any different from mixed martial arts for children? Is 6 years old too young for mixed martial arts? Does it teach kids to be violent or just competitive?[61]

Rules and Regulations

15. What types of rules and regulations should professional leagues have in place regarding violent behavior by athletes both on and off the field? What role should professional sports unions have in the administration of such matters?

16. Should leagues have gun control policies for players? Should a league be able to limit the possession of a weapon by a player?[62]

17. Should there be a special rule in high school football that protects the quarterback from injury? What type of rule is this: prospective or sportsmanship? What would be the purpose of such a rule?[63]

Civil and Criminal Sanctions

18. NFL player Plaxico Burress pled guilty to a weapons charge after shooting himself in a nightclub. He received a 2-year prison sentence.[64]

19. Hockey certainly has had its share of violence. Whether hockey violence is too extreme has been a matter of debate.[65]

20. Many hockey teams have an "enforcer" on their squad to ensure opposing players do not "mess" with their star players. Tie Domi was a noted enforcer in the NHL and once fought a fan in the penalty box.[66]

21. What should be done about violence in hockey? Should fighting be prohibited, or is it just too much a part of the game?[67]

22. Canada has been more aggressive than the United States in prosecuting violent athletes in the criminal courts.[68]

23. Marty McSorley was convicted of assaulting Vancouver Canucks' Donald Brasher in an on-ice incident. McSorley clearly understood his role in hockey, saying he just wanted to fight, not to hurt anyone.[69] Brasher suffered a grand mal seizure before regaining consciousness. McSorley was found guilty of assault and placed on criminal probation for 18 months.[70]

---

[61] See "Outside the Lines . . . for Kids," *ESPN.com*, July 19, 2008; *Also see*, G.J. Buse, "No Holds Barred Sports Fighting: A 10 Year Review of Mixed Martial Arts Competition," *British Journal of Sports Medicine* (February 9, 2006).

[62] See Lynn Zinser, "The N.F.L. Gun Culture," *New York Times*, December 1, 2008.

[63] See Thomas George, "Pro Football; N.F.L. Is Nearly Unanimous in Stand on Phoenix Super Bowl Issue," *New York Times*, March 21, 1991.

[64] John Eligon, "Burress Will Receive 2-Year Prison Sentence," *New York Times*, August 21, 2009.

[65] For a general discussion of violence in sports see Jeff Yates and William Gillespie, "The Problem of Sports Violence and the Criminal Prosecution Solution," *Cornell Journal of Law and Public Policy* 12, no. 145 (2002).

[66] See Arpon Basu, *NHL Enforcers: The Rough and Tough Guys of Hockey* (Montreal, Quebec, Canada: Overtime Books, 2006); "Leafs Win as Domi Fights Fan," *New York Times*, March 30, 2001.

[67] See Christine Brennan, "Latest Violence Calls Future of NHL into Question," *USA Today*, March 10, 2004.

[68] See *Regina v. Green*, 1 O.R. 591 (Ont. Prov. Ct. 1970).

[69] Tom Spousta, "Hockey: McSorley Says He Wants to Fight, Not Injure," *New York Times*, September 28, 2000.

[70] *Regina v. McSorley*, 2000 BCPC 117, at paragraph 21 (B.C. Prov. Ct.).

24. U.S. Representative Ronald Mottl of Ohio, a former baseball player, introduced the Sports Violence Act of 1980, but the bill failed to pass. Should there be a federal law dealing with this issue?[71]

25. The NFL has a "bounty rule," which fines any team that pays a player to target an opposing player for injury. Should all leagues impose such a rule? Can a team award players for "big hits" on the field without violating this rule?[72]

26. Baseball has its own version of violence. Interestingly enough, baseball is the only sport where all the players on the same team do not sit together on the bench.[73] Do you think separating teammates on the playing field decreases the chances of violence?

27. In one of the more infamous cases in baseball violence, pitcher Juan Marichal struck catcher John Roseboro in the head with a baseball bat. Marichal was later sued by Roseboro, and the case was settled for $6,000. Marichal was fined and suspended by the league.[74] Should baseball players who use bats as a weapon, during a game be charged criminally?

28. Violence in hockey can unfortunately occur off the ice as well.[75]

29. The commissioner of the NHL has said: "I think fighting has always reached whatever level is appropriate in the game and has been a part of the game. And I don't have a problem with that."[76] Do you agree with his statements? Is this an ethical or a proper view of violence in hockey by the commissioner of a sports league?[77]

Violence in Professional and Amateur Sports

30. A youth football league fired a coach after he was seen on videotape "leveling" a 13-year-old player from the opposing team. The coach was suspended for life.[78] Do you think this punishment was appropriate?

31. Some parents are unable to deal with a child's failure to excel in athletics. A parent attacked a coach after his daughter was cut from the basketball team. The coach went to the hospital as a result of the attack.[79]

32. Vince Lombardi may be the greatest football coach in the history of the NFL. He is reported to have said, "winning isn't everything, it's the only thing." Should that apply to youth sports as well? Where do you draw the line?[80]

---

[71] See Jeff Yates and William Gillespie, "The Problem of Sports Violence and the Criminal Prosecution Solution," *Cornell Journal of Law and Public Policy* 12, no. 145 (2002).

[72] See Thomas George, "N.F.L. Bounty-Hunting Dispute," *New York Times*, December 6, 1989.

[73] See Spike Vrusho, *Benchclearing: Baseball's Greatest Fights and Riots* (Guilford, CT: Lyon Press, 2008); "Rogers Doesn't Feel Tarnished by Accident," *South Florida Sun-Sentinel*, February 18, 2007.

[74] See "Tells His Side," *Chicago Tribune*, August 24, 1965.

[75] See *Commonwealth v. Junta*, 62 Mass. App. Ct. 120 (2004); "'Hockey Dad' Gets 6 to 10 Years for Fatal Beating," *CNN.com*, January 25, 2002.

[76] "Bettman: Fighting Part of the Game," *USA Today*, March 26, 2007.

[77] Also see "Should Violent Athletes Be Prosecuted?" *NPR*, March 2, 2000.

[78] "Football Coach Who Tackled Kid Gets Fired," *MSNBC.com*, September 7, 2006.

[79] See "Parent Attacks Coach After Daughter Cut from Team," *News Net*, November 10, 2005.

[80] See Eric Margenau, *Sports Without Pressure: A Guide for Parents and Coaches of Young Athletes* (New York: Gardner Press: 1990).

33. The Florida High School Athletic Association allows coaches, student-athletes, teams, officials, and spectators to complete an "exceptional sportsmanship report" for anyone who has done an exemplary job of displaying sportsmanship.[81]

34. The National Collegiate Athletic Association (NCAA) has established sportsmanship conduct penalties for on-the-field behavior. They range from a player removing his helmet while on the playing field, to making obscene gestures intended to incite the crowd, to pointing fingers at opponents, to prearranged or choreographed routines, or to a prolonged act where a player draws attention to himself. This includes praying in the end zone. A violation of the rule is a 15-yard penalty, with two penalties in the same game resulting in an ejection. What is the purpose behind these rules?[82] What if the celebration is done for religious purposes?

35. Ohio State's great football coach Woody Hayes once struck a cameraman during a 14–6 loss to Michigan. He was suspended for two games. His career was later marred by an incident in which he struck a Clemson player during a game.[83]

36. Temple coach John Cheney once directed a player to purposely injure another player.[84] What should be done to coaches who order "hits" on opposing players?

37. Should college coaches' contracts contain morals clause dealing with situations that occur both on and off the field, court, or ice? A typical morals clause in a coach's contract might stipulate that the coach be fired for the following reasons:
    — Dishonesty with employer or university
    — Acts of "moral depravity"
    — Conviction of a felony or drug-related misdemeanor
    — Intoxication
    — Being under the influence of illegal substances when performing duties under their contract[85]

38. Should a college coach be terminated for violent acts against a player? How would you define a violent act? Would your definition of violence also include emotional violence against players? Should a distinction be made between professional and amateur coaches for the purposes of discipline?[86]

39. In a rather unusual move, Texas Rangers reliever Frank Francisco tossed a chair into the stands and hit two fans in the head in the ninth inning of a game against the A's. He launched the chair used by the ball boy and hit a man in the face and broke a woman's nose. He was taken from the stadium directly to jail.[87]

---

[81] See 2009-2010 FHSAA Sportsmanship Manual.

[82] See Ivan Maisel, "Kicking Off Celebration Officiating," *Newsday*, August 27, 1997; Jeffrey C. True, "The NCAA Celebration Rule: A First Amendment Analysis," *Seton Hall Journal of Sports Law* (1997).

[83] See Alex Fineman, "Hayes Produced Champions, Controversy," *ESPN Classic*; "Big Ten Rebukes Hayes," *New York Times*, December 3, 1977.

[84] Jere Longman, "Chaney Trying to Get Back Inbounds," *New York Times*, February 25, 2005.

[85] See Porcher L. Taylor III, Fernando M. Pinguelo, and Timothy D. Cedrone, "The Reverse-Morals Clause: The Unique Way to Save Talent's Reputation and Money in a New Era of Corporate Crimes and Scandals," *Cordozo Arts & Entertainment Law Journal* 28, no. 1 (2010): 65.

[86] Cameron Jay Rains, "Sports Violence: A Matter of Societal Concern," *Notre Dame Law Review* 55 (1979–80): 796–813.

[87] "Rangers Pitcher Charged After Throwing Chair into Stands," *CBC Sports*, September 15, 2004.

40. Unfortunately, international athletics are subject to violence as well, with political over-tones.[88] At the 1972 Olympics, 11 Israeli athletes were killed in the Olympic Village. Millions of viewers watched the events unfold on television.[89]

41. Steroids and their use may contribute to aggressive behavior on the playing field. Professional leagues as well as amateur sports associations have taken extreme measures to try to prevent the use of steroids by players and student-athletes.[90] Former NFL lineman Lyle Alzado claims his "ticket" to the NFL was anabolic steroids. He became the symbol for the dangers of steroid abuse.[91] There is some evidence that steroid users are more likely to engage in aggressive behavior, sometimes referred to as "roid rage."[92]

42. Corporations typically place a morals clause in contracts as corporate protection. When companies hire athletes as spokespersons for their products or services, they seek to increase exposure of their product as well as increase revenue. The company also assumes the risk that the sports celebrity may get into some trouble along the way. A morals clause typically allow a corporation to cancel an agreement in the event the athlete engages in conduct that brings the corporation into a "bad light" or tarnishes its image.[93] Accusations of sexual assault of a woman in a hotel room caused Kobe Bryant to lose endorsements with McDonalds, Spalding, Coca-Cola, and Nutella.[94]

43. Violence has even erupted on the NASCAR circuit with drivers fighting each other on the track during and after races.[95]

44. Shaking hands before the game as a show of sportsmanship does not always produce the intended results. Oregon's LeGarrette Blount punched Boise State's Byron Hunt immediately after the Ducks' loss to the Broncos at the start of the 2009 season. Blount was suspended for the entire season as a result of his actions. Blount had led his teammates to shake hands with Boise State players before the game.[96]

45. ESPN lists the Tyson bite of Holyfield's ear as the most infamous moment in sports history.[97]

46. NBA player Vernon Maxwell had no row limit for hecklers, once going 12 rows deep in an NBA venue to punch a heckler. He was fined $20,000 and received a 10-game suspension.[98]

---

[88] See Joshua Robinson, "Runners Face Rising Violence in Kenya," *New York Times*, January 5, 2008.

[89] See "Munich Massacre Remembered," *ABC News*, May 9, 2002.

[90] For further study, see Nathan Jendrick, *Dunks, Doubles, Doping: How Steroids Are Killing American Athletics* (Guilford, CT: Lyon Press, 2006); Shaun Assael, "Steroid, Nation: Juiced Home Run Totals, Anti-Aging Miracles, and a Hercules in Every High School: The Secret History of America's True Drug Addiction," *ESPN.com*, 2007.

[91] See Mike Puma, "Not the Size of the Dog in the Fight," *ESPN.com*.

[92] See Will Dunham, "Steroid Users Seen Twice as Prone to Violence," *Reuters*, October 15, 2008.

[93] "Golfer Says Comments About Woods 'Misconstrued,'" *CNN Interactive*, April 21, 1997.

[94] Richard Sandomier, "Like Him or Not, Bryant the Brand Is Scoring, Too," *New York Times*, January 27, 2006. For further study, see Daniel Auerbach, "Morals Clauses as Corporate Protection in Athlete Endorsement Contracts," *DePaul Journal of Sports Law & Contemporary Problems* (Summer, 2005).

[95] See "Foyt and Luyendyk Fined for Fight," *New York Times*, July 11, 1997.

[96] Chadd Cripe, "LeGarrette Blount Apologizes for Punching Boise State's Byron Hunt," *Idaho Statesman*, September 4, 2009.

[97] "The Most Infamous Moments," *ESPN.com*, December 31, 2007.

[98] Jeff Merron, "Fighting Through the Years," *ESPN.com*, November 20, 2004.

47. NFL player Pat Tillman turned down a big contract with the NFL Arizona Cardinals to serve in the Iraq War. Tragically, he lost his life on the battlefield. He was only 27.[99]

48. For further study, see Charles Haray, "Aggressive Play or Criminal Assault? An In-Depth Look at Sports Violence and Criminal Liability," *Columbia Journal of Law & the Arts* (Winter 2002); Jenni Spies, "Only Orphans Should Be Allowed to Play Little League: How Parents Are Ruining Organized Youth Sports for Their Children and What Can Be Done About It," *Sports Lawyers Journal* (Spring 2006); Sean Bukowski, "Flag on the Play: 25 to Life for the Offense of Murder," *Vanderbilt Journal of Entertainment Law & Practice* (Winter, 2001).

49. At the amateur level, the Florida High School Athletic Association regulates unsportsman-like conduct and assesses a penalty for such conduct as follows:

> *Disqualification (ejection) for general unsportsmanlike conduct or flagrant foul.*
> (1) Student-Athlete. Suspend from competition for remainder of contest and all contests on all levels for the following seven days, but not less than the next two regularly scheduled contests (one contest in boys football).[100]

Is the penalty too harsh or too lenient? Why is the penalty for boys' football only one game?

50. What if the best player for a local youth soccer team has a sprained ankle and is going to play against your team, but his movement will be limited? As the coach of the opposing team, is it ethical to instruct your players to purposely tackle the star player around the ankles to attempt to put him out of the game? Would your answer be different if it were a professional game?[101]

Off-the-Field Violence

51. There has been much discussion about personal conduct policies in professional sports. Should all professional leagues have personal conduct policies?[102]

52. Some players have continued to commit violent acts after their playing days were over. Former MLB pitcher Ugueth Urbina was sentenced to 14 years in prison for the attempted murder of five workers on his family's ranch near Caracas, Venezuela.[103]

53. Author Don Yeager says it should be no surprise that so many NBA players are arrested. He deemed them adolescents "who are excessively paid and over hyped to play a boy's game while living in a cocoon where they are pampered, protected, and never told no."[104] Do you agree with his assessment? What are some of the root causes of athlete violence?[105]

---

[99] See Karen Crouse, "Tillman's Presence Is Still Strong," *New York Times*, January 31, 2009.

[100] Florida High School Athletic Association Rulebook.

[101] Randy Cohen, "Ankles Away," *New York Times*, June 3, 2001.

[102] See Mike Florio, "NFL Personal Conduct Policy Finally Making an Impact?" *Sporting News*, June 29, 2009.

[103] Associated Press, "Ex-Pitcher Urbina Sentenced to 14 Years for Attempted Murder," *CBS Sports*, March 28, 2007.

[104] Jeff Benedict, *Out of Bounds: Inside the NBA's Culture of Rape, Violence, and Crime* (New York: Perennial Currents, 2004): 216.

[105] See Joel Michael Ugolini, "Even a Violent Game Has Its Limits: A Look at the NFL's Responsibility for the Behavior of Its Players," *University of Toledo Law Review* (Fall 2007); Jeff Benedict and Don Yaeger, *Pros and Cons: The Criminals Who Play in the NFL* (New York: Warner Books, 1998).

54. Bennie Blades, former NFL player, once said, "It's going to be a lot harder for us to get out of trouble now. Three years ago, you smacked a girl around and people maybe said she asked for it. Now, whether she asked for it or not, they're going to haul you off."[106] Should the NFL take action against players for making similar statements? What does this say about some players' attitudes toward women? Blades paid $1 million in back child support in 2007.[107]

Hazing

55. What can be done to prevent further hazing incidents at the high school level or the collegiate level?[108]

56. What actions should an SMP take if confronted with a hazing situation?[109] A 1999 survey found that at least 80% of all college athletes were the subject of hazing.[110]

---

[106] Geoff Calkins, "Athletes and Domestic Violence," *Sun-Sentinel*, October 17, 1995.

[107] "In The Eyes of the State, Bennie Blades Is a Deadbeat Dad," *Detroit Free Press*, April 29, 2005. For further study, see W. Reed Moran, "NFL's Shields Tackles Domestic Abuse," *USA Today*, March 28, 2001.

[108] See Melissa Dixon, "Hazing in High School: Ending the Hidden Tradition," *Journal of Law and Education* 30 (2001): 357, 359–360.

[109] For further study, see "Public Posting of Illicit Photos Revives Hazing Issue," *USA Today*, May 19, 2006.

[110] "80% of College Athletes Victims of Hazing," *CNN.com*, August 30, 1999. See also Rehman Y. Abdulrehman, "The Cycle of Abuse in Sport Hazing: Is It Simply a Case of Boys Being Boys?" Dissertation, 2007; Sandra L. Kirby, "Running the Gauntlet: An Examination of Initiation/Hazing and Sexual Abuse in Sport," *Journal of Sexual Aggression* 8, no. 2 (July 2002); Joshua A. Sussberg, "Shattered Dreams: Hazing in College Athletics," *Cardozo Law Review* (2002–2003); Scott R. Rosner and R. Brian Crow, "Institutional Liability for Hazing in Interscholastic Sports," *Houston Law Review* (2002–2003); R. Brian Crow and Scott R. Rosner, "Institutional and Organizational Liability for Hazing in Intercollegiate and Professional Team Sports," *St. John's Law Review* (2002).

CHAPTER 7

THE ETHICS OF DRUG USE AND TESTING

INTRODUCTION

The use of performance-enhancing drugs (PED's) by athletes and drug testing has been one of the most debated ethical dilemmas in sports for the past few years. Debate regarding the use of steroids has become prevalent among professional athletes, coaches, trainers, student-athletes, parents, and school administrators. The ethics of drug use and testing has been written about, debated, litigated, and discussed in all forms of media. Every week there seems to be a new revelation about an athlete who has attempted to improve his or her performance through the use of PED's. Numerous sports associations including the Tour de France, the National Football League (U.S.), Ultimate Fighting Championship, NASCAR, the English Premier League, and the Professional Bowlers Association have instituted drug testing policies.[1] The overall purpose of a drug testing scheme is to prevent the use of artificial drugs by competitors and to ensure that the competition is fair to all participants.

Unfortunately, drug use and the use of performance-enhancing drugs in sports is not new. In 1971 it was reported that "Drug usage is quickly becoming as common among athletes as the wearing of white sweat socks."[2] Dave Meggyesy, a former National Football League player, quit the league in 1969, claiming it was "dehumanizing" because NFL trainers were no better than the average junkie.[3] In 1973, U.S. Senator Birch Bayh noted a huge increase in the use of drugs by athletes, including those in amateur sports, and specifically addressed the use of steroids among athletes.[4] The subject of drug use by athletes was reported in the *New York Times* in 1971 as follows:

The sport where the greatest variety as well as the greatest quantity of drugs are used is football— particularly professional football, although the use of drugs in football often extends all the way down

---

[1] For an overview of these policies and other sports associations see, "A Sports Fan's Guide to Drug Testing," *The Wall Street Journal Online*, November 12, 2009.
[2] Jack Scott, "It's Not How You Play the Game, but What Pill You Take," *New York Times*, October 17, 1971.
[3] "Meggyesy Charges Drugs Fed to Pros," *Washington Post*, November 3, 1970.
[4] "Athletic Drug Use Is Problem," *Chicago Tribune*, November 27, 1973.

to the Pop Warner Leagues. I recently had an irate and disgusted parent tell me how the star quarterback on his son's Pop Warner Team was given three injections of painkiller so he could play in the "championship" game. As startling as this may seem, it is really not surprising, for, from the players on the field to the coaches on the sidelines, Pop Warner league participants dress and behave as miniature replicas of their heroes in the college and professional ranks.

Realistically, however, the Lombardi philosophy that "winning is the only thing" is likely to continue as the dominant one in American athletics. As long as there is an inordinate emphasis on winning, athletes will continue using drugs or any other aid they believe will contribute to the likelihood of victory.[5]

Drug use is not a new problem, but many believe drug use—and, specifically, the use of performance-enhancing drugs—has increased in both the professional and amateur ranks in recent years. The use of performance-enhancing drugs among athletes poses multiple ethical dilemmas and raises numerous questions. The livelihood of the professional athlete depends on his or her achievement at the highest level. An athlete's career can be very short; therefore, many athletes are tempted to use performance-enhancing drugs to enhance their performance on the field. Professional athletes clearly understand the better they perform on the field of play, the greater potential they have to make more money. In today's competitive sports market, players want to hit more home runs, score more touchdowns, or jump higher than their competitors because their performance will most likely be directly tied to their next playing contract or endorsement deal.

In recent years it has almost become commonplace for sports stars to come forward and confess that they have used performance-enhancing drugs to improve their play. The list is long, but a few are noteworthy. Alex Rodriguez of the New York Yankees is the highest paid player in MLB and one of the most recognized athletes in the world. Initially, Rodriguez claimed he never used steroids[6] but later admitted he did in fact use steroids for a three-year period beginning in 2001 while playing for the American League Texas Rangers. During an interview he said, "Back then, [baseball] was a different culture. . . . It was very loose. I was young. I was stupid. I was naïve. And I wanted to prove to everyone that I was worth being one of the greatest players of all time. . . . I did take a banned substance. And for that, I am very sorry and deeply regretful."[7] Rodriguez has not been the only big name in sports to admit to the use of performance-enhancing drugs. Track star Marion Jones admitted steroid use when she was preparing for the 2000 Summer Olympic Games in Australia.[8] New York Yankees slugger Jason Giambi injected himself with human growth hormone in 2003 and admitted using steroids for several seasons. Although the Yankees could have terminated his playing contract for his drug use they chose not to do so.[9] Major league pitcher Roger Clemens is the subject of much debate when it comes to steroid use. Clemens denied any use of PED's and subsequently filed a lawsuit against his former trainer, Brian McNamee, for defamation, after McNamee claimed Clemens did use steroids during his playing days. The Clemens lawsuit was eventually dismissed.[10] Drug use in

---

[5] Jack Scott, "It's Not How You Play the Game, but What Pill You Take," *New York Times*, October 17, 1971.

[6] Associated Press, "A-Rod Steroids Report a Baseball Shocker," *CBS News*, February 7, 2009.

[7] "A-Rod Admits, Regrets Use of Performance Enhancing Drugs," *ESPN.com*, February 10, 2009.

[8] Amy Shipley, "Marion Jones Admits to Steroid Use," *Washington Post*, October 5, 2007.

[9] Scott Miller, "Giambi's Reported Steroid Use Admission Could Affect Yank's Deal," *CBS Sports*, December 2, 2004. Diana Taurasi's contract was terminated by Turkish Club Fenerbahce. Associated Press, "Taurasi has Turkish Contract Voided," *Fox Sports*, January 6, 2011.

[10] "Clemens' Lawsuit Against McNamee Dismissed," *Sporting News*, September 5, 2009.

sports has become the subject of several U.S. congressional hearings. President Barack Obama has even weighed in on the subject. The President said of Alex Rodriguez's admission of steroid use, "[it was] depressing news . . . and tarnishes an entire era in the national pastime."[11]

Before discussing whether using drugs to enhance athletic performance is ethical, it is important to establish what constitutes a "performance-enhancing drug" and how that determination is or should be made. The classification of substances as "performance enhancing" is not exactly clear cut. The term "performance-enhancing drugs" has been used to refer to a large group of drugs, including the following:

- Diuretics
- Sedatives
- Painkillers
- Stimulants
- Lean mass builders

A true definition can be difficult to obtain, and most definitions remain unclear. This can pose a problem for enforcement of a drug testing policy at the high school or collegiate levels or even in the professional ranks. What constitutes a performance-enhancing drug can also vary in each sport. A substance banned as a performance-enhancing drug in one sport may be allowed in another. This can lead to confusion over what is deemed a legal substance for a particular sport.

The issue of drugs in sports also calls into question the integrity of that particular sport. If existing rules prohibit the use of performance-enhancing drugs, is a player cheating if he or she takes them, or just breaking the rules like any other rule of the game?[12] Is it unethical or could it be considered engaging in unfair play if some players are using illegal drugs and others are not? Should athletes be able to use performance-enhancing drugs if they choose to with the full knowledge of the consequences of their use? If steroids are not physically harming anyone but the athlete, and the athlete is fully aware of the risks involved in taking PED's, should sport governing bodies still institute policies to prevent their use? Many argue that steroids do harm to other athletes by giving the user a competitive edge over other athletes. What if performance-enhancing drugs were available to all athletes and regulated by a sport's governing body? Under those circumstances, would the taking of PED's be considered cheating or unethical conduct?[13] If professional athletes were allowed to use performance-enhancing drugs during competition, do you believe that would influence younger athletes to use the same types of drugs? Would the pressure on athletes be increased toward the use of performance-enhancing drugs to obtain a college scholarship? Do you think the use of performance-enhancing drugs by professional athletes would be setting a bad example for younger athletes? How would that differ from an athlete who is in violation of a league's personal conduct policy? If the rules of a professional league prohibit the use of performance-enhancing drugs, should athletes compete against one another only in the context of those rules? Should an athlete's ability be measured solely

---

[11] Associated Press, "Obama Bemoans A-Rod Admission of Steroid Use," *ABC News*, 2009.

[12] See Nicolas Eber, "The Performance-Enhancing Drug Game Reconsidered," *Journal of Sports Economics* (December 21, 2007).

[13] See Thomas H. Murray, Willard Gaylin, and Ruth Macklin, *Feeling Good and Doing Better: Ethics and Nontherapeutic Drug Use* (Clifton, NJ: Humana Press, 1984).

by dedication, commitment, hard work, and training, without reference to the use of performance-enhancing drugs? If so, would it follow that an athlete's use of performance-enhancing drugs does not truly measure the competition between athletes, but instead measures the athlete's reaction to a certain substance rather than his or her true ability? What effect does the use of performance-enhancing drugs have on the process of athletic competition itself? What justification can be made for restricting the use of performance-enhancing drugs in athletic competition? These are all difficult ethical dilemmas to resolve.

When faced with ethical dilemmas and illegal behavior the wrongdoers are, many times, one step ahead of the regulators. If professional sports leagues allowed doping, do you believe they might alienate fans? If leagues were to allow drug use by athletes, would they be held legally responsible for the long-term health conditions of those athletes? Sports in America drive amateur and professional athletes to succeed, sometimes at all costs. With an overemphasis on winning, athletes are sometimes tempted to do whatever is necessary to enhance their performance and this can include taking illegal performance-enhancing drugs. Masking agents are sometimes used by athletes to prevent the detection of drugs in their system.[14]

Both the professional and amateur athlete is faced with ethical dilemmas in the area of drug use and testing:

1. If everyone else is taking them, does that provide greater incentive to an athlete to cheat, to ensure his or her place on a club?
2. The governing body for that competition will have promulgated rules for drug use. Is it considered unethical for an athlete not to keep a promise to stay drug free? If an athlete tells the coach, teammates, and governing body that he or she is "clean," when in fact the athlete is using drugs, is that an unethical act? Would you consider a broken promise to a teammate unethical or merely disloyal? What about personal responsibility to teammates, parents, and coaches?
3. Athletes do not always follow the rules of the sports in which they compete. Why should they be required to do so when it comes to taking PED's?
4. Under what circumstances should an athlete who has used illegal drugs be banned from further competition?
5. Should professional athletes ever be allowed to use human growth hormone (HGH) during competitions?
6. Should more severe penalties exist for those athletes who attempt to hide their drug use through masking agents or other forms of deception?
7. Should an athlete be allowed to do whatever he or she chooses to improve athletic performance as long as the athlete understands the health and legal risks involved?
8. Should an athlete always be responsible for what goes into his or her body?

Many athletes know how to avoid a positive drug test, cycling on and off banned substances to avoid being detected. Athletes can be pressured by society into making poor decisions; therefore, the sporting organization plays the role of decision maker for the athlete to ensure that he or she makes the right decision. Does a professional sports union fulfill its role in this regard?

---

[14] Lynn Zinser and Bill Pennington, "Another Suspension for Skeleton Team," *The New York Times*, January 11, 2006.

Education about the potential danger of illegal and banned substances can prevent harm to athletes now and in the future. Consider the following questions:

- What steps should be taken to educate kids in youth sports about the problems of banned and illegal drugs?
- What are the potential psychological side effects for adolescents who use anabolic steroids?[15]
- What comparisons can be made between an athlete's use of alcohol and use of illegal drugs? Should professional sports leagues and organizations make rules relating to both alcohol and illegal drugs for their players?[16]
- Should players incur the same suspension for excessive use of alcohol as they do for illegal drug use, illegal gambling, or domestic violence?
- How should a professional sports league's personnel be treated with regard to drug and alcohol use? Is it unethical to suspend a player for using marijuana but not suspend coaches, administrators or other office personnel for the crime of driving while intoxicated?[17]
- Do you believe if doping were legalized, it would lead to a more informed use of drugs in sports and an overall decline in health problems for the participants?
- What about having an "anything goes" professional league? Would fans object to the unnatural athletes, or would they flock to stadiums to see them perform at a "higher level"?
- Do you believe the use of performance-enhancing drugs violates the traditional notions of sportsmanship and fair play?
- Some argue that the aim of fair play through drug testing is a noble goal but that the science behind the tests needs to be more detailed and accurate to be effective. There are scientific problems dealing with drug testing at all levels. How does this affect the ethical dilemmas in drug testing?[18] Can drug testing regulations keep up with advancing technology to ensure the integrity of drug testing procedures?
- Who are the largest stakeholders when dealing with ethics in drug testing? In addition to ethical issues, what legal issues are present?
- Consider the following issues in deciding whether performance-enhancing drugs should be allowed in professional sports:
  1. Heath risks for all participants[19]
  2. The unfair advantage gained by a user of an illegal substance
  3. The effect advancing technology has on drug testing
  4. The overall drug testing effectiveness[20]
  5. The legalization of performance-enhancing drugs for selected sports

---

[15] See Reed Albergotti, "The Mystery of the Five Missing Tests," *Wall Street Journal*, August 7, 2010.

[16] "MLB Clubs Review Alcohol Policies in Wake of Hancock's," Death, *Sports Business Daily*, May 9, 2007.

[17] Mario Thevis, Andreas Thomas, Wilhelm Schänzer, "Mass Spectrometric Determination of Insulins and Their Degradation Products in Sports Drug Testing," *Mass Spectrometry Reviews*, Vol. 27, Issue 1, p. 35–50, 2008.

[18] See Mario Thevis and Wilhelm Schaenzer, "Mass Spectrometry in Sports Drug Testing: Structure Characterization and Analytical Assays," *Mass Spectrometry Reviews* (August 3, 2006).

[19] "Using anabolic-androgenic steroids (AAS) increases the risk of specific types of musculoskeletal injuries, according to an unprecedented survey of retired National Football League players." Steroids Linked to Musculoskeletal Injuries in Retired NFL Players, *Medical News Today*, February 21, 2009.

[20] Adam Rittenberg, "Iowa Admits to Flaws in Testing Program," *ESPN.com*, December 14, 2010.

6. How illegal drug use affects the topic of sportsmanship
7. Fan reaction to illegal drug use by players
8. Whether athletes actually function as role models in society[21]
9. Hall of Fame consideration for known illegal drug users

Some players who played in the steroids era of baseball have suffered the effect of others bad behavior. Jeff Bagwell was a great ballplayer for the Houston Astros and certainly should be enshired in Cooperstown. It was reported:

"[Jeff] Bagwell, who has never been linked in any way to performance-enhancing drugs, received 41.7 percent, which bodes well for him in the future. But Bagwell was likely a victim of suspicion. The kid who left the Red Sox organization in 1990 in a deal with Houston for reliever Larry Andersen went from gap hitter to power hitter and racked up some very impressive numbers in his long career. Bagwell denied he ever used anything—and if he didn't, we're sorry, but blame his peers, some of whom got caught and some of whom didn't, they're the ones who created the suspicion."[22]

THE ETHICS OF DRUG TESTING IN PROFESSIONAL SPORTS

No sport has wrestled more with the issues of PED's than the American national pastime of base-ball.[23] Baseball's "steroids era," ranging from approximately 1988 to the early 2000s, featured inflated statistics, monstrous home runs and some record-breaking moments. Mark McGuire and Sammy Sosa's home run duels brought millions of fans to the park. Mark McGuire said, "I definitely think we've brought the country together and helped make baseball a sport people care about and talk about again."[24] Some take a different viewpoint from McGuire's.[25] Barry Bonds's record-breaking season in 2001, in which he slugged 73 home runs, also packed stadiums. The hitters were in charge, driving the ERA of pitchers sky high. MLB National League MVP Ken Caminiti admitted he used performance-enhancing drugs in his MVP season in 1996.

Major League Baseball had a notion that some players were using performance-enhancing drugs but took relatively little action throughout the 1990s.[26] A labor dispute between players and manage-ment in 1994 cancelled the MLB World Series. After cancellation of the World Series, baseball needed all the goodwill it could generate. Fans began to come back to the game and all seemed right once again with baseball. However, a national scandal was looming right around the corner. The book, *Game of Shadows*, would change everything and eventually cause the commissioner of base-ball to investigate further, employing the knowledge and skill of a former U.S. Senator. The publica-tion of that book in 2006 exposed baseball's dark secret and uncovered a massive steroid scandal in baseball. The book, written by two investigative reporters for the *San Francisco Chronicle*, made BALCO (Bay Area Laboratory Co-Operative) common parlance in baseball circles and the sporting world. An excerpt from the book, appearing in *Sports Illustrated*, created a national stir. There were

---

[21] www.sportsanddrugs.procon.org.
[22] Nick Cafardo, "Effects of Steroids are Felt," *Boston Globe*, January 6, 2011.
[23] See "Speed Game: Amphetamines Should Have Been Part of New Plan," *Sports Illustrated*, January 18, 2005.
[24] David Leonhardt, "Myth of Men Who Saved Baseball," *New York Times*, March 30, 2005.
[25] Ibid.
[26] See generally "Part I: 1987–1994 Steroids Meets Baseball," *ESPN The Magazine Special Report; Who Knew?*.

demands for congressional hearings and an independent investigation to look into the allegations of massive steroid use claimed by the authors. The book gave details about the actions of Victor Conte, head of BALCO, and Greg Anderson, personal trainer for home run king Barry Bonds. It portrayed Conte as a big-time steroids dealer whose motto was "Cheat or Lose." In the book, the authors claimed Barry Bonds turned to steroids to improve his performance after watching Mark McGuire pass Roger Maris's home run record in 1998. Baseball had a culture of players using performance-enhancing drugs and as a result inflated statistics. Baseball wanted to ignore the rumors about Bonds just as it had done about McGuire and Sosa, but it could no longer do so, they were forced to act. Eventually the problem would lead to congressional hearings, criminal indictments and a detailed investigation by former U.S. Senator George Mitchell. Player and baseball executives were called to testify before Congress to discuss the problems of steroids in baseball.[27]

The Mitchell Report

The Mitchell Report may be the most damning and thorough report ever produced in the history of sports. Former U.S. Senator George Mitchell was requested by the Commissioner of Baseball to investigate drug use in baseball. The commissioner certainly got his money's worth, and maybe even more than he bargained for. On March 30, 2006, Commissioner Bud Selig requested Senator Mitchell to investigate allegations that many Major League Baseball players had used or were currently using steroids or other performance-enhancing drugs. Mitchell's charge from the commissioner was:

> ". . . to determine, as a factual matter, whether any Major League players associated with [the Bay Area Laboratory Co-Operative] or otherwise used steroids or other illegal performance enhancing substances at any point after the substances were banned by the 2002–2006 collective bargaining agreement."

The commissioner gave Senator Mitchell wide latitude to investigate and he was authorized, if necessary, to expand his investigation outside of the Bay Area Laboratory Co-Operative [BALCO] and "to follow the evidence wherever it may lead."[28] Senator Mitchell accepted the charge of Commissioner Selig with two caveats. First, he requested he be given total independence, both during the investigation and in preparing the report. Senator Mitchell stated he would only accept the task if he had "full freedom and authority to follow the evidence wherever it might lead."[29] Commissioner Selig agreed to the conditions set by the senator and the investigation began immediately.

At the outset of the investigation, Mitchell declared he would conduct a "deliberate and unbiased examination of the facts that would comport with American values of fairness."[30] Mitchell's goal in preparing the report was "to provide a thorough, accurate, and fair accounting of what [he] learned in [his] investigation about the illegal use of performance-enhancing substances by players in Major League Baseball."[31] He retained the law firm of DLA Piper US, LLP, to assist him in the investigation.

---

27 Michiko Kakutani, "Game of Shadows: Barry Bonds, BALCO and the Steroids Scandal That Rocked Professional Sports," *New York Times*, March 28, 2006.

28 See "Report to the Commissioner of Baseball of an Independent Investigation into the Illegal Use of Steroids and Other Performance Enhancing Substances by Players in Major League Baseball," Geroge J. Mitchell, DLA Piper US LLP. December 13, 2007.

29 Ibid.

30 Ibid.

31 Ibid.

Mitchell's investigation was extremely thorough. He and his team examined more than 115,000 pages of documents provided to them by a variety of sources, including the Office of the Commissioner of Baseball and all 30 major league teams. Another approximately 20,000 electronic documents provided by the league office and clubs were also reviewed by Senator Mitchell and his investigatory team. More than 700 witnesses were interviewed during the investigation, and more than 550 of those witnesses were "current or former club officials, managers, coaches, team physicians, athletic trainers, or resident security agents."[32] Sixteen individuals from the commissioner's office were interviewed, including Commissioner Bud Selig and baseball's Chief Operating Officer Robert DuPuy. Senator Mitchell and his staff attempted to contact almost 500 former players during the investigation. Only 68 players agreed to be interviewed. Mitchell also attempted to contact the Players' Association but stated in his report that "the Players Association was largely uncooperative."[33] He detailed the lack of cooperation of the Players' Association in his report. He stated that he asked each player to meet with him through their designated representative of the Players' Association so that each player would have a chance to respond to the allegations contained within the report. He noted "almost without exception they declined to meet or talk with me."[34]

Commissioner Bud Selig also agreed that the Mitchell Report would be made public when it was completed. The commissioner did, however, retain the right to determine whether any part of the investigation violated provisions of the Basic Agreement, which would include the joint drug program entered into between the owners and players in 2002. Senator Mitchell provided the commissioner's office with the report three days before it was made public. He also reported no material changes were made by the commissioner's office in the final report.

Senator Mitchell concluded that the use of anabolic steroids and other performance-enhancing substances was "widespread" in the game of baseball and threatened the integrity of the game itself. Mitchell further noted that although baseball's response to the crisis was slow to develop it did gain momentum after the institution of the 2002 drug testing program. Senator Mitchell found that at some point the players for all 30 major league teams were involved with performance-enhancing substances. The report named 78 players, most notably baseball's all-time home run leader Barry Bonds, and other notable players such as pitcher Roger Clemens, and Clemens's former teammate Andy Pettitte. All, Mitchell concluded, had used PED's at some time during their careers.

Senator Mitchell thought Major League Baseball was slow to react to the players' use of PED's and the "steroid era" in general.[35] Do you believe Major League Baseball acted quickly enough to deal with drug use by players? Does Major League Baseball or any other professional league owe an ethical duty to fans to ensure players are drug-free? If drug use is a crime and is illegal, is it, by definition, unethical? If baseball owners knew a crime was being committed on the field of play, did they have an ethical duty to act sooner? How much responsibility do you place on the players for baseball's steroids era?[36]

The Mitchell Report is hundreds of pages long and lists players that Senator Mitchell believed used illegal performance-enhancing drugs. In his report Senator Mitchell recommended to Commissioner Selig that no disciplinary action be taken against those players named. Do you agree with that recommendation? If players cheated and baseball can prove they took illegal substances, why should

---

[32] Ibid.
[33] Ibid.
[34] Ibid.
[35] "Mitchell Report: Baseball Slow to React to Players' Steroid Use," *ESPN.com*, December 14, 2007.
[36] See "A Fix Essay: Victims of the Steroids Era," *Wall Street Journal*, December 13, 2007.

they "skate free" if they violated league rules and broke the law? What message does that send to fans and other major league players who did not take steroids? Should every player named in the Mitchell Report have had his contract terminated by his club under the "good sportsmanship" clause of baseball's uniform player contract?[37]

Human growth hormone (HGH) has now become an issue with professional sports leagues as well.[38] The Major League Baseball Players Association (MLBPA) issued a statement on human growth hormone in 2010:

> Human growth hormone is banned under our Joint Drug Program. Discipline has been imposed against players who have been found to have used HGH. We do not test currently for HGH, because no scientifically validated urine test exists. Our program calls for immediate and automatic implementation of urine testing for HGH once a scientifically validated test is available. The Joint Program, negotiated several times with the Commissioner's Office, does not call for blood testing of players. Blood testing raises serious issues not associated with urine testing. Nonetheless, the Association has previously said that if a scientifically validated blood test for HGH was available, we would consider it. This week, a British rugby player was suspended as a result of a reported positive blood test for HGH. This development warrants investigation and scrutiny; we already have conferred with our experts on this matter, and with the Commissioner's Office, and we immediately began gathering additional information. However, a report of a single uncontested positive test does not scientifically validate a drug test. As press reports have suggested, there remains substantial debate in the testing community about the scientific validity of blood testing for HGH. And, as we understand it, even those who vouch for the scientific validity of this test acknowledge that it can detect use only 18–36 hours prior to collection.
>
> Putting these important issues aside, inherent in blood testing of athletes are concerns of health, safety, fairness and competition not associated with urine testing. We have conferred initially with the Commissioner's Office about this reported positive test, as we do regarding any development in this area. We look forward to continuing to jointly explore all questions associated with this testing—its scientific validity, its effectiveness in deterring use, its availability and the significant complications associated with blood testing, among others. The Association agrees with the Commissioner's Office that HGH use in baseball is not to be tolerated. We intend to act without delay to ascertain whether our Program can be improved as it relates to HGH. In so doing, however, we will not compromise the commitment to fairness on which our Program always has been premised.[39]

What should be done about HGH use in sports? What options do professional leagues have to deal with this issue? Should the issue of HGH be treated differently in professional leagues as opposed to amateur athletic associations?

CASE STUDY 7-1   *Steve Howe and his Addiction*

There was no doubt Steve Howe could play baseball, but he would also test the game's patience. There was also little doubt that he was haunted by personal demons that caused him severe heartache both on and off the diamond throughout his life. He was a two-time all Big Ten selection at the University of Michigan and was drafted in the first round of the 1979 baseball draft by the Los Angeles Dodgers. He paid immediate dividends for the

[37] See Major League Baseball, Uniform Player Contract, paragraph 7 (b)(1).
[38] Michael S. Schmidt, "Baseball Plans to Test for H.G.H. in Minors," *The New York Times*, February 24, 2010.
[39] MLBPA Press Release, New York, February 24, 2010.

Dodgers, winning the National League Rookie of the Year award in 1980. He saved a rookie-record 17 games in 1980 and gave up only one home run in 85 innings. In October of 1981, he won game 4 and saved game 6 of the World Series as the Dodgers beat the Yankees to win. In 1982, he was selected to the National League All-Star Team and led the Dodgers in appearances, saves, and ERA. At 24 years old, Steve Howe was a baseball star. He had won awards, been an all-star, and pitched in a World Series. His career was on the rise, but serious trouble was on the horizon. Howe would shuffle in and out of the game of baseball for the next 14 years, at times pitching well and at others battling personal problems. He would be given multiple chances to redeem himself while trying to shed the personal demons that hounded him throughout his life and his baseball career.

At the 1981 awards ceremony for the Rookie of the Year honors, Howe admitted he used cocaine in an effort to control his nervousness and excitement in receiving the award. His use of cocaine increased and continued throughout his entire baseball career. The 1981 baseball season was a strike-shortened season. In the second half of the 1981 season, Howe said he snorted "significant quantities" of cocaine but still managed to pitch pretty well because he had a "system." Beginning in 1982, Howe began to use cocaine during the season. Between the years 1982 and 1988, Howe was hospitalized six times for treatment of cocaine use. During the 1983 season, he was suspended twice by the team, fined $54,000 by the Dodgers, and placed on three years' probation. On May 28, 1983, he was suspended after admitting to drug use and placed in a treatment center until June 29.

Howe was suspended by Commissioner Bowie Kuhn for the entire 1984 season after he tested positive for cocaine during the off-season. Howe agreed not to play the 1984 season and to continue his probation and treatment for alcohol and drugs. In turn, Commissioner Kuhn removed Howe from baseball's suspended list to an inactive status. The commissioner's office issued a statement saying: "Steve continues in treatment, and there is unanimity of feeling among us, including Steve's medical advisers, that a return to baseball this season would not be appropriate. The most important thing for this young man is his long-range recovery." The Dodgers agreed they would forgo the $54,000 fine. The Dodgers request for repayment would have most likely been an exercise in futility anyway because Howe had recently filed for bankruptcy. Howe stated that one of the reasons he was forced to file for bankruptcy was his $1500 a week cocaine habit. The Dodgers did agree to loan Howe $10,000 a month for the remainder of the 1984 season as an advance on his 1985 salary.

Howe returned to the Dodgers for the 1985 season with great enthusiasm. Although he was no longer using cocaine, he was now drinking heavily. After Howe reported late to a game on June 30, 1985, the Dodgers took immediate action, giving him his unconditional release on July 3, 1985. He would once again relapse into cocaine use, and in September 1985, he entered the chemical dependency unit of St. Mary's Hospital in Minneapolis.

The future did not look bright for Steve Howe. Failing to sign on with a Major League club at the beginning of the 1986 season and still wanting to play baseball, he signed a contract with the San Jose Bees of the class-A California League. At 28 years old, Howe, once a National League Rookie of the Year and Major League All-Star, was playing single-A baseball. While with the Bees, Howe was suspended for what was deemed a "drug test discrepancy" but was reinstated by the club in June 1986. He admitted to using cocaine a few weeks later and was suspended for the remainder of the season. As a result of the suspension, Howe's name was placed on baseball's voluntarily retired list. Howe was seemingly on the bottom, having now been suspended from single-A baseball.

As the 1987 season began, Howe once again got the urge to play baseball. He started the 1987 season playing in Mexico and was surprised and eager when he was picked up by the Texas Rangers in July 1987. However, the Rangers had signed Howe without notifying the commissioner's office. When Commissioner Peter Ueberroth learned of the signing, he ordered Howe to play in the minor leagues before playing for the Rangers.

An addendum to Howe's contract with the Texas Rangers contained special provisions dealing with termination for drug use:

> e) The player and the Club ratify, adopt and incorporate herein . . . all of the terms and conditions of that certain "Texas Rangers After Care Program for Steve Howe" and in the event of a breach, violation, or transgression of

any of the covenants contained in the Program, the remedies set out in the Program (including but not limited to suspension and/or termination of this contract) shall be fully enforceable in all respects in accordance with their terms and supersede any and all other covenants or remedies contained in this Contract that relate to the subject matter of the Program.

Howe once again went back down to the minor leagues but was called up by the Rangers on August 6. Former Cleveland Indians great Sam McDowell was a certified alcohol counselor employed by the Rangers, and McDowell counseled Howe when he pitched for Texas. At the end of the 1987 season, Howe signed a two-year contract with the Rangers, which was to pay him $425,000 for 1988 and $500,000 for 1989, with the opportunity to earn more money through performance bonuses. Notwithstanding the proposed incentives, Howe's demons got the best of him once again. He tested positive for amphetamines in January 1988 and was given his unconditional release by the Rangers. From 1985 to 1987, Howe pitched for three teams and produced mediocre results. He was now 30 years old and a known drug user in baseball circles. It seemed like Steve Howe had worn out his baseball welcome.

Howe did not play organized baseball in 1988 or 1989, but he still had a burning desire to return to the game he loved. He wrote a letter to the commissioner on December 12, 1989, asking if he could return to baseball. The commissioner did not respond to the letter so the Players Association filed a grievance on Howe's behalf, seeking reinstatement. After some negotiations, the parties agreed to have Howe meet with the commissioner and two doctors, Dr. George DeLeon, a psychologist chosen by the Players Association, and Dr. Riordan, a psychiatrist chosen by the commissioner's office. After meeting with Howe, Dr. DeLeon made several observations about Howe, saying he was aware his recovery was a "lifetime process" and that a return to the game would "not constitute an unacceptable risk to relapse." Dr. Riordan disagreed with Dr. DeLeon, stating there would be a "high" risk that Howe would turn to substance abuse with therapy alone. He suggested a "very rigid" testing program, saying it was the only guarantee that Howe would not relapse into his previous bad habits. Dr. Riordan reported to the commissioner:

> We talked about the possibility of Steve giving a supervised urine sample every other day of his life as long as he may remain involved with organized baseball at any level, player, coach or manager. He acknowledged that he felt that this would be a reasonable strategy. I must emphasize that if this course were chosen and if he had a year or two of success, I would suspect that very likely Steve would come back demanding that this strategy be altered. It is my judgment that any altering of such a strategy, especially if it were successful, would be doomed to clinical failure. I believe that such a strategy must be linked to an absolute statement that a single dirty urine will mean his removal from organized baseball.[40]

After hearing all the evidence, the commissioner decided to give Howe one more "last chance." On March 10, 1990, the commissioner's decision to allow Howe to return to the game stated in part:

> Howe will be placed on probation, but permitted to return to Major League Baseball for the 1991 season if he agrees to participate in an aftercare program approved by the Commissioner's Office which includes drug testing, possibly as often as every other day if necessary, through the remainder of his career in Baseball. Howe may sign a Major League contract in the meantime, but he may play only in the minor leagues prior to the 1991 season. This result will afford Howe an opportunity to determine the effects a return to the game will have on his continued sobriety and could lead to a return to the major leagues. As Dr. Riordan recommended, Howe will be immediately removed from Baseball in the event of a positive drug test.[41]

The interpretation of what "one more last chance" meant, would later become an issue of interpretation in arbitration.

---

[40] Steve Howe Arbitration Opinion available though The Major League Baseball Players Association.
[41] Ibid.

Due to Howe's admitted past lies about his drug use, the commissioner decided Howe could play one year in the minor leagues and then have a chance to return to Major League Baseball with very stringent requirements for drug testing. It was back down to class-A ball where Howe played for Salinas in the Independent California League in 1990, compiling a 0–1 win–loss record with a 2.12 ERA. To the surprise of many, Howe appeared in the New York Yankees spring training camp in 1991 and asked the club for a tryout. He impressed the Yankees so much that they signed him to a contract. Howe pitched for the Yankees from early May until August 10, when he injured his elbow. He went 3–1 appearing in 37 games, saving 3 with a 1.68 ERA in 1991. Steve Howe was back. He had fought his way through the Mexican League, single-A baseball twice, and several years in which he never even played organized baseball. It seemed Howe had finally overcome his personal demons. At the end of the 1991 season, Howe left for his home in Whitefish, Montana, to enjoy the great outdoors and to revel in his return to the game he loved. He had just completed a successful season with a good club. On November 7, 1991, Howe signed a new contract with the Yankees for a salary of $600,000 plus incentives that could pay him as much as $2.3 million. Howe's return to baseball was a great comeback story and things were looking positive for Howe; however, once again, his success would be short-lived.

Howe's new contract required that he subject himself to drug testing, and if he tested positive, he could be terminated by the club. Howe's last drug test at the season's end was October 6, 1991. He was contacted by the president of comprehensive drug testing (CDT) on October 30 to arrange for some off-season testing. Howe said he wanted to talk to the Players Association before he agreed to be tested because he had not been tested in the previous off-season. When CDT did not hear back from Howe, the president of CDT called him on November 22, 1991, attempting to arrange for testing. Howe told her that his in-laws were in town and asked if the testing could be postponed again, and it was. He was finally tested on December 4, 6, 12, 13, 17, and 18.

On December 19, 1991, he was arrested for attempted possession of cocaine. Howe was charged with two federal misdemeanor counts for attempted possession of 1 gram of cocaine and possession of 2 grams of cocaine. He pled not guilty to both charges. On November 23, the day after he agreed with CDT that testing would begin on December 4, Howe had made arrangements to buy cocaine. When Commissioner Vincent heard the news about Howe, he stated: "I'm heartbroken. This is terrible news. I'm totally surprised and shocked. It's really disturbing if it's true. If it's true, it's a great tragedy."[42] Eventually, Howe pleaded guilty to attempted possession of cocaine and received three years' probation. He was also required to perform 100 hours of community service and to attend a substance abuse program.

Howe had paid for 2 grams of cocaine but never received it because the man he gave the money to, "J. J." (Jones), dropped the packet of cocaine in a pile of melting slush at the time of the "transaction." Howe later went back to J. J.'s house on several occasions to get the cocaine but discovered J. J. had been arrested. J. J. had told Howe if he was not around, Howe could try to contact Steve Boyd, an employee at a local used car dealership. Howe contacted Boyd about buying cocaine, and they met the next day at a car dealership. What Howe did not know was that Boyd was a government informant and was wearing a "wire." They agreed on a price of $100 a gram, and Boyd told Howe to come back later in the day to complete the deal. When Howe returned that same day, Boyd told him the cocaine was located in the visor of a pick-up truck in the car lot. Howe went to the truck and, when he reached for the cocaine in the visor, was surrounded by law enforcement agents and arrested. There was no evidence Howe ever used cocaine, only that he was trying to purchase it. Notwithstanding pending criminal charges, Howe started the 1992 season with the Yankees. On June 8, 1992, he entered a plea of guilty to the criminal charges and on that same day was suspended indefinitely from baseball by Commissioner Faye Vincent.

---

[42] Ibid.

The commissioner of baseball, Faye Vincent, suspended Howe for life from the game of baseball as a result of Howe's failure to control his cocaine habit. Howe, through the MLBPA, appealed the decision of the commissioner saying a lifetime ban was unfair even though Howe had previously been given a final warning by Commissioner Vincent. Did Howe overstay his welcome in baseball?

📖 **CASE 7-1** *In the Matter of Arbitration Between Major League Baseball Players Association and the Commissioner of Major League Baseball, Suspension of Steven Howe*

I fully understand Baseball's institutional interest and its need, in so far as possible, to keep its workplaces free of drugs and to deter drug use among players wherever it might occur. I also appreciate the pressures brought to bear on Baseball by those who only see the "athlete-as-hero." But those considerations, as important as they are, must be examined in the light of the just cause standard. Under that standard, Baseball's conduct, as well as Howe's, is subject to review.

In justifying his decision, the Commissioner told the Panel that Baseball had done all that could have been done and that Howe had simply "squandered" the many chances Baseball had given him. If Baseball had, in fact, done all it could, both before Howe's 1990 return to the game and after, the imposition of a lifetime ban would be more understandable. But it is obvious that reality and what the Commissioner perceived to be the case are quite different.

We now know that Howe has an underlying psychiatric disorder that was never diagnosed or treated; that this disorder has been a contributing factor to his use of drugs; and that, absent treatment for the condition, he remains vulnerable to such use.

We also know that in 1990 the Commissioner's medical adviser cautioned against Howe's return unless he was tested every other day of the year throughout his professional career and that Baseball did not heed this clear warning even though the Commissioner suggested in his March 1990 decision that such testing be imposed.

These two factors cast a very different light on the nature of the chance Howe was given in 1990 and, indeed, on the nature of the chances he had been given in earlier years.

It was clear from Dr. Riordan's report that in his expert view continuous testing, including testing in the off-season, was essential if Howe was to succeed in resisting drugs during his career while also seeking to overcome his addiction through therapeutic means. In his decision allowing Howe to return, the Commissioner quoted Dr. Riordan's report

at some length. The Commissioner's order that Howe play in the minors
for a year, his directions regarding testing and his declaration that
Howe would be immediately banned if he tested positive were all based
on Dr. Riordan's cautionary advice. But the stringent, year-round
testing requirement, as we have seen, was not implemented and Howe was
unfortunately set on a course without the strategic safeguard Dr.
Riordan considered indispensable to his success.

If that safeguard had been firmly in place and if Howe had never been
presented with an opportunity to vary its regularity, an opportunity
Dr. Riordan had clearly meant to foreclose, it is not at all likely,
given the certainty of detection such a regimen would have imposed,
that the events of December 19 would have occurred.

While Howe can certainly be faulted for seeking to delay testing at a
time of his admittedly increasing sense of vulnerability, the Office
of the Commissioner cannot escape its measure of responsibility for
what took place in 1991. Based on medical advice the Commissioner had
solicited, the need for continuous testing was obvious. To give Howe
"yet another chance" of returning to the game without implementing
those conditions was not, in my judgment, a fair shot at success.

Source: *Reprinted from Westlaw with permission of Thomson Reuters.*

The arbitrator overturned the commissioner's decision and allowed Howe back into baseball. Do you believe the arbitrator's decision makes a mockery of baseball's drug policy? Did the commissioner do enough to help Howe overcome his cocaine addiction? What types of rehabilitation programs should sports organizations provide for their players?

Should all professional sports associations institute drug testing programs and policies? What about sports such as tennis, boxing, baseball, football, badminton,[43] golf, and bowling? In 2007 the Professional Golfers Association (PGA) instituted a drug testing program.[44] In the following case, a PGA golf professional challenged the PGA drug testing program.

📖 CASE 7-2 *Barron v. PGA Tour, Inc.*

670 F.Supp.2d 674 (W.D. Tenn. 2009)

Doug Barron is a professional golfer who joined the PGA Tour in January
of 1995. In 1987, when he was eighteen years old, he was diagnosed
with mitral valve prolapse and was prescribed a beta blocker,

---

[43] For an international drug testing scheme for the sport of badminton see, Badminton Australia Anti-Doping Policy Updated Feb. 2010. Available at http://www.badminton.org.au/fileadmin/user_upload/pdfs/Anti_Doping_Documents/Badminton_Australia_Anti_Doping_Policy_Updated_Feb_2010.pdf.

[44] Bob Harig, "Drug Testing a Necessary Decision by PGA Tour," *ESPN.com*, July 1, 2008. Also see Larry Dorman, "L.P.G.A. to Start Testing for Performance-Enhancing Drugs," *New York Times*, November 15, 2007.

Propranolol, to treat the condition. Without Propranolol, Barron experiences a racing heartbeat and chest pains. In 2005, Barron was found to have low testosterone levels and was prescribed monthly doses of exogenous testosterone in order to maintain his testosterone level within the normal range. Side effects of low testosterone can include fatigue, lethargy, loss of sex drive, and a compromised immune system, resulting in an increased incidence of infection.

The PGA Tour establishes rules and policies that govern the conduct of golfers who participate in PGA and Nationwide Tour events. Golfers must pay dues to the PGA Tour and agree to abide by the rules and policies established by the PGA Tour in order to participate in PGA Tour events.

In 2008, the PGA Tour promulgated its Anti-Doping Program ("the Program"), and on July 3, 2008, the Program went into effect. The Program was developed in conjunction with the major golf tours and governing bodies around the world and incorporated input from leading experts in the field of anti-doping. The Program was modeled on the standards of the World Anti-Doping Agency and its Anti-Doping Code.

The Program contains a list of "Prohibited Substances and Methods," and included on this list of banned substances are Propranolol and exogenous testosterone. The Program allows players to apply for a Therapeutic Use Exemption ("TUE"). If granted, the TUE allows the player to use the substance despite its status on the list of banned substances. In order to obtain a TUE, the player must submit an application and supporting medical information. This information is submitted to a TUE Committee comprised of an independent medical advisor and one or more independent specialists of the medical advisor's choosing with experience in the area relevant to the player's illness or condition. The TUE Committee reviews the medical information and recommends to the PGA Tour whether to grant a TUE. Under the Program, a player may obtain a TUE if four criteria are met:

a. The player would experience a significant impairment to health if the *Prohibited Substance* or *Prohibited Method* were to be withheld in the course of treating an acute or chronic medical condition (the use of any *Prohibited Substance* or *Prohibited Method* to increase "low-normal" levels of any Endogenous hormone is not considered an acceptable therapeutic intervention); and

b. The therapeutic use of the *Prohibited Substance* or *Prohibited Method* would produce no additional enhancement of performance other than that which might be anticipated by a return to a state of normal health following the treatment of a legitimate medical condition; and

c. There is no reasonable therapeutic alternative to the use of the otherwise *Prohibited Substance* or *Prohibited Method*; and

d. The necessity for the use of the otherwise *Prohibited Substance* or *Prohibited Method* is not a consequence, wholly or in part, of a prior non-therapeutic use of any substance on the *PGA Tour Prohibited List*.

Prior to the effective date of the Program, on June 23, 2008, Barron submitted two TUE applications to the PGA Tour. The first application sought an exemption for the use of the beta blocker Propranolol. This application was reviewed by a TUE Committee consisting of a panel of doctors, including cardiologists. The application to use Propranolol was denied by the TUE Committee on October 10, 2008. Barron appealed the decision in accordance with the Program and the appeal was denied by the PGA Tour on October 22, 2008. Barron was instructed by the PGA Tour to begin weaning himself off of Propranolol. After his application was denied, Barron began reducing his dosage of Propranolol under a course of treatment prescribed by his medical doctor. He initially started the treatment with 160 milligrams of Propranolol, and by June of 2009, he had reduced his dosage to 40 milligrams.

The second application for a TUE sought an exemption for the use of testosterone. This application was reviewed by a TUE Committee consisting of a panel of doctors, including endocrinologists. At the request of the TUE Committee, Barron was reexamined by an independent endocrinologist. At the request of the independent endocrinologist, Barron stopped receiving monthly testosterone injections in October of 2008. The independent endocrinologist then took Barron's blood samples in November and December of 2008. The November test indicated Barron's Testosterone level was 325, while the December test indicated that it was 296. Both of these levels were within the normal range. The TUE Committee denied his application to use testosterone on January 21, 2009. Barron did not appeal the TUE Committee's decision.

Barron admits that, in early June of 2009, he received a single dose of exogenous testosterone from his medical doctor. Barron then played in the St. Jude Classic golf tournament in Memphis, Tennessee, which began on June 8, 2009. In conjunction with the tournament, he signed a tournament application form, confirming his understanding that he was required to abide by the Program. On June 11, 2009, Barron was tested in connection with his play in the tournament. His sample was found to contain evidence of Propranolol and testosterone. Barron did not dispute the test results and admitted to continued use of both Propranolol and testosterone. Following the positive tests, Barron provided additional medical information to the PGA Tour on July 23, 2009, and August 12, 2009. The TUE Committees reviewed the additional information provided by Barron and found it insufficient to justify TUEs for the use of Propranolol and testosterone.

On October 20, 2009, the Commissioner of the PGA Tour, Timothy W. Finchem, provided Barron with a written decision suspending him for one year from participating in PGA Tour or Nationwide Tour competitions and any related activities ("PGA Tour events"), from September 20, 2009, to September 20, 2010. In that letter, Commissioner Finchem wrote as follows:

> On June 23, 2008, you submitted a Therapeutic Use Exemption (TUE) application under the Program requesting that you be allowed to continue to use exogenous Testosterone and Propranolol. At that time, you were given full opportunity to medically justify your use of both substances. Your Therapeutic Use Exemption Application for Propranolol was denied by the PGA TOUR TUE Committee on October 10, 2008. You appealed that decision and your appeal was denied by Commissioner Finchem on October 22, 2008. Your application to use exogenous Testosterone was denied by the PGA TOUR TUE Committee on January 20, 2009. You did not choose to appeal that decision. As of October 23, 2008, you should have begun weaning off of Propranolol. As of January 21, 2009, you should have totally stopped using exogenous Testosterone. The PGA TOUR heard nothing further from you in 2009 concerning your use of Propranolol and exogenous Testosterone. We assumed, consistent with the denials of your Therapeutic Use Exemption applications, that your use of these Prohibited Substances had been discontinued.

> On June 11, 2009, you provided a doping control sample. That sample was found to contain evidence of both Propranolol and exogenous testosterone. That laboratory finding is not contested, since you have subsequently admitted continuing to use both substances. We invited you to submit any new medical information that might mitigate your continued use of these substances in total disregard of the denial of your TUE applications. You submitted additional information on July 23, 2009, and August 12, 2009. The information that you provided was reviewed by the PGA TOUR TUE Committee and again, no justification for your use of Propranolol or exogenous testosterone was found.

Pursuant to Section H(5) of the Program, Barron could have appealed the PGA Tour's ruling within seven days of receiving the notice of sanction. According to the PGA Tour, Commissioner Finchem told Barron during a telephone call that Barron "was unlikely to prevail in his appeal" and that "the third-party hearing officer would not be bound by the sanction imposed and . . . could impose a more significant sanction as a result of Mr. Barron's use of two banned substances and as a result of aggravated circumstances." According to Barron, the Commissioner said "in no uncertain terms that he would be wasting his time to appeal and that his punishment could be doubled if he appealed and lost." Barron did not appeal the suspension.

Pursuant to Section 2(M) of the Program, the PGA Tour notified Barron that it would issue a press release regarding his one-year suspension, and invited Barron to participate in the press release by proposing a statement to be read in conjunction with the PGA Tour's statement. On October 30, 2009, counsel for Barron sent a letter to Andrew B. Levinson, Executive Director of the Program, stating that Barron wanted the PGA Tour's press release to include the following statement: "Doug Barron disagrees with the PGA Tour's conclusion that he violated their Anti-Doping policy and the resulting sanction. All of the medications that were taken by Doug Barron were prescribed by his Medical Doctors for diagnosed medical conditions." The PGA Tour declined to release Barron's proposed statement, and instead, the following statement was released: "I would like to apologize for any negative perception of the TOUR or its players resulting from my suspension. I want my fellow TOUR members and the fans to know that I did not intend to gain an unfair competitive advantage or enhance my performance while on TOUR."

As a result of the one-year suspension, Barron alleges that the PGA Tour has violated Title III of the Americans with Disabilities Act, because he suffers from abnormally low testosterone, which causes him to have a reduced sex drive, experience fatigue, and have a compromised immune system, and that by refusing to allow him to take exogenous testosterone and suspending him for using it, the PGA Tour has discriminated against him based on his disability. Barron also alleges in his complaint that the Program is an unconscionable contract and therefore is void; that the PGA Tour has breached its duty of good faith and fair dealing by applying the TUE provisions and imposing the sanction against him in an arbitrary and capricious manner; that by issuing a press release that was misleading, the PGA Tour defamed him and placed him in a false light; and that the PGA Tour tortiously interfered with his prospective business endorsement opportunities.

Barron argues that he qualifies as being "disabled" under the ADA because he has a physical impairment (abnormally low Testosterone) that substantially limits a major life activity (engaging in sexual relations). The Sixth Circuit has not yet found that engaging in sexual activities is "a major life activity."

In addition to sexual relations, Barron also claims that his low testosterone causes fatigue and compromises his immune system. "Since fatigue in and of itself does not constitute an 'activity,' suffering from fatigue cannot qualify as a major life activity." A major bodily function, on the other hand, including functions of the immune system, is considered a major life activity. According to Barron's complaint, "low testosterone can prevent the body from healing at a normal rate and can further compromise a man's immune system, placing him at a higher risk of infection and illness," and Barron "experienced all of these symptoms.".

Source: *Reprinted from Westlaw with permission of Thomson Reuters.*

1. What is the rationale for the PGA to drug test their members?
2. PGA golfers do not have union representation. Should that be a consideration in the implementation of a drug testing program?
3. Under what circumstances should an individual's medical condition excuse him or her from drug testing procedures?
4. If you were the PGA commissioner, how would you make an ethical decision, concerning a player's disability and still maintain integrity for the drug testing program?
5. Do you agree with the press release issued by the PGA in this case?

Case 7-3, *Dimeo v. Griffin*, involves the heavily regulated sport of horse racing. In *Dimeo*, the issue was whether a provision in the drug testing scheme which called for random drug testing of all racing personnel, including outriders, parade marshals, starters, assistant starters, drivers, and jockeys, was an invasion of their privacy and too intrusive.

CASE 7-3 *Dimeo v. Griffin*

924 F.2d 664 (7th Cir. 1991)

It has long been labeled the sport of kings, but in this country some have come to regard it as the king of sports. Horse racing is now big business in which the state takes considerable interest. Not all involved are in it because of a love of horses. There have been problems generated because of the large sums of money involved in horse race gambling. Cheating and fixing followed gambling. It was not until the 1960s that a drug problem began to come into prominence. In 1968 the winner of the Kentucky Derby was disqualified after a post-race urine test of the horse, not the jockey, revealed the illegal use of a drug. Now the Illinois Racing Board ("Board"), which closely regulates horse racing on nine tracks, has perceived a new problem, the possible use and abuse of certain substances by the people directly involved in racing licensed as jockeys, drivers, outriders, parade marshals, starters, and assistant starters. The Board believes that drug use risks the safety of the people involved, impairs the state's financial interest in gambling proceeds, and causes the public to doubt the integrity of racing. Several members of the Jockeys' Guild ("Guild") in 1984 asked for Board assistance with the potential drug problem. Representatives of the Illinois Harness Horseman's Association were also consulted by the Board. The Board subsequently developed its own war on drugs by adopting a comprehensive drug rule which is now at issue.

The Board's antidrug program offended [Dimeo and other Board-approved licensees] [who claim the] . . . urine-testing rule[s] of the Board violated [their privacy].

I. HORSE RACING

Horse racing is one of the most ancient of sports. It is believed that chariots drawn by a four-horse team raced in the Olympic games of 700-40 B.C. Riders on single mounts also competed. The chariot drivers were the forerunners of today's harness drivers who now compete in lightweight sulkies drawn by standardbred horses. The Olympic bareback riders were the forerunners of today's jockeys now mounted on the backs of thoroughbreds competing at the run, a faster speed than the harness horse attains at a pace or a trot. In the reign of Richard the Lion-Hearted in England between 1189 and 1199, the first racing purse was offered. The first horse-racing trophy on this side of the Atlantic, however, was not awarded until 1665 in the colony of New York . . .

Jockeys riding thoroughbreds and drivers in sulkies behind standardbred harness horses are recognized, but the duties of the other licensees are less understood.

The outrider in thoroughbred racing is mounted and leads the horses from the paddock area, past the reviewing stands, and into the starting gate area for each race. The outrider makes sure the horses are led out in an orderly fashion without incident. If a horse throws its rider, as sometimes happens, and is running loose, the outrider is responsible for retrieving the horse. The term starting gate does not give an adequate picture of the structure used for starting a thoroughbred race. It is not one large gate stretching across the track. It is more like a series of connected, narrow short stalls, not much bigger than the horse which is led into it. When the horses are all in the gate and ready the electronically controlled door on each individual stall at the command of the starter opens simultaneously, and the race is on.

The parade marshal in harness racing performs much the same duties as the outrider in leading the horses to the starting positions, but the start of a harness race obviously cannot be done by the use of the stationary thoroughbred starting gate. A harness race is begun by the use of a moving pace car with retractable bars extending sideways from the back of the car. The starter rides elevated in the rear of the pace car facing backwards where he can observe the moving horses. The harness horses stride into place side-by-side behind the moving pace car and its extended bars. When moving at the proper gait and under control, the pace car barriers are retracted along the side of the car

by the starter and the pace car speeds out of the way to permit the
horses to move out in competition.

In a thoroughbred race there is a starter and assistant starters with
coordinating but different duties. The starter is located just outside
the infield rail and elevated where he can observe the horses in the
starting gate. He is responsible for ensuring that the horses are
properly loaded into their respective sections of the starting gate.
He observes their behavior to determine when a fair start is possible.
When the horses are all in proper position he releases the starting
gate. The assistant starters, however, are afoot on the track with the
responsibility of leading the individual horses into their respective
gate sections and to help the jockeys maintain control. An assistant
starter may enter into the gate and stand on a small side ledge where
he can help make sure the horse is under control with head up and
facing down the track. When the gate is opened the assistant starter
lets go of the horse turning it loose to run, raising his own arms in
the air. This shows there was no delay in a starter's release of a
horse possibly causing an unfair start.

[The] . . . revenue from wagers on horse racing [totals] above one
billion dollars per year in Illinois . . .

A. Random Testing

The Board determines the volume and frequency of random testing at
each race meet, as well as which selected racing programs are subject
to testing. The names of all licensees who appear as participants on
the official program are placed in a locked container secured by the
race stewards, the stewards being the onsite state supervisors of the
racing meet. A steward then may draw up to five names of licensees
from the container, with a representative of the Guild, the Illinois
Horseman's Benevolent and Protective Association, or the Illinois Harness Horseman's Association having been invited to witness the selection process. Following the drawing the stewards locate and notify the
licensees selected for random testing. Each licensee drawn must report
to the designated sample collection area and provide a urine sample to
the stewards or their designee before the last race on that day's
racing program . . .

No licensee is required to provide a sample more than three times in a
race meet . . .

B. Individualized-Suspicion Testing

Any particular licensee who is suspected to be in violation of the
Rule will receive written notice from the stewards stating that he or

she will be tested and giving the reason justifying the testing. Individualized-suspicion testing must be based on a finding that the licensee is under the influence of drugs as explained in the Guidelines . . .

C. Urine Collection and Testing Procedures

Any licensee selected for urine testing, either at random or because of individualized suspicion, must present himself or herself at the designated collection site . . .

If the initial screening reflects any positive reading, a Gas Chromatography/Mass Spectrometry ("GCMS") test is used to confirm the results. GCMS isolates an individual drug or metabolite and identifies it by a characteristic fragmentation pattern similar to a fingerprint. If the GCMS test confirms the sample as positive, both the resealed laboratory sample and the unsealed referee sample are retained by the laboratory in long-term frozen storage for at least one year . . .

IV. DISCUSSION

. . . The Board recognizes that an individual has a reasonable expectation of privacy in the ordinarily private act of urination and also in what a chemical analysis of a urine specimen may reveal . . .

The integrity of the race affects, among other things, not only who receives the winning purse but also the market reputation of the particular horse involved. The Board's integrity concerns are very important but the Board fails to explain why the criminal remedies for bribery, blackmail, race fixing, and other illegal activity are inadequate. Those ordinary criminal remedies not only punish, but also may deter the conduct purportedly affected by the Rule. Moreover, the sweep of the Rule is overly broad. The integrity risk is greatest with jockeys and drivers who can in various ways directly affect the race outcome. As to the other licensees, the starter might start the race before a particular horse was ready. The assistant starter might hold the horse slightly too long in the starting gate or do something else to distract the horse. The starts, however, are videotaped and [there is] little realistic opportunity for the starter or assistant starters to throw the race at that stage. In any event, that much of the government interest, though important, does not weigh enough when on the scale with [the privacy rights of the participants].

There is physical danger in horse racing to the horses and the participants. . . . The accidents are not shown to have any particular relationship to drug use by participants. Jockeys and drivers are at the greatest risk, but they are at risk in racing regardless of drug use. Drug use no doubt would increase that risk as alert, unimpaired, and physically fit participants are critical for the safety of themselves, others, and the horses . . .

Urine testing. . . has limited use for these purposes as it does not measure the licensees' present impairment, but only reveals that drugs were previously ingested and were in the person's system . . .

The other licensees are at less physical risk, outriders, parade marshals, starters, and assistant starters...

V. CONCLUSION

...There are good and valid reasons to strive to keep drugs out of horse racing . . . The Board along with all well-intentioned licensees, assuming the drug threat is as serious as the Board believes it to be, should be able to find a . . . way to accomplish an effective drug program. If not, horse racing may not long survive as the king of sports as it is viewed by some. It may even deteriorate into no sport at all.

Source: *Reprinted from Westlaw with permission of Thomson Reuters.*

1. Should jockeys and all others associated with horse racing be subject to drug testing?
2. Does the drug testing program infringe too much on the privacy of all involved?
3. Do you trust the chain of custody as described in the drug testing scheme?

THE ETHICS OF DRUG TESTING IN AMATEUR SPORTS

Interscholastic Athletics

Athletes at all levels are willing to use performance-enhancing drugs to gain an advantage even though it may be against the rules, and amateur athletes are no exception. With college scholarships at stake, high school athletes are facing growing pressure to perform at the highest level possible and hopefully gain that exclusive scholarship. A "win at all costs," attitude is prevalent among many high school coaches, administrators, parents, and student-athletes. Many times that attitude prevails over concerns for a student-athlete's health, academic progress, and integrity. High school coaches who want to move up to the collegiate coaching ranks need good players to win and a winning season can lead to a better coaching job. The pressure on coaches can be just as great as it is on the student-athletes. Amateur sports governing bodies have a legitimate and ethical interest in maintaining and establishing a sport's integrity and image. This is true at the interscholastic level as well as for professional sports. A sport which is infested by athletes using PED's can lose instant credibility and be subject to ethical and legal repercussions. It is essential for the integrity and ethical position for the sport, that the sport be seen as a "clean" sport.

Amateur athletics has its own set of ethical issues when dealing with drug use and testing. What drug testing procedures should be instituted at the interscholastic level and how should they be implemented? What students should be tested and how often? Is drug testing high school athletes even necessary?[45] Privacy issues are not usually present at the professional level when dealing with drug testing schemes and procedures but the amateur athlete does have privacy concerns under the law. Professional players are in unions who look out for their interests. Union representatives negotiate what they believe to be a fair drug testing program. However, the same is not usually true for the amateur athlete. If a student-athlete in one sport at a high school is tested, should student-athletes in all sports be tested? What about students involved in extracurricular activities which are not sports related? Should the policy apply to those students as well, to be ethical and fair to all?

In Case 7-4, the parents of a student-athlete challenged a high school drug testing program they believed to be unfair.

CASE 7-4 *Vernonia School District v. Acton*

515 U.S. 646 (1995)

. . . Vernonia School District 47J (District) operates one high school and three grade schools in the logging community of Vernonia, Oregon. As elsewhere in small-town America, school sports play a prominent role in the town's life, and student-athletes are admired in their schools and in the community.

Drugs had not been a major problem in Vernonia schools. In the mid-to-late 1980s, however, teachers and administrators observed a sharp increase in drug use. Students began to speak out about their attraction to the drug culture, and to boast that there was nothing the school could do about it. Along with more drugs came more disciplinary problems. Between 1988 and 1989 the number of disciplinary referrals in Vernonia schools rose to more than twice the number reported in the early 1980s, and several students were suspended. Students became increasingly rude during class; outbursts of profane language became common.

Not only were student-athletes included among the drug users but...athletes were the leaders of the drug culture. This caused the District's administrators particular concern, since drug use increases the risk of sports-related injury...The high school football and wrestling coach witnessed a severe sternum injury suffered by a wrestler, and various omissions of safety procedures and misexecutions by football players, all attributable in his belief to the effects of drug use.

Initially, the District responded to the drug problem by offering special classes, speakers, and presentations designed to deter drug use.

---

[45] Jeff Miller, "Steroid Testing Program for High School Athletes Shrink as State Cuts Funds," *DallasNews.com*, January 1, 2011.

It even brought in a specially trained dog to detect drugs, but the drug problem persisted . . .

> [T]he administration was at its wits end and . . . a large segment of the student body, particularly those involved in interscholastic athletics, was in a state of rebellion. Disciplinary actions had reached "epidemic proportions." The coincidence of an almost three-fold increase in classroom disruptions and disciplinary reports along with the staff's direct observations of students using drugs or glamorizing drug and alcohol use led the administration to the inescapable conclusion that the rebellion was being fueled by alcohol and drug abuse as well as the student's misperceptions about the drug culture.[46]

At that point, District officials began considering a drug-testing program. They held a parent "input night" to discuss the proposed Student Athlete Drug Policy (Policy), and the parents in attendance gave their unanimous approval. The school board approved the Policy for implementation in the fall of 1989. Its expressed purpose [was] to prevent student-athletes from using drugs, to protect their health and safety, and to provide drug users with assistance programs.

The Policy applie[d] to all students participating in interscholastic athletics. Students wishing to play sports must sign a form consenting to the testing and must obtain the written consent of their parents. Athletes are tested at the beginning of the season for their sport. In addition, once each week of the season the names of the athletes are placed in a "pool" from which a student, with the supervision of two adults, blindly draws the names of 10% of the athletes for random testing. Those selected are notified and tested that same day, if possible.

The student to be tested completes a specimen control form which bears an assigned number. Prescription medications that the student is taking must be identified by providing a copy of the prescription or a doctor's authorization. The student then enters an empty locker room accompanied by an adult monitor of the same sex. Each boy selected produces a sample at a urinal, remaining fully clothed with his back to the monitor, who stands approximately 12 to 15 feet behind the student. Monitors may (though do not always) watch the student while he produces the sample, and they listen for normal sounds of urination. Girls produce samples in an enclosed bathroom stall, so that they can be heard but not observed. After the sample is produced, it is given to the monitor, who checks it for temperature and tampering and then transfers it to a vial.

---

[46] Vernonia, 23 F.3d 1514 (1994).

The samples are sent to an independent laboratory, which routinely tests them for amphetamines, cocaine, and marijuana. Other drugs, such as LSD, may be screened at the request of the District, but the identity of a particular student does not determine which drugs will be tested. The laboratory's procedures are 99.94% accurate. The District follows strict procedures regarding the chain of custody and access to test results. The laboratory does not know the identity of the students whose samples it tests. It is authorized to mail written test reports only to the superintendent and to provide test results to District personnel by telephone only after the requesting official recites a code confirming his authority. Only the superintendent, principals, vice-principals, and athletic directors have access to test results, and the results are not kept for more than one year.

If a sample tests positive, a second test is administered as soon as possible to confirm the result. If the second test is negative, no further action is taken. If the second test is positive, the athlete's parents are notified, and the school principal convenes a meeting with the student and his parents, at which the student is given the option of (1) participating for six weeks in an assistance program that includes weekly urinalysis, or (2) suffering suspension from athletics for the remainder of the current season and the next athletic season. The student is then retested prior to the start of the next athletic season for which he or she is eligible. The Policy states that a second offense results in automatic imposition of option (2); a third offense in suspension for the remainder of the current season and the next two athletic seasons.

In the fall of 1991, James Acton, then a seventh grader, signed up to play football at one of the District's grade schools. He was denied participation, however, because he and his parents refused to sign the testing consent forms.

Source: *Reprinted from Westlaw with permission of Thomson Reuters.*

The Actons refused to sign the form saying it violated their son's privacy and also his constitutional rights.

1. What are primary concerns of a high school athletic association when dealing with a drug testing policy?
2. Were the drug testing procedures in *Vernonia* fair and ethical? How could they be improved?

CASE STUDY 7-2 *Drug Testing the Chess Team*

Should a school board's drug testing policy apply to student-athletes as well as all other students involved in school extracurricular activities? Under what circumstances should groups such as the The Fellowship of

Christian Athletes[47] or the future medical careers club be subject to drug testing? What about the school band or even the chess club?[48] Where would you draw the line with regard to drug testing high school students and student-athletes?[49]

Judge Monica Marlow has made some insightful comments on this issue:

> "Unlike participation in athletics, students participating in a math club, choir, band, symphony, or Future Farmers of America are not involved in routine regulation and scrutiny of their physical fitness and bodily condition . . . Unlike athletes, there is no evidence that drugs are used to enhance a student's flute playing, choir performance, chess playing, debating skills, math team skills, or farming skills."[50]

Dealing with student-athletes and parents can sometimes be a difficult task. What actions should have been taken by the athletic director and school administrators in the following case?

📖 CASE 7-5 *Doe v. Banos*

713 F.Supp.2d 404 (D. N.J.,2010)

In November 2006, the Haddonfield Board of Education (HBOE) adopted a policy addressing the use of drugs and alcohol by middle and high school students outside of school and unrelated to any school-sponsored activities. The Policy, referred to as the "24/7 Policy," prohibits students from consuming, possessing, or distributing drugs or alcohol, or attending any gatherings or activities where the presence of drugs or alcohol is reasonably likely to occur. For those students who violate it, the Policy mandates punishments, depending on the number of offenses, which may include suspension from extracurricular activities or the imposition of counseling or community service.

To effectuate the Policy, parents and students are required to sign a "Student Activities Permission Form" ("permission form" or "form"). Only by the parent and the student signing the form may the student then participate in an extracurricular activity. Relevant for purposes of this case, when a student signs the form, he or she affirms:

> I understand conduct regulations prohibit the use of tobacco in any form, drinking, possessing or providing alcoholic beverages and/or use, possession, or providing illegal drugs including anabolic steroids, at any time. The violation of these regulations will be dealt [with] according to the Haddonfield Board of Education Drug and Alcohol Policies . . .

---

[47] FCA.org
[48] "Judge Bars Drug Tests for Students in Band, Chess Club," *Los Angeles Times*, May 7, 2009.
[49] Greg Toppo, "High School Drug Testing Shows no Long-Term Effect on Use," *USA Today*, July 14, 2010.
[50] "Judge Bars Drug Tests for Students in Band, Chess Club," *Los Angeles Times*, May 7, 2009 citing to Judge Monica Marlow.

When a parent signs the form, he or she affirms: "I have received and read all the information regarding student participation in the inter-scholastic/co-curricular activities. I have also reviewed the HSD Alcohol & Drug Regulations." Correspondingly, a section of the Policy stipulates:

> All student participants in all extracurricular activities are to be made aware of the appropriate level of this policy and, as a condition of participation, each student in the Middle School and High School who participates in extracurricular activities and submits the necessary paperwork for participation in such activi-ties in connection with the student activity fee or other requirements, shall be deemed to agree to conform to this policy. *Similarly, the parent or guardian signature which accompanies the paperwork for participation in extracurricular activities will reflect the parent's/guardian's consent as well.*

On January 29, 2010, John Doe submitted a permission form allowing Jane Doe to play lacrosse. On the form, however, John Doe had scratched out the portion of the form informing Jane Doe that she would be subject to the Policy if she violates conduct regulations prohibiting drug or alcohol use. John Doe was told that the form, as modified, would not be accepted. In response to the school's refusal to accept the altered permission form, John Doe signed and submitted another form on February 24, 2010. This time, he attached to the form a cover letter in which he explained, in part: "You said that [Jane Doe] cannot play lacrosse unless the Student Activities Permission Form is filled out without alterations. I have enclosed a new form filled out without alterations. I believe the 24/7 policy is illegal and unenforceable but have filled out the form under duress."

On February 25, 2010, [HBOE's] counsel e-mailed John Doe's counsel, expressing concern over the use of the term "duress" and the possibil-ity that its inclusion could render the permission form unenforceable . . . Two days later, John Doe's counsel replied, in an e-mail, that [HBOE] was coercing John Doe to sign the form, and that "[m]y clients won't agree to be bound to a policy they believe to be illegal." Finally, on March 5, 2010, [HBOE's] counsel sent John Doe a letter explaining that the form he signed "under duress" was "invalid and unacceptable," and that Jane Doe would not be permitted to play lacrosse unless John Doe "either unconditionally sign[ed] a new per-mission form," [or] "rescind[ed] in writing [the] February 23, 2010 statement regarding signing the form under duress . . ."

Source: *Reprinted from Westlaw with permission of Thomson Reuters.*

1. Would you accept the student-athlete's revised version of the student activities permission form? If not, why not and on what basis?
2. What is the effect of accepting a revised form from a student-athlete or parent?
3. If you knew a student to be an outstanding role model, would you just accept the form and get rid of the headache? Why create problems when there are easy solutions?
4. Would you retain the opinion of a lawyer under these circumstances?
5. How could you handle this situation in a fair and ethical manner without resorting to legal action and a "take it or leave it" attitude when dealing with the parents of the student-athlete?

No resolution could be reached in Case 7-5 short of litigation. A federal court in New Jersey held that the school did not violate the student's rights by requiring her to sign an unaltered form. A court ruled in favor of the school district stating:

"[HBOE's] request for John Doe's signature on the permission form, and his unequivocal consent to the 24/7 Policy, was merely a reasonable effort to enforce the Policy uniformly as it applies to student-athletes. Barring Jane Doe from playing lacrosse was not imposed by [HBOE] as a *punishment* for or a *deterrent* to John Doe's dissent to the Policy. Not allowing Jane Doe to play was simply a consequence of the Policy's mandates, which require parental consent from all student-athletes on the lacrosse team.

[HBOE] were entitled to ask of John Doe the same thing they asked of all other parents—a legally valid permission form. Stated differently, . . . HBOE's conduct was designed not so much to compel or deter the father's *speech* as it was to elicit oral affirmation that his daughter's *conduct* would not violate the laws against drug use and underage drinking and that she would willingly join in a collective agreement with her teammates to remain drug and alcohol free during lacrosse season."

Source: *Reprinted from Westlaw with permission of Thomson Reuters.*

Drug Testing and the NCAA

Collegiate athletes are one step away from a professional career, although most will not become professional athletes. However, some student-athletes still take PED's to attempt to increase their performance on the playing field.[51] The NCAA has a drug testing program applicable to all student-athletes who participate in its member institutions' intercollegiate athletic programs. With more than 400,000 student-athletes participating in more than 20 sports, the NCAA has the world's largest athletic drug testing program.[52] The program is deemed a "strict liability program" and calls for a one-year suspension from participation in all NCAA sports if a student-athlete tests positive for a banned substance. The NCAA does provide a right of appeal to the student-athlete who tests positive.

Consider the following excerpts from the NCAA policy.

2010-11 NCAA Banned Drugs
    The NCAA bans the following classes of drugs:
    a. Stimulants;
    b. Anabolic Agents;

---

[51] See "Fifteen of 86 Football Players Test Positive for Drugs at North Texas," *ESPN.com*, October 28, 2008.
[52] See NCAA Eligibility Center, *2009–10 Guide for the College Bound Student Athlete.*

c. Alcohol and Beta Blockers (banned for rifle only);

d. Diuretics and Other Masking Agents;

e. Street Drugs;

f. Peptide Hormones and Analogues;

g. Anti-estrogens; and

h. Beta-2 Agonists.

Note: **Any substance chemically related to these classes is also banned.** The institution and the student-athlete shall be held accountable for all drugs within the banned drug class regardless of whether they have been specifically identified.

Drugs and Procedures Subject to Restrictions:

• Blood Doping.

• Local Anesthetics (under some conditions).

• Manipulation of Urine Samples.

• Beta-2 Agonists permitted only by prescription and inhalation.

• Caffeine—if concentrations in urine exceed 15 micrograms/ml.

NCAA Nutritional/Dietary Supplements Warning:

• Before consuming any nutritional/dietary supplement product, review the product and its label with your athletics department staff!

• Dietary supplements are not well regulated and may cause a positive drug test result.

• Student-athletes have tested positive and lost their eligibility using dietary supplements.

• Many dietary supplements are contaminated with banned drugs not listed on the label.

• Any product containing a dietary supplement ingredient is taken at your own risk.

Medical Exceptions

The NCAA recognizes that some banned substances are used for legitimate medical purposes. Accordingly, the NCAA allows exception to be made for those student-athletes with a documented medical history demonstrating the need for regular use of such a drug. Exceptions may be granted for substances included in the following classes of banned drugs: stimulants, anabolic agents, beta blockers, diuretics, peptide hormones, anti-estrogens, and beta-2 agonists.

Alcohol, Tobacco and Other Drug-Education Guidelines

The NCAA is committed to prevention of drug and alcohol abuse. NCAA Bylaw 30.5 requires the director of athletics or designee to educate student-athletes about NCAA banned substances and the products that may contain them. The following provides a framework for member schools to ensure they are conducting adequate drug education for all student-athletes. Each athletics department should conduct drug and alcohol education for all athletic teams, and target student-athletes who transfer mid-year. Athletic administrators, coaches, compliance officers and sports medicine personnel should also participate in drug education sessions. Campus colleagues working in alcohol and other drug prevention programs may provide additional support for athletic department efforts.

3.0. Causes for Loss of Eligibility

3.1. According to Bylaw 14.1.4.1, each academic year the student-athlete shall sign a form prescribed by the Committee on Competitive Safeguards and Medical Aspects of Sports in which the student-athlete consents to be tested for the use of drugs prohibited by NCAA legislation. Failure to complete and sign the consent form before practice or competition or before the Monday of the fourth week of classes, whichever date occurs first, shall result in the student-athlete's ineligibility for participation (i.e., practice and competition) in all intercollegiate athletics.

3.1.1. The institution shall administer the consent form individually to each student-athlete (including recruited partial qualifiers and non-qualifiers) each academic year.

3.2. All student-athletes found to be positive for a banned substance and/or metabolite are subject to loss of eligibility consistent with existing policies....

3.3. A student-athlete who refuses to sign the notification form or custody and control form, if any, fails to arrive at the collection station at the designated time without justification, fails to provide a urine sample according to protocol, leaves the collection station without authorization by the certified collector before providing a specimen according to protocol, or attempts to alter the integrity or validity of the urine specimen and/or collection process will be treated as if there was a positive for a banned substance other than a "street drug" as defined in Bylaw 31.2.3.

4.0. Drug Testing Selections.

4.1. The method for selecting championships, institutions or student-athletes to be tested will be recommended by the NCAA competitive safeguards committee, approved by the Executive Committee or the president acting for the Executive Committee in advance of the testing occasion, and implemented by the assigned certified collectors. All student-athletes are subject to testing.

4.2. Student-athletes who test positive will be tested at any subsequent NCAA championship or postseason bowl game at which they appear and at which drug testing is being conducted or at any subsequent year-round NCAA testing event.

4.3. Selection of Student-Athletes for Year-Round Testing on Campus.

4.3.1. Student-athletes competing in Divisions I and II sports are subject to year-round testing.

4.3.2. In year-round testing events, student-athletes may be selected on the basis of position, competitive ranking, athletics financial-aid status, playing time, an NCAA-approved random selection or any combination thereof.

6.0. Specimen Collection Procedures.

6.1. Only those persons authorized by the certified collector will be allowed in the collection station.

6.1.1. The certified collector may release a sick or injured student-athlete from the collection station or may release a student-athlete to return to competition or to meet academic obligations only after appropriate arrangements for having the student-athlete tested have been made and recorded by the certified collector.

7.0. Chain of Custody.

8.0. Laboratory Procedures, Notification of Results and Appeal Process.

9.0. Restoration of Eligibility.

Article 10.1 Unethical Conduct

Unethical conduct by a prospective or enrolled student-athlete or a current or former institutional staff member (e.g., coach, professor, tutor, teaching assistant, student manager, student trainer) may include, but is not limited to, the following:

Knowing involvement in providing a banned substance or impermissible supplement to student-athletes, or knowingly providing medications to student-athletes contrary to medical licensure, commonly accepted standards of care in sports medicine practice, or state and federal law. This provision shall not apply to banned substances for which the student-athlete has received a medical exception per Bylaw 31.2.3.5; however, the substance must be provided in accordance with medical licensure, commonly accepted standards of care and state or federal law;

14.1.4 Drug-Testing Consent Form.

14.1.4.1 Content and Purpose.

Each academic year, a student-athlete shall sign a form maintained by the Committee on Competitive Safeguards and Medical Aspects of Sports and approved by the Legislative Council in which the student consents to be tested for the use of drugs prohibited by NCAA legislation. Failure to complete and sign the consent form prior to practice or competition, or before the Monday of the fourth week of classes (whichever occurs first) shall result in the student-athlete's ineligibility for participation (practice and competition) in all intercollegiate athletics (see Constitution 3.2.4.7). Violations of this bylaw do not affect a student-athlete's eligibility if the violation occurred due to an institutional administrative error or oversight, and the student-athlete subsequently signs the form; however, the violation shall be considered an institutional violation per Constitution 2.8.1 . . .

Source: © *National Collegiate Athletic Association. 2011. All Rights Reserved.*

1. Does the NCAA provide a thorough drug testing policy? (See NCAA.org for full text of policy.)
2. What ethical issues for drug testing are prevalent at the collegiate level that are not present at the professional or interscholastic (high school) level?
3. Should NCAA member institutions perform their own drug testing of student-athletes in addition to those required of the NCAA?

Consider the following scenario in which a student-athlete objected to drug testing programs from both his university and the NCAA.

📖 CASE 7-6 *Bally v. Northeastern University*

403 Mass. 713 (1989)

David F. Bally commenced this action . . . challenging Northeastern University's drug testing program for student athletes on its intercollegiate athletic teams. Bally alleged that Northeastern's policy requiring student athletes to consent to drug testing as a condition of participating in intercollegiate sports violated his civil rights . . . and his right to privacy . . .

Bally is a student at Northeastern University . . . Until January, 1987, Bally was a member of the indoor and outdoor track teams, as well as the cross-country team. Northeastern places numerous conditions on participation in intercollegiate athletics,[FN1] including signing of a National Collegiate Athletic Association (NCAA)[FN2] student-athlete statement. The statement includes an NCAA drug testing consent form. In 1986, Northeastern began to require that varsity athletes also sign the university's drug testing consent form authorizing drug testing by urinalysis as a condition of participation in intercollegiate athletics.

FN1. Northeastern requires all student-athletes to undergo medical examinations before each academic year as a condition of participation in intercollegiate athletics. The examinations include the giving of blood and urine samples for medical testing purposes. The urine sample, however, is neither monitored nor tested for the presence of drugs.

FN2. The NCAA is a membership organization which governs and regulates the majority of intercollegiate competition among public and private colleges and universities in the United States. Northeastern is a member of the NCAA and must comply with NCAA requirements to be allowed to compete in NCAA events.

In November 1986, Bally signed the NCAA student-athlete statement for the 1986-1987 academic year. He later revoked it by a letter dated March 12, 1987. Bally refused to sign Northeastern's drug testing form, as well as the NCAA's drug testing consent form for the 1987-1988 academic year. Northeastern declared Bally ineligible to participate in the varsity indoor track and cross-country teams. Except for his refusal to sign the NCAA and Northeastern consent forms, Bally has met Northeastern's conditions for eligibility to compete in varsity sports.

Northeastern prohibits the use of those drugs which the NCAA has banned, including certain illicit drugs, some prescribed drugs, and some over-the-counter medications. The parties submitted, as part of their statement of agreed facts, a fifty-five page list of NCAA banned drugs. Northeastern's drug tests do not test for the presence of many of the drugs that the NCAA has banned. Northeastern's program requires that a student-athlete consent to drug testing, through urinalysis, during post-season competition as well as during the regular season. The program requires that student-athletes be tested once annually for certain drugs: viz., amphetamines, barbiturates, benzodiazepine, cannabinoid, cocaine, methaqualone, opiates, and phencyclidine. The program also mandates random testing throughout the academic year, and requires testing of athletes before any NCAA post-season competition. To date, Northeastern has only tested athletes participating in post-season NCAA competition. The random and post-season testing screen for the previously mentioned drugs, anabolic steroids (a substance which sometimes increases muscle mass and may enhance athletic performance), and testosterone. When presenting drug testing forms to student-athletes and asking for their signatures, an athletic director explains that students who refuse to sign the consent form will be ineligible to participate in intercollegiate sports, and may lose any athletic scholarships.

Northeastern cites as its reasons for instituting its drug testing program a desire: (a) to promote the health and physical safety of student athletes; (b) to promote fair intrateam and intercollegiate competition; and (c) to ensure that Northeastern student-athletes, as role models to other students and as representatives of Northeastern to the public, are not perceived as drug users.

The actual testing process requires that a monitor of the same sex as the student-athlete observe the athlete's urination when providing a urine specimen. This is the only means of ensuring that the athlete submits his or her own urine to be tested. Drug-free urine is commercially available and, without a monitor, could be substituted for the athlete's. The urine specimens are labeled by a number code. Only the director of Northeastern's Lane Health Center and Student Health Services has access to the identity of the specimen's donor. A specimen which tests positive will be retested, by using another portion of the same sample. Specimens which test negative on either the initial or second test are not tested further.

If both the initial and second tests are positive, another portion of the same urine sample will be tested by a different method. If this test is positive, the student athlete is notified and requested to confer with the director of the University's Lane Health Center and Student Health Services. The director decides whether to begin counselling the student. The student athlete is given follow-up testing. If a follow-up test is negative, the individualized process ends and the student is simply once again subject to further testing. If a follow-up test is positive, the student is suspended from the team; the athletic director, head coach, and student's parents are notified; and the student athlete is required to attend a formal drug counselling program as a condition of further athletic participation. The student-athlete is then tested at regular intervals and remains suspended from the team until he or she tests negative. If a student tests positive at any time after rejoining a team, he or she will be dismissed from the team for the entire academic year. Thereafter, any positive test result permanently bans the student from participating in intercollegiate athletics at Northeastern. At any point in the process, the student may appeal to the university's drug testing review and appeals committee.

Source: *Reprinted from Westlaw with permission of Thomson Reuters.*

1. Should NCAA member institutions drug test their student-athletes in addition to complying with the NCAA drug testing program?
2. Do you believe the Northeastern drug testing policy is fair to student-athletes?

NOTES AND DISCUSSION QUESTIONS

Introduction

1. Is the use of steroids by athletes unethical because it gives the user an advantage over his or her competitor? Is it unfair to the game itself by making the sport "easier"?

2. Competition in sports tests the ability of an athlete to run faster, jump higher, or perform better than the competitor. In what manner does the use of performance-enhancing drugs by an athlete taint the true competitive nature of an event?

3. Do you believe drug use in sports merely mirrors drug use in society in general?

4. Do you think steroid use will increase or decrease in the future at the professional level?

5. What causes athletes to use performance-enhancing drugs? Do you think increased competition at the professional amateur level causes an increase in steroid use by high school athletes?

6. Clearly there are health risks involved in taking steroids.[53] What programs should be put in place to educate young athletes about the dangers of steroid use?

The Ethics of Drug Testing in Professional Sports

7. Congress has attempted to get more involved in monitoring drug testing in professional sports. Is this a mistake?[54] Do you consider that too much "big brother"?[55]

8. What penalties should be assessed against athletes who use PED's to increase their performance?[56]

9. Should professional sports leagues treat recreational drug use such as cocaine and marijuana differently from the use of performance-enhancing drugs?

10. Some think Major League Baseball's new drug testing program is responsible for the "new era" of dominant pitching in the league. Do you agree?[57]

11. Is the prohibition against performance-enhancing drugs justified? Can you think of any arguments that may justify the use of performance-enhancing drugs in sports? What is unethical about using performance-enhancing drugs to attain excellence in sports and become a better athlete?

12. Should certain sports allow for the use of performance-enhancing drugs? What about the use of performance-enhancing drugs in professional wrestling where the "fix" is already in?[58] If professional wrestling is merely entertainment and participants fully understand the side effects of using performance-enhancing drugs, would their use be more acceptable or ethical than more traditional sporting events?[59]

13. Do athletes have a responsibility to make sure what they put in their body is legal?[60]

---

[53] See M. Parssinen and T. Seppala, "Steroid Use and Long-Term Health Risks in Former Athletes," *Sports Medicine* (February 1, 2002).

[54] See the Clean Sports Act of 2005 and The Drug Free Sporting Act, H.R. 1862, 109th Cong. (2005).

[55] See Michael S. Schmidt, "Clemens Lied to Congress About Doping, Indictment Charges," *New York Times*, August 19, 2010.

[56] See Paul H. Haagen, "Players Have Lost That Argument: Doping, Drug Testing, and Collective Bargaining," *New England Law Review* (2005–2006).

[57] See Mike Sielski, "Why Are Pitchers Dominating?" *Wall Street Journal*, June 12, 2010; Billy Witz, "For Ellis, a Long, Strange Trip to a No-Hitter," *New York Times*, September 4, 2010.

[58] See Tim Dahlberg, "Fake can be Very Real When Taking a Chair to the Head," *USA Today*, September 12, 2007. Also *see*, Jon Swartz, "High Death Rate Lingers Behind Fun Façade of Pro Wrestling," *USA TODAY*, March 12, 2004.

[59] See "Wrestling Deaths and Steroids," *USA Today*, March 12, 2004.

[60] Johnson, Kevin, "HGH Goes Beyond Athletes," *USA Today*, March 13, 2007. See "Olympic Athletes to Be Required to Take Medical Tests: Rule Would Curb Drug Stimulants," *New York Times*, May 9, 1967.

14. The world anti-doping agency publishes "The World Anti-Doping Code."[61] Review this code and compare it to a U.S. professional sports league drug testing policy. How are they different?

15. Canadian Ben Johnson won a gold medal at the 1988 Olympics in the 100-meter run but forfeited the medal three days later after he tested positive for the banned anabolic steroid Stanozolol.[62] Should all athletes be required to forfeit their awards if they test positive for illegal drug use?

16. How rigorous should criminal enforcement against athletes be for the use of PED's? Should all users be criminally prosecuted? Barry Bonds was the subject of a criminal indictment for steroid use arising out of the BALCO affair. Is it unethical to criminally charge some athletes but not others?

17. How rigorous should a players' association be in fighting on behalf of players who use drugs? Should they appeal a suspension of a player if the player confesses to illegal drug use?[63] Could you compare this to a lawyer representing a client he or she knows is guilty of the crime for which they are charged?

18. How many chances should a player get before being banned from a professional league for the use of performance-enhancing drugs?

19. What drugs should be tested for in a drug testing policy?

20. What penalty scheme would you develop for the use of performance-enhancing drugs in professional sports? What treatment should players receive for addiction?

21. Should different sports have different penalties for violators? For instance, should penalties in NASCAR be different from the penalties in the NFL or MLB?[64]

22. Should U.S. professional sports leagues adopt the same standards for drug use as those adopted at the international level such as the Olympics?[65]

23. How do the advancements in science affect ethical issues in drug testing?[66]

24. Do you agree with Major League Baseball's drug policy? What should be changed? Do you think the new drug testing program in baseball is harsh enough for its violators? If not, what is the appropriate discipline for violations of the policy? If you were drafting a drug policy for professional sports, what would you include?

25. NFL player Donte Stallworth was found guilty of involuntary manslaughter when he became intoxicated and killed a pedestrian with his automobile. He was suspended from the league for one season.[67] Should every league have a policy dealing with alcohol use by players as well as drug use?

---

[61] See code at www.wada.ama.org.

[62] Steve Wulf, "Scorecard: A Revealing Story," *SI Vault*, June 5, 1989.

[63] See David M. Wachutka, "Collective Bargaining Agreements in Professional Sports: The Proper Forum for Establishing Performance-Enhancing Drug Testing Policies," *Pepperdine Dispute Resolution Law Journal* (2007).

[64] See Tania Ganguli, "NASCAR Drug-Testing Policy Has Drivers on Edge," *Los Angeles Times*, May 16, 2009. Richard S. Chang, "Nascar Driver Fails Drug Test," *The New York Times*, May 1, 2009.

[65] See A. J. Perez, "Olympic Athletes Face New Drug Tests," *USA Today*, October 13, 2009. For further study on international drug testing, see Eoin Carolan, "The New WADA Code and the Search for a Policy Justification for Anti-Doping Rules," *Seton Hall Journal of Sports and Entertainment Law* (2006).

[66] See Angela Jo-Anne Schneider and Theodore Friedmann, *Gene Doping in Sports: The Science and Ethics of Genetically Modified Athletes* (Salt Lake City, UT: Academic Press, 2006).

[67] Judy Battista, "Stallworth Suspended for the Entire N.F.L. Season," *New York Times*, August 13, 2009.

26. In professional leagues, should it be left up to the bargaining process between management and labor to determine what constitutes a performance-enhancing drug?
27. What are the moral issues associated with illegal drug use in the sport of cycling?[68]
28. The BALCO situation also elicited major privacy concerns for professional athletes. In 2002, the U.S. government launched an investigation of the Bay Area Laboratory, and its alleged distribution of PED's to professional baseball players. During the investigation, federal agents seized voluminous electronic data that contained the names of hundreds of Major League Baseball players and athletes from other professional sports. The baseball players included star players Barry Bonds, David Ortiz, Manny Ramirez, Alex Rodriguez, and Sammy Sosa. This information was eventually leaked to the press. The government's "search" in that case dealt with the methods law enforcement officials may use to obtain digital evidence during an investigation.[69]

The Ethics of Drug Testing in Amateur Sports

29. What policies should be put in place at the high school level for the use of performance-enhancing drugs?[70]
30. At what age is it appropriate to begin testing student-athletes for performance-enhancing drugs?
31. Do you believe the use of performance-enhancing drugs by elite professional athletes encourages use at the amateur level?
32. Should every amateur athletic association adopt procedures similar to that of the NCAA? Under the NCAA's program a student-athlete must comply with the drug testing program as a condition of eligibility to participate.

---

[68] Reed Albergotti and Vanessa O'Connell, "Cyclist Armstrong Denies Doping," *The Wall Street Journal*, May 20, 2010.
[69] See United States v. Comprehensive Drug Testing, Inc., 513 F.3d 1085, 1089 (9th Cir. 2008). Also see, Derek Regensburger Bytes, BALCO, and Barry Bonds: An Exploration of the Law Concerning the Search and Seizure of Computer Files and an Analysis of the Ninth Circuit's Decision in *United States v. Comprehensive Drug Testing, Inc., Journal of Criminal Law and Criminology* (Summer 2007): 1151.
[70] See Tonya L. Dodge and James J. Jaccard, "The Effect of High School Sports Participation on the Use of Performance-Enhancing Substances in Young Adulthood," *Journal of Adolescent Health* (September 2006). See Paul Daugherty, "Should Athletes Be Allowed to Use Legal PED's? Sure, Why Not?" *SI.com*, August 5, 2010.

C H A P T E R   8

ETHICAL CONSIDERATIONS OF RACE IN SPORTS

INTRODUCTION

Racial issues have a long history in both professional and amateur sports.[1] Issues of race, equality, and discrimination are hotly debated in sports. Throughout the history of sports, race relations and discrimination have been topics of much discussion and debate. Racial discrimination in the United States in sports has deep historical roots. At many universities, African American student-athletes were not able to participate in sports until after World War II. Now, however, African American athletes dominate Division I-A collegiate basketball and football. Although African American athletes dominate the collegiate revenue-producing sports, some argue they are exploited and taken advantage of for financial reasons.[2] In many cases the large revenues produced by African American athletes are then used for purposes other than supporting the educational development of these student-athletes.

Racism has been a part of American sports since long before the beginning of baseball's Negro Leagues.[3] During the first half of the 20th century all professional athletes were Caucasian. Two noted scholars Michael J. Cozillo and Robert L. Hayman, Jr. have summarized the relationship between sports and racial issues,

"... how will we explain the unwritten but undeniable rule that governed much of American sports in the first half of the twentieth century: that players—all of them—had to be white? How will we explain vicious reaction to Jackie Robinson when he defied this convention, and how will we account for the iconic status that is—for better but sometimes worse—afforded him today? How will we comprehend the stunning racial disparities in the organization of American sports—where most ballplayers are black or Latino, but nearly all coaches and executives are white—or understand the integrity of the dispute over the treatment of college athletes in the "revenue-producing" sports, where minority ballplayers

---

[1] Kenneth Shropshire, *In Black and White: Race and Sports in America*, (NYU Press, 1998).
[2] See William C. Rhoden, *Forty Million Dollar Slaves* (New York: Three Rivers Press, 2006); Shaun Powell, *Souled Out? How Blacks Are Winning and Losing in Sports* (Champaign, IL; Human Kinetics, 2008).
[3] See Amy Bass, *In the Game* (New York: Palgrave Macmillan, 2005).

generate substantial funds for white dominated educational institutions that not atypically fail even to provide an education in return? Race in American sports: it is all about race in America."[4]

Major League Baseball player Curt Flood, who challenged baseball's reserve clause in the early 1970s was questioned by other players whether his antitrust lawsuit against baseball was "racially motivated."[5] Flood wrote about the racial hatred and unequal treatment he received while playing minor league baseball in the deep south in the 1950s. Racial animus continued against Flood even after he became a Major League All-Star for the St. Louis Cardinals.[6] Hall of Fame player Hank Aaron spoke of the hatred he encountered during his chase of Babe Ruth's home run record in 1974:[7]

The Sporting News: When did you realize you had a shot at Babe Ruth's record?

Aaron: I knew I had an outside chance after the 1972 strike ended. We came back, and I had a decent year. I had to stay healthy and be surrounded by great ballplayers.

TSN: As you were closing in on the Babe, when did you start feeling the pressure?

Aaron: This might sound like I'm bragging, but I never felt pressured. I never felt pressured because I felt the only way I could play baseball was to relax and do the best I could. I couldn't play under pressure.

TSN: How did you stay relaxed during that period?

Aaron: The record we are talking about now was not set in one year and it certainly wasn't going to be broken in one year. I felt like I had all year long to break the record. So I certainly wasn't going to let one game or one series or one month get me to the point where I was going to be pressured.

TSN: As you were approaching the record, what was the most disappointing experience you had on or off the field?

Aaron: That's a tough question. The closer I got to the record, people started thinking that it wasn't the most important record in baseball. Of course, there were other things. I just wished for a moment that I could have enjoyed it as much as Sammy Sosa and Mark McGuire enjoyed their chase last year.

TSN: The death threats and the letters from bigots are the reason you didn't enjoy the chase, right?

Aaron: The threats and all the controversy. My daughter was in college at Fisk University, and she wasn't able to enjoy it. And I had to put my two boys in private schools, so they weren't there to be bat boys. They weren't able to enjoy it. So I was deprived of a lot of things that really should have belonged to me and my family . . .

TSN: Since you said you are happy today, have you thrown away the hate mail?

---

[4] Robert L. Hayman and Michael J. Cozzillio, *Sports & Inequality* (Durham, NC: Carolina Academic Press, 2005), 111.

[5] See generally, Stuart L. Weiss, *The Curt Flood Story: The Man Behind the Myth (Sports and American Culture Series)*, (University of Missouri, 1st ed., 2007).

[6] Richard Carter, *Curt Flood: The Way It Is* (New York: Trident Press, 1971).

[7] Matt Spetalnick, "Bush: History will Judge if Bonds is True Home-Run King," *Reuters*, August 8, 2007. William C. Rhoden, "In Aaron's View, Bonds is Home Run King," *The New York Times*, February 15, 2009.

Aaron: No, I didn't. That will never be thrown away. That wasn't long ago. I don't need to remind myself of it, but we still have problems in this country. We still have hatred in this country. We still have to be reminded that things are not as good as we think they are.[8]

Brooklyn Dodgers' great Jackie Robinson broke Major League Baseball's color barrier in 1947 with the help of University of Michigan lawyer Branch Rickey.[9] Robinson spoke of his experiences in spring training in 1946, "We had a tough time getting to Daytona Beach...So we took a train to Jacksonville, and when we got there we found we'd have to go the rest of the way by bus. We didn't like the bus, and we particularly didn't like the back seat when there were empty seats near the center. Florida law designates where Negroes are to ride in public conveyances. The law says: "Black seat." We rode there."[10] Since baseball's integration in 1947, Major League Baseball has made significant efforts to ensure diversity within the American national pastime.[11]

CASE STUDY 8-1 *Race Relations in Baseball*

Al Campanis was the general manager of the Los Angeles Dodgers in 1981 and while being interviewed on ABC's *Nightline* by Ted Koppel was asked why baseball had so few black managers and general managers. Campanis created a firestorm of controversy with his responses:

Koppel: Mr. Campanis . . . you're an old friend of Jackie Robinson's, but it's a tough question for you. You're still in baseball. Why is it that there are no black managers, no black general managers, no black owners?

Campanis: Well, Mr. Koppel, there have been some black managers, but I really can't answer that question directly. The only thing I can say is that you have to pay your dues when you become a manager. Generally, you have to go to the minor leagues. There's not very much pay involved, and some of the better known black players have been able to get into other fields and make a pretty good living in that way.

Koppel: Yeah, but you know in your heart of hearts . . . you know that that's a lot of baloney. I mean, there are a lot of black players, there are a lot of great black baseball men who would dearly love to be in managerial positions, and I guess what I'm really asking you is to, you know, peel it away a little bit. Just tell me, why you think it is. Is there still that much prejudice in baseball today?

Campanis: No, I don't believe it's prejudice. I truly believe that they may not have some of the necessities to be, let's say, a field manager, or perhaps a general manager.

Koppel: Do you really believe that?

Campanis: Well, I don't say that all of them, but they certainly are short. How many quarterbacks do you have? How many pitchers do you have that are black?[12]

---

[8] William Ladson, "Q&A with Hank Aaron," *The Sporting News*, April 8, 1999.

[9] J. Gordon Hylton, "American Civil Rights Law and the Legacy of Jackie Robinson," *Marquettte Sports Law Journal* 8, no. 2 (1990): 387–399; Jules Tygiel, *Baseball's Great Experiment: Jackie Robinson* (New York: Oxford University Press, 2008).

[10] Steven A. Riess, *Major Problems in American Sport History: Documents and Essays, Edited By*, Thomas G. Paterson, Boston, MA: Houghton Mifflin Company, 1974) 373 citing to Jack R. Robinson and Wendell Smith, *Jackie Robinson: My Own Story* (New York: Greenberg, 1948), 65–68, 70–75, 79–80.

[11] "Study: MLB Gets 'A' for Racial Hiring," *UCF Today*, May 2, 2010; "MLB Gets First 'A-' in Racial Report Despite Fewer Black Players," *Sports Business Daily*, April 17, 2008. However, see Michael S. Schmidt, "Baseball's Praised Diversity Is Stranded at First Base," *New York Times*, August 11, 2010.

[12] Eric Johnson, "'Nightline' Classic: Al Campanis," *ABC News*, April 12, 2007. The List: Worst Cases of Foot-in-Mouth, Page 2, *ESPN.com*.

Campanis later apologized for his remarks. Noted Hall of Fame pitcher Don Newcombe, an African American, told the *Los Angeles Times*, "I do not believe Campanis has a prejudiced bone in his body" . . . "If Jackie were around today, I don't think he would appreciate what has happened to Al, because Al helped him and befriended him. He would tell Al, 'You just messed up and you've got to apologize,' and Al did apologize."[13]

The National Football League was integrated from 1920 to 1934, but in 1934 NFL owners entered into a "gentlemen's agreement" banning all African American players.[14] NBA superstar Bill Russell became the first African American coach in U.S. major professional sports when he became the head coach of the Boston Celtics in 1966. Since that time, continuing efforts have been made to combat discrimination in the coaching ranks in both professional and amateur sports. Discrimination in professional sports continues today in more subtle ways. For instance, the opportunities for minority candidates in the front offices of professional sports organizations are still extremely limited. Secondly, allegations of roster construction based on race continue to exist.[15] Finally, millions of white fans cheer African American student-athletes every year, but major college football programs continue to hire minority head coach candidates at a very slow pace.[16]

The 1936 Olympics in Berlin, Germany, were supposed to showcase the National Socialist government of Germany and exhibit Aryan supremacy; however, U.S. Olympian Jesse Owens, an African American, astounded the world as he won four gold medals. Adolf Hitler refused to shake hands with any black athletes at the 1936 Olympics, and did not attend any medal presentations for black athletes.[17]

One event in U.S. history in the 20th century brought race, sports, and culture together in a "perfect storm." The O.J. Simpson criminal trial was viewed by millions across America. A largely African American jury found Simpson not guilty of killing his wife and her friend, both were Caucasians. Simpson was a wildly successful college and professional football player, a popular figure in American culture and was a highly paid celebrity. He used his charm and fame to achieve movie stardom and a sports broadcasting career. Simpson was the first African American corporate spokesperson in America. In the 1960s, a Hertz car rental television commercial depicted Simpson dashing through an airport with a briefcase in his hand.[18] However, the night of June 12, 1994, would change Simpson's life and have a major impact on race relations in America. Simpson was charged with the murder of his wife, Nicole Brown Simpson, and her friend, Ronald Goldman. It seemed to be a rather "open and shut" case for the prosecution but celebrity lawyer Johnnie Cochran was able to convince a jury that Simpson was not guilty of all charges levied against him. The trial became a metaphor for racial issues in American society.[19] Although Simpson was found not guilty, many

---

[13] Ibid.

[14] Craig R. Coenen, *From Sandlots to the Super Bowl: The National Football League, 1920–1967* (University of Tennessee Press, 2005) p. 91.

[15] "The NFL and Race, by the Numbers," *Wall Street Journal*, January 2, 2009. See a breakdown of race for various positions for the 2008 NFL season at Judd Spicer, "NFL: A Study in Racial Separation by Position," *City Pages*, December 17, 2008.

[16] Neil Forrester, "The Elephant in the Locker Room: Does the National Football League Discriminate in the Hiring of Head Coaches?" *McGeorge Law Review* 34 (2003): 877.

[17] For further study see, Arnd Kruger and William Murray, *The Nazi Olympics* (Champaign, IL: University of Illinois Press, 2003).

[18] "Robert L. Stone, 87, Dies; Former Hertz Corp. Executive Hired O. J. Simpson for Famous TV Ads," *Los Angeles Times*, February 2, 2009.

[19] Walter T. Champion Jr., "The O.J. Trial as a Metaphor for Racism in Sports," *Thurgood Marshall Law Review* 33 (Fall 2007).

believed the jury came to the wrong conclusion and that Simpson was actually guilty of the murders. Because of Simpson's iconic stature in the sports world, the trial and its outcome were topics of discussion for both the African American and white communities. The verdict in the O.J. Simpson case had a profound effect on race relations in America.

RACE AND PROFESSIONAL SPORTS

Organized professional baseball essentially banned African American athletes from participation after 1899.[20] However, many major and minor league baseball players arranged exhibition games against black professional clubs. The Negro Leagues allowed black ballplayers an opportunity to play professional baseball. Many great Negro League baseball players never made it to baseball's major leagues because of discrimination.[21] The Negro League teams stayed in existence until the early 1960s. In Case 8-1 a program instituted by Major League Baseball created an ethical dilemma and a lawsuit relating to benefits provided to former Negro League players. Major League Baseball voluntarily decided to provide certain benefits for former Negro League players. Several retired professional baseball players, both Caucasian and Latino, sued Major League Baseball claiming a violation of Title VII of the Civil Rights Act of 1964 arguing their exclusion from the medical and supplemental income plans was discriminatory.

📖 **CASE 8-1**   *Moran v. Allan H. Selig, aka "Bud" Selig, as Commissioner of Major League Baseball*

---

447 F.3d 748 (9th Cir. 2006)

In October 2003, Mike Colbern, a retired Major League Baseball player, brought a class action on behalf of himself and other retired baseball players against Major League Baseball ("MLB") claiming . . . that MLB had (1) violated Title VII by excluding them from medical and supplemental income plans devised by MLB for former Negro League players . . . [Plaintiffs] are virtually all Caucasian former MLB players who played in the Major Leagues for less than four years between 1947 and 1979 and were accordingly denied MLB pension and medical benefits.

Until 1947, when Jackie Robinson broke the color barrier in the Major Leagues, African-Americans were not allowed to play Major League Baseball and could play only in the so-called "Negro Leagues," associations of professional baseball clubs composed exclusively of black players. These clubs terminated all operations in the early 1960s as a result of the absorption of African-Americans into MLB, and the Negro Leagues ceased to exist. With the coming of racial integration to baseball, the market for a separate league for minority players evaporated.

---

[20] See Rick Swaine, *The Integration of Major League Baseball* (Jefferson, NC; McFarland & Company, 2006).
[21] Generally see, www.nlbm.com.

Having lost their economic base, the former Negro Leagues were unable to offer any pension or medical benefits to their former players. In the 1990s, seeking to make partial amends for its exclusion of African-Americans prior to 1947, MLB voluntarily decided to provide certain benefits to former Negro League players. In 1993, MLB created a plan that provided medical coverage to former Negro League players ("Negro League Medical Plan"). In 1997, it adopted a supplemental income plan that provided an annual payment of $10,000 to eligible players ("Negro League Supplemental Income Plan"). Individuals who had played in the Negro Leagues prior to 1948, i.e., prior to African-Americans being allowed in the Major Leagues, were eligible for such payments. . . . these two plans are referred to collectively as the "Negro League Plans." Some of the eligible players had subsequently played in the Major Leagues for a period of time too short to qualify them for MLB's regular medical and pension plans and some had never played in the Major Leagues at all.

[Colbern] contends that MLB's provision of medical and supplemental income benefits to certain African-Americans, former Negro League players who played in the Major Leagues between 1947-1979 for too short a period to vest in the MLB medical and pension benefits plans-but not to [him]-constitutes unlawful discrimination on the basis of race.

Although some beneficiaries of the two Negro League Plans may have played MLB baseball for a relatively short period of time, eligibility for benefits is not based on such former employment with MLB or on any employment relationship between MLB and the recipients. Rather, to qualify for the Negro League Plans, a recipient need not be a former MLB player, only a former Negro League player. A former Negro League player who never played for an MLB team is eligible for the benefits even though he was never employed in any way by MLB or one of its clubs. Thus, although they resemble benefits typically conferred on the basis of an employment relationship, the Negro League Plans' benefits are not "part and parcel of the employment relationship" between recipients and MLB nor are they "incidents of employment" of the recipient by MLB. Because the supplemental income payments and medical benefits MLB provides to former Negro League players are not awarded on the basis of an employment relationship with MLB, but rather on the basis of participation in another entity to which MLB had no legal relationship, the receipt of these benefits cannot give rise to a valid Title VII claim. In other words, the fact that [Colbern and other Caucasian and Latino players] do not receive the same or substantially similar benefits as those provided under the Negro League Plans cannot be considered an "adverse employment action" because the provision of these benefits by the MLB is not an "employment action" at all.

. . . Although there are indeed some similarities between [Plaintiff's] circumstances and that of the players to whom they compare themselves, the two groups are not similar in "all material respects." Unlike the beneficiaries of the Negro League Plans, [Colbern and other Caucasian and Latino players] were never prevented from playing for an MLB team, and thus unable to acquire the necessary longevity, for reasons entirely independent of their ability to do the job (i.e., on account of their race). Nor did [Colbern] ever play in the Negro Leagues, a primary requirement for eligibility under the Negro League Plans.

MLB's absolute ban on African-American players before 1947 impeded those players from accumulating the necessary years of service in the Major Leagues to qualify for the medical and pension benefits under the terms of the MLB benefits plans in effect at the time.

. . . we hold that MLB had a legitimate, non-discriminatory and non-pretextual reason for awarding the pension and medical benefits to African-American players who qualified under the Plans . . .

The Negro League Plans were created to remedy specific discrimination that directly affected identifiable individuals and to compensate those individuals for injuries caused by that discrimination, specifically, for the loss of benefits by African-American baseball players-a loss that resulted from their inability to acquire the necessary years of playing time to qualify for MLB's pension and medical benefits. The decision to provide benefits under the Negro League Plans only to individuals, all African-Americans, who were injured by MLB's policy of excluding members of their race from playing MLB baseball does not discriminate against Caucasians. Not only were Caucasians the beneficiaries of the discriminatory policy; they had every opportunity under it to acquire eligibility for the MLB benefits. [Plaintiffs] were never the victims of discrimination and were never deprived, during any portion of their playing years, of an opportunity to acquire the longevity necessary to become eligible for MLB benefits; rather, they simply failed to do so. Although the players who qualify under the Negro League Plans are all African-American, it was African-Americans and not Caucasians who were discriminated against on the basis of their race. It is true that only players who played in the Negro Leagues are eligible to receive benefits under the Plans. It is also true, however, that the Negro Leagues were formed to provide the opportunity to play professional baseball to those who were otherwise excluded because of their race. There was no evidence, and it would strain credulity and one's sense of history, to suggest that [Colbern] or any other Caucasians sought entry to the Negro Leagues or would

have been willing to play baseball in that forum. In short, the Plans
were adopted for the specific purpose of providing benefits to those
who had been discriminated against by being denied the opportunity to
play MLB baseball and to qualify for MLB benefits.

To the extent that MLB sought to remedy in part its past discriminatory conduct, it acted honorably and decently and not out of an
improper or invidious motive. MLB has thus shown a legitimate, non-
discriminatory reason for its decision to provide benefits to former
Negro League Players, a reason that is not pretextual in any respect.

Source: *Reprinted from Westlaw with permission of Thomson Reuters.*

1. Do you believe the actions of Major League Baseball were justified in Case 8-1?
2. Were the Negro League players treated fairly under the plan or could have MLB done more for former Negro League players?
3. Do you believe the plan could be categorized as unethical?
4. How do you handle the claims of former players who believed the plan was unethical or unfair?

CASE STUDY 8-2 *American Football League All-Star Game, 1965*

Twenty-one black football players refused to play in the 1965 American Football League (AFL), All-Star Game in New Orleans because of race-related threats and insults they suffered in New Orleans. The 21 black players, more than a third of the players on the team, voted 13–8 not to play in the game. The players issued the following statement: "The American Football League is progressing in great strides, and the Negro players feel they are playing a vital role in the league's progression. They are being treated fairly in all cities in the league. . . . However, because of adverse conditions and discriminatory practices experienced by Negro Players while here in New Orleans, the players feel they cannot perform 100 percent as expected in the All-Star Game and be treated differently."[22]

As a result, AFL Commissioner Joe Foss announced that the game would be moved to Houston. The 1965 AFL All-Star Game not only showed the effect of racism on African American athletes but also displayed the courage of those players who were willing to stand against racism and hatred.[23]

Some would agree that NBA player Craig Hodges did not fit the mold of a typical professional athlete. In the following case, an NBA club terminated his contract. Hodges alleged that the club did so based on the fact that he was African American and because they did not like his political views.

CASE 8-2 *Hodges v. National Basketball Association*

1998 WL 26183

. . . . Craig Hodges is a former professional basketball player who
alleges that the National Basketball Association ("NBA") unlawfully
discriminated against him because of his race, in violation of § 1981

---

[22] David Barron, "Fighting Against Racial Slights," *Houston Chronicle*, January 16, 2005.
[23] "Was This Their Freedom Ride?" *S.I. Vault*, January 18, 1965.

of the Civil Rights Act, when it conspired to prevent him from acquiring an NBA Player contract.

Hodges, an African-American, was a professional basketball player in the NBA from 1981 until 1992. His career as a professional basketball player was marked with impressive accomplishments: twice he was the NBA three-point field goal champion, he won three consecutive Long Distance Shootout titles in 1989 through 1991. He was a member of the Chicago Bulls when the team won the NBA championship in 1991 and 1992, and at one time, he was the most accurate three-point shooter in NBA history. During his tenure with the NBA, Hodges was also "an outspoken African-American activist," who publicly criticized professional athletes who failed to use their wealth and influence to assist the poor. As a White House guest in 1991, Hodges came garbed in traditional African vestments and presented a letter to President Bush calling for an end to injustice toward the African American community. In 1992, Bulls' representatives conveyed to Hodges that they were embarrassed by these activities. When Hodges' contract with the Bulls expired after the 1992 championship and he became a free agent, the Bulls opted not to re-sign him. Despite his success in the NBA and his efforts to sign with another team, no team has granted Hodges even a tryout or an interview.

Hodges [alleged] that the NBA conspired to keep him from playing on any NBA team because he is black and his political activities were not welcomed by the NBA. Hodges argues that racial discrimination is at the root of the conspiracy, a conclusion supported by the fact that white players with backgrounds similar to his are free to express themselves politically without suffering any retaliation.

Source: *Reprinted from Westlaw with permission of Thomson Reuters.*

The *New York Times* reported the following with regard to the *Hodges* case:

. . . Phil Jackson, the Chicago Bulls' coach . . . [said] "I had the highest regard for Craig, though. He was a great team player, never caused any problems and I respected his views. I'm a spiritual man, and so is he. But I also found it strange that not a single team called to inquire about him. Usually, I get at least one call about a player we've decided not to sign. And yes, he couldn't play much defense, but a lot of guys in the league can't, but not many can shoot from his range, either."

In the lawsuit, Billy McKinney, the director of player personnel for the SuperSonics, who is black, is quoted as having first voiced interest in Hodges in 1992, and then shortly after backing away, telling Hodges he could do nothing because "brothers have families, if you know what I mean."

"I never heard of any conspiracy whatsoever," said Wayne Embry, the president and chief operating officer of the Cleveland Cavaliers, who is also black. "I'm sure I would have if there was one. And in a league that has about 80 percent black players, it's hard to charge racism." David Stern, the commissioner of the N.B.A., said that the idea of a conspiracy against Hodges is "ridiculous." "I was even at the White House when Craig wore the dashiki," he said. "I thought it looked great, and I told him so."

Perhaps more real than the allegations is the perception of discrimination, especially among some N.B.A. personnel. "It's well known through the league that there may be repercussions if you speak out too strongly on some sensitive issues," said Buck Williams, a forward for the Knicks and the respected head of the players association. "I don't know if Hodges lost his job because of it, but it is a burden when you carry the militant label he has."

Yet such star nonconformists as the bizarre Dennis Rodman and the frequently tasteless Charles Barkley are tolerated and even celebrated. Clearly, then, the dangers of expression in the N.B.A. have less to do with personal stances than with simply being a fringe player.[24]

1. Was Hodge's inability to secure employment based on his wearing traditional African garb to the White House and his expression of his faith or was it a result of his diminished skills?[25]
2. What facts would an SMP need to know to make this determination?
3. Does the fact that Phil Jackson says he usually gets calls about a player and he got none for Hodges, show a conspiracy to keep Hodges out of the league?

CASE STUDY 8-3   *Fuzzy Zoeller and Tiger Woods*

Fuzzy Zoeller was a good PGA professional. Unfortunately, he might be best remembered for his comments about fellow PGA golfer Tiger Woods than his ability as a ball striker. In 1997, Zoeller made the following comments about Woods dealing with The Masters golf tournament: "That little boy is driving well and he's putting well. He's doing everything it takes to win. So, you know what you guys do when he gets in here? You pat him on the back and say congratulations and enjoy it and tell him not to serve fried chicken next year. Got it?" [He added] . . . "or collard greens or whatever the hell they serve."

Zoeller said the remarks were a reference to the Champions Dinner, in which the previous year's winner gets to select the menu. "When I hosted the dinner I served fast-food hamburgers," Zoeller said. "It had nothing to do with black, white, purple, yellow, or green race. It had nothing to do with Tiger or his family or his golf game."[26]

1. Do you think Zoeller's comments were racist or just ignorant?
2. How should Tiger Woods have responded to these comments?
3. How should the PGA have handled this matter?
4. Do you think the word "boy," with reference to Tiger Woods, is a racist remark?[27]

CASE STUDY 8-4   *National Football League's Rooney Rule*

The NFL's Rooney Rule requires that all NFL team owners interview at least one minority candidate when a head coaching job in the league becomes available. Since the implementation of the rule, the number of minority head coaches has increased greatly. The NFL's Rooney Rule is a recent example of how sports leagues are attempting to address historical inequities. The following article discusses the rule in depth.

---

[24] Ira Berkow, "The Case of Hodges v. the N.B.A.," *The New York Times*, December 25, 1996.
[25] Ira Berkow, "The Case of Hodges v. the NBA," *The New York Times*, December 26, 1996.
[26] "Golfer Says Comments About Woods 'Misconstrued,'" *CNN Interactive*, April 21, 1997.
[27] Adam Liptak, "Appeals Courts in Atlanta Again Rejects Racial Discrimination Claim," *The New York Times*, September 6, 2010. (No racial overtones when a white supervisor repeatedly called an adult black male "boy.")

"African-Americans have...been the subject of discrimination in the coaching ranks . . . The NFL has been dilatory in its efforts to hire African-American head coaches. However, the NFL has recently made progress in this area. When Art Shell was hired by the Oakland Raiders in 1989, he became the first African-American coach in the NFL of the modern era. His record with the Raiders was a stellar 56-41 from 1989-1994. Prior to Shell, the NFL only had one African-American coach, Fritz Pollard. The 2006 NFL season ended in a Super Bowl match-up between the Indianapolis Colts and the Chicago Bears, with an African-American as head coach for both teams.

. . . [I]n December 2003, the Committee on Workplace Diversity issued a set of guidelines for teams to follow during the interviewing process. First, before the interview process began the team must prepare a job description which defined the role of the head coach and set forth the qualities they were looking for. Secondly, teams should put a search timeline in place indicating when key decisions must be made. The team should also ensure that they identify a "deep and diverse" pool of head coaching candidates. Fourth, the committee urged team owners to personally contact each candidate about the interview. Next, the committee informed teams that a request for an interview should comply with NFL anti-tampering rules. Sixth, invitations to interview for the position should be sent via letter from the club to the candidate. Seventh, the committee stated that interviewing by telephone was inadequate and was discouraged. Eighth, the same individual was not required to interview each applicant. Ninth, if candidates are refusing to interview for the position that information should be sent to the NFL Commissioner. Finally, the committee recommended no head coaching changes should occur during the season, however, if a club does fire its coach it could hire from within without engaging in the formal interview process. The NFL's Committee on Workplace Diversity also began a pilot program for coaching preparation.

Some have questioned the necessity of the Rooney Rule. Raider owner Al Davis was the first owner to hire an African-American coach in the modern era. At the same time he openly criticized the Rooney Rule.

"I'd say that the Raiders have done more against class consciousness and more for diversity than any person or group in sports, other than Jackie Robinson. That said, I find fault with the NFL program because it only addresses the process, not the reality. What good is putting a process in place if the results are still going to be unsatisfactory? The league means well. They want to do something. But it's easier to talk about this than to solve it."

Some have argued minority candidates will just serve as "token" candidates to be in compliance with the rule. Author Shaun Powell agrees:

The Rooney Rule, again despite its good intentions, is further proof
that you can't legislate hiring because, ultimately, owners and GMs
cannot be told whom to hire. Regardless of any watchdog group or
hiring procedure, people will ultimately settle on the person they're
most comfortable with."[28]

Source: *Reprinted from Westlaw with permission of Thomson Reuters.*

1. Do you believe the NFL's Rooney Rule functions as a private affirmative action policy?[29]
2. The Detroit Lions and team president Matt Millen were fined by the NFL for failing to comply with the Rooney Rule.[30]
3. Should the NCAA implement a version of the NFL's Rooney Rule based on its dismal hiring record for minorities?
4. What are the obstacles to such a proposed rule for the collegiate ranks?[31]

CASE STUDY 8-5 *Manager Dusty Baker, "Takes the Heat"*

Manager Dusty Baker took "heat" for making comments that Black and Hispanic players were better suited to play in the sun and heat than White players. He commented, "It's easier for most Latin guys and it's easier for most minority people because most of us come from heat . . . You don't find too many brothers in New Hampshire and Maine and the Upper Peninsula of Michigan . . . We were brought over here for the heat, right? Isn't that history? Weren't we brought over because we could take the heat?"[32] Noted sports psychologist Harry Edwards from the University of California-Berkeley deemed Baker's statements "unfortunate and not totally informed," but not "malicious." Edwards also stated, "If we didn't have a race issue in this country, that statement would have little or no consequence. But we do have a race issue."[33]

1. What do you make of Baker's comments?
2. Do you consider them racist or merely ignorant?

How could naming a race horse become an issue dealing with race and sports? It became an issue in the following case involving a horse owner who wanted to name his race horse, Sally Hemings.[34]

---

[28] Patrick K. Thornton, "The Legacy of Johnnie Cochran, Jr: The National Football League's Rooney Rule," *Thurgood Marshall Law Review*, Fall, 2007.

[29] Bram A. Maravent, "Is the Rooney Rule Affirmative Action? Analysing the NFL's Mandate to Its Clubs Regarding Coaching and Front Office Hires," *Sports Lawyers Journal* 13 (Spring 2006): 233.

[30] William C. Rhoden, "Sports of the Times," *New York Times*, July 31, 2003.

[31] See Joe Schad, "Houston Hires Sumlin, Eighth Minority in FBS," *ESPN*, December 13, 2007.

[32] Chuck Johnson, "Baker Stands by Heat Comments," *USA Today*, July 7, 2007.

[33] Ibid.

[34] Annette Gordon-Reed, *Thomas Jefferson and Sally Hemings: An American Controversy* (University of Virginia Press, 1998); Redmond v. The Jockey Club, C.A. 6 (Ky.), 2007.

CASE STUDY 8-6 *"What's in a Name?"*

What's in a name? that which we call a rose
By any other name would smell as sweet;
So Romeo would, were he not Romeo call'd,
Retain that dear perfection which he owes
Without that title.
WILLIAM SHAKESPEARE, ROMEO AND JULIET, act 2, sc. 2.

"What's in a name?" To Garrett Redmond, who desires to name his thoroughbred race horse "Sally Hemings," *everything* is in the name. When the Jockey Club, acting on behalf of the Kentucky Horse Racing Authority (KHRA), denied his request to register his horse under that name, Mr. Redmond protested. . . .

The Kentucky Horse Racing Authority (KHRA) is an independent state agency established by statute to "regulate the conduct of horse racing and pari-mutuel wagering on horse racing, and related activities within the Commonwealth of Kentucky." It has broad power over horse racing activities, including the "full authority to prescribe necessary and reasonable administrative regulations and conditions under which horse racing at a horse race meeting shall be conducted." One such regulation, pertinent to this case, is that "[n]o horse shall be entered or raced in this state unless duly registered and named in the registry office of the Jockey Club in New York."

The Jockey Club is the sole organization that registers and maintains records of thoroughbred horses in the United States, Canada, and Puerto Rico. It is a New York-based organization, established in 1894 and offering membership by invitation only, whose principal function is maintaining *The American Stud Book Principal Rules and Requirements,* which includes the universally-accepted rules and requirements for naming thoroughbred horses. Rule 6(A) states that "names will be assigned based upon availability and compliance with the naming rules as stated herein." Rule 6(F) identifies classes of names that are *not eligible* for use, including:

> . . . Rule 6(F)(6): Names of persons, unless written permission to use their name is on file with the Jockey Club.
> Rule 6(F)(7): Names of "famous" people no longer living, unless approval is granted by the Board of Stewards of the Jockey Club.
> Rule 6(F)(8): Names of "notorious" people.
> Rule 6(F)(13): Names that are suggestive or have a vulgar or obscene meaning; names considered in poor taste; or names that may be offensive to religious, political or ethnic groups.

Rule 6(G) gives the Jockey Club Registrar the absolute right to approve all name requests. Rule 20 provides the applicant the right to a hearing, upon payment of a $1,000 non-refundable fee.

When Mr. Redmond submitted the name "Sally Hemings" for his yearling filly in February 2004, the Jockey Club rejected it. A lengthy correspondence ensued, culminating in a telephone call in which the Jockey Club's president, Alan Marzelli, informed Mr. Redmond that the name is "in poor taste and may be offensive to religious, political or ethnic groups." Ultimately, Marzelli advised Mr. Redmond in writing that:

> [T]he name 'Sally Hemings' is not eligible for use under Rule 6(F) of The Principal Rules and Requirements of *The American Stud Book* as the name is considered by this office to be in poor taste and a name that may be offensive to religious, political or ethnic groups. . . . Furthermore, and as you are aware, the name of a 'famous' person no longer living is not eligible under Rule 6(F)(7), unless approval is granted by the Board of Stewards of The Jockey Club.

In short, because he has spent three years insisting that he has a constitutional right to name his horse "Sally Hemings" and that no other name will do, Mr. Redmond now finds himself, like the songster of the '70s, having "been through the desert on a horse with no name." If he really wants to race or breed this horse in Kentucky, Mr. Redmond will have to come up with a name that complies with the Jockey Club's rules. A quick look at the Jockey Club's Registry confirms that "Horse With No Name" is no longer available.

Dewey Bunnell, *A Horse with No Name,* on AMERICA (Warner Brothers 1972).

We note from outside the present record that Mr. Redmond's four-year-old filly made her racing debut on July 1, 2007, under the *temporary* name "Awaiting Justice," finishing fifth in a nine-horse field. *See* Churchill Downs Race Results, *available at* http://www.churchilldowns.com (last visited July 27, 2007); *see also* Jennie Rees, *Filly's Name is Some Affair,* Louisville (KY) Courier-Journal, June 30, 2007, available at http:// www.courier-journal. com (quoting Mr. Redmond as saying the name is "strictly temporary") (last visited July 27, 2007). Of course, the term "awaiting justice," being a temporary condition, would appear by its own implication to be necessarily temporary when used as a name.

Mr. Redmond appealed the decision to the Jockey Club Board of Stewards, objecting that it was arbitrary and unwarranted. The board rejected Mr. Redmond's arguments on appeal and concluded that the use of the name "may be offensive to persons of African descent and other ethnic groups, may be offensive to descendants of the specific people

involved, may have negative historical implications, may have negative
moral implications and may be degrading to ethnic groups and descendants of the people involved." The board also rejected the name based
on the prohibition against using the names of "famous person[s] no
longer living."

Source: Reprinted from Westlaw with permission of Thomson Reuters.

1. Was the jockey club correct in denying Mr. Redmond the use of his desired name for his race
   horse?
2. What other names do you believe would not be allowed under the policy?
3. Should an organization such as the jockey club be allowed to set its own rules as long as they
   are legal and ethical?
4. What ethical problems do you see with the implementation of this rule?
5. How many racing fans do you believe know who Sally Hemings was?[35]

CASE STUDY 8-7 *Rush Limbaugh Comments on NFL Quarterback Donovan McNabb*

Political commentator Rush Limbaugh is an outspoken individual; that is what he gets paid to do, to give
his opinion. In 2003, Limbaugh was hired by ESPN as an NFL analyst. As an analyst he made the following
comments regarding NFL quarterback Donovan McNabb:

> Sorry to say this, I don't think he's been that good from the get-go. . . . I think what we've had here is a little
> social concern in the NFL. The media has been very desirous that a black quarterback do well. There is a little
> hope invested in McNabb, and he got a lot of credit for the performance of this team that he didn't deserve.
> The defense carried this team.[36]

Limbaugh was forced to resign from ESPN because of his comments. Do you consider his comments
racist? In 2009 Limbaugh was considering becoming an owner in the St. Louis Rams NFL franchise. Some
objected to his ownership because of his comments about McNabb, including the NFLPA's executive director
Maurice Smith:

> I've spoken to the Commissioner [Roger Goodell] and I understand that this ownership consideration is in the
> early stages. But sport in America is at its best when it unifies, gives all of us reason to cheer, and when it tran-
> scends. Our sport does exactly that when it overcomes division and rejects discrimination and hatred.[37]

Do you agree with the union's position that Limbaugh should have been prevented from owning an NFL
franchise because of his comments about Donovan McNabb? It is ethical for the players union to take a position on ownership of a league franchise?

Making a "slip of the tongue" or an inappropriate remark does not always mean your career is over. Taking
an example from the other side of the aisle, U.S. Secretary of State Hillary Clinton, at a democratic fundraiser
in 2004, introduced a quote from Mahatma Gandhi by saying, "He ran a gas station down in St. Louis."[38] She
continued, "No, Mahatma Gandhi was a great leader of the 20th century." After being confronted about her

---

[35] Peter Nicolaisen, "Thomas Jefferson, Sally Hemings, and the Question of Race: An Ongoing Debate," *Journal of American Studies*, Vol. 37, Issue 01, May 8, 2003, pp. 99–118.
[36] "Limbaugh's Comments Touch Off Controversy," *ESPN.com*, October 1, 2003.
[37] Chris Mortensen, "Smith Sends E-Mail Detailing Opposition," *ESPN.com*, October 11, 2009.
[38] "Clinton Apologizes for Gandhi Remark," *The New York Times*, January 7, 2004.

remarks, she said she never meant to stereotype that certain ethnic groups were synonymous with operating a gas station.[39] She later apologized saying, "I have admired the work and life of Mahatma Gandhi and have spoken publicly about that many times . . . I truly regret if a lame attempt at humor suggested otherwise."[40]

How do you compare Secretary Clinton's remarks about Mahatma Gandhi with Limbaugh's comments about Donovan McNabb?

CASE STUDY 8-8 *Baseball and Immigration*

Immigration and specifically illegal immigration, is a tough political issue facing America. Many individuals and groups have differing viewpoints about immigration policy in the U.S. When the state of Arizona passed a controversial immigration bill,[41] the Major League Baseball Players Association issued a statement saying the law perpetuated racial profiling.[42] St. Louis Cardinals Manager Tony La Russa who doubles as an attorney, said he agreed with the law[43] stating, "I'm actually a supporter of what Arizona is doing . . . If the national government doesn't fix your problem, you've got a problem. You've got to fix it yourself. That's just part of the American way."[44]

1. Should a players association take a stand on immigration or any political issue for that matter, or should it restrict its concerns to issues directly relating to its sport?
2. Were La Russa's comments inappropriate or is he allowed to state his position?

CASE STUDY 8-9 *Interviewing Draft Prospects*

In any job interview an employer will certainly ask the prospective employee about his or her background to determine if the employee is a good fit for the company. The employer is entitled to do so within certain boundaries. The same is true in the sports industry with the same restrictions applicable. When potential draftee Dez Bryant was interviewed before the NFL draft by the Miami Dolphins, general manager Jeff Ireland asked Bryant several questions. One of the questions was whether Bryant's mother was a prostitute. Bryant's mother was only 15 when he was born, and she served time in jail for selling crack cocaine. In his defense, Ireland said, "My job is to find out as much information as possible about a player that I'm considering drafting. Sometimes that leads to asking in-depth questions. . . . Having said that, I talked to Dez Bryant and told him I used poor judgment in one of the questions I asked him. I certainly meant no disrespect and apologized to him."[45]

1. Was the interview "out of bounds" or was it legitimate, considering the amount of money NFL teams have to invest in their newly drafted players?
2. What other questions would you deem inappropriate by NFL teams to players during the interview process?
3. Should NFL teams be able to question players about their family history?

---

[39] Ibid.
[40] Jarrett Murphy, "Hillary Regrets Gandhi Joke," *CBS News*, January 7, 2004.
[41] Randal C. Archibold, "Arizona Enacts Stringent Law on Immigration," *The New York Times*, April 23, 2010.
[42] Michael O'Keeffe, "MLBPA Statement on Arizona's Immigration Law," *NY Daily News*, April 30, 2010.
[43] Patrick Saunders, "Immigration, Race and Baseball Are Inseparable," *Denver Post*, May 3, 2010.
[44] Jim McLennon, "Tony La Russa Backs Arizona Immigration Law," *SBNation.com*, July 1, 2010.
[45] Walt Bennett, "Defending the Dolphins: No Question Is Out of Bounds," *New York Times*, May 4, 2010.

4. As an SMP, how would you handle this situation?

5. What racial overtones are present in case study 8-9?

Title VII of the Civil Rights Act of 1964 prohibits racial discrimination in employment. In the following case, an NFL player sued the NFL and the commissioner claiming both retaliated against him after he claimed some rabid fans yelled racial epithets at him during an NFL game.

📖 CASE 8-3 *Cox v. National Football League*

29 F. Supp. 2d 463 (1998)

. . . Bryan Cox has sued his employer, the National Football League and its Commissioner, Paul Tagliabue, for retaliatory employment discrimination . . .

. . . Cox is a professional football player who has played for, and has been employed by, the Miami Dolphins and the Chicago Bears . . .

In July 1994 . . . Cox sought an injunction to order [the NFL] to institute policies that would prevent players from being subjected to the kind of racial epithets by fans that he was subjected to while entering Rich Stadium in Buffalo, New York, for a game on September 23, 1993 . . .

Within days after he filed the lawsuit, the NFL ordered Cox to participate in the NFL drug abuse program . . . Dr. Trop, who evaluated Cox for possible substance abuse, noted that Cox engaged in heavy drinking in December 1993, but that there was no evidence to support active substance abuse . . .

. . . shortly after Cox filed the lawsuit, the NFL Director of Communications released a statement which provided that the NFL has "implemented new security measures for the 1994 season to address [Bryan Cox's] concerns and to supplement previous procedure. . . . "The steps were taken in part because of the incident last season involving Bryan Cox which highlighted the issue of racial harassment of players and coaches by fans.". . .

The NFL maintains disciplinary policies and distributes a memorandum describing the policies annually with a "Message from the Commissioner." In a section entitled "Offense Against Game Official," the 1996 disciplinary memorandum, which Cox received, provides that "[p]layers, coaches, and other club personnel must maintain proper respect for game officials at all times" and that "[n]on-physical abuse of officials, including extreme profanity and other abusive language, is . . . prohibited." In a section entitled "Sportsmanship," the memorandum provides that: "every NFL game is broadcast on radio and television," "[t]he League and its participants are severely criticized whenever obscene or profane language or obscene gestures are carried or shown on the air," and "[s]erious incidents of this kind will warrant disciplinary action by the League."

On October 6, 1996, during a game between the Chicago Bears and Green Bay Packers and after a Packers touchdown, Cox threw his helmet to the ground under the goal post and three officials called a penalty on Cox for unsportsmanlike conduct. During the extra point attempt, Cox verbally abused game official Billy Smith by repeatedly shouting obscenities at him in a loud voice, calling him a "motherfucker," and then telling him to "suck my dick." Cox made obscene gestures toward Smith by "giving him the finger" several times while standing two to three feet from him. Cox's berating of Smith was broadcast live, his display of obscene gestures toward Smith was broadcast on replay by FOX television, and all of his conduct was visible to fans in Soldier Field.

Commissioner Tagliabue met with key NFL officials to review the incident and Jerry Seeman, Director of Officiating, Gene Washington, Director of Football Development, and Peter Hadhazy, Director of Football Operations, recommended suspension without pay due to Cox's repugnant treatment of a game official. Tagliabue determined that Cox's conduct represented "a unique set of circumstances" due to Cox's unusual and disturbing loss of control of his emotions, his unprovoked abuse of a game official, his continuing pattern of abuse toward officials as well as fans, and the NFL's past unsuccessful attempts to deter similar misconduct by Cox. Prior to October 1996, Cox had been disciplined for using profanity and making obscene gestures toward officials and fans. Based on the "totality of those circumstances," Tagliabue determined that Cox should be fined in an amount equal to his paycheck for one game, which was approximately $87,000.00.

On January 23, 1997, Cox filed a charge of discrimination with the Equal Employment Opportunity Commission (EEOC) stating that [the NFL and the commissioner] had retaliated against him in violation of Title VII... Cox [had] filed his Title VII discrimination suit against [NFL] in July 1994 and the NFL imposed the $87,500.00 fine in October 1996 . . .

. . . Regardless of the time lapse, Cox has failed to demonstrate that the NFL would not have fined him $87,500.00 but for his filing a discrimination case against defendants in 1994...

Source: *Reprinted from Westlaw with permission of Thomson Reuters.*

1. What steps should professional leagues take to ensure their players are free from racial hatred and taunting by fans before, during and after games?
2. If it can be proved that Cox was subjected to racial epithets, would his actions then be justified and ethical?

John Rocker was a left-handed relief pitcher for the Atlanta Braves and became the poster child for insensitivity. If not for a *Sports Illustrated* interview, Rocker may have gone into the annals of baseball as just another relatively successful baseball relief pitcher. During the interview, he disparaged multiple races and nationalities and as a result was disciplined by the commissioner of baseball under the best interests clause of the Major League Baseball Constitution. Rocker was a fiery left-hander with a 100 mph fastball and a competitive attitude, and he quickly developed into a star closer for the Atlanta Braves in the 1999 season. Rocker appeared on the scene very quickly for the Braves and soon developed a "friendly" rivalry with New York Met fans. The Mets were the chief rival of the Braves in the Eastern Division of the National League. Mets fans jeered Rocker, and he gave back as much as he got, sometimes working the crowd into a frenzy. His rivalry with Mets fans was well known throughout the league. Rocker was competitive, and it showed in his playing style. New York fans are very enthusiastic, and Rocker's antics would spur them to greater enthusiasm. Mets fans developed an ongoing feud with Rocker for most of the 1999 season as the Mets and Braves battled for the 1999 National League Championship (NLCS).

The Braves eventually prevailed over the Mets in the NLCS 4 games to 2. Sports fans began to turn their attention to football, basketball, and hockey while ball players left to play golf and spend time with their families. John Rocker, like many other players, waited in anticipation for the next season to begin. Rocker was asked by *Sports Illustrated* writer Ron Pearlman for an interview, and Rocker gave the interview as he drove around in his truck with Pearlman. Rocker was unaware of the impact the interview would have on his career, teammates, and the game of baseball. Rocker's interview with *Sports Illustrated* created a firestorm of controversy and initiated a very public debate about race relations and prejudice in America.

During the interview Rocker was asked a variety of questions and gave uncensored answers on a variety of "hot button" issues, some of which had little to do with baseball. The remarks that were published proved to be extremely controversial. In fairness to Rocker, he was promised by *Sports Illustrated* that some of his answers would be kept off the record, specifically his remarks concerning NBA player Latrell Sprewell.

📖 CASE 8-4 *In The Matter of Arbitration The Major League Baseball Players Association, Panel Decision No. 104, Grievance No. 2000-3, Player: John Rocker*

On January 31, 2000, Allan H. "Bud" Selig, the Commissioner of Baseball, imposed discipline on John Rocker, a pitcher for the Atlanta Braves, for having engaged in conduct not in the best interests of baseball. Selig specifically referred to "certain profoundly insensitive and arguably racist statements" made by Rocker that were reported in the December 27, 1999, issue of *Sports Illustrated*. Selig charged that: "Your comments in *Sports Illustrated* have harmed your reputation, have damaged the image and goodwill of Major League Baseball and the Atlanta Braves and have caused various other harms to the Club and the game."

The Association immediately filed a Notice of Grievance protesting that the discipline was without just cause. . . .

On March 1, 2000, the Chairman of the Panel issued the following Award:

Award

1. The decision of Commissioner Allan H. Selig to suspend John Rocker from Major and Minor League Spring Training in 2000, to suspend him, with pay, from Major League Baseball from opening day until May 1, 2000, to require that he make a $20,000 contribution to the NAACP or a similar organization dedicated to the goals of diversity, and to participate in a program of diversity training prior to his return as an active player, was without just cause.

2. Said suspension from Spring Training shall be rescinded. A suspension, with pay, from Major League Baseball from opening day until April 17 is sustained. A requirement of a $500.00 charitable contribution is sustained, as is a requirement that Rocker participate in an in-season program of diversity training, as established by Major League Baseball's Employee Assistance Program. . . .

Background

John Rocker, who is now 25 years old, began his minor league career in the Braves' organization in 1994. In 1999, he became the Braves' closer. His pitching performance during the 1999 regular season and the post-season was outstanding.

During the 1999 season, a mutual and growing antagonism developed between Rocker and the fans at Shea Stadium, the home of the New York Mets, Atlanta's principal rival in the National League East. Mets' fans used abusive and profane language and gestures to taunt Rocker, and he responded in kind.

The relationship between Rocker and the Mets' fans intensified after the Braves swept the Mets in a late September series at Shea. The two teams met again in the National League Championship Series. In the third game fans verbally attacked Rocker and he responded in kind . . . only quick and effective action by the New York Police Department prevented the fans from physically assaulting Rocker.

In the fourth game of the NLCS, his appearance triggered an immediate reaction by the Mets fans who loudly booed, and greeted him with obscenities and verbal abuse. Rocker responded by sticking out his tongue and yelling obscenities at the fans. . . .

On December 12, 1999, Rocker was interviewed by a reporter for *Sports Illustrated* . . . [who drove] around with Rocker. . . .

Rocker testified that he asked the reporter to keep certain remarks off the record and, with one exception, the reporter complied with his request.

On December 22, 1999, the *Sports Illustrated* article first appeared . . . it landed like a bombshell, creating a huge nationwide furor, which had not abated by the time of the arbitration hearing in early February 2000. The following excerpts are from the article. . . .

"So many dumb asses don't know how to drive in this town," he says. . . . Look! Look at this idiot! I guarantee you she's a Japanese woman." A Beige Toyota is jerking from lane to lane. The woman at the wheel is white. "How bad are Asian women at driving?"

John Rocker has opinions, and there's no way to sugarcoat them. They are politically incorrect, to say the least, and he likes to express them.

On ever playing for a New York team. . . . "Imagine having to take the [Number] 7 train to the ballpark, looking like you're [riding through] Beirut next to some kid with purple hair next to some queer with AIDS right next to some dude who just got out of jail for the fourth time right next to some 20-year-old mom with four kids. It's depressing."

On New York City itself: "The biggest thing I don't like about New York are the foreigners. I'm not a very big fan of foreigners." . . .

In passing, he calls an overweight black teammate "a fat monkey."

Immediately after publication of the article, the Braves issued a statement disassociating the Club from the viewpoints attributed to Rocker and Rocker issued a public apology. . . .

Source: *Reprinted from Westlaw with permission of Thomson Reuters.*

It is undisputed that negative racial comments reinforce racist stereotypes that demean not only the athletes but also the sports they play. In his *Sports Illustrated* interview, John Rocker uttered insensitive and racist statements. The punishment by the commissioner of baseball was partially based on the damage that Rocker's statements did to "the image and goodwill of Major League Baseball." Is that a sufficient reason for the commissioner to act? One can argue that Rocker was provoked, by fans some three months before the interview. Should this alleged provocation mitigate the punishment he received from the commissioner? The commissioner's suspension of Rocker and the amount of the fines were reduced by the arbitrator so that Rocker only lost two weeks of the season and paid only a $500 fine. Was this a just and fair penalty or was it too lenient or too harsh?

CASE STUDY 8-10 *Coach Bill Parcells and Secret Plays*

There is no doubt Bill Parcells is an excellent football coach and a motivator of players. He is a proven product in NFL circles. He was always admired for his ability to find unique ways to get the most out of his players. However, he was forced to apologize after making the following statement when talking to reporters during his team's mini camp in 2007, "No disrespect for the Orientals, but what we call Jap plays. OK. Surprise things."[46] John Tateishi of the Japanese-American Citizen's League, a national civil rights group said "Unfortunately, he [Parcells] is ignorant about racial slurs. I take great offense by what he said. Parcells ought to know

---

[46] "Delinquent Bill," *The Dallas Observer*, January 25, 2007.

better. He sorely needs more education on what is offensive and non-offensive to Japanese-Americans. I am shocked that he would say this."[47]

1. Do you believe Parcells's comments were racist or merely ignorant?
2. Should the NFL have suspended Parcells for his comments?
3. Should there be a different standard for coaches than players and owners for this type of conduct?

CASE STUDY 8-11   *Larry Bird—Larry Legend*

Larry Bird was one of the greatest players in the history of the NBA. "The Hick from French Lick"[48] made the following comments regarding the racial make up of the NBA, "You know, when I played, you had me and Kevin [McHale] and some others throughout the league. I think it's good for a fan base because, as we all know, the majority of the fans are white America. And if you just had a couple of white guys in there, you might get them a little excited. But it is a black man's game, and it will be forever. I mean, the greatest athletes in the world are African American."[49]

1. Do you consider Larry Bird's comments racist?
2. How should the NBA have handled his remarks?
3. Did the NBA overlook Bird's comments because he is "Larry Legend"?

CASE STUDY 8-12   *Baseball Owner Marge Schott*

Baseball club owner Marge Schott seemed to say the first thing that popped into her head. She was the first woman to own and operate a Major League Baseball team, the Cincinnati Reds. Schott was forced out of baseball temporarily because she embarrassed fellow owners and the game of baseball with her continued use of offensive racial and ethnic slurs. Why Marge Schott was commenting on Adolf Hitler is still a mystery but she did make the following statement about Hitler: "Everything you read, when he came [to power] he was good. . . . They built tremendous highways and got all the factories going. . . . Everybody knows he was good at the beginning but he just went too far."[50]

Schott's remarks drew a $25,000 fine and a one-year suspension from baseball. Was the punishment for Schott meted out by the commissioner appropriate? Other celebrities, for unknown reasons, have decided to comment upon Adolf Hitler as well.[51] A good policy is never to discuss Adolf Hitler unless you have a PhD in history.

---

[47] "Parcells Apologized for Making Ethnic Remarks," *ESPN.com*, June 7, 2004.
[48] "NBA Nicknames," *SI Vault, SI.com.*
[49] "Bird: NBA 'A Black Man's Game,'" *ESPN.com*, June 8, 2004.
[50] "Marge Schott's Comments on ESPN About Hitler," *Anti Defamation League,* Press Release, May 6, 1996;
    Richard Goldstein, "Marge Schott, Owner of Cincinnati Reds, Dies," *The New York Times*, March 2, 2004.
[51] "Jewish Group: Will Smith Didn't Praise Hitler," *USA Today*, December 26, 2007.

CASE STUDY 8-13   *Jimmy "The Greek" Snyder*

Jimmy "The Greek" Snyder was a very good sportscaster and very well known in the sports world. He was fired after 12 years as a CBS football analyst for remarks he made to a Washington, D.C. television reporter about the physical abilities of black and white athletes. Snyder said the black athlete is "bred to be the better athlete because, this goes all the way to the Civil War when . . . the slave owner would breed his big woman so that he would have a big black kid."[52] He later apologized for the comments.

CASE STUDY 8-14   *Michael Irvin*

Michael Irvin was an NFL wide receiver, not a very good television sports commentator, and certainly no historian. Consider the following exchange he had with noted sportscaster Dan Patrick in 2006 about the origin of the talents of Dallas Cowboys quarterback Tony Romo:

"[there must be] some brothers in that line somewhere . . . (laughs to himself) somewhere there are some brothers . . . I don't know who saw what, where . . . [maybe] his great, great, great, great Grandma ran over in the hood or something went down . . . (laughter)"

Dan Patrick, sensing disaster, jumps in and says, 'that's the only way to be a great athlete?'

Irvin comes back with, "No, that's not the only way . . . but it's certainly one way . . . [maybe his] great, great, great, great Grandma pulled one of them studs up outta the barn [and said] 'come here for a second' . . . back in the day . . . (more sinister laughter)"

Patrick steps in to defuse the situation by saying, "Alex Haley in 'Roots' on the Dan Patrick Show."

Source: *Bleacherreport.com*, October 6, 2008.

Irvin later apologized for his assessment of Romo's talents saying he was only joking. ESPN spokesman Mike Soltys stated, "Generalizations about heritage are inappropriate in jest, and what Michael said was wrong . . . We have spoken to Michael about it."[53] Are these racist comments? To his credit, Dan Patrick tried to soften his blow by saying no one is going to confuse Alex Haley with Michael Irvin.[54] Compare this to the comments made by Rush Limbaugh and Jimmy "the Greek" Snyder. Should Irvin have been fired by ESPN for his comments?

CASE STUDY 8-15   *NBA Player Stephen Jackson*

In 2005, the NBA announced the NBA dress code. The NBA excluded certain items:
"The following is a list of items that players are not allowed to wear at any time while on team or league business:

- Sleeveless shirts
- Shorts
- T-shirts, jerseys, or sports apparel (unless appropriate for the event (e.g., a basketball clinic), team-identified, and approved by the team)

---

[52] "Jimmy (the Greek) Snyder, 76, Is Dead; a Sports Oddsmaker," *The New York Times*, April 22, 1996.
[53] "Irvin on Comments: 'Inappropriate and Insensitive,'" *ESPN.com*, November 27, 2006.
[54] Ibid.

- Headgear of any kind while a player is sitting on the bench or in the stands at a game, during media interviews, or during a team or league event or appearance (unless appropriate for the event or appearance, team-identified, and approved by the team)
- **Chains, pendants, or medallions worn over the player's clothes** [Emphasis added]
- Sunglasses while indoors
- Headphones (other than on the team bus or plane, or in the team locker room)"[55]

Indiana Pacers guard Stephen Jackson contended that a league ban on chains worn over clothing was a "racist statement" from the NBA. He described the jewelry ban as "attacking young black males." He said, "I think it's a racist statement because a lot of the guys who are wearing chains are my age and are black," said Jackson, 27. "I wore all my jewelry today to let it be known that I'm upset with it. . . . I'll wear a suit every day. I think we do need to look more professional because it is a business. A lot of guys have gotten sloppy with the way they dress. But, it's one thing to [enforce a] dress code and it's another thing if you're attacking cultures, and that's what I think they're doing."[56]

What is your opinion of Stephen Jackson's comments? Do you consider the NBA's ban on chains a racist statement? Certainly, some adornments are associated with young males and are particular to certain ethnic, racial, or religious groups. Should the NBA have negotiated this issue with the players union first?[57]

Filmmaker and New York Knicks season ticket holder Spike Lee, supported the dress code 100 percent. Lee said: "If I was employed by an NBA team, I would have on a suit and tie . . . When you work in corporate America, you can't come to work with a do-rag, bling-bling, and what not . . . When you watch the NBA Draft . . . when their name gets called and they come on the stage and they shake David Stern's hand, what are they wearing? Suit and tie. I just think we've got to get back to some of the fundamentals."[58]

RACE AND AMATEUR SPORTS

Many racial issues are prevalent in youth and amateur sports as well.[59] The following cases and case studies explore issues dealing with violence based on race, racial issues in college and high school sports, and ethical dilemmas involving race with coaches.

CASE STUDY 8-16 *Olympic Protests*

John Carlos and Tommie Smith were exceptional athletes. Carlos won the bronze medal in the 200-meter race in the 1968 Olympics, and Smith took home the gold medal. When they received their medals on the

---

[55] See NBA Player Dress code, www.NBA.com, October 20, 2005.

[56] "One-Size-Fits-All Dress Code Draws Divergent Views," *ESPN*, October 19, 2002.

[57] Michael Lee, "New Dress Code Draws a Few Threads of Protest," *Washington Post*, October 20, 2005.

[58] S. Ronald, "Lee: NBA Dress Code Not 'Racist'" *Chicago Defender*, October 25, 2005.

[59] Timothy Davis, "Myth of the Superspade: The Persistence of Racism in College Athletics," *Fordham Urban Law Journal* 22 (1994–1995): 615; R. M. Sellers, "Racial Differences in the Predictors for Academic Achievement of Student-Athletes in Division I Revenue Producing Sports," *Sociology of Sports Journal* (1992); Davis Eitle, "Race, Culture Capital, and the Educational Effects of Participation in Sports," *University of Miami, Sociology of Education* 75 (April 2002): 123–146; Susan Tyler Eastman and Andrew C. Billings, "Biased Voices of Sports: Racial and Gender Stereotyping in College Basketball Announcing," *Howard Journal of Communications* 12, no. 4 (October 2001): 183–201.

Olympic victory podium, they stood with heads bowed and black gloves thrust skyward, signaling a "Black Power" salute, as the U.S. National Anthem was played. The event created a firestorm of controversy and is one of the more historic moments in Olympic history. "The two said they would make a token gesture . . . to protest racial discrimination in the United States."[60] Smith and Carlos were suspended by the U.S. Olympic Committee for making the black power salute on the victory stand during the playing of the national anthem.

Smith later said he prayed on the victory stand that he would not be shot. Both athletes were booed by the audience and both received over a hundred death threats for their Olympic protest. Smith and Carlos are alumni of San Jose State University. In 2005 a 20-foot sculpture honoring Smith and Carlos was unveiled on campus.[61]

1. Were the athletes acting properly in making their protest?
2. Is there a proper manner, place and time to make such a protest?

Racial taunting and racially stereotypical costumes at a high school basketball game are examples of racism, bad sportsmanship, and unethical decision making. That is what was present in the following case. How should the offending students in *Malcolm* be punished?

CASE 8-5 *Malcolm v. Novato Unified School District*

2002 WL 31770392

On February 13, 1998, San Marin hosted a basketball game against Tamalpais High School (Tam). Malcolm and Eaton are members of the Tam basketball team. Both are African-American. Prior to the start of the game, a group of approximately 12 to 20 San Marin students arrived at the game dressed in costumes. Though the exact description of the costumes varies, at least one student was wearing a "black afro wig" and some had on face paint.

While the Tam players were on the gym floor warming up, they heard unknown individuals chanting "[the n-word]." The chant was emanating from the direction of the costumed students. At first the players were unable to discern what was being chanted, but eventually they determined the group was chanting this racial slur. The players reported the chanting to their coach, who instructed them to return to the locker room. The coach reported the incident to Tam Assistant Principal Peg Regan, who reported the incident to San Marin Assistant Principal William Stiveson. Stiveson discussed the chant with the San Marin students and no further group chanting was heard during the game. Later in the game, however, a San Marin fan did yell the same racial slur at an African-American Tam player. The referee heard the shout and spoke with the Tam player and to a San Marin coach about the epithet. The players also saw a swastika drawn in pencil in the boys' bathroom next to the gym, and a San Marin student threatened to kill a Jewish student and his family. The players were also taunted in the parking lot after the game, although the taunts did not include racial slurs.

[60] "2 Accept Medals Wearing Black Gloves," *New York Times*, October 17, 1968.
[61] Hank Pellissier, "Black Power Statue," *The New York Times*, August 28, 2010.

When Stiveson was told at the game that San Marin fans were chanting the racial slur, he first claimed that the students were chanting "digger, digger digger." Nonetheless, he later confronted the fans sitting in the area from which the slur had emanated and told them of the allegation. The students denied chanting the slur and said that they were chanting "Yanger" for one of San Marin's players, Nick Yang. Yanger was a common chant at San Marin basketball games. Stiveson also inquired of a member of the NUSD Board of Trustees whether he had heard the chant, but the board member said that he had not. Stiveson also told Tassano about the allegation.

The next day, Stiveson and Tassano began their own investigation and received additional information from Tam Principal Ralph Gold. Stiveson and Tassano met with a number of students, including some of the students in the cheering section at the game, other students who attended the game and members of the basketball team, and encouraged them to come forward with any information regarding the chanting of the racial slur at the game. Stiveson and Tassano also discussed the matter with Officer John McCarthy, the school's resource officer who was present at the game, and Phillips and Whitburn, all of whom denied hearing the slur. Tassano held an emergency staff meeting to discuss the allegations and to gather information about the event. On February 25, 1998, Tassano forwarded a letter to Tam in which he apologized on behalf of San Marin for the incidents at the game. He also held two meetings with members of Tam's staff and its basketball team to apologize for the incident. On February 27, 1998, Stiveson issued an announcement to the student body, referencing the February 13th game, in which he reminded all students of the importance of sportsmanship and respect towards opposing teams and their fans. Approximately five weeks later, Whitburn informed Stiveson of a student who had admitted to using a racial slur at the game. Stiveson met with the student and suspended him for five days.

The NUSD received a complaint from Peg Regan about 10 days after the game. A subsequent complaint was received from a parent of a Tam student. Regan's complaint was referred to Michael Watenpaugh, the assistant superintendent, for investigation. Watenpaugh completed his investigation into the allegations and issued his report by March 27, 1998. Watenpaugh's investigation consisted of two interviews with Peg Regan; two interviews with Mike Evans, the Tam coach at the game; two interviews with Ralph Wilson, another Tam coach at the game; individual interviews with eight Tam basketball players who attended the game; an interview with Jeff Stewart, the referee who officiated the game; two interviews with Tassano; two interviews with Stiveson; two interviews with John Baker, the San Marin custodian responsible for removing the graffiti; individual interviews with six San Marin students who were seated in the area from which the slur emanated; an interview with Whitburn; and an interview with Phillips. He also reviewed various photographs and a videotape recording of the game. Based upon this investigation, he made a number of findings, including that the Tam players had heard the racial slur while warming up for the game and that Stiveson had mishandled the complaint once advised by Regan. Watenpaugh made eight recommendations regarding review and revision of the board's policies for workshops for staff and administrators concerning complaints of racial and sexual harassment. Based upon Watenpaugh's findings, [Stivenson was] issued a formal reprimand ... for having mishandled the situation initially and reminded Stiveson of the procedure by which he was to handle complaints of racial harassment in the future.

Concurrent with Watenpaugh's investigation, Joel Montero, another NUSD employee, met with the staff at San Marin to discuss the February 13th game. He stressed the importance of affording the students, personnel, and any visitors to the district a harassment-free environment and the importance of the staff's role in ensuring such an environment. He also discussed the district's antidiscrimination and harassment policy and conducted a workshop on dealing with discrimination and harassment complaints. Montero conducted a similar meeting with administrators in the district. Montero also planned a meeting between 15 Tam students and 15 San Marin students that was facilitated by a consultant with the Association of California School Administrators. Finally, Montero forwarded to Regan a letter on behalf of the district apologizing for the incident. A letter was also sent to parents in the district to inform them of the district's response to the allegation and to draw them into the efforts to ensure racial sensitivity throughout the district.

At an NUSD board meeting in May 1998, racism within the district was discussed. Members of the community addressed the board and school officials regarding their concerns about the handling of racial issues. The community was informed of a nine-point plan by the district to address racial issues in the future, including a zero-tolerance policy focusing on the responsibility of teachers and administrators to change attitudes within the district and a review of district hiring policies to attract a diverse staff.

Finally, in responding to this incident, the NUSD formed a diversity advisory committee made up of parents, administrators, and members of the community. This group was to provide recommendations on how to address issues of discrimination. In July 1998, the committee held a two-day retreat dealing with issues related to racism and diversity.

In October 1998, the NUSD adopted a policy expressing its expectations of student behavior and the responsibility of the district to protect students' rights to avoid hate crimes and racism. The policy was derived from California Department of Education publications.

In November 1998, the district adopted an equity action plan, designed to stop discrimination before it starts by teaching civility and acceptance. It provides for workshops to train teachers and school employees to confront prejudice. The plan was developed at the retreat of the diversity advisory committee and fine-tuned by the board. Also in November, an all-day diversity training workshop was held for staff and members of the community. In December 1998, the board approved distribution of "respect guidelines" to all students in the district.

Source: *Reprinted from Westlaw with permission of Thomson Reuters.*

1. Was an ethical decision-making process employed by NUSD?
2. Did NUSD perform a satisfactory investigation?
3. What could NUSD have done better to ensure that this situation does not occur again?
4. Did assistant principal William Stiveson do enough to investigate and handle this matter?

In the following case a high school football player was injured as a result of a racially motivated assault by another player.

CASE 8-6 *Priester v. Lowndes County*

354 F.3d 414 (5th Cir. 2004)

. . . On September 14, 1999, Terry, an African-American tenth-grade student at New Hope High School, sustained a serious eye injury during football practice allegedly caused by a white teammate Eli Ward. Leading up to the injury, Ward slapped Terry on the back of the head and derided him in the locker room and during warm-up drills on matters such as his weight and race. On previous occasions, the head football coach Rick Cahalane subjected Terry to numerous racial epithets and derogatory comments concerning his weight.[FN2] After hearing such comments from Cahalane, Ward used the same derogatory terms toward Terry. The day of the injury, Ward also approached Terry and, without provocation, hit him on the helmet with a rock. Terry was also hit in a similar manner by another fellow player. Cahalane allegedly heard the statements and witnessed the assaults, but he did nothing to protect Terry or take the necessary actions that could stop or prevent the recurrence of the incident. Terry's mother witnessed these events and immediately informed the high school principal, who said he would handle the problem in the morning.

FN2. The record shows that Terry Priester was subjected to such derogatory terms as "[n-word]" and "fat black ass."

In the midst of a full-contact drill during football practice, the injury occurred subsequent to Terry's successful block of Ward. In response, Cahalane walked over to Ward to "get on to him" about the previous play. While Cahalane and Ward talked, Ward apparently looked at Terry throughout the conversation. Immediately following the conversation, Ward told Terry that he "had something for him." On the next play from scrimmage, Terry alleges that Ward lunged toward him, thrust his hands through his helmet, and gouged his eye. Terry's injury resulted in permanent damage including a torn right lower eyelid, a laceration to his lower punctum and caniliculus (tear duct), chronic tearing, and blurry vision. The school's response was two-fold. First, upon interviewing the coaches and players, New Hope High School principal Mike Halford compiled a report of the incident. In the report, however, no one admitted seeing anyone hit Terry. Second, the school declined to pay Terry's medical bills.

Source: *Reprinted from Westlaw with permission of Thomson Reuters.*

1. What course of action should the coach have taken in this case?
2. Should the school discipline the coach considering his overall conduct, as well as his failure to act in the best interests of his student-athletes?
3. What restitution is owed to Terry and his parents?

Review the following report produced by the Institute for Diversity and Ethics in Sports, the University of Central Florida. What are your overall impressions of the findings of the executive summary?

CASE STUDY 8-17 *The 2009 Racial and Gender Report Card*

Executive Summary[62]

Orlando, FL . . . March 11, 2010

The 2008 Racial and Gender Report Card for College Sport showed that NCAA member institutions and their conferences lost ground for both their record for gender hiring practices and hiring practices by race. In fact, college sport had the lowest grade for racial hiring practices in 2008.

Every other year, the NCAA releases a new *NCAA Race and Gender Demographics of NCAA Member Conferences Personnel Report* and *NCAA Race and Gender Demographics of NCAA Member Institutions Athletic Personnel*. In previous years, these reports were used to examine the racial and gender demographics of NCAA head and assistant coaches, athletics directors across all divisions, associate and assistant athletics directors, senior woman administrators, academic advisors, compliance coordinators and managers for business development, fund-raising, facilities, marketing, ticket sales and media relations and an array

---

[62] Richard Lapchick, with Alejandra Diaz Calderon, Charles Harless, and Ashley Turner, "College Sport," March 11, 2010.

of assistants and support staff. This year represented the in-between year in terms of the NCAA releasing racial and gender demographic data via these reports. Lacking these NCAA-issued reports, The Institute for Diversity and Ethics in Sports (TIDES) was unable to issue College Sport a new overall grade for 2009. . . .

The commitment to fostering opportunities for women and people of color at the collegiate level was evidenced the last several years under the leadership of the late NCAA president Myles Brand. Brand hired Charlotte Westerhaus in 2005 to be the NCAA Vice-President for Diversity and Inclusion. The creation of the Office of Diversity and Inclusion and the diversity programs it created reflect this dedication. In terms of expanding opportunities in sport for women and people of color, the greatest prospects exist in college sport rather than at the professional sport level because of the sheer number of jobs available. However, the record shows there is still significant room for improvement.

The Institute for Diversity and Ethics in Sport (TIDES) at the University of Central Florida publishes the *Racial and Gender Report Card* to indicate areas of improvement, stagnation and regression in the racial and gender composition of professional and college sports personnel and to contribute to the improvement of integration in front office and college athletics department positions.

It is imperative that sports teams play the best athletes they have available to win games. TIDES strives to emphasize the value of diversity to athletic departments when they choose their team on the court and in the department. Diversity initiatives such as diversity management training can help change attitudes and increase the applicant pool for open positions. It is clearly the choice of the institution regarding which applicant is the best fit for their department, but TIDES wants to illustrate how important it is to have a diverse organization involving individuals who happen to be of a different race or gender. This element of diversity can provide a different perspective, and possibly a competitive advantage for a win in the board room as well as on the athletic fields of play.

Report Highlights for 2009

University Leadership Positions at Football Bowl Subdivision Institutions

- Positive gains were made by women and African-Americans in the role of university president at the 120 FBS Institutions. There are 22 female presidents, an increase of 0.8 percentage points, and four African-Americans, also representing a 0.8 percentage point increase.

- There was a noticeable decline in the number of Latino presidents, as representation fell 1.7 percentage points. 93.3 percent of FBS university presidents were white, an increase of 0.8 percentage points from last year's study. There was one Asian president (0.8 percent) but there were no Native American university presidents.
- The level of diversity within the athletic director position at FBS schools has stayed constant from last year's study, as 16 (13.3 percent) people of color hold this position. However, this total does not include any women of color.
- With the addition of four new African-American head coaches at FBS schools (Ron English, Eastern Michigan University; Mike Haywood, Miami University [Ohio]; Mike Locksley, University of New Mexico; DeWayne Walker, New Mexico State University), the overall number of African-American head coaches from 2008 increased from six to seven.
- The nine coaches of color in the 2009 season represented the highest number and percentage of coaches of color ever at FBS schools.
- There were six African-American coaches hired after the completion of the 2009 season, which brings the total number of coaches of color at FBS institutions to a record 15 in 2010. This included coaches in the ACC, SEC and Big East.
- Of the 268 offensive and defensive coordinators in the FBS, there was one less African-American coordinator from last year's total of 31 while there was an increase of one coordinator in both the Latino and Asian demographics, respectively.
- According to the *Chronicle of Higher Education*, 9.4 percent of full-time faculty members at FBS schools are Asian, which is more than the combined percentage of African-American, Latino, and Native Americans (7.7 percent).

NCAA Headquarters

- At the high levels of NCAA headquarters in the EVP/SVP/VP positions, the number of people of color and women remained at three and four, respectively. African-Americans are the only people of color to be represented at this level, accounting for 16.7 percent of the positions. Women held 22.2 percent of the positions.
- The percentages increased for people of color who hold posts at the managing director/director level. People of color increased by 0.8 percentage points to 24.3 percent, which represents the largest total percentage of racial minorities to occupy these posts since data was first recorded in 1998. The highest percentage gain from last year to this year was seen in the Latino demographic, as Latinos held 4.3 percent of positions at this level, up 1.4 percentage points. Women held 41.4 percent of these positions, an increase of 0.3 percentage points.
- At the NCAA administrator level, the percentage of people of color dropped 1.1 percentage points from last year even though there was no net loss in total number of minorities holding these positions. The number

of white administrators increased by 10, thus causing the shift in percentages. Women held 53.2 percent at the NCAA administrator level, down by 1.7 percentage points.

* 95 percent of support staff positions are occupied by women, an increase of 0.4 percentage points from last year and leading to the highest percentage ever of women in this role. Nineteen percent were held by people of color.

Richard Lapchick
Chair of DeVos Sport Business Management Program and Director, Institute for Diversity and Ethics in Sport, University of Central Florida.
Source: *Courtesy of Richard Lapchick, National Consortium for Academics and Sports.*

CASE STUDY 8-18 *Paul Hornung*

Paul Hornung was football's "golden boy." He is a dedicated alumnus of the University of Notre Dame. On a Detroit radio station in 2004 he said that to compete in football in the upper echelon, Notre Dame had to get the black athlete so that meant easing up on its academic standards. He said "You can't play a schedule like that unless you have the black athlete today. You just can't do it, and it's very, very tough, still, to get into Notre Dame. They just don't understand it, yet they want to win."[63] Notre Dame spokesperson, Matthew Storin, said the university disagreed with Hornung and that Hornung's statements were "generally insensitive and specifically insulting to our past and current African-American student-athletes."[64]

Do you consider Hornung's remarks racist? Former NFL standout Tim Brown, also a Notre Dame alumnus, said Hornung was not a racist and defended Hornung's character. Hornung later apologized for his comments. Should Notre Dame bar him from all future sporting events because of his remarks?

Many decisions at the intercollegiate level in sports are difficult and require an ethical decision making process for the SMP. At the university level, coaches and athletic directors will not always see "eye to eye" on every issue. That was the situation in the following case involving a famous basketball coach and an athletic director of a major university.

📖 CASE 8-7 *Richardson v. Sugg*

325 F.Supp.2d 919 (E.D.Ark.,2004)

The two primary protagonists in this real life drama are Nolan Richardson, Jr., the former Head Basketball Coach at the University of

---

[63] "Hornung: Irish Should Still Lower Standards," *ESPN.com*, March 30, 2004.
[64] Ibid.

Arkansas, Fayetteville, and J. Frank Broyles, the Athletic Director (AD) of the institution...

Nolan Richardson, Jr., is an African-American who was employed by the University of Arkansas at Fayetteville (UAF) as the men's head basketball coach from 1985 until his firing, which was effective on March 1, 2002 . . .

In 1985, Richardson was hired as the first African-American to serve as a Head Coach at UAF...

[Richardson] alleges that he was fired because of his race, and because he spoke out on matters of public concern (race) . . .

[The issue in the case was] . . . Whether Broyles's use of the word "[n-word]" at the Hawgs Illustrated banquet should be viewed as a "stray remark" or as direct evidence of racial animus.

It is important to consider the context in which Broyles's statements were made.

Broyles and Richardson talked about Richardon's duties, or lack of duties, as AAD. On December 20, 1999, Richardson wrote Broyles complaining that he did not want to be a "token" AAD. He attached a copy of a press release citing a study of the substantial racial disparity in the numbers of African-Americans employed in intercollegiate athletic departments. The study, released December 9, 1999, excluded traditionally black schools. It found that, of 899 NCAA schools, only 125 of the 2,498 people who held the three core management titles were black. The essence of Richardson's letter was simply that he did not want to be counted for purposes of affirmative action if he did not have substantive duties.

On December 23, 1999, Broyles wrote Richardson that he would respond after the holidays.

On January 15, 2000, Richardson, during a press conference, complained again about his "token" status as AAD, stating that he should not be counted among the 5 percent of African-Americans holding core position in management in the National Association of Black Colleges (NABC) study because he had no duties and received no additional pay. Richardson's complaints were reported in the Arkansas Democrat-Gazette . . .

. . . On January 17, 2000, Richardson again complained about the issue in an article in the Springdale Morning News. When reminded by the reporter that other Caucasian AAD's had not been "overly involved" in administrative duties, Richardson responded that:

"Those guys can go ahead and stay that way because they've got guys their color doing things for them. What about me? Who sits in that hallway up there to represent us? I don't. Do I help make decisions? No, sir. I've never been asked a question, I've never been in a meeting. So why use me as an AAD for affirmative action? I'm not an Uncle Tom."

On January 25, 2000, with still no response from Broyles, Richardson wrote a second letter to him, this time complaining about the disparity in pay between his assistant coaches and the assistant football coaches. In this letter, Richardson reminded Broyles that he had raised the issue in a 1997 letter, and that the disparity in pay had become even greater since Nutt had replaced Ford as head football coach in 1998. In 1997, Broyles had justified the difference by citing experience. Richardson reminded Broyles that, with the passage of time, his assistant, Mike Anderson, now had greater experience than any of Nutt's assistants, so experience could no longer be used to justify disparate treatment.

On February 17, 2000, Broyles responded to Richardson's letter and admitted that there were pay disparities between assistant football coaches and assistant basketball coaches. This time, Broyles attempted to justify the pay disparity, not because of experience, but because it was "required by the marketplace.". . .

. . . That same day, Richardson called Wally Hall, the Sports Editor for the Arkansas Democrat-Gazette to complain about the manner in which the Democrat-Gazette had portrayed his son's involvement in the departure of a basketball player. Richardson testified that, during this conversation, he called Wally Hall a "redneck."

The next day, February 18, 2000, Hall described this conversation in his column, and wrote that Richardson had called the fans "redneck SOB's." That morning, after reading the article, Jim Lindsey, a former member of the UAF Board of Trustees and the Foundation, and a former star player for Coach Broyles, received a call from a Caucasian Razorback fan in eastern Arkansas, who reported that the "redneck-SOB" statement had caused a firestorm among fans in Eastern Arkansas. Lindsey, Broyles' friend and confidant, called Broyles, to discuss the article and the phone call. Lindsey told Broyles that he believed the statements justified terminating Richardson for cause.

That same night, Hawgs Illustrated, a Razorback fan magazine published by Clay Henry, held a banquet to honor senior Razorback football players. Broyles sat at the table with Henry, Paul Eells (sports anchor for the local ABC Affiliate, KATV and Host of the TV show "Rollin' with Nolan"), and Nate Allen (sportswriter), among others, all of whom are Caucasian. According to Henry, during the dinner, Broyles asked Henry if he would do a column in Hawgs Illustrated equating Richardson's calling a fan a "redneck SOB" to a Caucasian person calling

Richardson a "[n-word]." Henry testified that he was surprised at Broyles's use of the word "[n-word]" and at Broyles's request that Henry write the column. He told Broyles that Hawgs Illustrated had an aversion to controversy.

Paul Eels was seated by Coach Broyles at this banquet. Although Eels was not engaged in conversation with him at that time, Eels clearly heard the part regarding "redneck SOB's" and "[n-word]." Eels testified that he was shocked. He also testified that he heard it as a direct statement by Broyles, and not as Broyles' quoting someone else. Eels pointed out, however, that he was not engaged in the conversation with Broyles when he heard the "[n-word]." Whether a quote or a direct statement, Broyles testified that he regretted making the remark . . .

It should ring out loudly and clearly-an African-American calling a Caucasian person a redneck is nowise the same as a Caucasian person calling an African-American "[the n-word]." Although some may argue that there is no real difference, they are wrong, and I suspect they know it. I think the following analysis makes this point well:

What about words like "honky," "redneck," and "cracker"? While those words can be harmful epithets in certain contexts, some have argued that such words are not comparably damaging to whites as are epithets hurled against people of color and other so-called minorities. In the view of two commentators:

The word "honky" is more a badge of respect than a put down. "Cracker," although disrespectful, still implies power, as does "redneck." The fact is that terms like "[the n-word]," "spick," "faggot," and "kike" evoke and reinforce entire cultural histories of oppression and subordination. They remind the target that his or her group has always been and remains unequal in status to the majority group. Even the most highly educated, professional class African-American or Latino knows that he or she is vulnerable to the slur, the muttered expression, the fishy glance on boarding the bus, knows that his degree, his accomplishments, his well-tailored suit are no armor against mistreatment at the hands of the least educated white.

But not only is there no correlate, no hate speech aimed at whites, there is no means by which persons of color and others can respond effectively to this form of speech within the current paradigm. Our culture has developed a host of narratives, mottoes, and presuppositions that render it difficult for the minority victim to talk back in individual cases, and to mobilize effectively against hate speech in general. These include: feelings are minor; words only hurt if you let them; rise above it; don't be so sensitive; don't be so humorless; talk back-show some backbone. Stated or unstated narratives like these form part of the linguistic and narrative field on which minority

victims have to play in responding to taunts and epithets, and of
course limit the efficacy of any such response.

[Broyles] has argued that [his] banquet comments two years before the
firing are "too remote" and "stray" to support an inference that [he]
harbored racial hostility toward Richardson.

Source: *Reprinted from Westlaw with permission of Thomson Reuters.*

Coach Richardson was adamant that Frank Broyles's use of the n-word at the banquet showed Broyles's true colors and that Richardson was fired by the University of Arkansas based on his race, and not for any other reason. A court disagreed with him, finding in favor of the University and Broyles. A *Sports Illustrated* article discussed Nolan Richardson's background and shed some insight on the case:

"While there's no denying that Richardson has experienced racism in its ugliest forms—growing up, he would cross the border to dine at restaurants in Mexico rather than eat in El Paso's segregated establishments—his frequent and somewhat haphazard charges of racism through the years have detracted from a Hall of Fame career. (He's the only coach to have won a national junior college title, an NIT championship and an NCAA crown.) "If I was white, and I did what I've done here, they'd build statues to me," he said in 1994, the year Arkansas won the national title. At a press conference on Feb. 25 Richardson said, "I know for a fact that I do not play on the same level as the other coaches around this school play on." The problem with that is that Richardson was the highest-paid coach at Arkansas, making $260,000 a year more than football coach Houston Nutt."[65]

In Case 8-8, a collegiate basketball coach had the idea that his use of the n-word during a half-time speech, would motivate his players to perform better on the court. He was fired for his use of the word on campus.

📖 CASE 8-8 *Dambrot v. Central Michigan University*

55 F.3d 1177 (6th Cir. 1995)

On May 12, 1991, [Keith] Dambrot became the head coach of the Central
Michigan University men's basketball team . . . This lawsuit arises
from events which occurred during the 1992-93 men's basketball season.

The 1992 CMU men's basketball team was made up of eleven African
Americans and three Caucasians. The team's full-time coaching staff
included two assistant coaches, Derrick McDowell (an African American)
and Barry Markwart (a Caucasian). The part-time coaching staff included
one voluntary graduate assistant, Chip Wilde (a Caucasian), three managers (all Caucasian), and a professional trainer (a Caucasian).

In January of 1993, Dambrot used the "[n-word]" during a locker room
session with his players and coaching staff either during the halftime

---

[65] Grant Wahl, "Nolan Richardson's Charges of Racism Sealed his Fate and Left Arkansas in Disarray," *Sports Illustrated*, March 11, 2002.

or at the end of a basketball game in which the team lost to Miami University of Ohio. According to Dambrot's testimony, Dambrot told the players they hadn't been playing very hard and then said "Do you mind if I use the N word?" After one or some of the players apparently indicated it was okay, Dambrot said "you know we need to have more [n-word] on our team. . . . Coach McDowell is a [n-word], . . . Sand[er] Scott who's an academic All-American, a Caucasian, I said Sand[er] Scott is a [n-word]. He's hard nose, [sic] he's tough, et cetera." He testified he intended to use the term in a "positive and reinforcing" manner. The players often referred to each other using the N-word during games and around campus and in the locker room. Dambrot stated he used the word in the same manner in which the play-ers used the term amongst themselves, "to connote a person who is fearless, mentally strong and tough."

Prior to the January incident, the record shows Dambrot had used the N-word on at least one other occasion. In November, Dambrot apparently addressed the team after a practice and said he wanted the players to "play like [n-word] on the court" and wished he had more [n-word] on the basketball court. He then said he did not want the team to act like [n-word] in the classroom. When asked why he made these state-ments Dambrot stated:

Well, that's really a very easy question for me to answer, because we had had an incident early in the year where we had five or six basket-ball players, some of our bigger kids on our team, in a math class. And our kids were aggressive, tough, you know, a little bit loud, abrasive. And the lady was intimidated, because it was the first year that she ever had taught. And they almost got kicked out of the math class. A matter of fact, Dave Keilitz, myself, Pat Podoll, Doug Nance, who is the faculty rep, and then the head of the department,-I don't remember his name-the math department, met and discussed the situa-tion. And it was my feeling that you can't be aggressive, tough, hard-nosed, abrasive in class, or you're going to get thrown out of classes, especially at a school like Central Michigan where the fac-ulty members don't understand a lot about black people or have many black people in class. And I think our players understood what I meant by, "Don't be [n-word] in the classroom."

The news Dambrot had used the N-word in the locker room incident became known to persons outside the basketball team. In February 1993, Keilitz interviewed members of the men's basketball team at Dambrot's request. Keilitz reported all the African American players he interviewed said they were not offended by the coach's use of the term. At some point after those interviews, a former member of the men's basketball team, Shannon Norris, complained to the university's affirmative action offi-cer, Angela Haddad, regarding Dambrot's use of the N-word during the

November incident. The affirmative action officer confronted Dambrot who admitted using the word but stated he used it in a positive manner. The officer viewed Dambrot's use of the word as a violation of the university's discriminatory harassment policy and recommended Dambrot be disciplined. Dambrot accepted the proposed disciplinary action in lieu of a more formal investigation and was suspended without pay for five days.

News of the locker room incident spread through the campus after Dambrot was suspended. An article in the student newspaper was printed in which Dambrot told his side of the story. The statement was characterized by the district court as "considerably more explanatory and defensive than apologetic in tone." Students staged a demonstration and local, regional, and national news media reported accounts of the incident at CMU.

On April 12, 1993, Keilitz, the athletic director, informed Dambrot he would not be retained as head coach for the 1993–94 season. The university stated that it believed Dambrot was no longer capable of effectively leading the men's basketball program.

Dambrot instituted a lawsuit on April 19, 1993, alleging . . . he was fired because he used the term "n-word," and the termination violated his First Amendment rights to free speech and academic freedom. Several members of the basketball team joined the lawsuit . . .

Dambrot's use of the N-word is even further away from the marketplace of ideas and the concept of academic freedom because his position as coach is somewhat different from that of the average classroom teacher. Unlike the classroom teacher whose primary role is to guide students through the discussion and debate of various viewpoints in a particular discipline, Dambrot's role as a coach is to train his student athletes how to win on the court. The plays and strategies are seldom up for debate. Execution of the coach's will is paramount. Moreover, the coach controls who plays and for how long, placing a disincentive on any debate with the coach's ideas which might have taken place.

While Dambrot argues and we accept as true that he intended to use the term in a positive and reinforcing manner, Dambrot's total message to the players is disturbing. Corey Henderson, one of the players on the 1992–93 team touched on the concern in his deposition testimony.

Question: What did that phrasing that he had wanted you to play like [n-word] on the basketball floor but not be [n-word] in the classroom mean to you as a students? [sic]

Answer: I really am not sure. Because in the context he was trying to use it in, I mean, [n-word] I guess as a-he wanted us-I guess he wanted us to play harder, I suppose, and I didn't understand why if it was good enough on the court then why it wasn't good enough in the classroom.

```
I mean, I was kind of shocked that he used that word being a coach and
all because he-I didn't think that was appropriate for him to use that
word, him or any coach, talking to a group of mostly young adult black
males. I didn't think it was right for him to use that word.

But then I was kind of disgusted when he said not being one in the
classroom. I didn't understand why it was good enough on the court but
not good enough in the classroom.

Source: Reprinted from Westlaw with permission of Thomson Reuters.
```

1. How should the athletic director at Central Michigan have handled the situation?
2. Does it make any difference that the student-athletes on the team supported the coach?
3. What if coach Dambrot had made the same comments to student-athletes at a historically all black university? How should his actions be viewed then?
4. As an SMP what kind of training would you have implemented for the coach or the team to ensure this never occurs again?

Dr. Alvin Poussaint of Harvard Medical School and entertainer Bill Cosby would vehemently disagree with coach Dambrot's use of the word. They assert the following in response to the use of the "n-word" in society:

Among its other charms, gangsta rap promotes the widespread use of the N-word to sell CDs among people of all ethnic groups. In fact, the audience for gangsta rap is made up predominantly of white youth, who get a vicarious thrill from participating in a black thug fantasy, including the degradation of women. Black youth, as well as some misguided adults, have defended the use of the N-word, suggesting they are somehow making it a positive term.

Don't fall for that nonsense. The N-word is a vile symbol of our oppression by slave masters. It was the word that empowered lynch mobs and emboldened them to mutilate black bodies. Remember Emmitt Till, the fourteen-year-old boy lynched in 1955 for whistling at a white woman in Mississippi? The N-word may have been the last word he ever heard. You don't honor his memory by trivializing it. You can't change its meaning by saying "nigga" instead of "[n-word]."

How many times have we heard angry black kids denounce their black foes in the most vile and derogatory fashion: "I'll kick your ass, [n-word]" or " You [n-word] son of a bitch." There is nothing cute about this. The N-word still has a negative connotation, which suggests both self-hatred and the projection of the same hate against other black people, including the "bitches" and "hos" who represent their mothers and sisters.[66]

CASE STUDY 8-19 *Radio Talk Show Host, Don Imus*

Don Imus was a world-famous radio talk-show host. He is famous for his "cutting-edge style" and his "grainy" voice. During a broadcast of his radio program in 2007, Imus made some very controversial statements

---

[66] Alvin F. Poussaint, MD, and Bill Cosby, *Come on People: On the Path from Victims to Victors* (Nashville, TN: Thomas Nelson, 2007), 144–145.

concerning the Rutgers University women's basketball team. Those comments thrust Imus and his radio show into the national spotlight. Significant portions of his radio show transcript that day stated the following:

> **Don Imus**: So, I watched the basketball game last night between—a little bit of Rutgers and Tennessee, the women's final.
>
> **Sid Rosenberg**: Yeah, Tennessee won last night—seventh championship for [Tennessee coach] Pat Summitt, I-Man. They beat Rutgers by 13 points.
>
> **Imus**: That's some rough girls from Rutgers. Man, they got tattoos and—
>
> **Bernard McGuirk**: Some hard-core hos.
>
> **Imus**: That's some nappy-headed hos there. I'm gonna tell you that now, man, that's some—woo. And the girls from Tennessee, they all look cute, you know, so, like—kinda like—I don't know.
>
> **McGuirk**: A Spike Lee thing.
>
> **Imus**: Yeah.
>
> **McGuirk**: The Jigaboos vs. the Wannabes—that movie that he had.
>
> **Imus**: I don't know if I'd have wanted to beat Rutgers or not, but they did, right?
>
> **Rosenberg**: It was a tough watch. The more I look at Rutgers, they look exactly like the Toronto Raptors.[67]

In response to Imus's racial remarks, the president of Rutgers University, Dr. Richard L. McCormick stated:

> "Last week our university family was focused on celebrating the amazing performance of our Scarlet Knights women's basketball team in the NCAA tournament. The team brought pride and excitement to our university and captured the hearts of people across the state and the nation. Our student-athletes and their coach deserved to feel immensely proud of what they had just accomplished, but they had that moment stolen away by the racist, sexist remarks of radio personality Don Imus and his colleagues.
>
> Mr. Imus's shocking comments last week were despicable and deeply hurtful to our students, our coach, and their families. They were also offensive to every member of the Rutgers community, as well as to people across the nation. Racism and sexism have no place in our society and are completely at odds with our values as a university that celebrates diversity and civility."[68]

The Rutgers women's basketball team had no forum or public access to respond to Imus's comments.[69]

1. Should that also be a consideration in determining how to handle this situation?
2. How do you categorize the remarks made by Don Imus?
3. Are they stereotypical, or just a guy on the radio who happens to have a job saying uninteresting stuff?

---

[67] "Imus Calls Rutgers' Women's Basketball Team; Nappy-Headed 'Hos' / MSNBC Distances Itself," *Fishbowl NY*, April 6, 2007.

[68] "Denouncing Don Imus's Appalling Remarks," *Office of the President, Letters to the Rutgers Community, http://president.rutgers.edu/letter_040907.shtml*, April 9, 2007.

[69] Terry McDonell, "The High Road, Depth of Character from Robinson to Rutgers," *S.I. Vault*, April 23, 2007.

NOTES AND DISCUSSION QUESTIONS

Race and Professional Sports

1. Hate crimes have statutorily enhanced punishment.[70] Do you believe race-based stereotyping, profiling and harassment in sports should also be viewed as a hate crime?
2. Is Major League Baseball doing enough to honor the stars of the Negro Leagues?[71]
3. The Negro Leagues were unable to provide adequate and comparable pension and medical benefits. Major League Baseball has attempted to make partial amends for its exclusion of African American athletes prior to 1947 by voluntarily providing certain benefits, including medical coverage and supplemental income to former Negro League players. Should baseball provide the same benefits to former Negro League players that current retirees of baseball receive?
4. Do you think Fuzzy Zoeller's comments about Tiger Woods were merely overblown or racist?
5. The NFL's Rooney Rule mandates that every NFL team interview at least one minority candidate upon the vacancy of a head coaching position or be subjected to a significant monetary fine. The rule has achieved unchartered success in the NFL. However, criticism remains that it promotes tokenism and operates as a form of reverse discrimination. Should the Rooney Rule be used to promote racial equality in hiring African American and other minority candidates in the college ranks similar to what has been done at the professional level? How would you define a minority under a collegiate rule similar to that of the NFL's Rooney Rule?
6. Allen Iverson was an eleven-time NBA All-Star, notwithstanding his lack of "practice."[72] Iverson a.k.a. "Jewelz," doubled as a rapper and issued a song "40 Bars," which included the following lyrics: "Get murdered in a second in the first degree; / Come to me with faggot tendencies; / You'll be sleeping where the maggots be . . . ; / Die reaching for heat, leave you leaking in the street; / [n-word] screaming he was a good boy ever since he was born; / But fuck it he gone; / Life must go on; / [n-word] don't live that long."

   After the song's release, many civil rights groups, gay and lesbian groups, as well as NBA Commissioner David Stern, voiced displeasure with both Iverson, his musical career and his controversial lyrics. The commissioner strongly encouraged Iverson to rewrite the song in a less offensive tone, which he did. What actions, if any, should have been taken against Iverson for his controversial lyrics?[73] Does the fact that it happened "off the court" make a difference?

Race and Amateur Sports

7. It is alleged that Frank Broyles used the n-word at the *Hawgs Illustrated* banquet when discussing coach Richardson. Should the use of this word in and of itself be sufficient to prove

---

[70] See, Connecticut Hate Law Crime, Conn. Gen. Stat. §§ 53a-181j- 53a- 181l.

[71] For an excellent historical overview of the Negro Leagues see, Lawrence D. Hogan, *Shades of Glory: The Negro Leagues and the Story of African-American Baseball* (Washington, DC: National Geographic Society, January 31, 2006).

[72] Joannie C. Gerstner, "Can Iverson Say Practice in Turkish?" *The New York Times*, October 26, 2010.

[73] Chris Sheridan, "NBA's Iverson to Change Offensive Rap Lyrics," *ABC NEWS*, New York, October 13, 2006.

the existence of racism, regardless of the context of the use of the word?[74] The court in the *Richardson* case did not think so.

8. Some universities have changed their team names or mascots in response to pressure exerted by the NCAA. Stanford University renamed its team from the Indians to The Cardinal, and Marquette University changed from the Warriors to the Golden Eagles. The Washington Wizards in the NBA were originally the Bullets. The Houston Astros were called the Colt .45's from 1962 to 1965. In August 2005, the NCAA stated that any school using a Native American mascot would be prevented from hosting future postseason events. Major college football is not affected because there is no official NCAA tournament. The NCAA later announced that approval from American Indian tribes would be a primary factor in giving approval for schools that wanted to use Native American nicknames and mascots in postseason play. Florida State University sought approval from two Seminole groups to use their name for university sports teams. The NCAA subsequently removed these names from the list of banned mascots and team names.[75] How do you view the debate over the use of Native American mascots? What other school mascots and traditions might people find offensive? Greyhounds? Demons? Pirates? The Red Raiders (Texas Tech U. mascot mimics the use of a handgun, source: www.texastech.com.).

9. For further study dealing with race and its intersection with sports, see Angela J. Murphy, "Life Stories of Black Male and Female Professionals: An Inquiry into the Salience of Race and Sports," *The Journal of Men's Studies* (February 19, 2007); J. F. McElvogue, "Racial Segregation in America Sport," *International Review of Sport Sociology* (1970); Kenneth L. Shropshire, *In Black and White: Race and Sports in America* (New York: NYU Press, 1996); John Milton Hoberma, *Darwin's Athletes: How Sport Has Damaged Black America and Preserved the Myth of Race* (Boston, MA: Mariner Books, 1997); Douglas Booth, *The Race Game: Sports and Politics in South Africa* (London, UK: Frank Cass Publishers, 1998).

---

[74] Michael Klein, "Trial Set for Firing Over use of 'n' Word," *Philadelphia Inquirer*, January 5, 2011. ". . . federal jury will be asked to decide whether it is acceptable for an African American person, but not a white person, to use the 'n' word in a workplace."

[75] Aaron Goldstein, "Intentional Infliction of Emotional Distress: Another Attempt at Eliminating Native American Mascots," *Journal of Gender, Race and Justice* (1999–2000): 689. See also Brian R. Moushegian, "Native American Mascots' Last Stand? Legal Difficulties in Eliminating Public University Use of Native American Mascots," *Villanova Sports & Entertainment Law Journal* 13 (2006): 465; Kenneth B. Franklin, "A Brave Attempt: Can the National Collegiate Athletic Association Sanction Colleges and Universities with Native American Mascots?" *Journal of Intellectual Property Law* 13 (2005–2006): 435.

CHAPTER 9

THE ETHICAL
DUTIES OF
SPORTS AGENTS

INTRODUCTION

Long before "show me the money" became a well-worn phrase, ethical dilemmas were present in the sports agent business.[1] The profession of the sports agent is not a new one. Charles C. "Cash and Carry" Pyle represented athletes in the early part of the 19th century,[2] including football star Harold "Red" Grange. Early baseball Hall of Famer and Columbia Law School graduate John Montgomery Ward was the driving force behind the formation of an early baseball players' union, The Brotherhood, in 1890. Ward was the leader of The Brotherhood, which formed the Players League, an organization run solely by the players. Ward represented many early ballplayers in legal matters and in contract disputes with clubs.[3]

Although there have been sports agents throughout the history of sports, agents did not begin to garner national attention until the 1960s and 1970s. The Andy Messersmith and Dave McNally arbitration cases in baseball in 1975 granted all Major League Baseball players free agency, and many players began to hire agents to represent their interests after the arbitration decision. Player salaries skyrocketed in sports in the 1980s, and this trend has continued to the present day, creating a market for sports agents. Player agents stepped in and began to negotiate lucrative player and endorsement contracts. Agents are now a mainstay of the sports industry.

Unfortunately, sports agents have not always had the best reputation. As in any profession, a small group of unethical individuals can make it tough for ethical agents to succeed.[4] Josh Luchs, at the age of twenty, became the youngest contract advisor ever certified by the NFLPA. He represented more than 60

---

[1] In the 1990s sport agents were given a Hollywood spotlight when Tom Cruise starred as *Jerry McGuire*, the fictional NFL agent representing an Arizona Cardinals wide receiver who possessed a good dose of talent, confidence, and attitude.

[2] Jim Reisler, *Cash and Carry: The Spectacular Rise and Hard Fall of C.C. Pyle, America's First Sports Agent*, McFarland Publishing, 2008.

[3] See generally, David Stevens, *Baseball's Radical for All Seasons: A Biography of John Montgomery Ward*, The Scarecrow Press, Inc., 1998.

[4] See Hannah Karp, "Sports Agent Donates $5 Million to Syracuse," *Wall Street Journal*, April 22, 2008.

NFL players over the course of his career. However, by his own admission he did it unethically and illegally. In 2010, the NFLPA revoked his agent certification. In that same year, Luchs gave an interview to *Sports Illustrated* in which he detailed his career as an NFL agent. In his confession Luchs stated:

> Why am I doing this? Why am I telling everything? There are a few small reasons and one big one. People should know how the agent business really works, how widespread the inducements to players are and how players have their hands out. It isn't just the big, bad agents making them take money. People think the NFLPA is monitoring agents, but it is mostly powerless. People should also be aware of all that an agent does for his clients. Catering to their needs can be an all-consuming job. But those are the small reasons. Recently, my nine-year-old daughter got an iTouch, and she has figured out how to get on the Internet. My six-year-old is not far behind. At some point, they are going to Google their daddy's name, and before this story they would have found only page after page of stuff saying how I was suspended. I was a good agent and I took care of my players. I don't want my career to be defined by that suspension.[5]

University of Alabama head football coach, Nick Saban, said the following about unethical agents, "I don't think it's anything but greed that's creating it right now on behalf of the agents . . . The agents that do this—and I hate to say this, but how are they any better than a pimp? . . . I have no respect for people who do that to young people. None. How would you feel if they did it to your child?"[6] Sports agents can come from many disciplines and industries including business, law, finance, accounting, and engineering. However, many sports agents are lawyers, and, well deserved or not, lawyers have suffered from a negative reputation in American society.

If an agent can sign a star player to a representation agreement, the agent could receive a large fee for negotiating just one contract. This has led to vicious competition between agents attempting to get clients. Unscrupulous, unethical, and cutthroat methods have been employed by some sports agents to obtain clients. In recent years some steps have been taken in sports organizations to clean up unethical activity.[7]

Responsibilities

Agents owe certain responsibilities and ethical duties to the principal, the athlete. Agents have a duty to perform and carry out their duties in good faith on behalf of the principal and they also must avoid all potential and actual conflicts of interest. For instance, sports agents should not gamble on their own clients to win sporting events.[8] Agents have a duty of confidentiality and a duty to account for all funds handled on behalf of the principal. Sports agents act as a fiduciary on behalf of an athlete and should always keep the client's best interests in mind. Agents operate in a position of trust much like the patient-physician relationship, or a stockbroker with a financial client. One of the most significant duties of sports agents is their obligation of undivided loyalty and duty to act in good faith during the representation process. In essence, agents must be honest, credible, trustworthy, and capable of performing the duties of an agent.

---

[5] George Dohrmann, "Confessions of an Agent," *Sports Illustrated*, October 18, 2010.

[6] Associated Press, "Alabama Coach Nick Saban Compares Unscrupulous Agents to a 'Pimp,'" *ESPN.com*, July 22, 2010.

[7] Dave Solomon, "Sports Agents Need to Be Held Accountable," *New Haven Register*, July 25, 2010.

[8] Joe Drape, "IMG's Forstmann Gambled on College Sports, Suit Alleges," *The New York Times*, November 30, 2010.

An agent may be called upon to perform many duties on behalf of a client. Negotiating a player's contract with a club may just be the beginning of a long-term relationship with the agent being involved in all aspects of a player's career. An agent also may negotiate endorsement contracts, perform legal work (if a lawyer), arrange for investment counseling, provide career planning advice, protect and promote the public image of the athlete, and counsel the athlete about matters of everyday life, if necessary.

In the following case, a player refused to pay his agent a fee, claiming his agent failed to do his job properly while representing the player.

CASE 9-1 *Zinn v. Parrish*

644 F.2d 360 (7th Cir. 1981)

For over two decades . . . Zinn had been engaged in the business of managing professional athletes. He stated that he was a pioneer in bringing to the attention of various pro-football teams the availability of talented players at small black colleges in the South. In the Spring of 1970, Parrish's coach at Lincoln University approached Zinn and informed him that Parrish had been picked by the Cincinnati Bengals in the annual National Football League draft of college seniors, and asked him if he would help Parrish in negotiating the contract. After Zinn contacted Parrish, the latter signed a one-year "Professional Management Contract" with Zinn in the Spring of 1970, pursuant to which Zinn helped Parrish negotiate the terms of his rookie contract with the Bengals, receiving as his commission 10% of Parrish's $16,500 salary. On April 10, 1971 Parrish signed the contract at issue in this case, which differed from the 1970 contract only insofar as it was automatically renewed from year to year unless one of the parties terminated it by 30 days' written notice to the other party. There were no other restrictions placed on the power of either party to terminate the contract.

Under the 1971 contract, Zinn obligated himself to use "reasonable efforts" to procure pro-football employment for Parrish, and, at Parrish's request, to "act" in furtherance of Parrish's interest by: (a) negotiating job contracts; (b) furnishing advice on business investments; (c) securing professional tax advice at no added cost; and (d) obtaining endorsement contracts. It was further provided that Zinn's services would include, "at my request efforts to secure for me gainful off-season employment," for which Zinn would receive no additional compensation, "unless such employment (was) in the line of endorsements, marketing and the like," in which case Zinn would receive a 10% commission on the gross amount. If Parrish failed to pay Zinn amounts due under the contract, Parrish authorized "the club or clubs that are obligated to pay me to pay to you instead all monies and other considerations due me from which you can deduct your 10% and any other monies due you. . . ."

Over the course of Parrish's tenure with the Bengals, Zinn negotiated base salaries for him of $18,500 in 1971; $27,000 in 1972; $35,000 in 1973 (plus a $6,500 signing bonus); and a $250,000 series of contracts covering the four seasons commencing in 1974 (plus a $30,000 signing bonus). The 1974-77 contracts with the Bengals were signed at a time when efforts were being made by the newly-formed World Football League to persuade players in the NFL to "jump" to the WFL to play on one of its teams. By the end of [the] 1973 season Parrish had become recognized as one of the more valuable players in the NFL. He was twice selected for the Pro Bowl game, and named by Sporting News as one of the best cornerbacks in the league. Towards the end of the 1973 season, the Bengals approached Parrish with an offer of better contract terms than he had earlier been receiving. By way of exploring alternatives in the WFL, Zinn entered into preliminary discussions with the Jacksonville Sharks in early 1974, but decided not to pursue the matter once he ascertained that the Sharks were in a shaky financial position. In retrospect, Zinn's and Parrish's decision to continue negotiating and finally sign with the Bengals was a sound one, for the Sharks and the rest of the WFL with them folded in 1975 due to a lack of funds.

Shortly after signing the 1974 series of contracts, Parrish informed Zinn by telephone that he "no longer needed his services." By letter dated October 16, 1975, Parrish reiterated this position, and added that he had no intention of paying Zinn a 10% commission on those contracts . . . Zinn claims that the total was at least $304,500 including bonus and performance clauses. The 1971 contract by its terms entitled Zinn to 10% of the total amount as each installment was paid, and Zinn claims that he has only received $4,300 of the amounts due him . . .

In addition to negotiating the Bengals contracts, Zinn performed a number of other services at Parrish's request. In 1972 he assisted him in purchasing a residence as well as a four-unit apartment building to be used for rental income; he also helped to manage the apartment building. That same year Zinn negotiated an endorsement contract for Parrish with All-Pro Graphics, Inc., under which Parrish received a percentage from the sales of "Lemar Parrish" t-shirts, sweatshirts, beach towels, key chains, etc. The record shows that Zinn made a number of unsuccessful efforts at obtaining similar endorsement income from stores with which Parrish did business in Ohio. He also tried, unsuccessfully, to obtain an appearance for Parrish on The Mike Douglas Show. Zinn arranged for Parrish's taxes to be prepared each year by H & R Block.

The evidence showed that, despite his efforts, Zinn was unable to obtain off-season employment for Parrish. In this connection, however, it was Zinn's advice to Parrish that he return to school during the off-season months in order to finish his college degree, against the time when he would no longer be able to play football. With respect to Zinn's obligation to provide Parrish with advice on "business investments," he complied first, by assisting in the purchase of the apartment building; and second, by forwarding to Parrish the stock purchase recommendations of certain other individuals, after screening the suggestions himself. There was no evidence that Zinn ever forwarded such recommendations to any of his other clients; he testified that he only did so for Parrish.

In summing up Zinn's performance under the contract, Parrish testified as follows:

Question: Did you ever ask Zinn to do anything for you, to your knowledge, that he didn't try to do?

Answer: I shall say not, no.

Source: *Reprinted from Westlaw with permission of Thomson Reuters.*

Did the agent fulfill his ethical obligations to the client in *Zinn*? What else could he have done on Parrish's behalf?

CASE STUDY 9-1 *Hiring an Agent*

Major League pitcher Matt Morris fired his agent and negotiated his own contract, a $27 million deal for four years. Morris said the St. Louis Cardinals sent him a deal that was fair so he signed it. Others players who have negotiated their own contracts are Alan Trammell of the Detroit Tigers, Mike Singletary of the Chicago Bears, and Danny Ainge of the Boston Celtics.[9]

1. Should players negotiate their own contracts?
2. Should teams negotiate with a player without an agent?
3. Is it fair to the player to be unrepresented when negotiating a multimillion dollar contract?

Len Bias was a great college basketball player and was selected in the first round of the 1986 NBA draft by the Boston Celtics, but Bias would never play a game in the NBA. He died of a cocaine overdose just two days after he was drafted by the Celtics.[10] Prior to the draft, he selected a well known sports agency to represent him, Advantage International Inc. After his death, Bias's estate filed a lawsuit against Advantage International saying they had failed to represent Len Bias properly.

---

[9] James, Caryn, "Of Athletes and Agents (Oh, and Money, Too)," *New York Times*, August 10, 1996; Brian Berger, "Making a Case for Doing Away with Full-Time Agents," Sports Business Radio, November 19, 2007.

[10] Keith Harriston and Sally Jenkins, "Maryland Basketball Star Len Bias is Dead at 22," *Washington Post*, June 20, 1986.

📖 CASE 9-2   *Bias v. Advantage International*

905 F.2d 1558 (D.C. Cir. 1990)

On April 7, 1986, after the close of his college basketball career, [Len] Bias entered into a representation agreement with Advantage whereby Advantage agreed to advise and represent Bias in his affairs. Fentress was the particular Advantage representative servicing the Bias account. On June 17 of that year Bias was picked by the Boston Celtics in the first round of the National Basketball Association draft. On the morning of June 19, 1986, Bias died of cocaine intoxication. The Estate sued Advantage and Fentress for two separate injuries allegedly arising out of the representation arrangement between Bias and [Advantage].

First, the Estate alleges that, prior to Bias's death, Bias and his parents directed Fentress to obtain a one-million dollar life insurance policy on Bias's life, that Fentress represented to Bias and Bias's parents that he had secured such a policy, and that in reliance on Fentress's assurances, Bias's parents did not independently seek to buy an insurance policy on Bias's life. Although [Advantage] did obtain increased disability coverage for Bias, in a one-million dollar disability insurance policy with an accidental death rider, they did not secure any life insurance coverage for Bias prior to his death.

Second, on June 18, 1986, the day after he was drafted by the Boston Celtics, Bias, through and with Fentress, entered into negotiations with Reebok International, Ltd. ("Reebok") concerning a potential endorsement contract. The Estate alleges that after several hours of negotiations Fentress requested that Bias and his father leave so that Fentress could continue negotiating with Reebok representatives in private. The Estate alleges that Fentress then began negotiating a proposed package deal with Reebok on behalf of not just Bias, but also other players represented by Advantage. The Estate contends that Fentress breached a duty to Bias by negotiating on behalf of other players, and that because Fentress opened up these broader negotiations he was unable to complete the negotiations for Bias on June 18. The Estate claims that as a result of Fentress's actions, on June 19, when Bias died, Bias had no contract with Reebok. The Estate alleges that the contract that Bias would have obtained would have provided for an unconditional lump sum payment which Bias would have received up front.

Source: *Reprinted from Westlaw with permission of Thomson Reuters.*

1. In *Bias*, did the agent fulfill all his ethical obligations to his client?

2. If not, what else could he have done?

3. Did the agent violate his duty of loyalty to Bias by negotiating on behalf of several clients at one time?

4. The agent told Bias and his parents that he was able to obtain a life insurance policy but actually failed to do so. Even though a court would later rule the agent's failure to obtain the policy was irrelevant because Bias would not have passed a life insurance physical, should the agent still be held accountable because he lied to his client?

CASE STUDY 9-2 *NFL Contract for Ricky Williams*

Every NFL first-round draft pick, understands the importance of retaining an experienced agent who knows his or her way around the NFL and can negotiate a multi-million dollar contract successfully. Notwithstanding this sound advice, Heisman Trophy winner Ricky Williams chose to hire well-known rapper Master P. (Percy Robert Miller) to represent him. Through Master P., Williams was represented by Leland Hardy for his contract negotiations with the New Orleans Saints. Williams was the lone draft pick of the Saints, and instead of securing a contract with guaranteed money up front, his agent negotiated a contract which was noted by most experienced NFL agents to be heavily in favor of the team.[11] Hardy constructed a rookie deal for Williams which has subsequently been used in law schools and business schools as a model for bad contracts."[12] Two weeks after Williams signed his contract, his agent failed an open-book, take-home exam given to agents by the NFLPA.[13] The agent was suspended from representing players until he could pass the exam. The contract was a disaster for Williams, and he eventually hired agent Leigh Steinberg to re-negotiate his contract.[14]

Competition Among Agents

Much like other industries, the sports agent business can be an unethical and a dirty business at times. There are very few professional athletes to represent. There are many agents seeking just a few clients with very large sums of money at stake for both the player and the agent. This scenario has led to fierce competition among agents. Some agents will do whatever it takes to sign a client, even if that means engaging in unethical conduct to sign a new player, such as stealing clients from other agents or breaking rules and regulations they are required to abide by. Many unethical agents will try to "persuade" players to sign contracts with them even though the player may be already represented by an agent.

In the following case, one agent sued another for intentional interference with a contract.

---

[11] Jason Cole, "Williams Should Have Gotten Better Deal," *Yahoo! Sports*, September 5, 2008.

[12] Ibid.

[13] Kenneth L. Shropshire, Timothy Davis, *The Business of Sports Agents*, 2nd Edition, University of Pennsylvania Press, 2nd Edition, May 28, 2008.

[14] Karen Crouse, "Pro Football, Ricky Williams Steps Carefully Toward Return," *New York Times*, July 11, 2005; Jason Cole, "Williams Should Have Gotten Better Deal," *Yahoo! Sports*, September 5, 2008. For more tales about Ricky Williams, see Hannah Gordon, "In The Replay Booth: Looking at Appeals of Arbitration Decision in Sports Through Miami Dolphins v. Williams," *Harvard Negotiation Law Review* (Spring 2007).

📖 **CASE 9-3** *Rosenhaus v. Star Sports, Inc.*

---

929 So.2d 40 (3rd Cir. 2006)

Star Sports, Inc. ("Star"), filed a multi-count complaint . . . against Drew Rosenhaus, Jason Rosenhaus, and Rosenhaus Sports Representation, Inc., alleging intentional interference with an advantageous business relationship and tortious interference with a contractual right. The complaint alleges that Star is in the business of providing marketing and related services to professional football players in the National Football League, and that Drew and Jason Rosenhaus are both certified Contract Advisors with the National Football League Players Association. The complaint alleges that Star entered into a written contract referred to as a "Marketing Agreement" with Anquan Boldin, a professional football player in the NFL, wherein Star was to be Boldin's exclusive agent for marketing and related services. The complaint also alleges that Drew and Jason Rosenhaus intentionally and unjustifiably interfered with this Marketing Agreement by directly soliciting Boldin to have Jason and Drew Rosenhaus and/or Rosenhaus Sports Representation, Inc., represent him in his marketing endeavors and to exclude Star from representing him.

Source: *Reprinted from Westlaw with permission of Thomson Reuters.*

A court eventually found in favor of Rosenhaus. What restrictions should be placed on agents about contacting players who already have an agent?

In the following situation, one agent sued another agent claiming he was defamed by the second agent. Smith sued Condon, alleging that Condon had told potential clients that Smith "played the race card" during his negotiations with NFL teams and that NFL general managers were getting tired of it. Condon denied all of the allegations and prevail against Smith.

📖 **CASE 9-4** *Smith v. IMG Worldwide, Inc.*

2006 WL 3302485 (2006)

[Smith] and Condon are professional sports agents. [Smith] founded All Pro Sports and Entertainment, Inc. ("All Pro") in 1987. Condon is the President of IMG Football, which is a division of IMG. [Smith] alleged that a recent decline in his representation of high-end players is directly attributable to Condon's repeated defamatory statements to prospective professional players that [Smith] uses the "race card" in contract negotiations with NFL clubs. Condon denied having any conversations with prospective professional football players about [Smith] or [Smith]'s relationships with NFL general managers.

In November and December 2000, [Smith] and Condon were competing for a contract to represent Walker, an offensive lineman at the University of Florida and a prospective professional football player. [Smith] asserted that, in the course of the competition to sign Walker, Condon told Walker that [Smith] alienated general managers of NFL clubs because he "plays the race card in negotiating contracts." [Smith] testified at his deposition that the alleged defamation involving Walker was communicated to him in a telephone conversation with Walker one day after Condon spoke with Walker. According to [Smith], Walker said that:

> he had been advised that general managers did not like dealing with [Smith] because [Smith] played the race card in negotiations. . . . [Walker said] that Tom Condon had advised him . . . that [he] better be careful with dealing with [Smith] because [Smith] play[ed] the race card.

Additionally, Kenneth Anderson, a former employee of [Smith]'s company, and Peter Schaffer, [Smith]'s law and business partner, testified that Walker told them that Condon told Walker that he should not sign with [Smith] because [Smith] "play[s] the race card." Walker has no memory of anyone at IMG, including Condon, making comments to him about [Smith] playing the "race card."

In January 2002, [Smith] and Condon were competing for a contract to represent Bryant, a highly-skilled wide receiver from the University of Pittsburgh and a prospective professional football player. [Smith] alleges that, during a meeting with Bryant and Sanders in January 2002, Condon said that "Bryant needed to be careful about retaining [Smith] as his agent because [Smith] . . . 'plays the race card' in his negotiations with NFL clubs." While recruiting Bryant, Condon visited Sanders's home in Pittsburgh in January 2002. Sanders, who advised Bryant in choosing an agent, testified that Condon commented on [Smith]'s use of race in contract negotiations during that meeting. According to Sanders, Condon said:

> 'Hey, you know something else you got to be careful with Lamont [Smith] he plays the race card and a lot of the general manager[s] are getting tired of that. I know the [general manager] at Tennessee is tired of it, and, you know, that's not a good thing.'

Although [Smith] alleges that the comments were made to Bryant and Sanders, Sanders testified that Bryant was not present when Condon

made these remarks. Sanders further testified that he did not
"specifically" relay Condon's remarks to Bryant, but that Condon's
remarks "fed into how [he] presented" race issues to Bryant and Bryant's
high school coach. According to Sanders, when he heard Condon's
remarks, he kept them to himself and did not repeat them to anyone
until he mentioned them to [Smith] at the Cowboys' training facility
in July 2002. Eventually, Bryant signed with [Smith] and was selected
in the second round of the 2002 NFL Draft by the Dallas Cowboys.

Source: *Reprinted from Westlaw with permission of Thomson Reuters.*

The court dismissed the case against Condon. Condon has long been considered one of the top agents in sports; in fact, he was listed number one in 2008.[15] In 2006 Condon was named the most powerful agent in American Football by *The Sporting News*.

Terminating a representation agreement with a sports agent can usually be done by a player by giving proper notice to the agent. Some players skip from agent to agent trying to find the right agent to meet their needs. That is what happened in the following case.

CASE 9-5 *Speakers of Sport, Inc. v. ProServ, Inc.*

178 F.3d 862 (7th Cir. 1999)

. . . The essential facts, construed as favorably to [Speaker of
Sports, Inc., "Speakers"] as the record will permit, are as follows.
Ivan Rodriguez, a highly successful catcher with the Texas Rangers
baseball team, in 1991 signed the first of several one-year contracts
making Speakers his agent. ProServ wanted to expand its representation
of baseball players and to this end invited Rodriguez to its office in
Washington and there promised that it would get him between $2 and
$4 million in endorsements if he signed with ProServ—which he did, ter-
minating his contract (which was terminable at will) with Speakers.
This was in 1995. ProServ failed to obtain significant endorsements for
Rodriguez and after just one year he switched to another agent who the
following year landed him a five-year $42 million contract with the
Rangers. Speakers brought this suit a few months later, charging that
the promise of endorsements that ProServ had made to Rodriguez was
fraudulent and had induced him to terminate his contract with Speakers.

. . . Speakers could not sue Rodriguez for breach of contract, because
he had not broken their contract, which was, as we said, terminable at
will. Nor, therefore, could it accuse ProServ of inducing a breach of
contract. . . . But Speakers did have a contract with Rodriguez, and
inducing the termination of a contract, even when the termination is

---

[15] "The 20 Most Influential Sports Agents," *Sports Business Journal* (August 18, 2008).

not a breach because the contract is terminable at will, can still be
actionable under the tort law of Illinois, either as an interference
with prospective economic advantage, or as an interference with the
contract at will itself. . . .

There is in general nothing wrong with one sports agent trying to take a
client from another if this can be done without precipitating a breach
of contract. That is the process known as competition, which though
painful, fierce, frequently ruthless, sometimes Darwinian in its piti-
lessness, is the cornerstone of our highly successful economic system.

Source: *Reprinted from Westlaw with permission of Thomson Reuters.*

When is it ethical for a player to terminate a representation contract with an agent? Did ProServ
violate any ethical duty it had to its client in *Speakers*?

LAWYERS AS SPORTS AGENTS

Sports agents are not required to be lawyers, but attorneys do comprise a large percentage of
sports agents. However, the two are not always an easy fit, sometimes creating a convoluted set of
questions and ethical predicaments for the merging of the two professions. Lawyers are trained in
many of the skills necessary to be a successful sports agent. Lawyers have extensive training in contract interpretation and negotiations in law school. Agents who are not attorneys do not have many
of the same ethical and legal restrictions that lawyers may have. Attorneys are held to a higher standard than agents who are not attorneys because of the Model Rules of Professional Conduct, an ethics
code that makes attorneys more accountable to their clients.[16] If a client is dissatisfied with the representation of a sports agent who is also a lawyer, the client could file a grievance with the state bar
association against the sports agent–lawyer, in addition to filing a civil lawsuit for damages. A
lawyer who fails to comply with the ethics code for lawyers is subject to discipline, fines, and possibly disbarment from the practice of law.

One example of an ethical dilemma for an attorney–agent deals with handling conflicts of interest.
If an attorney who is working as a sports agent has a conflict of interest, which regulations or rules
should apply in resolving the conflict? An attorney is governed by a code of ethics that he or she must
abide by. Is it that code that should be consulted to resolve the conflict, or should the traditional principles of agency law apply? An agent who is not a lawyer is bound by the general principles of
agency law, but a lawyer will be governed by both the professional rules of conduct for attorneys and
agency law.

One of the glaring ethical issues that has been raised in the agent business is the advantage
a non-attorney has over an attorney in attempting to sign new clients. The non-attorney is not
bound by client solicitation restrictions as attorneys are, and therefore, would seem to have an
advantage over the attorney–agent in the recruitment of new clients. Attorney ethical rules prohibit
solicitation of new clients and state: "A lawyer shall not by in-person or live telephone contact or
solicit professional employment from a prospective client with whom the lawyer has no family
or prior professional relationship when a significant motive for the lawyer's doing so is the lawyer's

---

[16] See generally, Ronald D. Rotunda, *Legal Ethics in a Nutshell, 3rd Ed.*, Thomson West, 2007.

pecuniary gain."[17] This ethical rule makes it very difficult for the lawyer to compete with the non-lawyer in the recruiting of new athlete clients. If a lawyer has to wait for the potential client to contact him or her, the lawyer will most likely not get as many new clients as a non-lawyer. Some lawyers have attempted to maneuver around the rule by operating a sports management company in addition to a law firm and performing the recruiting aspects of the business through the sports management company.

There are some advantages in hiring an agent who is also an attorney. Attorneys are more likely to have malpractice insurance coverage in the event of agent negligence, whereas a non-lawyer sports agent may not have liability insurance to cover a judgment if a player sues the non-attorney agent for negligence or breach of contract.

Attorney Discipline

In the following case, an attorney who was working as a sports agent was disciplined by a state bar association for his improper actions.

CASE 9-6   *In the Matter of Henley*

478 S.E.2d 134 (1994)

The underlying facts are undisputed. From the fall of 1992 until early 1993 . . . Fredrick J. Henley, Jr., represented Todd Kelly, a 1992 member of the University of Tennessee football team and a 1993 first round draft choice for a National Football League team. In this same time period, Henley entered into an agreement with Bienstock Sports in New York whereby Henley would assist Bienstock in recruiting Kelly as its client. Under the agreement, if Kelly became a client of Bien-stock, Henley would receive one-third of any commissions paid by Kelly to Bienstock. Bienstock gave Henley $5,000 in expenses and loaned him an additional $25,000. Following Henley's successful recruitment of Kelly, Bienstock sent Henley a statement crediting him for the kick-back on Kelly's commission payment and deducting the amount Henley owed Bienstock in loans.

Based on the foregoing, the State Bar filed a formal complaint against Henley charging him with violations of various professional standards under Bar Rule 4-102(d), including Standard 30 (representing a client where the attorney has a financial interest, without fully disclosing that interest, and obtaining written consent or giving written notice), and Standard 40 (accepting compensation for legal service from one other than the client without the client's consent after full disclosure).

The record shows Henley violated Standard 30 by failing to give Kelly written notice of the full extent of Henley's own financial interest in

---

[17] Model Rules of Professional Conduct, Rule 7.3(a).

Bienstock Sports' obtaining Kelly as its client, or obtaining Kelly's written consent to Henley's representation notwithstanding Henley's financial interests. We find unpersuasive Henley's contention that no discipline is appropriate because his client requested that Henley represent him, and was aware of the loans and expenses provided by Bienstock Sports to Henley. There is no evidence that Henley disclosed the kickback arrangement between him and Bienstock Sports which is the very essence of Henley's conflict in this case. Neither is there evidence of either written notice to Kelly, nor written consent by Kelly following Henley's full disclosure of his financial interest as required by Standard 30. These requirements are not mere formalities. Rather, they are crucial safeguards. A lawyer's representation of a client where the lawyer has a financial or personal interest which will or reasonably may affect the lawyer's professional judgment illustrates one of the most blatant appearances of impropriety. The requirements of full disclosure and written notice to or consent from the client are intended to insure to some extent both that a client will receive professional legal services, and that a lawyer may be protected should he or she choose the risky course of representing a client despite the lawyer's potentially conflicting personal or financial interest. By failing to meet these requirements, Henley violated Standard 30. Likewise, Henley violated Standard 40, precluding a lawyer's acceptance of compensation or anything of value from one other than the client relating to the representation of the client, without obtaining the client's consent after the lawyer's full disclosure.

In mitigation we note that at the time of the conduct involved in this disciplinary matter, Henley was a relatively recent member of the State Bar, having been admitted to practice in 1990. While not a mitigating factor per se, we note that the client states he was not harmed by Henley's conduct. Contrary to Henley's arguments, the fact that the client is a close friend of Henley's and does not object to Henley's conduct does not negate Henley's violations of professional standards. In aggravation, we note that Henley has been previously disciplined and suspended from the practice of law, for failing to provide discovery to the Bar in another proceeding. In this proceeding also, Henley has obstructed the disciplinary proceedings by intentionally failing to comply with the special master's order on discovery, resulting in the sanction of striking his answer. Henley has consistently refused to acknowledge the wrongful nature of his conduct. In light of Henley's violations in this matter, and having considered the mitigating and aggravating factors above, a 90-day suspension from the practice of law is appropriate.

Source: *Reprinted from Westlaw with permission of Thomson Reuters.*

Was Henley's penalty sufficient for his wrongful actions? Should Henley be disbarred for his actions?

The following case dealt with issues relating to lawyers and sports agents.

📖 CASE 9-7 *Wright v. Bonds*

117 F.3d 1427 (9th Cir. 1997)

Section 1510 of the California Labor Code requires all athlete agents
to register with the Labor Commissioner. Wright, who never registered,
claims he was exempt because he was a lawyer. *See* Cal. Lab.Code
§ 1500(b) (defining "athlete agent" not to include California Bar members "when acting as legal counsel"). However, Wright was not acting
as Bonds' legal counsel. Not only would some provisions of the Wright-
Bonds contract have been illegal if entered into between a lawyer and
client, but the contract specifically excluded legal work. Wright also
used the stationery of his sports management firm—as opposed to his
law firm—in corresponding with Bonds. Wright's argument that lawyers
need never register renders the "when acting as legal counsel"
language in section 1500 meaningless. The contract is void, see Cal.
Lab.Code §1546 . . .

Source: *Reprinted from Westlaw with permission of Thomson Reuters.*

In the following case, an attorney sought an opinion from the bar association regarding his dual
role as an attorney and sports agent.

📖 CASE 9-8 Illinois State Bar Association-ISBA Advisory Opinion on Professional Conduct

IL. Adv. Op. 700, 1980 WL 130464

ISBA Advisory Opinions on Professional Conduct are prepared as an educational service to members of the ISBA. While the Opinions express
the ISBA interpretation of the Illinois Rules of Professional Conduct
and other relevant materials in response to a specific hypothesized
fact situation, they do not have the weight of law and should not be
relied upon as a substitute for individual legal advice.

Digest: It is professionally improper for an attorney to initiate private communications with coaches and athletic directors to inform them
that he engages in the practice of "sports law" and is available to
represent clients.

It is professionally proper to handle "player representation" from the
attorney's law office.

Ref: Rule 2-103(a)ABA EC 2-8

Facts

Attorney has a "sports law" practice and represents athletes in con-tract negotiations. The athletes he represents are handled through his law office from which he conducts a private law practice.

Question

May the attorney advise college athletic directors and coaches of his "sports law" practice and representation of athletes without naming any specific athletes that he represents, and inform the athletic directors and coaches that he is "available"? Secondly, may the "player representation" be carried on in the attorney's law office?

Opinion

Rule 2-103(a) of the Illinois Code of Professional Responsibility . . . provides:

> "A lawyer shall not by private communication . . . directly or through a representative, recommend or solicit employment of himself, his partner or his associate for pecuniary gain or other benefit and shall not for that purpose initiate contact with a prospective client." . . .

EC 2-8 of Canon 2 of the Code of Professional Responsibility of the American Bar Association provides in part as follows:

> "Selection of a lawyer by a lay person should be made on an informed basis. Advice and recommendation of their parties—relative, friends, acquaintances, business associates, or other lawyers—and disclosure of relevant information about the lawyer and his practice may be helpful. A lay person is best served if the recommendation is disinterested and informed. In order that the recommendation be disinterested, a lawyer should not seek to influence another to recommend his employment."

Advising coaches and athletic directors that one practices "sports law" and represents athletes in contract negotiations and is "available" would appear to be designed to encourage the coaches and directors to recommend the attorney to the athletes under their charge. The committee is of the opinion, therefore, that the initia-tion of communications by an attorney to coaches and athletic direc-tors to inform them of the attorney's availability to represent athletes would be professionally improper.

The second question presented deals with whether an attorney may handle "player representation" from the same office in which he engages in the general practice of law. It would appear, therefore, that the attorney making this inquiry questions whether the representation of athletes is actually the practice of law in that it may include a wide range of business counseling, as well as contract negotiation. This doubt could be prompted by the fact that nonlawyers frequently engage in these activities.

The committee is of the opinion that, when an attorney engaged in the private practice of law represents a client in contract negotiations and general business counseling, these activities constitute the practice of law and it would be professionally proper to handle them from the same office in which he engages in the general practice of law.

Source: *Reprinted from Westlaw with permission of Thomson Reuters.*

Conflict of Interest

The following case is the quintessential case in sports ethics dealing with conflict of interest. It is rudimentary that a team owner should not also be working as an agent, much less on the same deal.

📖 CASE 9-9 *The Detroit Lions, Inc. v. Argovitz*

580 F.Supp. 542 (6th Cir. Mich. 1984)

The plot for this Saturday afternoon serial began when Billy Sims, having signed a contract with the Houston Gamblers on July 1, 1983, signed a second contract with the Detroit Lions on December 16, 1983. On December 18, 1983, the Detroit Lions, Inc. (Lions) and Billy R. Sims filed a complaint in the Oakland County Circuit Court seeking a judicial determination that the July 1, 1983, contract between Sims and the Houston Gamblers, Inc. (Gamblers) is invalid because Jerry Argovitz (Argovitz) breached his fiduciary duty when negotiating the Gamblers' contract and because the contract was otherwise tainted by fraud and misrepresentation . . .

Sometime in February or March 1983, Argovitz told Sims that he had applied for a Houston franchise in the newly formed United States Football League (USFL). In May 1983, Sims attended a press conference in Houston at which Argovitz announced that his application for a franchise had been approved. The evidence persuades us that Sims did not know the extent of Argovitz's interest in the Gamblers. He did not know the amount of Argovitz's original investment, or that Argovitz was obligated for 29 percent of a $1.5 million letter of credit, or that Argovitz was the president of the Gamblers' Corporation at an annual salary of $275,000 and 5 percent the yearly cash flow. [Argovitz] could not justifiably expect Sims to comprehend the ramifications of Argovitz's interest in the Gamblers or the manner in which that interest would create an untenable conflict of interest, a conflict that would inevitably breach Argovitz's fiduciary duty to Sims. Argovitz knew, or should have known, that he could not act as Sims' agent under any circumstances when dealing with the Gamblers. Even the USFL Constitution itself prohibits a holder of any interest in a member club from acting "as the contracting agent or representative for any player."

Pending the approval of his application for a USFL franchise in Houston, Argovitz continued his negotiations with the Lions on behalf of Sims. On April 5, 1983, Argovitz offered Sims' services to the Lions for $6 million over a four-year period. The offer included a demand for a $1 million interest-free loan to be repaid over 10 years, and for skill and injury guarantees for three years. The Lions quickly responded with a counter offer on April 7, 1983, in the face amount of $1.5 million over a five-year period with additional incentives not relevant here. The negotiating process was working. The Lions were trying to determine what Argovitz really believed the market value for Sims really was. On May 3, 1983, with his Gamblers franchise assured, Argovitz significantly reduced his offer to the Lions. He now offered Sims to the Lions for $3 million over a four-year period, one-half of the amount of his April 5, 1983, offer. Argovitz's May 3rd offer included a demand for $50,000 to permit Sims to purchase an annuity. Argovitz also dropped his previous demand for skill guarantees. The May 10, 1983, offer submitted by the Lions brought the parties much closer.

On May 30, 1983, Argovitz asked for $3.5 million over a five-year period. This offer included an interest-free loan and injury protection insurance but made no demand for skill guarantees. The May 30 offer now requested $400,000 to allow Sims to purchase an annuity. On June 1, 1983, Argovitz and the Lions were only $500,000 apart. We find that the negotiations between the Lions and Argovitz were progressing normally, not laterally as Argovitz represented to Sims. The Lions were not "dragging their feet." Throughout the entire month of June 1983, Mr. Frederick Nash, the Lions' skilled negotiator and a fastidious lawyer, was involved in investigating the possibility of providing an attractive annuity for Sims and at the same time doing his best to avoid the granting of either skill or injury guarantees. The evidence establishes that on June 22, 1983, the Lions and Argovitz were very close to reaching an agreement on the value of Sims' services.

Apparently, in the midst of his negotiations with the Lions and with his Gamblers franchise in hand, Argovitz decided that he would seek an offer from the Gamblers. Mr. Bernard Lerner, one of Argovitz's partners in the Gamblers agreed to negotiate a contract with Sims. Since Lerner admitted that he had no knowledge whatsoever about football, we must infer that Argovitz at the very least told Lerner the amount of money required to sign Sims and further pressed upon Lerner the Gamblers' absolute need to obtain Sims' services. In the Gamblers' organization, only Argovitz knew the value of Sims' services and how critical it was for the Gamblers to obtain Sims. In Argovitz's words, Sims would make the Gamblers' franchise.

On June 29, 1983, at Lerner's behest, Sims and his wife went to Houston to negotiate with a team that was partially owned by his own agent. When Sims arrived in Houston, he believed that the Lions organization was not negotiating in good faith; that it was not really interested in his services. His ego was bruised and his emotional outlook toward the Lions was visible to Burrough and Argovitz. Clearly, virtually all the information that Sims had up to that date came from Argovitz. Sims and the Gamblers did not discuss a future contract on the night of June 29th. The negotiations began on the morning of June 30, 1983, and ended that afternoon. At the morning meeting, Lerner offered Sims a $3.5 million five-year contract, which included three years of skill and injury guarantees. The offer included a $500,000 loan at an interest rate of 1 percent over prime. It was from this loan that Argovitz planned to receive the $100,000 balance of his fee for acting as an agent in negotiating a contract with his own team. Burrough testified that Sims would have accepted that offer on the spot because he was finally receiving the guarantee that he had been requesting from the Lions, guarantees that Argovitz dropped without too much quarrel. Argovitz and Burrough took Sims and his wife into another room to discuss the offer. Argovitz did tell Sims that he thought the Lions would match the Gamblers financial package and asked Sims whether he (Argovitz) should telephone the Lions. But, it is clear from the evidence that neither Sims nor Burrough believed that the Lions would match the offer. We find that Sims told Argovitz not to call the Lions for purely emotional reasons. As we have noted, Sims believed that the Lions' organization was not that interested in him and his pride was wounded. Burrough clearly admitted that he was aware of the emotional basis for Sims' decision not to have Argovitz phone the Lions, and we must conclude from the extremely close relationship between Argovitz and Sims that Argovitz knew it as well. When Sims went back to Lerner's office, he agreed to become a Gambler on the terms offered. At that moment, Argovitz irreparably breached his fiduciary duty. As agent for Sims he had the duty to telephone the Lions, receive its final offer, and present the terms of both offers to Sims. Then and only then could it be said that Sims made an intelligent and knowing decision to accept the Gamblers' offer.

During these negotiations at the Gamblers' office, Mr. Nash of the Lions telephoned Argovitz, but even though Argovitz was at his office, he declined to accept the telephone call. Argovitz tried to return Nash's call after Sims had accepted the Gamblers' offer, but it was after 5 p.m. and Nash had left for the July 4th weekend. When he declined to accept Mr. Nash's call, Argovitz's breach of his fiduciary duty became even more pronounced. Following Nash's example, Argovitz left for his weekend trip, leaving his principal to sign the contracts with the Gamblers the next day, July 1, 1983. [Argovitz], assert[s] that neither Argovitz nor Burrough can be held responsible for following Sims' instruction not to contact the Lions on June 30, 1983. Although it is generally true that an agent is not liable for losses occurring as a result of following his principal's instructions, the rule of law is not applicable when the agent has placed himself in a position adverse to that of his principal.

During the evening of June 30, 1983, Burrough struggled with the fact that they had not presented the Gamblers' offer to the Lions. He knew, as does the court, that Argovitz now had the wedge that he needed to bring finality to the Lions' negotiations. Burrough was acutely aware of the fact that Sims' actions were emotionally motivated and realized that the responsibility for Sims' future rested with him. We view with some disdain the fact that Argovitz had, in effect, delegated his entire fiduciary responsibility on the eve of his principal's most important career decision. On July 1, 1983, it was Lerner who gave lip service to Argovitz's conspicuous conflict of interest. It was Lerner, not Argovitz, who advised Sims that Argovitz's position with the Gamblers presented a conflict of interest and that Sims could, if he wished, obtain an attorney or another agent. Argovitz, upon whom Sims had relied for the past four years, was not even there. Burrough, conscious of Sims' emotional responses, never advised Sims to wait until he had talked with the Lions before making a final decision. Argovitz's conflict of interest and self dealing put him in the position where he would not even use the wedge he now had to negotiate with the Lions, a wedge that is the dream of every agent. Two expert witnesses testified that an agent should telephone a team that he has been negotiating with once he has an offer in hand. Mr. Woolf, [expert for Detroit club], testified that an offer from another team is probably the most important factor in negotiations. Mr. Lustig, [expert for Argovitz], believed that it was prudent for him to telephone the Buffalo Bills and inform that organization of the Gamblers' offer to Jim Kelly, despite the fact that he believed the Bills had already made its best offer to his principal. The evidence here convinces us that Argovitz's negotiations with the Lions were ongoing and it had not made its final offer. Argovitz did not follow the common practice described by both expert witnesses. He did not do this because he knew that the Lions would not leave Sims without a contract and he further knew that if he made that type of call Sims would be lost to the Gamblers, a team he owned.

On November 12, 1983, when Sims was in Houston for the Lions game with the Houston Oilers, Argovitz asked Sims to come to his home and sign certain papers. He represented to Sims that certain papers of his contract had been mistakenly overlooked and now needed to be signed. Included among those papers he asked Sims to sign was a waiver of any claim that Sims might have against Argovitz for his blatant breach of his fiduciary duty brought on by his glaring conflict of interest. Sims did not receive independent advice with regard to the wisdom of signing such a waiver. Despite having sold his agency business in September, Argovitz did not even tell Sims' new agent of his intention to have Sims sign a waiver. Nevertheless, Sims, an unsophisticated young man, signed the waiver. This is another example of the questionable conduct on the part of Argovitz who still had business management obligations to Sims. In spite of his fiduciary relationship he had Sims sign a waiver without advising him to obtain independent counseling.

The parties submitted a great deal of evidence and argued a number of peripheral issues. Although most of the issues were not determinative factors in our decision, they do demonstrate that Argovitz had a history of fulfilling his fiduciary duties in an irresponsible manner. One cannot help but wonder whether Argovitz took his fiduciary duty seriously. For example, after investing approximately $76,000 of Sims' money, Argovitz, with or without the prior knowledge of his principal, received a finder's fee. Despite the fact that Sims paid Argovitz a 2 percent fee, Argovitz accepted $3800 from a person with whom he invested Sims' money. In March 1983, Argovitz had all of his veteran players, including Sims, sign a new agency contract with less favorable payment terms for the players even though they already had an ongoing agency agreement with him. He did this after he sold his entire agency business to Career Sports. Finally, Argovitz was prepared to take the remainder of his 5 percent agency fee for negotiating Sims' contract with the Gamblers from monies the Gamblers loaned to Sims at an interest rate of 1 percent over prime. It mattered little to Argovitz that Sims would have to pay interest on the $100,000 that Argovitz was ready to accept. While these practices by Argovitz are troublesome, we do not find them decisive in examining Argovitz's conduct while negotiating the Gamblers' contract on June 30 and July 1, 1983. We find this circumstantial evidence useful only insofar as it has aided the court in understanding the manner in which these parties conducted business.

We are mindful that Sims was less than forthright when testifying before the court . . . We remain persuaded that on balance, Argovitz's breach of his fiduciary duty was so egregious that a court of equity cannot permit him to benefit by his own wrongful breach. We conclude that Argovitz's conduct in negotiating Sims' contract with the Gamblers rendered it invalid.

The relationship between a principal and agent is fiduciary in nature, and as such imposes a duty of loyalty, good faith, and fair and honest dealing on the agent.

A fiduciary relationship arises not only from a formal principal-agent relationship, but also from informal relationships of trust and confidence.

In light of the express agency agreement, and the relationship between Sims and Argovitz, Argovitz clearly owed Sims the fiduciary duties of an agent . . .

An agent's duty of loyalty requires that he not have a personal stake that conflicts with the principal's interest in a transaction in which he represents his principal.

(T)he principal is entitled to the best efforts and unbiased judgment of his agent. . . .

A fiduciary violates the prohibition against self-dealing not only by dealing with himself on his principal's behalf, but also by dealing on his principal's behalf with a third party in which he has an interest, such as a partnership in which he is a member.

Where an agent has an interest adverse to that of his principal in a transaction in which he purports to act on behalf of his principal, the transaction is voidable by the principal unless the agent disclosed all material facts within the agent's knowledge that might affect the principal's judgment.

The mere fact that the contract is fair to the principal does not deny the principal the right to rescind the contract when it was negotiated by an agent in violation of the prohibition against self-dealing. . . .

Once it has been shown that an agent had an interest in a transaction involving his principal antagonistic to the principal's interest, fraud on the part of the agent is presumed. The burden of proof then rests upon the agent to show that his principal had full knowledge, not only of the fact that the agent was interested, but also of every material fact known to the agent which might affect the principal and that having such knowledge, the principal freely consented to the transaction.

It is not sufficient for the agent merely to inform the principal that he has an interest that conflicts with the principal's interest. Rather, he must inform the principal "of all facts that come to his knowledge that are or may be material or which might affect his principal's rights or interests or influence the action he takes."

Argovitz clearly had a personal interest in signing Sims with the Gamblers that was adverse to Sims' interest-he had an ownership interest in the Gamblers and thus would profit if the Gamblers were profitable, and would incur substantial personal liabilities should the Gamblers not be financially successful. Since this showing has been made, fraud on Argovitz's . . . part is presumed, and the Gamblers' contract must be rescinded unless Argovitz has shown by a preponderance of the evidence that he informed Sims of every material fact that might have influenced Sims' decision whether or not to sign the Gamblers' contract.

We conclude that Argovitz has failed to show . . . either: (1) that he informed Sims of the following facts, or (2) that these facts would not have influenced Sims' decision whether to sign the Gamblers' contract:

a. The relative values of the Gamblers' contract and the Lions' offer that Argovitz knew could be obtained.
b. That there was significant financial differences between the USFL and the NFL not only in terms of the relative financial stability of the Leagues, but also in terms of the fringe benefits available to Sims.
c. Argovitz's 29 percent ownership in the Gamblers; Argovitz's $275,000 annual salary with the Gamblers; Argovitz's five percent interest in the cash flow of the Gamblers.
d. That both Argovitz and Burrough failed to even attempt to obtain for Sims valuable contract clauses which they had given to [NFL player Jim] Kelly on behalf of the Gamblers.
e. That Sims had great leverage, and Argovitz was not encouraging a bidding war that could have advantageous results for Sims.

. . . We are dismayed by Argovitz's egregious conduct. The careless fashion in which Argovitz went about ascertaining the highest price for Sims' service convinces us of the wisdom of the maxim: no man can faithfully serve two masters whose interests are in conflict.

Source: *Reprinted from Westlaw with permission of Thomson Reuters.*

CASE STUDY 9-3 *Conflict of Interest 1*

The National Football League Players Association (NFLPA) suspended agent Neil Conrich for a conflict of interest in 2005. Conrich violated the union's conflict of interest policy when he went to work for General Motors in a lawsuit brought by the estate of a deceased NFL player, Derrick Thomas. Conrich testified in a deposition and created reports for GM but never testified at the trial. He was suspended for one year. He appealed the suspension but lost.[18]

CASE STUDY 9-4 *Conflict of Interest 2*

Assume an agent represents two NBA players who play the same position and are both unrestricted free agents and are able to sign with any NBA club. During negotiations with an NBA club, the agent is told by the general manager of the club that salary cap considerations only allow the signing of one star player. Does the agent have an irreconcilable conflict of interest in this scenario? What are the agent's ethical duties in this case?

[18] Liz Mullen, "NFL, Player Agent Neil Conrich Begins One-Year Suspension," *Street & Smith's Sports Business Daily*, August 10, 2005.

What about an agent who is told by a team that his client, Player A, needs to take a salary cut to make room for Player B on the squad and the agent represents both players? What conflict of interest issues arise under those circumstances? Can the agent continue to represent both players under the circumstances?

FEE STRUCTURES OF AGENTS

The topic of agent fees can raise many ethical and legal concerns amongst players, leagues, agents, and administrators. Agent fees can be determined by the league, as in the NFL, or left to the marketplace like MLB. The following case deals with the always sticky situation of agent fees. Well known sports agent Bob Woolf was sued after a professional hockey player claimed Woolf took more of a fee than he was entitled to.

📖 CASE 9-10 *Brown v. Woolf*

554 F.Supp. 1206 (7th Cir. 1983)

[Brown] seeks compensatory and punitive damages and the imposition of a trust on a fee [Woolf] allegedly received, all stemming from [Woolf]'s alleged constructive fraud and breach of fiduciary duty in the negotiation of a contract for the 1974-75 hockey season for [Brown] who was a professional hockey player. [Brown] alleges that prior to the 1973-74 season he had engaged the services of [Woolf], a well known sports attorney and agent, who represents many professional athletes, has authored a book, and has appeared in the media in connection with such representation, to negotiate a contract for him with the Pittsburgh Penguins of the National Hockey League. [Brown] had a professionally successful season that year under the contract [Woolf] negotiated for him and accordingly again engaged [Woolf]'s services prior to the 1974-75 season. During the negotiations in July 1974, the Penguins offered [Brown] a two-year contract at $80,000.00 per year but [Brown] rejected the offer allegedly because [Woolf] asserted that he could obtain a better, long-term, no-cut contract with a deferred compensation feature with the Indianapolis Racers, which at the time was a new team in a new league. On July 31, 1974, [Brown] signed a five-year contract with the Racers. Thereafter, it is alleged the Racers began having financial difficulties. [Brown] avers that Woolf continued to represent [Brown] and negotiated two reductions in [Brown]'s compensation including the loss of a retirement fund at the same time [Woolf] was attempting to get his own fee payment from the Racers. Ultimately the Racers' assets were seized and the organizers defaulted on their obligations to [Brown]. He avers that he received only $185,000.00 of the total $800,000.00 compensation under the Racer contract but that [Woolf] received his full $40,000.00 fee (5% of the contract) from the Racers.

```
[Brown] alleges that [Woolf] made numerous material misrepresentations
upon which he relied both during the negotiation of the Racer contract
and at the time of the subsequent modifications. [Brown] further avers
that [Woolf] breached his fiduciary duty to [Brown] by failing to con-
duct any investigation into the financial stability of the Racers, fail-
ing to investigate possible consequences of the deferred compensation
package in the Racers' contract, failing to obtain guarantees or collat-
eral, and by negotiating reductions in [Brown]'s compensation from the
Racers while insisting on receiving all of his own. [Brown] theorizes
that such conduct amounts to a prima facie case of constructive fraud
for which he should receive compensatory and punitive damages and have a
trust impressed on the $40,000.00 fee [Woolf] received from the Racers.
```

Source: *Reprinted from Westlaw with permission of Thomson Reuters.*

1. Was Woolf's fee structure ethical?
2. How much money should Woolf be entitled to?
3. Did the agent breach his fiduciary duty to his client?

CASE STUDY 9-5   *Agent Fees*

How much should sports agents charge their clients? Should unions regulate the fee structure between players and agents? Agent fees in baseball are not regulated by MLB but are individually negotiated between player and agent. Agents in MLB can only charge a fee if the agent negotiates a fee above the minimum salary set forth for a player in the Basic Agreement.[19] The National Football League allows a contract advisor (agent) to take a fee on a league minimum contract even though the player would have been entitled to the minimum salary without the services of an agent.

Which fee structure is better for the player? What about charging an hourly fee for work performed on behalf of a player?

THE REGULATION OF SPORTS AGENTS

Numerous entities have attempted to regulate sports agents, attempting to keep unethical and criminal conduct of agents out of the sports industry. Agents are now regulated and monitored from a variety of sources. The NCAA was the first to regulate player-agents. Players' unions, legislative bodies, state attorney generals, and universities have stepped forward as well, in an attempt to curb the unethical conduct of agents.[20]

Union Regulations

Players' unions along with other entities regulate and monitor the activities and conduct of sports agents. Unions have an interest in making sure that union members are being adequately and

---

[19] See, MLBPA Regulations Governing Player Agents, Sec. 4:F.
[20] Kenneth L. Shropshire and Timothy Davis, *The Business of Sports Agents* (Philadelphia, PA; University of Pennsylvania Press, 2008).

properly represented. Unions have taken a myriad of actions to ensure that agents are properly prepared to represent professional athletes. Unions can require agents to have a certain education level or possess comparable business experience to be a certified agent. They can perform criminal background checks on agents, require agents to pass an exam to become a certified agent, and also set desirable fee structures. Unions have a lot of input about who can be an agent. They also possess the power to certify or decertify an agent for improper conduct.

The NFLPA has by far been the most aggressive organization in regulating the conduct of agents. The suspensions of contract advisors David Dunn and Carl Poston provide examples of the NFLPA's regulatory power. In 2006 the NFLPA voted to suspend Poston for allegedly signing a contract for a client without first reading the contract.[21] Poston sued the NFLPA, seeking to have his suspension overturned.[22] The case became the subject of congressional activity.[23]

In the following case study a former lawyer for Major League Baseball sought to be a players' agent but was turned down by the Players' Union.

CASE STUDY 9-6 *Barry Rona and Collusion in Major League Baseball, 1985–1989*

In *Barry Rona and Major League Baseball Players' Association* (Arbitration 1993), the Major League Players' Union rejected Barry Rona's application under section 2(c) of its regulations, which allowed the union to refuse certification to anyone whose conduct "may adversely affect his credibility [or] integrity . . . to serve in a representative and/or fiduciary capacity on behalf of players." The arbitrator stated:

> [T]he Arbitrator finds that the Players Association acted arbitrarily and capriciously in rejecting Rona's application.
>
> The Players Association's conclusion that Rona was part of the collusion in the 1985 and 1986 free agent markets because he was a leading figure in the PRC [Player Relations Committee] is fundamentally at odds with the Code's very clear position that lawyers do not act unethically merely because they represent individuals or institutions that are found to have engaged in wrongful activities. And there is no evidence, nor any finding by Chairman Roberts or Chairman Nicholau that it was or should have been obvious to Rona that his clients were acting "merely for the purpose of harassing or maliciously injuring any person." . . . On the contrary, he expressed his "concerns" to his clients, asked them directly whether they were involved in collusion to destroy the free agent markets in 1985 and 1986 and, when they replied negatively, allowed them to so testify under oath before the Roberts and Nicholau Panels. Rona acted entirely properly . . . in allowing his clients to have their day in court to attempt under oath to refute the circumstantial evidence that they were engaged in collusion can hardly be termed taking a "frivolous legal position." . . . This Arbitrator believes that these are not even close questions. For the foregoing reasons the Arbitrator concludes that the Players Association's rejection of Rona's application because of his alleged involvement in the 1985 and 1986 collusion was arbitrary and capricious.

---

[21] Liz Mullen, "NFLPA Files Complaint Against Arrington's Agent," *Sports Business Journal* 14 (January 23, 2006).

[22] *Carl Poston v. NFL Players Association*, United States District Court Southern District of New York, 06 Civ. 2249 (BSJ).

[23] Letter to the Honorable Henry Hyde and the Honorable Sheila Jackson Lee dated July 14, 2006, from NFLPA president, Eugene Upshaw. See also, "Testimony of Richard A. Berthelsen, General Counsel NFL Player Association before Committee on Commercial and Administrative Law," Committee on the Judiciary, U.S. House of Representatives, December 7, 2006. For further study, see Patrick Connors, John Genzale, Richard Hilliard, Brian Mackler, and Rachel Newman-Baker, "Panel III: Ethics and Sports: Agents Regulation," *Fordham Intellectual Property, Media and Entertainment Law Journal* (Winter 2004).

The union rejected the application of Barry Rona, stating he was an integral part of the collusion by baseball owners in the 1980s to keep player salaries down in MLB. Rona was able to convince an arbitrator otherwise. Do you believe the arbitrator was correct in this decision? Could a former general manager of a team become an agent? What about a sports agent who leaves the players' side to go to the management side of sports? What ethical and legal ramifications does this pose? What issues of confidentiality do these scenarios present?

What ethical duties does a union owe to its members? That was the question explored in Case 9-11.

📖 CASE 9-11   *Peterson v. Kennedy*

771 F.2d 1244 (9th Cir. Cal. 1985)

James Peterson played college football at San Diego State University. After graduating with a physical education degree in 1973, Peterson was drafted by the Los Angeles Rams of the National Football League (NFL). He played for the Rams until 1976, at which time he was traded to the Tampa Bay Buccaneers.

In the summer of 1976, Peterson signed three separate one-year contracts with Tampa Bay for the 1976, 1977, and 1978 football seasons. Each of the contracts contained a standard clause providing that if Peterson were unable to play professional football because of an injury incurred in the performance of services under that contract, the club would continue to pay him his full salary during the remainder of the contract term. In addition, the club agreed to Peterson's request to include a special "injury protection" clause in the 1977 contract. That clause specified that if Peterson were unable to play football in either 1977 or 1978 because of a football-related injury, he would receive the full salary to which he was entitled for the year or years that the injury prevented him from playing. Each of the contracts also contained a provision authorizing the ballclub to terminate the agreement if, in the opinion of the head coach, Peterson's level of performance was "unsatisfactory" as compared to that of other members of the club's squad of players.

Peterson's contracts incorporated the terms of the collective bargaining agreement entered into between the NFLPA and the NFL Management Council. The collective bargaining agreement contemplated two distinct grievance procedures by which a player could contest a club's decision to terminate his contract. An "injury grievance" was the proper procedure to be employed by a player seeking to enforce a club's contractual obligation to pay his salary when he incurred an injury in the performance of his services under the contract. A "non-injury" grievance was the appropriate means to resolve all other disputes involving the enforcement of a player's contract. An injury grievance was required to be filed within 20 days of the date on which the dispute arose, a non-injury grievance within 60 days of that date.

Peterson was injured in the third game of the 1976 football season. He had surgery on his right knee and was sidelined for the rest of the season. The club honored its contractual obligation to pay Peterson's salary over the balance of the 1976 season. After his surgery, Peterson underwent a medically supervised rehabilitation program. He reported to the Tampa Bay pre-season camp in mid-July, 1977. After passing a physical examination administered by the team's physician, Peterson participated fully in all practices and drills during the first seven or eight days of training camp.

The club's records reveal that on July 22, 1977, Peterson was verbally advised that he had been "cut" from the team and placed on waivers. Peterson received written notification that his 1977 and 1978 contracts had been terminated on July 25, 1977.

Peterson believed that he was cut from the team because of reduced mobility attributable to the knee injury that he suffered in the 1976 season. He claimed that, under the "injury protection" clause of the 1977 contract, the club remained obligated to pay him his full salary for both the 1977 and 1978 football seasons. The club disagreed. Its officials told Peterson that he had been released because he lacked sufficient skill to make the team, not because of his knee injury, and that he was therefore not entitled to payment under the "injury protection" clause.

Source: *Reprinted from Westlaw with permission of Thomson Reuters.*

In Case 9-11, what action should the union take on Peterson's behalf?

In the following arbitration case, an agent had his license revoked by the players' union after he publicly criticized the NBPA during a two-month lockout in the 1998–99 NBA season.

CASE 9-12 *In the Matter of the Agent Certification Application of Stephen M. Woods (Opinion and Award)*

On January 5, 1999, two days before an agreement was reached to end the lockout imposed by the NBA, the NBPA Committee on Agent Regulation, acting under the "emergency circumstance" clause of Section 2E of the Regulations, invalidated the certification of Agent Stephen Woods. That action was grounded in Section 3 B(m), which provides that discipline, ranging from a reprimand to decertification, may be imposed for conduct "which reflects adversely on [an individual's] fitness as a player agent or jeopardizes the effective representation of player agents."

In a 19-page specification Woods was charged with a number of acts which, in the Committee's estimation, harmed the Union's bargaining position in the negotiations that occurred during the long lockout. Included were such acts as publicly seeking to undermine the Union's bargaining position after being warned to desist; repeatedly issuing misleading statements, both to the press and in a sports column of which he was the author; publicly and offensively attacking NBA players, including the Union leadership; engaging in activity that created an actual or potential conflict of interest with the effective representation of NBA players by revealing as a columnist confidential information he had obtained as an agent; billing the NBPA for a hotel room at a meeting of players to which he was not invited; and making misrepresentations in his 1994 application for certification.

Woods denied all the charges and appealed his decertification.

Source: *Reprinted from Westlaw with permission of Thomson Reuters.*

CASE STUDY 9-7   *Agent Exam*

Should a sports agent be required to pass a written exam to be able to represent players in a professional league?[24] If the agent does not pass on the first try, how many times should he or she be able to re-take the exam? What should a potential agent be tested on? Should there be a minimum passing score for certificate?[25]

In the following case, a player-agent challenged the NBA's agent certification system.

📖 CASE 9-13   *Collins v. National Basketball Players Association*

850 F. Supp 1468 (D. Col. 1992)

Like other sports and entertainment unions, the NBPA believes that the collective good of the entire represented group is maximized when individualized salary negotiations occur within a framework that permits players to exert leverage based on their unique skills and personal contributions. The NBPA therefore has authorized the players or their individually selected agents to negotiate individual compensation packages. This delegation of representational authority to individual players and their agents has always been limited solely to the authority to negotiate individual compensation packages, and to

---

[24] Darren Rovell, "Students Learn About Legal Issues, Negotiations," *ESPN.com*, June 9, 2005.
[25] See NFLPA Regulations Governing Contract Advisors, Sec. 2: Certification.

enforce them through the grievance-arbitration procedure established by the NBPA-NBA Agreement.

Player agents were unregulated by the NBPA before 1986. By the mid-1980s, a substantial number of players had complained to the officers of the NBPA about agent abuses. Specifically, players complained that the agents imposed high and non-uniform fees for negotiation services, insisted on the execution of open-ended powers of attorney giving the agents broad powers over players' professional and financial decisions, failed to keep players apprised of the status of negotiations with NBA teams, failed to submit itemized bills for fees and services, and, in some cases, had conflicts of interest arising out of representing coaches and/or general managers of NBA teams as well as players. Many players believed they were bound by contract not to dismiss their agents regardless of dissatisfaction with their services and fees, because the agents had insisted on the execution of long-term agreements. Some agents offered money and other inducements to players, their families and coaches to obtain player clients.

In response to these abuses, the NBPA established the Regulations, a comprehensive system of agent certification and regulation, to insure that players would receive agent services that meet minimum standards of quality at uniform rates. First, the Regulations provide that a player agent may not conduct individual contract negotiations unless he signs the "Standard Player Agent Contract" promulgated by the Committee. The "Standard Player Agent Contract" limits player agent fees by prohibiting any fee or commission on any contract which entitles the player to the minimum salary and by limiting agent fees on all contracts. Second, the Regulations contain a "code of conduct" which specifically prohibits an agent from providing or offering money or anything of value to a player, a member of a player's family or a player's high school or college coach for the purpose of inducing the player to use that agent's services. The code also prohibits agents from engaging in conduct that constitutes an actual or apparent conflict of interest (such as serving as an agent for a player while also representing an NBA team, general manager or head coach), engaging in any unlawful conduct involving dishonesty, fraud, deceit, misrepresentation, or engaging in any other conduct that reflects adversely on his fitness to serve in a fiduciary capacity as a player agent or jeopardizes the effective representation of NBA players.

Third, the Regulations restrict the representation of players to individuals who are certified player agents, and set up a program for the certification of agents who are then bound by the Regulations' fee restrictions and code of conduct. Prospective player agents must file the "Applications for Certification as an NBPA Player Agent" with the Committee. The Committee is authorized to conduct any informal investigation that it deems appropriate to determine whether to issue certification and may deny certification to any applicant:

(1) Upon . . . determining that the applicant has made false or misleading statements of a material nature in the Application;

(2) Upon . . . determining that the applicant has ever misappropriated funds, or engaged in other specific fraud, which would render him unfit to serve in a fiduciary capacity on behalf of players;

(3) Upon . . . determining that the applicant has engaged in any other conduct that significantly impacts adversely on his credibility, integrity or competence to serve in a fiduciary capacity on behalf of players; or

(4) Upon . . . determining that the applicant is unwilling to swear or affirm that he will comply with these Regulations and any amendments thereto and that he will abide by the fee structure contained in the standard form player-agent contract incorporated into these Regulations.

Regulations, Section 2C.

Any prospective agent whose application for certification is denied may appeal that denial by filing a timely demand for arbitration. The arbitration procedure incorporates by reference the Voluntary Labor Arbitration Rules of the American Arbitration Association, and includes the right to be represented by counsel, to cross-examine the Committee's witnesses, to present testimonial and documentary evidence and to receive a transcript. The arbitrator is empowered to order certification if he determines, based on the evidence, that the Committee did not meet its burden of establishing a basis for denying certification. The arbitrator's decision is final and binding on all parties and is not subject to judicial review. The NBPA's selected arbitrator, George Nicolau, is experienced and highly qualified in handling labor relations in the sports industry. He is currently the chairman of the arbitration panel for the Major League Baseball and the Major League Baseball Players Association and the contract arbitrator for the Major Indoor Soccer League and Major Indoor Soccer League Players Association. The NBPA player representatives of each NBA team approved the Regulations which became effective on March 7, 1986.

After unilaterally promulgating the Regulations, the NBPA obtained, in arms length collective bargaining, the NBA's agreement to prohibit all member teams from negotiating individual player salary contracts with any agent who was not certified by the NBPA.

Collins was an agent for several NBA players from 1974 until 1986. Collins applied for and received certification in 1986 soon after the Regulations took effect. In late 1986 or early 1987, he voluntarily ceased functioning as a player agent because of a lawsuit filed against him by a former NBA player client, Kareem Abdul-Jabbar, the former center of the Los Angeles Lakers, but retained his certification. Collins said he would not resume agent activities until he was exonerated of all charges in the pending lawsuit. In that case, Abdul-Jabbar, together with Ain Jeem, Inc. a corporation Abdul-Jabbar had established, alleged that Collins had committed numerous serious breaches of the fiduciary duty he owed as an agent to Abdul-Jabbar. The alleged breaches included mishandling of Abdul-Jabbar's federal and state income tax returns which caused Abdul-Jabbar to pay approximately $300,000 in interest charges and late penalties; improvidently investing Abdul-Jabbar's money; mismanaging Abdul-Jabbar's assets; and transferring funds from Abdul-Jabbar's accounts without permission to the accounts of other players who were also Collins' clients. Collins' certification was revoked because he failed to pay agent dues and failed to attend at least one agent seminar as required by the Regulations.

Collins submitted an application to be recertified as a player agent. His application noted that there was still pending against him another lawsuit filed by another NBA player, Lucius Allen, and that eight of his former player clients—Abdul-Jabbar, Alex English, Lucius Allen, Rickey Sobers, Terry Cummings, Ralph Sampson, Rudy Hackett and Brad Davis—had discharged him by the end of 1986.

By letter dated December 14, 1990, the Committee issued its decision denying Collins certification as a player agent. The letter explained that based on the allegations against him by Abdul-Jabbar and the information gathered by the Committee, the Committee concluded that Collins was unfit to serve in a fiduciary capacity on behalf of NBA players and that he made false or misleading statements to the Committee concerning a relevant subject in connection with the investigation into his application. Specifically, the Committee found: (1) Collins violated fiduciary duties to his former client Kareem Abdul-Jabbar and Ain Jeem, Inc. in his preparation and filing of federal and state tax returns, causing penalties and interest in excess of $300,000 to be imposed on Mr. Abdul-Jabbar and the corporation. (2) In handling the financial and business affairs of Mr. Abdul-Jabbar and other players, Collins acknowledged commingling funds from one account to another without authorization and resulting in losses of over $200,000 to Mr. Abdul-Jabbar. (3) Collins ignored requests by Mr. Abdul-Jabbar to invest money in safe investments, and invested in speculative ventures, many of which produced negative investment results. (4) In December 1985, Collins converted a corporate indebtedness of approximately $290,000 into a personal obligation of Mr. Abdul-Jabbar's without his approval. He also caused Mr. Abdul-Jabbar to execute loan documents relating to several investments making him jointly and severally liable for repaying loans. (5) Collins told the Committee that

he had not filed his own Federal income taxes for the four year period
1986 through 1989 (even though he admitted earning over $300,000 in
1986). (6) Collins falsely represented to the Committee that Mr. Abdul-
Jabbar paid $300,000 of Collins indebtedness to the Bank of California
in connection with settling a lawsuit filed by Mr. Abdul-Jabbar and
Ain-Jeem against Collins.

Source: *Reprinted from Westlaw with permission of Thomson Reuters.*

Were the NBPA actions against Collins ethical and fair? What ethical guidelines should be included in an agent regulatory scheme?

State Law

In many states, athlete agents must register with the state where they reside and also pay a fee to recruit potential clients within the state. States provide a list of eligible sports agents to universities who in turn allow the agent on campus to interview student-athletes. If the agent's name does not appear on the certified state list, the agent cannot recruit student-athletes in that state. In many states an application must be completed by the potential athlete agent before he or she can become certified. The application sometimes requires a fee, and renewal of the license also requires a fee. For example, the annual filing fee in the State of Texas is $1,000.[26] The athlete agent registration in the State of Texas requires the applicant to provide information relating to the following before the applicant can be considered for certification by the state:

- Entity name and type
- Background and employment experience
- References
- Athlete representation experience
- Additional persons who recruit or solicit athletes
- Financially interested parties

University Regulations

Universities and colleges have also established rules and regulations for agents who desire to interview student-athletes on campus.[27] Universities do not want agents to violate the law during the recruitment process and potentially create legal and ethical problems for the university. Therefore, universities closely monitor the activities of sports agents on their campuses. The following is a sample university policy dealing with agents and student-athletes:

The University requires that all agents and their interactions with the University's student-athletes comply with the following policies:

---

[26] Athlete Agents Act, Tex. Occupations Code § 2051.001 et.seq.
[27] See, http://gofrogs.cstv.com/compliance/compliance-agents.html (Texas Christian University).

1. Any contact with a University student-athlete with eligibility remaining must be arranged through the University's Athletic Director for Compliance and Eligibility.
2. The Athletic Director for Compliance will advise the agent in the event a student-athlete requests an interview with that player agent. The location and time of the interview program will also be communicated to the player agent by a representative of the Office of Compliance.
3. Agents and their runners and/or representatives are prohibited from any type or form of contact (including but not limited to phone calls, letters, email messages, fax messages, text, Twitter, and communications in person) not made under the supervision and assistance of the Athletic Director for Compliance and Eligibility with a student-athlete, their spouse, parents, or legal guardian while that student-athlete remains eligible for intercollegiate competition.
4. All agents are required to direct all correspondence to the University's Athletic Director for Compliance and Eligibility where each student-athlete has a file.
5. In the event a student-athlete, their parents, or legal guardians contact an agent to arrange a discussion of that agent's qualification or proficiency in the marketing of the student-athlete's athletic ability or reputation, that agent is not permitted to discuss that agent's services until after the agent has given notice of the proposed discussion to the University's Associate Athletic Director for Compliance and Eligibility.
6. All agents interested in representing a student-athlete from the University are required to register with the University Athletic Director for Compliance and Eligibility.

The University will establish dates on which interviews may be held with University student-athletes during the academic year.

National Collegiate Athletic Association (NCAA)

What role should the NCAA play in regulating sports agents? They have published the following list of questions that student-athletes should ask of potential football agents:

1. Where and when did you graduate from law school?
2. If you are not a lawyer, what are your educational credentials?
3. Have you ever been disbarred, suspended, reprimanded, censured or otherwise disciplined or disqualified as an attorney or as a member of any other profession?
4. Are there currently any complaints or charges pending against you regarding your conduct as an attorney or as a member of any other profession?
5. Have you ever been implicated or investigated for any violations of NCAA or professional league rules?
6. Are you an NFLPA certified contract advisor?
7. Did you take the NFLPA Collective Bargaining Agreement Test? What was your score? If you did not take the test, why not?
8. Do you have ownership interests in your company?
9. Can you supply me with a list of current and former clients?
10. What services do you offer to your clients other than contract negotiations (financial planning, tax advice, etc.)? Do you mind if I use my own accountant or financial planner?
11. Who will be negotiating my contract?
12. How many clients have you lost, what was the reason for their departure? Can you provide me with a list of their phone numbers?
13. Who do you consider to be your top clients?

14. What have you done to advance the careers of your clients on and off the field?
15. Do you provide an annual statement to your clients? May I see an example?
16. How do you keep your clients informed of charges?
17. What is your fee structure? Are your fees negotiable?
18. How and when are you to be paid?
19. What is the duration of the agreement?
20. What are the procedures for terminating the agreement?
21. What happens to our agreement if I fail to make the team; if I am waived; or if I get injured?
22. If I am likely to be a free agent, how can you help maximize my chances of making a team?
23. Do you have any connections with NFL Europe, the CFL, or the Arena Football League?
24. Have you ever had a dispute with a client and if so, how was it resolved?[28]

CRIMINAL ACTS OF AGENTS

The criminal acts of sports agents have become widely known through media reports. Reports of agents mismanaging and misappropriating the fortunes of players have become headline news, as have reports of agents who pay amateur players and bestow gifts on potential clients who are still amateur athletes. All this activity has created new ethical issues in the sports agent business, and some agents have been prosecuted for criminal behavior. Some state statutes regulate the conduct of professional sports agents by the imposition of criminal sanctions and fines. The Miller-Ayala Athlete Agent Act (State of California) provides for the following enforcement penalties:

> An athlete agent or his representative or employee who violates the California Agent Athlete Law is guilty of a misdemeanor, and shall be punished by:

- a fine of not more than fifty thousand dollars ($50,000), or
- imprisonment in a county jail not exceeding one year, or
- both that fine and imprisonment.

The court also may suspend or revoke the convicted individual's privilege to conduct the business of athlete agent.[29]

Norby Walters and Lloyd Bloom were able to sign 58 college football players to representation agreements. They also "loaned" money to amateur players. All but two of their clients fired them after the players graduated from college. Walters and Bloom were eventually found guilty of criminal charges arising out of their activities.

📖 CASE 9-14 *Walters v. Fullwood*

```
675 F.Supp. 155 (S.D.N.Y. 1987)

. . . Brent Fullwood . . . was an outstanding running back with the
University of Auburn football team in Alabama. His success in the
highly competitive Southeastern Athletic Conference marked him as a
```

---

[28] NCAA.org.
[29] Miller-Ayala Athlete Agents Act, Business and Professions Code, Division 8 Special Business Regulations, Chapter 2.5 Athlete Agents.

top professional prospect. At an unspecified time during his senior
year at Auburn, Fullwood entered into an agreement with W.S. & E., a New
York corporation ("the W.S. & E. agreement"). The agreement was dated
January 2, 1987, the day after the last game of Fullwood's college
football career, and the first day he could sign such a contract without forfeiting his amateur status under sec. 3-1-(c) of the N.C.A.A.
Constitution. . . . The contract was arranged and signed for the corporation by [Lloyd] Bloom, and granted W.S. & E. the exclusive right
to represent Fullwood as agent to negotiate with professional football
teams after the spring draft of the National Football League
("N.F.L."). [Norby] Walters and Bloom were the corporate officers and
sole shareholders of W.S. & E. As a provisionally certified N.F.L.
Players' Association ("N.F.L.P.A.") contract advisor, Bloom was subject to the regulations of that body governing agents ("N.F.L.P.A.
Agents' Regulations"), which require the arbitration of most disputes
between players and contract advisors.

On August 20, 1986, W.S. & E. paid $4,000 to Fullwood, who then exe-
cuted a promissory note [for Walters and Bloom] for that amount. . . .
At various times throughout the 1986 season, [Walters and Bloom] sent
to Fullwood or his family further payments that totaled $4,038.

. . . While neither [Walters and Bloom] nor [Fullwood] have specifically admitted that the W.S. & E. agency agreement was postdated, they
have conspicuously avoided identifying the actual date it was signed.
There is a powerful inference that the agreement was actually signed
before or during the college football season, perhaps contemporaneously with the August 20 promissory note, and unethically postdated as
in other cases involving [Walters and Bloom]. No argument or evidence
has been presented to dispel this inference, and the Court believes
the parties deliberately postdated the contract January 2. Even if
this likelihood is not accepted, it is conceded by all parties and
proven by documentary evidence that a security interest was granted on
Fullwood's future earnings from professional football, by the express
terms of the promissory note of August 20, 1986.

At some point prior to the N.F.L. spring 1987 draft, Fullwood repudi-
ated his agreement with W.S. & E., and chose to be represented by
[agent] George Kickliter, an attorney in Auburn, Alabama. As anticipated, Fullwood was taken early in the N.F.L. draft. The Green Bay
Packers selected him as the fourth player in the first round; he
signed a contract with them, and currently is playing in his rookie
season in the N.F.L.

Source: *Reprinted from Westlaw with permission of Thomson Reuters.*

In the following case the U.S. government sued an agent for his unethical and illegal acts over
his dealing with amateur athletes.

CASE 9-15   *United States v. Piggie*

303 F.3d 923 (8th Cir. 2002)

In the mid to late 1990's, Myron Piggie (Piggie) created and pursued a secret scheme to pay talented high school athletes to play basketball for his "amateur" summer team. Because the athletes intended to play college basketball, the scheme produced multiple violations of National Collegiate Athletic Association (NCAA) rules which require college athletes to be amateurs. Piggie pled guilty to one count of conspiracy to commit mail and wire fraud and one count of failure to file an income tax return.

Between 1995 and 1999, Myron Piggie devised a scheme to assemble elite high school basketball players and compensate them for their participation on his traveling Amateur Athletic Union (AAU) basketball team, known first as the Children's Mercy Hospital 76ers and later as the KC Rebels. The payments were designed to retain top athletes on his team, gain access to sports agents, obtain profitable sponsorship contracts, and forge ongoing relationships with players to his benefit when the athletes joined the National Basketball Association (NBA).

The pre-sentence report shows Piggie realized at least $677,760 in income through his scheme. In the plea agreement, Piggie concedes that, as a result of his fraud, he received a total of $420,401 between 1995 and 1998. Piggie received at least $184,435 from team owner Tom Grant, $159,866 from team sponsor Nike, and $76,100 from sports agents Jerome Stanley and Kevin Poston. He further planned on receiving a portion of his players' compensation when they became professional athletes.

Piggie received a gross income of approximately $99,100 from these sources during the 1998 calendar year, and he knowingly and willfully failed to file a tax return by April 15, 1999. Piggie also failed to file income tax returns in 1995, 1996, and 1997. In the plea agreement, the parties stipulated to a total tax loss of $67,662.69 for the period of 1995 to 1998.

Piggie took portions of the money he was receiving as the coach of this elite AAU team and made payments to the high school athletes in a clandestine manner, frequently hiding the money in Nike shoe boxes. All of the parties intended to keep the payments a secret from authorities. During the conspiracy, Piggie paid Jaron Rush $17,000, Korleone Young (Young) $14,000, Corey Maggette (Maggette) $2,000, Kareem Rush $2,300, and Andre Williams (Williams) $200.

After accepting Piggie's payments to play AAU basketball, Jaron Rush, Maggette, Kareem Rush, and Williams submitted false and fraudulent

Student-Athlete Statements to the universities where they were to play intercollegiate basketball. These four athletes falsely certified that they had not previously received payments to play basketball. The athletes delivered through the U.S. Postal Service signed letters of intent asserting their eligibility. Based upon the false assertions that these athletes were eligible amateurs, the University of California, Los Angeles (UCLA); Duke University (Duke); the University of Missouri-Columbia (Missouri); and Oklahoma State University (OSU) (collectively Universities) awarded scholarships to these athletes, enrolled them in classes, and allowed them to play on NCAA basketball teams.

NCAA regulations permit universities to award only thirteen basketball scholarships per year. When Piggie's payments to these players were discovered, the Universities became subject to NCAA penalties. Each school lost the use of one of the thirteen scholarships and lost the value of each player's participation due to the player's NCAA-required suspension. The scholarships were forfeited, and the Universities lost the opportunity to award the scholarships to other top amateur athletes, who had actual eligibility to play intercollegiate basketball. In 1999 and 2000, UCLA lost the benefit of playing Jaron Rush, the $44,862.88 scholarship awarded to him, and also forfeited $42,339 in tournament revenue; Missouri lost the benefit of playing Kareem Rush, and the $9,388.92 scholarship awarded to him; and OSU lost the benefit of playing Williams and the $12,180 scholarship awarded to him. Duke provided Maggette with a $32,696 scholarship for the 1998-1999 season based upon the false assertion that he was an eligible amateur. As a result of the ineligible athlete's participation, the validity of Duke's entire 1998-1999 season was called into question.

NCAA regulations also required each of the four Universities involved to conduct costly internal investigations after Piggie's scheme was discovered. UCLA spent $59,225.36 on the NCAA-mandated investigation of Jaron Rush, Duke spent $12,704.39 on the NCAA-mandated investigation of Maggette, Missouri spent $10,609 on the NCAA-mandated investigation of Kareem Rush, and OSU spent $21,877.24 on the NCAA-mandated investigation of Williams. The total monetary loss to the Universities was $245,882.79. The scandal following the disclosure of Piggie's scheme caused further intangible harms to the Universities including adverse publicity, diminished alumni support, merchandise sales losses, and other revenue losses.

Pembroke Hill High School (Pembroke), where Jaron and Kareem Rush played high school basketball, sustained a loss of $10,733.89 in investigative costs and forfeiture of property as a result of the conspiracy. Pembroke was placed on probation by the State of Missouri after the violations of Jaron and Kareem Rush were discovered and a mandatory investigation of the matter was concluded.

After Piggie's guilty plea, the district court sentenced him to 37 months imprisonment, three years supervised release, and $324,279.87 in restitution.

Source: *Reprinted from Westlaw with permission of Thomson Reuters.*

In *Lounsbury* an uncertified sports agent sued a former player and his agent claiming the player "took him for a ride" and promised the uncertified agent that he could represent him when he began his professional career.

CASE 9-16 *Lounsbury v. Camby*

2003 WL 22792348

. . . John Lounsbury initiated an action against Camby and ProServ, Inc. ("ProServ"). Lounsbury alleges that, while a student at the University of Massachusetts and a member of its basketball team, Camby promised that he would sign an exclusive agency contract with [Lounsbury] when he ended his collegiate career if Lounsbury provided Camby, his friends and family with money, gifts, gratuities and services. At the time of the alleged agreement, Lounsbury was not a certified agent and therefore was not authorized, in accordance with the collective bargaining agreement between the Players Association and the National Basketball Association (NBA), to represent Camby in contract negotiations with any NBA team. In 1996 Camby signed an exclusive agency contract with ProServ to represent him in contract negotiations with the NBA team that drafted Camby...Lounsbury alleges that Camby breached his oral contract with him by signing with ProServ and that ProServ tortuously interfered with his agreement with Camby.

ProServ states that Lounsbury is basing his action...on conduct that violates Connecticut civil and criminal law with respect to prohibited acts of athlete agents. In Connecticut General Statutes § 20-555, Prohibited Acts are defined as:

> An [athlete-agent] shall not:
> (1) Publish or cause to be published any false, fraudulent or misleading information, representation, notice or advertisement or give any false information or make any false promises or representations to any person concerning any employment;
> (2) Divide fees with or receive compensation from a professional sports league or franchise or its representative or employee;
> (3) Enter into any agreement, written or oral, by which the athlete agent offers anything of value to any employee of an institution of higher education located in this state in return for the referral of any athletes by that employee;

(4) Enter into an oral or written agent contract or professional sport services contract with an athlete before the athlete's eligibility for collegiate athletics expires; or

(5) Give, offer or promise anything of value to an athlete, his guardian or to any member of the athlete's immediate family before the athlete's eligibility for collegiate athletics expires.

The statutory civil and criminal penalties for failing to comply with § 20-555 include,

(a)(1) The Commissioner of Consumer Protection may, after notice and conducting a hearing . . . revoke or suspend any certificate of registration.

(2) The commissioner shall revoke any such certificate of registration held by any person.

(b) The Commissioner of Consumer Protection may, after notice and conducting a hearing . . . order restitution or impose a civil penalty, or both. . . . Any civil penalty imposed by the commissioner under this subsection shall not exceed one thousand dollars plus the amount of profits derived as a result of the violation minus any amount paid as restitution.

(d) In addition to any other remedy provided any person who violates any provision shall [also] be guilty of a class B misdemeanor.

Source: *Reprinted from Westlaw with permission of Thomson Reuters.*

Marcus Camby later admitted to having taken thousands of dollars in cash from agents in violation of NCAA rules while at the University of Massachusetts. Agents supplied him with "money, jewelry, rental cars and prostitutes," which he accepted and sometimes even requested. He left UMass after his junior year of college and with the help of ProServ, negotiated a 3-year $8 million contract as the number 2 pick in the 1996 NBA draft. Camby admitted that while at an electronic store with John Lounsbury in March 1995 he asked the agent to buy him a stereo for his birthday which Lounsbury bought on the spot for $1,066.00.[30] To what extent should Marcus Camby be held responsible for his actions? Is Camby as culpable as his uncertified agent for what transpired?

NOTES AND DISCUSSION QUESTIONS

Introduction

1. What standard must agents meet to fulfill their duties to a client? In *Zinn v. Parrish*, what else could the agent have done to fulfill his duties to the client? Did the agent act ethically in his representation of the player? Did the player act in an unethical manner?

---

[30] Phil Taylor, Tangled Web: Marcus was Both Victim and Villain in his Illicit Dealings with Agents While at UMass, *Sports Illustrated*, September 15, 1997.

2. In *Bias v. Advantage International, Inc.*, did the agent breach his fiduciary duty to his client? How long should it take an agent to negotiate an endorsement contract? What actions should the league or other entity have taken against the agent for Len Bias under the circumstances?

3. Describe the essential functions of a sports agent. What ethical guidelines should an agent follow?

4. Should there be a uniform code of ethics for sports agents? If so, what would it include?[31]

5. Under what circumstances should an agent refer a client to an attorney or another agent?

6. Is it ever right to lie during negotiations? Can failing to tell the "whole truth" be part of a negotiating strategy? Should an agent ever represent that he or she has an offer from another club when in fact this is not true, solely to improve the client's negotiating position?[32]

7. Under what circumstances should an agent advise his client to "hold out"? If a player is legally bound under a contract to play, does an agent engage in an unethical act by advising the player to hold out for more money notwithstanding the player's contractual obligations? Would the agent be advising the player to breach his or her contract?

8. How does a sports agent properly resolve a conflict of interest situation?[33]

9. How should a court decide *Rosenhaus v. Star Sports, Inc.*? What other factors do you need to know to decide this case?

10. Do you believe race is a factor when athletes consider hiring an agent? Only a relatively small percentage of African American athletes use African American sports agents.[34]

11. Former NBA star Scottie Pippen prevailed against his former financial advisor Robert Lunn and won a judgment of $11.8 million. Pippen never recovered any of the money because his former advisor filed for bankruptcy after the judgment.[35] Baseball great Sandy Koufax lost a substantial amount of money due to the fraudulent actions of Bernard Madoff.[36] Actors and entertainers are not immune from the criminal activities of agents and financial advisors. Kevin Bacon lost a small fortune to Bernard Madoff.[37] Many players have filed civil lawsuits against agents in attempts to recover what they lost. Kareem Abdul-Jabbar lost millions to an agent.[38]

Lawyers as Sport Agents

12. Should all agents be required to be lawyers? What advantages do lawyers have in representing a player? Are there any disadvantages?

---

[31] For further study , see Lori K. Miller, "A Uniform Code to Regulate Athlete Agents," *Journal of Sports & Social Issues* 16, no. 2 (1992): 93, 102.

[32] See generally, Ron Simon, *The Game Behind the Game, Negotiating in the Big Leagues* (Stillwater, MN: Voyageur Press, 1993).

[33] See generally, Melissa Neiman, "Fair Game: Ethical Consideration in Negotiation by Sports Agents," University of Houston Law Center, August 2007, available through the Social Science Research Network.

[34] James G. Sammataro, "Business and Brotherhood, Can They Coincide? A Search into Why Black Athletes Do Not Hire Black Agents," *Howard Law Journal* 42 (Spring 1999): 535.

[35] Geoff Dougherty, "Chicago Bulls' Scottie Pippen Wins Judgment over Investment Advice," *Chicago Tribune*, November 24, 2004, B1.

[36] Thomas Zambino and Larry Mcshane, "Sandy Koufax, John Malkovich Among Bernie Madoff Victims as Court Filings Are Released," *New York Daily News*, February 5, 2009.

[37] Jake Coyle, "King, Malkovich Among Madoff Investor List Names," *ABC News*, 2009.

[38] Kim Murphy, "$55 Million Action Alleges Financial Mismanagement," *Los Angeles Times*, July 19, 1986.

13. In *Brown v. Woolf*, the agent took his entire fee even though the player did not receive the full amount of the contract. Would that ever be acceptable? Should an agent only get paid when and if the player gets paid?

14. In *Detroit Lions, Inc. v. Argovitz*, the court found that Argovitz had breached his duty to his client regarding conflict of interest. How did he do that? How should an agent resolve a conflict of interest? What about representing a coach and a player on the same team?

Fee Structures of Agents

15. Most professional leagues set fees for agents. The NFL contract advisor fee is 3% unless the player and the advisor agree otherwise. A player's "juice" sometimes allows a player to negotiate a lower agent's fee. Some NFL star players have been able to reduce the agent's fee to as low as 1%.[39] Should players be able to negotiate directly with an agent about a fee or should it be set by the union?

16. Should a league be able to regulate the financial advisors of players as well as agents? The NFL publishes guidelines on the regulations of financial advisors.[40]

The Regulation of Sports Agents

17. In *Atwater et.al. v. The National Football League Players Association, et.al.*,[41] several former NFL players sued the NFLPA saying they breached a duty owed to him by negligently performing background checks on financial advisors.[42] Should all professional leagues perform criminal background checks on prospective agents?[43]

18. Should professional leagues also check the credit scores of potential agents and financial advisors? Many employers now check credit scores of new employees. As reported in *The Wall Street Journal*: "Concerned about rising rates of employee theft and fiduciary issues, more employers are conducting credit background checks on applicants for some positions. Companies say the financial information can offer insight into a candidate's level of responsibility."[44]

19. Should non-lawyer agents be bound by the same rules as sports agents who are lawyers?

20. The University of Southern California sued sports agent Robert Caron for what they deemed to be improper contact with student-athletes. He allegedly gave student-athletes airline tickets, rent money, and phone cards for promises of future representation. The case was eventually settled for $50,000.[45]

---

[39] www.nflplayers.com, Agents Fees can dip Below 3 Percent, *www.nflplayers.com*, May 6, 2008.

[40] See, "Securities and Exchange Commission, No-Action Letter under: Investment Advisers Act of 1940-Sections 202(a)(11); 206(4) and Rule 206(4)-3, National Football League Players Association," January 25, 2002, Response of the Office of Chief Counsel Division of Investment Manager, No. 2002-1251421, National Football League Players Association.

[41] U.S. Dist. LEXIS 23371 (N.D. Ga. Mar 29, 2007).

[42] Harry Weber, "NFLPA Countersues Players Who Want Money They Lost in Hedge Fund," *USA Today*, May 1, 2007.

[43] Liz Mullem, "NFL Agents to Get Criminal Check," *Sports Business Journal* (March 25, 2002).

[44] Kristen McNamara, "Bad Credit Derails Job Seekers," *Wall Street Journal*, March 16, 2010.

[45] "College Football; Agent Agrees to Settle Suit," *New York Times*, October 14, 1995.

21. What organizations are in the best position to regulate the sports agent industry?[46]
22. What ethical duties do universities have to assist student-athletes in the proper selection of an agent? Many universities hold an agent day on campus so registered agents can come to the university campus and be interviewed by student-athletes who are contemplating a professional career.[47] How should colleges and universities go about regulating agents? How would it differ from union regulations? From state regulations?
23. The NCAA was the first entity to institute a regulatory scheme for sports agents. What ethical responsibilities do they owe student-athletes in instructing them regarding the selection of an agent?
24. Should unions require agents to carry malpractice insurance during the representation process with a player? What types of misconduct might constitute malpractice or breach of a fiduciary duty on the part of an agent?
25. Most sports unions can decertify an agent for misconduct. What type of misconduct would require league intervention? What about an agent who files for personal bankruptcy? What about an agent who is charged with or convicted of drunk driving or domestic violence? Should a league be able to regulate an agent's conduct off the field?
26. What qualifications should an agent possess? Should agents be required to have a college degree? What about a graduate degree? What level of negotiating experience should the agent possess?
27. Discuss the primary duties of a sports agent. What duties might an agent have aside from negotiation of a player's contract?
28. Why do leagues require Standard Representation Agreements (SRA's) between a player and an agent? Why not allow each player to negotiate whatever agreement he or she can with an agent? Why would a league want all agreements to be uniform?[48]
29. Should leagues require agents to attend continuing education seminars to be updated on matters related to the league and players' rights?
30. How should leagues regulate disputes between agents and players?
31. Should there be a limit on the number of agents a league can certify? In the NFL a contract advisor must negotiate an NFL player contract every three years or lose his or her certification. Is this a good rule? What effects would this rule have on the ethical activities of agents as a body?
32. Leigh Steinberg sued his former employee David Dunn after Dunn left the firm taking multiple clients. After a five-week trial, a jury ordered Dunn and his company to pay Steinberg's firm $44.7 million in damages. A California appellate court later vacated the award. The NFLPA had suspended Dunn for two years beginning in 2003 based on evidence revealed at the trial. His bankruptcy filing suspended the NFLPA's disciplinary action against him. Dunn filed bankruptcy as a result of the jury's verdict. Dunn eventually agreed to an 18-month suspension from the NFL.[49]

---

[46] Jim Tanner, "Leave Congress Out of Fix for Unethical Sports Agents," *USATODAY.com*, August 5, 2010.

[47] See, www.rolltide.com.

[48] See NFLPA.org.

[49] *Steinberg Moorad & Dunn Inc. v. Dunn*, 136 Fed App 6 (9th Cir 2005); Liz Mullen, "David Dunn Agrees to 18-Month Suspension," *Sports Business Daily*, November 22, 2006.

33. Many states require lawyers to pass an ethics exam in addition to a bar exam to become attorneys. Should sports agents have to pass both a test to become a certified agent and an ethics exam? If it is good enough for a lawyer, why not require it of a sports agents?

34. Becoming a free agent can be a player's biggest payday, that is, unless the player's agent misses the filing deadline for free agency. That is what happened to Cleveland Browns wide receiver Dennis Northcutt. NFLPA contract advisor Jerome Stanley was suspended by the NFLPA for his failure to file by the deadline.[50] What actions should be taken against agents who are merely negligent as opposed to intentionally breaking a duty of trust owed to the client?

Criminal Acts of Agents

35. Gus Dominguez was the subject of the first ever indictment of a sports agent for smuggling major league prospects out of Cuba.[51] "The trial, the first of its kind in which a baseball agent was charged with alien smuggling, lasted seven days and exposed a shadowy underworld of the baseball industry. In court testimony, an admitted drug felon said Dominguez paid him to orchestrate a smuggling operation in 2004 that brought five Cuban baseball players to a beach in the Florida Keys."[52]

36. Agent Finn Rothman was ordered to pay restitution of $197,000 to a former New York Giants player after he defrauded several players. He pled guilty to grand larceny and was sentenced to 3 to 9 years in prison.[53]

37. Would it be a good idea to establish a "hotline" for alleged ethical violations of sports agents? What ethical problems would the hotline itself pose?[54]

38. Sports agent Norby Walters was sentenced to five years in prison and Lloyd Bloom received a three-year sentence.[55] Were these sentences fair in light of their unethical and criminal conduct?

---

[50] Mark Maske, "NFLPA Taking Steps to Discipline Agents," *Washington Post*, November 9, 2004.

[51] Associated Press, "Convicted Sports Agent Faces Decades in Prison," *ESPN.com*, April 13, 2007.

[52] Tim Arango, "Gus Dominguez Convicted of Smuggling Cuban Baseball Players into US," *Havana Journal*, April 13, 2007.

[53] Robert Kessler, "Man Gets Prison Time for Cheating Giants Player, Agent," *News Day*, August 21, 2009.

[54] J. Brian Ewing, "Hotline to Target Athletics Recruiting," *News-Record.com*, August 26, 2009.

[55] Steve Fiffer, "Two Sports Agents Get Prison Terms," *New York Times*, June 20, 1989.

WOMEN IN SPORTS, DISCRIMINATION, AND TITLE IX

INTRODUCTION

American women have faced many historical challenges. Like many minorities, women have been subjected to discrimination, but not because of their race, color, or national origin, but solely because of their gender. This discriminatory attitude toward women has permeated virtually every aspect of American society, from business to politics to the sports world. However, in the past few decades, women have seen many changes in the roles they play in society. Women have held a variety of leadership positions in all aspects of society and have become major political figures,[1] leading business executives, attorneys, and educators. In the sports world, women have become announcers, participants, sports lawyers, team executives, and sports agents. Notwithstanding the substantial progress that has been made, women executives in sports still face many hurdles and a glass ceiling still exists at certain levels of sport.[2] For example, as of January 2008, only about 11% of vice president positions or higher at the 122 professional sports franchises were filled by women.[3]

Fortunately, the role of women in sports has increased in recent years. Girls are participating more than ever in sports at the amateur levels, and colleges and universities are promoting women's sports at an increasing rate. In 1972, only 1 in 27 girls in secondary schools participated in sports or about 300,000 girls. In 2008, almost 3 million girls participated in high school athletics, or about 1 in 3. Nonetheless, women today continue to face many obstacles and barriers in the sports field. Many times

---

[1] Nancy Pelosi, the highest ranking woman in the history of the U.S. government has stated: "I didn't run as a woman . . . I presented my credentials as an experienced legislator, skilled organizer, astute politician. I didn't want anyone to vote for me or against me because I was a woman. But the fact that I am a woman is a giant bonus." "Pelosi said her political ascent is meaningful because it had been difficult for women to rise in power in the U.S. Congress." Ellen Guettler, The 108th Congress: Crisis and Conflict, Representative Nancy Pelosi (D-Calif.), *Online NewsHour*, www.pbs.org.

[2] Hannah Clark, "Are Women Happy Under the Glass Ceiling?," *Forbes.com*, March 8, 2006; AJ Porter, "Women Cracking the Glass Ceiling in Sports . . . ," *Bleacher Report*, March 7, 2009; "Larry Blustein, Northwestern Football Makes History!," *The Miami Herald*, September 24, 2010.

[3] See Shira Springer, "Facing a Power Shortage, Women Executives Still Struggling to Reach Top with Sports Teams," *Boston Globe*, January 18, 2008.

women and girls are still subject to physical and emotional abuse, sexual harassment, and discrimination, whether as a team executive, sports professional, or tragically, even as Little League participants.

Prior to the 1970s, women had very few opportunities to participate in athletics, and there were virtually no opportunities for women in the coaching or administrative ranks of sport. Historically, several arguments were offered in support of the spurious theory that women were not suited for or capable of successfully competing athletically with or against men. Women were falsely stereotyped as being too delicate, frail, or weak to participate in sports. Because of this traditional, but obviously misguided perspective, females of all ages have historically been denied athletic opportunities. In 1972 virtually no colleges offered women's sports scholarships, and women's participation in sports was restricted many times to being a mere bystander.

It has also been asserted that men consistently outperform women and that they are physiologically superior to women. Although it is true that the anatomical composition of males and females is quite different, studies have shown that each has advantages and disadvantages.[4] One study, in particular, described the differences between the sexes in relation to athletics and concluded that due to the structure of the male body, a man has an advantage over a woman in throwing, striking, and physically explosive types of events, whereas the female, due to her body proportions, enjoys advantages in balance, stability, and flexibility. It is undisputed that women can participate in competitive sports at the highest levels.

Some have argued that the separation of the sexes is necessary to prevent physical and psychological injury to girls and women. Unfortunately, this outdated argument perpetuates the stereotype of the "weak woman" who is unable to cope with the competitive nature associated with athletics.[5] Furthermore, it has been argued that "tradition" in sports requires separate teams.[6] Finally, many, unfortunately, have paid homage to the stereotype that girls should not be involved in sports in any manner on a competitive level with boys. Schools have not historically allocated an equal amount of funding for female athletic programs and have discriminated against girls by providing better schedules, better fields, and better equipment for boys. Boys also traditionally have been given a wider selection of sports to play than girls.

Nonetheless, in the past two decades the number of women participating in sports programs and the amount of money expended in support of women's athletics have increased dramatically. Furthermore, women's professional sports leagues have become very popular. There are several reasons for this development in athletics for women, one of which is the changing societal attitude toward women in general. This has included women's own perceptions about their athletic capabilities and participation. One helpful hand has come from the National Collegiate Athletic Association (NCAA), which is committed to providing equal athletic opportunities without regard to gender, and they have been true to this goal over a long period of time.

---

[4] See M. Barnekow-Bergkvist, G. Hedberg, U. Janlert, E. Jansson, "Physical Activity Patterns in Men and Women at the Ages of 16 and 34 and Development of Physical Activity from Adolescence to Adulthood," *Scandinavian Journal of Medicine & Science in Sports*, Vol. 6, Issue 6, pp. 359–370, December 1996.

[5] Jennifer L. Knight and Traci A. Giulano, "He's a Laker; She's a 'Looker': The Consequences of Gender-Stereotypical Portrayals of Male and Female Athletes by the Printed Media," *Behavioral Science, Sex Roles*, Volume 45, Number 3–4, 217–229.

[6] See generally, www.womenssportsfoundation.org.

There has been a growing interest in female sports by spectators and fans at both the professional and amateur levels.[7] Local and national media coverage of female athletic events has also greatly increased. The women's NCAA "Final Four" in basketball is very popular as is the "Frozen Four" in women's hockey.[8] Media coverage for the women's NCAA Final Four in basketball has increased greatly. The number of media credentials issued for the women's NCAA Final Four in 1982 was only 37. That number grew to 557 for the women's NCAA Final Four in St. Louis in 2009.[9]

Although girls in amateur sports have achieved some great success, many have been treated like "second class" citizens during their athletic careers. Progress has been made in recent years, and increased funding for women's athletics at the high school and collegiate levels has expanded athletic opportunities for women and girls. All these issues are encouraging and indicate a positive movement toward more female involvement in sports at all levels. Still, some significant considerations need to be addressed. As women reach more competitive levels, they will begin to face the same pressures to succeed that men face and will experience the same pressures to prevail in the competitive world of sports.[10]

CASE STUDY 10-1   *Erin Andrews and an Invasion of Privacy*

Erin Andrews is an excellent sports reporter. She had worked her way up the ranks of sports reporting, achieving great success after leaving the University of Florida. Unfortunately, Andrews was the target of a criminal who surreptitiously shot a video of her walking through her hotel room naked. The video spread like wildfire on the Internet. Legal counsel for Andrews and ESPN moved quickly to have the video removed and to have this individual prosecuted. Andrews later appeared on the *Oprah Winfrey Show*, saying it would be her first and last interview about the subject. She described the situation as "a nightmare" and believed that her career as a sportscaster would end. Andrews said she was devastated by the invasion of her privacy. She was told by law enforcement agencies that she was going to have to deal with the issue because there was virtually no way to remove the pictures from the Internet.[11] She is still a very successful sports reporter.

The Ethics of Eligibility and Athletic Opportunities for Women

Erin Israel was a fierce baseball player and a Little League All-Star. Her high school in West Virginia had a girls' softball team, but Erin wanted to play baseball. If her school maintained a separate girls' team in the same or a related sport, the rules said that a girl could not play on the boys' team. The question presented was whether baseball and softball were "substantial equivalents."

---

[7] Reed Albergoti, "The Dunk That Made History," *Wall Street Journal*, March 20, 2007.

[8] Harvey Araton, "The Top 10 Reasons to Cover the Women's Final Four," *New York Times*, April 6, 2008.

[9] See, NCAA.org.

[10] Mary Lou Sheffer and Brad Schultz, "Double Standard: Why Women Have Trouble Getting Jobs in Local Television Sports," *Journal of Sports Media*, Volume 2, 2007, pp. 77–101.

[11] Jerry Crowe, "Erin Andrews Video Controversy is a Low Point," *Chicago Tribune*, July 23, 2009; Viv Bernstein, "Erin Andrews and the Ugliness of Judging Beauty," *Fox News*, July 22, 2009; Michael Hiestand, "YouTube Clips Can't Tell Story of Erin Andrews," *USA Today*, April 15, 2008.

📖 CASE 10-1   *Israel v. West Virginia Secondary Schools Activities Commission*

388 S.E.2d 480 (1989)

Ms. Israel has a great deal of experience playing baseball. She began playing baseball at the age of six in the local park and recreation league where she learned the basic fundamentals of the game. At the age of nine, Ms. Israel progressed into the Little League system. Her Little League coach testified that Ms. Israel's skills were always above average. He stated that "[s]he was very aggressive, understood the game, its concepts, and its technique." While playing Little League, Ms. Israel was nominated for every all-star team. At the age of thirteen, she became the first female to ever play on a Pony League team in Pleasants County. When Ms. Israel was a freshman at St. Marys High School, and expressed a desire to play on the all-male baseball team, the high school baseball coach told her he had no objections to her playing for him and promised to give her a fair tryout. In February, 1984, Ms. Israel tried out for the all-male high school baseball team. She was prohibited from playing on the team because of a regulation promulgated by the Secondary Schools Activities Commission (SSAC).

Rule No. 3.9, which provides:

"If a school maintains separate teams in the same or related sports (example: baseball or softball) for girls and boys during the school year, regardless of the sports season, girls may not participate on boys' teams and boys may not participate on girls' teams. However, should a school not maintain separate teams in the same or related sports for boys and girls, then boys and girls may participate on the same team except in contact sports such as football and wrestling."

Shortly after Ms. Israel tried out to play on the baseball team, she was informed by St. Marys' assistant principal that she was ineligible to play on the baseball team because St. Marys had a girls' softball team. The assistant principal explained that if the school allowed Ms. Israel to play baseball, it would be in violation of Rule 3.9 and would be barred from playing in state tournaments. After numerous futile efforts to have the rule changed through the internal mechanisms provided by the SSAC, Ms. Israel filed a complaint with the Human Rights Commission.

From the record in this case, we find that the games of baseball and softball are not substantially equivalent. There is, of course, a superficial similarity between the games because both utilize a similar format. However, when the rules are analyzed, there is a substantial disparity in the equipment used and in the skill level required.

The difference begins with the size of the ball and its delivery, and differences continue throughout. The softball is larger and must be thrown underhanded, which forecloses the different types of pitching that can be accomplished in the overhand throw of a baseball.

Source: *Reprinted from Westlaw with permission of Thomson Reuters.*

1. Should Ms. Israel be allowed to play on the boys' team?
2. Do you agree with Rule 3.9?
3. Do you consider any rule that discriminates based on gender as opposed to skill unethical?

GENDER DISCRIMINATION AND ABUSE AGAINST WOMEN IN SPORTS

Gender Discrimination

Discrimination against women and girls has historically taken many forms. Gender discrimination is both unethical and illegal and can be remedied through the court system to attempt to prevent future discriminatory behavior. Historically, girls' sports team have typically suffered inequalities in the following areas and more at all levels of sports:

- Publicity for sports teams or individual athletes
- Medical services provided to the team or athlete (trainers, etc.)
- Travel expenses
- Scheduling
- Operating expenses and funds for athletic competition
- Recruiting budgets
- Provision of equipment and facilities
- Number of coaches
- Payment to coaches
- Access to facilities and quality of facilities

The general rule in both contact and non-contact sports is that when only one team is available, both sexes must be allowed to try out for and play on the team. In the majority of cases involving non-contact sports in which no women's team is available, the trend is to allow women to participate on the men's team. If there is ample opportunity for women to compete on their own, courts appear less apt to allow women to compete with men in contact sports. The HEW regulations under Title IX permit an athletic department that receives federal funds to maintain separate teams for each sex if selection for the teams is based on competitive skill or if the sport involved is a contact sport. The competitive skill exception applies to most programs because athletics, by their very nature, are based on individual skill. Therefore, separate teams are permissible for most sports. If no team is sponsored for one gender in a particular sport and the excluded gender has had a history of limited opportunities in that sport, the excluded sex must be permitted to try out for that team.

Under Title IX, contact sports include boxing, wrestling, rugby, ice hockey, football, basketball, and other sports in which the purpose or major activity involves bodily contact. In some cases, baseball and soccer have also been determined to be contact sports.

Women and girls have had to overcome many obstacles in their quest to achieve equality in the sporting world at all levels. In the following case the issue was whether a woman could play on a college football team. Why not? Many women have done it and have been successful at it.[12] In the following case, placekicker Heather Sue Mercer was "kicked off" the Duke University football team. She then sued the university based on discrimination for their actions.

📖 CASE 10-2 *Mercer v. Duke University*

190 F.3d 643 (1999)

. . . Duke University operates a Division I college football team. During the period . . . (1994-98), . . . Fred Goldsmith was head coach of the Duke Football team and . . . Heather Sue Mercer was a student at the school.

Before attending Duke, Mercer was an all-state kicker at Yorktown Heights High School in Yorktown Heights, New York. Upon enrolling at Duke in the fall of 1994, Mercer tried out for the Duke football team as a walk-on kicker. Mercer was the first—and to date, only—woman to try out for the team. Mercer did not initially make the team, and instead served as a manager during the 1994 season; however, she regularly attended practices in the fall of 1994 and participated in conditioning drills the following spring.

In April 1995, the seniors on the team selected Mercer to participate in the Blue-White Game, an intrasquad scrimmage played each spring. In that game, Mercer kicked the winning 28-yard field goal, giving the Blue team a 24-22 victory. The kick was subsequently shown on ESPN, the cable television sports network. Soon after the game, Goldsmith told the news media that Mercer was on the Duke football team, and Fred Chatham, the Duke kicking coach, told Mercer herself that she had made the team. Also, Mike Cragg, the Duke sports information director, asked Mercer to participate in a number of interviews with newspaper, radio, and television reporters, including one with representatives from "The Tonight Show."

Although Mercer did not play in any games during the 1995 season, she again regularly attended practices in the fall and participated in conditioning drills the following spring. Mercer was also officially listed by Duke as a member of the Duke football team on the team roster filed with the NCAA and was pictured in the Duke football yearbook.

During this latter period, Mercer alleges that she was the subject of discriminatory treatment by Duke. Specifically, she claims that

---

[12] Katie Hnida, *Still Kicking: My Dramatic Journey as the First Woman to Play Division One College Football* (New York: Scribner, 2006).

Goldsmith did not permit her to attend summer camp, refused to allow her to dress for games or sit on the sidelines during games, and gave her fewer opportunities to participate in practices than other walk-on kickers. In addition, Mercer claims that Goldsmith made a number of offensive comments to her, including asking her why she was interested in football, wondering why she did not prefer to participate in beauty pageants rather than football, and suggesting that she sit in the stands with her boyfriend rather than on the sidelines.

At the beginning of the 1996 season, Goldsmith informed Mercer that he was dropping her from the team. Mercer alleges that Goldsmith's decision to exclude her from the team was on the basis of her sex because Goldsmith allowed other, less qualified walk-on kickers to remain on the team. Mercer attempted to participate in conditioning drills the following spring, but Goldsmith asked her to leave because the drills were only for members of the team. Goldsmith told Mercer, however, that she could try out for the team again in the fall.

On September 16, 1997, rather than try out for the team again, Mercer filed suit against Duke and Goldsmith, alleging sex discrimination.

Source: *Reprinted from Westlaw with permission of Thomson Reuters.*

1. Were coach Goldsmith's actions unethical or merely boorish?
2. Describe coach Goldsmith's ethical decision-making process.
3. What actions should Duke University have taken against coach Goldsmith, if any?

Why are there not any Major League Baseball women umpires? If women are able to perform the tasks of an umpire and are good enough to compete, shouldn't Major League Baseball allow them on the field as an umpire? Unbeknownst to many, baseball has a history of women umpires. The Baseball Hall of Fame recognizes Amanda Clement as the first women to umpire a baseball game. She umpired for six years at the semi-pro level, umpiring her first game in 1904 when she was only 16 years old. Clement was 5ft 10in. and worked her way through Yankton College and The University of Nebraska earning $15 to $25 for umpiring games.[13] Her solid reputation as an umpire spread, and she became a huge gate attraction. It was reported she received more than 60 marriage offers from players, but never married. Clement was regarded as an umpire who was fair and who knew the rules and she was also multi-talented. She later worked as a justice of the peace, a newspaper reporter, a social worker, and taught at the University of Wyoming.

No woman has yet made it as an umpire in the major leagues. Although many have tried, Pam Postema gave it her best shot. She encountered a glass ceiling and had to fight it out in court with MLB. They eventually settled the case with her on a confidential basis.

---

[13] Sharon L. Roan, "No One Yelled 'Kill The Ump' When Amanda Clement was a Man in Blue," *Sports Illustrated*, April 5, 1982.

📖 **CASE 10-3** *Postema v. National League of Professional Baseball Clubs (MLB)*

---

799 F.Supp. 1475 (S.D. New York 1992)

Pamela Postema, a California resident, is a former professional baseball umpire.

After graduating from umpiring school with the rank of 17th in a class of 130 students, [Postema] began work in 1977 as a professional baseball umpire in the Gulf Coast League, a rookie league. At that time, she was the fourth woman ever to umpire a professional baseball game. [Postema] worked in the Gulf Coast League during 1977 and 1978. In 1979, she was promoted to the Class A Florida State League, where she umpired during the 1979 and 1980 seasons. In 1981, [Postema] was promoted to the AA Texas League, and she umpired there in 1981 and 1982. She was the first woman to ever umpire a professional baseball game above the Class A level.

In 1983, [Postema] was promoted to the AAA Pacific Coast League, where she umpired from 1983 to 1986. In 1987, her contract was acquired by Triple-A, and she umpired in that league from 1987 until her discharge in 1989.

[Postema] alleges that during her employment as a Triple-A umpire, [MLB] conferred on her significant duties and responsibilities, including the following:

- In 1987, [Postema] was the home plate umpire for the Hall of Fame exhibition game between the New York Yankees and the Atlanta Braves.
- In 1988, [Postema] was selected to umpire the Venezuela All Star game.
- In 1988 and 1989, [Postema] was the chief of her umpiring crew, with ultimate responsibility for its umpiring calls and performance.
- In 1988 and 1989, [Postema] was appointed to umpire Major League spring training games.
- In 1989, [Postema] was the home plate umpire for the first Triple-A Minor League All Star Game.
- In 1989, [Postema] was asked by Triple-A to become a supervisor for umpires in the minor league system.
- From 1987 to 1989, [Postema] received high praise from qualified and experienced baseball people, including Chuck Tanner, Tom Trebelhorn, Hal Lanier, and Roger Craig, all current or former managers of Major League teams.

Notwithstanding these responsibilities and honors, [Postema] alleges that throughout her career as a minor league umpire she was subjected to continual, repeated, and offensive acts of sexual harassment and gender discrimination. Such acts included the following:

- On numerous occasions, players and managers addressed her with a four-letter word beginning with the letter "c" that refers to female genitalia.
- Players and managers repeatedly told [Postema] that her proper role was cooking, cleaning, keeping house, or some other form of "women's work," rather than umpiring.
- Bob Knepper, a pitcher with the Houston Astros, told the press that although [Postema] was a good umpire, to have her as a major league umpire would be an affront to God and contrary to the teachings of the Bible.
- During arguments with players and managers, [Postema] was spat upon and was subjected to verbal and physical abuse to a greater degree than male umpires.
- In 1987, the manager of the Nashville Hounds kissed [Postema] on the lips when he handed her his lineup card.
- At a Major League spring training game in 1988, Chuck Tanner, then the manager of the Pittsburgh Pirates, asked [Postema] if she would like a kiss when he gave her his lineup card.
- Although [Postema] was well known throughout baseball as an excellent ball and strike umpire, she was directed and required by Ed Vargo, the Supervisor of Umpiring for the National League, to change her stance and technique to resemble those used by him during his career. No such requirement was placed on male umpires.

[Postema] continually took action against such conduct through warnings, ejections, and reports. Although the existence of such conduct was well known throughout baseball, no one in a position of authority, including [MLB], took action to correct, stop, or prevent such conduct.

[Postema] alleges that at the time she began her service with Triple-A, she was fully qualified to be a Major League umpire, and she had repeatedly made known to [MLB] her desire for employment in the Major Leagues. While she was not promoted to or hired by the National League or American League, male umpires having inferior experience, qualifications, and abilities were repeatedly and frequently promoted and hired by the National and American Leagues.

[Postema] alleges that in 1988 and 1989, "events came to a head" in her effort to become a Major League umpire. Specifically, in July 1987, Dick Butler, then Special Assistant to the President of the American League and the former supervisor of umpires for the American League, told *Newsday* that for [Postema] to become a Major League umpire:

"She realizes that she has to be better than the fellow next to her. She's got to be better because of the fact that she's a girl. I'm not saying it's fair, but it exists and she's not going to change it."

These comments were widely reported in the media, including in the *Los Angeles Times*. [MLB] neither issued any statements contradicting, retracting, or correcting Butler's statements, took any remedial or disciplinary action with respect to Butler, nor otherwise said or did anything to communicate that Butler had not stated the true position of professional baseball. . .

On May 14, 1989, Larry Napp, Assistant Supervisor of Umpires for the American League, told the *Richmond Times-Dispatch* that [Postema] would never become a Major League umpire. He stated:

"She's a nice person, and she knows the rules. But the thing is, she's got to do the job twice as good as the guy. . .

[MLB] neither issued any statements contradicting, retracting, or correcting Napp's statements, took any remedial or disciplinary action with respect to Napp, nor otherwise said or did anything to communicate that Napp had not stated the true position of professional baseball. . .

During the 1989 season, Ed Vargo required [Postema] to adopt the above mentioned changes in her umpiring technique.

[Postema] alleges that during the 1989 season, [MLB] either ignored or criticized her. She and her partner were the only two of the nine minor league umpires invited to 1989 spring training who were not given the opportunity to fill in for ill or vacationing Major League umpires, an opportunity which was given to male umpires with inferior abilities, experience, and qualifications. At the end of the 1989 season, [Postema] received an unfairly negative written performance evaluation which alleged that she had a "bad attitude." Prior to 1989, [Postema] had never received a written performance evaluation.

On November 6, 1989, Triple-A discharged and unconditionally released [Postema] from her employment as an umpire. The reason for [Postema's] discharge was that the National League and American League were not interested in considering her for employment as a Major League umpire. [Postema] alleges that the sole reason for her discharge, for her inability to obtain a job in the Major Leagues [is] intentional discrimination on the basis of gender [by MLB].

Source: *Reprinted from Westlaw with permission of Thomson Reuters.*

1. Do you believe Postema was discriminated against in Case 10-3?
2. Would training women at the high school levels to become umpires assist in creating more of an interest in the umpire position for women?
3. Is MLB doing enough to encourage women to become umpires? If not, what more could be done?

CASE STUDY 10-2   *Sarah Thomas—NCAA Referee*

NCAA Division I football has an outstanding woman referee. Sarah Thomas is a major college football referee. She commented on her position, "Most of the time they are so focused on what they are doing, they don't notice me . . . and that is what every other official strives for. Our best games are the ones that no one knows we're there." She has also worked the New Orleans Saints training camp, and her name comes up often as a candidate for an NFL job.[14]

Discrimination against women has historically permeated every aspect of the sports business and exists in the coaching ranks as well. There have been many successful women coaches, but historically most sports programs have been controlled and administrated by men. Women have been underrepresented at the highest levels of power in sports. Many reasons have been given for this, including that men have well-established connections to assist them in job searches, that professional development opportunities are minimal for women, and that many sports organizations are insensitive to the family responsibilities of coaches and administrators. Furthermore, most of the hiring at the highest levels of education is done by men and many times men are hesitant to hire a woman in a position such as athletic director or coach for a variety of reasons. This has led to discrimination against women in the coaching ranks. In Case 10-4 a woman basketball coach claims she was discriminated against.

CASE 10-4   *Bowers v. Baylor University*

862 F.Supp. 142 (W.D. Texas 1994)

Pam Bowers ("Bowers"), was hired by Baylor University ("Baylor") to coach its women's basketball team in 1979. In 1989, Bowers began to complain about the disparate allocation of resources in the men's and women's basketball programs, including but not limited to the disparate terms and conditions of her employment versus the terms and conditions of employment by and between Baylor and the men's basketball coach. Her first contact with the Office of Civil Rights of the Department of Education was in March of 1989, and Baylor was aware of [Bowers] complaints at or about the same time.

Bowers' employment was initially terminated by Baylor in 1993. Bowers alleges that the termination was premised on alleged violations of NCAA and Southwest Conference rules, and that her win-loss record was not even mentioned. After her termination, Bowers filed a complaint with the Office of Civil Rights and the Equal Employment Opportunity Commission. Immediately after filing the complaint, Bowers was notified that she would be reinstated (1) on the same terms under which she had been employed the previous 14 years, or (2) on a two-year written contract. Bowers alleges that she was forced to accept the

---

[14] Joe Drape, "Earning Her Stripes in College Football," *New York Times*, September 19, 2009.

```
first offer because the terms of the written contract were vague and
ambiguous and Baylor refused to discuss them.
```

```
Despite her reinstatement, Bowers continued to pursue her employment
complaints with the federal agencies. In an employment evaluation of
August 30, 1993, Bowers' win-loss record was mentioned, and she was
informed that she needed to achieve a winning season. On or about
March 28, 1994, Bowers was notified in writing that her employment
would be terminated as of May 31, 1994, because of her unsuccessful
win-loss record throughout her employment at Baylor.
```

Source: *Reprinted from Westlaw with permission of Thomson Reuters.*

1. Do you believe Bowers was discriminated against?
2. What other information would you need to make this determination?

Sexual Harassment of Women in Sports

Sexual harassment consists of unwelcomed sexual advances, requests for sexual favors, and other physical and verbal conduct.[15] Sexual harassment is prevalent throughout society and in the workplace.[16] It is a violation of the law and in some cases can be criminally prosecuted. Unfortunately, it is present in the sports world as well. There is little doubt that sexual harassment in sports deters girls and women from participating and developing as athletes. The development of sexual harassment policies by organizations will help to deter sexual harassment.[17] SMPs should take a leadership role in establishing policies that clearly indicate sexual harassment will not be tolerated in any manner, under any circumstances in the workplace.

It is clear that consensual sex or a romantic relationship between a coach and a student-athlete compromises the professional integrity of the coach and harms the student-athlete. It can result in termination of employment for the coach and may subject the coach and the university to penalties from an athletic association or other governing body. It could also lead to legal action against the university, high school, or coach.[18] Coaches are in the position of authority over student-athletes, including making recommendations that further an athlete's goals. Opportunities for a coach to abuse his or her power and sexually exploit an athlete are inherent in this relationship. Many times "voluntary consent" by the athlete is at best suspect and calls the coach's moral judgment into question. These types of relationships also create unworkable conflict of interest situations.

Legal and administrative remedies are available to those who have been harassed, and a coach may be subject to criminal charges depending on the age of the athlete.[19] Sexual harassment has severe consequences for its victims and for the sports organization. It lowers the self-esteem of girls and women and impairs the functioning capacity of its victims to experience full athletic participation. Sexual harassment destroys the atmosphere of mutual respect and trust between a coach and the

---

[15] See generally, www.eeoc.gov.

[16] Steve Stecklow, "Sexual-Harassment Cases Plague U.N.," *Washington Street Journal*, May 21, 2009.

[17] Ben Worthen and Pui-Wing Tam, "H-P Chief Quits in Scandal," *Washington Street Journal*, August 7, 2010.

[18] Doug Lederman, "North Carolina and Coach Settle Sexual Harassment Suit," *Inside Higher Ed*, January 15, 2008.

[19] Geoff Liesik, "Former Coach Gets Prison for Sex With Student," *Deseret News*, October 1, 2009.

athlete and may make girls and women reluctant to accept employment or a leadership role in sports. Administrators responsible for the oversight of coaches and athletic programs should take such charges seriously and educate and address all issues of sexual harassment that may occur in the sports organization. Examples of sexual harassment include the following:

- A coach who sexually intimidates an athlete. For example, when a coach unnecessarily and continually holds an athlete in the process of explaining a correct technique.
- An athlete's selection on a team becomes dependent on compliance with an implied sexual proposition.
- A team whose acceptance or initiation rituals require that the athlete perform demeaning physical acts of a sexual nature.
- A coach who requests or requires sexual favors as a way of influencing decision making.
- An employer who demands sexual favors from an employee in the course of employment during normal working hours or at work-related activities such as training courses, conferences, field trips, work functions, and office parties.

In Case 10-5, a woman employee sued, saying she was sexually harassed by members of the Detroit Tigers baseball team while on the club's private jet.

CASE 10-5 *Kesner v. Little Caesars Enterprises, Inc.*

2002 WL 1480800 (2002)

[Kesner] alleges that she was harassed by members of the Detroit Tigers. [Kesner] alleges that the harassment started on her first flight with the Tigers in April 2000, when a group of players were looking at pornographic material on one of the player's laptop computer. She alleges that the computer was positioned in a way that allowed [Kesner], as well as at least one other flight attendant, Jenifer Campbell, to witness it. [Kesner] alleges that the harassment was thereafter continued. For instance, she alleges that some of the players repeatedly called her pejorative and profane names, such as "bitch," "cunt," and "hide." She alleges that some players would make comments with sexual innuendos. For example, [Kesner] alleges that when she would ask players if they wanted a dessert, players would occasionally reply by asking whether she had any "cooter pie" or "hair pie." Or else, she alleges that two players, Doug Brocail and Gregg Jefferies, asked her whether she would give her husband a "blowjob in a van?" [Kesner] also alleges that some of the players would touch or rub against her breasts and buttocks in a manner that she thought was inappropriate, and that made her uncomfortable.

[Kesner] alleges that the harassment from the players culminated in July 2000. Before the airplane took off, [Kesner] alleges that she noticed a player, Jeff Weaver, walk out of the lavatory. She saw a smoke cloud and smelled burnt marijuana following him out of the lavatory, and saw ashes inside the lavatory. [Kesner] alleges that she approached Weaver and Matt Anderson, who were sitting next to each other, and told them that smoking marijuana was not permitted on the flight. She alleges that Anderson responded by barking profanities at her, and calling her a "stupid bitch." Later that flight, she alleges that another player, Bobby Higginson, confronted and chastised her for reporting the marijuana smoking. A third player, Brad Ausmus, also confronted [Kesner], and allegedly called her a "dumb bitch" for reporting the marijuana smoking incident. [Kesner] alleges that she was treated this way by the players because of her gender, and that she had never seen the players treat her male counterparts on the flight crew in the same manner.

[Kesner's] complaints extend beyond the treatment she received from the players; she alleges that she was mistreated by other members of the flight crew as well. [Kesner] alleges that two pilots, Al Long and Pat White, repeatedly touched her in a manner that she thought was "inappropriate," including repeatedly touching her breasts with their hands, and that a third pilot, Rob Mintari, touched her buttocks with his hands on three separate occasions.

[Kesner] had many difficulties with Mintari, who was the chief pilot. [Kesner] alleges that Mintari personally disliked [Kesner], and stated that he would fire her if he had the chance.

Source: *Reprinted from Westlaw with permission of Thomson Reuters.*

What actions should the club take against its players for their highly inappropriate and illegal conduct?

Abuse and Violence Against Women in Sports

Abuse in any form harms and prevents women and girls from participating and developing as athletes and as individuals. Cases of extreme abuse can psychologically damage girls and women athletes and keep them from ever participating. Organizations that set policies dealing with abuse against women in sports are likely to decrease the frequency of such abuse. Coaches are in a position of authority over women athletes in interscholastic athletics and can affect their performance. They hold a position of power over the student-athlete. If this power is abused, it can lead to the abuse of the woman athlete. A variety of different kinds of abuses can occur in sports against girls and women. Abuse can appear as sexual harassment, mental or physical abuse, emotional abuse, unreasonable confinement or excessive punishment. Sports organizations and bodies should formulate and enforce policies dealing with all types of abuse. Issues dealing with abuse of women athletes also apply to athletic trainers, school administrators, sports officials, and sports information personnel.

The most common types of verbal abuses are name calling, making disparaging comments about a player's performance, swearing at players or officials, or making any comments that demean or devalue a woman athlete. Emotional abuse can be as simple as having unrealistic expectations for a woman or girl athlete, keeping women athletes from playing in games because of assumed limits or underdeveloped skills, or issuing threats against players. Physical abuse occurs when a coach or other individual touches a player in a way that causes physical pain. It can include excessive exercise, denial of fluids, or using unreasonable requests as a form of punishment. "Bullying" can take many forms and can be verbal, physical, or psychological.[20] Hazing is another kind of abuse and can take a variety of forms against women.[21]

Any abuse whatsoever by a coach demeans and devalues the woman athlete and should not be tolerated. Abuse has dire consequences for both the coach and the victim. Examples of abuse can include the following:

- A coach putting the success of a team on the shoulders of one "superstar."
- Slapping, grabbing, spitting, shoving, hitting, or throwing equipment.
- A coach demanding that players run around the track until they vomit or pass out.
- "Punishment type" practices for losing games after playing poorly.
- Instances in which coaches or other players know about or are participants in any harmful or degrading initiation rituals involving new players. Examples of these rituals include running through a line of players who assault the player, performing lewd acts, being forced to drink excessive amounts of alcohol, or any act that demeans or devalues a player.
- Referring to a woman athlete's body parts. This can also constitute sexual harassment.
- Comparing women's teams to the men's teams and insinuating that the men's teams are better or have more skill.
- Using derogatory terms for women athletes such as "chicks," "hotties," "sweetie," "babes," "bitches," or any other term which demeans or diminishes a female athlete.
- Violating the privacy rights of women athletes.

A coach can play an important role in the development of young athletes and especially young women athletes. A coach must be trustworthy. Most coaches work hard to develop young athletes' self-worth, confidence, and athletic ability. However, a few individuals abuse their position of power and look for a chance to take sexual advantage of women or girl athletes. Criminal penalties are in place for sexual abuse of women athletes. A civil lawsuit can also be brought against a coach or a school for damages in cases of sexual abuse.

Sexual abuse falls into two categories:

Noncontact: "Flashing or exposing sexual body parts to a young athlete, watching intrusively as a young athlete changes or showers, speaking or communicating sexually/seductively with a young athlete, showing pornographic films, magazines or photographs to young athletes; having young athletes participate in the creation of pornographic materials, forcing a young athlete to watch a sexual act performed by others; objectifying or ridiculing a young athlete's body parts."

Contact: "Kissing or holding a young athlete in a sexual manner; touching a young athlete's sexual body parts or forcing a young athlete to touch another person's sexual parts; penetrating a young athlete anally or vaginally with objects or fingers; having vaginal, anal or oral intercourse with a young athlete."[22]

---

[20] Kayan Brown, "Crunch Time: Confronting Coaching Bullying," *Women's Sports Foundation*, August 13, 2008.
[21] Elizabeth J. Allan, Ph.D., "Transforming Hazing Cultures," www.mpr.org, Spring 2004.
[22] See "Coach Notes: Preventing Sexual Abuse of Children in Sport, Making It Safer," www.mhp.gov.on.ca.

In Case 10-6, a coach was criminally charged for sexual harassment and for engaging in sexual intercourse with a female athlete.

📖 CASE 10-6 *State of Montana v. Thompson*

243 Mont. 28, 792 P.2d 1103 (1990)

On May 25, 1989, Gerald Roy Thompson was charged with two counts of sexual intercourse without consent and one count of sexual assault.

Gerald Roy Thompson, the principal and boys basketball coach at Hobson High School, was accused of two counts of sexual intercourse without consent, and one count of sexual assault.

Count I

On or between September, 1986 and January, 1987 in Judith Basin County, Montana, [Thompson] knowingly had sexual intercourse without consent with a person of the opposite sex; namely Jane Doe, by threatening Jane Doe that she would not graduate from high school and forced Jane Doe to engage in an act of oral sexual intercourse.

Count II

On or between February, 1987 and June, 1987 in Judith Basin County, Montana, [Thompson] knowingly had sexual intercourse without consent with a person of the opposite sex; namely Jane Doe, by threatening Jane Doe that she would not graduate from high school and forced Jane Doe to engage in an act of oral sexual intercourse.

The affidavits filed in support . . . contained facts and allegations supporting the two counts of sexual intercourse without consent. In essence, they alleged that the threats "caused Jane Doe great psychological pain and fear."

The State contended that fear of the power of Thompson and his authority to keep her from graduating forced Jane Doe into silence until after she graduated from high school in June of 1987. On November 25, 1988, Jane Doe filed a letter with the Hobson School Board describing the activities against her by Thompson. After investigations by both the school board and the Judith Basin County prosecutor's office, the prosecutor filed an information on May 25, 1989. The information charged Thompson with two counts of sexual intercourse without consent, both felonies, and with one count of attempted sexual assault, a felony.

The State in its information and accompanying affidavit complain that Thompson deprived Jane Doe of consent to the sexual act by threatening that he would prevent her from graduating from high school. The threat required, is "a threat of imminent death, bodily injury, or kidnapping to be inflicted on anyone. . . ." A threat one will not graduate from high school is not one of the threats listed. . . . The State argues that the definition "threat of bodily injury" includes psychological impairment. Unfortunately, the statute sets forth bodily injury, not psychological impairment. A threat that eventually leads to psychological impairment is not sufficient. The statute only addresses the results of three specific kinds of threats, and psychological impairment is not one of them.

Source: *Reprinted from Westlaw with permission of Thomson Reuters.*

CASE STUDY 10-3   *Erin Andrews 2*

While ESPN reporter Erin Andrews was reporting a game on the sidelines for ESPN, USC linebacker Rey Maualuga came up behind Andrews and made highly inappropriate gestures and body movements toward her, then walked away. He later apologized to her for his behavior. USC suspended him from the team for a short period of time. The *Los Angeles Times* thought the video of the incident was so inappropriate that it posted the following message on its web site: "This post previously contained a video showing the USC linebacker and ESPN sideline reporter Erin Andrews. A reference in the post described his actions on the Rose Bowl sideline as 'dancing' with Andrews. Maualuga later apologized to Andrews. The video has since been removed once it was deemed inappropriate based on *Times* standards and practices, and should not have been posted."[23]

1. What can be done to stop this type of offensive and unethical behavior in the future by athletes?

CASE 10-7   *Special Olympics Florida, Inc. v. Showalter*

6 So.3d 662, (2009)

The central question in this case is whether [The Special Olympics] may be found liable for the acts of one of its volunteers who molested . . . two developmentally disabled adults, in a bowling center parking lot.

[The Special Olympics] is a nonprofit organization that "[p]rovide[s] sports training and competition for persons with . . . disabilities, [and] ongoing opportunities to participate with their families and the community." All of [Special Olympics]'s activities are run by county coordinators, who are volunteers, as are the coaches and others who assist in operating the programs. [Special Olympics] has approximately 34 paid staff members throughout Florida and as many as 17,000 volunteers. Margaret Showalter and Nancy Vasil, are both developmentally

---

[23] Adam Rose, "All Things Trojan: Rey Maualuga Dances with Erin Andrews," *Los Angeles Times*, January 3, 2009.

disabled adults who participate as athletes in [Special Olympics]'s events. Ms. Showalter is apparently somewhat self-reliant, although a social worker resides with her. Ms. Vasil lives with her father, who is her guardian.

One of [Special Olympics]'s organized activities, in which [Showalter and Vasil] participate, is an annual bowling competition. The athletes practice between August and November each year and then participate in county, regional, and state competitions. [Special Olympics] arranged with Colonial Lanes, a public bowling center in Orange County, to conduct much of its bowling activity there. Practices were scheduled to begin every Saturday at 1:30 p.m. and the athletes were instructed to arrive no earlier than 1:00 p.m. However, the athletes widely ignored this instruction. As a consequence, volunteers routinely arrived at practices early because they anticipated that the athletes would arrive early and need supervision.

On October 25, 2003, the day of the molestations, bowling practice was scheduled for 1:30 p.m. On the same day and at the same facility, [Special Olympics] also scheduled physicals for some of the athletes, beginning at 10:00 a.m. [Special Olympics] had announced the physicals at a prior event via loudspeaker . . . [Showalter and Vasil] knew they were not scheduled for physicals, but they both arrived early to socialize before practice. Ms. Showalter travelled to the bowling center using public transportation. Ms. Vasil's father dropped her off at the bowling alley at 10:00 a.m. Although Ms. Vasil's father was aware that practice started at 1:30 p.m., he assumed, based on past experience that someone from Special Olympics would be there to supervise.

Another early arriver to the October 25 practice was the accused molester, 79-year-old James McDonald, who had been involved with [Special Olympics] for many years in several capacities. As his son was an athlete, Mr. McDonald participated in events as a parent. He was also a registered volunteer. In this capacity, he had been head bowling coach from the 1980s until 1994, at which time he stepped down as head coach due to accusations that he had molested another athlete and her sister. The incidents were investigated by the police, but the charges were dropped two years later.

Evidence was presented that Mr. McDonald's volunteer application remained on file until after the molestations involved in this case. According to routine practice, this suggested that Mr. McDonald's volunteer status had not been terminated. He continued to attend practices and events regularly, even arriving early to help all the athletes, not just his son. Louise Newton, the successor bowling coach, admitted that Mr. McDonald was still there every week acting like he was in charge. As she stated: "I guess it was hard [for Mr. McDonald] to let go." After the instant molestations, [Special Olympics] sent a letter to Mr. McDonald banning him from attendance at events, but stating that "there will be an investigation and [Special Olympics] shall either reinstate your volunteer duties and opportunities or we shall have to determine an appropriate course of action . . . depending on the outcome of the investigation." Mr. McDonald apparently heeded the directive as he did not attend any of [Special Olympics] events up to the date of trial in 2007.

In addition to the accusations that Mr. McDonald had previously molested an athlete and her sister in 1994, other allegations against Mr. McDonald were brought to [Special Olympics] attention prior to October 25, 2003. Between 1994 and 2003, one of the [Special Olympics athletes] reported to Ms. Newton that Mr. McDonald had molested her on more than one occasion, albeit not in connection with any of [Special Olympics] events. During this same time period, Ms. Newton was also informed that Mr. McDonald attended dances conducted for developmentally disabled adults (not associated with [Special Olympics] activities) where he escorted attendees to and from his van. Ms. Newton discussed these issues with Mr. McDonald but accepted his denial of claims of wrongdoing. She did, however, caution him to avoid taking developmentally disadvantaged people to his van because it appeared inappropriate. At some point in the year 2000 or 2001, Ms. Newton began keeping a "closer eye" on Mr. McDonald and had a discussion with Charlotte Day, [Special Olympics] county coordinator, about whether he was a liability. Ms. Newton did not, however, warn anyone else associated with [Special Olympics] or the athletes' parents or guardians about any suspicions concerning Mr. McDonald.

Other than to accept Mr. McDonald's resignation as head bowling coach, [Special Olympics] did nothing to limit his involvement with its activities. In fact, most people within the [Special Olympics] organization gave no apparent credit to the accusations against Mr. McDonald. For example, the county coordinator in 1994, Jane Fournier, did nothing to investigate the 1994 incident, assuming that because prosecutors dropped the charges two years later, Mr. McDonald was cleared of wrongdoing. When Charlotte Day took over as county coordinator in 1998, Ms. Fournier told her that the 1994 incident had been unfounded. Consequently, Ms. Day did not investigate the charges in any way. The county co-coordinator, Patricia Webb, although aware of many of the allegations against Mr. McDonald, concluded that he was "completely harmless."

On the day of the instant molestations, Ms. Webb arrived at the bowling center shortly after 10 a.m. to assist a volunteer physician with performing the physicals. Meanwhile, Mr. McDonald lured [Showalter and Vasil] outside to his van where he subsequently molested them, one after the other, either in or near his van. At some point in time, Ms. Webb looked out the window into the parking lot and saw Mr. McDonald molesting [Showalter and Vasil]. While she was summoning police to report the incident, Mr. McDonald molested the other [Showalter and Vasil]. He was subsequently arrested, and his culpability is not herein disputed.

. . . [Showalter and Vasil] assert that [Special Olympics] was under a duty to protect them or control Mr. McDonald, or both, so as to prevent the foreseeable conduct of Mr. McDonald, and [Special Olympics] failure to do so amounted to negligence. The jury returned a verdict for each [Showalter and Vasil]. . .

Source: *Reprinted from Westlaw with permission of Thomson Reuters.*

1. To what extent was the Special Olympics at fault in this case?

2. What policies should have been in force to prevent these tragic circumstances?

CASE STUDY 10-4 *Jets Fans*

In 2007 it was reported that rowdy New York Jets fans would gather at halftime on a pedestrian ramp at the stadium and "chant obscenities" at women to encourage them to expose their breasts.[24] The team issued a statement saying:

"We expect our fans to comply with all rules at the stadium, and the vast majority do. For those who don't, we expect and encourage N.J.S.E.A. security to take appropriate action."[25]

1. What actions should the league take against the fans? The New York Jets football club?

2. How should the club or league enforce a fan code of conduct when dealing with these issues?

CASE STUDY 10-5 *Elizabeth*

Elizabeth plays in a mixed sports team in a lower grade competition. In a particular match Elizabeth believed she was subjected to sexual harassment by way of a touch on the genital area that she claimed was premeditated by two male players. What should she do? What action should league officials take?

CASE STUDY 10-6 *Jennifer*

Jennifer volunteered to be an official for an upcoming athletic event with her local athletic club. She was sexually harassed by the male volunteer coordinator at the club. The behavior included sex-based insults and innuendos, intrusive questions about her personal life, and repeated requests to go out on a date. Jennifer asked

---

[24] "Zero Tolerance on Harassment," *New York Times*, December 16, 2007; Associated Press, "Lawmaker Wants to Rein in Jets Fans," *CNNSI.com*, November 20, 2007.

[25] David Picker, "At Jets Game, a Halftime Ritual of Harassment," *The New York Times*, November 20, 2007.

that the behavior cease as she felt intimidated and humiliated and stated that she would complain to a member of the club's board should the behavior continue. The next day Jennifer was informed that her services as a volunteer were no longer needed. What should she do?

CASE STUDY 10-7 *Hazing*

Morton Ranch High School cheerleaders had a ritual of "kidnapping" junior varsity members from their homes, blindfolding them, binding their hands and mouths with duct tape, and tossing them into a swimming pool.

"Five former members of a Houston-area varsity cheerleading squad were placed on probation after being arrested on suspicion of hazing junior varsity cheerleaders who claimed they were pushed into a swimming pool, bound and blindfolded, on July 25, the *Houston Chronicle* reported."[26]

---

1. How should this matter be handled?
2. What punishment should be rendered against the cheerleaders?[27]

TITLE IX

Introduction

Proponents of women's rights sought a federal legislative remedy to reverse sex discrimination in education. The Title IX statute provides in part the following remedy:

No person in the United States shall, on the basis of sex, be excluded from participation in, be denied the benefits of, or be subjected to discrimination under any education program or activity receiving federal financial assistance.

The act prohibits any federally funded education program from discriminating on the basis of gender. It forbids discrimination in any program, organization, or agency that receives federal funds. Title IX applies to primary and secondary schools as well. The objective of the statute was to give women an equal opportunity to develop their skills and to apply those skills. This act, as enforced by the Department of Health, Education, and Welfare, is limited to discrimination against participants of federally funded educational programs. Title IX applies to the admissions policies of institutions of vocational, professional, graduate, and undergraduate education. Title IX applies to policies and practices, other than admissions in all educational programs, including athletic programs, that receive federal funds.

Exceptions to Title IX include educational institutions that traditionally admit members of only one sex, institutions that train individuals for military service, and institutions whose compliance with Title IX would violate religious benefits.

Many problems have arisen in regard to the scope of the statute's application and have led to extensive debate about the application of Title IX. The following case discusses how Title IX has greatly

---

[26] Melissa Vargas Wethe, "Katy Cheerleaders Avoid Hazing Trial Updated with a North Texas Twist," *Houston Crime Examiner*, December 24, 2008.

[27] Ibid.

increased the opportunities for women in sports. Brown University women student-athletes sued the university, arguing Brown violated Title IX.

Cases in Title IX

📖 CASE 10-8 *Cohen v. Brown University*

101 F.3d 155 (1st Cir. 1996)

This is a class action lawsuit charging Brown University, and its athletics director with discrimination against women in the operation of its intercollegiate athletics program, in violation of Title IX. The . . . class comprises all present, future, and potential Brown University women students who participate, seek to participate, and/or are deterred from participating in intercollegiate athletics funded by Brown.

This suit was initiated in response to the demotion in May 1991 of Brown's women's gymnastics and volleyball teams from university-funded varsity status to donor-funded varsity status. Contemporaneously, Brown demoted two men's teams, water polo and golf, from university-funded to donor-funded varsity status. As a consequence of these demotions, all four teams lost, not only their university funding, but most of the support and privileges that accompany university-funded varsity status at Brown . . .

There can be no doubt that Title IX has changed the face of women's sports as well as our society's interest in and attitude toward women athletes and women's sports. In addition, there is ample evidence that increased athletics participation opportunities for women and young girls, available as a result of Title IX enforcement, have had salutary effects in other areas of societal concern.

One need look no further than the impressive performances of our country's women athletes in the 1996 Olympic Summer Games to see that Title IX has had a dramatic and positive impact on the capabilities of our women athletes, particularly in team sports. These Olympians represent the first full generation of women to grow up under the aegis of Title IX. The unprecedented success of these athletes is due, in no small measure, to Title IX's beneficent effects on women's sports, as the athletes themselves have acknowledged time and again. What stimulated this remarkable change in the quality of women's athletic competition was not a sudden, anomalous upsurge in women's interest in sports, but the enforcement of Title IX's mandate of gender equity in sports.

Source: *Reprinted from Westlaw with permission of Thomson Reuters.*

In the following case, individuals claimed Temple University engaged in unlawful gender discrimination.

📖 CASE 10-9 *Haffer v. Temple University of the Commonwealth System of Higher Education*

678 F. Supp. 517, 1987

This is a class action alleging unlawful gender discrimination in Temple University's intercollegiate athletic program. The class consists of "[a]ll current women students at Temple University who participate, or who are or have been deterred from participating because of sex discrimination in Temple's intercollegiate athletic program." [The plaintiffs'] claims focus on three basic areas: (a) the extent to which Temple affords women students fewer "opportunities to compete" in intercollegiate athletics; (b) the alleged disparity in resources allocated to the men's and women's intercollegiate athletic programs; and (c) the alleged disparity in the allocation of financial aid to male and female student athletes.

The plaintiffs' complaint is that, despite the fact that Temple's student body is approximately fifty percent female, approximately one-third of the participants in Temple's intercollegiate athletic program are women. Figures produced by [Temple] reveal that approximately 450 men and 200 women participate in Temple's intercollegiate athletic program. That is, by sponsoring more women's teams and/or fewer men's teams, Temple could increase the participation rate of females in the University's athletic program to 50, 75, or even 100%.

Plaintiffs claim that the differences in expenditures for the men's and women's intercollegiate athletic programs violate [the law]. Temple presently spends approximately $2,100 more per male student athlete than per female student athlete.

In addition, some evidence suggests that each of the women's teams engages in fund raising, while only the men's crew and baseball teams raise funds . . . . There is conflicting evidence regarding which teams find it necessary to engage in fund raising. A finding that substantially all of the women's teams and few of the men's teams engage in fund raising would support plaintiffs' claim of disparate impact in the area of expenditures.

[Temple] argue[s] that there is no gender discrimination because the women student athletes outperform the men student athletes and the "expenditure patterns reflect Temple's policy of operating a unified athletics program while promoting at a higher level its three revenue producing teams."

Plaintiffs claim that [Temple] discriminate[s] against women student athletes regarding team travel. In 1985-86, Temple spent $423,908 on team travel for men's teams, and $162,110 on team travel for women's teams. In 1984-85, the relevant figures were $349,492 for the men's teams and $145,297 for the women's teams. The per capita figures also favor the men. Plaintiffs have produced evidence that when a men's and a women's team travel to the same destination, the men's team receives superior treatment. For example, during the 1984-85 season, the men's and women's basketball teams played at the University of Rhode Island. The men's team flew to their game; the women's team took a bus. There is also evidence that various women's teams must raise funds to travel to certain competitions. Temple argues that the mode of travel depends on distance, the size of the team, and the coach's preference.

There are also factual disputes over the accommodations [Temple] offers student athletes on team trips. . . . Temple's "policy is to house 3 players in a room, 1 to a bed, except for the football and 2 basketball teams." Players on these teams are housed 2 to a room, 1 to a bed. There is also evidence that "Temple's policy is one student per bed and two students per room" and that some coaches deviate from this policy. Plaintiffs have presented evidence that the women's badminton and softball teams have been housed 4 to a room, and that the women's swim team was housed 5 to a room. The present record provides conflicting accounts of Temple's policy and is unclear regarding the actual room assignments.

Plaintiffs allege that [Temple] provide[s] male athletes with superior support in the areas of uniforms, equipment, including locker rooms, and supplies. In 1985-86, Temple spent $100,669 on uniforms, equipment and supplies for men's teams, and $33,318 on the women's teams. In 1984-85, the figures were $85,491 on men's teams, and $43,735 on the women's teams. However, as average expenditures vary widely from team to team and year to year, it is difficult to interpret the significance of the figures introduced. However, it seems clear that, assuming male student athletes receive adequate uniforms, equipment and supplies, the female student athletes must likewise receive adequate uniforms, equipment and supplies.

Plaintiffs allege that [Temple] provide[s] superior housing and dining facilities to male student athletes. As to dining facilities, plaintiffs point to evidence that the men's football team has a training table, but that no women's team has a training table. The un-contradicted record establishes that the head coaches of the men's football team, women's field hockey, and the women's volleyball teams select the menu to be served to their players during preseason camp. There is no evidence that any women's team requested, but did not receive, a training table.

Temple provides off-campus housing for student athletes who practice or compete during school vacation periods. This is called "holiday living." Plaintiffs allege that holiday living expenditures favor male student athletes. [Temple has] introduced evidence that the average expenditure for holiday living for the women's teams was higher than the comparable figure for the men's program.

Plaintiffs allege that [Temple] provide[s] superior publicity to the men's athletic teams. There is evidence that, in 1985-86, [Temple] spent $189,688 on the football and men's basketball teams, and $0 on the women's teams. Over the last three years, [Temple] spent $410,672 to publicize the football and men's basketball teams, $1,580 to promote sports generally, and $945 to promote the women's lacrosse team. There is evidence that men's teams receive more publicity than do the women's teams.

[Temple] attempt[s] to justify these spending disparities on the grounds that they "represent an outgrowth of Temple's aim to promote the three revenue producing sports," and that Temple supports the teams with the greatest spectator interest. In the context of the expenditures claim, Temple argued that it treated the women's basketball team as a revenue sport. . . .

Source: *Reprinted from Westlaw with permission of Thomson Reuters.*

NOTES AND DISCUSSION QUESTIONS

Introduction

1. How have women historically been discriminated against in sports?[28]
2. Historically, men's attitudes toward women in sports have not helped in the progress of women's sports. Former MLB player Keith Hernandez made disparaging comments about the presence of women in Major League dugouts. During the broadcast of a New York Mets game he told his broadcast partner, "I won't say that women belong in the kitchen, but they don't belong in the dugout." He later apologized.[29]
3. Former Formula One president Bernie Ecclestone has never been one to curtail his remarks to fit societal demands. After female racer Danica Patrick finished in fourth place in the Indianapolis 500, Ecclestone commented: "You know I've got one of those wonderful ideas . . . women should be dressed in white like all the other domestic appliances."[30] He also later made some very controversial remarks about Hitler, saying "He got things done," while expressing a preference for strong leadership.[31]
4. How can attitudes about women in sports be changed?[32]

---

[28] See Paula Lavigne, "Pregnant Athletes Don't Have to Sit Out," *ESPN*, November 29, 2009.
[29] "Hernandez Offers Apology," *New York Times*, April 24, 2006.
[30] "Ecclestone Repeats 'Domestic Appliance' Quip," *ESPN.com*, June 22, 2005.
[31] Associated Press, "Auto Racing: Ecclestone Is Criticized," *New York Times*, July 5, 2009.
[32] See Javier Espinosa, "Women Boxers Have an Eye on Olympic Ring," *Wall Street Journal*, July 14, 2010.

5. How can boys and girls in youth programs be taught to respect and value girls' participation in youth sports?

6. Linda Cohn has been one of the premier sportscasters for ESPN for many years. She became a diehard sports fan and was the goalie for her college ice hockey team.[33]

Gender Discrimination and Abuse Against Women in Sports

7. Melissa Ludtke brought a civil rights lawsuit to prevent the New York Yankees from enforcing a policy by baseball Commissioner Bowie Kuhn that prevented women from entering the clubhouse after a game. Ludtke worked for *Sports Illustrated* as a reporter and was assigned to cover the 1977 World Series between the Yankees and the Dodgers. Before the series began, the Dodgers told Ludtke she was free to enter the clubhouse after the game. However, the commissioner said she was not allowed to immediately enter the clubhouse, even though her male counterparts were. The commissioner did make special arrangements for Ludtke to interview players after the game. Some ballplayers were offended by the policy and supported Ludtke, particularly Yankees slugger Reggie Jackson.[34]

8. A jury found that the NBA discriminated against a woman referee, Sandra Ortiz-Del Valle, when they failed to hire her as a referee. Even though the NBA had a woman referee at the time, Ortiz-Del Valle was able to prevail in front of a jury.[35] In 1998 a jury awarded her $7.85 million after she had been passed over several times for an NBA referee position. The jury awarded her $100,000 for lost wages, $750,000 in mental pain and emotional distress, and $7 million in punitive damages. A federal judge reduced the award to $350,000.[36]

   The National Basketball Association took a giant step forward when they hired Dee Kanter and Violet Palmer as NBA referees in 1997. Palmer said, "When I started my fourth season, I could kind of see the heads not turn anymore. . . . I could see players come up to me and just talk."[37] Palmer has proven that she can referee at the highest level of the sport and is one of the best in the world at what she does.

9. On December 26, 1974, the Federal Little League Baseball Charter was amended by Pub. L. No. 93–551 (December 26, 1974, 88 Stat. 1744, 93 Congress). The amended charter deleted the word "boys" from each place it appeared in the original charter and replaced it with "young people." The phrase "citizenship, sportsmanship and manhood" was replaced with "citizenship and sportsmanship." The stated purpose of the amendment was to indicate that Little League "shall be open to girls as well as boys." Approximately 5 million girls have participated in Little League Baseball and Softball since 1970.

10. In *Mercer v. Duke University* the jury awarded $2 million in punitive damages to Heather Sue Mercer for her claim of discrimination against Duke University. The U.S. Court of Appeals overturned the award.

---

[33] Linda Cohn, "Cohn-Head: A No-Holds-Barred Account of Breaking into the Boys' Club," *The Globe Pequot Press*, 2008.

[34] Ludtke v. Kuhn, 461 F. Supp. 86 (S.D.N.Y. 1978)

[35] Benjamin Weiser, "Pro Basketball, Jury Tells N.B.A. to Pay Female Referee $7.85 Million," *New York Times*, April 10, 1998.

[36] Ibid.

[37] Ibid.

11. Is it ethical to pay a women's basketball coach at a major university less than the men's basketball coach? What about a noted women's basketball program like the University of Tennessee or Old Dominion? Should the women's coach make more than the men's coach because the women's program is more popular on campus?[38]

12. There is unfortunately a substantial record of men's violence against women both at the collegiate and professional levels. Many factors could be the driving force behind this behavior. Domestic violence has become such an issue in the NBA and it has now made its way into the collective bargaining agreement.[39]

13. Famous MLB umpire Harry Wendelstedt has noted, "I have no doubt that someday there'll be a woman umpire in the major leagues; I just hope I'm the one who trains her."[40]

Title IX

14. How has Title IX affected women's participation in sports?[41]

15. Is it fair to disband men's teams in favor of women's teams for Title IX purposes?

16. What place should the generation of revenue play in Title IX? If women's sports are not generating as much revenue as men's sports, how should that be viewed under Title IX?

---

[38] Dick Patrick, "Raising Salaries Increase Pressure on Top Women's Coaches," *USA Today*, March 8, 2007.

[39] Todd W. Crosset, James Ptacek, Mark A. McDonald, and Jeffrey R. Benedict, "Male Student-Athletes and Violence Against Women," *Violence Against Women* 2, no. 2 (1996): 163–179; Elizabeth A. Gage, "Gender Attitudes and Sexual Behaviors," *Violence Against Women* 14, no. 9 (2008): 1014–1032.

[40] Anna Quindlen, "Public and Private; The Cement Floor," *New York Times*, August 28, 1999; Kristin Walseth, "Young Women and Sport: the Impact of Identity Work," *Leisure Studies* 25, no. 1 (January 2006).

[41] See Wendy Olson, "Beyond Title IX: Toward an Agenda for Women and Sports in the 1990's," *Yale Law Journal & Feminism* 3 (1990–91): 105; Jane English, "Sex Equality in Sports," *Philosophy and Public Affairs* 7, no. 3 (Spring 1978): 269–277.

C H A P T E R   1 1

ETHICAL CONSIDERATIONS FOR INTELLECTUAL PROPERTY IN SPORTS

INTRODUCTION

Intellectual property rights have become a major issue for sport franchises, owners, players, and universities. The theft of intellectual property has become a "sport" in and of itself both in the United States and on the international level. The piracy of intellectual property and stopping the flow of knock-off goods has become a major problem for U.S. companies in the international marketplace.[1] The theft of intellectual property, which can include the trade secrets of a corporation, poses a serious and direct threat to the continued survival of any business, including those in the sports industries. If a competitor, a former employee, or any other entity obtains a company's trade secrets or infringes a company's trademark or a copyright, millions of dollars can be lost with merely the click of a mouse.

Knock-off goods are ubiquitous in the marketplace and are unfortunately many times, freely available to consumers. A seller of black market goods can be difficult to detect and apprehend. They are often not held accountable by any law enforcement agency or governing body for their criminal actions.[2] Many individuals freely operate in the marketplace without serious restrictions or repercussions of their illegal actions. With the amount of infringement of intellectual property occurring on a worldwide basis, it is almost impossible to monitor all aspects of the ownership of intellectual property rights. Through a connected world, much intellectual property theft occurs online via illegal downloads and copying materials from the Internet. Corporations spend millions of dollars and thousands of hours of employee time monitoring foreign markets and industry sectors for the possible theft of their valued intellectual property rights. Some corporations are successful in fending off infringers and thieves while others are not.

The sporting world is no different. Professional sports franchises attempt to protect their logos and trademarks through the enforcement of copyright and trademark laws and by "policing" their marks. If they do not value their mark, the mark may be encroached upon by others. Professional teams

---

[1] Laurie J. Flynn, "U.S. Discloses Moves to Stop Piracy of Intellectual Property," *New York Times*, September 22, 2005.

[2] "Black Market Fears over Replica Football Shirts," *MarketWatch*, June 29, 2007.

enter into multi-million dollar licensing agreements with sponsors for the sale of merchandise. The licensing of intellectual property is a big business; therefore, the license agreement must be monitored and enforced to ensure that the licensee is using the licensed intellectual property within the scope of the agreement.[3]

Similar to corporations, professional athletes must take the necessary steps to protect their image and right of publicity. Many famous athletes have made millions of dollars through the endorsement of products. To protect their right of publicity and contractual agreements, athletes must also "police" or monitor the use, authorized or unauthorized, of their image to ensure their rights are not being infringed upon and to further protect their image.

Universities and amateur athletic associations have intellectual property concerns as well.[4] They must monitor and protect their intellectual property on a global basis to prevent others from diluting or tarnishing their images and logos.

The NFL's Super Bowl is the most watched sporting event in the world on a yearly basis.[5] The NFL sells in excess of $125 million in Super Bowl merchandise every year. The league is a merchandising behemoth, entering into contracts with numerous licensees who are contractually authorized to sell NFL branded goods. However, many unlicensed vendors venture into the marketplace and attempt to profit from the goodwill of the NFL's intellectual property and from the images of its star players. Many individuals sell knock-off goods and illegal merchandise without the approval of the NFL, and, in simple terms, steal money from the coffers of the NFL. In 2007 "Operation Gridiron" was put in place with authorities cooperating together from the U.S. Immigration and Customs Enforcement, Detroit Police Department, and the NFL. They partnered together for a street sweep of unlicensed NFL goods during the week of the 2007 Super Bowl. As a result authorities impounded approximately $5 million worth of unlicensed NFL merchandise.[6] At the 2010 Super Bowl, federal and local authorities in South Florida seized 8,615 counterfeit items of Super Bowl memorabilia.[7] Similar to any other major corporation, the NFL must continue to police their intellectual property to stop criminals who steal their goodwill and profits.

The theft of intellectual property has become a major concern in the sports business, costing owners millions of dollars per year in lost profits. Civil and criminal penalties are in place for the infringer and thieves, but legal remedies may not always adequately compensate the owners of intellectual property for the losses they suffered. It can be difficult to track down the infringer or thief or to locate the source of the counterfeit goods.[8]

The Internet had revolutionized the way fans view and participate in sports, and has created new and extremely difficult ethical and legal challenges for the sports industry. "Real-time" gamecasts on the Internet, fantasy websites using player statistics, digital technology, and streaming videos all have

---

[3] "Sponsorship, Advertising & Marketing, Licensing Company Sues Nike, Baseball HOF over Jordan Line," *Street & Smith's Sports Business Daily*, June 25, 2009.

[4] "Artist, 'Bama Collide Over Trademark Issue," *National Public Radio*, www.npr.org, October 29, 2005. (University of Alabama sued an artist for infringement for lifelike depictions of Alabama football players.)

[5] Associated Press, "Super Bowl XLIV was Most Watched Program in History," *Foxsports.com*, February 8, 2010.

[6] Royal W. Craig, "With Sports Big Business, Trademark Theft Keeping Courtrooms Busy," *Baltimore Business Journal* (February 23, 2007).

[7] Michael David, "Feds Seize $400,000 in Counterfeit Super Bowl Memorabilia," *NBC Sports*, February 18, 2010.

[8] See, Steven N. Geise, "A Whole New Ballgame: The Application of Trademark Law to Sports Mark Litigation," *Seton Hall Journal of Sports Law* 5 (1995): 553.

created new issues for the owners of intellectual property. It is sometimes difficult, if not impossible, to keep pace with advancing technology, and the sports business is no exception. Many copyright violations occur through new technologies that are beyond the control of the copyright owners.

The NFL complained about TiVo to the Federal Communication Commission in 2005 because TiVo was allegedly allowing the unauthorized television distribution of NFL games in areas that had been blacked out due to lack of ticket sales. The feature that was in dispute was called "TiVo guard," which had been created for the purposes of controlling copyright piracy. The two sports giants eventually resolved their dispute.

In Case 11-1, the sale of counterfeit merchandise,[9] baseball gloves, was at issue. The seller of the gloves was charged with a crime for his involvement.

CASE 11-1 *State of Utah v. Ted Frampton*

737 P. 2d 183 (1987)

In March 1983, [Frampton] offered to sell several baseball gloves to Chris Larsen, the manager of Al's Sporting Goods in Logan, Utah. [Frampton] offered to sell the gloves for $50 each. The gloves bore the Wilson A2000 mark, and [Frampton] represented that they were genuine Wilson gloves. Upon examining them, however, Larsen concluded that they were counterfeit and declined to buy any. When Larsen told [Frampton] the gloves were counterfeit, [he] insisted they were genuine Wilson gloves. A day or so later, Steve Hansen, an employee of Al's Sporting Goods, went to [Frampton]'s place of business and bought a baseball glove from [Frampton] for $50. This glove also bore the Wilson A2000 mark, and [Frampton] represented that it was a genuine Wilson glove. While at [Frampton]'s business, Hansen also observed a box filled with thirty-five to fifty additional gloves. According to Hansen and others, the glove he bought was not a genuine Wilson glove, but was an inferior imitation. Hansen's purchase was made under the supervision of the Logan City police, who were investigating [Frampton] in response to a complaint by Wilson Sporting Goods.

As part of the police investigation, Larsen had a recorded telephone conversation with [Frampton] ... During the conversation, Larsen negotiated the purchase of eleven gloves at $40 each. [Frampton] told Larsen the gloves were Wilson A2000 gloves, which were made in Korea. Larsen responded that he had contacted Wilson Sporting Goods and had been told that all A2000's were made in the United States. Furthermore, he told [Frampton] that he could not get the gloves from Wilson for a similar price. Also in March 1983, two advertisements appeared in local newspapers offering the A2000 glove for sale at [Frampton]'s place of business for $50 each.

---

[9] Brian Stelter and Brad Stone, "Digital Pirates Winning Battle with Studios," *The New York Times*, February 4, 2009.

On March 10, 1983, the Logan City police conducted a search of [Frampton]'s business. Pursuant to that search, police seized thirty-eight baseball gloves bearing the Wilson A2000 mark. A Wilson Sporting Goods representative examined the gloves and determined that they were counterfeit.

In this case, [Frampton] possessed (with intent to sell) baseball gloves which are undisputedly modern commercially manufactured products. These gloves were made so that they would appear to have value because of their source, and not only because they were made by Wilson Sporting Goods. [Frampton] represented that the mitts were genuine Wilson gloves. One of the A2000's promotional qualities exploited by Wilson was that A2000s, at least at the time of the charged offenses, were only made in the United States. Because [Frampton] sold or possessed such goods, he was properly charged.

Source: *Reprinted from Westlaw with permission of Thomson Reuters.*

1. Should there be government regulation of infringement of intellectual property?[10]
2. Should there be criminal penalties if a person sells knock-off goods? If so, what should they be?

CASE STUDY 11-1   *Top Cops or "Over the Top"?*

In 2007 MLB sent a letter to Sports Station, a uniform supplier for youth baseball leagues saying Sports Station should stop using the names of big league teams on uniforms they produced. MLB requested they pay a licensing fee for use of the big league names. MLB agreed not to sue the supplier after they agreed to discontinue use of the MLB marks.[11]

1. Should Major League Baseball teams be "cracking down" on Little League Baseball teams for infringement of intellectual property?
2. If MLB has a legal duty to make sure others do not use their intellectual property without their permission, should they then police their mark against all parties, including youth sports teams?

THE ETHICS OF COPYRIGHT OWNERSHIP AND USE

Introduction

The theft of copyrighted material has increased dramatically in the last few years. With the advent of the Internet, copyright owners now have grave concerns over the unauthorized use and infringement of their intellectual property rights.[12] The electronic age has made information immediately available

---

[10] See, "Reporting Intellectual Property Crime: A Guide for Victims of Copyright and Trademark Infringement," *Royal Canadian Mounted Police*, www.rcmp-grc.gc.ca.
[11] *SouthtownStar Reporting*, Tinley Park, Illinois May 25, 2008.
[12] Pamela Samuelson, "Will the Copyright Office Be Obsolete in the Twenty-First Century?" *Cardozo Arts & Entertainment Law Journal* 13 (1994–95): 55.

and access to copyrighted material relatively easy. This has made theft and infringement of copyrighted material much easier for criminals. Damages arising from piracy and related crimes has grown exponentially as better technology has been developed. It is now much easier to reproduce higher quality copies of copyrighted works. Digital technology allows users to make multiple perfect copies in an instant with little investment. Disgruntled employees, a dissatisfied customer, or for that matter any Internet user has the opportunity to inflict great harm to a corporation's copyrighted material, many times with just a click of a mouse.[13]

Copyrights can be granted for literary works, music, lyrics, art work, statues, poems, paintings, software, choreography works, along with a few other works.[14] A copyright can exist "[i]n original works of authorship fixed in any tangible medium of expression. . . ."[15] A work of authorship must be original and to be protected under copyright law must possess a modicum of creativity. If a party violates any of the exclusive rights of the copyright owner, infringement has occurred unless the party can present a viable defense or a legal reason for use of the material. The fair use defense under copyright law can be used to avoid an infringement claim by an owner of the copyright material. To prove a copyright infringement case a copyright owner must show "(1) ownership of a valid copyright; and (2) copying of a constituent element of the work that is original."[16] If a party independently creates a work, that is not an infringement.

A copyright owner rarely possesses direct proof of a copyright violation but instead must prove that another party copied the work by showing that they had access to the owner's copyrighted work and that the two works are substantially similar. The term "substantially similar" is subject to interpretation and can provide for ethical and legal concerns about the use of and ownership of copyrighted material.

CASE STUDY 11-2   *"The Juice" and Dr. Seuss*

Two parties that most individuals would never consider in the same context are O.J. Simpson and Dr. Seuss. One is a famous author known worldwide and the other a former Heisman Trophy winner that is currently incarcerated.[17] Dr. Seuss Enterprises brought a lawsuit against a publisher who allegedly infringed Dr. Seuss's copyrighted work. Penguin Books used copyrighted material from Dr. Seuss Enterprises in a book about the most famous criminal case of the 20th century, the O.J. Simpson murder trial. Simpson, a member of the NFL Hall of Fame, was charged but found not guilty for the murder of his ex-wife and her friend Ron Goldman. Penguin published a book titled *The Cat Not in the Hat! A Parody by Dr. Juice*. The book asserted that it was taking a "fresh look" at the O.J. Simpson double murder trial. The book used the famous writing style created by Theodore S. Geisel, better known to the world as Dr. Seuss. Penguin argued that the book was a parody and therefore, not an infringement. One of Dr. Seuss's most famous lines was, "one fish / two fish / red fish / blue fish, Black fish / blue fish / old fish / new fish" while in Penguin's book there was a slightly difficult line, "one knife? / two knife? / red knife / dead wife."[18]

---

13 Faye Rice, "How Copycats Steal Billions, Foreign Theft of Ideas and Innovations, From Hit Songs to Computer Software, Has Become a Huge Headache for American Business. Wise Companies Have Learned to Fight Back," *CNN Money*, April 22, 1991.

14 17 U.S.C. §102.

15 17 U.S.C. §102.

16 *Feist Publications, Inc. v. Rural Tel. Serv. Co.*, 499 U.S. 340, 361 (1990).

17 Steve Fries, "O.J. Simpson gets 9 Years in Prison," *The New York Times*, December 5, 2008.

18 *Penguin Books, USA, Inc. v. Dr. Seuss Enterprises*, 924 F. Supp. 1559 (S.D. Cal. 1996).

Copyright Ownership

A club logo can define a sports franchise, especially when it is in the National Football League. Many fans associate a team with its logo. NFL goods and merchandise are extremely popular with fans and create substantial amounts of goodwill for teams and the league. They also generate millions of dollars in revenue for the league and its players.[19] Most NFL fans can easily recognize the star on the helmet of the Dallas Cowboys football club to represent the NFL Cowboys even though the words Dallas or Cowboys do not appear. The NFL Miami Dolphins logo has a dolphin wearing a football helmet, the San Diego Chargers have a lightning bolt, and the Indianapolis Colts a horseshoe. The NFL's Pittsburgh Steelers logo is based on the American Iron and Steel Institute (AISI).[20] The logo was first used as a part of a major marketing campaign to educate consumers about how important steel was in the customer's daily life. At the collegiate level, the University of Texas (Longhorns) made a record $8.2 million in licensing royalties in 2005–2006 with the University of Michigan (Wolverines) finishing second.[21] Both universities possess strong intellectual property rights. When the NFL Cleveland Browns moved to Baltimore, they needed a new logo to market the team. What better logo than a raven! The name alludes to the famous poem, "The Raven," by Edgar Allen Poe.[22] In fact, the official mascot of the Baltimore Ravens is named "Poe." Frederick Bouchat thought he had a great idea for a logo for the new Baltimore team. He presented the idea, but it was rejected. After learning that the team adopted a very similar logo, Bouchat alleged the idea for the logo was stolen from him by the club.

📖 CASE 11-2 *Bouchat v. Baltimore Ravens, Inc.*

214 F. 3d 350 (4th Cir. 2000)

Frederick Bouchat is an amateur artist. He has a ninth grade education, and now works as a front entrance security guard at the State of Maryland office building on St. Paul Street in Baltimore. Bouchat often showed his artwork to people passing through the building's main entrance.

As news of an NFL team for Baltimore spread in 1995, Bouchat created drawings and designs for the team based on his favorite possible team name—the Ravens. Bouchat created a helmet design and affixed his creation to a miniature football helmet. Bouchat gave the design and helmet to Eugene Conti, a state official who worked in the St. Paul Street office building. Conti kept the helmet displayed in his office.

---

[19] Sanjay Jose Mullick, "Browns to Baltimore: Franchise Free Agency and the New Economics of the NFL," *Marquette Sports Law Journal* 7 (1996–1997): 1.
[20] The Story Behind the Pittsburgh Steelers Logo: How AISI's Steelmark Made it to the Super Bowl, *American Iron and Steel Institute*, www.steel.org, January 30, 2006. "Back in the early 60s, the Steelers had to petition AISI in order to change the word "Steel" inside the Steelmark to "Steelers" before the logo was complete." Ibid.
[21] Associated Press, "Longhorns Hook Record Merchandising Revenue," *ESPN.com*, August 26, 2006.
[22] Ian Urbina, "Baltimore Has Poe; Philadelphia Wants Him," *New York Times*, September 5, 2008.

Bouchat showed other team drawings to employees of the building, and gave two drawings away as holiday gifts in December of 1995.

Conti asked a colleague to arrange a meeting between Bouchat (an enthusiastic Baltimore fan) and John Moag, chairman of the Maryland Stadium Authority (the man who brought the team to Baltimore) in order to include a story about Bouchat in the employee newsletter. On March 28, 1996, Bouchat was taken to meet Moag at Moag's law office on Pratt Street. The Ravens, and David Modell (the team's owner) occupied the same office suite in the Pratt Street building as a temporary space at this time.

At the meeting, photos were taken and Moag told Bouchat that the team was going to be named the Ravens. When Bouchat described his drawings, Moag told Bouchat to send his drawings along, and Moag would give them to the Ravens for consideration. The next day, Bouchat got permission from his supervisor to use the office fax machine in order to send his drawings to Moag at the Maryland Stadium Authority (MSA). Jan Drabeck, Bouchat's immediate supervisor, showed Bouchat how to use the fax machine.

On April 1 or 2, 1996, Bouchat faxed his drawings to the MSA. He received a fax confirmation but did not retain the printed confirmation receipt. One of the drawings Bouchat faxed to the M.S.A. was his shield drawing.

On April 2, 1996, Modell met with the NFL Properties Design Director to discuss the development of a Ravens logo. Thereafter, Modell communicated with the design team concerning the logo project. The Ravens unveiled their new logo in June of 1996. The new Ravens logo was a Raven holding a shield.

Bouchat and several of his co-workers immediately recognized the new logo as Bouchat's work. Bouchat contacted a lawyer, and in August of 1996 he obtained copyright registration for his shield drawing. . . . Also see Higgings, Brian, *Bouchat Sues Ravens, NFL Over "Flying B" Design*, Maryland Intellectual Property Law Blog, February 18, 2008.

Source: *Reprinted from Westlaw with permission of Thomson Reuters.*

1. Do you think that the Baltimore Ravens club stole the idea from Bouchat?[23]
2. What should Bouchat have done to protect his idea from others stealing it?

Fair Use of Copyrighted Material

Not all uses of copyrighted material are considered infringing. The fair use defense to copyright law allows use of copyrighted material under certain circumstances, notwithstanding the copyright

---

[23] "Appeals Court Rules Against Ravens in Logo Dispute," *ABC News*, September 2, 2010.

owner's exclusive rights. The fair use doctrine can be used to resolve potential conflicts between copyright ownership and free speech. Essentially, individuals may avoid liability based on a fair use of the work. The doctrine is founded on principles of fairness and prevents the strict application of the copyright laws when that application would be deemed unfair.

Copyrights are prevalent in sports and entertainment. In Case 11-3, famous entertainer Carol Burnett had a disagreement with the television program *Family Guy* over a portrayal of her image on the show. Carol Burnett was loved by millions, but so is *Family Guy*. These two cultural behemoths disagreed over *Family Guy*'s raunchy portrayal of Ms. Burnett in one of its episodes.

📖 CASE 11-3 *Burnett v. Twentieth Century Fox Film Corporation*

491 F.Supp.2d 962 (C.D.Cal.,2007)

Family Guy is a half-hour, animated, comedy television program broadcast on primetime and geared toward an adult audience. The show bor-
rows heavily from popular culture, following the exploits of the
Griffin family and friends in the fictional suburb of Quahog, Rhode
Island. Family Guy routinely puts cartoon versions of celebrities in
awkward, ridiculous, and absurd situations in order to lampoon and
parody those public figures and to poke fun at society's general fas-
cination with celebrity and pop culture.

On or about April 23, 2006, Fox aired an episode of "Family Guy" entitled "Peterotica." Near the beginning of the episode, the Griffin
family patriarch, Peter Griffin, an "Archie Bunker"-like character,
enters a porn shop with his friends. Upon entering, Peter remarks that
the porn shop is cleaner than he expected. One of Peter's friends
explains that "Carol Burnett works part time as a janitor." The screen
then switches for less than five seconds to an animated figure resem-
bling the "Charwoman" from the Carol Burnett Show, mopping the floor
next to seven "blow-up dolls," a rack of "XXX" movies, and a curtained
room with a sign above it reading "Video Booths." As the "Charwoman"
mops, a "slightly altered version of Carol's Theme from The Carol Burnett Show is playing." The scene switches back to Peter and his
friends. One of the friends remarks: "You know, when she tugged her
ear at the end of that show, she was really saying goodnight to her
mom." Another friend responds, "I wonder what she tugged to say goodnight to her dad," finishing with a comic's explanation, "Oh!"

Source: *Reprinted from Westlaw with permission of Thomson Reuters.*

1. Just because *Family Guy* could legally portray Ms. Burnett in the way they did, should they have done so?

2. If they knew Ms. Burnett never had an incestuous relationship with her father, should the producers still go forward with the show?

Case 11-4 deals with the use of real-time technology on the Internet. When this type of technology first emerged, it became immensely popular with sports fans and net users. Real-time information was also available on TV, and many stations had sports tickers scrolling across the bottom of the screen to update viewers on games and sports news. There was a huge demand by fans for this immediate sports information. Previously, the only way to find scores was to turn on the radio, TV, or to look in the paper the next morning.

Motorola teamed up with STATS, Inc. to create "SportsTrax," a wireless paging device that provided users with up-to-the-minute information about any sports event in progress. STATS, Inc. hired people all over the country to watch games and send the updates to a satellite, which would then transmit that information to anyone who had a SportsTrax pager. In addition to scores and stats, the pager displayed graphics of a basketball court, or football or baseball field, to illustrate where the ball was in play at that exact moment. Motorola also created a website as a companion to SportsTrax, relaying the same information as the pager to users. The selling point was that fans would be able to "attend" any game they wanted to without buying tickets or sitting in front of the TV or radio all day. The pager and website were marketed and broadcast games without the permission of any sports leagues, TV stations, or radio stations. The NBA objected to the actions of Motorola as seen in the next case.

📖 CASE 11-4 *NBA v. Motorola*

105 F.3d 841 (2d Cir. 1997)

```
Motorola manufactures and markets the SportsTrax paging device while
STATS supplies the game information that is transmitted to the pagers.
The product became available to the public in January 1996, at a
retail price of about $200. SportsTrax's pager has an inch-and-a-half
by inch-and-a-half screen and operates in four basic modes: current,
"statistics," "final scores" and "demonstration." It is the "current"
mode that gives rise to the present dispute. In that mode, SportsTrax
displays the following information on NBA games in progress: (i) the
teams playing; (ii) score changes; (iii) the team in possession of the
ball; (iv) whether the team is in the free-throw bonus; (v) the quar-
ter of the game; and (vi) time remaining in the quarter. The informa-
tion is updated every two to three minutes, with more frequent updates
near the end of the first half and the end of the game. There is a lag
of approximately two or three minutes between events in the game
itself and when the information appears on the pager screen. Sports-
Trax's operation relies on a "data feed" supplied by STATS reporters
who watch the games on television or listen to them on the radio. The
reporters key into a personal computer changes in the score and other
information such as successful and missed shots, fouls, and clock
updates. The information is relayed by modem to STATS's host computer,
which compiles, analyzes, and formats the data for retransmission. The
information is then sent to a common carrier, which then sends it via
satellite to various local FM radio networks that in turn emit the
signal received by the individual SportsTrax pagers.
```

Starting in January 1996, users who accessed STATS's AOL site, typically via a modem attached to a home computer, were provided with
slightly more comprehensive and detailed real-time game information
than is displayed on a SportsTrax pager. On the AOL site, game scores
are updated every 15 seconds to a minute, and the player and team statistics are updated each minute.

Source: *Reprinted from Westlaw with permission of Thomson Reuters.*

The NBA complained that Motorola was engaging in unfair competition by taking the information and distributing it to users. Considering the advanced technology currently available, is the
NBA v. Motorola case now moot?

THE ETHICS OF TRADEMARK OWNERSHIP AND USE

Introduction

Trademarks are a mainstay of U.S. culture and are ubiquitous in the business marketplace.
Trademarks can be extremely valuable, defining the business, and establishing goodwill and a good
reputation for the company. McDonald's has "the Golden Arches," Nike a Swoosh, and Coca-Cola
trademarks are recognized globally. A trademark can be a word, a name, a symbol, or a device used
by a manufacturer or merchant to identify its goods and to help distinguish the goods from other merchants' goods.[24] The basis of trademark law lies in the concept of unfair competition between merchants.[25] If a seller uses a mark that is similar to one already in use, the seller of the goods could be
liable for a buyer's confusion between the two products or services. In 1946 Congress passed the
Lanham Act, which governs trademark use and provides for their protection and registration. Trademark law and ethics deals with balancing the rights between trademark owners and others who want
to use the mark or a similar trademark. One of the primary purposes behind trademarks is to prevent
"consumer confusion."[26] Consumers are not always able to examine in detail, goods or services
before purchasing them to determine the quality and source of those goods, therefore the consumer
must rely on trademarks to ensure the quality of goods and services.

Sports organizations and players are also concerned about trademark rights. The theft or infringement of a club's trademark or a player's identity can mean a loss of millions of dollars and may tarnish or disparage the organization or the athlete's reputation.[27] Trademark counterfeiting is the most
egregious form of trademark infringement. A counterfeiter intentionally uses a trademark identical
to or substantially indistinguishable from a registered trademark to illegally profit from the goodwill
that a trademark represents. In essence, the intentional infringer is stealing from the trademark owner
through loss of sales and profits and additionally is harming the reputation of the owner of the mark.
Knock-off goods are typically of lesser quality than genuine goods. Sub-par goods can tarnish the

---

[24] 15 U.S.C. §1127.
[25] "The Rational Basis of Trademark Protection," *Harvard Law Review* 4, no. 6 (April, 1927): 813–833.
[26] *See generally*, http://cyber.law.harvard.edu.
[27] Laura Lee Stapleton and Matt McMurphy, "The Professional Athlete's Right of Publicity," *Marquette Sports Law
Journal* 10 (1999–2000).

actual mark and may cause a business to lose customers. Some counterfeiters are deterred through fines, civil lawsuits, criminal sanctions, and court orders for the seizure of the counterfeit goods, but that is not always the case. Some thieves are confident they will never get caught.

Companies spend millions of dollars attempting to find the right saying, jingle, or picture (or combination thereof) to attract customers to their product or use of their service. Once a successful mark is established, others may try to copy or infringe upon the mark in an attempt to draw customers away.

If an owner of a business has established name recognition and goodwill through the use and subsequent recognition of a trademark, the owner certainly has a stake in ensuring that the trademark is protected. The owner will do everything possible to make sure no one steals the mark, infringes upon it, or uses it in an obscene or unwholesome way.

Trademark Infringement: "Likelihood of Confusion," The Theft of Trademarks

For a trademark owner to prevail in a trademark infringement lawsuit, the owner of the mark must show (1) ownership of a protectable mark and (2) likelihood of consumer confusion.[28] Case 11-5 dealt with media giant ESPN and a TV show they created and produced titled *Playmakers*. Play-Makers LLC, an athlete management agency, contended that ESPN's use of the mark threatened to damage the LLC's goodwill associated with the mark through possible confusion between the television series and the LLC's athletic management services. The LLC was concerned that the TV show would create a negative association with their mark, PlayMakers.

📖 CASE 11-5   *PlayMakers, LLC v. ESPN, Inc.*

297 F.Supp.2d 1277 (2003)

This is a case of alleged trademark infringement. PlayMakers, LLC ("the LLC") is a small "sports agency" whose services include representation of athletes in contract negotiations with professional sports teams, procurement of endorsement and appearance contracts, and professional sports career guidance. ESPN is a multimedia sports entertainment cable network that specializes in broadcasting sporting events, commentary, and sports-related entertainment television series . . . ESPN promotes and airs a dramatic series called "Playmakers," which touts its behind-the-scenes look at the lives of professional football players . . .

On August 26, 2003, "Playmakers" ran its series debut. The program depicts professional football players both on and off (mostly off) the field, and includes scenes of football players using steroids, womanizing, using illegal drugs, and generally being discriminatory. Although the first season ended on November 11, 2003, ESPN intends to re-air the first season episodes, and to air future seasons of new episodes . . .

---

[28] *Fuddruckers, Inc. v. Doc's B.R. Others, Inc.*, 826 F.2d 837, 841 (9th Cir. 1987).

. . . The LLC has provided documentation of its registration of its "PLAYMAKERS" mark. The first is a "word-mark" for "agency services, namely, representing and advising professional athletes and aspiring professional athletes in contract negotiations with professional sports teams and in endorsements and appearances." The second is a "word plus design" mark in the same class and description. Both marks have now become "incontestable," affording conclusive evidence of the validity of the LLC's "PLAYMAKERS" mark, its ownership of the mark, and its exclusive right to use the mark *in connection with the services identified.*

Source: *Reprinted from Westlaw with permission of Thomson Reuters.*

CASE STUDY 11-3 *"How Bout' Dem Cowboys!"*[29]

What sports club or organization would be so arrogant as to claim they were "America's team"? The NFL's Dallas Cowboys have done just that. How can one sports team claim to represent the sporting interests of an entire nation? After all, there are approximately 120 professional sports franchises in North America and many more collegiate sports teams, so how can one team be singled out as the team America claims as its own? The Dallas Cowboys of the National Football League have been making that claim for many years. Any sports franchise laying claim to the phrase "America's team" must be the winningest team and a perennial champion, correct? Well, that does not describe the recent fate of the Dallas Cowboys franchise.

In *Dallas Cowboys v. America's Team Properties, Inc.*, the Cowboys sought to cement their legal claim to the phrase "America's team." The Cowboys sued America's Team Properties . . . claiming they were entitled to rights in the phrase "America's team" and had been using it as a service mark and trademark since 1979. The Cowboys were first referred to as America's team in 1978 by Bob Ryan, an editor at NFL Films. In 1978 the Cowboys used the term in commerce by titling their 1978 season highlight film, "America's Team." A 1979–1980 Cowboys calendar referred to the term, as did an NFL Films videocassette showing the Cowboys' seasons from 1975 through 1979. National Football League Properties (NFLP) sold silver coins with "America's Team" engraving between 1986 and 1990. The club used the term in a variety of publications in the 1980s and 1990s, and in 1991 sold t-shirts with the words "America's team." In 2003 NFL Films released a DVD collection titled *The Dallas Cowboys: The Complete History of America's Team, 1960–2003*. Many media outlets have referred to the Cowboys as America's team. When the NFL announced its 2007 schedule, it noted the term when referring to the Cowboys; however, not all agree that the Cowboys are so popular. Colorful former Houston Oilers head coach Bum Phillips said, "They may be America's team . . . but we're Texas's team." HBO sports has also referred to the Cowboys using the same term. *Sports Illustrated* dubbed them America's team in 1994.[30]

---

[29] Michael K. Ozanian, "How 'Bout Them Cowboys?," *Forbes.com.* September 13, 2007.
[30] See, *Dallas Cowboys Football Club, LTD and NFL Properties LLC v. America's Team Properties, Inc.* In the United States District Court for the Northern District of Texas Dallas Division, Civil Action No. 306-CV-1906K, October 16, 2006.

CASE STUDY 11-4 *Bullets to Wizards*

Harlem Wizards Entertainment Basketball, Inc. ("Harlem Wizards") is a theatrical basketball organization that performs "show basketball" in the tradition established by the world famous Harlem Globetrotters. The Capital Bullets Basketball Club, commonly known as the "Washington Bullets," is a member team of the National Basketball Association ("NBA"), the world's preeminent professional basketball league. On February 22, 1996, the Washington Bullets publicly announced that beginning in the 1997–1998 NBA season, the team would formally change its name to the Washington Wizards. Soon after, the Harlem Wizards filed a lawsuit against the Washington Bullets, alleging that the proposed name change infringed its trademark.[31]

CASE 11-6 *Young, Jr. v. Vannerson*

612 F. Supp. 2d 829 (S.D. Tex 2009)

This is a trademark dispute over rights to the marks "VY" and "INVINCE-ABLE." Young, a professional football player, asserts that he is widely known by his initials—"VY"—and nickname—"Invincible." In this suit, [he] assert that the defendants have engaged in substantial preparations to sell products using these marks. Young asserts that he is a senior user of the marks and has a common-law ownership interest in the trademark rights. [He] seek[s] a permanent injunction and a declaration that [he] have the exclusive right to use the marks VY and INVINCEABLE, that [his] use of these marks does not infringe any possible rights of the defendants, and that the defendants have no rights in these marks.

Young is a professional football player for the National Football League's ("NFL") Tennessee Titans. He played high school football in Houston, Texas, and was named National Player of the Year by *Student Sports Magazine* in 2001. Young played college football at the University of Texas ("UT") from 2002 to 2006. As a collegiate athlete, Young licensed his name and likeness to UT "to promote their entertainment services and football program." Young asserts that he became widely known as "VY" and "INVINCEABLE" during his "highly publicized collegiate football career." He asserts that UT protected his name and likeness by sending cease-and-desist letters to entities using the names "VY" and "INVINCEABLE." In 2005, his final season at UT, Young received several national awards, including college player of the year and the Davey O'Brien Quarterback Award, and was named a Heisman Trophy finalist and runner-up. On January 4, 2006, Young led UT to a BCS National Championship with a victory in the Rose Bowl. Young

[31] "Harlem Wizards Simply Won't See the Big Picture," *Washington Post*, August 28, 1996. See also Mitchell J. Nathanson, "What's in a Name or, Better Yet, What's It Worth?: Cities, Sports Teams and the Right of Publicity," *Villanova School of Law, School of Law Working Paper Series* 91 (2007).

scored the winning touchdown, was named the Rose Bowl's Most Valuable
Player, and was featured on the cover of a commemorative issue of
Sports Illustrated. After being selected by the Titans as the third
overall pick in the 2006 NFL draft, Young was named the NFL's Offensive Rookie of the Year. [Young] assert[s] that Young "has become one
of the most recognizable figures in professional football." He is featured on the cover of "Madden 2008," a video game produced by EA
Sports. Young "currently has endorsement contracts wherein he has
licensed his name and likeness," including his "proprietary rights to
his nicknames and his abbreviated name," to various entities, including Vincent Young, Inc.

Source: *Reprinted from Westlaw with permission of Thomson Reuters.*

Do you believe Young is entitled to the use of the trademarks?[32]

Trademark Dilution and Tarnishment

Trademark dilution is the "whittling away" of the distinctiveness or goodwill of a mark. Many
states have anti-dilution laws to prevent merchants from "free riding" on the goodwill of others. The
Federal Trademark Dilution Act of 1995 (FTDA) provides owners of famous trademarks some protection against those parties diluting or tarnishing their trademark. Corporations not only have to be
concerned about their trademarks being stolen and infringed but also must concern themselves with
the goodwill of the mark being diluted or tarnished.

The Heisman Trophy is one of the most recognizable and treasured awards in sports, second only
to Lord Stanley's Cup, given to the winning team in the NHL playoffs.[33] The Heisman Trophy is
given to college football's most outstanding player every year. In the following case the Heisman
Trust sought to protect their mark against an alleged infringer.

📖 CASE 11-7   *The Heisman Trophy Trust v. Smack Apparel Co.*

595 F. Supp. 2d 320 (2009)

The Heisman Trophy Trust ("The Heisman Trust") brought this action
alleging that Smack Apparel Company ("Smack Apparel") breached a settlement agreement with The Heisman Trust, and continues to infringe
and dilute The Heisman Trust's trademarks.

The Heisman Trust is a registered not-for-profit trust charged with
supporting public charities, especially those that support and encourage student athletics; providing scholarships; and promoting youth
physical fitness in high school and college. The Heisman Trust owns
the rights for all intellectual property relating to the Heisman

---

[32] Adjunct professor of Sports Law at South Texas College of Law, Michael Flint, has called Young the "greatest
college quarterback of all time."

[33] John P. Wise, "Heisman is Cool, but Stanley Cup Still Best Trophy," *bleachreport.com*, December 14, 2009.

Trophy. These rights were transferred to it by The Downtown Athletic Club of New York City, Inc. (the "Downtown Athletic Club"), the organization that was originally responsible for awarding the Heisman Trophy.

The Heisman Trophy is awarded each year in recognition of an outstanding college football player. The presentation of the award is generally preceded by coverage from national television networks, newspapers, magazines, and radio talk shows, and the award itself is presented on ESPN television network, with millions of viewers watching. The Heisman Trust owns the following federal trademark and service mark registrations relating to the Heisman Trophy (the "Heisman Marks"):

1. HEISMAN MEMORIAL TROPHY, U.S. Trademark Reg. No. 936,853, dated June 27, 1972, for "promoting interest, excellence and sportsmanship in intercollegiate football through the medium of an annual award";
2. HEISMAN MEMORIAL TROPHY AND DESIGN, U.S. Trademark Reg. No. 936,852, dated June 27, 1972, for "promoting interest, excellence and sportsmanship in intercollegiate football through the medium of an annual award";
3. HEISMAN TROPHY AWARD, U.S. Trademark Reg. No. 1,397,161, dated June 10, 1986, for "promoting interest, excellence and sportsmanship in intercollegiate football through the medium of an annual award";
4. HEISMAN TROPHY, U.S. Trademark Reg. No. 3,139,387, dated September 5, 2006, for "promoting interest, excellence and sportsmanship in intercollegiate football through the medium of an annual award";
5. HEISMAN TROPHY, U.S. Trademark Reg. No. 3,477,047, dated July 29, 2008, for "clothing, namely T-shirts and hats";
6. HEISMAN, U.S. Trademark Reg. No. 1,397,160, dated June 10, 1986, for "promoting interest, excellence and sportsmanship in intercollegiate football through the medium of an annual award";
7. HEISMAN, U.S. Trademark Reg. No. 3,388,826, dated February 26, 2008, for "video games, namely video game software, interactive video game programs, and video game discs";
8. HEISMAN, U.S. Trademark Reg. No. 3,311,769, dated October 16, 2007, for "footballs"; and
9. HEISMAN, U.S. Trademark Reg. No. 3,331,298, dated November 6, 2007, for "shirts, sweat shirts, hats, visors and jackets".

The Heisman Trust alleges that it has also acquired common law trademark rights through its extensive use of its registered and unregistered trademarks. The Heisman Trust spends more than $650,000 each year advertising and promoting the Heisman Trophy and the Heisman Marks, and it has licensed the use of the Heisman Marks to various third parties, including Reebok International Ltd. ("Reebok"), in exchange for royalty and other payments.

Smack Apparel is a clothing manufacturer that sells principally to retailers and operates a website through which it also sells its apparel. The Heisman Trust alleges that Smack Apparel first made unlawful use of the Heisman Marks in 1999, when a college football player who was a candidate for the Heisman Trophy that year was arrested for shoplifting. Smack Apparel produced a T-shirt with the word "Heistman" and a depiction of the football player from the Heisman Trophy statuette holding a shopping bag in his hand.

In 2000, Smack Apparel entered into a settlement agreement (the "Settlement Agreement") with the Downtown Athletic Club. In the Settlement Agreement, Smack Apparel stipulated that it would "cease and permanently refrain from manufacturing, displaying, selling or offering for sale any clothing or other merchandise bearing the [Heisman] Marks, or confusingly similar marks, and from displaying or otherwise using the [Heisman] Marks, or confusingly similar marks, on or in connection with any website." Smack Apparel also agreed that a breach of the Settlement Agreement "would result in continuing material and irreparable harm, and because it would be difficult or impossible to establish the full monetary value of such damage," the holder of the Heisman Marks "shall be entitled to injunctive relief."

In the years since the Settlement Agreement, Smack Apparel has occasionally produced T-shirts promoting the candidacies of potential Heisman Trophy winners, including one series of T-shirts in 2002, and another in 2007. In the fall of 2008, Smack Apparel produced thirteen varieties of Heisman Trophy-related T-shirts. The Heisman Trust then filed the underlying suit, alleging breach of contract (referring to the Settlement Agreement), as well as trademark infringement and dilution. . . .

The Smack Apparel T-shirts also use a font that is virtually identical to the font used on the T-shirts licensed by The Heisman Trust and on The Heisman Trust's website.

Source: *Reprinted from Westlaw with permission of Thomson Reuters.*

1. Do you consider the word "Heistman" trademark dilution or tarnishment?
2. Could "Heistman" be considered a parody?

Parody

Sometimes a party will make fun of a copyright or trademark through the use of a parody or spoof. Even though the mark is being used, it may not be an infringement of the mark.[34] The First

---

[34] See, *Hershey Company et al v. Art Van Furniture, Inc.*, Case No. 08-cv-14463 (E.D. Mich. Oct. 21, 2008). "Parody is protected under the First Amendment, but in this case the court didn't buy Art Van's argument that its truck design was a protected parody of Hershey's product packaging." Ibid.

Amendment to the U.S. Constitution can be a factor in determining whether parody can be a proper defense to the use of a trademark. Trademark infringement is concerned with the consumer being confused by the use of the mark, but that is not the case with a parody.[35] To operate as a parody, the mark must merely "conjure up" or suggest the owner's trademark to the consumer.

What if a parody is vulgar, obscene, or done in "poor taste"? Should that stop the individual from using the mark as a parody? In the case study that follows, the Dallas Cowboys football club was once again involved. However, this time it was their famous cheerleaders who were the target of a parodist.

CASE STUDY 11-5 *Dallas Cowboys Cheerleaders*

The famous cheerleaders sued a company that made a 90-minute "film" titled "Debbie Does Dallas." The company asserted that the "film" was a parody or satire and they were therefore entitled to the "fair use" defense. In discussing the fair use defense in the context of parody or satire, one court stated:

> In the present case, there is no content, by way of story line or otherwise, which could conceivably place the movie Debbie Does Dallas within any definition of parody or satire. The purpose of the movie has nothing to do with humor; it has nothing to do with a commentary, either by ridicule or otherwise, upon the Dallas Cowboys Cheerleaders. There is basically nothing to the movie Debbie Does Dallas, except a series of depictions of sex acts. The other phases of the movie the dialogue and the "narrative" are simply momentary and artificial settings for the depiction of the sex acts. The associations with the Dallas Cowboys Cheerleaders obviously play an important role in the film and in the advertising; but this is a role that has nothing to do with parody or satire. The purpose is simply to use the attracting power and fame of the Dallas Cowboys Cheerleaders to draw customers for the sexual "performances" in the film. The obvious intent of defendant Zaffarano and the others responsible for this film is to cash in upon the favorable public image of the Dallas Cheerleaders, including the image of a particular quality of feminine beauty and character.[36]

1. How is parody to be determined?
2. Who should decide?
3. Were the use of trademarks in Case 11-5 a fair use?

Trademarks and Domain Names

What happens when a famous trademark is being used as a domain name by another party? What if an individual obtains a domain name fraudulently and tries to sell it? Is that considered stealing of intellectual property? Cybersquatting has been defined as "involv[ing] the registration as domain names of well-known trademarks by non-trademark holders who then try to sell the names back to the trademark owners."[37] In essence, the purchaser of the domain name holds another party (many times a famous person) as a commercial "hostage." The most important tool for fighting cybersquatting is the Anticybersquatting Consumer Protection Act of 1999 (ACPA). Individuals may attempt to register an athlete or entertainer's domain name or name similar to it and use it as a fan website. Many cybersquatters have purchased the domain names of athletes and entertainers in hopes of making a

---

[35] Moana Weir, "Making Sense of Copyright Law Relating to Parody: A Moral Rights Perspective," *Monash University Law Review* 18 (1992): 194.

[36] *Dallas Cowboys Cheerleaders, Inc. v. Pussycat Cinema, Ltd.*, 467 F. Supp. 366 (D.C.N.Y. 1979). Also see Geri J. Yonover, "The Precarious Balance: Moral Rights, Parody, and Fair Use," *Cardozo Arts & Entertainment Law Journal* 14 (1996): 79.

[37] *Sporty's Farm v. Sportsman's Mkt., Inc.*, 202 F.3d 489, 493 (2nd Cir. 2000).

profit by selling the name back to them. However, some cybersquatters have successfully defended the use of the domain name on First Amendment grounds.

Many athletes have had tussles with individuals who have taken the athlete's name, a part of the athlete's name, or even his or her nickname, for use in a domain name. Courts and arbitration panels have had to decide whether the taking of an athlete's name in the form of a domain name is a violation of the athlete's right of publicity, a violation of trademark law, or both. Does an athlete have trademark protection in his or her name?

Tiger Woods is not used to losing, but he did lose a battle at the National Arbitration Forum over the registration of his newborn son's domain name. The dispute was over the domain name <charlieaxelwoods.com>. Woods owns a U.S. Trademark for "Tiger Woods." Tiger claimed that the registrant of his son's name offered the domain name for sale on eBay on February 18, 2009, just nine days after the birth of Tiger's son, trying to cash in on the name of his famous father, Tiger Woods.

> 📖 **CASE 11-8** *Eldrick 'Tiger' Woods, for Itself, Tiger Woods and His Minor Child, Charlie Axel Woods v. Josh Whitford*

Claim Number: FA0905001263352 (2009)

Decision

Parties

[The] Complainant is Eldrick 'Tiger' Woods, for itself, Tiger Woods minor child, Charlie Axel Woods. The Respondent is Josh Whitford.

Registrar and Disputed Domain Name

The domain name at issue is <charlieaxelwoods.com>, registered with Godaddy.com, Inc.

Relief Sought

[Woods] requests that the domain name be transferred from [Whitford to him].

Parties' Contentions

A. Complainant

. . . Eldrick 'Tiger' Woods (Tiger Woods) is one of the world's best known sports personalities, "via the titanic amount of global exposure he receives in television broadcasts and Internet coverage of golf tournaments, exhibitions and charity events. . . ."

TIGER WOODS is the subject of U.S. Trademark Registration. . . .

Charlie Axel Woods is the second child of Tiger Woods and his wife Elin Nordgren. Charlie Axel Woods was born on February 8, 2009, which

event was announced and widely reported around the world in all forms
of media. The disputed domain name, <charlieaxelwoods.com>, was registered on February 9, 2009, the day after Charlie Axel Woods was born.

[Woods] asserts that the disputed domain name is confusingly similar
to the registered and common law trademarks in which [he] has rights.
[He] asserts that TIGER WOODS "has acquired distinctiveness and such a
high degree of secondary association in the mind of the public that
even if the name were not trademarked, common law trademark rights
would certainly exist. . . ."

[Woods] further alleges that the disputed domain name, less the ".com"
extension, is identical to [his] minor child's name. . . .

[He] contends that [Whitford] has no rights or legitimate interests in
the subject domain name. [Woods] maintains that: (1) there is no
relationship between [Whitford] and Charlie Axel Woods or [Woods];
(2) <charlieaxelwoods.com> does not correspond to [Whitford]'s given
name, Josh Whitford; (3) at no time has [Woods] assigned, granted,
licensed, sold, authorized or otherwise agreed to [Whitford]'s use of
the mark CHARLIE AXEL WOODS; and (4) [Whitford] is not using the domain
name in connection with any bona fide use or making any legitimate
noncommercial or fair use of the domain name.

With respect to the issue of "bad faith" registration and use, [Woods]
highlights the fact that the domain name was registered the day after
Charlie Axel Woods was born. [Woods] further asserts that [Whitford]
registered and is holding the domain name primarily, if not exclusively, for the purpose of selling or otherwise transferring the
domain name to [him], or to a third party, for consideration in excess
of [Whitford]'s out-of-pocket costs directly related to the registration of the subject domain name. To support this allegation, [Woods]
notes that [Whitford] offered the <charlieaxelwoods.com> domain name
registration for sale on eBay on February 18, 2009 (nine days after
the birth of Charlie Axel Woods). The listing description states, in
part, as follows: "This is your chance to own the domain to a future
golf legend or use it in some way to extord (sic) the current golf
legend for some extra cash (not highly recomended (sic) seeing he has
lots of money and lawyers). I personally feel someone much more into
golf would appreciate the address much more than myself. I am not
really sure why I bought the domain, but since I am loosing (sic) my
job on the 1st of April anything sounded like a good idea." . . . the
WHOIS record for the disputed domain name directs users to the eBay
listing.

[Woods] also refer(s) to a February 18, 2009, email sent by [Whitford]
to members of the Tiger Woods Community, an official online Internet
club, indicating that [Whitford] had advised Tiger Woods to register

his son's name before announcing the name to the public. "Now that domain name will be worth Millions in the future," [Whitford] predicted.

According to [Woods], "[Whitford]'s use of the charlieaxelwoods.com domain name inherently has the potential to confuse Internet users who encounter that name, and when an Internet user tries to visit what he or she reasonably believes will be a legitimate web site about or concerning [Woods] and/or CHARLIE AXEL WOODS instead finds that there is no web site for that domain name and instead are sent to [Whitford]'s personal commercial web site at www.joshwhitford.com." [Whitford]'s website consists of a blog dedicated to unconventional marketing techniques.

B. [Whitford]

[He] asserts that the disputed domain name is not confusingly similar to any registered or common law trademarks in which [Woods] has rights. While conceding that TIGER WOODS is a registered mark, [Whitford] contends that Tiger Woods has no inherent right to the <charlieaxelwoods.com> domain name. "A birth does not create a trademark or entitlement to a domain name."

[Whitford] also contends that he is using the domain name in a *bona fide* legitimate noncommercial manner as a fan page and did not register the domain name for the purpose of selling or transferring it to [Woods]. He states that his eBay listing for the domain name was satire. [Whitford] further argues that [Woods] has failed to show any damaging, impairing or blemishing effects due to [his] registration of the <charlieaxelwoods.com> domain name.

Findings

The Panel finds that the disputed domain name is not identical or confusingly similar to a trademark or service mark in which [Woods] has rights.

. . . in the opinion of the Panel, the alphanumeric string constituting the <charlieaxelwoods.com> domain name is not sufficiently similar to the TIGER WOODS mark.

On the other hand, there is no question but that the <charlieaxelwoods.com> domain name is, for all intents and purposes, identical to the term "Charlie Axel Woods." The key issue to be decided, however, is whether the personal name "Charlie Axel Woods" is protectable as a common law trademark or service mark. The Panel concludes that it is not.

[Woods] baldly asserts that "Charlie Axel Woods" is a common law trademark but has presented no evidence that "Charlie Axel Woods" has been

used in connection with the commercial offering of goods or services
or that the personal name in question has acquired secondary meaning
as the source of such goods or services. Accordingly, the Panel finds
that [Woods does] not have trademark or service mark rights in the
name "Charlie Axel Woods."

Source: *Reprinted from Westlaw with permission of Thomson Reuters.*

Tiger Woods also brought a claim over his daughter's domain name <samalexiswoods.com>. The registrant failed to submit a response to Tiger's claim and the name was transferred.[38] Woods has also won the right to <tigerwoodscoursedesign.com> and <tigerwoodsdesign.com>.[39]

Abandonment of Trademarks

An owner of a mark can abandon a mark if the owner fails to use it for three years or more with no intention of future use of the mark.[40] Once it is abandoned, the trademark owner has no further rights. Otherwise they are free to take the mark and use it.[41] After reading Case 11-9, can you determine what "abandon" means?

📖 **CASE 11-9** *Hawaii-Pacific Apparel Group, Inc. v. Cleveland Browns Football Company LLC and National Football League Properties, Inc.*

---

418 F. Supp.2d 501 (S.D.N.Y. 2006)

In 1984, Browns players and fans started to refer to the team's
defense—and, eventually, the team's fans—as the "Dawg Pound." The
phrase caught on quickly, and, in part as a result of the notoriety of
the Dawg Pound, in the mid-eighties NFLP considered Cleveland to be a
"hot market," as Browns-related merchandise was selling particularly
well. In 1985, to capitalize on this market, NFLP asked the Browns to
register the marks CLEVELAND BROWNS DOGS and CLEVELAND BROWNS DAWGS
with the State of Ohio Trademark Office. CLEVELAND BROWNS DAWGS—a mark
bearing those words and a design of three dogs in football uniforms—
was eventually officially registered by the State of Ohio in 1988, as
was a similar design for CLEVELAND BROWNS DOGS. Each of these trademark registrations expired ten years after the date of its issuance.

---

[38] National Arbitration Forum Decision, Claim Number: FA 0904001256681.

[39] National Arbitration Forum Decision, Claim Number: FA: 0608000772899; National Arbitration Forum Decision, Claim Number: FA: 0608000772886.

[40] Cornell University Law School, Legal Information Institute, Abandonment (of trademark), http://topics.law.cornell.edu.

[41] Stephen L. Carter, "The Trouble with Trademark," *Yale Law Journal* 99 (1989–1990): 759.

One of the functions of NFLP was to license the trademarks of the NFL and its teams to third parties via licensing agreements. NFLP referred to these marks as "NFL Marks," and broke them down into five categories:

- "League Marks," which included marks such as "National Football League," "NFL," "Super Bowl," "Pro Bowl," and the like;
- "Club Marks," which included the names, symbols, designs, and colors of the various NFL teams;
- "Huddles," which included copyrighted team mascots, helmet designs, and other indicia of the teams;
- "Superstars," which included special designs including Club Marks and the personal likenesses of one or more NFL players; and
- "Game Day," which were special design treatments of the Club Marks marketed in connection with the term "Game Day" and/or the League Marks.

NFLP considered DAWG POUND to be a Club Mark, and licensed its use to various third parties. Prior to 1994, NFLP accepted licensing fees for at least the following merchandise that used the phrase "Dawg Pound" in some form:

- *T-Shirts:* in 1989, Trench Manufacturing Co. sold 176 units of officially licensed t-shirts bearing the words "DAWG POUND" for a total of $15,108.60.
- *Christmas Cards:* Cleveland-area Hallmark stores sold Christmas cards, copyrighted 1989 and 1990, that featured the DAWG POUND mark. One such card depicted Santa Claus standing in front of a group of anthropomorphized dogs sitting in football stadium bleachers behind a banner that reads "CLEVELAND DAWG POUND." Another such card depicted Santa Claus sitting in a recliner watching a Browns game with a dog wearing a "BROWNS DAWG POUND" sweatshirt. Both cards displayed the familiar NFL shield on the back with the words "Officially Licensed Product."
- *Posters:* In 1993, Andrew Noch & Associates received a license from NFLP to manufacture and distribute a poster depicting a photograph of Municipal Stadium with the words "The Dawg Pound" underneath the photograph. Noch sold these posters to various retailers, including ten copies to a retailer called A.I.M. Enterprises, Inc., on February 16, 1994.
- *Logos:* Logo-7, Inc., an apparel manufacturer later acquired by Tultex Corporation and then Reebok International Ltd., created graphic designs for use on its apparel, which were submitted to NFLP for its approval. NFLP received licensing fees for Browns-related logos bearing the word DAWG, including one in 1989 with "DAWG POUND" over a picture of a bulldog and the words "CLEVELAND BROWNS." Logo-7 sold $123,241.70 worth of merchandise bearing the words DAWG or DAWG POUND in 1989 and 1990.
- *Other Apparel:* In 1992 and 1993, Nutmeg Mills, Inc., a sports apparel manufacturer, submitted various designs to NFLP for approval for use on Nutmeg's apparel, including an image of a bulldog wearing a football helmet and jersey sitting in front of a doghouse with the words "DAWG POUND." The entire image is contained between the words "Cleveland Browns."

At least sixty units of clothing bearing the DAWG POUND mark were shipped to JCPenney, among other retailers.

While all this was happening, HP was founded in 1986 by Donald Shepherd (its president and sole shareholder) and began to manufacture and distribute apparel bearing phrases such as "DAWG POUND," "LIL DAWG POUND," and "TOP DAWG" in the early and mid-nineties, after Shepherd's teenage son was given the nickname "Top Dawg" by members of his baseball team in 1991. In March of 1994, HP attempted to register the DAWG POUND mark with the PTO (alleging a date of first use in commerce of March 1994), but NFLP opposed the registration and the mark was never registered. Shepherd, who had no interest in football, was not aware until NFLP opposed the DAWG POUND registration that the words DAWG and DAWG POUND were commonly used to refer to the fans of the Cleveland Browns.

In 1995, the Browns franchise moved to Baltimore and became the franchise now known as the Baltimore Ravens. There was thus no longer a "Dawg Pound" in Cleveland, in the sense that the Browns were no longer in existence.

During this period when there was no "Dawg Pound," HP sold its apparel in national chains, and since 1991 its total revenue from DAWG-related merchandise (including DAWG POUND merchandise) is approximately $10 million.

In 1999, the Browns and the "Dawg Pound" returned to Cleveland. On March 26, the Browns and NFLP—which had never registered or attempted to register DAWG POUND prior to this—filed an intent-to-use application with the PTO for the DAWG POUND mark. In August of 1999, the application was rejected on account of its similarity to, and corresponding likelihood of confusion with, HP's LIL DAWG POUND mark, which had been successfully registered in 1996. On March 29, 2000, HP's counsel sent a letter to the Browns and NFLP, demanding that they immediately cease and desist using the DAWG POUND mark.

Source: *Reprinted from Westlaw with permission of Thomson Reuters.*

ETHICS IN LICENSING AND SPONSORSHIP AGREEMENTS

Sports marketing now dominates our culture. The licensing of intellectual property has become a billion-dollar venture worldwide. Corporations view events as a way to expand their products globally. Teams, leagues, and players possess logos, names, nicknames, memorabilia, designs, characters, and other forms of intellectual property, which they must protect, usually through the trademark or copyright laws or through a right of publicity claim for players.

Licensing at the collegiate level is big business as well. The NCAA conducts 88 championships a year. They have extensive licensing and marketing programs that make use of NCAA marks. They have instituted an "NCAA Trademark Protective Program." They own many marks; here are some of the marks the NCAA constantly monitors:

65 Teams . . . One Dream™
And Then There Were Four®
College World Series®
Final 4®
Frozen Four®
It's More Than A Game®
March Madness®
Middle School Madness®
Midnight Madness®
Men's Elite Eight®
Men's Final Four™
Men's Frozen Four®
The Big Dance®
The Final Four®
The Greatest Show on Dirt®
The Road Ends Here®
The Road to Atlanta™
The Road to Cary™
The Road to Cleveland™
The Road to Detroit™
The Road to Indianapolis®
The Road to Minneapolis™
The Road to New Orleans™
The Road to Omaha®
The Road to San Antonio™
The Road to San Diego™
The Road to St. Louis™
The Road to the Final Four®
We are the Game®
Women's Frozen Four®

1. What is the best way for the NCAA to protect their trademarks?
2. Which of their trademarks is most valuable?

CASE STUDY 11-6   *Michael Vick's Jersey for Pets*

Michael Vick's troubles with the NFL are well known. When he first got into trouble for participating in dog fighting, the NFL suspended the sale of "Vick-related merchandise" on NFL.com. The NFL said selling his merchandise was "not appropriate under the circumstances."[42] After Vick returned to the NFL from prison, the

---

NFL began to sell jerseys that fans could custom order for their pets.[43] An NFL spokesman said, "as far as putting it on the dog product, he's working with humane societies, working to educate others on this issue so we don't see a problem."[44] In September 2009 Michael Vick's jersey was the top jersey in sales in the NFL.[45]

1. Should the NFL allow the sale of Vick's "pet jerseys" considering they suspended Michael Vick from the league for his involvement with dog fighting, a felony?
2. Was the NFL merely seeking a good marketing opportunity with the jerseys?

PROTECTING THE ATHLETE'S IMAGE AND RIGHT OF PUBLICITY

Famous athletes possess a commercial value in their name and likeness. Companies pay large amounts of money to athletes for their endorsement; therefore, athletes must make every effort to protect the use of their image and likeness.

CASE 11-10 *Ali v. Playgirl, Inc.*

447 F.Supp. 723 (1978)

. . . Muhammad Ali until recently the heavyweight boxing champion of the world, has brought this . . . action for . . . damages against Playgirl, Inc., for their alleged unauthorized printing, publication and distribution of an objectionable portrait of Ali in the February, 1978, issue of *Playgirl Magazine* ("Playgirl"), a monthly magazine published by Playgirl, Inc. . . . The portrait complained of depicts a nude black man seated in the corner of a boxing ring and is claimed to be unmistakably recognizable as . . . Ali. He alleges that the publication of this picture constitutes, a violation of his rights under the New York Civil Rights Law and of his related common law "right of publicity". . . .

Even a cursory inspection of the picture which is the subject of this action strongly suggests that the facial characteristics of the black male portrayed are those of Muhammad Ali. The cheekbones, broad nose and wideset brown eyes, together with the distinctive smile and close cropped black hair are recognizable as the features [of Ali], one of the most widely known athletes of our time. In addition, the figure depicted is seated on a stool in the corner of a boxing ring with both hands taped and outstretched resting on the ropes on either side. Although the picture is captioned "Mystery Man," the identification of the individual as Ali is further implied by an accompanying verse

---

[43] "Fans Can Get Custom Vick Jerseys for Their Dogs," *NBCSports.msnbc.com*, August 20, 2009.
[44] Sean Leahy, "NFL Selling Michael Vick Jersey Customized for Dogs," *USA Today*, August 20, 2009.
[45] Donna Goodison, "Michael Vick, Tops in Jersey Sales," *Boston Herald*, September 9, 2009.

```
which refers to the figure as "the Greatest." This court may take
judicial notice that ... Ali has regularly claimed that appellation
for himself and that his efforts to identify himself in the public
mind as "the Greatest" have been so successful that he is regularly
identified as such in the news media.
```

```
Source: Reprinted from Westlaw with permission of Thomson Reuters.
```

Should an athlete be able to protect a self-designated nickname such as "The Greatest"?

When Albert Pujols slams a 500-foot home run, who owns the statistic of the home run he has created with his bat? Is it Albert Pujols? Is it Major League Baseball? His employer, the St. Louis Cardinals baseball club? Who has ownership of player performance statistics is a difficult question. With large amounts of money at stake, Major League Baseball wanted its piece of the action in the fantasy game industry.

Each year more than 8 million baseball fans gather before the regular season begins and draft their fantasy teams. As the season progresses, the owners pretend they are a general manager: trading, waiving, and picking up new players along the way to try to win. The outcome of each fantasy team and player is tied to the actual, on-field performance of Major League Baseball players. The information utilized by fantasy leagues is publicly available for everyone who wants to locate it. It is simply the information from the box scores printed in the daily sports page or found on multiple websites. With the growth of the industry to its current size, fantasy providers do more than just provide the names and numbers. The industry treats its fantasy owners as if they were actual team officials. Although there are now fantasy games for almost all major sports, baseball began the phenomenon many years ago. With the advent of the Internet, fantasy sports has turned into a commercialized, money-making machine that allows millions to play every season.[46]

In Case 11-11, a former licensee of MLB fantasy games, C.B.C., thought it should no longer have to pay for information readily available to the general public and so easily located in the public domain. The Major League Baseball Players Association disagreed, arguing fantasy games' providers should have to pay for the information.

📖 CASE 11-11   *C.B.C. Distribution and Marketing, Inc. v. Major League Baseball*

```
443 F.Supp.2d 1077 (7th Cir. 2006)
```

```
The Players' Association is the bargaining representative for Major
League baseball players and is comprised of almost all persons who are
employed as Major League baseball players. Advanced Media was formed
in 2000 by various owners of Major League Baseball teams to serve as the
```

---

[46] See Patrick K. Thornton and Christopher James, "Down Two Strikes, Is Major League Baseball Already Out?: How the 8th Circuit Balked to Protect the Right of Publicity in C.B.C. v. MLB, Advanced Media," *South Texas Law Review* 50, no. 2 (Winter 2008); www.deepleagues.com.

interactive media and Internet arm of Major League Baseball. As part of its responsibilities, Advanced Media is in charge of running Major League Baseball's Internet site, MLB.com.

CBC, which uses the trade name CDM Fantasy Sports . . . markets, distributes, and sells fantasy sports products, including fantasy baseball games accessible over the Internet . . .

. . . CBC currently offers eleven fantasy baseball games, two mid-season fantasy baseball games, and one fantasy baseball playoff game. CBC provides lists of Major League baseball players for selection by participants in its games. Game participants pay fees to CBC to play its games and pay additional amounts to trade players. Prior to the start of the professional baseball season participants form their teams by "drafting" players from various Major League baseball teams. Participants or "owners" compete against other fantasy owners who have drafted their own teams. The success of one's fantasy team over the course of the baseball season is dependent on one's chosen players' actual performances on their respective actual teams.

In addition to fantasy sports games, CBC's website provides up-to-date information on each player to assist game participants in selecting players for and trading players on their fantasy teams. This information includes information which is typically found in box scores in newspapers such as players' batting averages, at bats, hits, runs, doubles, triples, home runs, etc . . .

Source: *Reprinted from Westlaw with permission of Thomson Reuters.*

Do players have a right of publicity in the statistics they create?

In the following case a famous MLB pitcher was upset by how he was depicted in an alcohol ad that appeared in *Sports Illustrated* magazine.

📖 CASE 11-12 *Don Newcombe v. Coors Brewing Company*

157 F.3d 686 (9th Cir. 1997)

[Donald] Newcombe is a former Major League Baseball All-Star who pitched for the Brooklyn Dodgers and other teams from 1949 until 1960. He had previously starred in the so-called Negro leagues and was one of the first African-American players to play in the major leagues after Jackie Robinson broke the color barrier in 1947. Newcombe is the only player in Major League history to have won the Most Valuable Player Award, the Cy Young Award, and the Rookie of the Year Award. He was a four-time member of the National League All Star Team, he batted over .300 in four different seasons, and had the most wins of any pitcher in the National League in 1950, 1951, 1955, and 1956.

Newcombe's baseball career was cut short due to his service in the Army and a personal battle with alcohol. He is a recovering alcoholic and he has devoted a substantial amount of time using his fame to advocate the dangers of alcohol, including serving as a spokesperson for the National Institute on Drug and Alcohol Abuse pursuant to presidential appointments by Richard Nixon, Gerald Ford, and Ronald Reagan. He is currently the Director of Community Relations with the Los Angeles Dodgers, where he continues an active role in fighting alcohol abuse.

Killian's Irish Red Beer, owned by Coors Brewing Co., published an advertisement in the February 1994 *Sports Illustrated* "swimsuit edition" that featured a drawing of an old-time baseball game. The drawing was on the left half of the full-page advertisement while the right half was filled with text and a picture of a glass of beer. The baseball scene focused on a pitcher in the windup position and the background included a single infielder and an old-fashioned outfield fence. The players' uniforms did not depict an actual team, and the background did not depict an actual stadium. However, Newcombe, along with family, friends, and former teammates, immediately recognized the pitcher featured in the advertisement as Newcombe in his playing days...

While denying that the pitcher in the advertisement was a "likeness" of Newcombe, Coors admitted that the drawing in the color advertisement was based on a newspaper photograph of Newcombe pitching in the 1949 World Series. The drawing and the newspaper photograph are virtually identical, as though the black and white newspaper photo had been traced and colored in. The only major differences between the newspaper photograph of Newcombe and the drawing of him are that the pitcher's uniform number has been changed from "36" to "39," and the bill of the hat in the drawing is a different color from the rest of the hat. Otherwise, the drawing in the advertisement appears to be an exact replica of the newspaper photograph of Newcombe.

Newcombe contends that [both Coors and SI] violated his right of privacy and used his likeness and identity to their commercial advantage in violation of his statutory rights and common law right of privacy. California has long recognized a common law right of privacy for the protection of a person's name and likeness against appropriation by others for their advantage.

Cal. Civ.Code §3344 provides in relevant part, "Any person who knowingly uses another's name, voice, signature, photograph, or likeness, in any manner . . . for purposes of advertising . . . without such person's prior consent . . . shall be liable for any damages sustained by the person."

. . . we hold that in order to constitute Newcombe's likeness, the pitcher depicted in the advertisement must be readily identifiable as Newcombe.

Having viewed the advertisement . . . we note that the drawing in the advertisement and the newspaper photograph of Newcombe upon which the drawing was based are virtually identical. The pitcher's stance, proportions, and shape are identical to the newspaper photograph of Newcombe; even the styling of the uniform is identical, right down to the wrinkles in the pants. [Coors and SI] maintain that stance alone cannot suffice to render a person readily identifiable, and that even if it could, the drawing of the pitcher in the advertisement was essentially generic and could have been any one of thousands of people who have taken to the pitcher's mound to throw a baseball. We disagree.

It may be the case that Newcombe's stance is essentially generic, but based on the record before us, Newcombe is the only one who has such a stance. The record contains pictures of other pitchers in the windup position but none of these pitchers has a stance similar to Newcombe's, thus giving us no basis to reach the conclusion proposed by [Coors and SI] that the pitcher in the advertisement is "generic."

In addition to the identifiability of the pitcher in the advertisement as Newcombe based on the pitcher's stance, the pitcher's skin is moderately dark, which is quite similar to Newcombe's skin color. A jury could rationally find from this that Newcombe was readily identifiable, even though his facial features were not entirely visible . . . the uniform number in the advertisement ("39") is only slightly different than Newcombe's number ("36")-the first number is the same and the second number is simply inverted and the advertisement utilized the same block style numbers that were used on Newcombe's jersey-and it is arguable that the similarity in numbers could either consciously or subconsciously conjure up images of Newcombe. Also, we do not find persuasive the fact that the coloring of the bill of the hat in the advertisement is different, in light of the fact that the rest of the uniform is identical to the uniform in the newspaper photograph of Newcombe.

Source: *Reprinted from Westlaw with permission of Thomson Reuters.*

1. In *Newcombe v. Coors,* did Coors have a duty—ethical or legal or otherwise—to find out who the player was in the picture?
2. Did *Sports Illustrated* violate media ethics by publishing the ad?

CASE STUDY 11-7   *College Athletes*

Sam Keller, former Nebraska and Arizona state quarterback, filed a lawsuit alleging the NCAA and EA Sports were using his collegiate likeness and image in college sports video games. Because NCAA student-athletes are not allowed to receive compensation for their athletic ability, he argued that NCAA and EA sports should not be able to gain from the use of his image.[47]

---

1. Should amateur athletes be paid for use of their image and likeness?

NOTES AND DISCUSSION QUESTIONS

Introduction

1. What actions should be taken against those who steal, knock off, or otherwise infringe upon the intellectual property of another?
2. What steps should corporations take to protect their intellectual property?
3. What steps should corporations take to protect their intellectual property on the Internet?
4. Why are intellectual property rights so important to professional sports franchises?
5. How is intellectual property valued?[48]
6. Which form of intellectual property—trademarks, copyrights, trade secrets, or patents— do you believe are most important to a professional sports franchise?
7. In what ways can the theft of intellectual property damage a business?
8. Athletic shoes seem to be a favorite target for counterfeiters. In 2006 Germany seized almost 1 million pairs of knock-off Nike sneakers. The shoes were valued at $500,000.00. The goods had been shipped from Asia to Hamburg, Germany.[49]
9. Should counterfeiters be put in jail?[50]
10. In 2008 the NFL sent "Cease and Desist" letters to churches that had intended to host Super Bowl parties. They warned churches that showing games on television screens bigger than 55 inches violated the NFL's copyright.[51] Is this just the NFL being the bully on the block, or should they "police" their mark to this extent?
11. In May 2008, the Maricopa County attorney's office filed criminal complaints against three men accused of selling counterfeit NFL merchandise on the eve of Super Bowl XLII. The goods were valued at $500,000. The NFL has taken a hard line on counterfeiters and has enlisted the help of local law enforcement officials to enforce their intellectual property rights.[52]

---

[47] Steve Wieberg, "Ex-QB Sues NCAA, EA Sports over Use of Athletes' Likenesses," *USA Today*, May 7, 2009. Also see Matthew G. Matzkin, "Getting Played: How the Video Game Industry Violates College Athletes' Rights of Publicity by Not Paying for Their Likeness," *Loyola of Los Angeles Entertainment Law Review* 21 (2000–2001): 227.

[48] See Gordon V. Smith, and Russell L. Parr, *Valuation of Intellectual Property and Intangible Assets*, 3d ed. (Hoboken, NJ: John Wiley & Sons, Inc., 2000).

[49] Associated Press, "Germany Seizes Nearly 1M Knockoff Nikes," *Washington Post*, November 14, 2006.

[50] See Mark A. Lemley, "Property, Intellectual Property, and Free Riding," *Texas Law Review* 83 (2004–2005: 1031).

[51] Marcus Baram, "NFL Sacks Church Super Bowl Parties," *ABC News*, February 2, 2008; Alexandra Alter, "God vs. Gridiron," *Wall Street Journal*, February 2, 2008.

[52] Lily Leung, "Criminal Complaints Filed for Fake NFL Goods," *Arizona Republic*, May 18, 2008; Mike Dodd, "More than $300,000 Worth of Counterfeit Goods Seized," *USA Today*, February 4, 2008.

12. Kyle Mathins pled guilty to selling counterfeit NFL goods on eBay. He sold more than 8,600 NFL jerseys worth almost $400,000. He faced a maximum of 10 years in prison for trafficking in counterfeit goods.[53]
13. In the fall of 2006 the NFL demanded that YouTube remove video clips of NFL games and highlights posted on their website. The NFL argued that YouTube was infringing its copyright. Should YouTube have been required to remove the NFL clips from its website?[54]

Copyright Ownership and Use

14. Intellectual property law covers many types of property claims. A New York chef filed a lawsuit in 2007 charging a competitive oyster bar copied "each and every element of her bar." She alleged Ed's Lobster Bar stole her intellectual property.[55]

The Ethics of Trademark Ownership and Use

15. A party has a duty to protect and police its trademark to ensure no one else is using the mark. In 2006 Texas A&M University filed a lawsuit over the NFL Seattle Seahawks' use of what they believed to be an infringement of their noted "12th Man" trademark. Does it make a difference that the Seahawks are a professional team and the Aggies are collegiate? Are the Aggies just being "poor sports"?[56]
16. Intellectual property rights can come in all forms. In 2007 the Colorado Rockies filed an application with the patent and trademark office for "Rocktober"; a term used to identify the club's playoff run. They sought exclusive rights for "Rocktober" for use on stuffed animals, bobblehead dolls, and similar items.[57]
17. The NFL shot down the sales of t-shirts that said "Yes, We Did," with a picture of the Lombardi Trophy and a black and gold "Six Burgh," after the Steelers sixth Super Bowl win. A cease and desist order stated that the picture of the NFL's Lombardi Trophy violated the NFL trademark and copyright rights. Is this too much "policing"? Should the NFL try to establish some goodwill with fans or stop them from using the marks?[58]
18. The NFL wanted to trademark "The Big Game," but Cal and Stanford objected, saying they had played in "The Big Game" since 1897.[59]

53 "Maryland Man Pleads Guilty to Selling Stolen Stamps and Counterfeit NFL Goods on e-Bay," *U.S. Immigration and Customs Enforcement*, September 8, 2009.
54 For further study, see Ay R. Mellow, "And the Ruling on the Field Is Fair: A Fair Use Analysis of Uploading NFL Videos onto YouTube and Why the NFL Should License Its Material to the Website," *Southern California Interdisciplinary Law Journal* (Fall 2007); *Also see*, "Law Professor Wendy Seltzer Takes on the NFL," *Wall Street Journal*, March 21, 2007.
55 Pete Wells, "Chef Sues Over Intellectual Property (the Menu)," *New York Times*, June 27, 2007.
56 Associated Press, "Texas A&M Unhappy Seattle Fans Called '12th Man,'" *ESPN*, January 28, 2006.
57 Associated Press, "Rockies Seek Trademark Protection for 'Rocktober,'" *ESPN.com*, October 19, 2007.
58 "NFL Orders Cease-and-Desist to Pittsburgh Retailer over SB Gear," *Sports Business Daily*, February 6, 2009.
59 Tom Fitzgerald, "NFL Marketers Want 'Big Game' Trademark," *San Francisco Gate*, March 1, 2007; Craig Mendle, "On Watching 'The Big Game,'" *Forbes.com*, February 1, 2008.

19. In 2008, the New England Patriots filed for trademark protection for the terms "19–0" and "19–0 The Perfect Season." The Patriots lost the 2008 Super Bowl to the New York Giants. The *New York Post* was so confident that the Giants would beat the Pats that they applied for their own trademark, "18–1," application number 77385477.[60]

20. Trademarks that are considered scandalous or immoral cannot be registered, if they give offense to the conscience or moral feelings or are "shocking" to the sense of decency or propriety. For example, a trademark "Old Glory Condom Corp." along with a picture of a condom decorated with stars and stripes suggesting the American flag, was not considered either "scandalous" or "immoral." However, a design of a defecating dog and the word "bullshit" for handbags were considered scandalous and immoral. Who should decide what is scandalous or immoral?[61] Should it depend upon the industry and the consuming public?

21. In *Stop the Olympic Prison [SOP] v. United States Olympic Committee*,[62] [SOP] used the five interlocking rings symbol of the Olympic Games in its "Stop the Olympic Prison" poster as part of their protest against converting the Olympic Village at Lake Placid into a prison after the 1980 Olympic Games. A New York court held that this use was not a dilution of the Olympic mark.[63]

22. A trademark can be held for as long as the owner desires, so long as the owner does not abandon the mark. What are the ethical concerns around holding intellectual property in perpetuity? Should there be limitations on the length that intellectual property can be held?[64]

23. In *Steinberg, Moorad & Dunn, Inc. v. David L. Dunn and Athletes First LLC*,[65] well-known sports agent Leigh Steinberg sued his former employee David Dunn when Dunn left the firm and took clients with him. He sued Dunn and his corporation on a variety of legal theories, including breach of contract and trade secret misappropriation. The court of appeals found in favor of Dunn. The appeals court stated the following in finding against [Steinberg]'s claims for trade secret misappropriation: ". . . the client list information was available to all agents. Thus, this information was not a protectable trade secret in this case."[66]

24. Barry Zito, a MLB star pitcher had his domain name registered by another party. Zito was able to wrestle away his domain name, <barryzito.com>, from the registrant. In an arbitration decision *Barry Zito v. Stan Andruszkiewicz*,[67] in Claim Number: FA0207000114773 (2002), the panel found Mr. Zito had built up a "commercial value" in his name and was entitled to the return of the domain name.

---

[60] Jessica Fargen, "Pats Try to Trademark Perfection," *Boston Herald*, February 1, 2008.

[61] *In re old Glory Condom Corp.*, Trademark Trial and Appeals Board, March 3, 1992.

[62] 489 F. Supp. 1112 (1980).

[63] Robert Kravitz, "Trademarks, Speech, and the Gay Olympics Case," *Boston University Law Review* 69 (1989): 131.

[64] See Sean H. Brogan, "Who Are These 'Colts?': The Likelihood of Confusion, Consumer Survey Evidence, and Trademark Abandonment in Indianapolis Colts, Inc. v. Metropolitan Baltimore Football Club, LTD.," *Marquette Sports Law Journal* 7 (1996–1997): 39.

[65] 136 Fed.Appx. 6 (9th Cir. 2005).

[66] See also Liz Mullen "Steinberg Case: Secret Agent's Tale," *Sports Business Journal* (June 18, 2001).

[67] www.barry-zito.com

25. In 2008 the MLBPA sued Steiner Sports Marketing, saying the seller of memorabilia was selling the jerseys of Boston Red Sox players with authentic signatures. The players wanted the court to confiscate all counterfeited materials.[68]

26. At the 2009 Super Bowl, U.S. Customs, the Tampa Police Department, and the NFL seized 826 pieces of Super Bowl XLIII counterfeit merchandise valued at $115,978 along with $1 million worth of non-NFL counterfeit merchandise.[69]

Ethics in Licensing and Sponsorship Agreements

27. Colleges and universities have had to battle over the use of their trademarks against infringers.[70]

28. A professional wrestling promoter sued the manufacturer of t-shirts and related consumer merchandise for copyright infringement, trademark infringement and dilution, trade dress infringement, and related state-law torts. The manufacturer made "dogified" caricatures of the promoter's copyrighted characters (e.g., "The Rock"). A Court held that the accused merchandise did not violate the wrestling characters' publicity rights.[71]

Protecting the Athlete's Image and Right of Publicity

29. Pitcher Nolan Ryan was sued by a Texas couple who claimed he breached a contract for the exclusive right to sell the likeness of his pitching hand.[72]

30. New England star quarterback Tom Brady sued Yahoo! over the use of his image to promote fantasy football games. Brady said Yahoo! used his photo without his permission in a September 2006 *Sports Illustrated* ad and in its banner ads on Yahoo![73]

31. Kareem Abdul-Jabbar was a great NBA player, maybe the greatest. His "sky hook" dominated the league for many years. Should he capitalize on his "Sky Hook" and be able to use the term in marketing? In fact, that is exactly what he did. Abdul-Jabbar stated he hopes to use proceeds from "Sky Hook" apparel sales to raise money for schools.[74]

32. The NFLPA dealt with fantasy sports leagues in *CBS Interactive Inc. v. National Football League Players Association, Inc.* Should football statistics be treated any differently from baseball statistics with dealing with the right of publicity?

33. James "Cool Papa" Bell was a well-known baseball player who played in the Negro Leagues from 1922 to 1950 and was inducted into the Baseball Hall of Fame in 1974.

---

[68] Leslie Gevitz and Toni Reinhold, "Baseball Players Sue Steiner Sports over Trademark," *Reuters*, May 16, 2008.

[69] "Super Bowl: ICE, TPD, NFL Team to Seize Counterfeit Jerseys, T-Shirts . . .," *Imperial Valley News*, January 29, 2009.

[70] *Texas Tech University v. Speigelberg*, 461 F.Supp.2d 510 (N.D. Tex. 2006) (Disputes over "Red Raider" trademarks); *Board of Trustees University of Arkansas v. Professional Therapy Services, Inc.*, 873 F.Supp. 1280 (W.D. Ark. 1995) (Dispute over Razorback logo).

[71] David A. Kessler, Greenberg & Traurig, McLean, Virginia, "2004 Summer Intellectual Property Law Conference: The Parody Defense: Is Anyone Still Laughing?" American Bar Association, Section of Intellectual Property Law, June 16–20, 2004, Toronto, Ontario.

[72] Associated Press, "Ryan Is Sued over a Show of Hands," *New York Times*, July 23, 1992.

[73] "Tom Brady: Yahoo! In Illegal Procedure," *CNNMoney.com*, December 8, 2006.

[74] Don Walker, "Does Kareem Own 'Sky Hook'?" *Milwaukee Journal Sentinel*, June 1, 2009.

Once inducted, he gave the Baseball Hall of Fame permission to use his likeness. Following his death, his daughter granted permission to use his likeness to several different companies. However, in 2001 and 2004, Topps released some baseball trading cards with Bell on them without getting permission from Bell's daughter. His daughter also claimed that there was information on the cards that was both false and derogatory. The right of publicity claim was barred by the statute of limitations.[75]

34. In January 2010, Shaquille O'Neal sued a Las Vegas company over the word, "Shaqtus." When O'Neal played for the Phoenix Suns, he was known as "the Big Cactus" and "the Big Shaqtus."[76] Do you consider this an infringement upon Shaq's right of publicity? Do you consider this stealing?

---

[75] Clay Luraschi, "Topps Settles Lawsuit over Cool Papa Bell Cards," *Reuters*, November 14, 2008.
[76] Steve Green, "Company Sues in LV over Alleged Shaquille O'Neal Trademark Infringement," *Las Vegas Sun*, January 18, 2010.

CHAPTER 12

ETHICAL CONSIDERATIONS
IN SPORTS MEDIA

SPORTS AND THE MEDIA

Sports and the media have always been interrelated. Individuals have been reading and writing about sporting events for over a century.[1] Whether a fan is checking the box score of his or her favorite team in a newspaper or other source, or gathering news about a favorite sports star, individuals are interested in getting information about the sporting life and those who play sports.[2]

Historically, fans followed only their local teams; however, technology has now made sports a global business. Fans all over the world follow a variety of sporting events, teams, players, and coaches. Americans watch Australian Rules football (footy), the National Football League is popular in Japan, the National Hockey League plays games in Europe, and football (soccer) is a global sport. With the explosion of coverage by the sports media on an international basis, teams such as Real Madrid, the New York Yankees, Manchester United, and the Detroit Red Wings have become international franchises followed by millions of fans around the globe.

Before cable television, sports programming consisted of a relatively few sporting events on the weekend with Major League Baseball's game of the week operating as the cornerstone of sports programming. Now sports fans can proudly sit in front of a big screen television for hours on end, and watch a myriad of sporting events, 24 hours a day, seven days a week. Cable television, and more specifically ESPN, has transformed sports reporting, production, and the viewing of sports in the last three decades. Sports fans now have multiple channels exclusively dedicated to sports programming and offering many different sports from around the world. Who would want to watch sports 24 hours a day, seven days a week? Evidently, millions of people, because that is exactly what has transpired in today's sports media bonanza. ESPN now has multiple channels showing sports from many different countries. Television, radio, Internet, print media, and other forms of media are able to deliver sports programming to rabid fans.

---

[1] See David Remnick, *The Only Game in Town: Sportswriting from the New Yorker* (New York: Random House, 2010).
[2] See David Halberstam, *The Best American Sports Writing of the Century* (Boston, MA: Mariner Books, 1999); "The Best Sportswriting of 2008," *Wall Street Journal*, January 2, 2009.

All these various forms of media deliver a constant stream of sporting events, news, and information to viewers. The wide range of sports they broadcast includes the traditional four major U.S. sports, baseball, hockey, football (American), and basketball, and also includes many other sports such as weightlifting, competitive cheerleading, lumberjacking, spelling bees, bowling, track and field, poker tournaments, tennis, volleyball, and hunting and fishing. Media outlets not only deliver the games and the events themselves but also ancillary programming such as pre- and postgame shows, fantasy game shows, coaches' shows, and draft programs, all exploring every conceivable angle of a particular sporting event.

Drafts for professional leagues used to be something a fan would read about in the newspaper days or even weeks later, but ESPN has turned the NFL draft and other sports drafts into a "must see" event for sports fans. Radio shows abound with sports talk and sports news. Callers and hosts discuss every conceivable angle of the sport and players. Professional sports leagues understand that fans want to view the games so they developed their own broadcast venues. MLB "Extra Innings," NHL "Center Ice," MLS "Direct Kick," NBA "League Pass," and the NFL Network are all exclusively dedicated to showing programming from each particular league. Collegiate athletic conferences have quickly followed, establishing their own programming including the Big Ten Network.[3] The University of Texas at Austin is the first university with its own television network, dedicated exclusively to showing Longhorn athletic events.[4]

Sports programming and news are now delivered through a variety of forms of media. Fewer fans are getting their news from the daily newspaper, instead choosing the Internet and other nontraditional media sources to gather their sports information. Sports fans are retrieving their sports, news, scores, and information from Internet websites, blogs, Twitter, text messages, and cable television. Print media now takes a backseat to other forms of media that can deliver the sports news much quicker to the fan. At one time only the local sportswriter was able to express opinions about local sports teams and players, but a variety of individuals are now involved in the media process and have the ability to have input on a variety of issues. Fans have always had their own opinions on what a team or professional player should do to improve their skills or chances of winning, that is not new. However, technological advances have provided fans with easier access to voice comments, concerns, and recommendations to general managers, coaches, and players. Players have blogs and send out tweets and coaches do the same. Call-in radio shows and local television programs also offer access to sports fans. University athletic directors make themselves available to alumni and students on the web or through a blog. Fans (some who have nothing intelligent to say whatsoever) have also gained access to the sports forum through the Internet, text messaging, and via a variety of handheld devices. In short, if a sports fan wants to watch, listen, comment, or follow sports, numerous media platforms are now available.

Ethical dilemmas exist for all those involved in the sports media process. In 2010, ESPN was faced with ethical concerns when dealing with basketball's biggest star.

CASE STUDY 12-1   *"The Decision"*

When NBA star LeBron James became a free agent, his decision to join the NBA's Miami Heat became a media circus. ESPN aired a one-hour special about James, called "The Decision," and James used the program

---

[3] www.bigtennetwork.com

[4] Chris Duncan, *"Longhorns Get Own TV Network,"* theeagle.com, Bryan-College Station Texas, February 20, 2011.

to announce that he was joining the NBA's Miami Heat. James's sports marketing company suggested to ESPN that the show's advertisers would donate money to the Boys and Girls Clubs of America, a favorite charity of Mr. James.[5]

The *Washington Post* reported:

> The most troubling aspect of the whole ill-conceived mess was ESPN's willingness to hand over an hour of prime-time television to an egomaniacal athlete the network should be covering as a news story. After all, James's final choice of teams already had previously been reported and confirmed by several other news outlets, including ESPN's own man, Chris Broussard. Wasn't that enough?[6]

1. Was ESPN's agreement to air "The Decision" a violation of media ethics?
2. Did ESPN lose its editorial independence by airing the program?[7]

CASE STUDY 12-2   *2010 Olympic Luge Controversy*

Deciding what should be shown to the viewing public can be a difficult task. Media outlets are now showered with images, and with technological advances, are now able to capture a moment in time that would have been impossible just a few years ago. Controversy sells, and the media clearly understands that concept. Money and ratings are important to media outlets, and exploiting a controversy could bring more viewers to that outlet.

In the 2010 Olympics, a Georgian Luger was tragically killed during an Olympic training run. NBC decided to show the footage of the death of the athlete. NBC News anchor Brian Williams gave the following warning before showing the footage: "We owe folks a warning here . . . these pictures are very tough for some people to watch." Could the story have been told just as well without showing the fatal accident of the athlete? *USA Today* stated:

> News organizations frequently weigh the imperative of depicting the reality of the world they cover with concerns about whether images would be too disturbing for the public. In this case, the network warned viewers and used the video. NBC, in a departure from its usual policy of holding onto video because it is the U.S. Olympics rightsholder, let other networks use it.[8]

1. Should such a tragic event be shown on television?
2. Was it poor judgment or a breach of journalistic ethics on behalf of NBC to show such an event?
3. What considerations should be given to the family of the athlete before showing the event?
4. Was it a necessary part of the story to show an athlete being killed on television?

---

[5] "ESPN's Internal Watchdog Slams Network's LeBron James Special," *Wall Street Journal*, July 21, 2010. Richard Deitsch, "MEDIA CIRCUS," *Sports Illustrated*, July 9, 2010.
[6] Leonard Shapiro, "Coverage of LeBron James's Decision Brings ESPN's Integrity Into Question Yet Again," *The Washington Post*, July 13, 2010.
[7] Ibid.
[8] David Bauder, "Networks Criticized for Video of Fatal Luge Accident at Olympics," *USA Today*, February 13, 2010.

MEDIA ETHICS

Ethics, and in particular journalistic ethics, is not a new field. Ethics in journalism has been a subject of debate for many years.[9] Reporters don't always get it right—consider 1948 U.S. presidential candidate Thomas Dewey.[10] Reporting the facts of a story can sometimes be difficult, as writers and reporters try to determine the truth. Reporters and writers wield a great deal of power and can, with just a few words, reveal a devastating truth or a bold-faced lie. The press has a remarkable degree of freedom in the United States. The media can control the fate of nations and important people in society. Along with that power the media also has ethical duties and responsibilities to fulfill. Media outlets have a responsibility to perform journalism in accordance with the highest standards, and to avoid all potential and actual conflicts of interest.[11]

Integrity is an essential quality for any journalist or media outlet. Simply put, media outlets and their employees must produce accurate information. A journalist must be trusted to produce a quality product. Reporters, editors, and producers who prepare stories, graphics, and interactive media must do so in a manner consistent with ethical standards.

The cornerstone of any reporting is accuracy. If the news and stories produced are not accurate, a media outlet will lose credibility with the viewing public and may be out of business due to multiple lawsuits. Any interpretation from the facts of a story must be a reasonable interpretation, not merely the opinion of a writer or producer, and must be based on a fair interpretation of the facts. Reporters, editors, and writers must be committed to the concept of fairness in the pursuit of any story.

No individual can be totally objective; everyone brings their own experiences, background, and education to a situation, and this may influence their viewpoint of a story. However, some basic principles of fairness do exist. Fairness translates to completeness. No story is fair if it is incomplete or fails to attempt to present both sides of an issue. No story should omit significant facts that would shed light on the truthfulness of the story. Furthermore, news reporting should never exclude important facts at the expense of irrelevant information. If a story misleads or deceives a reader, it should not be told. The concept of fairness means being straightforward with the reader. Certain essential questions should be asked before a news story is released:

1. Does the story present both sides of the issue?
2. Were both sides of the dispute given a chance for equal input in the story?
3. Does the story show bias in any way?
4. Does the story deceive the reader or viewer in any way?
5. Was every reasonable effort made to determine the truth of the matter?

Recognizing and avoiding conflicts of interest are essential to the integrity of any media outlet. Writers, producers, and employees of media outlets should not accept gifts or any form of preferential treatment when covering a story. It is the essence of journalistic integrity to show independence. Reporters must fully understand their role and the trust they have been given to report a story fairly and accurately.

---

[9] Cooper Rollow, "Sportscasters Debate TV Sports' Ethics, Style," *Chicago Tribune*, June 9, 1977.

[10] Thomas Mallon, *Dewey Defeats Truman: A Novel* (New York: Picador, 1997).

[11] See Lawrence A. Wenner, *MediaSport* (New York: Routledge, 1998). Also see, Lee Witkins and Clifford G. Christians, *The Handbook of Mass Media Ethics* (New York: Routledge, 2008).

In our technological age, a news story can be transmitted instantaneously. Media outlets have immense power to tell a story and persuade. It is essential they get it right to avoid damage to their own reputation or to those who are the subject of the story.

It is also essential that reporters not make the news, only report the news. Writers should be able to distinguish between advocacy and news reporting. Furthermore, during the news gathering process, reporters must be careful not to misrepresent their identity. They should be truthful and forthright with all individuals they interview while investigating a story.

Accuracy should be the major goal of any media outlet. Any significant errors of facts, or omission of facts, should be promptly corrected in a responsible and an ethical manner, making it clear that the media outlet was at fault in reporting the story. Media outlets should publish, in an acceptable manner to all parties involved, a proper retraction to set the record straight, accepting responsibility for their actions.[12]

A recent example of failed reporting occurred in the sport of baseball. Because of the suspicion of steroid use by players, commissioner Bud Selig solicited former U.S. Senator George Mitchell to investigate and issue a report about drug use in America's national pastime. The Mitchell Report contained the names of many MLB players that former Senator Mitchell said used performance enhancing drugs. When the report was released, St. Louis Cardinals star Albert Pujols was not named in the report as a player who used PED's. However, that did not prevent WNBC-TV in New York from reporting on its website that Pujols was listed in the Mitchell Report as a user of PED's. KTVU, a St. Louis television station, picked up the story and also reported that Pujols appeared in the report as a user of PED's. It was also incorrectly reported that MLB player Johnny Damon was listed in the Mitchell Report. After being named in the report many MLB players confessed that they did in fact use illegal drugs. Reporting that players were in the report, when in fact they were not, could cause major legal problems for the media outlets who engaged in false reporting and rumors as well as creating substantial ethical dilemmas. Pujols's agent issued the following statement on his behalf:

"It has come to my attention that several national and local news outlets have published false reports that associated my name with the Mitchell Report. I have never disrespected, nor cheated the game of baseball and knew without a doubt that my name would not be mentioned in the official investigation. . . . I would like to express how upset and disappointed I am over the reckless reporting that took place this morning. It has caused me and my family a lot of senseless aggravation due to their inaccurate information.". . . "What concerns me, is the effect this has had on my family and that my character and values have now been questioned due to the media's lack of accuracy in their reporting. I have never had a problem with the media when they do their job correctly, whether it is positive or negative—just as long as they report truthfully."[13]

"I would like to thank my fans for their continued support and never doubting my integrity. God has blessed me and allowed me to play a game that I would never take for granted."

The New York station issued an apology to Pujols.[14] What other actions should they have taken to correct their mistake?

---

[12] Nicholas Wade, "3 Harvard Researchers Retract a Claim on the Aging of Stem Cells," *The New York Times*, October 14; 2010; William Safire, "Retraction," *The New York Times*, June 12, 2005.

[13] "Pujols Reacts upon Hearing Name on Rumored List," *ESPN.com*, December 14, 2007.

[14] Associated Press, "Pujols Bans TV Station That Erred Naming Him in Mitchell Report," *ESPN.com*, January 21, 2008.

CASE STUDY 12-3 *A Proper Retraction*

In 2009, *Sports Illustrated* reported that Boston College football player B.J. Raji had tested positive for drug use at the NFL combine, but they were wrong; Raji had not tested positive. After discovering their error, they issued the following retraction:

> **"Correction: BC's Raji not on NFL's Drug List**
> An si.com report posted earlier this month incorrectly stated that Boston College defensive tackle B.J. Raji's name would appear on the NFL's list of players who tested positive for drugs at the NFL Scouting Combine in February. We regret the error."[15]

1. Do you consider the retraction satisfactory?
2. How could *Sports Illustrated* have made the retraction more effective?
3. Should they have issued a formal apology directly to the Boston College player?[16]
4. Should they have also sent the retraction directly to Raji's potential employers, all 30 NFL teams?

Plagiarism is one of the unforgivable sins of the journalist. All producers, reporters, and writers should fully understand the concepts and principles surrounding plagiarism.[17] Materials taken from other sources must be given their proper attribution. No work should be passed off as original if it has been copied from another source.[18] Plagiarism can lead to lawsuits and sometimes even a criminal conviction.[19] Taking another individual's idea without giving proper credit can devastate the credibility of a journalist, reporter, or media outlet and is clearly an ethical violation.[20]

Media sources should make every effort to disclose the source of their information whenever possible. However, if a journalist promises to protect the identity of an informant, every effort should be made to keep the identity of the source confidential.

When producing and delivering a story, every effort should be made to abstain from showing profanity, violence, or indecent behavior unless it can be shown to be an essential part of the story that needs to be told.

The first and primary goal of any news media outlet should be to tell the truth. Sometimes the truth is hard to define and even tougher to find. Reporters may discover competing versions of the truth and the versions must be reconciled whenever possible. Images are a major part of reporting and of truth-seeking, particularly in light of advanced technology in reporting. People remember what they see long after what they hear. A media outlet's depiction of images must always be genuine and truthful. No objects or pictures should ever be rearranged, distorted, or removed from a scene in an

---

[15] "Correction: BC's Raji not on NFL's Drug List," *Sports Illustrated*, April 21, 2009.

[16] For further study, see Elad Peled, "Constitutionalizing Mandatory Retraction in Defamation Law," *Hastings Communications and Entertainment Law Journal* 30 (2007).

[17] See Marc Santora, "Columbia Professor in Noose Case Is Fired on Plagiarism Charges," *The New York Times*, June 24, 2008.

[18] Katherine Q. Seelye, "Sportswriter at Massachusetts Paper Is Fired for Plagiarism," *The New York Times*, February 4, 2005.

[19] Trip Gabriel, "Plagiarism Lines Blur for Students in Digital Age," *The New York Times*, August 1, 2010.

[20] Dan Former, "WSJ Freelancer Plagiarized Column, Attributed Stolen Quotes to Fake People," *Business Insider*, December 3, 2009. See also "Goodwin Withdraws from Pulitzer Judging," *CNN.com*, March 5, 2002.

attempt to tell a story. It is essential that images surrounding the story never be staged or posed. The use of a picture, image, or video must be done in a manner that advances the fairness of the story being told. Enhancing an image for technical clarity is permissible if done fairly and when consistent with the overall objective of the story being told.

When reporting a story, writers should always refrain from stereotyping based on age, gender, national origin, religion, sexual orientation, geography, disability, physical appearance, or social status. It is essential that media outlets treat every individual with respect and dignity.

CASE STUDY 12-4   *"Broadway Joe" in Primetime*

Joe Namath was a showman and a great football player in the AFL and NFL. In December 2003, Namath was being interviewed by ESPN's Suzy Kolber during a Monday night football game. As the interview progressed, it was clear that Namath was intoxicated. The interview was paused while the camera went back to the action on the field. After the next play, the interview continued with Namath still clearly intoxicated. He then asked Kolber if he could kiss her. Kolber did the best she could under the circumstances to deal with the situation, saying she would take Namath's statement as a compliment. ESPN executive Jeff Drake stated, "If we had known definitively (Namath) was in that kind of state, we wouldn't have conducted the interview." Namath later apologized to Kolber and ESPN, and the apology was accepted.[21]

1. Once the broadcaster determined Namath was drunk, did the broadcaster have an ethical obligation to terminate the interview and not place Namath back on camera?

CASE STUDY 12-5   *Media Ethics: Role Models*

Any fan of the NFL has been exposed (sometimes unfortunately) to NFL wide receivers Terrell Owens ("T. O.") and Chad Johnson ("Ocho Cinco"). A lesser known athlete is NBA star Tim Duncan but why is he a lesser known superstar considering his stellar accomplishments? All Duncan has done is win four NBA championships, be named NBA finals MVP three times, win two league MVP awards, earn NBA Rookie of the Year, honors, be voted to 12 All-Star games and 13 all-NBA defense teams. Not too bad for a basketball player who is not usually the subject of a national media campaign.

One noted writer said this about Tim Duncan:

"Whenever there's a story done on Tim Duncan, it always comes with a preface: That Tim isn't like the rest of those guys, He's not from Harlem. He's from the Caribbean," said Earl Smith, a professor at Wake Forest, where Duncan attended college. "I would argue that Tim Duncan, who's plain vanilla, has no media appeal. I don't think the media is looking for that kind of black athlete. If they scratch the surface, they're supposed to find something. You know, 'he came from a single parent household, ran with a gang, raised by adoptive white parents,' something like that. When they don't find that person, they take a pass, because nobody wants to read about those folks. So I always wonder, Where's the story about the player who doesn't carry all that baggage?"[22]

---

[21] Rudy Martzke, "Embarrassed Namath Apologizes to Kolber," *USA Today*, December 23, 2003; Associated Press, "Still Broadway Joe," *SI.com*, December 21, 2003.

[22] Shaun Powell, *"Souled Out?"* First Edition, Human Kinetics, 2007. p. 191.

1. Does the sports media community as a whole focus too much on the athletes who market themselves rather than those who don't seek the limelight?
2. Should the sports media focus on the overwhelming majority of athletes who never have any personal problems and are contributing to their community rather that the few who engage in bad behavior?
3. Is the media just giving sports fans what they want?

CASE STUDY 12-6 *Reporter Reports on Golfer Michelle Wie*

A simple proposition in the media industry is that a reporter should never become the story or even part of the story. In 2005 golfer Michelle Wie was disqualified from the Samsung World Championship when a *Sports Illustrated* reporter alerted a LPGA official that Wie had allegedly violated tournament rules by taking an illegal drop during the event. The reporter was *Sports Illustrated* senior writer Michael Bamberger. Bamberger had spent a year caddying on the PGA tour. He said, "I don't think she cheated. I think she was simply hasty." Before reporting her, he first went to Wie and discussed the situation with her. He said, "I felt the correct thing was to go to Michelle first. I wanted to hear what she had to say. That's a reporter's first obligation."[23]

1. Did Bamberger act ethically in reporting Wie's actions on the golf course?
2. Should Bamberger have merely written a story about Wie's alleged violation of the rules instead of turning her in?
3. Is it ever proper for a reporter to step out of his or her role as a reporter and become a "self-appointed referee" as Bamberger did?

THE ETHICS OF FAIR REPORTING AND DEFAMATION

Many times a story will reveal facts and circumstances that are not flattering to the individual who is the subject of the story. A media outlet must make a decision about what stories should be told and which ones are not newsworthy. In the sporting world, a newsworthy story could be an injury to a star athlete, the gambling problems of an owner, the negotiation of a new collective bargaining agreement for a professional league, or any other relevant or significant news about a sport and those who play it. A closer call for a media outlet is whether to cover a story that may be more personal in nature but still concerns a sports star or a team. Media professionals should be concerned with the privacy rights of those people who are the subject of their reporting and furthermore, must ensure that their rights are respected while they are reporting on a newsworthy story.

Coaching and leading a major college football program can be a high-profile job, especially if that job is at the University of Alabama. Historically, Alabama has been one of college football's winningest programs. Mike Price was hired as the new football coach at the university but would never coach a game for the Crimson Tide. Price's antics at a local establishment created a media frenzy and eventually cost him his head coaching job. Price sued Time, Inc. for a story that appeared in *Sports Illustrated* magazine. The issue was to what extent could *Sports Illustrated* and their writer be forced

---

[23] Alan Shipnuck, "Steep Drop," *SI Vault*, October 24, 2005.

to reveal a confidential source for an article that was published about coach Price and his activities at a Florida night club.

📖 **CASE 12-1** *Price v. Time, Inc.*

416 F.3d 1327 (11th Cir. 2005)

In the Spring of 2003 Mike Price was head coach of the University of Alabama's Crimson Tide football team. Given the near-fanatical following that college football has in the South, the head coach at a major university is a powerful figure. However, as Archbishop Tillotson observed three centuries ago, "they, who are in highest places, and have the most power . . . have the least liberty, because they are most observed."[FN1] If Price was unaware of that paradox when he became the Crimson Tide's coach, he learned it the hard way a few months later in the aftermath of a trip he took to Pensacola, Florida.

[FN1]Thomas Birch, The Life of Dr. John Tillotson Compiled Chiefly from His Original Papers and Letters, in 1 The Works of the Most Reverend Dr. John Tillotson, Lord Archbishop of Canterbury lxxix (London, J. & R. Tonson et al. 1752).

While in Pensacola to participate in a pro-am golf tournament, Price, a married man, visited an establishment known as "Artey's Angels." The name is more than a little ironic because the women who dance there are not angels in the religious sense and, when he went, Price was not following the better angels of his nature in any sense. Scandal ensued, and as often happens in our society, litigation followed closely on the heels of scandal.

[The issue in the case is] whether *Sports Illustrated* magazine and one of its writers are protected under Alabama law or by the federal Constitution from being compelled to reveal the confidential source for an article they published about Price and his activities in Pensacola . . . The federal constitutional question involves application of the First Amendment qualified reporter's privilege, which in this case comes down to one factor: whether Price has made all reasonable efforts to discover the identity of the confidential source in ways other than by forcing *Sports Illustrated* and its writer to divulge it . . . we conclude that *Sports Illustrated* is not a newspaper for purposes of Alabama's shield law, but we also conclude that Price has not yet exhausted all reasonable efforts to discover through other means the identity of the confidential source.

Don Yaeger is a reporter for *Sports Illustrated*, a weekly magazine published by Time, Inc., which contains sports-related features, reports, opinions, and advertisements. The issue of *Sports Illustrated* that hit the newsstands on May 8, 2003 (but actually bore the date of

May 12, 2003) contained an article written by Yaeger entitled, "Bad Behavior: How He Met His Destiny At A Strip Club." The "he" in the title refers to Price, and the "Destiny" reference is a double-entendre playing off the stage name of one of the strippers at Artey's Angels. The *Sports Illustrated* article itself recounts allegations of boorish behavior and sexual misconduct by Price in the months following his ascension to the position of head football coach at the University of Alabama. The article indicates that it relies on confidential sources for the most salacious parts of its content.

One of the incidents described in the article involves sexual advances Price allegedly made, shortly after he was hired in late 2002, towards some unnamed female students in a bar and at an apartment complex in Tuscaloosa, Alabama, where the University is located. The parties refer to this as "the Tuscaloosa incident." . . . Price's counsel informed us that since . . . he has uncovered by other means the identity of the confidential sources for the reporting about the Tuscaloosa incident . . .

Price has not yet discovered the identity of the confidential source for the article's reporting on "the Pensacola incident," . . . The article states that shortly after arriving in Pensacola, Florida, on the afternoon of April 16, 2003, Price went to a strip club called "Artey's Angels." It says that he spent most of his time with a dancer named Lori "Destiny" Boudreaux, who is quoted in the article as saying that Price bought her drinks, tipped her $60 for "semiprivate" dances, and touched her inappropriately during those dances, which was against the house rules. Price told Destiny that he had a room at a hotel in town and that he wanted her to meet him there later that night.

The article also alleges that Price visited Artey's a second time, later on the same day, after he had left the golf tournament's sponsor dinner early. The article says that while sitting at the bar in Artey's, Price was "kissing and fondling a waitress until a reminder from the deejay prompted him to stop." It describes how he continued to buy several hundred dollars worth of drinks and dances until about midnight, and finally invited two dancers back to his hotel room where the three of them supposedly had sex. The article includes this description of what allegedly occurred at Price's hotel room:

At about midnight [after leaving the club] Price headed back to the hotel. He eventually met up with two women, both of whom he had earlier propositioned for sex, according to one of the women, who agreed to speak to SI about the hotel-room liaison on the condition that her name not be used. The woman, who declined comment when asked if she was paid for the evening, said that the threesome engaged "in some pretty aggressive sex." She said that at one point she and her female companion decided to add a little levity to the activity: "We started screaming 'Roll Tide!' and he was yelling back, 'It's rolling baby, it's rolling.'"

On May 3, 2003, five days before the article was published, Yaeger called Price to get his response to the allegations about the Pensacola incident. Yaeger asked Price if it was true that "both Jennifer (Eaton) and 'Destiny,'" two exotic dancers from Artey's Angels, "met [him] back at the hotel" after he left the club. Price expressed surprise at the allegations and asked Yaeger who had told him that. Price denied having sex with any woman in his hotel room that night. He said the allegations were "[c]ompletely not true." When asked if he had invited anyone back to his hotel room, Price said "[a]bsolutely not." Although Price initially declined to comment when Yaeger asked if he had awakened the next morning with "at least one woman," Price did tell Yaeger "[t]hat story you heard is completely false." When told by Yaeger that Jennifer and Destiny claimed he had paid them $500 plus a "healthy" tip for sex, Price responded: "Well, someone bought 'em, bought 'em off because it's a lie. A flat lie."

On May 6, 2003, only two days before the magazine appeared on the newsstands, Yaeger went on the popular radio show of Paul Finebaum, a sportswriter in Birmingham, Alabama to discuss the upcoming article. Yaeger told listeners about Price's alleged hijinks in Tuscaloosa and Pensacola. The parties agree that the statements Yaeger made on the radio show are not materially different from what he said in the article.

Based on Yaeger's comments on the Finebaum show and the published article, Price sued Yaeger and Time, which is *Sports Illustrated*'s publisher and parent company [for] . . . libel, slander, and outrageous conduct . . .

. . . Price labels as "false and defamatory" most of the allegations in the *Sports Illustrated* article. He does admit visiting Artey's Angels once while in Pensacola for the golf tournament, but he denies everything else . . . Price vehemently denies having sex with anyone mentioned in the article.

Price [says *Sports Illustrated*] "knew or had reason to know" of the "falsity and lack of verified or factual support" for Yaeger's story, and that they published the account of the incidents in Tuscaloosa and Pensacola "knowing of its sensationalizing sting and falsity with malice by intent and/or reckless disregard for the truth in an effort to increase sales and profit to the[ir] benefit." Price [says *Sports Illustrated*] "created this sensational and provocative article in a malicious effort to publish untruths that were assigned to purported

anonymous sources and without a full and fair investigation into the
truth or veracity of the [facts in the article] in an effort to get the
story to press as quickly as possible regardless of its truth and defamatory content so it would explode into the newsstands." . . . Price claims
that [Sports Illustrated] maliciously defamed him either by lying about
having a confidential source, or by relying exclusively on a confidential source that they knew, or should have known, to be untrustworthy.

Source: *Reprinted from Westlaw with permission of Thomson Reuters.*

1. What is the reasoning behind allowing reporters to use materials in a news story that are gathered from confidential sources?[24]
2. Under what circumstances should a media outlet be forced to reveal the confidential sources of a story?
3. Do you think *Sports Illustrated* and writer Don Yaeger treated coach Price ethically and fairly in their reporting of all events?
4. Do you think coach Price's "activities" were newsworthy because of his position at the university or do you consider them a private matter not worthy of reporting?
5. If Coach Price's contract contained a morals clause, would that change your answer?
6. Would your decision about whether the matter was newsworthy change if the university was a private institution rather than a state university?

In the following case, an NBA player sued Time, Inc., a famous sports writer, and a legendary coach about an article that appeared in *Sports Illustrated*. The player, Neil Johnston, claimed he was defamed by the article. The writer, George Plimpton, claimed Johnston had been destroyed "psycho-logically" by NBA great Bill Russell. For further study, read the entire *Sports Illustrated* article[25] and determine if what George Plimpton wrote was a fair and accurate recording of the events.

CASE 12-2   *Johnston v. Time, Inc., et al.*

321 F.Supp. 837 (M.D.N.C. 1970)

This is an action for libel brought against Time, Inc., Arnold 'Red'
Auerbach and George Plimpton, to recover damages resulting from an article appearing in the December 23, 1968, issue of *Sports Illustrated*. The
allegedly libelous statements were printed in connection with a cover
story on Bill Russell, star center for the Boston Celtics professional
basketball team. George Plimpton, the author of the article, chose a
format which included interviews with various people in the sporting
world who had come into contact with Russell. Among those he selected
was 'Red' Auerbach, coach of the Boston Celtics, to whom is attributed
the following statement upon which [Johnston] bases this action:

---

[24] See Jane Kirtley, "A Magazine Is Not a Newspaper," *American Journalism Review* (October/November 2005).
[25] See full text of article at George Plimpton, "Sportsman of the Year Bill Russell," *SI Vault*, December 23, 1968.

'* * * That's a word you can use about him (Russell)—he 'destroyed'
players. You take Neil Johnston—a good set shot and a great sweeping
hook shot, a big long-armed guy who played for Philly and was the
leading scorer in the NBA the year before. Russell destroyed him. He
destroyed him psychologically as well, so that he practically ran him
out of organized basketball. He blocked so many shots that Johnston
began throwing his hook farther and farther from the basket. It was
ludicrous, and the guys along the bench began to laugh, maybe in
relief that they didn't have to worry about such a guy themselves.'

Source: *Reprinted from Westlaw with permission of Thomson Reuters.*

1. Do you think the *Sports Illustrated* article falls under the category of fair reporting?
2. Do you consider what coach Auerbach said or what George Plimpton wrote, either defamatory or unethical?
3. This case was decided in 1970. Would this case be decided differently today?
4. Bill Russell was arguably one of the greatest NBA defensive players of all time. Does this justify the article and the comments made about Johnston?[26]

Crime dominates the lead story on many news broadcasts. When an athlete is charged with a crime, media outlets should be careful about how they report the story. How they portray the athlete can be significant for both ethical and legal reasons. Under the U.S. legal system an individual is presumed innocent until proven guilty and media outlets should report with that principle in mind. Former major leaguer John Montefusco was irate about how he was portrayed by ESPN after he was charged with criminal conduct toward his wife. He sued the media behemoth claiming they unfairly compared him to another athlete who had been charged with a crime, O.J. Simpson.

📖 CASE 12-3 *Montefusco v. ESPN, Inc.*

2002 WL 31108927

John Montefusco, formerly a Major League Baseball pitcher for the San
Francisco Giants, the Atlanta Braves, and the New York Yankees, and once
the National League's "Rookie of the Year," was the subject of a telecast by the ESPN sports news show, "SportsCenter." In the SportsCenter
telecast, ESPN described criminal proceedings in New Jersey concerning
charges against Montefusco by his ex-wife, Doris Montefusco, of sexual
and physical violence. Doris Montefusco charged Montefusco with rape,
threatened murder, and three attempts to seriously injure her with
extreme indifference to human life. The ESPN broadcast noted that a jury
found Montefusco not guilty of eighteen felony counts, but convicted him
of assault and criminal trespass. Several times throughout the telecast,

---

[26] See "ESPN and Bill Bradley," *ESPN College Basketball Encyclopedia: The Complete History of the Men's Game* (ESPN, 2009): 75; Also see, Frank Deford, "The Ring Leader," *SI Vault*, May 10, 1999 (arguing Russell was also the greatest team player of all time).

Montefusco's case was analogized to that of O.J. Simpson, "another ex-
athlete accused of domestic violence." Montefusco sued ESPN for defamation and made a claim for false light invasion of privacy. Both the
defamation claim and the false light claim were based on identical
grounds. Montefusco argues that the comparison with Simpson implies that
Montefusco is guilty of the crimes of which he was acquitted.

Source: *Reprinted from Westlaw with permission of Thomson Reuters.*

1. Was ESPN's comparison of Montefusco to O.J. Simpson a fair comparison?
2. Do you consider this a newsworthy story?
3. Are all alleged criminal activities of athletes "fair game" for the media? Under what circumstances would they not be?
4. Is an athlete's paternity case a newsworthy story? What about a divorce case or a lawsuit involving sexual harassment of an owner, player, or sportscaster?

In holding in favor of ESPN the court stated:

In the instant case, none of the statements made in the sports news
broadcast were defamatory: all of the statements related to the criminal charges were factually accurate, as was the comparison of Montefusco's case to Simpson's...

Pursuant to New Jersey's "fair report privilege," ESPN's presentation
was "accurate and complete," and did not mislead viewers as to the
Simpson case or Montefusco's circumstances.

Source: *Reprinted from Westlaw with permission of Thomson Reuters.*

In Case 12-4, a famous surfer was dissatisfied with the way he was portrayed in a *Sports Illustrated*
article so he sued the magazine for defamation.

CASE 12-4 *Virgil v. Sports Illustrated*

424 F.Supp. 1286, (S.D. 1976)

The facts themselves, putting out cigarettes in his mouth and diving
off stairs to impress women, hurting himself in order to collect unem-
ployment so as to have time for bodysurfing at the Wedge during
summer, fighting in gang fights as a youngster, and eating insects are
not sufficiently offensive to reach the very high level of offensiveness necessary . . . to lose newsworthiness protection. . . . The
above facts are generally unflattering and perhaps embarrassing, but
they are simply not offensive to the degree of morbidity or sensation-
alism. In fact they connote nearly as strong a positive image as they

do a negative one. On the one hand Mr. Virgil can be seen as a juvenile exhibitionist, but on the other hand he also comes across as the
tough, aggressive maverick, an archtypal character occupying a
respected place in the American consciousness. Given this ambiguity as
to whether or not the facts disclosed are offensive at all, no reasonable juror could conclude that they were highly offensive.

. . . Along with the facts complained of Sports Illustrated included
directly therewith Mr. Virgil's retrospective, more mature, perception
and explanation of them. Mr. Virgil was quoted as saying:

"I guess I used to live a pretty reckless life. I think I might have
been drunk most of the time. . . . I'm not sure a lot of the things
I've done weren't pure lunacy."

Any negative impression a reader might have of Mike Virgil would be
tempered considerably by Virgil's own admissions that in hindsight he
may have been acting a bit crazily.

. . . For highly offensive facts, i. e. those having a degree of
offensiveness equivalent to "morbid and sensational," to be denied
protection as newsworthy, the revelation of them must be "for its own
sake." Both parties agree that body surfing at the Wedge is a matter
of legitimate public interest, and it cannot be doubted that Mike
Virgil's unique prowess at the same is also of legitimate public
interest. Any reasonable person reading the *Sports Illustrated* article
would have to conclude that the personal facts concerning Mike Virgil
were included as a legitimate journalistic attempt to explain Virgil's
extremely daring and dangerous style of body surfing at the Wedge.

Source: *Reprinted from Westlaw with permission of Thomson Reuters.*

1. Do you agree that "body surfing at the Wedge" or Mr. Virgil's "unique prowess" are matters
of legitimate public interest?
2. What standards should be employed to make such a decision?
3. Can a matter of public interest be defined differently in sports reporting than elsewhere?

Sports talk radio is very popular. Sports fans call and debate everything from a player's performance on the field to his or her personal life. At times, the topics seem to have no boundaries. Many
times, what is said can be highly inappropriate, even bordering on defamation. Can a radio talk
show host ever go too far in commenting on a team or player? Yes, they can, *see* Don Imus, Chapter 8
on Ethical Considerations of Race in Sports. It is clear that fans and sports casters alike have varying opinions on the skill levels of professional sports players. Many times fans' comments about a
sports star's abilities insightful, can be very cruel and harsh.

In Case 12-5, a well-known radio talk show host was sued by an owner of an NBA team after the
broadcaster continuously took the owner to task over his operation of the NBA's Cleveland Cavaliers.

📖 **CASE 12-5** *Stepien v. Franklin*

528 N.E.2d 1324 (1988)

The area of sports is a traditional haven for cajoling, invective, and hyperbole; therefore, a reasonable listener to a sports talk program is on notice that the host's descriptions of a sports public figure as, *inter alia*, "stupid," "dumb," "buffoon," "nincompoop," "scum," "a cancer," "an obscenity," "gutless liar," "unmitigated liar," "pathological liar," "egomaniac," "nuts," "crazy," "irrational," "suicidal," and "lunatic" are statements of opinion which are constitutionally protected.

Public figures, having thrust themselves into the public eye, cannot prevent others from criticizing or insulting them for their acts or deeds.

Theodore J. Stepien ("Stepien") is the former President of the Cleveland Professional Basketball Company, more commonly known as the Cleveland Cavaliers. The Cleveland Cavaliers is a professional basketball franchise operated under the auspices of the National Basketball Association ("NBA"). [Stepien's] tenure as President of the Cavaliers began in June 1980 and he remained in that position until the team was sold to George and Gordon Gund in May 1983.

Peter J. Franklin ("Franklin") is the host of a radio sports talk show known as "Sportsline." During the period in question, Sportsline was regularly broadcast Monday through Friday, 7:00 p.m. to midnight, unless it was pre-empted by a live sports event. Franklin principally employed an audience call-in format—listeners are encouraged to call in and give their opinions and/or solicit Franklin's opinion about sports. Sportsline is entertainment, designed to encourage and capitalize on the considerable public interest in professional sports.

The style of radio and television personalities who host talk shows such as Sportsline varies widely, from the erudite analysis of William F. Buckley to the insults of Joan Rivers. Franklin's style, which is immediately apparent from listening to his show, is an extreme version of the "insult" genre of entertainment. Franklin is often loud, opinionated, rude, abrasive, obnoxious, and insulting. In a manner reminiscent of the popular comedian Don Rickles, Franklin frequently hangs up on his callers and/or calls them insulting names.

The period when Stepien was the President of the Cavaliers, June 1980 to May 1983, is also the time period in which the alleged slander and emotional distress took place.

[Stepien], after becoming President of the Cavaliers, immediately began an aggressive style of management that involved making numerous player transactions and staff appointments. [Stepien] went through more than fifty players and six coaches in two and one-half years, including the hiring and firing of one coach twice. This aggressive style of management and the lack of the Cavaliers' success thereafter resulted in [Stepien] receiving a great deal of unfavorable criticism in the press, nationally and locally.

The factual background specifically relevant to the alleged defamatory statements can be broken down into three general topics:

1. National Basketball Association's moratoriums on trading;
2. The finances of the Cavaliers; and
3. The proposed sale of the team and move to Toronto.

Many of Franklin's alleged defamatory statements complained of herein consisted of those that challenged [Stepien's] ability to manage an NBA team. These remarks by Franklin involved Cavaliers' player trans-actions and the league's subsequent reaction to them. In November 1980, the Cavaliers engaged in the above-stated trades that resulted in the team's trading away several first-round draft choices. These trades were criticized by most observers and fans as being detrimental to the Cavaliers. In response, the NBA Commissioner imposed a restric-tion referred to as a "moratorium on trades" involving the Cavaliers. The restriction permitted the team to make trades, but only upon con-sulting with the league office and obtaining final approval. After a short while, the moratorium was lifted, but in February 1983, a second moratorium occurred. This restriction required the Cavaliers to give the NBA twenty-four hours to consider any trade and was apparently motivated by the NBA's concern that the Cavaliers' troubles might lead them to make unwise player transactions in order to raise operating capital. The Cavaliers' financial problems were acute. [Stepien] con-sidered many options to alleviate this problem. Between January and April 1983, [Stepien] explored several possibilities including selling the team to out-of-town buyers, selling the team to a local buyer, or retaining ownership and moving the team to Toronto. During this period, the media harshly criticized [Stepien] for not completing the sale and for proposing that the team move away from Cleveland.

There is no question that during [Stepien's] three-year period of own-ership of the Cavaliers, Franklin was a harsh and critical commenta-tor. His descriptions of [Stepien], extracted from tapes of the show provided to this court, include: "stupid," "dumb," "buffoon," "nincom-poop," "scum," "a cancer," "an obscenity," "gutless liar," "unmiti-gated liar," "pathological liar," "egomaniac," "nuts," "crazy," "irrational," "suicidal," "lunatic," etc.

Source: *Reprinted from Westlaw with permission of Thomson Reuters.*

1. Do you consider Franklin's remarks fair reporting of the facts?

2. Does the fact that Franklin said them over a three-year period make any difference?

3. Is this just a situation of a sports commentator giving his honest opinion about the running of a local franchise, or did he cross the line?

One scholar noted the following about sports commentator Pete Franklin and his opinions on the Cleveland Indians Major League Baseball team:

> Franklin's attacks on the Indians franchise could be merciless, though to be fair, were often quite accurate. The team was mired in mismanagement and presented itself more often than not as being a player or two away from winning it all. In actuality, the team was mortgaging its future by selling out its player development system at an astonishing rate in favor of young players with questionable skills and a bevy of well-known but past-their-prime veterans who offered little on the field.[27]

He also said,

> [A]lthough Franklin could be brusque as well as childlike, those who knew him off-mike would also maintain that he could be positively charming. . . . When pressed on the subject, Nick Mileti—the Cleveland sports magnate of the 1970s who targeted Franklin specifically to anchor his newly purchased 50,000 watt station—said that off-air Franklin was "the sweetest man who ever lived," . . . noting well that "[he] turned into a killer" once the microphones were turned on, a refrain heard time and again by peers and associates.[28]

CASE STUDY 12-7   *Media Accuracy and Ethics*

Assume a media outlet has been producing a story about a university's athletic program and the lack of academic success achieved by its student-athletes. The athletic director for the university calls the media outlet and wants to see the final product before it goes on the air, citing concerns over accuracy and wanting to ensure that the university and its student-athletes are portrayed accurately and fairly. Should the media outlet allow the athletic director access? If not, what alternatives could be offered to be fair?

RACE, IDENTITY, AND STEREOTYPING IN SPORTS MEDIA

Media outlets have a duty to ensure fairness in all their reporting and to refrain from engaging in stereotyping of athletes. Racial stereotyping, gender bias, and prejudice arise from an overgeneralization about characteristics or behaviors of whole groups that are then inaccurately applied to the individuals within those groups. Professional and amateur athletes come from a variety of backgrounds and are of different races, cultures, and national origins. Media outlets, and specifically sports broadcasters, must ensure that reporting and production of sporting events are done with this in mind.

---

[27] See Joel Nathan Rosen, "The Mouth Roars No Longer: Pete Franklin, Sports Talk, and Cleveland Indians Baseball, 1967–1987," *NINE: A Journal of Baseball History and Culture* 15, no. 1 (Fall 2006): 13–26.

[28] Ibid.

The African American Athlete

The issue of race and specifically how African American athletes and other minorities are depicted in the media has become the subject of much debate.[29] Filmmaker Spike Lee donated over $700,000 to start a sports journalism program at his alma mater, Morehouse College.[30] In support of his generous donation Lee stated:

> "Too often . . . black athletes are portrayed in the media as "one-dimensional, selfish, immature and poor citizens" because of the lack of African American media representation. "Too long we have been on the field, but not in charge of generating the images of our athletes," . . . The solution . . . is to "train black sports journalists who would be willing to interact with athletes and describe them as people."[31]

An individual's skin color and how he or she is portrayed by the media can be a volatile topic and can, and has, created controversy. One such controversy occurred involving a famous ex-athlete, O.J. Simpson. *Time* magazine created a huge national controversy when it intentionally darkened a photograph of O.J. Simpson on its cover in June 1994 during the O.J. Simpson criminal trial.[32] Simpson was on trial at the time for allegedly killing his ex-wife Nicole Simpson (Caucasian) and her friend Ron Goldman (Caucasian).

How African American athletes are portrayed in the media can create a stereotypical image for the African American community as a whole. Well-known author and intellectual Shaun Powell has addressed this issue using former NFL and MLB player Deion Sanders "(Neon Deion)" as an example:

> Certainly, *Sports Illustrated* had shown the black athlete in a gazillion different ways over the decades, almost always honorable or respectable or decent. The magazine does not have a history, shameful or otherwise, of exploiting the black athlete negatively. Muhammad Ali, for example, the most covered athlete in the magazine's history, could usually be seen as the essence of black power, putting a fist to someone's face. Michael Jordan, number 2 on the list, was the picture of grace and greatness. And so on. But along came Deion Sanders, with all his blinging and jingling, and *Sports Illustrated* couldn't resist. Sanders wasn't about to be caught dead in a Brooks Brothers suit, although that certainly would have been a twist for him at that time in his professional life. Deion had to be neon. He had to be true to the game. He had to keep it real. And *Sports Illustrated* had to have that cover.
>
> It didn't matter that Sanders dressed the way most drug dealers dressed, or once did anyway. Back in his humble Fort Myers, Florida, neighborhood, Sanders was all about living up to a cartoonish character he created for the purpose of self-promotion and making money, and selfishly, he posed in a way to flaunt this image. And *Sports Illustrated*, given the green light by Sanders, a black man, figured everything was okay. It was a partnership, then. An immature black athlete, blinded by fame, chose to

[29] Andrew C. Billings, "Portraying Tiger Woods: Characterization of 'Black' Athlete in a 'White' Sport," *Howard Journal of Communication*, Volume 14, Issue 1, January 2003, pages 29–37.

[30] Black College Wire, "Spike Lee Donates Money for Sports Journalism Program at Morehouse," *The Panther, The Student Publication of Prairie View A&M University*, February 14, 2007.

[31] Ibid. Also see, Richard Lapchick, "Who's Covering Whom? Sports Sections Lag in Diversity," *ESPN.com*, June 22, 2006. "Diversity is an imperative for the media. When the media covers sports with staffs that don't come close to mirroring the percentages of people of color and women in the workforce—and, especially, that don't reflect the percentage of the people they're covering—it exacerbates the problem." Ibid.

[32] Christo Lassitter, "The O. J. Simpson Verdict: A Lesson in Black and White," *Michigan Journal of Race and the Law* 1(1960): 69. Also see Tiffany O'Callaghan, "The Politics of Perceiving Skin Color," *TIME Healthland*, November 23, 2009.

dress this way. A magazine, looking for a provocative cover that would catch the eye, tried to capture the essence of the subject at hand.

Each benefited from the other, and in the process, the sensitive image of the black athlete, if not the black race took another kick in the groin.[33]

Do you agree with Shaun Powell's assessment of Sanders and the media? Was Sanders merely marketing himself and his image, attempting to get the most out of a short professional sports career? Powell makes the point that the black community is overrepresented by athletes and entertainers in the mainstream media and therefore more visible to society in general. He asserts that the African American community as a whole is stereotyped as the young rich African American athlete. Do you agree with his assessment? African Americans make up a relatively small percentage of the U.S. population, but make up the majority of NFL and NBA players.[34] That can result in the African American athlete being overemphasized in the media and the viewing public sometimes only viewing African Americans as being athletic and nothing more.[35]

Author Casey Gane-McCalla has also stated:

Black athletes are usually given credit for their "natural athleticism," while whites are credited for their "hard work," "discipline," and "knowledge of the game"; as if Black athletes are naturally given the gift of great athleticism, and white people become great athletes through hard work, discipline, and intelligence.

Every Black athlete who is successful has worked very hard and is knowledgeable of their sport. Every white athlete who is successful has natural athletic ability.

The problem with stereotypes in sports is that they often lead to general stereotypes. If you say "white men can't jump," why not "Black men can't read defenses"? And if Black men can't read defenses, maybe they can't read books either?

Sports stereotypes have a real effect in the real world. Most employers are not concerned with employees' natural athletic abilities, so stereotypes of African-Americans being athletically superior for the most part do not help Blacks in the real world. However, the stereotypes of whites being hard working, disciplined, and smart are helpful to them in finding employment.

One of the most prevalent stereotypes in sports is that of the Black quarterback. Both Rush Limbaugh and former sports commentator, Jimmy the Greek, have caught flack for their philosophies on African-American quarterbacks. Jimmy's explanation of how blacks were bred for physical skill but whites were bred for intelligence was blatant racism, but there have been many more subtle ways at insinuating the same point.

Former NFL M.V.P. Steve McNair played for a small Black college because every major college recruited him to play defensive back rather than quarterback, his natural position. Many African-Americans are discouraged from playing quarterback and asked to play other positions in high school, college, and the professional ranks. How many other black M.V.P.-caliber quarterbacks were forced to play other positions because coaches didn't feel Blacks made good quarterbacks?

---

[33] Shaun Powell, "Souled Out? How Blacks Are Winning and Losing in Sports," *Human Kinetics* (2008): 186–188.

[34] Susan Tyler Eastman and Andrew C. Billings, "Biased Voices of Sports: Racial and Gender Stereotyping in College Basketball Announcing," *The Howard Journal of Communication* (2001).

[35] Ibid. For further study see, Jane P. Sheldon, Toby Epstein Jayaratne, and Elizabeth M. Petty, "White Americans' Genetic Explanations for a Perceived Race Difference in Athleticism: The Relation to Prejudice Toward and Stereotyping of Blacks," *The Online Journal of Sports Psychology*, Volume 9, Issue 3, September 2007.

Biological factors do not compel people from certain races to excel in certain sports. Cultural factors do. China produces a lot of good Ping-Pong players because Ping-Pong is part of Chinese culture. Kenya produces a lot of marathon winners because long distance running is part of their culture. Jamaica produces sprinters because track and field has become a strong part of their culture and national identity. Baseball has become a big part of Latin American culture and subsequently several of baseball's top players come from Latin America. Basketball is a big part of African-American culture, so a good deal of players in the NBA are African-American.

Sports stereotypes are made to be broken. Athletic basketball players are popping up all over the world from all different backgrounds, from Argentina to Turkey, from Kenya to China. Boxing, once a sport dominated by African-Americans, is now being dominated by boxers of other ethnicities from all around the world. Russians are dominating the heavyweight division, and a Filipino, Manny Pacqiao, will fight an Englishman, Ricky Hatton, for the title of best fighter, pound for pound (at least while Floyd Mayweather is retired).

While no Black quarterback has won a Super Bowl since Doug Williams proved Jimmy the Greek wrong in 1988, two of the last three Super Bowl winning coaches have been African-American. This goes even further to disprove Jimmy the Greek's theory, given that African-Americans have excelled at coach, the most cerebral position of all.

Despite all the stereotypes of Black athletes not being intelligent or caring about their education, an African American, Myron Rolle, has become the first major U.S. athlete to win the Rhodes Scholarship since Bill Bradley. He bypassed a career in the NFL to get an education from Oxford University, one of the world's most prestigious schools.[36]

1. Do you agree with the assessments made by Mr. Gane-McCalla?

2. How can stereotyping be avoided by the sports media?

For many years it was an unspoken rule in the National Football League that African American players could not play the position of quarterback. NFL player Warren Moon (African American) was not drafted into the NFL based on this myth. He graduated from the University of Washington, would later star in the NFL and eventually make it to the Pro Football Hall of Fame.[37] There are now many successful African American quarterbacks in the NFL. Do you believe professional sports players are stereotyped with regard to particular positions on teams? If so, what role does the media play in that regard?

Shaun Powell has also stated:

"To be honest with you, the media really doesn't harp that much on the responsible athletes, black athletes of which there are many, by the way, and it seems to really play up to emphasize the—those small numbers who insist on being unprofessional and the like."[38]

Do you agree with his assessment?

---

[36] See Casey Gane-McCalla, "Athletic Blacks vs. Smart Whites: Why Sports Stereotypes are Wrong," *Huffington Post*, April 19, 2009. Also see, Kimberly Nash, *Perceptions on Race and Profiling in the NFL*, Bleacher Report, April 29, 2009.

[37] See Andrew C. Billings, "Depicting the Quarterback in Black and White: A Content Analysis of College and Professional Football Broadcast Commentary," *Howard Journal of Communications* 15, no. 4 (October 2004): 201–210; David Niven, "Race, Quarterbacks, and the Media: Testing the Rush Limbaugh Hypothesis," *Journal of Black Studies* 35, no. 5 (May 2005): 684–694; Jennifer Byrd, "Is Stereotypical Coverage of African-American Athletes as Dead as Disco?: An Analysis of NFL Quarterbacks in the Pages of *Sports Illustrated*," *Journal of Sports Media* 2 (2007).

[38] Blacks Winning and Losing in Sports, *www.npr.org*, October 4, 2007.

CASE STUDY 12-8 *Media Ethics and Tiger Woods*

Anchor Kelly Tilghman was suspended by the Golf Channel for two weeks after a comment she made on air about Tiger Woods. During a conversation with golfer Nick Faldo, discussing young players who could challenge Woods, Tilghman made a statement that they should "lynch [Tiger Woods] in a back alley." The Golf Channel stated that "there is simply no place on our network for offensive language like this." The Reverend Al Sharpton demanded that she be fired immediately.

Tilghman was the first female play-by-play announcer in PGA history. Mark Steinberg, Woods's agent said that it was a non-issue and considered the matter closed. Tilghman later apologized for the remark.[39]

1. By making the statement, did Tilghman improperly interject herself into the story?

ETHICS AND SOCIAL MEDIA IN SPORTS

The term *social media* did not exist just a few years ago but is now a common phrase in the business community. Social media is essentially a platform that enables the dissemination of information through Internet tools such as Twitter, Facebook, LinkedIn, and MySpace. Social media can include news and information that is posted by the user and can take many different forms, including forums, blogs, websites, podcasts, and message boards. How information is gathered, transcribed, and reported has changed immensely with advancing technologies. Information that may have taken weeks or even months to gather, verify, and distribute can now be compiled and distributed to millions of viewers or readers instantaneously. Information moves quickly through a myriad of modern communication devices available to people on a global basis. Advanced technologies can be used for both good and bad applications. Fair and accurate reporting is essential to any story, and with information moving quickly along the information highway, verifying the truth of a story and fact-checking can become a much more difficult task. One wrong statement or impression can be transmitted to numerous individuals who in turn can transmit that information to others, and this can lead to unfairly damaging the reputation of an innocent person.[40] Many media outlets have social media policies in an effort to ensure that journalistic ethics are also upheld in the social media environment.[41] Broadcasting giant ESPN issues its own social media guidelines and Rob King, editor-in-chief of ESPN.com, made the following comments about the policy:

It's an important opportunity to reiterate to folks that this technology is the equivalent of a live microphone. In that respect, it should be treated with some measure of awareness about how it represents those individuals who are forward-facing talent and how it represents how ESPN wants to connect with the audience. There's a lot of education that goes along with it. Anyone who's ever had a tweet re-tweeted to an

---

[39] "Golf Channel Anchor Apologizes for 'Lynch' Remark About Tiger," *ESPN.com*, January 17, 2008.
[40] "Entrepreneurs Question Value of Social Media," *Wall Street Journal*, March 15, 2010.
[41] Katie Rolnick, "NPR Joins the Pack of Media Outlets Issuing Social Media Guidelines," *NPR.org*, October 25, 2009.

audience knows that it can be presented in ways that you might never have understood or intended when you originally articulated those 140 characters.[42]

Technological advances have enabled more sports fans to participate and contribute to the discourse, but unfortunately the comments of many individuals can go unchecked.[43] A media professional must abide by ethical rules when reporting on a story. The same standard is not always applicable to those who may have a variety of social media applications at their fingertips. An individual fan can distribute information instantaneously but is not held to the same standard as a media professional. They are, of course, still subject to the law and its requirements, but with so many individuals having access to information, it is inevitable that damaging information will go unchecked and eventually be transmitted. Newspapers and other traditional forms of publishing have editors who review and analyze a story before it is published. The same cannot be said for many nontraditional forms of media.

Sports teams and players are using social media just like any other business or celebrity.[44] Leagues, teams, and players understand the value of connecting with fans and many have used social media platforms to further promote their brands, sell tickets, and provide more exposure to star players. However, many individuals do not have time to use social media applications.[45] Along with that exposure however, comes responsibility. The NBA and the NCAA have issued social media guidelines to attempt to regulate social media use by players and student-athletes. Not surprisingly, NBA Dallas Mavericks owner Mark Cuban was issued the NBA's first fine under the NBA social media policy when he tweeted a complaint about NBA referees.[46]

Miami Heat star Dwyane Wade has more than 100,000 followers on twitter. He said:

> When you come to work, you come to work . . . you can tweet before, you can tweet after. It's not addicting like where I'm going to take a bathroom break, go downstairs and tweet. I think people take it a little too far with that. But I think it's very good to have communication with your fans personally. A lot of people, you can see them in a different light.[47]

The NFL's Washington Redskins banned Twitter from their practices because of the distraction it brought to the team.[48] Many teams have also announced a stricter ban on social networking than the league requires, calling it "team time." Players see the social media world as a way to promote themselves, some call it marketing, but as a team member and employee of the club, a player must abide by all team rules and keep the team's interest ahead of the player's interest. It is never a good idea to say the first thing that comes to mind. A tweet in the hands of the wrong person can lead to disaster. In 2009 former Kansas City Chiefs running back Larry Johnson tweeted a gay slur when referring to his head coach.[49] He was suspended and fined for his actions.

---

[42] "ESPN.com's Rob King Discusses Guidelines for Use of Social Media," *Sports Business Daily*, August 5, 2009.

[43] Luke Jerod Kummer, "A Boston Newspaper Prints What the Local Bloggers Write," *The New York Times*, May 7, 2007.

[44] See generally, Lon Safko, *The Social Media Bible: Tactics, Tools, and Strategies for Business Success* (Hoboken, NJ: Wiley, 2010).

[45] "Millionaires Have No Time for Facebook," *The Wall Street Journal*, October 20, 2010.

[46] Marc Stein, "NBA Social Media Guidelines Out," *ESPN.com*, September 30, 2009.

[47] Associated Press, "Heat ban Twitter During 'Office Hours,'" *ESPN.com*, September 28, 2009.

[48] "Washington Redskins Latest Team to Ban Twittering from Practice Fields," *TBD.com*, September 16, 2010.

[49] "Johnson Uses Slurs for Haley, Reporters," *ESPN.com*, October 26, 2009.

CASE STUDY 12-9   *Facebook, MySpace and Other Social Media Sites*

A University of Texas student-athlete was dismissed from the university's football team for making disturbing comments about U.S. President Barack Obama on his Facebook page.[50] The student-athlete's page stated in part, "All the hunters gather up, we have a (slur) in the White House."[51]

---

1. Should universities and high schools be able to limit and monitor what student-athletes post on social networking websites or do you consider that too overreaching and an invasion of privacy?[52]
2. What about free speech rights for student-athletes?
3. Should professional teams also have social networking policies as well?

ETHICS AND ATHLETE PRIVACY

In today's media-driven world, it is clear, star professional athletes are public figures. Millions of fans follow sports teams and their players on the field, the Internet, on television, and a variety of other places, both on and off the field. They seem to want to know every excruciating detail, both professionally and personally, about their sports stars. American society loves celebrities, and athletes are celebrities. The issue becomes at what point is an athlete's private life off limits to the media and fans? Certainly, the private life of Tiger Woods was exposed to the entire world when he engaged in extramarital affairs. His actions and their repercussions received worldwide attention. They were debated endlessly by "talking heads" in all forms of media. What did his actions have to do with his ability to play golf? Is the media overstepping its bounds by reporting such behavior? Should the private lives of athletes be off limits to reporters, if the actions of the athlete have nothing to do with the sport?

Which of the following would you argue are not "newsworthy" events of an athlete and should not be reported?

1. A professional or amateur athlete is charged with domestic violence.
2. A professional or amateur athlete takes an illegal drug.
3. A professional or amateur athlete engages in an extramarital affair.
4. A professional or amateur athlete gets a divorce from their spouse.
5. A professional or amateur athlete is charged with driving under the influence of alcohol.
6. A professional or amateur athlete donates no money to charity.
7. A professional or amateur athlete gambles in Las Vegas as a "hobby."
8. A professional or amateur athlete's religious views.
9. A professional or amateur athlete's family member has a serious disease.
10. A professional or amateur athlete fails to pay taxes.

---

[50] As of 2011 Facebook has over 500 million active users. http://www.facebook.com/press/info.php?statistics.

[51] David DeBolt, "U. of Texas Kicks Football Player Off Team for Anti-Obama Comment on Facebook," *The Chronicle of Higher Education*, September 14, 2008.

[52] Sarah Netter, "Suspension over Sexy Slumber Party Photos Leads to ACLU Lawsuit," *ABC News*; November 2, 2009; Danielle Canada, "Oregon Football Player Kicked Off Team for Facebook Status," *hiphopwired.com*, February 22, 2010.

Brett Favre is one of the greatest quarterbacks in NFL history. He has thrown more than 500 touchdown passes. In 2010 Favre became the subject of an NFL investigation after it was alleged he sent pictures of his private anatomy to a New York Jets female employee when Favre played for the Jets in 2008. The sports website deadspin.com posted photos, text messages, and voice mails it had obtained by paying an undisclosed party. 3.2 million people viewed the photos and listened to the calls. This represented a fivefold increase in the website's usual weekly traffic.[53] *The New York Times* writer David Carr stated the issue well:

> While we were not the first people to use the Internet to look at another person's privates, something more pernicious and tawdry was under way. Newsrooms all over America have ethics policies they fuss over and debate, but all those strictures and best intentions are really beside the point once a sensational story rings the bell.
>
> Deadspin violated a promise to a source, then paid for the photos and voice mails that it asserted were from Favre. But the "news" spread throughout other media organizations despite a lack of information about the provenance of the photos or the motivations of the source (both Favre and the woman who is said to have sent the photos have refused to comment).[54]

Favre refused to cooperate with the NFL during the investigation and was subsequently fined $50,000 by the league for failing to cooperate with the commissioner's office.[55] Favre was later sued for sexual harassment by former Jets employees.[56]

1. Did Deadspin act ethically in reporting the story?
2. If it is a newsworthy story, is it only newsworthy because it involves a famous NFL quarterback?
3. Does it change your viewpoint if it is determined Favre's actions constituted sexual harassment under New York law?

CASE STUDY 12-10 *More LeBron James and ESPN*

Evidently, it is true, what happens in Vegas, stays in Vegas! ESPN chose to remove from its website a story detailing LeBron James's visit to Las Vegas with his friends. Reporter Arash Markazi wrote a story about James and his friends; however, it was determined Markazi never properly identified himself as a reporter. ESPN pulled the story from its website saying:

> "We looked into the situation thoroughly and found that Arash did not properly identify himself as a reporter or clearly state his intentions to write a story. As a result, we are not comfortable with the content, even in an edited version, because of the manner in which the story was reported. We've been discussing the situation with Arash and he completely understands."[57]

[53] David Carr, "When Salacious Is Irresistible," *The New York Times*, October 17, 2010.
[54] Ibid.
[55] "Favre Fined $50,000, not Suspended in Sterger Case," *CBSSports.com*, December 29, 2010.
[56] Andrea Canning, Jessica Hopper and Katie Morison, "Brett Favre Sexual Harassment Suit the 'Tip of the Iceberg'?" *ABC News*, January 4, 2010.
[57] Statement of ESPN digital media vice president and editor in chief Rob King as reported in Dan Devine, "ESPN Won't Republish LeBron-In-Las Vegas Story due to Ethics Breach," *Yahoo! Sport*, July 30, 2010.

CASE STUDY 12-11 *Fair or Foul Questions?*

Reporters ask questions, it's what they do. Some questions are well thought out and some are not. There is no doubt Tiger Woods has had his personal struggles, as all individuals do. The media has been "on the case," keeping the public updated on Tiger's activities in every excruciating detail. Before the 2010 Ryder Cup, a British reporter asked him: "You don't win majors anymore. . . . You don't win regular tournaments anymore. And you are about to be deposed by Europeans as the world No. 1, or [by] Phil Mickelson. Where is the Ryder Cup now that you're an ordinary golfer?"

Tiger's response was: "I remember you're the same one at the British Open who asked me that, too. . . . I hope you're having a good week."[58]

1. Did the reporter draw too much attention to himself by asking the questions?
2. Do you consider the questions insulting or just part of the sports landscape in today's sports media driven world?
3. From the viewpoint of a journalist, what is the point or desired result of the question posed by the reporter?

In Case 12-6, media outlets reported on a story involving the sexual molestation of members of a Little League Baseball team. Privacy issues became a major concern for coaches and team members because of the reporting of the story.

CASE 12-6 *M.G. v. Time Warner, Inc.*

89 Cal.App.4th 623 (2001)

In September 1999, *Sports Illustrated* and an HBO television program, Real Sports, used the 1997 team photograph of a Little League team to illustrate stories about adult coaches who sexually molest youths playing team sports. [Plaintiffs], all of whom appear in the photograph, were formerly players or coaches on the Little League team. The team's manager, Norman Watson, pleaded guilty to molesting five children he had coached in Little League. [Plaintiffs] have sued Time Warner [Parent company of HBO].

The 10 [Plaintiffs] were eight players and two coaches for a Little League team in Highland, California. Norman Watson was the team's manager in 1996 and 1997, until it was discovered in September 1997 that he had a long history of sexually abusing children, beginning with a molestation conviction in 1971. Watson pleaded guilty in April 1998.

In September 1999, *Sports Illustrated* published a cover story, *Every Parent's Nightmare*, on incidents of child molestation in youth sports. Using Watson as one example, the article reported Watson had "pleaded guilty to 39 counts of lewd acts with children, four boys and a girl,

---

[58] Gene Wojciechowski, "For Once, Tiger *Needs* the Ryder Cup," *ESPN.com*, September 28, 2010.

that had occurred between 1990 and 1996, when Watson was a San Bernardino Little League coach and umpire and the five kids were all playing in the league." Watson was further described as having "spent most of his 54 years sexually preying on children . . . [m]ost of . . . whom he first met through his work in Little League."

Accompanying the article was a team photograph of 18 people, including the 10 [Plaintiffs] in this case. The photograph featured a sign board reading: "East Baseline S P 1997." (We use only the team's initials to preserve its members from further notoriety.) The photograph also bore a caption: "A *fixture*, Watson (center, in black) coached for years not far from a hospital where he'd been incarcerated as a molester."

Also in September 1999, HBO broadcast a similar report on child molesters in youth sports. The story discussed Watson and his involvement with [Plaintiffs'] team. The story employed a fleeting shot of the team photograph.

The *Sports Illustrated* article and the HBO program did not name any of the people shown in the team photograph except Watson. The article did not identify any of Watson's victims by his or her real name. Two victims were identified by pseudonyms. One player, who is not a [Plaintiff] was interviewed on the HBO program, apparently using his real name . . . four of the eight [Plaintiffs] had been molested by Watson and four had not.

First, [Plaintiffs] themselves are of three different types: the four players who were Watson's victims, four players who escaped being molested, and two adult assistant coaches who also appeared in the team photograph. Second, two different publications are involved, the *Sports Illustrated* article and the television program. Depending on which category of [Plaintiffs] and which publication are involved, a different theory of liability may apply.

The parties seem to agree that disclosure of information connecting a person with sexual molestation potentially may offend a reasonable person. But Time Warner argues that the photograph of [Plaintiffs] was not private and its publication met the test of newsworthiness. [Plaintiffs] of course, assert the photograph was private and was not newsworthy.

As to what constitutes a private fact, Time Warner asserts the information was not private because plaintiffs had played a public sport and the team photograph had been taken on a public baseball field. Furthermore, during the two years after Watson was found out, it had been widely reported that Watson had coached a Little League team, occasionally identified as the S P, and that Watson had admitted molesting Little League players. Time Warner maintains that [their] use of the team photographs disclosed only information that was

already publicly known: ". . . Norman Watson, a convicted child molester, had coached the East Baseline S P."

[Plaintiffs] counter that their identities, as coaches or players on
Watson's team, were not revealed in any of the coverage of the Watson
case until the publication of the team photograph, an event which publicly linked [Plaintiffs] with child molestation as either victims,
perpetrators, or collaborators. [Plaintiffs] stated that, immediately
after the article and the program appeared, they were teased and
harassed at school and called "gay," "faggot," "queer," and one of
"Norm's boys." As a consequence, the [Plaintiffs'] academic performances suffered. Some of them were forced to quit school, to transfer,
or to be home-schooled. The two coaches have stated they were
"ridiculed, questioned, and harassed" and received crank phone calls
accusing them of being molesters or of condoning molestation.

Time Warner apparently equates "private" with "secret" and urges any
information not concealed has been made public. But the claim of a
right of privacy is not "'so much one of total secrecy as it is of the
right to *define* one's circle of intimacy—to choose who shall see
beneath the quotidian mask.'" Information disclosed to a few people
may remain private.

In the present case, none of the previous media coverage specifically
identified [Plaintiffs] as team members. Nor, as the trial court
observed, is there evidence in the record that the team photograph was
ever widely circulated. . . . But [Plaintiffs] maintain the photograph
was intended to be private, only for dissemination among family and
friends. Although [Plaintiffs] do not know how Time Warner acquired
the photograph, they never consented to its use.

"An analysis measuring newsworthiness of facts about an otherwise private person involuntarily involved in an event of public interest by
their relevance to a newsworthy subject matter incorporates considerable deference to reporters and editors, avoiding the likelihood of
unconstitutional interference with the freedom of the press to report
truthfully on matters of legitimate public interest. In general, it is
not for a court or jury to say how a particular story is best covered.
The constitutional privilege to publish truthful material 'ceases to
operate only when an editor abuses his broad discretion to publish
matters that are of legitimate public interest.' By confining our
interference to extreme cases, the courts 'avoid unduly limiting . . .
the exercise of effective editorial judgment.'

"On the other hand, no mode of analyzing newsworthiness can be applied
mechanically or without consideration of its proper boundaries. To
observe that the newsworthiness of private facts about a person involuntarily thrust into the public eye depends, in the ordinary case, on

the existence of a logical nexus between the newsworthy event or activity and the facts revealed is not to deny that the balance of free press and privacy interests may require a different conclusion when the intrusiveness of the revelation is greatly disproportionate to its relevance. Intensely personal or intimate revelations might not, in a given case, be considered newsworthy, especially where they bear only slight relevance to a topic of legitimate public concern."

Furthermore, the article and the program in themselves demonstrate the team members' faces should have been concealed. Although the program showed footage of boys playing baseball, it did not show their faces but photographed them without their faces showing. In the program and the article, the victims were given pseudonyms unless they consented to using their real names. Nor is this case analogous to one in which a news documentary used the first name of a rape victim and a picture of her house. The intrusion here, in which the children's faces were revealed, is far greater and outweighs the values of journalistic impact and credibility.

Source: *Reprinted from Westlaw with permission of Thomson Reuters.*

1. Was the privacy of the coaches or players properly protected in Case 12-6?
2. Do you agree with the case's definition of newsworthy?
3. How should a media professional treat individuals who are thrust into the spotlight?
4. How should a media professional approach a story involving children, such as this one?

NOTES AND DISCUSSION QUESTIONS

Sports and the Media

1. What are the essential elements of a journalistic ethics policy?
2. How can a media outlet ensure that it is publishing a true and accurate version of the facts of every newsworthy story?
3. What ethical obligations do media professionals have to supply the public with stories that are wholesome and good?
4. Why are there not more media stories about the good things athletes do in the community?[59]

Media Ethics

5. ESPN commentator Tony Kornheiser is known for his sarcastic approach to sports reporting. He created a media "storm" when he commented on one of his colleagues, Hannah Storm's, wardrobe on his radio show. He said about Storm: "I know she's very good, and I'm not supposed to be critical of ESPN people, so I won't but Hannah Storm, come on

---

[59] Tim Layden, "New Orleans Saints' Drew Brees Named SI's Sportsman of the Year," *Sports Illustrated*, November 30, 2010.

now! Stop! What are you doing? . . . She's got on red go-go boots and a Catholic-school plaid skirt. Way too short for somebody in her 40s—or maybe early 50s by now. She's got on her typically very, very tight skirt. She looks like she has a sausage casing wrapping around her upper body."[60]

He later apologized: "I'm a troll; look at me. . . . I have no right to insult what anyone else looks like, what anyone else wears."[61] He was suspended by the network for his comments. His comments were certainly inappropriate and degrading to his colleague.

6. ESPN football analyst Bob Griese was suspended for one week when he said Colombian NASCAR driver Juan Pablo Montoya was "out having a taco" when asked why he was not on a list of drivers.[62] Was that a fair punishment? Montoya did not comment, only saying he never heard of Griese.

7. Superstar David Beckham demanded a front page retraction from a U.S. celebrity gossip magazine after it was reported that he allegedly slept with a prostitute. His agent said: "The allegations that have been made are completely untrue and totally ridiculous as the magazine was clearly told before publication . . . sadly we live in a world where a magazine can print lies and believe they can get away with it. We are taking legal action against the magazine."[63]

8. Publishers have legal concerns as well ethical duties. In *Way v. Boy Scouts of America*,[64] a 12-year-old boy was killed when a rifle accidentally discharged. His mother sued the Boy Scouts of America, claiming that a 1988 edition of *Boys Life* magazine containing an advertising supplement for shooting sports was the cause of his death. The supplement presented information about the "power, speed, sounds, and ammunition, with images promoting and conveying the fun and excitement of shooting to boys the ages of [plaintiff's son]." The mother claimed there were limited references to the safety of shooting. The court said:

> Given the pervasiveness of firearms in society, we conclude that encouragement of safe and responsible use of firearms by minors in conjunction with Boy Scouts and other supervised activities is of significant social utility. Also included in our consideration of the social utility of publishing the supplement is our recognition of the pervasiveness of advertising in society and the important role it plays. . . . The weight we attach to the social utility of advertising in this case is further strengthened by the fact that the supplement provided useful information about lawful products. . . .
>
> . . . a risk utility analysis leads us to conclude that the firearms supplement did not create a duty on the part of [the Scouts] to either refrain from publishing the supplement or add warnings about the danger of firearms and ammunition.

9. It has been argued that one of the dominant messages in sports programming is that many aggressive athletes are praised and rewarded. Sports highlights are always shown for the

---

[60] Helen Kennedy, "ESPN Suspends Tony Kornheiser for Comments About SportsCenter Anchor Hannah Storm's Wardrobe," *My Daily News*, February 23, 2010.

[61] Ibid.

[62] Associated Press, "ESPN's Griese Suspended 1 Week," *ESPN.com*, October 26, 2009.

[63] John Plunkett, "David Beckham to Demand Front-Page Retraction from *In Touch* Magazine," *Guardian.co.uk*, September 23, 2010.

[64] 856 S.W. 2d 230 (1993).

"toughest hits" or "best fights." Sports commentators will commonly use phrases such as the following:

- The players are doing "battle."
- A player is "killing" his opponent.
- A team is going on the "attack mode."
- An offensive is "explosive."
- "Battle lines" have been drawn.

Are these types of references suitable for younger viewers? Boys watch sporting events at a much higher rate than girls do.[65] What kind of messages are they sending to those young men who are watching about how they should play sports? Is there a correlation between athletes who engage in criminal acts off the field and violent play on the field? Should there be a parental rating system for certain sporting events?

The Ethics of Fair Reporting and Defamation

10. Is Robert Dee the worst tennis player in the world? Evidently several newspapers thought so, publishing articles calling him the "world's worst player" after the 21-year-old professional tennis player lost 54 consecutive matches. Dee sued several newspapers for libel, saying his reputation was damaged and the newspapers should issue a retraction.[66]

11. Certainly newspapers should make sure they have the correct information before printing it. A story needs to be verified. The *New York Times* reported that James Stewart, a former star running back for the University of Miami, had failed a drug test given by the NFL. His attorney stated: "It's libel to take a young man about to start a pro career to have his name go forward as a marijuana user, when in fact he is not."[67] Stewart played in the NFL for the Minnesota Vikings.

12. Many times the target of a story will go on the offensive. In 2009, ESPN's show *Outside the Lines* did a segment on Florida State's academic scandal among its student-athletes. FSU denied all the charges made by ESPN. FSU e-mailed a letter to its supporters, stating in part:

> Dear Florida State Supporters:
>
> I want to let you know about an upcoming ESPN "Outside the Lines" television program that we know will portray the academic profile of student-athletes and the admissions and retention process at the Florida State University in a negative way. The promotions for this program already have shown that it contains false information.
>
> Therefore, I and other top administrators have called and e-mailed Vince Doria, vice president of News at ESPN who has oversight of "Outside the Lines," to report our concerns and urge the network not to air this program. That e-mail follows, and we encourage you to read it."[68]

If a party believes he or she is unjustly depicted in a story, should that party go on the offensive as FSU did? When is that not a good course of action to take?

---

[65] Mike Messner, Darnell Hunt, and Michele Dunbar, "Boys to Men: Sports Media," *Children Now*, 1999.

[66] Ben Dowell, "British Tennis Player Sues Three Papers," *Guardian.co.uk.*, June 11, 2008.

[67] Alan Goldfarb. "Ex-Miami Player Sues *Times* for Libel," *The New York Times*, March 30, 1995.

[68] "Florida State Tries to Pre-Empt ESPN's 'Outside the Lines,'" *Tampabay.com*, December 2009.

13. A media outlet should never issue a report solely based on rumors.[69] The *New York Times* had addressed this issue when an issue occurred in Olympic figure skating.

> "If a sporting event is rigged, that is news. The bigger the sport, the bigger the news. So when tens of millions of people saw a sprightly Canadian figure-skating pair perform flawlessly in their Olympic event, only to be judged inferior to an elegant but wobbly Russian pair, the journalists' task was clear: find out if the fix was in.
>
> But was the ensuing coverage more scrupulous than the pairs judging? Or does figure-skating journalism, like figure-skating judging, have its own folkways and methods of attribution, inscrutable to those who report on government, business, or other fraud-prone venues?
>
> So it seems. For most of the week, the rule widely followed was: if you have heard it, report it. And while many early reports were borne out—the French judge in the competition was dismissed on Friday for failure to rule impartially—the sources that reporters used to look into vote-trading accusations seemed, at times, obscure. Among them were:
> - "Unsubstantiated reports" (*Agence France-Presse*)
> - "Various reports, citing unnamed sources" (*USA Today*)
> - "Speculation" (*The Chicago Tribune*)
> - "Rumors" (CNN)
>
> The inescapable lesson seems to be that rigorous attribution rules are relaxed when journalists are reporting accusations of corrupt deals in a world like figure skating, which has a reputation for unsavory dealings. If that logic holds, many Washington reporters may ask their editors to lighten up."[70]

Do you believe media outlets can sometimes be more concerned with ratings and getting the "scoop" than reporting an accurate story?

14. Media ethics require a retraction when a story is wrong or misleading. The law also addresses this issue. Florida law states the following with regard to a retraction:

> "(1) If it appears upon the trial that said article or broadcast was published in good faith; that its falsity was due to an honest mistake of the facts; that there were reasonable grounds for believing that the statements in said article or broadcast were true; and that, within the period of time specified in subsection (2), a full and fair correction, apology, or retraction was, in the case of a newspaper or periodical, published in the same editions or corresponding issues of the newspaper or periodical in which said article appeared and in as conspicuous place and type as said original article or, in the case of a broadcast, the correction, apology, or retraction was broadcast at a comparable time, then the plaintiff in such case shall recover only actual damages.
>
> (2) Full and fair correction, apology, or retraction shall be made:
> > (a) In the case of a broadcast or a daily or weekly newspaper or periodical, within 10 days after service of notice;
> >
> > (b) In the case of a newspaper or periodical published semimonthly, within 20 days after service of notice;

[69] In general see, Robert E. Cooper, *Libel and the Reporting of Rumor*, Yale Law Journal, 1982.

[70] Felicity Barringer, "The News Media; Sports Reporting: Rules on Rumors," *The New York Times*, January 3, 2008.

(c) In the case of a newspaper or periodical published monthly, within 45 days after service of notice; and

(d) In the case of a newspaper or periodical published less frequently than monthly, in the next issue, provided notice is served no later than 45 days prior to such publication."

How do the ethical duties of a media outlet correlate with the law?

15. Everyone likes a good joke unless, of course, they are the target of that joke. In one of the most famous cases of parody, the Reverend Jerry Falwell sued *Penthouse* magazine for their portrayal of Reverend Falwell as having an incestuous relationship with his own mother in an outhouse. Is that going too far?[71] Where should the line be drawn when deciding issues of parody and the media?[72]

Race, Identity, and Stereotyping in Sports Media

16. Do you believe it is racial stereotyping of an African American athlete for an announcer to refer to his or her "natural athleticism" while referring to a Caucasian athlete as being a "smart player"?[73]

17. For further study in this area, see John Hoberman, *Darwin's Athletes: How Sports Has Damaged Black America and Preserved the Myth of Race* (Boston, MA: Mariner Books, 1997); Garu Sailes, *African Americans in Sport* (New Brunswick, NJ:Transaction Publishers, 1998); Cynthia D. Bond, "Laws of Race/Laws of Representation: The Construction of Race and Law in Contemporary American Film," *Texas Review of Entertainment & Sports Law* (Spring 2010); Brian Carroll, "The Black Press and the Integration of Professional Baseball, a Content Analysis of Shifts in Coverage, 1945–1948," *Journal of Sports Media* 3, no. 2 (Fall 2008):,61–87. C. Keith Harrison, Suzenne Malia Lawrence, Michael Plecha, Scott J. Bukstein, and Neza K. Janson, "Stereotypes and Stigmas of College Athletes in Tank McNamara's Cartoon Strip: Fact or Fiction?," *Journal of Issues in Intercollegiate Athletics* (2009).

Ethics and Social Media in Sports

18. How do you define social media?

19. How has social media affected the reporting of sports?

20. Should amateur athletic associations have social networking policies?[74]

21. Italian Footy Star Alessandro del Piero sued Facebook over a fake profile that contained his name and had links to Nazi propaganda websites.[75]

22. What should be contained in a professional sports league's Twitter policy?

---

[71] *Hustler Magazine v. Falwell*, 485 US 46; 108 S. Ct 876; 99 L. Ed 2d 41. See also Robert C. Post, "The Constitutional Concept of Public Discourse, Outrageous Opinion, Democratic Deliberation, and Hustler Magazine. Falwell," *Harvard Law Review* 103, no. 3 (January 1990).

[72] Charles C. Goetsh, "Parody as Free Speech- The Replacement of the Fair Doctrine by First Amendment Protection," 3 W. *New Eng. L. Rev.* 39, 1980–1981. See also, Jacqueline D. Lipton, "Commerce Versus Commentary: Gripe Sites, Parody, and the First Amendment in Cyberspace," *Washington University Law Review*, Vol. 84, Number 6, 2006.

[73] Casey Gane-McCalla, "Athletic Blacks vs. Smart Whites: Why Sports Stereotypes are Wrong," *Huffington Post*, April 19, 2009. See, Kimberly Nash, *Perceptions on Race and Profiling in the NFL*, Bleacher Report, April 29, 2009.

[74] Allegra M. Richards, "NCAA Clarifies Facebook Policy," *The Harvard Crimson*, March 14, 2007.

[75] John Leyden, "Footy Star Sues Facebook over Fake Fascist Profile," *The Register*, February 9, 2009.

23. Tony La Russa, attorney-at-law, is also the manager of the St. Louis Cardinals of Major League Baseball. La Russa sued the social networking site Twitter, claiming that an unauthorized page, which purportedly came from La Russa, used his name to make light of drunk driving and two St. Louis Cardinals pitchers who died. In 2007, La Russa had pled guilty to a misdemeanor charge of driving under the influence. One tweet post said "lost 2 out of 3, but we made it out of Chicago without one drunk driving incident or dead pitcher." La Russa sued, claiming emotional distress and that the fake page harmed his reputation.[76]

24. How do ethics for reporters and writers in traditional media differ from those for reporters in the social media area?

25. Coverage of the Paralympic Games has been limited to a great extent. Does the media give enough exposure to disabled athletes who are participants in sports or is there a void in reporting on individuals with disabilities?[77]

26. White males still dominate the "play-by-play" or color commentary of games in the NHL, NBA, NFL, and MLB.[78] What can be done to improve diversity among those ranks? Would a rule similar to the NFL's Rooney Rule be a viable option in the sports media business?

27. For further study, see Brett Hutchins and David Rowe, "Reconfiguring Media Sports for the Online World: An Inquiry into 'Sports News and Digital Media,'" *International Journal of Communication* 4 (2010): 696–718; Benjamin T. Hickman, "Old Law, New Technology: The First Amendment's Application When Sports Teams and Leagues Attempt to Regulate New Media," *Communications Lawyer* (July, 2010). Arthur A. Raney and Jennings Bryant, *Handbook of Sports and Media* (Mahwah, NJ: Earlbaum Associates, 2006); K. Tim Wulfemeyer, "Ethics in Sports Journalism: Tightening Up the Code," *Journal of Mass Media Ethics* 1, no. 1 (Autumn 1985); Sarah K. Fleish, "The Ethics of Legal Commentary: A Reconsideration of the Need for an Ethical Code in Light of the Duke Lacrosse Matter," *Georgetown Journal of Legal Ethics* (Summer, 2007); Thomas P. Oates and John Pauly, "Sports Journalism as Moral and Ethical Discourse," *Journal of Mass Media Ethics* 22, no. 4(2007): 332–347; Brad Schultz, *Sports Media, Second Edition: Reporting, Producing, and Planning* (Boston, MA: Focal Press, 2005).

Ethics and Athlete Privacy

28. Is every professional athlete a public figure? If so, how can the athlete argue that his or her conduct should be kept private?

29. What is the best way for an athlete to protect his or her privacy?

30. What limits should be placed upon the media with regard to reporting on an athlete's private affairs?

---

[76] Jim Salter, "Tony La Russa Sues Twitter over Alleged Fake Page," *ABC News*, 2009.

[77] Anne V. Golden, "An Analysis of the Dissimilar Coverage of the 2002 Olympics and Paralympics: Frenzied Pack Journalism Versus the Empty Press Room," *Disability Studies Quarterly*, Vol. 23, No. 3/4, Summer/Fall 2003.

[78] Anthony M. Meale, *Colorblind or Blinded by Color? An Analysis of Race and Gender Stereotyping Among College Basketball Broadcasters*, OhioLINK ETD Center, 2008.

Ethical Guidelines for The Sports Management Professional (SMP)

CHAPTER 1 ETHICAL CONCEPTS IN SPORTS

1. Have all employees develop a personal statement of ethics.
2. Create hypothetical ethical dilemmas for managers and employees to debate and explain within the organization.
3. Develop an ethical statement for your organization.
4. Develop a mission statement that delineates the ethical viewpoint of the company.

CHAPTER 2 SPORTSMANSHIP AND GAMESMANSHIP

1. Strive to win and play aggressively while treating one's opponent and officials with respect and civility.
2. Do not exhibit behavior that shows a lack of respect for opponents, officials, opposing coaches, or the integrity of the game, including the following:
   a. Do not taunt an opponent.
   b. Do not disrespect the opposing team, officials, or coaches.
   c. Do not engage in unnecessary roughness.
   d. Do not use profanity.
   e. Do not berate and belittle officials or opponents.
   f. No fighting, kicking, or throwing objects at officials, opposing players, or the opposing coach.
3. Understand that "trash talking" is inappropriate for youth sports.
4. Understand that strategic fouling is inappropriate for youth sports.
5. At the professional level, trash talking should not be profane, racist, sexist, bigoted, or personal.
6. Trash talking should not perpetuate stereotypes in any form or manner.
7. Victory celebrations should not be tasteless, taunt the opponent, or be excessive.

8. Establish "captain clinics" for captains of sports teams. In these clinics, teach leadership skills, sportsmanship, and sports ethics.
9. Have team captains present what they learned at the clinic to all team members. This will produce accountability for all team members.
10. Amateur athletic associations should post rules and regulations online for all to view. Keep accurate records to ensure all participants in the sport have read the rules and regulations. Before an athlete can participate, the athlete must complete a statement saying he or she has read all the rules and regulations and will faithfully abide by them.
11. Have an athlete, who is an exceptional role model in the community, speak to a youth sports organization about true sportsmanship.
12. Promote a good sportsmanship award as much as the most valuable player award at all levels of amateur sports.
13. Produce a video with participants in the league discussing good sportsmanship. Distribute the video free to all participants.

CHAPTER 3 GAMBLING IN SPORTS

1. Thou Shalt Not Gamble!
2. Gambling is not good for sports because it diminishes and tarnishes the game's integrity.
3. Remember friendly wagers are not always so "friendly."
4. Report any illegal gambling activity to the proper authorities.
5. Athletes should never associate with gamblers.
6. Gambling diminishes the ethical sense of fair play of a sport.

CHAPTER 4 ETHICS FOR PARTICIPANTS, COACHES, AND SPORTS OFFICIALS

1. Amateur sports associations should have a policy handbook that sets forth detailed rules that regulate conduct of all participants, umpires, coaches, and parents.
2. When necessary, enforce criminal sanctions against a participant or fan who becomes violent or engages in conduct that could lead to violence.
3. Parents, coaches, and participants should never scream at or demean officials.
4. Each participant should know the rules and customs of the game.
5. Participants must not allow their emotions to cloud their better judgment.
6. Be a good sportsman! Remember, it's only a game!
7. Games have rules to eliminate the possibility of unnecessary violence. Have a good understanding of what constitutes unnecessary violence in a particular sport.
8. Never go beyond the boundaries of acceptable behavior in sport.
9. Coaches should not unjustly argue calls with sports officials.
10. Have amateur coaches sign a code of conduct statement.
11. Coaches should always deal with their athletes in a positive and fair manner.
12. Coaches should never encourage, coax, or urge students to punish fellow students.
13. Coaches should be properly trained to properly instruct students.
14. Coaches should remain in control at all times, both on and off the field.

15. Coaches should be careful not to overemphasize the importance of a win or loss, keeping in mind that it is just a game.
16. Coaches should be honest and forthright about their credentials.
17. Coaches should remember they are role models to their team.
18. Have a coaching clinic for new coaches at the amateur level to instruct them on how to deal with violence issues.
19. School districts should place a morals clause in every coach's contract outlining the required ethical conduct.
20. Never let coaches participate with players in a practice session; it can only lead to something bad.
21. Require sexual harassment training for both male and female coaches.
22. Educate coaches about hazing, bullying, and both psychological and emotional abuse.
23. Provide coaches with information, training, and continuing education about how power and dependence can influence relationships and lead to abusive behavior.
24. Actively screen all applicants for coaching and volunteer positions.
25. Explain the policy on verbal, physical, and psychological abuse between coaches and athletes in all pre-employment interviews with prospective employees.
26. A coach should not use profanity or personal attacks in a misguided attempt to motivate athletes under his or her care.
27. Sports officials should be neutral and unbiased.
28. Sports officials should not gamble.

CHAPTER 5 ETHICAL CONSIDERATIONS FOR PARENTS AND FANS

1. Parents should know all the rules and regulations of the amateur sports organizations in which their children participate.
2. Amateur participants and parents should be required to pass a sportsmanship test before they can compete.
3. Have all parents and fans sign a statement saying they will abide by a code of conduct.
4. Perform criminal background checks on all parents who participate.
5. Establish a parent code of conduct.
6. Award a sportsmanship trophy to parents and fans as well as to the participants to promote good behavior in the stands.
7. Establish a fan code of conduct.
8. Warn and discipline unruly fans when required.

CHAPTER 6 VIOLENCE IN SPORTS

1. If a game is becoming violent between the participants, the game should be stopped immediately.
2. If a participant commits a flagrant foul or engages in conduct that could be considered a violent act, the player should be suspended for the remainder of the game and should be subject to the proper disciplinary measures.

3. All amateur participants should be required to shake hands after the game to create a more accountable environment between the participants. If it is good enough for the National Hockey League, it should be good enough for amateur sports.
4. At the professional level, players should be disciplined if they engage in a violent act on or off the field.
5. Require anger management classes for any player who needs assistance in controlling his or her anger.
6. Provide counseling to any player, participant, or coach who may have shown violent tendencies either on or off the field.
7. Punish violent athletes at both the professional and amateur levels.
8. Treat violence by athletes seriously, and take a "no tolerance" stance toward coaches and athletes who commit violent acts on or off the field.

CHAPTER 7 THE ETHICS OF DRUG USE AND TESTING

1. Recognize the privacy concerns of student-athletes.
2. Know the relevant state and federal laws concerning drug testing.
3. Ensure that a proper chain of custody is followed for specimen collection.
4. Fully understand and comprehend the drug testing program of your athletic association.
5. Have a good understanding of what substances are banned under the drug testing program.
6. Ensure that any disciplinary measures assessed against any individuals who violate the drug testing program are applied fairly to all individuals
7. At the professional level, understand the role of the union in any drug testing program.

CHAPTER 8 ETHICAL CONSIDERATIONS OF RACE IN SPORTS

1. Treat all student-athletes equally regardless of race, skin color, national origin, sexual orientation, or disability.
2. Work hard to understand another's point of view.
3. Know the historical significance that race has played in sports.
4. Be familiar with and understand the issues surrounding race in sports. Understand the NFL's Rooney Rule and read the Race and Gender Report Card published by the University of Central Florida, and any other issues that affect your particular sport.
5. As an SMP, possess a good understanding of the employment laws relating to the interviewing process.
6. Refrain from making any comments that would, in any way, demean or ridicule another individual's race, skin color, sex, national origin, sexual preference, or disability.
7. Never make jokes about another person's race, even if you think they are funny.
8. As an SMP, have a good understanding of the background of employees to gain a greater understanding of how they view the world.

9. As an SMP, perform a self-evaluation to determine whether you have any "hidden agendas," stereotypical viewpoints or perspectives, or have unconscious bias toward individuals of other races or religions that may affect your ethical decision-making process.

10. When conducting a meeting as an SMP, be aware of all individuals who are present. Conduct the meeting in a professional and forthright manner and steer away from making any comments regarding race that could be deemed inappropriate. If you are hesitant about saying it, do not say it.

11. Use appropriate language when describing an individual's race, disability, sexual orientation, and other sensitive issues.

CHAPTER 9 THE ETHICAL DUTIES OF SPORTS AGENTS

1. Agents should establish a trust relationship with clients and always tell clients the entire truth so clients can make informed decisions about their sports career.

2. Agents should never breach the confidence of a client.

3. Agents should keep a client informed of all matters concerning the client.

4. Agents should fulfill all their duties in good faith and give their best efforts to clients to avoid any disputes.

5. Agents shall negotiate on behalf of the client with integrity and honesty and never place the client in a "bad light" in the press.

6. Agents should realize when they are incapable of performing a client's request and refer the client to an expert in the area.

7. Agents should immediately disclose any conflicts of interest to the client.

8. Agents should never lie, conceal, or misrepresent information to a client or opposing party during negotiations.

9. Agents should be familiar with the collective bargaining agreement of each sport they are involved in and how it affects their clients.

10. Agents should be able to account for all funds handled on the client's behalf.

11. Lawyers who are agents should have an understanding of the rules of professional responsibility and how they interact with the rules and regulations concerning sports agents.

12. Lawyers who are agents should follow and comply with all rules regarding professional responsibility.

13. Lawyers should resolve all conflicts of interest according to the rules of professional responsibility.

14. Lawyers who are agents should never solicit a client for sports representation.

15. Agents should have a written fee agreement and have a clear understanding of their duties for the client.

16. Agents should keep current on all new regulations that are passed by regulatory bodies.

17. If an agent has an ethical concern, he or she should contact the agents' regulatory body for clarification.

18. Agents should never interfere with a player who is under contract with another agent.

19. Agents should never pay or bestow gifts on amateur student-athletes.

CHAPTER 10 WOMEN IN SPORTS, DISCRIMINATION, AND TITLE IX

1. Educate boys and girls at an early age about gender equity issues and their proper application in sports.
2. Educate boys and girls that what is fair for the boys' team is also fair for the girls' team.
3. Encourage girls to participate in sports at an early age if they have the desire to play.
4. Train participants, coaches, trainers, and all others involved in athletics to never ridicule or demean a girls' team or a girl participant in any manner whatsoever.
5. Allow girls to participate in a variety of sports at an early age to spark their interest in sports.
6. Encourage girls in youth sports to participate in all areas of sports including umpiring, scorekeeping, announcing, athlete training, and coaching in addition to playing sports!
7. Establish programs that bring boys and girls together for a shared sports experience to break down traditional viewpoints regarding a girl's role in sports.
8. Establish programs for women and girls who want to be coaches and sports officials.
9. Address any discriminatory practices towards women or girls participating in a sports organization immediately.
10. Teach all participants to be advocates for women athletes, coaches, and administrators.
11. Educate all involved about the historic discrimination in sports against women athletes.
12. Where appropriate, prepare and publish a gender equity report card delineating the percentage of women involved in the sport.
13. Have a well-known female athlete, coach, announcer, or sports executive speak to the youth sports organization about her experience in sports.
14. High school athletic associations should establish sexual harassment policies for all employees and athletes.
15. Educate employees and students about the sexual harassment policy.
16. Encourage staff and students to come forward with discrimination issues and concerns.
17. Establish a primary contact who will handle all sexual harassment complaints.
18. Apply sexual harassment policies equally to all employees and students.
19. Develop a complaint procedure for women athletes to report abusive behavior.
20. Formulate written policies for the administration and implementation of policies dealing with verbal and physical abuse of women athletes.
21. Ensure procedures for reporting all forms of abuse to protect the privacy of all athletes.
22. Require all new employees to sign a statement saying they agree not to engage in any physical or psychological abuse or sexual harassment of women athletes or coaches.
23. Schools should perform an initial assessment to evaluate whether they are in compliance with Title IX.
24. Develop a survey to be completed by the school's female students to identify areas of athletic interest.
25. Examine and monitor non-interscholastic sports such as intramurals, club sports, and physical education classes to note trends in female participation.
26. Schools should make a commitment to fairness to all athletes as they begin to examine the budget to see how fairness goals can be met.
27. Search for innovative methods to provide benefits to women's teams that help in establishing overall equity.
28. Have coaches of men's and women's teams meet to plan joint fund-raising activities for coaches.

29. Review salary scales of all coaches and athletic administrators for any discrepancies.
30. If a girl wants to try out for a boys' team, meet with the girl and the coach to discuss the issue, and allow a fair tryout. Videotape the tryout.
31. For girls on boys' teams, discuss specific needs for locker room facilities and traveling accommodations.
32. At the amateur level, review the schedule and start times of all athletic teams.
33. At the amateur level, establish a schedule so when one team is away the other is home.
34. At the amateur level, alternate starting times if boy/girl doubleheaders are scheduled.
35. Appoint Title IX coordinators for each educational institution and school district to organize efforts to comply with the law, investigate complaints, and publicize information on patterns of compliance with Title IX.
36. Provide all members of the school community, including students, parents, faculty, and staff, with information about Title IX protections.
37. Provide professional development and training to educators and administrators about approaches to counteracting gender stereotyping and sex discrimination.
38. Ensure that female and male students have equal opportunities to participate in athletics and other types of educational programs, where one sex is underrepresented.

CHAPTER 11 ETHICAL CONSIDERATIONS FOR INTELLECTUAL PROPERTY IN SPORTS

1. File for trademark protection immediately. This protects your property. Register your trademark in all countries where you plan to do business.
2. Have all employees sign confidentiality agreements during their employment if they have access to a company's intellectual property.
3. Have licensees of intellectual property rights sign confidentiality agreements that they will protect intellectual property rights of the company, only disclosing confidential information to necessary parties.
4. Use your trademark!
5. "Police" your mark. Do not let others use it without seeking permission.
6. Consult a trademark attorney to register your mark and to fend off possible counterfeiters.
7. Develop brand protection or an anti-counterfeiting program within your company.
8. Train key personnel on how to recognize when a trademark or brand is being wrongfully exploited, infringed upon, diluted, or tarnished.
9. If you suspect a trademark is counterfeit, contact the certification agency to determine its legitimacy.
10. Review the anti-counterfeiting program of Underwriters Laboratories (UL) for further tips on how to protect intellectual property.

CHAPTER 12 ETHICAL CONSIDERATIONS IN SPORTS MEDIA

1. Sports reporters should be fair and accurate.
2. Sports reporters should remain objective.
3. Sports reporters should verify their sources.

4. Sports reporters should be careful to avoid stereotyping with regard to race, disability, gender, national origin, and sexual orientation.

5. Sports reporters should be respectful of the privacy of individuals.

6. Media outlets should be aware they owe a duty to report only significant matters of interest to the public that are newsworthy.

7. When a mistake has been made in reporting, media outlets should publish a retraction in the same manner and with the same scope as they first reported the story.

8. When a matter is discussed "off the record," it needs to stay off the record.

9. Media outlets should always cover stories that promote the good of the sport and the individuals who play it.

10. Ratings should never be the driving force behind a story.

BIBLIOGRAPHY

ARTICLES

Rehman Y. Abdulrehman, "The Cycle of Abuse in Sport Hazing: Is It Simply a Case of Boys Being Boys?" PhD dissertation, University of Manitoba, Canada, 2007.

American Gaming Association, "Sports Wagering Industry Information Fact Sheets: Industry Issues," February 4, 2009.

Kyle J. Anderson and David A. Pierce, "Officiating Bias: The Effect of Foul Differential on Foul Calls in NCAA Basketball," *Journal of Sports Sciences* 27, no. 7 (May 2009) 687–694.

Penelope Andrews, "Violence Against Women in South Africa: The Role of Culture and the Limitations of the Law," *Temple Political & Civil Rights Law Review* 8 (1998–1999): 425.

Daniel Auerbach, "Morals Clauses as Corporate Protection in Athlete Endorsement Contracts," *DePaul Journal of Sports Law & Contemporary Problems* 3 (Summer 2005).

N. J. Balmer, A. M. Nevill, and A. M. Lane, "Do Judges Enhance Home Advantage in European Championship Boxing?" *Journal of Sports Sciences* 23, no. 4 (April 2005): 409–416.

Subhajit Basu and Richard Jones, "Regulating Cyberstalking," *Journal of Information, Law, and Technology* 2 (February 2007).

Howard P. Benard, "Little League Fun, Big League Liability," *Marquette Sports Law Journal* 8, no. 1 (1997–1998): 93–97.

Dan Bernhardt and Steven Heston, "Point Shaving in College Basketball: A Cautionary Tale for Forensic Economics," *Economic Inquiry* 48, no. 1 (January 2010): 14–25.

William Blake, "Umpires as Legal Realists," *Social Science Research Network*, no. 178 (July 23, 2010).

Cynthia D. Bond, "Laws of Race/Laws of Representation: The Construction of Race and Law in Contemporary American Film," *Texas Review of Entertainment & Sports Law* 11 (Spring 2010): 219.

Timothy J. Brailsford, Philip K. Gray, Stephen A. Easton, and Stephen F. Gray, "The Efficiency of Australian Football Betting Markets," *Australian Journal of Management* 20, no. 2 (December 1995): 167–197.

Mike Brewster, "Bill Veeck: A Baseball Mastermind," *Bloomberg Business Week*, October 27, 2004.

Joy D. Bringer, Celia H. Brackenridge, and Lynne H. Johnston, "Defining Appropriateness in Coach-Athlete Sexual Relationships: The Voice of Coaches," *Journal of Sexual Aggression* 8, no. 2 (July 2002): 83–98.

Sean H. Brogan, "Who Are These 'Colts'?: The Likelihood of Confusion, Consumer Survey Evidence, and Trademark Abandonment in Indianapolis Colts, Inc. v. Metropolitan Baltimore Football Club, LTD.," *Marquette Sports Law Journal* 7 (1996–1997): 39.

Kidd Bruce and Peter Donnelly, "Human Rights in Sports," *International Review for the Sociology of Sports* 35 (September 2010): 131–148.

Sean Bukowski, "Flag on the Play: 25 to Life for the Offense of Murder," *Vanderbilt Journal of Entertainment Law & Practice* 3 (Winter 2001): 106.

Babatunde Buraimo, David Forrest, and Robert Simmons, "The 12th Man?: Refereeing Bias in English and German Soccer," *Journal of the Royal Statistical Society* 173, no. 2 (April 2010): 431–449.

Ian Burstein, "Liability for Injuries Suffered in the Course of Recreational Sports: Application of the Negligence Standard," *University of Detroit Mercy Law Review* 71 (1994): 993.

G. J. Buse, "No Holds Barred Sports Fighting: A 10 Year Review of Mixed Martial Arts Competition," *British Journal of Sports Medicine* (February 9, 2006).

Jennifer Byrd, "Is Stereotypical Coverage of African-American Athletes as Dead as Disco?: An Analysis of NFL Quarterbacks in the Pages of Sports Illustrated," *Journal of Sports Media* 2 (2007): 1–28.

Anthony N. Cabot and Robert D. Faiss, "Sports Gambling in the Cyberspace Era," *Chapman Law Review* 5z (2002): 1–45.

Clay Calvert and Robert D. Richards, "Fans and the First Amendment: Cheering and Jeering in College Sports," *Virginia Sports and Entertainment Law Journal* 4 (2004–2005): 1.

Eoin Carolan, "The New WADA Code and the Search for a Policy Justification for Anti-Doping Rules," *Seton Hall Journal of Sports and Entertainment Law* (2006).

Brian Carroll, "The Black Press and the Integration of Professional Baseball: A Content Analysis of Shifts in Coverage, 1945–1948," *Journal of Sports Media* 3, no. 2 (Fall 2008): 61–87.

Michael S. Carroll, Daniel P. Connaughton, John O. Spengler, and James J. Zhang, "Case Law Analysis Regarding High School and Collegiate Liability for Hazing," *European Sports Management Quarterly* 9, no. 4 (December 2009): 389–410.

Walter Champion, "The O. J. Trial as a Metaphor for Racism in Sports," *Thurgood Marshall Law Review* 33 (Fall 2007): 157.

Linda Cohn, "Cohn-Head: A No-Holds-Barred Account of Breaking into the Boys' Club," *The Globe Pequot Press*, 2008.

Patrick Connors, John Genzale, Richard Hilliard, Brian Mackler, and Rachel Newman-Baker, "Panel III: Ethics and Sports: Agents Regulation," *Fordham Intellectual Property, Media and Entertainment Law Journal* 14 (Winter 2004): 747–791.

Mark Conrad, "Fleeting Expletives and Sports Broadcasts: A Legal Nightmare Needs a Safe Harbor," *Journal of Legal Aspects in Sport* 18 (2008): 175.

Royal W. Craig, "With Sports Big Business, Trademark Theft Keeping Courtrooms Busy," *Baltimore Business Journal* (February 23, 2007).

Michael E. Cross, Jay Basten, Erin Marie Hendrick, Brian Kristofic, and Evan J. Schaffer, "Student-Athletes and Gambling: An Analysis of Attitudes Towards Risk-Taking," *Journal of Gambling Studies* 14, no. 4 (Winter 1998): 431–439.

Tood W. Crosset, James Ptacek, Mark A. McDonald, and Jeffrey R. Benedict, "Male Student-Athletes and Violence Against Women," *Violence Against Women* 2, no. 2 (1996): 163–179.

R. Brian Crow and Scott R. Rosner, "Institutional and Organizational Liability for Hazing in Intercollegiate and Professional Team Sports," *St. John's Law Review* 39 (2002): 275.

Paulo David, "Young Athletes and Competitive Sports: Exploit and Exploitation," *International Journal of Children's Rights* 7 (1999): 53–81.

Timothy Davis, "Myth of the Superspade: The Persistence of Racism in College Athletics," *Fordham Urban Law Journal* 22 (1994–1995): 615.

Danielle Deak, "Out of Bounds: How Sexual Abuse of Athletes at the Hands of Their Coaches Is Costing the World of Sports Millions," *Seton Hall Journal of Sport Law* 9 (1999): 171.

Samara Kalk Derby, "Legislation Pushes for Funding to Treat Gambling Addicts," *Madison State Journal* (November 29, 2009).

Louis J. DeVoto, "Injury on the Golf Course: Regardless of Your Handicap, Escaping Liability Is Par for the Course," *University of Toledo Law Review* 24 (1992–1993): 859.

Michael Dillingham, "Steroids, Sports, and the Ethics of Winning," Santa Clara University, Markkula Center for Applied Ethics, August 25, 2004.

Melissa Dixon, "Hazing in High School: Ending the Hidden Tradition," *Journal of Law and Education* 30 (2001): 357.

Tonya L. Dodge and James J. Jaccard, "The Effect of High School Sports Participation on the Use of Performance-Enhancing Substances in Young Adulthood," *Journal of Adolescent Health* 39 (September 2006): 367–373.

Sheryle Bergmann Drewe, "Coaches, Ethics, and Autonomy," *Sport, Education, and Society* 5, no. 2 (October 2000): 147–162.

Will Dunham, "Steroid Users Seen Twice as Prone to Violence," *Reuters*, October 15, 2008.

Susan Tyler Eastman and Andrew C. Billings, "Biased Voices of Sports: Racial and Gender Stereotyping in College Basketball Announcing," *Howard Journal of Communications* 12, no. 4 (October 2001): 183–201.

Nicolas Eber, "The Performance-Enhancing Drug Game Reconsidered," *Journal of Sports Economics* 9, no. 3 (December 21, 2007): 318–327.

Marc Edelman, "How to Prevent High School Hazing: A Legal, Social, and Ethical Primer," *North Dakota Law Review* 81 (2005).

Davis Eitle, "Race, Culture Capital, and the Educational Effects of Participation in Sports," *University of Miami, Sociology of Education* 75 (April 2002): 123–46.

D. Stanley Eitzen, "Ethical Problems in American Sport," *Journal of Sport and Social Issues* 12, no. 1 (1988): 17–20.

John W. Emerson, Miki Seltzer, and David Lin, "Assessing Judging Bias: An Example From the 2000 Olympic Games," *The American Statistician* 63, no. 2 (May 1, 2009): 124–131.

Jane English, "Sex Equality in Sports," *Philosophy and Public Affairs* 7, no. 3 (Spring 1978): 269–277.

J. Rice Ferreille Jr., "Combating the Lure of Impropriety in Professional Sports Industries: The Desirability of Treating a Playbook as a Legally Enforceable Trade Secret," *Journal of Intellectual Property Law*, 11 (2003–2004): 149.

Dianna K. Fiore, "Parental Rage and Violence in Youth Sports: How Can We Prevent Soccer Moms and Hockey Dads from Interfering in Youth Sports and Causing Games to End in Fistfights Rather Than Handshakes," *Villanova Sports and Entertainment Law Journal* 10 (2003): 103.

Sarah K. Fleish, "The Ethics of Legal Commentary: A Reconsideration of the Need for an Ethical Code in Light of the Duke Lacrosse Matter," *Georgetown Journal of Legal Ethics* 20 (Summer 2007): 599.

Neil Forrester, "The Elephant in the Locker Room: Does the National Football League Discriminate in the Hiring of Head Coaches?" *McGeorge Law Review* 34 (2003): 877.

Kenneth B. Franklin, "A Brave Attempt: Can the National Collegiate Athletic Association Sanction Colleges and Universities With Native American Mascots?" *Journal of Intellectual Property Law* 13 (2005–2006): 435.

Elizabeth A. Gage, "Gender Attitudes and Sexual Behaviors," *Violence Against Women* 14, no. 9 (2008): 1014–1032.

Steven N. Geise, "A Whole New Ballgame: The Application of Trademark Law to Sports Mark Litigation," *Seton Hall Journal of Sport Law* 5 (1995): 553.

Leslie Gevitz and Toni Reinhold, "Baseball Players Sue Steiner Sports over Trademark," *Reuters*, May 16, 2008.

Michael Gibbons and Dana Campbell, "Liability of Recreation and Competitive Sport Organizations for Sexual Assaults on Children by Administrators, Coaches, and Volunteers," *Journal of Legal Aspects in Sport*, 13 (2002–2003): 185.

Jonathan Gibbs, "Point Shaving in the NBA: An Economic Analysis of the National Basketball Association's Point Spread Betting Market," PhD dissertation, Stanford University, May 11, 2007.

Alison Go, "Athletes Show Huge Gaps in SAT Scores," *U.S. News & World Report*, December 30, 2008.

Jonah Goldberg, "Just Like Ozzie and Harriet: When Hollywood Liberals 'Settle Down,'" *National Review*, December 18, 2000.

Aaron Goldstein, "Intentional Infliction of Emotional Distress: Another Attempt at Eliminating Native American Mascots," *Journal of Gender, Race and Justice*, 3 (1999–2000): 689.

Brent J. Goodfellow, "Betting on the Future of Sports: Why Gambling Should Be Left Off the Field of Play," *Willamette Sports Law Journal* 2, no. 2 (Fall 2005): 21–43.

Hannah Gordon, "In the Replay Booth: Looking at Appeals of Arbitration Decision in Sports Through Miami Dolphins v. Williams," *Harvard Negotiation Law Review* 12 (Spring 2007): 503.

Martin Greenberg, "Sports Law Practice," *Lexis Law Publishing* (1993).

Paul H. Haagen, "Players Have Lost That Argument: Doping, Drug Testing, and Collective Bargaining," *New England Law Review* 40 (2005–2006): 831–849.

Charles Haray, "Aggressive Play or Criminal Assault? An In-Depth Look at Sports Violence and Criminal Liability," *Columbia Journal of Law & the Arts* 25 (Winter 2002): 195.

Nick Harris, "Revealed: Biased Rugby Referees in Both Codes Hand Big Advantage to Own Countries," *Sporting Intelligence*, July 29, 2010.

G. S. Heinzmann, "Parental Violence in Youth Sports: Facts, Myths and Videotape," *National Recreation and Parks Association* (March 2002).

Benjamin T. Hickman, "Old Law, New Technology: The First Amendment's Application When Sports Teams and Leagues Attempt to Regulate New Media," *Communications Lawyer*, July 2010.

Warren D. Hill and John E. Clark, "Sports, Gambling, and Government: America's First Social Compact?" *American Anthropologist* 103, no. 2 (June 2001): 331–345.

Earl F. Hoerner, "Safety in American Football," *ASTM International*, 1997.

Lawrence D. Hogan, "Shades of Glory: The Negro Leagues and the Story of African-American Baseball," *National Geographic*, First Printing Edition (January 31, 2006).

Samuel J. Horovitz, "If You Ain't Cheating You Ain't Trying: Spygate and the Legal Implications of Trying Too Hard," *Texas Intellectual Property Law Journal* 17 (2008–2009): 305.

Mary A. Hums, Carol A. Barr, and Laurie Gullion, "The Ethical Issues Confronting Managers in the Sports Industry," *Journal of Business Ethics* 20, no. 1 (1999): 51–66.

Thomas R. Hurst and James N. Knight, "Coaches' Liability for Athletes' Injuries and Deaths," *Seton Hall Journal of Sports Law* 13 (2003): 27.

Brett Hutchins and David Rowe, "Reconfiguring Media Sports for the Online World: An Inquiry into 'Sports News and Digital Media,'" *International Journal of Communication* 4 (2010): 696–718.

J. Gordon Hylton, "American Civil Rights Law and the Legacy of Jackie Robinson," *Marquette Sports Law Journal* 8 (1998): 387.

Robin Insley, Lucia Mok, and Tim Swartz, "Issues Related to Sports Gambling," *Australia & New Zealand Journal of Statistics* 46, no. 2 (June 2004): 219–232.

Anna L. Jefferson, "The NFL and Domestic Violence: The Commissioner's Power to Punish Domestic Abusers," *Seton Hall Journal of Sports Law* 7 (1997): 353.

James W. Keating, "Sportsmanship as a Moral Category," *Ethics* 75, no. 1 (October 1964): 29.

David A. Kessler, Greenberg Traurig, and Virginia McLean, "The Parody Defense: Is Anyone Still Laughing?" Intellectual Property Law Conference, American Bar Association, Toronto, Ontario, June 16–20, 2004.

Lynn Kidman, Alex McKenzie, and Bridget McKenzie, "The Nature and Target of Parents' Comments During Youth Sport Competitions," *Journal of Sport Behavior* 22 (1999): 1.

John Warren Kindt and Thomas Asmar, "College and Amateur Sports Gambling: Gambling Away Our Youth," *Sports and Entertainment Law Journal* 8 (2001–2002): 221–252.

Sandra L. Kirby, "Running the Gauntlet: An Examination of Initiation/Hazing and Sexual Abuse in Sport," *Journal of Sexual Aggression* 8, no. 2 (July 2002): 49–68.

Jane Kirtley, "A Magazine Is Not a Newspaper," *American Journalism Review* (October/November 2005).

Kelly B. Koenig, "Mahmoud Abdul-Rauf's Suspension for Refusing to Stand for the National Anthem: A 'Free Throw' for the NBA and Denver Nuggets, or a 'Slam Dunk' Violation of Abdul-Rauf's Title VII Rights?" *Washington University Law Quarterly* 76 (Spring 1998): 377.

Allan Korpela, "Tort Liability of Public Schools and Institutions of Higher Learning for Injuries Results from Lack or Insufficiency of Supervision," *American Law Reports* 36 (1971): 330.

Andrew M. Lane, Alan M. Nevill, Nahid S. Ahmad, and Nigel Balmer, "Soccer Referee Decision-Making: 'Shall I Blow the Whistle?'" *Journal of Sports Science and Medicine* 5 (June 1, 2006): 243–253.

J. D. Larsen and D. W. Rainey, "Judgment Bias in Baseball Umpires' First Base Calls: A Computer Simulation," *Journal of Sport and Exercise Psychology* 13, no. 1 (1991): 75–59.

Christo Lassitter, "The O. J. Simpson Verdict: A Lesson in Black and White," *Michigan Journal of Race & the Law* 1 (1960): 69.

Daniel E. Lazaroff, "Golfers' Tort Liability: A Critique of an Emerging Standard," *Hastings Commercial and Entertainment Law Journal* 24 (2001–2002): 317.

Trisha Leahy, Grace Pretty, and Gershon Tenenbaum, "Prevalence of Sexual Abuse in Organised Competitive Sport in Australia," *Journal of Sexual Aggression* 8, no. 2 (July 2002): 16–36.

Mark A. Lemley, "Property, Intellectual Property, and Free Riding," *Texas Law Review* 83 (2004–2005): 1031.

Richard Lempert, "Error Behind the Plate and in the Law, *Southern California Law Review* 59 (1985–1986): 407–422.

Gill Lines, "Villains, Fools or Heroes? Sports Stars as Role Models for Young People," *Leisure Studies* 20, no. 4 (October 2001): 285–303.

Robert I. Lockwood, "The Best Interests of the League: Referee Betting Scandal Brings Commissioner Authority and Collective Bargaining Back to the Front Court in the NBA," *Sports Lawyers Journal* 15 (Spring 2008): 138.

Jeanne M. Logsdon and Donna J. Wood, "Global Business Citizenship and Voluntary Codes of Ethical Conduct," *Journal of Business Ethics* 59, nos. 1–2 (2005): 55–67.

Anthony C. Luke and Michael F. Bergeron, "Heat Injury Prevention Practices in High School Football," *Clinical Journal of Sport Medicine* 17, no. 6 (November 2007).

Clay Luraschi, "Topps Settles Lawsuit over Cool Papa Bell Cards," *Reuters*, November 14, 2008.

Bram A. Maravent, "Is the Rooney Rule Affirmative Action? Analysing the NFL's Mandate to Its Clubs Regarding Coaching and Front Office Hires," *Sports Lawyers Journal* 13 (Spring 2006): 233.

S. Marino, "People Who Cheat at Golf Cheat in Business," *Industry Week*, 1998.

Matthew G. Matzkin, "Getting Played: How the Video Game Industry Violates College Athletes' Rights of Publicity by Not Paying for Their Likeness," *Loyola of Los Angeles Entertainment Law Review* 21 (2000–2001): 227.

Michael Mayer, "Stepping in to Step Out of Liability: The Proper Standard of Liability for Referees in Foreseeable Judgment-Call Situations," *DePaul Journal of Sports Law and Contemporary Problems*, 3 Issue 1 (Summer 2005).

Thomas J. McCarthy and Paul M. Anderson, "Protection of the Athletes Identity: The Right of Publicity, Endorsements and Domain Names," *Marquette Sports and Law Review* 11 (2000–2001): 195.

Andrew McCasky and Kenneth Biedzynski, "A Guide to the Legal Liability of Coaches for a Sports Participant's Injuries," *Seton Hall Journal Sport Law* 6 (1996): 12–13.

J. F. McElvogue, "Racial Segregation in American Sport," *International Review of Sport Sociology* 6, no. 4 (1970): 393–400.

Ay R. Mellow, "And the Ruling on the Field Is Fair: A Fair Use Analysis of Uploading NFL Videos onto YouTube and Why the NFL Should License Its Material to the Website," *Southern California Interdisciplinary Law Journal* 17 (Fall 2007): 173.

Mike Messner, Darnell Hunt, and Michele Dunbar, "Boys to Men: Sports Media," *Children Now*, 1999.

Andrew Metrick, "March Madness? Strategic Behavior in NCAA Basketball Tournament Betting Pools," *Journal of Economic Behavior & Organization* 30, no. 2 (August 1996): 159–172.

Lori K. Miller, "A Uniform Code to Regulate Athlete Agents," *Journal of Sports & Social Issues* 16, no. 2 (1992): 93–102.

Lori K. Miller and Cathryn L. Claussen, "Online Sports Gambling: Regulation or Prohibition?" *Journal of Legal Aspects in Sport* 11, Issue 2 (2001): 99–134.

Helen Moffett, "'These Women, They Force Us to Rape Them': Rape as Narrative of Social Control in Post-Apartheid South Africa," *Journal of South African Studies* 32, no. 1 (March 2006): 129–144.

Sally Monaghan, Jeffrey Derevensky, and Alyssa Sklar, "Impact of Gambling Advertisements and Marketing on Children and Adolescents: Policy Recommendations to Minimize Harm," *Journal of Gambling Issues* 22 (December 2008): 252–274.

Brian R. Moushegian, "Native American Mascots' Last Stand? Legal Difficulties in Eliminating Public University Use of Native American Mascots," *Villanova Sports & Entertainment Law Journal* 13 (2006): 465.

Liz Mullen, "NFLPA Files Complaint Against Arrington's Agent," *Sports Business Journal* 14 (January 23, 2006).

Sanjay Jose Mullick, "Browns to Baltimore: Franchise Free Agency and the New Economics of the NFL," *Marquette Sports Law Journal* 7 (1996–1997): 1.

Angela J. Murphy, "Life Stories of Black Male and Female Professionals: An Inquiry into the Salience of Race and Sports," *The Journal of Men's Studies* 13, no. 3 (February 19, 2007): 313–325.

Tony D. Myers, Nigel J. Balmer, Alan M. Nevill, and Yahya Al-Nakeeb, "Evidence of Nationalistic Bias in Muay-Thai," *Journal of Sports Science and Medicine* 5 (July 2006): 21–27.

Juha Nasi and Pasi Sajasalo, "Consolidation by Game-Playing: A Gamesmanship Inquiry into the Forestry Industry," *The Evolution of Competitive Strategies in Global Forestry Industry*, World Forest 4, no. 3 (2006): 225–256.

Bruce Neckers, "Cheating," *Michigan Bar Journal* (September 2002).

Melissa Neiman, "Fair Game: Ethical Consideration in Negotiation by Sports Agents," *University of Houston Law Center* (August 2007).

David Niven, "Race, Quarterbacks, and the Media: Testing the Rush Limbaugh Hypothesis," *Florida Atlantic University* 35, no. 5 (September 1, 2010): 684–694.

Thomas P. Oates and John Pauly, "Sports Journalism as Moral and Ethical Discourse," *Journal of Mass Media Ethics* 22, no. 4 (2007): 332–347.

Tiffany O'Callaghan, "The Politics of Perceiving Skin Color," *TIME Healthland*, November 23, 2009.

Thomas J. Ostertag, "From Shoeless Joe to Charley Hustle: Major League Baseball's Continuing Crusade Against Sports Gambling," *Seton Hall Journal of Sport Law* 2 (1992): 19.

John Ourand and Michael Smith, "Fox Likely Partner for Future University of Texas Network," *Austin Business Journal* (October 11, 2010).

M. Parssinen and T. Seppala, "Steroid Use and Long-Term Health Risks in Former Athletes," *Sports Medicine* 32, no. 2 (February 1, 2002): 83–94.

Daphne Patai, "Gamesmanship and Androcentrism in Orwell's 1984," *PMLA* 97, no. 5 (October 1982): 856–870.

Elad Peled, "Constitutionalizing Mandatory Retraction in Defamation Law," *Hastings Communications and Entertainment Law Journal* 30 (2007).

Per Pettersson-Lidbom and Mikael Priks, "Behavior Under Social Pressure: Empty Italian Stadiums and Referee Bias," *Economic Letters*, February 17, 2009.

Deborah Posel, "Scandal of Manhood: 'Baby Rape' and the Politicization of Sexual Violence in Post-Apartheid South Africa," *Culture Health & Sexuality* 7, no. 3 (May 2005): 239–252.

Robert C. Post, "The Constitutional Concept of Public Discourse, Outrageous Opinion, Democratic Deliberation, and Hustler Magazine." *Harvard Law Review* 103, no. 3 (January 1990): 601.

Charles S. Prebish, "'Heavenly Father, Divine Goalie': Sport and Religion," *The Antioch Review* 42, no. 3 (Summer 1984): 306–318.

Joseph Price and Justin Wolfers, "Racial Discrimination Among NBA Referees," *National Bureau of Economic Research* 125, no. 4 (May 2, 2007): 1859–1882.

David W. Rainey, Janet D. Larsen, Alan Stephenson, and Torry Olson, "Normative Rules Among Umpires: The 'Phantom Tag' at Second Base," *Journal of Sport Behavior* 16 (1993).

D. Rainey and G. Schweickert, "Fans' Evaluations of Major League Baseball Umpires' Performances and Perceptions of Appropriate Behavior," *Journal of Sport Behavior* 13, no. 2 (1990): 122–129.

Cameron Jay Rains, "Sports Violence: A Matter of Societal Concern," *Notre Dame Law Review* 55 (1979–1980): 796.

Allegra M. Richards, "NCAA Clarifies Facebook Policy," *The Harvard Crimson*, March 14, 2007.

Joel Nathan Rosen, "The Mouth Roars No Longer: Pete Franklin, Sports Talk, and Cleveland Indians Baseball, 1967, 1987," *NINE: A Journal of Baseball History and Culture* 15, no. 1 (Fall 2006): 13–26.

Scott R. Rosner and R. Brian Crow, "Institutional Liability for Hazing in Interscholastic Sports," *Houston Law Review* 39, no. 2 (2002–2003).

Kirkley L. Russell, "A Qualitative Investigation of Confidence of Novice and Experienced American Legion Baseball Umpires," PhD dissertation, Capella University, 137 (2007).

James G. Sammataro, "Business and Brotherhood, Can They Coincide? A Search into Why Black Athletes Do Not Hire Black Agents," *Howard Law Journal* 42 (Spring 1999): 535.

Kimberly S. Schimmel, C. Lee Harrington, and Denise D. Bielby, "Keep Your Fans to Yourself: The Disjuncture Between Sport Studies' and Pop Culture Studies' Perspectives on Fandom," *Sport in Society* 10, no. 4 (July 2007): 580–600.

R. M. Sellers, "Racial Differences in the Predictors for Academic Achievement of Student-Athletes in Division I Revenue Producing Sports," *Sociology of Sports Journal* 9, no. 1 (1992): 48–59.

Hela Sheth and Kathy M. Babiak, "Beyond the Game: Perceptions and Practices of Corporate Social Responsibility in the Professional Sport Industry," *Journal of Business Ethics* 91, no. 3 (2010): 433–450.

Hee-Joon Shin and Joeng-Woong Baik, "Vicarious Liability Against University and Coach," *Journal of Physical Education, Recreation, and Dance* 75 (2004).

Neil S. Siegel, "Umpires at Bat: On Integration and Legitimation," *Constitutional Commentary* 24 (2007): 182.

Tom Silverstein, "Favre, Millen Had Talk, but QB Insists He Wasn't Trying to Sabotage Packers," *Journal Sentinel*, October 22, 2008.

Jonathan Singer, "Keep It Clean: How Public Universities May Constitutionally Enforce Policies Limiting Student Speech at College Basketball Games," *University of Baltimore Law Review* 39 (Winter 2010): 299.

Aaron J. Slavin, "The 'Las Vegas Loophole' and the Current Push in Congress Towards a Blanket Prohibition on Collegiate Sports Gambling," *University of Miami Business Law Review* 10 (2002): 715.

Horton Smith, "What the PGA Is," *USGA Journal and Turf Management* (April 1951).

William Spain, "The World Cup: Biggest Gambling Event in History?" *MarketWatch*, June 1, 2010.

Jenni Spies, "Only Orphans Should Be Allowed to Play Little League: How Parents Are Ruining Organized Youth Sports for Their Children and What Can Be Done About It," *Sports Lawyers Journal* 13 (Spring 2006): 275.

Jeffrey Standen, "The Beauty of Bets: Wagers as Compensation for Professional Athletes," *Willamette Law Review* 42 (2006): 640–641.

Katlin Stinespring, "The Art of Sports Heckling," *The Charleston Gazette*, June 11, 2010.

Frederick R. Struckmeyer, "God and Gamesmanship," *Religious Studies* 7, no. 3 (September 1971): 233–243.

Joshua A. Sussberg, "Shattered Dreams: Hazing in College Athletics," *Cardozo Law Review* 24, no. 3 (2002–2003): 1421.

Matthias Sutter and Martin G. Kocher, "Favoritism of Agents: The Case of Referees' Home Bias," *Journal of Economic Psychology* 25, no. 4 (August 2004): 461–469.

Porcher L. Taylor III, Fernando M. Pinguelo, and Timothy D. Cedrone, "The Reverse-Morals Clause: The Unique Way to Save Talent's Reputation and Money in a New Era of Corporate Crimes and Scandals," *Arts & Entertainment Law Journal* 28 (2010): 65.

Mario Thevis and Wilhelm Schaenzer, "Mass Spectrometry in Sports Drug Testing: Structure Characterization and Analytical Assays," *Mass Spectrometry Reviews* Vol. 43 issue 7 (August 3, 2006): 892–902.

Michael J. Thompson, "Give Me $25 and Derek Jeter for $26: Do Fantasy Sports Leagues Constitute Gambling?" *Sports Lawyers Journal* 8 (Spring 2001): 21–25.

Patrick Thornton, "Rewriting Hockey's Unwritten Rules: Moore v. Bertuzzi," *Maine Law Review* 61, no. 1 (2009): 205.

Patrick K. Thornton, "The Limits of the Fair Use Doctrine: The Family Guy Ko's Carol Burnett in a Battle of Cultural Icons," *University of Baltimore Intellectual Property Law Journal* 17, no. 1 (Fall 2008): 79.

Patrick K. Thornton and Christopher James, "Down Two Strikes, Is Major League Baseball Already Out?: How the 8th Circuit Balked to Protect the Right of Publicity in C.B.C. v. MLB," *South Texas Law Review* 50, no. 2 (Winter 2008): 173.

Kelley Tiffany, "Cheering Speech at State University Athletic Events: How Do You Regulate Spectator Sportsmanship?" *Sports Law Journal* 14 (2007), 111.

Jim Tootle, "Bill Veeck and James Thurber: The Literary Origins of the Midget Pinch Hitter," *NINE: A Journal of Baseball History and Culture* 10, no. 2 (Spring 2002): 110–119.

Jeffrey C. True, "The NCAA Celebration Rule: A First Amendment Analysis," *Seton Hall Journal of Sports Law* 7 (1997): 129.

Joel Michael Ugolini, "Even a Violent Game Has Its Limits: A Look at the NFL's Responsibility for the Behavior of Its Players," *University of Toledo Law Review* 39 (Fall 2007): 41.

David Q. Voigt, "America's Manufactured Villain: The Baseball Umpire," *The Journal of Popular Culture* 5, no. 1 (Summer 1970): 1–21.

David M. Wachutka, "Collective Bargaining Agreements in Professional Sports: The Proper Forum for Establishing Performance-Enhancing Drug Testing Policies," *Pepperdine Dispute Resolution Law Journal* 8 (2007): 147.

Don Walker, "Does Kareem Own 'Sky Hook'?" *Journal Interactive* (June 1, 2009).

Kristin Walseth, "Young Women and Sport: the Impact of Identity Work," *Leisure Studies* 25, no. 1 (January 2006): 75–94.

Howard M. Wasserman, "Cheers, Profanity, and Free Speech in College Sports," PhD dissertation, Florida International University, August 9, 2004.

Geoffrey G. Watson, "Games, Socialization and Parental Values: Social Class Differences in Parental Evaluation of Little League Baseball," *International Review for the Sociology of Sport* 12, no. 1 (1977): 17–48.

Ge Weizhuo, "Study on Baseball Umpire Selection from Psychological Characteristics," *Journal of Tianjin Institute of Physical Education* (1995).

Joshua H. Whitman, "Winning at All Costs: Using Law and Economics to Determine the Proper Role of Government in Regulating the Use of Performance-Enhancing Drugs in Professional Sports," *University of Illinois Law Review* 45 (2008): 459.

Darryl C. Wilson, "Let Them Do Drugs: A Commentary on Random Efforts at Shot Blocking in the Sports Drug Game," *Florida Coastal Law Review* 8, no. 53 (Fall 2006).

Bethany P. Withers, "The Integrity of the Game: Professional Athletes and Domestic Violence," *Journal of Sports and Entertainment Law* 1, no. 1 (Spring 2010): 145–172.

Justin Wolfers, "Point Shaving: Corruption in NCAA Basketball," *American Economic Review* 96, no. 2 (May 2006): 279–283.

K. Tim Wulfemeyer, "Ethics in Sports Journalism: Tightening Up the Code," *Journal of Mass Media Ethics* 1, no. 1 (Autumn 1985).

Jeff Yates (with William Gillespie), "The Problem of Sports Violence and the Criminal Prosecution Solution," *Cornell Journal of Law and Public Policy* 12 (2002): 145.

Aaron S. J. Zelinsky, "The Justice as Commissioner: Benching the Judge-Umpire Analogy," *Yale Law Journal* 119 (March 4, 2010): 113.

BOOKS

The American Heritage Dictionary, New College Edition (Boston, MA: Houghton Mifflin, 1976).

Amy Bass, *In the Game* (New York: Palgrave MacMillan, 2005).

Arpon Basu, *NHL Enforcers: The Rough and Tough Guys of Hockey* (Montreal, Quebec, Canada: Overtime Books, 2006).

Jim Becker, Andy Mayer, Rick Wolff, and Barrie Maguire, *Golf Dirty Tricks: 50 Ways to Lie, Cheat, and Steal Your Way to Victory* (Bellevue, WA: Becker & Mayer, 1994).

Jeff Benedict, *Out of Bounds: Inside the NBA's Culture of Rape, Violence, and Crime* (New York: Perennial Currents, 2004).

Jeff Benedict, *Public Heroes, Private Felons: Athletes and Crimes Against Women* (Lebanon, NH: Northeastern University Press, 1997).

Jeff Benedict and Don Yaeger, *Pros and Cons: The Criminals Who Play in the NFL* (New York: Warner Books, 1998).

Ross Bernstein, *The Code: Baseball's Unwritten Rules and Its Ignore-at-Your-Own-Risk Code of Conduct* (Chicago, IL: Triumph Books, 2008).

Tommy Boone, *Basic Issues in Sports Ethics: The Many Ways of Cheating* (Lewiston, NY: Edwin Mellen Press, 2009).

Douglas Booth, *The Race Game: Sports and Politics in South Africa* (New York: Routledge, 1998).

Dana Brooks and Ronald Althouse, *Diversity and Social Justice in College Sports: Sport Management and the Student-Athlete* (Morgantown, WV: Fitness Information Technology, 2007).

Richard Carter, *Curt Flood: The Way It Is* (New York: Trident Press, 1971).

Walter Champion, *Fundamentals of Sports Law* (St. Paul, MN: Thomson West, 2004).

Joy Theresa DeSensi and Danny Rosenberg, *Ethics and Morality in Sport Management* (Morgantown, WV: Fitness Information Technology, 2003).

Paul Dickson, *The Dickson Baseball Dictionary Third Edition* (New York: W.W. Norton & Company, 2009).

Les Edgerton, *Surviving Little League: For Players, Parents, and Coaches* (New York: Taylor Trade Publishing, 2004).

Jon Entire, *Taboo: Why Black Athletes Dominate Sports and Why We're Afraid to Talk About It* (New York: PublicAffairs, 1999).

Christopher H. Evans and William R. Herzog II, *The Faith of 50 Million* (Louisville, KY: Westminster John Knox Press, 2002).

Joel Fish and Susan Magee, *101 Ways to Be a Terrific Sports Parent* (New York: Fireside, 2003).

Peter A. French, *Ethics and College Sports: Ethics, Sports, and the University (Issues in Academic Ethics)* (Lanham, MD: Rowman & Littlefield Publishers, 2004).

Theodore Friedmann, *Gene Doping in Sports: The Science and Ethics of Genetically Modified Athletes* (Salt Lake City, UT: Academic Press, 2006).

Margaret Gatz, Michael A. Messner, and Sandra J. Ball-Rokeach, *Paradoxes of Youth and Sport* (New York: State University of New York Press, 2002).

Bob Gibson, Reggie Jackson, and Lonnie Wheeler, *Sixty Feet, Six Inches: A Hall of Fame Pitcher & a Hall of Fame Hitter Talk About How the Game Is Played* (Garden City, NY: Doubleday, 2009).

Daniel E. Ginsburg, *The Fix Is In: A History of Baseball Gambling and Game Fixing Scandals* (Jefferson, NC: McFarland and Co., 2004).

David Halberstam, *The Best American Sports Writing of the Century* (Boston, MA: Mariner Books, 1999).

Betty Lehan Harragan, *Games Mother Never Taught You: Corporate Gamesmanship for Women* (New York: Warner Books, 1978).

Katie Hnida, *Still Kicking: My Dramatic Journey as the First Woman to Play Division One College Football* (New York: Scribner, 2006).

John Milton Hoberma, *Darwin's Athletes: How Sport Has Damaged Black America and Preserved the Myth of Race* (Boston, MA: Mariner Books, 1997).

Frederick E. Hoxie, *Encyclopedia of North American Indians* (Boston, MA: Houghton Mifflin Harcourt, 1996).

Nathan Jendrick, *Dunks, Doubles, Doping: How Steroids Are Killing American Athletics* (Guilford, CT: Lyons Press, 2006).

Arnd Kruger and William Murray, *The Nazi Olympics* (Champaign, IL: University of Illinois Press, 2003).

Paul Blumenau Lyons, *The Greatest Gambling Stories Ever Told: Thirty-One Unforgettable Tales of Risk and Reward* (Guilford, CT: Lyons Press, 2004).

Thomas Mallon, *Dewey Defeats Truman: A Novel* (New York: Picador, 1997).

Eric Margenau, *Sports Without Pressure: A Guide for Parents and Coaches of Young Athletes* (New York: Routledge, 1990).

Christy Mathewson, *Pitching in a Pinch: Or, Baseball from the Inside* (Lincoln, NE: University of Nebraska Press, 1994).

Francois-Xavier Mbopi-Keou, *Health and Sports in Africa: A Challenge for Development* (Esher, Surrey, UK: John Libbey Eurotext, 2008).

Anne McDonald Maier, *Mother Love, Deadly Love: The Texas Cheerleader Murder Plot* (New York: Carol Publishing Corporation, 1992).

J. Reid Meloy, Lorraine Sheridan, and Jens Hoffmann, *Stalking, Threatening, and Attacking Public Figures: A Psychological and Behavioral Analysis* (New York: Oxford University Press, 2008).

William J. Morgan, *Ethics in Sport* (Champaign, IL: Human Kinetics, 2007).

Thomas H. Murray, Willard Gaylin, and Ruth Macklin, *Feeling Good and Doing Better: Ethics and Nontherapeutic Drug Use* (Clifton, NJ: Humana Press, 1984).

Arnold Palmer and Steve Eubanks, *Playing By the Rules* (New York: Atria Books, 2002).

Stephen Potter, *The Theory and Practice of Gamesmanship: Or the Art of Winning Games Without Actually Cheating* (Kingston, RI: Moyel Bell, 1998).

Shaun Powell, *Souled Out? How Blacks Are Winning and Losing in Sports* (Champaign, IL: Human Kinetics, 2008).

Eugene F. Provenzo, John P. Renaud, and Asterie Baker Provenzo, *Encyclopedia of the Social and Cultural Foundations of Education*, Vol. 2 (New York: Sage Publications, 2008).

Jonathan Rand, *300 Pounds of Attitude: The Wildest Stories and Craziest Characters the NFL Has Ever Seen* (Guilford, CT: Lyons Press, 2006).

Arthur A. Raney and Jennings Bryant, *Handbook of Sports and Media* (Mahwah, NJ: Earlbaum Associates, 2006).

David Remnick, *The Only Game in Town: Sportswriting from the New Yorker* (New York: Random House, 2010).

William C. Rhoden, *Forty Million Dollar Slaves* (New York: Three Rivers Press, 2006).

Charley Rosen, *Scandals of 1951: How the Gamblers Almost Killed College Basketball* (New York: Holt, Rinehart and Winston, 1978).

Lon Safko, *The Social Media Bible: Tactics, Tools, and Strategies for Business Success* (Hoboken, NJ: Wiley, 2010).

Garu Sailes, *African Americans in Sport* (New Brunswick, NJ: Transaction Publishers, 1998).

Brad Schultz, *Sports Media, Second Edition: Reporting, Producing, and Planning* (Boston, MA: Focal Press, 2005).

Kenneth L. Shropshire, *In Black and White: Race and Sports in America* (New York: New York University Press, 1996).

Kenneth L. Shropshire and Timothy Davis, *The Business of Sports Agents* (Philadelphia, PA: University of Pennsylvania Press, 2008).

Robert L. Simon, *Fair Play: The Ethics of Sport* (Boulder, CO: Westview Press, 2003).

Ron Simon, *The Game Behind the Game, Negotiating in the Big Leagues* (Stillwater, MN: Voyager Press, 1993).

Gordon V. Smith and Russell L. Parr, *Valuation of Intellectual Property and Intangible Assets*, 3d ed. (Hoboken, NJ: John Wiley & Sons, 2000).

Mike Sowell, *The Pitch That Killed* (Hoboken, NJ: John Wiley & Sons, 1994).

Murray Sperber, *Beer and Circus: How Big-Time College Sports Is Crippling Undergraduate Education* (New York: Holt Paperbacks, 2001).

Rick Swaine, *The Integration of Major League Baseball* (Jefferson, NC: McFarland & Company, 2006).

Tom Swift, *Chief Bender's Burden: The Silent Struggle of a Baseball Star* (Lincoln, NE: Bison Books, 2010).

Claudio Tamburrini, *Values in Sport: Elitism, Nationalism, Gender Equality and the Scientific Manufacturing of Winners (Ethics and Sport)* (New York: Taylor & Francis, 2000).

Rick Telander, *The Hundred Yard Lie: The Corruption of College Football and What We Can Do to Stop It* (Champaign, IL: University of Illinois Press, 1989).

Jason Turbow and Michael Duca, *The Baseball Codes: Beanballs, Sign Stealing, and Bench-Clearing Brawls: The Unwritten Rules of America's Pastime* (New York: Pantheon, 2010).

Jules Tygiel, *Baseball's Great Experiment: Jackie Robinson* (New York: Oxford University Press, 2008).

Don Van Natta, *First Off the Tee: Presidential Hackers, Duffers, and Cheaters from Taft to Bush* (Boston, MA: Little, Brown, & Co., 2003).

Bill Veeck, *Veeck—As in Wreck: The Autobiography of Bill Veeck* (Chicago, IL: University of Chicago Press, 2001).

Spike Vrusho, *Benchclearing: Baseball's Greatest Fights and Riots* (Guilford, CT: Lyons Press, 2008).

Lawrence A. Wenner, *Mediasport* (New York: Routledge, 1998).

Lee Witkins and Clifford G. Christians, *The Handbook of Mass Media Ethics* (New York: Routledge, 2008).

James Wolfe and Mary Ann Presman, *Curse? There Ain't No Stinking Chicago Cub Curse and Other Stories About Sports and Gamesmanship* (Charleston, SC: BookSurge Publishing, 2009).

Fran Zimniuch, *Crooked: A History of Cheating in Sports* (New York: Taylor Trade Publishing, 2009).

Derek Zumsteg, *The Cheater's Guide to Baseball* (Boston, MA: Houghton Mifflin, 2007).

CASES AND ARBITRATION DECISIONS

Ali v. Playgirl, Inc.
Muhammad Ali v. The State Athletic Commission
Atlanta Baseball Co. v. Lawrence
Avila v. Citrus Community College District
Babych v. McRae
Baker v. Farmingdale Union Free School District
Baker v. Trinity-Pawling School
Bally v. Northeastern University
Barron v. PGA Tour, Inc.
Bias v. Advantage International
Bouchat v. Baltimore Ravens, Incorporated
Bourque v. Duplechin
Bowers v. Baylor University
Brahatcek v. Millard School District
Brantley v. Bowling Green School
Brown v. National Football League
Brown v. Woolf
Burnett v. Twentieth Century Fox Film
C.B.C. Distribution and Marketing, Inc. v. Major League Baseball
Carabba v. The Anacortes School District
Carrigan v. Roussell
Cohen v. Brown University
Collins v. NBPBA
Collins v. Resto
Collins v. State of New York
Cox v. National Football League

Dambrot v. Central Michigan University

The Detroit Lions, Inc. v. Argovitz

Doe v. Banos

Donnell v. Spring Sports, Inc.

Eldrick 'Tiger' Woods, for itself, Tiger Woods and his minor child, Charlie Axel Woods v. Josh Whitford

Erica Eneman and Amy Nadler v. Pat Richter

Gauvin v. Clark

Gustaveson v. Gregg

Haben v. Anderson

Hackbart v. Cincinnati Bengals

Haffer v. Temple University of the Commonwealth System of Higher Education

Hagan v. Houston Independent School District

Hale v. Antoniou

Hawaii-Pacific Apparel Group, Inc. v. Cleveland and Browns Football Company LLC and National Football League Properties, Inc.

Haymon v. Auburn Community Non-Profit Baseball Association, Inc.

The Heisman Trophy Trust v. Smack Apparel Co.

Hills v. Bridgeview Little League Association

Hodges v. National Basketball Association

Hustler Magazine v. Falwell *In re old Glory Condom Corp.*, Trademark Trial and Appeals Board, March 3, 1992.

In the Matter of Arbitration Between Major League Baseball Players Association and the Commissioner of Major League Baseball, Suspension of Steven Howe

In the Matter of Arbitration the Major League Baseball Association Panel Decision No. 104, Grievance No. 2000–3, Player: John Rocker ISBA Advisory Opinion on Professional Conduct, Opinion No. 700.

Israel v. West Virginia Secondary Schools Activities Commission

Joe Montana, Jr. v. San Jose Mercury News, Inc.

Johnson v. Time, Inc.

Kesner v. Little Caesars Enterprises, Inc.

Koffman v. Garnett

Ladd v. Uecker and Milwaukee Brewers Baseball Club

Larry Spacek and Steve Ramsey v. Thea Clark Charles

Lestina v. Jerger

Lounsbury v. Camby

Lowery v. Euverard

M.G. v. Time Warner, Inc.

Malcolm v. Novato Unified School District Matter of Henley

Mayer v. Belichick

McKichan v. St. Louis Hockey Club

Mercer v. Duke University

Molinas v. National Basketball Association

Montefusco v. ESPN, Inc.

Nancy Moore and Garry Moore v. Willis Independent School District and Alan Beene
Moran v. Allan H. Selig, aka "Bud" Selig, as Commissioner of Major League Baseball
Nabozny v. Barnhill
NBA v. Motorola
Peterson v. Kennedy
Playmakers, LLC. v. ESPN, Inc.
Postema v. National League of Professional Baseball Clubs
Price v. Time, Inc.
Priester v. Lowndes County
Reaume v. Jefferson Middle School
Regina v. Edward Joseph Green
Richardson v. Sugg
Rickert v. Midland Lutheran College
Rose v. Giamatti
Rosenhaus v. Star Sports, Inc.
Kevin Ross v. Creighton University
Raymond Santopietro, Jr. v. City of New Haven
Simmons v. Baltimore Orioles, Inc.
Smith v. IMG Worldwide, Inc.
Speakers of Sports, Inc. v. Proserv, INC.
Special Olympics Florida, Inc. v. Showalter
Sporty's Farm v. Sportsman's Mkt., Inc.
Sprewell v. Golden State Warriors
State of Colorado v. Nathan Hall
State of Iowa v. William Maurice Floyd
State of Montana v. Thompson
State of Utah v. Ted Frampton
Stephen v. Franklin
Strock v. USA Cycling, Inc.
Thomas v. Special Olympics Missouri, Inc.
United States v. Piggie
University of Texas at Austin v. KST Electric, Ltd.
United States v. James Battista
Valentine v. National Sports Services (NSS), Smashmouth Sports, Scott Spreitzer, Jim Feist
Vendrell v. School District No. 26C, Malheur County
Vernonia School District v. Acton
Virgil v. Sports Illustrated
Walters v. Fullwood
Way v. Boy Scouts of America
Welch v. Dunsmuir Joint Union High School District
Wildman v. Marshalltown School District
Wright v. Bonds
Young, Jr. v. Vannerson
Zinn v. Parrish

MEDIA

Eight Men Out
Field of Dreams
The Fan

WEBSITES

ABCNews.com
BleacherReport.com
Bombasticsports.com
Cardinals.com
CBSNews.com
CNKI.com.cn
CNN.com
ESPN.com
ESPNsoccernet.com
Fanhouse.com
Forbes.com
FoxNews.com
Freep.com
Guardian.Co.Uk
KATU.com
KCBY.com
KSL.com
KTVB.com
LittleLeague.org
MarketWatch
MLB.com
MLive.com
MSNBC.com
NBA.com
NBCSports.com
News-Record.com
nhlhotglove.com
NPR.org
Salon.com
SI.com
SILive.com
Tampabay.com
TBD.com
Telegraph.co.uk
TribuneSport.com
WKRN.com

www.cces.ca
www.parentstv.org
www.rolltide.com
www.sportsanddrugs.procon.org
www.wada.ama.org
Youthsports.Rutgers.edu

NEWSPAPERS

Arizona Republic
Atlanta Journal-Constitution
The Atlantic
The Badger Herald
Baltimore Sun
Bloomberg Business Week
The Boston Channel
The Boston Globe
Boston Herald
Business Insider
Chicago Daily Tribune
Chicago Tribune
Christian Post
Cincinnati Enquirer
Cricket Suite
The Daily Examiner
The Daily Orange
The Dallas Observer
Denver Post
Denver Rocky Mountain News
Detroit Free Press
Doncaster Today
Fort Worth Star Telegram
The Grand Rapids Press
Heritage Newspaper
Houston Chronicle
Huffington Post
Idaho Statesman
Imperial Valley News
International Herald Tribune
Las Vegas Sun
Lawyers Weekly
Literary Digest
Los Angeles Times
Manila Times

Maryland Business Daily Record
MaxPreps High School Sports
Minneapolis Star-Tribune
The New Haven Register
New York Times
Newsday
The News-Herald
Post Gazette
Pittsburgh Post-Gazette
The Register
The Rice Thresher
San Diego Union-Tribune
The Seattle Times
South Florida Sun-Sentinel
Sports Business Daily
Sports Illustrated
Sports Illustrated Vault
The Star Ledger
Sun-Sentinel
The Sydney Morning Herald
Wall Street Journal
Time Magazine
UCF Today
United Press International
USA Today

MAGAZINES

Hockey Digest
Reader's Digest
Smart Money
The Sporting News
Street & Smith's Sports Business Daily

MISCELLANEOUS SOURCES

Anabolic Steroid Abuse, National Institute on Drug Abuse Research Report, U.S. Department of
    Health and Human Services & National Institutes of Health Florida High School Athletic
    Association Rulebook.
In re old Glory Condom Corp., Trademark Trial and Appeals Board, March 3, 1992.
ISBA Advisory Opinion on Professional Conduct, Opinion No. 700.
Major League Baseball Rules 2010.

Jeanette S. Martin and Lillian H. Chaney, "Sports Etiquette," *Proceedings of the 2007 Association for Business Communication Annual Convention.*

NCAA Eligibility Center, *2009–10 Guide for the College Bound Student Athlete.*

Brian Soebbing and Daniel Mason, "Protecting Integrity in Professional Sports Leagues: Preserving Uncertainty of Outcome," *2008 North American Society for Sport Management Conference*, May 29, 2008.

CASE INDEX

INDEX